PETER M. DALY is a member of the Department of German at McGill University.

The symbolic mode of thought and expression that produced the mixed art form of the emblem also informs and shapes much of the literature of the sixteenth and seventeenth centuries. This study explores the relationship between the emblem proper and the literature of England and Germany during the period.

The book proceeds from a definition of the emblem, based on a critical theory which has received little attention among English and Romance scholars, to a detailed analysis of the form and function of emblematic imagery in a variety of literary forms. The chapters following move into specific discussions of the structural affinities between emblems and poetry, drama, and fiction.

The emblem-books are important as a cross-reference for the meaning of motifs in literature. They indicate what educated men knew about nature, history, and mythology and, furthermore, how they interpreted this knowledge. It is not only as a mode of thought but also as an art form that the emblem offers a valuable perspective on the purely verbal art of literature. Emblematic structure and imagery function as a formal, shaping principle in literature in all its genres and forms. Imaginatively conceived, carefully researched, and clearly presented, this book makes connections which will enrich the field of comparative studies.

PETER M. DALY

Literature in the Light of the Emblem

Structural Parallels between the Emblem and
Literature in the Sixteenth and Seventeenth Centuries

UNIVERSITY OF TORONTO PRESS
Toronto Buffalo London

© University of Toronto Press 1979
Toronto Buffalo London
Printed in Canada

Library of Congress Cataloging in Publication Data

Daly, Peter Maurice.
   Literature in the light of the emblem.
   Bibliography: p.
   Includes indexes.
   1. Emblems – History and criticism. 2. German
literature – Early modern, 1500–1700 – History and
criticism. 3. English literature – Early modern,
1500–1700 – History and criticism. I. Title.

   PN6348.5.D3   809'.91'5   79-11863
   ISBN 0-8020-5390-4

To JOAN

sometime emblematic widow

Contents

PREFACE ix

ABBREVIATIONS xiii

1

The Emblem 3
Definitions and Descriptions of Emblem-Books 3
Forerunners of the Emblem 9
Recent Developments in Emblem Theory 36

2

The Word-Emblem 54
The Emblem-Book as a Source of Poetic Imagery 55
The Emblem-Book as a Parallel for the Word-Emblem 60
Towards a Phenomenology and Typology of the Word-Emblem 64
The Forms of the Word-Emblem 94

3

Emblematic Poetry 103
Copies or Imitations of Emblems in Poetry 103
The Word-Emblem as the Foundation of a Poem 104
The Word-Emblem as a Controlling or Unifying Element in Poetry 107
The Emblematic Poem 113
The Pattern Poem 123

4

Emblematic Drama 134
The Emblematic Word in Drama 134
The Emblematic Character 143
The Emblematic Stage 149
Drama as Extended Emblem 162

5

Emblematic Narrative Prose 168
The Emblematic World-View of the Novel 168
Emblematic Imagery 169
The Emblematic Episode 171
Emblematic Narrative Structure 176
The Emblematic Frontispiece 180

6

Conclusion 185

NOTES 189

SELECTED BIBLIOGRAPHY 224
Critical Studies 224
Selection of Works in English on German Baroque Literature 232
Recent Comparative Studies of European Literature of the Sixteenth and
Seventeenth Centuries 232
Translations of European Poetry of the Sixteenth and Seventeenth Centuries 233

INDEX OF NAMES 235

INDEX OF EMBLEM MOTIFS 241

Preface

This book is the result of my attempts to inform myself about emblematic literature, a subject that first caught my attention when I was completing a dissertation in 1962 on the metaphoric language of the baroque poetess Catharina Regina von Greiffenberg. Initially I was struck by similarities between poetic images and motifs in emblem-books, but it soon became apparent that something like an emblematic structural principle was at work in many different ways in German and English poetry of the sixteenth and seventeenth centuries. I wanted to learn more. The well-known studies of Henry Green, Mario Praz, and Rosemary Freeman had much to offer – a wealth of material and many brilliant insights – but they did not deal comprehensively with literature in the light of the emblem. Albrecht Schöne's study *Emblematik und Drama im Zeitalter des Barock* (Stuttgart, 1964; 2nd ed 1968) provided a more substantial theory of the emblem, and his analysis of the drama of the period laid a sounder foundation for an investigation of emblematic literature in general. As I read on, casting further afield, I found that I was organizing my reading into a kind of *Forschungsbericht*, or critical survey. It also became necessary to keep referring to a basic theory of the emblem and its counterpart in literature in order to decide whether a given article or book was really dealing with an emblematic structure, or some other form of allegory or symbolism.

Chapter 1 offers an account of the emblem, which has provided me with a basis for a construct of the verbal emblem, or word-emblem as I prefer to call it. Chapter 2 considers the forms and functions of emblematic imagery in a variety of literary forms. The next three chapters attempt to deal with structural affinities between the emblem and poetry, drama, and prose fiction. In these chapters I pay less attention to imagery, since it is discussed more fully in Chapter 2.

This book is offered as a critical introduction to the study of emblematic structure in the purely verbal art of literature. It sets about the task by reviewing a selection of the criticism on the subject. I do not pretend to have dealt exhaustively or definitively with the topic. My decision to limit myself to English and German discussions of literature written largely in those two languages was dictated by immediate personal interest and my own linguistic limitations. I have not reviewed the treatment of the subject by such writers as Robert J. Clements,[1] nor have I tried to incorporate the findings of other scholars of Romance literatures, for two reasons. First, it would have expanded the focus of my investigation in a direction I did not desire, and the richness of the material would have broken the bounds of the monograph I proposed. Secondly, the basis for the modern theory of the emblem comes from the German scholar Schöne whose work, although well-known among German scholars and a smaller number of students of comparative literature, is hardly known to English and Romance scholars; therefore, little was to be gained in the introductory chapter by going yet further afield, and this chapter lays the groundwork for my analysis of emblematic structures in literature proper. It was tempting to try to include the Netherlands, because in many respects the Dutch led the way, especially in the writing and printing of emblems. Theirs was a major contribution to the development of the love emblem as well as the moral and stoic emblem collections. In terms of technique Dutch graphic artists and printers were in advance of their English counterparts, a situation instanced by George Wither's adoption of Gabriel Rollenhagen's plates for his *Collection of Emblemes* (1635). Zesen's translation of van Veen's *Moralia Horatiana* (1607) made a veritable stoic emblem-book available to a wider reading public in Germany. However, in the end I resisted the temptation, since I am not offering a history of the development of emblematic structures, but rather a critical account of various emblematic modes and forms in literary works.

Although I have limited my scope to English and German, I hope that my findings will also be of interest to readers of other European literatures of the sixteenth and seventeenth centuries. I do not assume that all the structures described in this book will necessarily be discovered in the same form and to the same extent everywhere during the period under review. The evidence is, however, incontrovertible that German and English literature of the sixteenth and seventeenth centuries owes much to the emblematic attitude of mind and emblematic principles of composition.

The emblem did not die out at the end of the seventeenth century.[2] A glance at the bibliographies of Goethe, Brentano, and Eichendorff, Coleridge, Wordsworth, and Blake will show that many scholars believe that emblematic echoes may be discovered in the writings of these poets. However, because new problems of definition and evidence arise for these later periods,[3] I decided to limit my investigation to the 'age of the emblem.'

It is always a pleasure to acknowledge one's gratitude to those who have helped in one way or another. High on my list comes Joseph Leighton of Bristol University: I profited from his critical reading of the manuscript, and also enjoyed many hours discussing various aspects of baroque literature with him. My thanks are also due to the University of Manitoba and The Canada Council who provided me with research funds, and, above all, time in the form of a sabbatical leave during the academic year 1972–3 to write this book. This book has been published with the help of a grant from the Canadian Federation for the Humanities, using funds provided by the Social Sciences and Humanities Research Council of Canada, and a grant to University of Toronto Press from the Andrew W. Mellon Foundation. I should also like to thank the many libraries in North America and Europe for their co-operation in sending me materials of various kinds. Finally, I wish to express my thanks to *Mosaic*, *Neophilologus*, and *Wascana Review* for permission to use materials contained in articles of mine published by these journals. With minor exceptions I have not dealt with the critical literature appearing after 1973.

PMD

Abbreviations

A	*Anglia*
AfdA	*Anzeiger für deutsches Altertum*
ASnS	*Archiv für das Studium der neueren Sprachen*
B	*Baconia*
CA	*Coat of Arms*
CL	*Comparative Literature*
Cri	*The Criterion*
CG	*Colloquia Germanica*
DubR	*Dublin Review*
DVJs	*Deutsche Vierteljahrsschrift für Literaturwissenschaft und Geistesgeschichte*
Emblemata	Arthur Henkel and Albrecht Schöne, *Emblemata, Handbuch zur Sinnbildkunst des XVI. und XVII. Jahrhunderts* (Stuttgart, 1967)
E	*English*
ELH	*English Literary History*
ES	*English Studies*
ESt	*Englische Studien*
Euph	*Euphorion*
FG	Georg Phillipp Harsdörffer, *Frauenzimmer Gesprächspiele*, ed Irmgard Bottcher (Tübingen, 1968–9)
Fs	*Festschrift*
GgA	*Göttingische gelehrte Anzeigen*
GLL	*German Life and Letters*
GQ	*German Quarterly*
GR	*Germanic Review*
GRM	*Germanisch-Romanische Monatsschrift*
HLQ	*Huntingdon Library Quarterly*

JEGP	*Journal of English and Germanic Philology*
JHI	*Journal of the History of Ideas*
JWCI	*Journal of the Warburg and Courtauld Institutes*
L'EC	*L'Esprit Createur*
M	*Mosaic*
MLN	*Modern Language Notes*
MLQ	*Modern Language Quarterly*
MLR	*Modern Language Review*
MP	*Modern Philology*
NM	*Neuphilologische Mitteilungen*
Neoph	*Neophilologus*
N&Q	*Notes and Queries*
PEGS	*Publications of the English Goethe Society*
PMLA	*Publications of the Modern Language Association of America*
PQ	*Philological Quarterly*
RD	*Renaissance Drama*
rde	*rowohlts deutsche enzyklopädie*
RES	*Review of English Studies*
RL	*Reallexikon der deutschen Literaturgeschichte*
RQ	*Renaissance Quarterly*
SP	*Studies in Philology*
SQ	*Shakespeare Quarterly*
SR	*Studies in the Renaissance*
TBS	*Transactions of the Bibliographical Society*
TQ	*Texas Quarterly*
WascR	*Wascana Review*
ZdP	*Zeitschrift für deutsche Philologie*
ZfdAdL	*Zeitschrift für deutsches Altertum und deutsche Literatur*
ZrP	*Zeitschrift für romanische Philologie*

LITERATURE IN THE LIGHT OF THE EMBLEM

1

The Emblem

In a stimulating article on emblem literature published in 1946 Henri Stegemeier expressed the hope 'that the term *Emblem* need not be again and again defined by everyone who today discusses the subject ...'[1] With the wealth of new insights into the nature and history of the emblem we are nearer to a definitive account which would obviate the need to define the term,[2] but that account has yet to be written. In the meantime it is advisable to define the term in order to avoid misunderstanding. By emblematic literature I do not mean the emblem-books proper, but rather the verbal art of literature which reveals those qualities associated with emblem-books.

Since the term 'emblematic' is derived from emblem-books, it seems appropriate to make some introductory comments on that subject before proceeding to literature *per se*. In my view it has become necessary to find an inclusive and neutral description of emblematic forms, since attitudes ranging from enthusiasm through amusement to hostility have accompanied the application of the epithet 'emblematic' to literature. Criticism and rejection of emblematic literature usually stem from a misunderstanding or from too narrow a conception of the emblems themselves. In this century some critics have denounced the emblem as 'a degenerate form of allegory'[3] and one of allegory's 'bastard children';[4] others have condemned it with monotonous regularity as 'arbitrary' and 'capricious.'

One of the hazards of literary scholarship is that of definition. One can but agree with Marc F. Bertonasco: 'Literary scholarship still lacks a satisfactory system of imagistic classification as well as a truly definitive study of the nature of symbolic imagery.'[5] To some extent the difficulty lies in our limited terminology. Loosely speaking, the emblem is a form of allegorical or symbolical expression, but its relation to allegory, symbolism, metaphor, and conceit is difficult to establish. This is partly because the same terms have been used with different things in mind: allegory and symbol have been discussed in their aesthetic, rhetorical, ontological, semantic, linguistic, and grammatical contexts.[6] Confusion tends to arise when a writer uses one of these image terms without making explicit its frame of reference, so that, for example, the reader is not sure whether 'simile' is intended rhetorically or semantically. The difference may be important, because a rhetorician's simile is not necessarily a semanticist's, and *vice versa*. A rhetorically oriented critic like Heinrich Lausberg[7] might well accept as metaphor the following image (I use the word as an umbrella term): 'Harbour, stepmother of ships.' A semantic critic like Philip Wheelwright, less interested in grammatical or rhetorical structures, would call the same image a simile, since it conveys to him but one meaning, whereas in his definition metaphor is characterized by plurisignation.[8]

Reliable definitions grow out of careful observation which is then used to modify the first impressions that led to the initial hypothesis. A complicating factor in defining emblematics is the quantity and variety of works calling themselves emblem-books. This can make first impressions unreliable – one gets quite a different idea of what an emblem is from Alciatus's *Emblematum liber* than from Michael Maier's *Atalanta fugiens*. Mario Praz's bibliography[9] lists over six hundred authors, most of whom produced more than one emblem-book which, in turn, were often enlarged, reprinted, and translated into several languages. The variety of emblem-books is astounding; taken together they reveal a nearly complete panoply of renaissance interests and experience. There are military, amorous, and religious emblem-books; collections that are moral, political, and didactic (imparting information on any and every subject); emblem-books that are entertaining and simply decorative. Like any other genre, emblem-books did not remain static, but underwent a development; in short, they too have a history, although it has yet to be written. Furthermore, national differences play a certain role in the development of emblem-books in spite of the fact that there was a great deal of international collaboration in their production.[10]

The various kinds of illustrated literature that preceded the emblem-books and were assimilated by them in varying degrees contribute in large measure to their richness and variety, and also complicate any discussion of the origin and definition of emblem-books. Illustrated broad sheets,[11] dance-of-death sequences, *biblia pauperum*, book illustrations, tituli, illustrated fables,[12] and Greek epigrams should be mentioned. When we add to this list of illustrated literary forerunners the even more important tradition of heraldry and devices, hieroglyphics and medieval Bible allegory and symbolism, then the scope of the emblem-book is more clearly sketched and the problem of definition may be appreciated. As Stegemeier observed: 'It is, actually, difficult to make a definition of the term complete and inclusive; *emblem* has meant such a variety of things to so many different men, that this at first is confusing' (p 27). And this confusion, or at least uncertainty, may be encountered even among early emblem-writers. Johann Fischart, who was well acquainted with contemporary theories of the emblem and *impresa*, provided the foreword to Mathias Holtzwart's collection *Emblematum Tyrocinia* (Straßburg, 1581). Written in German for a more general reading public, the foreword takes up historical questions of the origin of the emblem and the uses to which it may be put. As the editors of a recent edition of Holtzwart's emblems state, the introduction 'reveals the uncertainty which continued to exist at this time concerning the origin and meaning of the emblem, and which was the reason why this genre could develop in most diverse variants.'[13] The 'confusion' which Stegemeier noted in 1946, has, in my view, not been completely cleared up in modern studies of the emblematic tradition. Stegemeier observes in a footnote that Thompson,[14] Praz, and others give adequate definitions of emblem terminology, and to those names must now be added, among others, those of Rosemary Freeman,[15] Heckscher and Wirth,[16] Albrecht Schöne[17] and Dietrich Jöns[18] with their book-length contributions, and Dieter Sulzer,[19] Hessel Miedema,[20] Holger Homann,[21] Wolfgang Harms,[22] and Sibylle Penkert[23] with their substantial articles. There is no dearth of excellent scholarship, but there remain areas of substantial disagreement. It is perhaps only natural that modern critics offer divergent, at times contradictory definitions and accounts, since critics have approached the emblem from different angles, with different assumptions and perspectives. Several tendencies are discernible. Ludwig Volkmann[24] and Karl Giehlow[25] have stressed the role of hieroglyphics, whereas at a time when mannerism was being rediscovered Praz focused on the device, epigram, and conceit. This latter direction was taken up by Gustav René Hocke,[26] who has gone so far as to equate the emblem with mannerism. In so doing he has exaggerated the role of wit in the creation of emblems and overemphasized the enigmatic nature of the picture, which lead him to the conclusion that the function of the motto is to decipher an otherwise insoluble emblem riddle. Heckscher and Wirth also take a similar view (cf cols 88–96).[27] The iconographical research of Panofsky[28] and writers associated with the Warburg Institute has tended to concentrate on the motif content of emblems and has been basically literary in perspective. Emblems are used as ancillary materials in the interpretation of larger works of art, in the pursuit of themes and motifs, and the resulting criticism frequently resembles the *topos*-criticism of literary studies. This being the case, iconographical scholarship has not produced any systematic studies of the emblem as a form or genre in its own right, nor has such an approach been conducive to the establishment of an adequate theory of the emblem. Panofsky's own description of the emblem is not very helpful. He describes Alciatus's emblem-book as 'the first and most famous of the countless collections of illustrated epigrams, or epigrammatic paraphrases of images.'[29] Similarly, literary studies have tended to use emblems as either sources or parallels for images, structures, or effects in the purely verbal art of literature. And while much of value has emerged from some of these studies, little if any light has been shed on the emblem as a genre, or on individual emblem-books in their own right.

If Heckscher and Wirth stress the element of wit and enigma in the emblem, Schöne plays down these aspects, insisting on the necessary relationship between word (i.e., meaning) and picture, which derives from the tradition of medieval bestiaries and hieroglyphics, a tradition in which objects are intended to convey inherent meanings (pp 26–30, 45–50). Jöns emphasizes the tradition of religious exegesis in the emblem as a mode of thought ('Denkform'), while insisting on the neutrality of the form in the Alciatus type of emblem as an artistic form ('Kunstform'). On the whole, the general and descriptive accounts of the emblem (Praz, de Vries,[30] and Freeman) have made way for more specific and at times more normative definitions (Heckscher and Wirth, Schöne, and Jöns).

There is no disagreement among the leading critics about the presence in emblems of devices and hieroglyphics, Christian, classical, and natural symbols, and literary conceits. Opinions differ on the extent of that presence and on the primary question of whether all these motifs are 'emblematic' in any precise sense. At best the 'precise sense' is derived from an analysis of characteristic emblems, but already the selection of characteristic emblems presumes a hypothesis. The sheer quantity of emblems is enough to inundate both the individual and teams of scholars, so that as yet it is not possible to test methodically and accurately any single hypothesis against a large enough body of emblems. A task for the computer perhaps? But it should be borne in mind that any such analysis, whether carried out by man or machine, depends on a prior interpretation and classification of the emblems.

As is well known, the emblem is composed of three parts for which the Latin names seem most useful: *inscriptio, pictura,* and *subscriptio.*[31] A short motto or quotation introduces the emblem. It is usually printed above the *pictura,* and it functions as the *inscriptio.* The *pictura* itself may depict one or several objects, persons, events, or actions, in some instances set against an imaginary or real background (cf Daniel Meisner, *Politisches Schatzkästlein* [Frankfurt am Main, 1623–6] with its engravings of cities as backdrop to the emblematic objects shown in the foreground). Some of the objects are real (i.e., found in the world of man or nature), others are imaginary, which does not imply that during the seventeenth century they were necessarily considered fictitious. These objects are found in organic and inorganic combinations, or real and unreal combinations – provided no value judgment about the truth or value of the emblem is implied by the words 'real' and 'unreal.' Beneath the *pictura* comes a prose or verse quotation from some learned source or from the emblematist himself, which functions as a *subscriptio*. On the facing page it is not uncommon to find an explanatory poem in the vernacular tongue of the emblematist.

Perhaps the time is right for a synthesized definition of the emblem,[32] which would need as a prelude a sharply focused analysis of both the philosophical and phenomenological basis of the emblem (which, or better, whose?). Bearing in mind the substantial disagreements between Heckscher and Wirth and Miedema,[33] it is hardly surprising to find Heckscher and Bunker observe: 'At some point it would be desirable to re-open – pace Miedema – the discussion of the theory of the emblem.[34] Penkert recently echoed Reinhold Grimm's call for a critical comparison ('Auseinandersetzung') between the views of Schöne and Jöns on the subject (p 111, n 48).[35]

Any attempt to produce a systematic theory of the emblem would probably need to answer such questions as:

1 What are the content and origin of the *pictura*; what is its relation to reality, if any?
2 What are the content, origin, and purpose of the *inscriptio* and *subscriptio*?
3 What functional relationship exists between *pictura* and *scriptura*, i.e., between thing (pictured) and meaning (expressed in words)? How is the synthesis effected?
4 What is the overriding purpose of the emblem-book?[36]

When these questions have been satisfactorily answered for a sufficiently large number of emblem-books, then a reliable theory of the emblem can be advanced and a history of emblematics undertaken. A history of emblem theory, such as we may shortly expect from Dieter Sulzer,[37] which stresses the emblematists' prefaces in which they express their intentions and describe their methods of composition, will contribute a great deal to a history of emblematics. But that contribution may well require some modifications when set against the results of an interpretation of emblem-books as outlined above. Without engaging in a preliminary discussion of allegory, symbolism, and metaphor, the following minimal description of the emblem might serve as a basis on which to build:

emblems are composed of pictures and words; a meaningful relationship between the two is intended; the manner of communication is connotative rather than denotative. This neutral description of the emblem as a finished artefact makes no assumptions about either the primacy of *pictura* or *scriptura*,[38] or the nature of the relationship between the two. It refuses to prejudge any generic affiliations with symbol, allegory, or metaphor, and it implies nothing about the emblem's relationship to literature, the visual arts, or other mixed art forms.

Ideally a definition of the emblem would be based on an analysis of the first and most influential of all emblem-books, Alciatus's *Emblematum liber*, and the results applied to others thereafter. It could begin with the classification of *picturae* according to motifs (cf Stegemeier, p 33, n 33), and their origins in classical myth and allegory, biblical and Christian tradition, medieval nature lore, Horapollo and hieroglyphics, heraldry and devices, and literary conceits, e.g., Petrarchistic and Hellenistic erotic conceits (cf Praz, p 44). Of course, at times it would be difficult to assign the given motif to one area, because a heraldic device and a moral emblem may use the same motif from the sphere of hieroglyphics (cf Praz, p 79). Questions of origin and influence are even more complicated in the field of literature, where both the emblem-book and the literary work frequently have the same outside source, so that, in the absence of a notation by the poet, it is always difficult and usually impossible to establish the emblem-book as a source for the poet. With the classification of Alciatus's *picturae* complete, a list could then be compiled of the *inscriptiones* and *subscriptiones* according to basic idea conveyed and source (where determinable), and also an index made of significant words.[39]

This analysis of Alciatus would conclude with a cautious investigation of the relationship of word to picture. Allegations that there is 'no necessary likeness' between an image and its meaning assume too much, and epithets like 'capricious,' 'far-fetched,' 'zufällig,' and 'willkürlich' are value judgments which reveal more about the taste of the critics who sit in judgment of emblematics than about emblem-books. What is required is an unbiased attempt to describe the relationship of picture and meaning, which would need to speak in neutral terms of single signation and plurisignation, noting that meanings may derive from unpictured qualities of the object portrayed, in other words, that they may be inherent. It should refer to distance between object and meaning, and discuss the nature of the combination of meanings and objects.

There is yet no one study which fully takes into account the variety of emblem-books in terms of their phenomenology, ontology, and semantics, their relationship to illustrated forerunners, and finally their historical development. A judicious selection of the findings of Volkmann, Giehlow, Praz,

Freeman, Heckscher and Wirth, Schöne, and Jöns would provide a solid basis for such a work.

In the following pages I shall attempt to review what I consider the most important literature on the subject of the relation of emblem to many of the other forms which, like tributaries, feed the mainstream of the emblem.

FORERUNNERS OF THE EMBLEM

The Greek epigram[40]

Alciatus's model was first and foremost the Greek epigram, as found in the *Anthologia palatina cum planudeis* (cf Praz, p 31), which Alciatus was translating in the early 1520s. It is from this period that the first reference to a collection of emblems dates. Praz summarizes the relationship of emblem to epigram in the following words: 'Emblems are therefore things (representations of objects) which illustrate a conceit; epigrams are words (a conceit) which illustrate objects (such as a work of art, a votive offering, a tomb). The two are therefore complementary, so much so that many epigrams in the *Greek Anthology* written for statues are emblems in all but name' (pp 22–3).

According to a number of scholars no less than 50 of Alciatus's 212 emblems (see illustration 1) can be traced to translations or imitations of Greek epigrams (cf Praz, pp 25–6). Praz finds further substantiation for this thesis in the discovery of the vestiges of the epigrams now contained in the *Planudean Anthology* on the walls of a Pomepeian house, each of which is illustrated by a painting. 'It follows that between an emblem of Alciati and an epigram of the *Anthology* there is a difference only in name' (p 25). Without denying the presence of Greek epigrams in Alciatus's emblems Schöne doubts the validity of Praz's conclusions, since Schöne sees structural differences between the emblem, which in his view is characterized by the 'priority of idea in the picture' ('ideelle Priorität des Bildes'), and Pompeian illustrations, which assume the reverse, namely the primacy of words in the epigram (cf Schöne, pp 24–5). For Schöne the Greek epigram is 'merely a beginning' (p 26).

In Rosenfeld's view Alciatus's combination of Greek epigram and emblematic device was something of a mistake: 'The use for emblematic purposes was nevertheless an impossibility, since interpretations were applied to the pictorial works, whereas in emblem-books meanings are read out of the picture.'[41]

Renaissance collections of 'loci communes'

Another important source for the textual parts of the emblem is provided by those endless collections of *loci communes* or commonplace books, which played such a large role in the cultural and educational life of the Renaissance

In uictoriam dolo partam.

Aiacis tumulum lachrymis ego perluo uirtus,
Heu misera albentes dilacerata comas.
Scilicet hoc restabat adhuc,ut iudice græco
Vincerer,& caussa stet potiore dolus.

Illustration 1
From Andreas Alciatus, *Emblematvm libellvs* (Paris, 1542)

and the Baroque. If the *Planudean Anthology* was, indeed, Alciatus's model both in terms of much of the material rendered in the new form, as well as an influence on the form itself, then Erasmus's *Adagia* were a decided influence on many of the texts of Alciatus's emblem. The *Adagia* were published initially in 1500, a fuller edition appearing in 1520 at Venice from the famous house of Aldus, which was later to publish a number of outstanding editions of Alciatus's emblems. Claude Mignault, learned commentator of Alciatus's emblems, was the first to demonstrate this influence of Erasmus's *Adagia*, a subject taken up by Henry Green[42] and most recently by Virginia Woods Callahan.[43]

It is well known that Erasmus and Alciatus were friends who held each other in high esteem; as Christian humanists they shared many opinions in matters of ethics and religion. Callahan, in the critical edition of the 1621 collection of emblems that she is preparing,[44] will also endeavour to uncover 'the influence of the other writings of Erasmus and the impact of Alciati's personal connections with him on the form and matter of his Emblem Book' (p 133). She argues that the emblems are a 'distillation of the Alciati-Erasmus friendship' (p 136), and she illustrates her thesis with an interpretation of emblem CXXXVIII 'The Twelve Labours of Hercules' (pp 136–7; see illustration 2).

Hieroglyphics[45]

Volkmann and Giehlow have demonstrated that Alciatus's *Emblematum liber* arose in part at least out of the humanist interest in hieroglyphics. It is important at the outset to recognize that the renaissance conception of the Egyptian hieroglyphs was in fact a misconception. The renaissance humanists believed that each picture sign represented a word, that is, they took the hieroglyphs for ideograms. The truth is more complicated. From the very beginnings of hieroglyphic writing, which dates back to the time immediately preceding the unification of the Upper and Lower Kingdoms of Egypt (3200 BC), the picture signs of common objects 'were used as graphic elements with the sound value of the Egyptian word for the object they represented' (Iversen, p 12). For instance, as an ideogram the picture of a mace conveyed the idea of the mace as an instrument, but as a phonogram it also had the sound value for the Egyptian word for mace which was ḥd. As a phonetic system the Egyptian hieroglyphic code was deficient in vowels. Thus ḥd could mean 'white,' 'silver,' and 'damage.' However, in time this and other deficiencies were overcome.

During the Renaissance Egyptian hieroglyphs were regarded as an ideographical form of writing used by Egyptian priests to shadow forth enigmatically divine wisdom. The term 'hieroglyph' is inseparably linked with the name of Horapollo (Horus, or Orus Apollo). Nothing can be said with certainty about the author of this most influential collection of hieroglyphics. The manuscript was discovered on the Greek island of Andros in 1419 by the priest Christo-

Illustration 2
From Andreas Alciatus, *Emblemata* (Lyon, 1551)

Spernit auaritiam, nec rapto aut foenore gaudet.
Vincit, foemineos spoliatq, insignibus actus.
Expurgat sordes, & cultum mentibus addit.
Illicitos odit coitus, abigitq, nocentes.
Barbaries, feritasq, dat impia denique poenam.
Vnius virtus collectos dissipat hostes.
Inuehit in patriam externis bona plurima ab oris.
Docta per ora virū volat, & non interit vnquam.

phorus de' Buondelmonti and taken to Florence. A brief introduction states that the book was originally written in Egyptian by Horapollo from Nilopolis and was subsequently translated into Greek by a certain Philippos, who remains a mystery. Iversen dates the work to the fourth century AD (cf p 47); more recently Schöne has suggested that it was probably compiled in the second half of the fifth century (cf p 35). The inclusion of Greek names and some Greek allusions suggests that the Horapollo is of Alexandrian provenance, since Alexandria was a melting-pot of Greek and Egyptian culture.

The Horapollo consists of two books containing 70 and 119 chapters respectively; each chapter deals with one hieroglyph. The heading describes the hieroglyph, e.g., a falcon, or its meaning, e.g., eternity. There is no reference whatsoever to the phonetic aspects of Egyptian hieroglyphic writing, which helps to account for the humanists' misconception of the very nature and purpose of ancient Egyptian hieroglyphs. Volkmann states quite categorically that Horapollo contains merely an interpretation of the so-called enigmatic hieroglyphs, which were frequently drawn from the artificial ideograms of a later period (cf p 8). On the other hand, Iversen, an Egyptologist, contends that there is a fundamental element of truth in the greater part of Horapollo's explanations. 'Almost all of the allegorical expoundings can more or less directly be traced back either to the actual hieroglyphical meaning of the signs, or be explained from one of their specific employments as graphic signs' (p 48). We are more concerned with object-related significance, that is with the hieroglyph as ideogram, and it is interesting to note that Horapollo is right when he says that goose signifies 'son' (1.53), because the goose is believed to love its offspring more than any other animal. Vulture expresses the notion 'mother,' because male vultures do not exist (1.11). The ear of an ox means 'hearing' (1.47); the hare signifies 'what is open' (1.26). In every case there is not only an ideogramatic correlation with ordinary hieroglyphic writing, but also a phonetic correspondence. The words for goose and son were homonyms in Egyptian, as were 'vulture' and 'mother.' Iversen concludes: 'If, as a matter of fact, Horapollo had confined himself to state quite simply that the pictures of the goose, vulture, the ear and the hare were used in the writing of the words for "son," "mother," "hear" and "open," he would actually have been right in all cases' (p 48).

Volkmann lists the following as some of the most important and frequently encountered hieroglyphs: the eel = spiteful man; eye and sceptre = Osiris; female bear licking her young = an originally unformed person; bee = people subject to a king; elephant = strong (or honest) man; fire and water = purity; two hippopotamus hooves = injustice; hawk = god, excellence, victory, quick execution; dog with regal robe = magistracy or judge; ibis = heart; flying crane = man who knows of heavenly things; crane carrying a stone = watchful man on his guard against his enemies; crocodile = rapacious or furious man; lion = anger; frontal parts of lion = strength; man without head, or man's feet walking on water = that which is impossible; papyrus bundle = descendant of old family; phoenix = soul or rebirth; salamander = man burned in the fire; snake hiding its tail = time; snake biting its tail = world; bull = moderated courage; stork = someone who loves his parents; goat = reproductive power (cf pp 87–8).

Horapollo also describes a number of alleged hieroglyphs which never occur in any form of Egyptian art or writing, such as 'a lion eating a monkey' (II.76) or 'a horse's carcass' (II.44); these were probably the author's own invention.

The scholars of the Renaissance wrongly believed that in the Horapollo they had discovered a key to the meaning of the ancient Egyptian hieroglyphics inscribed on obelisks and other monuments, whereas they were really 'a secret kind of writing dating from Hellenist times ... which could in no way lead to an understanding of actual Egyptian hieroglyphics' (Schöne, p 35).[46] These hieroglyphs flowed into the mainstream of the emblem both directly through the original Greek version of Horapollo, first printed in 1505, and translated into Latin in 1517 (there were thirty subsequent editions), and indirectly through the tributaries of medieval Christian allegory, the most important work of this kind being *Physiologus* (cf Iverson, p 48; Jöns, p 10) and the books of devices (cf Praz, pp 59, 79ff). As the examples of the goose for 'son' and vulture for 'mother' indicate, the relationship of sign to meaning in Horapollo is always of an allegorical nature, or we might now say of an emblematic nature, in so far as a fact or belief concerning the object or creature is the basis of the associated meaning. This mode of thought is the basis of the *Physiologus* and the bestiary tradition; Iversen goes so far as to describe it as 'exactly the same sort of "philosophical" reasoning which we find later in the Physiologus and the bestiaries of the Middle Ages' (p 48). For instance, both Horapollo and *Physiologus* inform us that the lion sleeps with its eyes open. The descriptions of the beaver, the lion, the pelican, the phoenix, and the stork in *Physiologus* all correspond with the accounts in Horapollo. This will make it difficult, and usually impossible, to determine the actual origin of an emblem based upon such a motif, unless the emblem-writer has named his source.

Earlier the Greeks had shown an interest in the Egyptian hieroglyphs. Plato, Herodotus, Plutarch, Pliny, Clement of Alexandria, Plotinus, Lucan, Diodorus all make reference to the hieroglyphic system which embodied wisdom in picture signs. The Greeks were not concerned with the phonetic aspects of the language, only with the symbolic system, which they viewed in the light of their own theory of Platonic ideas. As Iversen puts it: 'what interested the

Greeks was not Egyptian writing at all; but from their own ''Platonic'' interpretation of the relation between sign and meaning in Egyptian hieroglyphs, grew the idea of the existence of a true symbolic system of writing in which abstract notions and ideas could be expressed by means of concrete pictures of material objects' (p 49). The attitude of the Greeks helped to determine and reinforce the attitude of renaissance humanists. The leader of the Platonic academy in Florence, Marsilio Ficino, studied many of the relevant texts, including the Horapollo, and came to the conclusion that the priests in Egypt had used not letter characters but the figures of whole animals, plants, and trees to express profound wisdom; at the same time, in a clearly Platonic sense, he regarded the hieroglyphs as the reflections of divine ideas in the things themselves. One of the examples he cites is that of the snake biting its tail which embodies the concept of time. In general the influence of Egyptian hieroglyphs was conceptual rather than stylistic.

The earliest impact of hieroglyphic studies is to be found in the graphic and plastic arts of the Renaissance. The scholar and artist Leon Battista Alberti was well acquainted with many of the texts and actual obelisks, and this knowledge informs the discussions and illustrations of his ten-volume work on architecture. There is an important passage in the Eighth book of Alberti's *Ten Books on Architecture*:

> The Egyptians employed symbols in the following manner: they carved an eye, by which they understood God; a vulture for Nature; a Bee for King; a circle for Time; an ox for Peace, and the like. And their reason for expressing their sense by these symbols was, that words were understood only by the respective nations that talked the language, and therefore inscriptions in common characters must in a short time be lost: as it has actually happened to our Etruscan characters: for among the ruins of several towns, castles and burial-places I have seen tombstones dug up with inscriptions on them ... in Etruscan characters which ... nobody can understand. And the same, the Egyptians supposed, must be the case with all sorts of writing whatsoever; but the manner of expressing their sense which they used upon these occasions, by symbols, they thought must always be understood by learned men of all nations, to whom alone they were of the opinion that things of moment were fit to be communicated.[47]

As Dieckmann[48] suggests, Alberti's new contribution to the renaissance discussion of hieroglyphs lies in his emphasis on their universal significance, which rests upon a Platonic assumption. In Platonic theory ideas were believed to exist independent of their expression in different languages. Alberti also points to the use of hieroglyphs by the Romans to record the accomplishments of their great men in paintings and architecture. Wittkower gives an instance of Roman hieroglyphs in the temple frieze of the fifteenth-century church of San Lorenzo Fuori le Mura which was studied by renaissance artists and the writer Fra Francesco Colonna whose romance *Hypnerotomachia Poliphili* abounds in hieroglyphic inventions.[49]

We find the first evidence of renaissance hieroglyphics, however, in medals and coins. It is no coincidence that a medal printed for Alberti is hieroglyphic in content and intent. It depicts a winged eye with the Ciceronian inscription 'Quid tum?' ('what then?'), often interpreted as meaning after death. According to Diodorus the eye represents God the Judge, the wings of a hawk stand for speed; the whole has been regarded as signifying preparedness to be called swiftly before God's throne of judgment.[50] The medal is an *impresa* or device.

One of the first literary works, richly illustrated, to deal fairly systematically with the hieroglyph was Colonna's *Hypnerotomachia Poliphili*, which probably dates back to the 1460s but was first published in 1499.[51] The title means something like Poliphilo's dream-fight with Eros. The complicated novel tells the story of Poliphilo's pursuit of his divine Polia in dream. She herself is an allegorical personification of antiquity. The scene is set in pastoral landscapes of fauns and nymphs, gardens and forests dotted with monuments and picturesque ruins. Egypt is a kind of wonderland. Colonna's hieroglyphs and their inscriptions were considered genuine, although in fact they were essentially re-creations of his imagination, an imagination largely inspired by other imitations of hieroglyphs. Wittkower writes: 'The innocent frieze in San Lorenzo[52] with sacrificial implements stimulated Francesco Colonna to most extraordinary inventions. For instance, he describes fourteen hieroglyphs one after the other on the base of a mausoleum, illustrates them, and winds up with a coherent reading in Latin of their meaning which may be translated thus, 'Sacrifice your toil generously to the God of nature. Little by little you will then subject your soul to God, and He will take you into His firm protection, mercifully govern your life and preserve it unharmed' (pp 71–2). One small detail of a frieze on a bridge must suffice to indicate the nature of these renaissance hieroglyphs (see illustration 3). The pattern has three motifs: a circle, and a dolphin wound around the shaft of an anchor. This exemplifies the motto of Augustus, 'semper festina tarde.' The circle means 'always,' the dolphin 'hurry,' and the anchor stands for 'rest' or 'peace.' This same device of dolphin and anchor was adopted by the Venetian publisher Aldus Manutius. It also occurs in Alciatus where the motif receives a moral-political interpretation.

Hieroglyphs gain currency in German through the influence of the humanists gathered at the court of Maximilian. The most famous Horapollo manuscript is that translated into Latin by Pirckheimer and illustrated by Dürer. It was

Illustration 3
Architectural detail from a frieze on a bridge, depicted and interpreted by
Francesca Colonna in his *Hypnerotomachia Poliphili* (1499)

presented to the Emperor in 1514. Doubtless the most celebrated hieroglyphic
monument is Dürer's *Triumphal Arch of Maximilian* with its famous hieroglyphic portrait of the Emperor (see illustration 4). One cannot do better than
quote Panofsky's translation, with its parenthetical references, of the explanatory text of Stabius and Pirckheimer.

> Maximilian [the Emperor himself] – a prince [dog draped with stole] of great piety
> [star above the Emperor's crown], most magnanimous, powerful and courageous
> [lion], ennobled by imperishable and eternal fame [basilisk on the Emperor's crown],
> descending from ancient lineage [the sheaf of papyrus on which he is seated], Roman
> Emperor [eagles embroidered in the cloth of honor], endowed with all the gifts of
> nature and possessed of art and learning [dew descending from the sky] and master of
> a great part of the terrestrial globe [snake encircling the scepter] – has with warlike
> virtue and great discretion [bull] won a shining victory [falcon on the orb] over the
> mighty king here indicated [cock on a serpent, meaning the King of France], and
> thereby watchfully protected himself [crane raising its foot] from the stratagems of
> said enemy, which has been deemed impossible [feet walking through water by
> themselves] by all mankind.[53]

With the exception of the cock, which is a symbol of France, all the hieroglyphs
derive from Horapollo.

One of the earliest humanist links between renaissance hieroglyphics and
Christian allegory was forged by Pierus Valerianus, whose *Hieroglyphica, sive
de sacris Aegyptiorum aliarumque gentium literis* (Basel, 1556) combines both
hieroglyphics and the medieval nature symbolism of bestiaries, lapidaries, and
the *Physiologus* (cf Volkmann, pp 35–40; Praz, p 24; Jöns, pp 9–10). About a
century later the German Jesuit Athanasius Kircher published a number of
works dealing with the ancient Egyptian hieroglyphs. Much earlier in his life
Kircher had become fascinated with hieroglyphs and his ambition was to
decipher the enigmatic code. The opportunity presented itself in 1650, when

Illustration 4
Hieroglyphic portrait of Emperor Maximilian 1
Detail from Albrecht Dürer's woodcut of the *Triumphal Arch of Maximilian* (1515)

Pope Innocent x charged Kircher with the responsibility for restoring and erecting the recently discovered Pamphilian obelisk. Kircher was also asked to publish a description and interpretation of the hieroglyphs on the monument. Kircher had one of the most universal minds of the seventeenth century; as one of the latter-day heirs of the Renaissance he sought to integrate all human knowledge from religion, philosophy, science, history, and art into one theological system based on a neo-platonized Christianity. Christ and his religion were for Kircher the supreme manifestation of divine truth, but this same truth was already prefigured in all earlier religions and philosophies. He found support for this view in the assertions of the Greeks that Zeus was Osiris, Cybele was Isis, and Apollo was Horus. Given the inclination of the seventeenth century to think in analogies and correspondencies, it was only natural for a man like Kircher to see a relationship between these early theological systems and cosmological order: Osiris, male principle and king of heaven, is identified as the source of all with the sun; Isis, female principle and queen of heaven, is identified with the moon. But nature is also related to this cosmic and theological order: Kircher identified iron with the destructive principle of Seth or Typhon (cf Iversen, p 95). Iversen concludes:

> Each concept and idea, each substance and element, and each phenomenon was, therefore, a divine manifestation of an ubiquitous God, the all-pervading soul of the universe. But the true connection between the phenomena and their divine originator was the mystic secret of existence, and it could only be understood by divine inspiration, by means of an esoteric knowledge and understanding of the symbolical nature of things ... His interest in Egyptology was, therefore, based on the conviction that the Egyptians were the first to have understood this fundamental truth, over which the whole of their religion and their philosophy had been formed. The Greeks had also understood it, but the Egyptians were the only people who had taken the final consequence and invented a system of symbolic writing to express it, and this writing was the hieroglyphs. (P 95)

Athanasius Kircher is now beginning to receive the attention he deserves. His neo-platonic *interpretatio christiana* of the hieroglyphs was influential in integrating hieroglyphic motifs into the emblematic mode of thought.

In their drive for knowledge the European humanists were attracted to a study of hieroglyphics primarily because they promised to unlock the *sapientia veterum* or *priscorum theologia* which primeval man had handed down in the form of pictures to protect them against profanation (cf Jöns, pp 7ff). No matter how odd, unreal, or enigmatic the pictures might be, the renaissance humanist believed them to hold hidden truth or wisdom; they did not appear 'as a capricious invention with no validity' (Schöne, p 38). Seen in this way, the hieroglyphic is related to the emblem in terms of meaning,[54] and it was a welcome discovery to the humanist with his emblematic turn of mind, which sought significance in all things. Hieroglyphics also satisfied the decorative needs of the Renaissance. They were recommended to artists as decorative motifs and to poets as a source of poetic invention (cf Jöns, 13).

Impresa[55]

The *impresa* has only two parts where the emblem has three. In spite of all the pedantic squabbling of sixteenth- and seventeenth-century Italian theorists,[56] the basic form and content of the *impresa* are not hard to define: the *pictura* contains only one or two motifs and its *inscriptio* may not contain more than three words, unless, as Paulo Giovio observes, it is in verse. In an *impresa* the *pictura* depicts such things as the salamander thriving in fire, the eagle gazing at the sun, and the phoenix reborn in the fire. According to contemporary authorities, the pictures should be true, noble, and strange (cf Praz, p 62); but there was room for such hyperboles as the winged stag. However, known errors and fictions, other than those hyperbolically intended, were to be excluded from the *impresa* (cf Praz, p 69).

The *inscriptio* should express a noble thought (cf Praz, p 70); but, according to Giovio, not directly so that every plebeian would understand it. An exclusive and esoteric intention, which derives from the practical purposes of the *impresa*. speaks from Giovio's instructions: it was a personal badge, 'a symbolical representation of a purpose, a wish, a line of conduct ...' (Praz, p 58), invented by the princes of church and state, and later adopted by academics for themselves and their societies.

Giovio listed five rules for the perfect *impresa*:

1 that the *impresa* should have just proportion between body (*pictura*) and soul (*inscriptio*);
2 that it should not be so obscure as to require a Sybil to interpret it;
3 that it makes a fine show representing things pleasant to the eye;
4 that the human figure should not appear in it;
5 that the motto be brief and in a different language from that of the author of the *impresa*, so that the sentiments should be somewhat concealed, but not obscure and misleading.[57]

Critics differ in their interpretations of Giovio's contention that there should be a just proportion between picture and motto similar to that between body and soul. Is this a formal or ontological and semantic statement? In his discussion of Georg Philipp Harsdörffer's identical definition of the emblem (which he traces to Giovio) Schöne writes: '[Harsdörffer's] formulation ... suggests that one think of the *res significans* and *significatio* in the same firm relationship to each other that obtains between body and soul' (Schöne, p 23).[58] Schöne is thinking of the semantic relationship between picture and motto, which he insists is 'firm' (*fest*), necessary, and, by implication, not capricious. Jöns, on the other hand, holds that Giovio's definitions are 'of a purely formal kind ... In this comparison there is no suggestion of an objectively valid relation between image and motto in the sense of an *analogia entis* between thing and meaning' (p 20).[59] Jöns also discusses the Harsdörffer passage cited by Schöne and concludes: 'A firm relationship between *res significans* and *significatio* is not implied by this terminology' (p 21n).[60] Then again, Sulzer places the 'body-soul' formulation within the wider context of renaissance anthropology and philosophy in which the major debate centred on the dual nature of man as half beast and half angel, and on his dignity (cf Sulzer, pp 33–4). To this it might be added that the renaissance belief that the exterior human form reflected the inner spiritual being – a belief which, among other things, plays such a telling role in renaissance love poetry, both profane and religious – lends further credence to Schöne's view that the body-soul formula has semantic implications.

This particular facet of the theory of the *impresa* has some bearing on emblematic literature, since it concerns the relation of image to meaning, which has long been a bone of contention.

The veiled and enigmatic character of the *impresa* is the subject of some disagreement, as might be expected. Again, as with the emblem, in some respects the heir of the *impresa*, the question of obscurity concerns the relationship of *pictura* and *scriptura*. Jean Hagstrum finds that in the *impresa* 'a cryptic and almost occult graphic representation was usually accompanied by an equally cryptic *mot* or posy'[61] which suggests that words and pictures present parallel riddles. Praz holds that motto and picture 'reciprocally interpret each other' (Praz, p 58), and Schöne likewise speaks of the 'interpretative function' of the *inscriptio* (Schöne, p 43; cf Jöns, p 19). On the subject of obscurity it may be well to remind ourselves again of what should be obvious. Obscurity is a relative matter: what one twentieth-century reader finds cryptic may have been clear to Giovio's contemporaries for whom the *impresa* was intended. Furthermore, as we have seen, clarity and directness were not expected of the *impresa*, the understanding of which was a matter of intellectual effort. Giovio insists that the sense of the *impresa* be hidden, but not obscure or ambiguous.

On the relation of *impresa* to emblem, Sulzer goes so far as to assert that the emblem is a 'variety of the *impresa*' and that Alciatus's contemporaries did not find the threefold structure of the emblem revolutionary, but rather viewed the epigram (i.e., *subscriptio*) as a piece of additional poetic commentary without recognizing fully its function (Sulzer, p 40). Since both *impresa* and emblem frequently draw on the same body of motifs and meanings, and since the emblem may confine itself to one or two motifs, there are no defining differences between emblem and *impresa* in terms of content and form, with the exception of the absence of *subscriptio* in the *impresa*. The basic difference is one of purpose. The *impresa* represents the 'principle of individuation' (Sulzer, p 35); it was used by one person only 'as the expression of a personal aim' (Schöne, p 45). The word itself comes from the Italian for 'undertaking,'[62] which underlines the functional purpose of the *impresa*. The emblem, on the other hand, is addressed to a larger audience, its message is general, and it fulfils a didactic, decorative, or entertaining function, or any combination of these. Estienne succinctly states the functional difference between emblem and *impresa* as follows: 'And their difference is taken from this, that the words of the *Embleme* may demonstrate things universall, and hold the rank of morall precepts, which may as wel serve for all the word [world?], as for the proper author of the *Embleme*' (Blount's translation, p 25).

One example may illustrate the difference. The motif of the phoenix was associated with such concepts as 'uniqueness,' 'regeneration,' and 'indestructibility.' The motif becomes an *impresa* when an individual chooses this motif and one of these concepts to express a personal intention. Paradin's *Devises heroiques* (Lyon, 1557) contains the *impresa* of Eleanor of Austria, Dowager Queen of France, who chose the motto 'Unica semper avis' to stand above the picture of a phoenix surrounded by fire (p 89; see illustration 5). Reusner employs the same motif with exactly the same *inscriptio*, but his *subscriptio* makes it clear that what had been in Paradin an *impresa* is now an emblem of Christ's death and resurrection. A general religious truth is made manifest through the 'fact of nature' of the phoenix. Camerarius also uses the phoenix in the flames with the *inscriptio* 'Vita mihi mors est' to embody the same message of resurrection, only here it is not applied to Christ, but rather by implication to the general reader (cf *Emblemata*, col 795).

With Heinrich Wölfflin's[63] categories in mind, Praz suggests that a distinction may be drawn in terms of open and closed form, the *impresa* with its prescriptive rules being the closed form, and the emblem with its greater freedom of development the open form (cf Praz, p 81).[64]

Be that as it may, and notwithstanding all the learned distinctions advanced

Vnica semper auis.

Comme le Phenix est à iamais seul et unique Oiseau *Theophraste.*
au monde de son espece. Aussi sont les tresbonnes cho-
ses de merueilleuse rarité, & bien cler semecs. Deuise
que porte Madame Alienor d'Austriche, Royne douai-
riere de France.

Illustration 5
From Claude Paradin, *Devises heroïqves* (Lyon, 1557)

during the heyday of the production of books of *impresa* and emblems, the fact remains that the two genres are and were difficult to distinguish from each other (cf Jöns, p 19). So much so that Rollenhagen evidently considered them synonymous, giving his book the title *Nucleus Emblematum selectissimorum, quae Itali vulgo Impresas vocant* (Cologne, 1611–13). In spite of Taurellus's discussion of emblematics in the foreward to his *Emblemata physico-ethica* (Nürnberg, 1595), the book itself is a 'mixture of the *impresa* and the emblem' (Sulzer, p 45).

Commemorative medals[65]

During the Renaissance medals were frequently struck to commemorate the deeds and accomplishments of great men, or to celebrate their high qualities of mind and spirit. Estienne suggests that the purpose of medals rests in their 'setting forth, as in a tablet, their most heroick actions and hopes ... yet there are some of them that resemble our *Devises*, as that of *Vespatian*, where there is a Daulphin about an anchor' (Blount's translation, p 19). Both in purpose and in form such medals often show strong affinities with the *impresa*. To begin with, the medal has only two parts, a brief motto and a central motif or symbolic complex comprising a limited number of separate motifs. Unlike the emblem, which addresses itself to a wide audience, the renaissance medal, like the *impresa*, was directed or dedicated to one person, and it was probably understood by only a small circle of the educated elite. Wittkower suggests that such medals 'were meant to remain dark and mysterious to the public at large' (p 74). Alberti's medal with its winged eye, which has already been alluded to,[66] is a good example (see illustration 6). There seems to be some doubt as to whether the motto 'Quid tum' necessarily refers to that which follows death, since Alberti's own commentary indicates that the laurel wreath denotes glory and joy, the winged eye God's omniscience and also the injunction to man to be as intellectually alert as possible. Whichever of the two meanings was intended, and I see no reason to rule out the possibility that both were purposed, as Alberti gives two different senses of the winged eye, the medal celebrates the great artist Alberti and it must have remained an enigma to the ordinary man, combining, as it does, hieroglyph with *impresa*.[67]

Such motifs as the phoenix, salamander, ermine, and eagle were all employed in hieroglyphs, *impresa*, heraldry, medals, and the emblem. Whereas historically all these forms predate the emergence of the first printed emblems in 1531, as the sixteenth century progressed we find instances of emblems being used in the design of medals, thus reversing the direction of dependence. Camerarius's emblems were incorporated into medals struck to honour Duke Heinrich Julius von Braunschweig-Wolfenbüttel. The civic

Illustration 6
Alberti's medal 'Quid tum.
Reproduced by courtesy
of the Trustees of the British
Museum

museum of Brunswick has a collection of medals, seven of which are described in a catalogue and compared with the original Camerarius emblems.[68] Those bearing dates were struck between 1610 and 1614. One example must suffice to illustrate the relationship. An undated medal with the motto 'Prospiciente Deo' features a tree with three branches in full leaf that have grown from graftings; in front of the tree a hare eats a plant. On the reverse side we read 'A grafting thrives when it has rain, wind, and sun; he grows large to his satisfaction for whom God and fortune coincide.'[69] The catalogue suggests that the three graftings symbolize the three territories of Hohenstein (1593), Grubenhagen (1596), and Blankenburg-Regenstein (1599) which the Duke had 'inherited' and over the succession to which he was still engaged in a number of law suits. The medal thus expresses the hope that the three territories may be happily integrated into his state.

Heraldry[70]

A number of critics have made passing reference to heraldic motifs and colours in emblems, but – with the exception of Heckscher and Wirth[71] – no systematic study of the relationship of heraldry to emblematics exists, although as Crompton has noted: 'Heraldry was firmly ... allied with the growing emblem tradition.'[72] The relationship would appear all the more relevant when one considers the overlap between heraldry and the *impresa*, an important precursor of the emblem. In purpose and in the choice of such motifs as flowers and animals, heraldry and *impresa* have much in common. They are both directly related to the individual, his family and fortunes. From the roses of Lancaster and York, through the sun and sunflower of France's King Henry IV and Queen Margaret, to the eagle of the Habsburgs, many similarities may be observed. In the sphere of 'applied' ('angewandte') or non-literary ('außerliterarische') emblematics there are many striking instances of the convergence of heraldry with *impresa* and emblem. In the residence of the then recently ennobled Eggenberg family in Graz the emblems featuring the relationship of eagle and sun represent a conscious political programme, designed to associate the Eggenberg family with the Kaiser as his loyal advisers.[73] As Wolfgang Harms comments: 'The emblem fulfils in such a case a function similar to that of the heraldic sign of a coat-of-arms laying claim to some desired possession.'[74]

Harms has studied the use of emblems as interior decorations in Schloß Weißenstein in Pommersfelden.[75] This private residence was designed and built by the powerful Lothar Franz von Schönborn, Archbishop and Electoral Prince of Mainz, Bishop of Bamberg and Erzkanzler of the German Reich. The frequent use of eagle and sun emblems had earlier been construed as an 'imperial programme' ('Kaiserprogrammatik,' cited in Harms and Freytag, p 137). Whereas that is true of the eagle-sun emblems in the residence of the Eggenberg family in Graz, Harms shows that the Schönborn lions and the imperial eagle represent a programme of self-awareness and self-glorification. The lion was the heraldic animal of the Schönborn family as the eagle was of the Habsburgs, a situation that is reflected in the necrologue for Lothar Franz, where we read 'Leo tunc Aquilam coronavit.' It is a historical fact that Schönborn was instrumental in securing the election of Charles VI as Emperor, and actually crowned him in 1711. In one emblem a heraldically stylized lion confronts seven natural lions. The number seven indicates the seven nephews of Lothar Franz, and the motto 'Sibi similes' (they are – or should be – like him) may be interpreted as the self-confident expectation of a powerful prince of church and state that his nephews will follow in his path to the greater glory of the Schönborn family (see illustration 7). Harms regards similar eagle emblems as approaching the heraldic identification of 'thing' and person thereby intended, whereby certain non-heraldic allegorical dimensions of meaning of the emblematic 'thing' are maintained.[76] The emblematic self-portrayal of Lothar Franz crosses 'the dividing lines between the emblem, the art of the *impresa* and heraldry and thereby between objective and subjective picture-related expression,' as Harms rightly observes (Harms and Freytag, p 153).[77]

Stegemeier suggests that the relationship of heraldry to the emblem deserves closer attention (p 33). Such an investigation might attempt to establish the extent to which heraldic motifs and colours are found in both the heroic device and the emblem, and furthermore, try to ascertain whether heraldic principles govern the organization and distribution of individual motifs in emblems. This might well be a fruitful field when one considers the attention Harsdörffer pays to heraldry in his *Frauenzimmer Gesprächspiele*,[78] and what is more, the close proximity of discussions of heraldry to conversations on emblems (*FG*, VII, 78–138).

Henry Peacham utilized a number of heraldic signs and indeed whole coats-of-arms in his *Minerva Britanna* (London, 1612). Many are *impresas* in which the *subscriptio* is merely a description of the device together with complimentary words about the bearer. An instance is the *impresa* of the Earl of Essex with the motto 'Par nulla figura dolori' inscribed in an empty shield, indicating that nothing can 'resemble' or portray his grief and sorrow.[79] The majority in Peacham's collection are moral emblems. There are, however, some instances of the almost emblematic use of heraldic signs. Emblem no. 15 (see illustration 8), dedicated 'To the most Christian King Lovis, XIII. King of Fravnce and Navarre,' has at its centre the three fleurs-de-lis of France. The *subscriptio*

Illustration 7
The Schönborn lions, emblematic wall decoration at Schloß Weißenstein,
Pommersfelden. Reproduced by permission of Wilhelm Fink Verlag

Henricus IV Galliarum Rex.
In Herum exurgis Ravillac.

Anagram: Henr-
IIII. occiſi a
ſcaleſtiſſimo illo
Ravillac. G.F.

M OST Chriſtian King, if yet haſt turn'd away,
   Thoſe kindly rivers, from thy royall eies
For Fathers loſſe, this little view I pray
Our Muſe reſcrues from his late Exequies:
   The leaſt of littles, yea though leſſe it be,
   It's thine, and ſigne, of her loues loyaltie.

Which, whereſoe're preſented to thy view,
(For all thinges teach vs) thinke a heavenly mind
Is meant vnto thee, by that cullour Blew,
The Gold, the golden plentie thou doſt find;
   The number of thy '* Heaven-ſent Lillies, three,
   Is concord's ground, the ſweeteſt harmonie.

* Tria lilia cœli-
tus delata. S:
Clithoveo.

Vnita

Illustration 8
From Henry Peacham, *Minerva Britanna* (London, 1612)

names the motif and the heraldic colours blue and gold, which are not discernible in the black and white printing, but Peacham's interpretation is emblematic, indeed, typological, rather than heraldic. The colour blue indicates 'a heavenly mind,' gold stands for 'plentie,' and the three 'Heaven-sent Lillies' represent 'concord' and 'sweetest harmonie.' In a parenthetical aside Peacham gives expression to a characteristically emblematic view of the universe, namely that whatever is presented to eyesight carries significance for the beholder, as he says: '(For all things teach vs).' The stanza reads:

Which, wheresoe're presented to thy view,
(For all thinges teach vs) thinke a heavenly mind
Is meant vnto thee, by that cullour Blew,
The Gold, the golden plentie thou dost find;
    The number of thy Heaven-sent Lillies, three,
    Is concord's ground, the sweetest harmonie.

Peacham's reference to blue revealing 'a heavenly mind' may be interpreted in a general sense as meaning that notions of God or providence are everywhere conveyed to the thoughtful man by that colour.[80] However, the words 'a heavenly mind / *Is meant vnto thee*, by that cullour Blew' (emphasis added) are ambiguous and can also be construed as referring to King Louis himself. A 'Christian King,' as he is called in the dedication, Louis is encouraged to have 'a heavenly mind' himself, i.e., to think heavenly thoughts[81] in a manner appropriate to a Christian ruler. Such a ruler may then well expect to find 'plenty' in his realm, especially when it is founded on 'concord's ground.' Seen in this light, Peacham is holding up a mirror to King Louis, reflecting the virtues of the true prince, in this case, virtues to which he is already committed by inheriting the heraldic coat-of-arms of France. Spiritual and temporal concerns should unite in the ruler and unity and prosperity will be the result. In Peacham's hands a heraldic sign receives a far-ranging emblematic application in moral and spiritual terms.

According to Heckscher and Wirth early examples of heraldry are not emblematic in the proper sense, because 'there was no intrinsic connection between the picture of the coat-of-arms and its motto ... Such a connection only arose after a certain loosening of the heraldic form ... made it possible to incorporate impulses from the art of devices' (col 133).[82] Indeed, Heckscher and Wirth speculate that this development may have occurred under the influence of the growing interest in emblems. This would, in fact, reverse the order of dependence, suggesting that the chicken came before the egg – that the emblem fed the heraldic coat of arms with motifs. It remains to be seen what effect heraldic motifs have in the development of the emblem genre, which lays claim to objectivity and general validity. As Harms suggests, one could begin with the emblems of Zincgref and the emblematically structured broadsides of the Thirty Years War,[83] and I would add that Peacham also merits consideration in this regard.

Medieval nature symbolism[84]

Praz was one of the first to draw attention, if briefly, to the 'emblematic ... mentality ... of the Middle Ages with their bestiaries, lapidaries and allegories' (pp 12, 24). Heckscher and Wirth speak of the 'close intellectual relationship' ('enge geistige Verwandtschaft,' col 130) of such medieval compendia to emblem-books. However, it is to Albrecht Schöne that we are indebted for a fuller account of the relationship of medieval nature allegory – or symbolism, if the term be preferred – to emblematic art.

The typological exegesis of the Middle Ages presumed an ordered and meaningful universe, created by God to reveal himself and his plan for the salvation of man. Both the medieval allegorist and the renaissance emblematist held that everything that exists points to meanings beyond the things themselves, or as Schöne puts it: 'that which exists at the same time carries significance' (p 48).[85] The higher spiritual sense, which the Scriptures and creation convey, was separated out in medieval exegesis into three layers of meaning: *sensus mysticus* or *allegoricus*, *sensus moralis* or *tropologicus*, and *sensus anagogicus*.[86]

The relationship of meaning to created thing is not arbitrary or capricious in this world-view, because meanings derive from a quality or formal aspect of the object. A single object like the sun could be seen from twenty different points of view, connoting twenty different meanings. These meanings could be good or bad depending on the qualities involved. The lion could mean Christ, because it sleeps with its eyes open; or the devil, because of its blood-lust; or the blasphemous heretic, because of its evil-smelling mouth; or the upright Christian, because of its courage (cf Ohly, p 7). Animals and flowers, in short, everything, can be interpreted in this way, as Harsdörffer says 'good or ill' (*FG*, 1, 89), in recognition of their inherent good or evil qualities (cf Schöne, pp. 49–50; Jöns, pp 31 ff).

Since each *res* is at the same time a *res significans*, there develops a 'network of world-encompassing relations and meanings' (Schöne, pp 49–50).[87] Of the three spiritual senses the emblematists developed, in Schöne's view, the tropological or moral sense, which, however, not only determines man's behaviour in social and worldly affairs, but also guides him towards salvation (p 48). As Jöns observes: 'In the Baroque moral values and salvation were still linked together' (p 51).[88] Jöns stresses more the religious sense, in both the theoretical and interpretative parts of his book.

Rosemary Freeman is doubtless correct in saying that the medieval conception of the world was disappearing in the sixteenth century, and with it the 'unified allegorical conception of the meaning of life' (p 20) contained in the much quoted words of Alan of Lille:

> Omnis mundi creatura
> quasi liber et pictura
>   nobis est in speculum,
>   nostrae vitae, nostrae sortis,
>   nostrae status, nostrae mortis,
>   fidele signaculum.

For many English and German poets of the later sixteenth and seventeenth centuries the great circle was broken; however allegorical patterns of thought continued, and among Christian writers typological thinking lived on to enrich the meditational practices of believers of all denominations. Heckscher and Wirth are thus on the right track when they observe that 'the products of medieval typological thinking enriched the works of the emblematists' (col 127).[89] Unfortunately they then proceed to assert that the analogical thought of the Middle Ages has no place in the scientific thinking of the modern period (the Age of the Baroque), which confuses the discussion in a number of ways. It oversimplifies the nature of 'scientific thought' by implying the objective and impersonally calculating approach of twentieth-century science, which does not fully describe the manner of a Giordano Bruno or a Galileo; in addition, by any definition 'scientific thought' does not adequately characterize either the conceptions or interests of the majority of poets and emblematists of the period.[90] Bertonasco offers a more accurate description: 'In early seventeenth century England it was possible for the first time to look upon material objects in a manner *exclusively* "scientific" or "objective," but it was still possible to regard these same objects as analogues of spiritual realities' (p 24).

Wolfgang Harms has shown that the 'New Philosophy' associated with such names as Copernicus and Descartes had little impact on the eschatological way of thinking and world-view of large sections of the public. Indeed emblematic attitudes of mind as well as relicts of emblematic knowledge may be discovered in didactic and scientific writings down into the nineteenth century.[91] In many scholarly and didactic works, as well as in emblem-books, we find both the modern scientific interest and the analogical method at work at one and the same time. Harms demonstrates how, in the writings of the chemist Johann Rudolf Glauber, inherited exegetical attitudes frequently underlay modern scientific description.[92]

There are many examples that indicate the persistence with which traditional information concerning nature, which would not stand any scientific test, was still accepted as true and allegorized. Erasmus Franciscus, indefatigable writer of long, emblematically embellished meditational works, could apparently in all seriousness elaborate on the 'pharmaceutical fact' that crocodile's teeth, when filled with incense and hung about the human body, act as a remedy against common fever. He notes Pliny's report that after five days the patient is cured. Franciscus transfers this curing of a physical condition from the body to the ailing soul. The 'crocodile's teeth of eternal death,' i.e., fear of eternal death, when imbued with the 'incense of prayer,' act as an antidote to the 'soul-fever,' which is sin.[93] For Franciscus this is not metaphor. He begins by first describing the treatment of fever with crocodile's teeth, and then proceeds to apply the process to the spiritual life.

Franciscus evidently believed in the efficacy of crocodile's teeth, but what happens if the emblem-writer no longer gives credence to supposed facts he has inherited from humanist or religious tradition? Quoting the Altdorf professor of medicine and the natural sciences, Nicolaus Taurellus, Schöne suggests that, where the truth and credibility of the motif is called into question, the motif loses its emblematic quality as *res significans*; it is no longer suitable for the emblem (pp 28–30). There is some indication, however, that certain emblem-writers and theoreticians held a somewhat different view on the matter of truth and the emblem. It comes down to the question: Which frame of reference for truth is the emblem-writer appealing to? More precisely: What happens when two systems of truth collide; when a fact is deemed to be true according to one system but false according to another? Estienne confronts this question head on in his *Treatise on the Making of Devises*. The author is clearly committed to the idea of truth, and, whereas the poet may exercise poetic license, i.e., 'feigne and metamorphize at pleasure' (p 45), the writers of devices are 'obliged to be strict observers of the truth' (p 45). Estienne envisages a situation where an object of nature is said to be true according to religious and humanist tradition, but false when questioned empirically:

Here we must also observe, that it is lawful to use the propriety of a naturall subject, be it animal, plant, fruit, or other thing, according to the generall approbation or received opinion of ancient Authors, though the Modernes have lately discovered it to be false, because the comparison which is grounded upon a quality, reputed true by the generality, though indeed it be false, shall be more universally received, and better understood, then if it were grounded upon a true property, which nevertheless were held false, and which were altogether unknowne to the greater part of the learned. (P 46)

What decides the contest is not 'truth,' but rather considerations of communication and reception. Estienne gives two instances. The first is the phoenix: 'Thus the Holy Fathers did use the comparison of the Phoenix to prove the Resurrection of Jesus Christ' (p 46). Estienne implies that at least a small part of the 'learned' no longer believe in the fabulous creature. The second example is of the bear 'who (according to the generall opinion) brings forth her young ones like a lump of flesh, without forme or distinction of members, untill with long licking, she renders them perfect and polished; though *Johannes Bodinus* hath lately proved the contrary in his Historicall Treatise' (p 46).

Bible exegesis[94]
In his treatment of the emblem as a 'mode of thought' Jöns lays particular stress on the role of medieval symbolism ('Ding- und Bild-Symbolik') and the allegorical interpretation of the Bible (cf pp 29–40). The basis of this allegorizing is the conviction that the words of the Holy Scriptures, unlike those of secular literature, possess not only a literal, but also a higher spiritual sense, the *sensus spiritualis* or *sensus mysticus*. However, this spiritual sense is not contained within the word itself, but resides in the content of the word, or the object to which the word refers. This is the medieval distinction between *vox* (sound of the word) and *res* (word content). This exegetical interpretation was extended from the scriptural word to everything in nature (Jöns, pp 30 ff). Jöns traces this medieval and essentially Catholic tradition through the Protestant Reformation and establishes the extent to which the method was applied to the interpretation of reality, noting the role allegorical interpretation played in the educational system as a standard feature in the instruction of rhetoric. In attitude and formal composition the medieval allegorical dictionaries have much in common with the emblem-books, not to mention the bestiaries of the *Physiologus* type. In every case the object is first described with all its qualities, to which are added individual interpretations. Again Jöns insists that there is nothing capricious about this procedure (p 40).[95]

Classical mythology[96]
Setting aside Greek epigrams from the *Planudean Anthology*, there is still the question of the role of classical mythology in the emblem-books. Figures like

Tantalus, Icarus, Medea, Hercules performing many labours, Cadmus sowing the dragon's teeth, Paris and the three goddesses, and many others appear in the emblem-books and are interpreted in many different ways. They tend to stand paradigmatically for particular virtues or vices, or lines of conduct. In other words, they typify a particular human experience, which is used for didactic purposes. See illustration 9.

For Schöne mythology can possess 'potential facticity,' which for him is an essential criterion of the emblem (p 28); when this is not the case, 'the emblem in its strict form is dissolved and an allegorical variant is produced' (p 30).[97] Jöns concurs in this view and would appear to wish to include Alciatus and secular love emblems in the category of 'allegorical variant,' doubting whether one can still speak in these cases of a picture with *res significans* (p 57n).

RECENT DEVELOPMENTS IN EMBLEM THEORY

I have endeavoured to sketch briefly the most important roots of the emblem. Clearly what is now needed is a synthesizing, yet critical, definition of the emblem which would take into account all the traditions and forms that led to its creation. For the present it will suffice to outline recent developments in the theory of the emblem, which will shed some light on the application of the term 'emblematic' to European literature. It can be shown that the negative attitude of many earlier critics – negative in that they characterize the emblem as the capricious imposition of meaning on objects and pictures – derives from a limited conception of the emblem that overstresses hieroglyphics, without acknowledging the renaissance belief that these same hieroglyphics contain keys to hidden wisdom. In addition, a negative view may arise from a one-sided equation of the emblem with the mannerist conceit, especially when the latter implies a negative value judgment.

The revaluation of the emblem that has been going on in German studies for over a decade is associated with the names Albrecht Schöne and Dietrich Jöns. Schöne's theory of the emblem, first published in article form in 1963,[98] was included in his *Emblematik und Drama im Zeitalter des Barock* (Munich, 1964, 2nd ed 1968), and incorporated into the introduction of the *Emblemata*; it quickly established itself as the standard work on the subject. However, it has been largely neglected outside Germanistic circles,[99] presumably because no translation exists. Schöne and Jöns began working on the emblem more or less at the same time, during the early sixties. Since, independent of each other, they were viewing the emblem in the light of medieval typological thought and the tradition of biblical exegesis that carried over into the seventeenth century, it is inevitable that they should be in fundamental agreement on most essential

AVARITIA.

Auaritia.

Heu miſer in medÿs ſitiens ſtat Tantalus vndis,
Et poma eſuriens proxima, habere nequit.
Nomine mutato de te id dicetur auare,
Qui, quaſi non habeas, non ſrueris quod habes.

Illustration 9
From Andreas Alciatus, *Emblemata* (Lyon, 1551)

matters. Furthermore, both acknowledge an indebtedness to Friedrich Ohly, whose essay 'Vom geistigen Sinn des Wortes im Mittelalter'[100] has also been influential in baroque studies.

In dealing with the theories of Schöne and Jöns I shall concentrate on the functional relationship of words and pictured motifs, and on the semantics of the emblem, because these are central to any theory of the emblem, and have important implications for the purely verbal art of literature.

The view that the function of the *subscriptio* is to resolve the enigma produced by the combination of *inscriptio* and *pictura* was widely shared by scholars. It was succinctly stated by Heckscher and Wirth in their book-length article in the *Reallexikon zur deutschen Kunstgeschichte*: 'In the emblem one is dealing with the combination of the word of the lemma with the picture of the icon which produces an enigma, the resolution of which is made possible by the epigram' (vol v, col 95).[101] Schöne rejects this narrow view because it does not describe the functional relationships found in many emblems. In its place he offers a characterization that is at once broader and more elastic; the function of the individual parts of the emblem is a 'dual function of representation and interpretation':

> One is probably more likely to do justice to the variety of forms if one characterizes the emblem in the direction that its three-part structure corresponds to a dual function of representation and interpretation, description, and explanation. Inasmuch as the *inscriptio* appears only as an object-related title, it can contribute to the representational function of the *pictura* as can the *subscriptio* – if part of the epigram merely describes the picture or depicts more exhaustively what is presented by the *pictura*. On the other hand, the *inscriptio* can also participate in the interpretative function of the *subscriptio*, or that part of the *subscriptio* directed towards interpretation; through its sententious abbreviation the *inscriptio* can, in relation to the *pictura*, take on the character of an enigma that requires a solution in the *subscriptio*. Finally, in isolated instances the *pictura* itself can contribute to the epigram's interpretation of that which is depicted, when, for example, an action in the background of the picture with the same meaning helps to explain the sense of action in the foreground. (P 21)[102]

> The dual function of representation and interpretation, description and explanation, which the tripartite construction of the emblem assumes, is based upon the fact that that which is depicted means more than it portrays. The *res picta* of the emblem is endowed with the power to refer beyond itself; it is a *res significans*. (P 22)[103]

It emerges from these quotations that Schöne's characterization of the emblem embraces formal, ontological, semantic, and functional elements. While remaining clear in focus and conception, it is broader and more tolerant than any view advanced to date.

In the past the most serious adverse criticism of the emblem has centred on the relationship of *pictura* to *scriptura*, i.e., the relationship of visual motif to its meaning, thing to thought, or to the application of that meaning. What relationships exist in the following randomly chosen examples? The *pictura* of an eagle shot with an arrow flighted with its own feathers means self-caused destruction.[104] The ivy which strangles the tree around which it has been able to grow signifies ingratitude.[105] The same motif could embody the concept of selfless love, or self-sacrifice.[106] For the greater part of this century readers have judged such emblems to be arbitrary. Of the emblematic imagery in the poetry of Quarles and Herbert Rosemary Freeman has observed: 'there was never any necessary likeness between the picture and its meaning.'[107] For Freeman, Herbert's 'method is always to evolve meaning by creating likenesses; the likenesses are rarely inherent or to be seen from the outset' (p 159). German critics have also missed what they are wont to call 'die eigentliche Bedeutung,' the real, natural, or inherent meaning. Behind the conception of 'necessary likeness' lurks a modern notion of organic or natural relationships and the more complex modern symbol.

Schöne argues that the 'dual function of representation and interpretation' assumes the symbolic status of the pictured motif, which is not merely a *res picta* but a *res significans*:

> That which transcends the *res picta*, which the picture refers to and which the *inscriptio*, in interpreting the picture, seeks to put into words, is called by Harsdörffer ... 'the soul of the emblem, whose translator is the caption [motto and epigram] and whose body is the picture or figure [*pictura*] itself.' His formulation, which derives from Paolo Giovio's definition of the *impresa*, suggests thinking of the *res significans* and the *significatio* in the same close relationship that exists between body and soul, and correspondingly it suggests understanding all interpretation through *inscriptio* and *subscriptio* as grasping a pre-existent and unchangeable meaning. (Pp 22–3)[108]

In Schöne's view the emblem has a special ontological status, and by comparison with the Greek picture-epigram of the *Anthologia Graeca* the emblem has 'a different level of reality':

> it and only it represents directly, in a graphic way, that which will then be interpreted by the emblematic *subscriptio*, in that the latter makes manifest the *significatio* which is contained in the *pictura* and which transcends the *res picta*. Thus every

emblem is a contribution to the elucidation, interpretation, and exposition of reality. (P 26)[109]

It follows that the *pictura* is central and primary in that the reader perceives the picture first; this Schöne calls 'the priority of the picture':

> It is therefore of no consequence whether the *subscriptio* was present first, as was the Greek epigram in the case of Alciatus, or whether later emblematists proceed from the *pictura* and then add the epigram: the emblem places the picture that is to be interpreted ahead of the interpretation deriving from the *subscriptio* and requires the reader and viewer to accept the priority of the picture. (P 26)[110]

Schöne proceeds to characterize the priority of the *pictura* more closely, shifting attention from the reader to emblematist, from reception to creation, in describing what he later names the 'priority of idea in the emblematic *pictura*' (p 28). In many cases we know that the emblematist was inspired by an actual observation. Taurellus describes how he discovered the meaning inherent in growing corn: as he was walking through a field he noticed how some ears of corn pointed downwards, while others stretched proudly up towards the heavens. The reason was clear to him: the empty husks were light and those filled with corn heavy and pointing downwards. He interpreted this as meaning true knowledge makes a man humble, whereas imagined learning leads to pride. Taurellus later incorporated this *pictura* and its meaning into an emblem in his *Emblemata physico-ethica* (see illustration 10).[111]

Schöne shows how the 'priority of idea in the emblematic *pictura*' (creator's perception) and the primacy of *pictura* (reader's reception) both hinge on the credibility of the motif, and this credibility depends on its 'facticity' or 'potential facticity' (p 28):

> Thus the *pictura* and the textual parts of the emblem that participate in its representative function depict either what actually exists or may possibly exist – something that is admittedly not always visible, or not yet visible, but could at any time appear on man's horizon or in his sphere of experience. Besides the priority of idea in the emblematic *pictura* (vis-à-vis the *subscriptio*), indeed the precondition of such primacy is the potential facticity of the image content, which determines the emblem. (P 28)[112]

This 'potential facticity' refers primarily to the attitude of the creative emblematist. Schöne also shows that classical authority frequently lent credibility to motifs which could not be factually verified (pp 27–8). However, when

Levitate superbit, & extae.
Ad Christophorum Paulum Gugel Norib.

Cernis ut optatis fæcunda est messibus æstas:
    Et dominum quanto fænore ditet ager.
Una sed ecce alias supereminet inter aristas :
    Quæ celsa erectum tollit ad astra caput.
Scilicet hac multis, at inanibus aucta locellis
    Effertur: dum nil quo retrahatur, habet.
Quem levis assurgens effert doctrina, superbis.
    Nam scit, qui doctum se putat esse, nihil.

A 5   Insunt

Illustration 10
From Nicolaus Taurellus, *Emblemata physico-ethica* (Nürnberg, 1595)

the credibility of a motif was called into question, the motif no longer appeared in an emblem (cf Schöne, p 27).

If 'potential facticity' and 'priority of idea in the emblematic *pictura*' are essential criteria of the emblem, what is the basis of this mode of thought? Renaissance hieroglyphics? Medieval exegesis, typology, and allegory? Neoplatonic theory?

Jöns and Schöne concur in that both see the medieval typological and exegetical tradition as the essential root of the emblem. This recognition, which Schöne shares with Praz, leads him to conclude that 'the relation between the symbolism of the Middle Ages and the emblem' may be traced to a 'related mode of perception' (p 46). Schöne elaborates:

> If it is correct that the emblematic picture is characterized by potential facticity and priority of idea vis-à-vis the interpretative text, which discovers in it a higher meaning, unlocks an inherent significance, then one will have to trace this back to the typological exegesis and the allegorical procedures of medieval theology which understood everything created as an indication of the Creator, and sought to reveal the significance implanted into things by God, to uncover their christological relevance directed towards the divine centre of meaning. *Omnis mundi creatura, / Quasi liber, et pictura / Nobis est, et speculum*, wrote Alan of Lille in the twelfth century. (P 47)[113]

> According to patristic-scholastic doctrine of the fourfold meaning of the Scriptures medieval exegesis had differentiated between a literal and spiritual meaning: the *sensus litteralis seu historicus* and the *sensus spiritualis*, subdividing the spiritual sense into a *sensus allegoricus*, a *sensus tropologicus*, and a *sensus anagogicus*. Above all, the interest in the *sensus tropologicus* appears to survive in the emblematists' conception and interpretation of the world. It [the *sensus tropologicus*] refers to the significance of things and facts for the individual and his destiny, for his path to salvation and his conduct in the world. In this sense, the emblematic mode still conceives of all that exists as at the same time embodying significance. Everything existing in the *historia naturalis vel artificialis* incorporated by the huge encyclopaedia of emblematic works and reflected in their *res pictae* points, as *res significans*, beyond itself, its transcendant meaning in its tropological sense determined in the *subscriptio*. (Pp 47–8)[114]

The individual meanings associated with creatures and things may be thought of as 'true,' since they derive from the form or qualities of the creatures and objects named. The diamond is hard, bright, and valuable. There is a direct and factual relationship between these qualities and the abstract meanings 'hardness,' 'brightness' or 'beauty,' and 'value.' But there are other meanings deriving from certain qualities of the diamond which science no longer regards as true, but which were accepted at the time. It was believed that the diamond resists fire, iron, and the chisel, and that only the blood of a goat would soften it.[115] This general meaning was frequently applied to Christ and his redeeming blood (see illustration 11).

The erroneous view that emblematic images are necessarily contrived or arbitrary may result from the modern reader's confusion when confronted with an image carrying different, at times contradictory, meanings. Of the snake Harsdörffer observes: 'The interpretation is frequently doubtful, and, as was said earlier of the lion, it can be good or evil. The snake is an image of cleverness, poisonous slander, and when it has its tail in its mouth, it is a representation of eternity' (FG, VII, 98).[116]

Nature can be interpreted in this way because the observer recognizes good and evil qualities in the objects of nature. Although the meaning read out of nature was derived from essential qualities, it was not always easy to depict those qualities in such a way as to make their inherent meanings accessible. Recognition of meaning depends on an understanding of the thing portrayed. Harsdörffer comments 'that one cannot judge an emblem without first having thoroughly studied the nature and qualities of the figures, which are often hidden and cannot be depicted; hence the meaning of the emblem becomes difficult and obscure' (FG, IV, 244).[117] In stressing the active participation on the part of the reader, whose knowledge of the properties of things portrayed in the emblem is assumed by the emblem writer, Harsdörffer is in agreement with established opinion. Edgar Wind has pointed out that Erasmus makes a similar observation regarding the content of hieroglyphs which 'presupposed in the reader a full acquaintance with the properties of each animal, plant, or thing represented.'[118] In another context Harsdörffer suggests that the 'comparison ... must not be drawn with accidental, but rather with essential, qualities of a thing' (FG, VII, 39).[119] Here once more Harsdörffer is allying himself with received opinion. Estienne made a point of identifying the properties of objects depicted in the impresas he discussed, and he states quite categorically: 'You must have a care that (in placing the figures of naturall subjects) you doe not destroy their essential properties, or that (for expressing your conceptions) you doe not name their proper quality, by abusing the use of them.'[120] And this because, in Estienne's view, the writers of emblems 'are obliged to be strict observers of the truth.'[121] Similarly, Christian exegetes from the time of Augustine stressed how important is the knowledge

True Vertue, *firme, will always bide,*
By *whatſoever* ſuffrings *tride.*

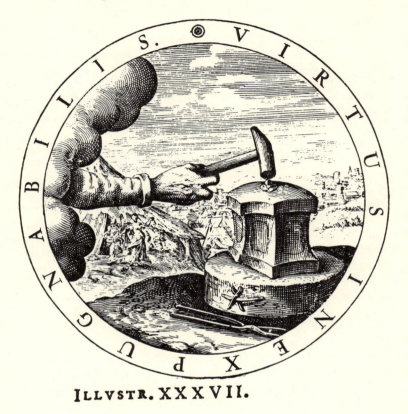

ILLVSTR. XXXVII.

Illustration 11
From George Wither, *A Collection of Emblemes* (London, 1635)

ILLVSTR. XXXVII.

This is a well-knowne *Figure*, fignifying,
A man, whofe *Vertues* will abide the trying :
For, by the nature of the *Diamond ftone*,
(Which, *Violence*, can no way worke upon)
That *Patience*, and *long-fuffering* is intended,
Which will not bee with *Injuries* offended;
Nor yeeld to any bafe dejectedneffe,
Although fome bruifing *Pow'r*, the fame oppreffe ;
Or, fuch hard *ftreights*, as theirs, that hamm'rings feele,
Betwixt an *Anvile*, and a *Sledge* of Steele.

None ever had a perfect *Vertue*, yet,
But, that moft *Prettous-ftone*, which God hath fet
On his right hand, in *beaming-Majeftie*,
Vpon the *Ring* of bleft *ETERNITIE*.
And, this, is that impenitrable *Stone*,
The *Serpent* could not leave impreffion on,
(Nor figne of any *Path-way*) by temptations,
Or, by the pow'r of·fly infinuations :
Which wondrous *Myfterie* was of thofe *five*,
Whofe depth King *Solomon* could never dive.

Good *God* ! vouchfafe, ev'n for that *Diamond-fake*,
That, I may of his *pretioufneffe*, partake,
In all my *Trialls*; make mee alwayes able
To bide them, with a minde impenitrable,
How hard, or oft fo'ere, thofe *hamm'rings* bee,
Wherewith, *Afflictions* muft *new fafhion* mee.
And, as the common *Diamonds* polifh'd are,
By their owne duft; fo, let my *errours* weare
Each other out ; And, when that I am pure,
Give mee the *Luftre, Lord*, that will endure.

Truth,

of the natural properties of things named in the Scriptures. Augustine himself writes:

> an imperfect knowledge of things causes figurative passages to be obscure; for example, when we do not recognize the nature of the animals, minerals, plants, or other things which are very often represented in the Scriptures for the sake of an analogy. It is well known that a serpent exposes its whole body, rather than its head, to those attacking it, and how clearly that explains the Lord's meaning when he directed us to be 'wise as serpents.' [See illustration 12.] We should, therefore, expose our body to persecutors, rather than our head, which is Christ. Thus, the Christian faith, the head so to speak, may not be killed in us, as it would be if, preserving our body, we were to reject God! ... A knowledge of the nature of the serpent, therefore, explains many analogies which Holy Scripture habitually makes from that animal; so a lack of knowledge about other animals to which Scripture no less frequently alludes for comparisons hinders a reader very much.
> (*The Fathers of the Church* II: *Saint Augustine* IV, 'Christian Instruction,' trans John J. Gavigan OSA [Washington, 1947], pp 82–3)

The meanings associated with the pictured motif, which were regarded as inherent in nature, are objective and general; however, they allow of specific application. The hare which sleeps with one eye open is for Camerarius an emblem of exemplary vigilance,[122] whereas for de la Perrière[123] it signifies the bad conscience which cannot sleep (see illustration 13). It is perhaps unwise to speak of the arbitrary imposition of meaning upon object, unless 'arbitrary' is related to Harsdörffer's sense of 'essential qualities.'

Sulzer argues that the characteristically three-part form of the emblem may have something to do with the renaissance pre-occupation with the philosophical question of universals. Quoting Albertus Magnus, Sulzer juxtaposes the philosophical problem and the form of the emblem. *Universalia sunt*:

ante rem	cf emblem *inscriptio* (general and abstract meaning)
in re	cf emblem *pictura* (concrete and visual particulars)
post rem	cf emblem *subscriptio* (application of general idea) (Cf Sulzer, p 39)

Such a suggestion is, of course, in harmony with the conception of the emblem as a mode of knowledge with its roots in medieval allegorical exegesis. In an essay on the baroque style of Crashaw T.O. Beachcroft[124] has likewise spoken of the emblem as a 'fragment of medieval realism' (p 421) which he relates to Platonic theories of universals: 'Taking an instance from nature and revealing an occult divine meaning is symptomatic of believing that absolutes exist before

Voyant liurer l'affaut iournellement,
Il est befoin de s'armer de prudence,
Ainfi qu'auons de Chrift enfeignement,
Qui eft feul chef, & noftre fapience.
Quand le ferpent void le bras qui s'auance
Pour le meurtrir, & que fa vie y pend,
N'a de fon corps, ains du chef fouuenance.
Aprenons donc prudence du ferpent.

Un

Illustration 12
From Georgette de Montenay, *Emblemes ov devises chrestiennes* (Lyon, 1571)

Illustration 13
From Guillaume de la Perrière, *Le Theatre des bons engins* (Paris, 1539)

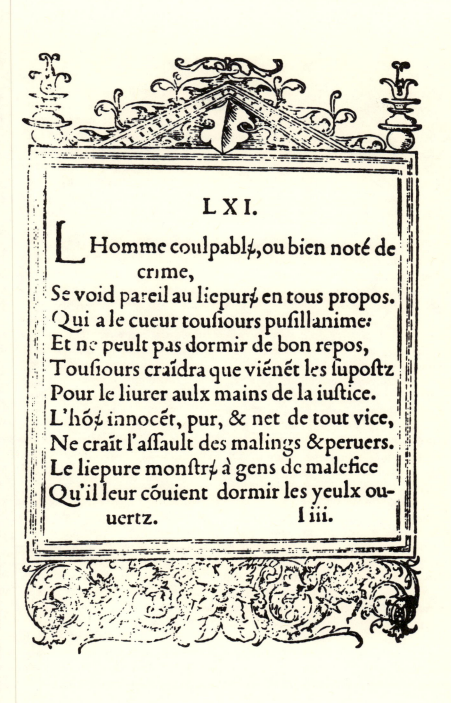

LXI.

L'Homme coulpablɇ, ou bien noté de crime,
Se void pareil au liepurɇ en tous propos.
Qui a le cueur touſiours puſillanime:
Et nɇ peult pas dormir de bon repos,
Touſiours craídra que viénét les ſupoſtz
Pour le liurer aulx mains de la iuſtice.
L'hóɇ innocét, pur, & net de tout vice,
Ne craít l'aſſault des malings & peruers.
Le liepure monſtrɇ à gens de malefice
Qu'il leur cóuient dormir les yeulx ou-
uertz.   I iii.

particulars. Henry More, the Cambridge Platonist, in discussing Emblems, says that "primordials are spermatical, not mechanical", and that is another way of saying "Universalia ante rem" ' (p 421). This renaissance preoccupation with universals in a broadly Platonic sense evidently merges with the medieval concern for allegorical exegesis, and the emblem was frequently a vehicle for their conjunction. Notions of universal ideas, the image of the great chain of being, and Nature regarded as God's Second Book are but different articulations of a sense of underlying order; and where that order was crumbling for whatever reason, emblems function as re-affirmations of the desired, if threatened, order.

Details aside, the only substantial criticism of Schöne's emblem theory which I am aware of comes from Reinhold Grimm and concerns the relationship of emblem to conceit.[125] As this disagreement bears more on the definition of the conceit than of the emblem, it does not undermine the foundation of Schöne's theory. Grimm points to an inconsistency in Schöne's account: on the one hand, Schöne contrasts the emblem with the deceptive unemblematic conceit (Schöne, p 115), and on the other, he associates the two (cf p 39, and *Emblemata*, xvi). Schöne writes: 'In many cases the emblematic *subscriptio* approaches ... the figure of the conceit, which connects by means of ingenious, acute paralogisms images and concepts widely different or even mutually exclusive to produce surprising, intellectually pointed comparisons, correspondences, or confrontations' (p 39).[126]

In order to determine whether the separation of the two phenomena is justified, Grimm takes a historical approach, enquiring how the Baroque understood the conceit and its relation to the emblem (pp 396–404). In his *Tratato degli emblemi* (1670) Tesauro argues that *impresa* and emblem are essentially conceited; both have 'corpo significante' and 'concetto significato,' they are conceited in form and substance, and like the conceit they operate 'per modo di argometo.' 'Emblems, writes the author, are ingenious syllogisms, "però che la simiglianza della proprietà significante, con la proprietà significata ha una tacita virtù entimematica." Thus they belong to the domain of Acutezza or Argutezza, "gran madre d'ogni 'ngegnoso concetto" ...' (p 399).[127] The mention of 'argomenti' and 'virtu entimematica' indicates that Tesauro's basis is Aristotelian rhetoric, although his elucidations are in fact an extension of Aristotle's enthymeme, which was merely a rhetorical form of the logical syllogism. Grimm demonstrates that the enthymeme is not necessarily 'logically imperfect,' although it is certainly a compressed figure; he argues that Aristotle distinguishes between logical and rhetorical syllogisms according to content rather than form – dialectics dealing with truths, and rhetoric with probabilities. Although Tesauro may go beyond Aristotle in his interpretation of the 'enthymema urbanum,' stressing elegant, witty, and ingenious inventions, Grimm doubts whether Hocke and Schöne are justified in calling conceits 'paralogisms' and 'alogical sophisms.' After discussing a number of passages from Tesauro which on the surface appear to lend support to Hocke's views, Grimm concludes:

> The conscious illusion, in so far as one can speak in those terms at all, stands unequivocally in the service of truth and partakes of the same 'metaphysical relations' [Jöns, p 49] which also inform the emblem. [128] Emblem like conceit, indeed the whole image-art of the Baroque, converges in Tesauro's words: 'Quanto ha il mondo d'ingegnoso, o è Iddio è da Dio.' [Trattatisti, p 24]. If then one speaks, without closer differentiation, of 'paralogisms,' 'false conclusions,' and 'sophisms,' one awakens impressions, which, put mildly, are misleading and in Hocke's case can lead to complete distortion. (Pp 404-5) [129]

In a perceptive essay on 'Metaphysical Poetry and the Poetic of Correspondencies' [130] Joseph Mazzeo has come to similar conclusions regarding the nature and function of the conceit; and this also after a fairly detailed analysis of Italian theory, in this instance Pallavicino's. He writes: 'The conceit was the instrument for [the] poetic exploration of reality' (p 231). However, in his article entitled 'A Critique of Some Modern Theories of Metaphysical Poetry' [131] Mazzeo rejects any attempt to link the conceit and emblem, [132] largely because the baroque theorists he discussed made little or no connection between the two, and treated emblem and *impresa* as incidental topics in the analysis of metaphor (cf p 92). It is not my purpose to enter the lists in the cause of the relationship of emblem to metaphysical poetry – Mazzeo is probably right in denying any simple causal connection between the two; however, it seems to me that his understanding of the conceit is greater than his appreciation of the emblem (cf p 94), leading him to exaggerate the incompatibility of the two, and generally to underestimate the significance of what he terms a 'secondary cultural phenomenon ... the emblem habit' (p 93).

The introductory chapters of Jöns's monograph on Andreas Gryphius *Das 'Sinnen-Bild'. Studien zur allegorischen Bildlichkeit bei Andreas Gryphius* (Stuttgart, 1966) represent a theory of the emblem that in most essential respects harmonizes with Schöne's theory. Jöns distinguishes between the emblem as an 'art form' and as a 'mode of thought.' [133] Taking Alciatus as his model, Jöns defines the relationship of the three parts of the emblem as 'art form' as follows: 'Between the motto and the picture there existed a more or less hidden relationship in meaning which the epigram illuminated' (p 3). [134] For Jöns the 'formal law' of the emblem is 'a relationship of tension between *pictura* and meaning resulting from the desire to create an enigma' (p 28),[135] whereby there is no necessary or inherent connection between picture and meaning (cf p 28). Creation of meaning is a function of the ingenious *inventio* of the emblem writer, who is the sole authority, 'without asserting any necessary relationship between picture and meaning that extends beyond the aesthetic' (p 23 ;[136] cf also pp 20–1, 28).

At this point Schöne and Jöns appear to part company. Schöne insists on the 'potential facticity' and inherent thing-meaning relationships as *the* characteristics of the emblem. Jöns's rejection of this definition, however, applies only to the emblem as 'art form.' As a 'mode of thought' (cf pp 28–58) Jöns also emphasizes that with its allegorical roots in the Middle Ages the emblem is an instrument of knowledge, a way of interpreting reality, the basis of which is the Christian medieval belief in the significance of the qualities of things (cf p 56). If the cosmos is a system of correspondences and analogies in which each object carries meaning imprinted in its very qualities by God at creation, then the interpretation of reality – the meanings read out of individual objects – is not capricious and accidental; it is not an invention of the poet,[137] but a recognition of an inherent meaning. Here Schöne and Jöns are in complete agreement. Furthermore, no critic has challenged this assumption, which represents a significant departure from the traditional English view as stated by Rosemary Freeman, whose study is still the basis of much English criticism.

The question naturally arises as to the relationship of the emblem as 'art form,' characterized by an 'absolute neutrality of form' (p 56) and a certain 'veiling for the sake of the pleasure of unveiling,[138] to the emblem as a 'mode of thought,' which Jöns describes as the 'final realization of a spiritual interpretation of the world based on Christian allegory' (p 56).[139] Jöns sees the relationship between emblematic form and mode of thought as follows: 'And if this allegorical thinking uses the emblematic art form as invented by Alciatus then it does so as a means to achieve clarity and greater effect' (p 57).[140]

Grimm expresses reservations about whether the absolute neutrality of the emblem form constitutes a statement about the essential nature of the emblem (cf p 386). He senses 'an inner contradiction between content and form, between spiritual and worldly, historical and theoretical findings and theses' (p 386).[141] From a structuralist point of view the emblem genre is neutral, as is every other genre for that matter. Although using one term "emblematic" for two different sets of particulars, each with a different series of characteristics – for both 'form' and 'mode of thought' – leads to difficulties both in theory and in application, I find no logical contradiction here. The suggestion is that the emblematic form is ideally suited to the emblematic way of thinking, but it can serve other purposes. The general thrust of Grimm's criticism, however, appears to be that

Jöns has concentrated one-sidedly on the theological-allegorical basis of the emblematic attitude to the world, thereby underrating the importance of the secular rhetorical tradition and the concetto aspects (cf p 386). [142]

The theories of Schöne and Jöns represent a considerable enrichment in our understanding of the phenomenology of the emblem. They also provide a firmer methodological basis for an examination of the purely verbal art of literature in the light of emblematics.

2

The Word-Emblem

The sceptic may ask whether there is such a thing as emblematic literature at all. Dieter Mehl 'raises the general question whether an emblem that is merely quoted in the text can be called an emblem in the true sense any more, a question that applies to many of the "emblems" in Elizabethan drama that have been listed by scholars.'[1] Mehl does not answer the question he quite properly raises; instead he is content to assert that it is important 'to train one's ear to discover emblematic associations' and recognize the 'function' of emblematic imagery (p 44). Dieter Sulzer gives his reasons for doubting whether the term can be usefully applied to literary texts: 'In so doing no consideration is given to the question whether it is at all meaningful to speak of emblems in the case of texts, since comparable literary *topoi* lack the constituent that language must first imitate: the pictura' (pp 39–40).[2] He also quotes with approval André Jolles's observation: 'Emblem, like symbol, has been given the general meaning of *Sinnbild* [a synonym for emblem or symbol]. In our view it is ... not an image, but an object' (p 40).[3] This is not a very purposeful distinction, since neither the visual emblem nor the verbal symbol, allegory, or word-emblem portrays an object ('Gegenstand') directly. In an emblem the object in its three-dimensional plasticity is conveyed through the visual medium of a picture, whereas in literature it is conveyed through the verbal medium of words. The major difference lies in the medium. But perhaps this is splitting hairs.

　　Whether or not terms are useful depends on the precision with which they are defined. Definitions should be sufficiently precise to permit the discovery of differences as well as similarities. To borrow a phrase from John Shearman: 'the value of any such term as ours varies in inverse proportion to the number of diverse phenomena it is made to embrace.'[4] The term 'emblematic' can be a valuable label, but its indiscriminate usage is bringing it into some disrepute.

By a word-emblem I mean a verbal image that has qualities associated with emblems. As emblematic motifs were widely employed in every literary genre,[5] and as they come closest in form and structure to emblems, it seems advisable to begin here. Surprisingly numerous are the essays dealing with the emblematic imagery of poets who lived from the sixteenth to the late nineteenth centuries. Most critics have been interested to a greater or lesser extent in using the emblem-books as sources or parallels for such imagery. The difficulties of such an investigation have frequently been stressed. A similarity, or indeed an exact correspondence, between an emblem and a poetic image does not necessarily indicate any dependence or direct influence, since, as we know, both may have been inspired by the same common source. Camerarius (cf *Emblemata*, col 335), de la Perrière (cf *Emblemata*, col 335), and the poet Martin Opitz[6] all make specific reference to saffron which, when rubbed, gives off fragrance, and this is interpreted to mean 'virtue in misfortune.' On the one hand, the emblem-books of both Camerarius and de la Perrière predate the Opitz poem, thus allowing for dependence, but on the other hand, there are many classical sources for the motif and its meaning that predate both poet and emblematists. Indeed, the problem of defining 'emblem' by reference to the motifs and materials depicted in the *pictura* is further aggravated by the fact that emblems include literary *topoi* used both before the introduction of emblem-books and after they ceased to be a cultural force. Peter Demetz has provided ample evidence of this in the case of the elm and vine, a common marriage *topos*.[7] The same is true of many mythological and Christian symbols. The problem of source and influence is discussed at some length by Mario Praz, (*Studies in Seventeenth-Century Imagery*, pp 206, 208, 210, 214), Heckscher and Wirth (col 125), Schöne (pp 60–3), and Jöns (pp 60–4).

THE EMBLEM-BOOK AS A SOURCE OF POETIC IMAGERY

It might perhaps be expected that much of the criticism written between 1920 and 1950, frequently conceived in the spirit of positivism, attempts to ferret out emblem-book sources for poetic images. A typical example is A.H.R. Fairchild's[8] note on *Macbeth*, in which the author argues that Alciatus's emblem with its picture of an eye set into the palm of a hand (Held ed, no. 37 [*Emblemata*, col 1010]) 'may well have been momentarily in Shakespeare's mind' as he wrote the words 'The eye wink at the hand.' Henry Green's *Shakespeare and the Emblem Writers* (London, 1870) is quoted in support of the search for emblem sources.[9]

A particularly naive instance of positivistic source-hunting may be found in

Edward D. Johnson's short essay on Shakespeare's use of the emblem-books.[10] In his introductory paragraph the author states: 'From the emblem writers he [Shakespeare] appears to have derived many of the mythological allusions and expressions which are found in the Plays' (p 145). It is, however, only the most obvious surface similarities that have attracted Johnson's attention. He quotes *Henry V* (III.vii), in which the Dauphin praises his horse Pegasus with the words 'he bounds from the earth, he trots the air,' comparing it with an emblem in Nicolas Reusner which has a similar picture. No closer identification of the source is given. Johnson offers another lame example of such an alleged source relationship from *The Tempest* (III.iii):

> And then, in dreaming
> The clouds methought would open, and shew us riches
> Ready to drop on me.

This is supposed to derive from an emblem in Dirck Volckertozoon Coornhert's *Recht Ghebruyck Ende Misbruyck van Eydlichen Have* (Leyden, 1585) in which a poor man receives a bag of gold and a rich man an empty bowl from two hands appearing from the clouds. Johnson's treatment of classical mythology is no more convincing. A picture of Orpheus charming animals by playing the harp to them in Constau[11] is supposed to be the source for the Orpheus references in *The Merchant of Venice* (v.i), *Two Gentlemen of Verona* (III.ii), and *Henry VIII* (III.i). In each case the similarity rests solely on the mention of Orpheus and the power of his music. Johnson also believes that Alciatus's picture of Opportunity standing on a wheel floating on the waves is the source for *Julius Caesar* (IV.iii), where 'We find almost exactly the same thought … expressed in the words':

> There is a tide in the affairs of men,
> Which taken at the flood leads on to fortune.   (Quoted on p 146)

The article continues, mentioning Actaeon, Medea, Aeneas as further examples. Although in his introductory paragraph Johnson is at pains to take the edge off certainty with such verbs as 'seems' and 'appears,' both the title and body of the essay make it clear that he does assume that the emblem-books are the source for the images. Such studies contribute very little to our understanding of literature.

An instructive example of the difficulties encountered by source-hunters is contained in W.S. Hoole's essay on Middleton's *Your Give Gallants*.[12] In the play one of the characters is hired to prepare suitable devices for the five gallants, each a master in his chosen field of gallantry. Hoole's attempt to find sources led him to investigate forty-one volumes of *impresa* and emblems, only to discover no exact duplication, though certain similarities did appear.

Lloyd Goldman's essay on Daniel's Delia sonnets and the emblem tradition,[13] with its interest in motif similarities and structural parallels, follows in the line of Henry Green and Rosemary Freeman. It is Goldman's contention that 'Daniel seized upon the idea of the English sonnet that Surrey had invented, in order to produce a Petrarchan sequence of verbalized emblems' (p 50). Goldman discovers in Daniel's sonnets the five specific properties of the device (cf p 53): the device was to include no more than three figures, and Daniel's sonnets are always divided into three quatrains; no sonnet ever contains more than three conceits; the conceits are treated in the logical but imaginative manner required of the device; the gnomic quality of the motto is also reproduced in Daniel's aphoristic final couplets, which must be considered as a single unit. All this sounds promising, if perhaps a little too perfect.

In order to document his statement that Daniel's Petrarchistic sonnets are verbalized emblems Goldman suggests that we turn first to the emblem-books (cf p 54). On the basis of Geoffrey Whitney's *A Choice of Emblemes* (1586) and the interpretations of Green and Freeman, Goldman advances three characteristics of English emblem-books. First: 'Their verse interpreted the emblems' devices in a literary fashion, often imposing upon them a symbolism and a significance of arbitrary nature' (p 54). Secondly, the symbols of emblem-books were 'often conventional or traditional and easily adaptable to the impersonal themes of the emblems' (p 54). This may be true, but it is of little help in defining the nature of the emblematic tradition. Thirdly, 'the nature and treatment of each emblem had to be, and was, simple, fitting both the verse and the device – which tended to be self-contained statements' (p 54).[14] I find this sentence syntactically confused; to what does the word 'fitting' refer? The observation that an emblem is simple is not particularly illuminating and not completely true. Does Goldman mean that it contains one motif? Or that the meaning conveyed pictorially by the motif is simple in the sense of easy to understand, or mathematically single, i.e., a single signation as opposed to plurisignation?

Goldman then proceeds to assert that: 'Almost every important conceit found in Daniel's sonnets, it seems to me, either is an interpretation of, is suggested by, or is constructed in the manner of an emblem' (p 54). In other words the emblem-books provide either a source or a parallel for every important conceit. This again sound promising, however, the burden of proof falls upon the writer. Goldman's prime example of a 'controlling conceit' (p 55), the use of which 'seems to be based ultimately on ... an emblem' (p 55), is the phrase 'my Vultur-gnawne hart' (sonnet 15). Goldman describes Prometheus emblems from Alciatus, Aneau, Whitney, and Reusner in which he finds that the poems interpreting the emblems 'foist arbitrary symbols on the details of his punishment' (p 56). Like the explanatory poems in the emblem-books, Daniel's poem is 'simple, self-contained, and impersonal in the way it treats the punishment of Prometheus *per se*, and in the manner in which it depends on the stylized picture of Prometheus' predicament as it is found in the devices of the emblematists' (p 57). If this description is intended to demonstrate the emblematic quality of Daniel's sonnet, it is unsuccessful, because statements such as 'simple, self-contained and impersonal' are not defining characteristics since they apply equally to other forms of verbal image. If Daniel's conceit were in fact 'stylized ... as it is found in the devices of the emblematists,' we might have a more satisfactory description. However, I am not persuaded that the phrase 'Vultur-gnawne hart' is stylized.

Goldman next proceeds to enumerate no fewer than twenty-one further conceits which he traces back to their 'parallel ideas as figures in the devices recorded by Whitney and others' (p 58). However, he admits that, like the conceit of the 'Vultur-gnawne hart,' the other twenty-one may not derive ultimately from emblem-books. None the less, he is convinced that they are all 'employed in a manner similar to that of the device and conceit of Prometheus and the vulture' (p 58), by which he means 'the type of stylized presentation of action' (p 59). Among the twenty-two motifs listed, no fewer than nine are taken from classical mythology; these include Actaeon, Sisyphus, Fortuna, Prometheus, Nemesis, Icarus, Narcissus, Fame, and Hercules.[15] When we consider how reluctant Schöne and Jöns are to accept such classical materials as emblematic, the probability that poetic conceits employing the same figures are emblems in any proper sense of the term is somewhat remote. In conclusion, Goldman's essay contains the mixture of perceptive structural comment, erroneous generalization about the arbitrary nature of emblems, and the problematic inclusion of classical motifs as emblems that has characterized much English scholarship.

One of the few convincing source studies is Dietrich Jöns's essay on Grimmelshausen,[16] which opens with a succinct repetition of his definition of the emblem as 'art form' and 'mode of thought.' He begins by drawing attention to examples of 'spiritual nature contemplation' in *Simpliciccimus* and the *Vogelnest*. On his desert island the hermit Simplex, who lacks meditational works, recalls the example of a holy man to whom the whole world was a great book in which all things taught spiritual lessons. In like manner the apple reminds Simplex of the fall of man, the fire of hell, and so on. For the heroes of both novels such religious emblematizing is a preparation for, or consequence of, conversion.

Jöns relates two examples of the religious word-emblem – flower bulbs connoting hope, and the activity of bees and spiders which from the same flowers draw honey and poison respectively – to 'emblematic parallels' (p 386) in the works of Johann Saubert and Jakob von Bruck. In fact he illustrates the emblematic tradition of the spider–bee motif by quoting Picinelli, Valerianus, and Palladius. He concludes that these things of nature are mirrors of generally valid truths (p 388), and not simply 'Exempla.' The function of these emblems is to provide the reader with moral criteria against which to judge the actions of the characters of the novel. Jöns is careful to stress that 'emblem' is used here in the sense of 'mode of thought' (p 388), and that 'the criteria for the identification of an emblematic source are very often inadequate' (p 388). [17]

None the less, Jöns has discovered a precise emblematic source for three sayings in Simplicissimus in Zincgref's Sapientia picta. All three instances are to be found in the satirical dream allegory of the tree. The emblems depict a young bull leading a herd, an oil lamp burning at night, and an holm-oak in a storm. In each case Grimmelshausen quotes the interpretative verses of the emblem with only minor alterations in the text of his novel, and the manner in which he does so indicates that he had a copy of Sapientia picta at hand while he was writing Simplicissimus (cf p 391).

The critic is greatly aided in his pursuit of sources by a knowledge of which books the writer in question actually possessed, and even more so by the marginal notes and other indications which some poets thoughtfully added concerning their sources. Some English and German dramatists are particularly helpful in this regard. It is known that Ben Jonson possessed a copy of Nicolas Caussin's De Symbolica Aegyptiorum Sapientia (Paris, 1634) which contains a reprint of Horapollo. Furthermore, Jonson acknowledges his indebtedness to Cesure Ripa's Iconologia in several masques. Don C. Allen's essay on Jonson and the hieroglyphics [18] is primarily concerned with the use to which Jonson put Ripa's and Valerianus's hieroglyphics in his masques. Allen describes Jonson's use of Ripa as follows: 'Sometimes he takes over Ripa's description verbatim; sometimes he combines the parts of two descriptions; sometimes he takes over part of Ripa's description and adds to it matter drawn from other sources or of his own invention; and sometimes he invents a new character on Ripa's pattern' (cf p 296).

The question of Jonson's sources is taken up by Allen H. Gilbert in a book-length study entitled The Symbolic Persons in the Masques of Ben Jonson (Durham, North Carolina, 1948). Much of the symbolism in the masques takes the form of allegories of virtues and vices, who are 'so dressed and provided with attributes as to tell the spectator their qualities' (p 3). Ripa's Iconologia provides a 'key to the allegorical art of the seventeenth century' (p 3). Gilbert appears to be in basic agreement with Allen on both the extent and the manner of Jonson's use of Ripa's work (cf p 7). In his introductory chapter Gilbert explains Jonson's use of the terms 'hieroglyphic,' 'emblem,' and *'imprese,'* providing illustrations of each. The major part of the book (pp 30–258) takes the form of an alphabetical catalogue of the allegorical, mythological, and historical persons who appear in Jonson's masques and entertainments. Each figure is described and compared with possible iconological and hieroglyphical sources, and Ripa's is the name most commonly cited.

Schöne devotes the first chapter 'Hinweise bei den schlesischen Dramatikern' ('References by Silesian dramatists' pp 3–14) of his *Emblematik und Drama im Zeitalter des Barock* to examples of dramatic imagery which certain Silesian dramatists gloss with reference to emblem-books. Schöne reports that Lohenstein makes overt reference to Saavedra no fewer than fourteen times in the notes which the dramatist appended to his plays, and in this Lohenstein is no exception (cf p 7). Gryphius, Hallmann, and Haugwitz cite Saavedra, Typotius, Isselburg, and Camerarius among others (cf pp 8–14). A number of source studies which identify with greater or lesser success emblem-book sources for poetic imagery are given on pp 203–4.[19]

THE EMBLEM-BOOK AS A PARALLEL FOR THE WORD-EMBLEM

Roger Sharrock's essay 'Bunyan and the English Emblem Writers'[20] takes up an intermediary position between the pursuit of sources and the search for parallels. In discussing Bunyan's debt to emblem literature Sharrock stresses that he is a 'man with a strong visual imagination and a mind that delighted in pictures and "similitudes"' (p 106). He notes that much of the symbolism of *The Holy War* 'is part of that desire to find infinite meaning in the most ordinary things which is also present in the emblem writers' (p 106). The emblem habit reinforced a figurative attitude towards religious truth which went back to the medieval sermon. Bunyan is an artist of 'archetypal similitudes ... much of his imagery is borrowed from the world of the emblem books' (p 106). For example, the Interpreter's House in *The Pilgrim's Progress* is a kind of emblem theatre, devoted to a series of emblem pictures. Although Sharrock believes that it is 'safe to assume Bunyan's knowledge of Quarles, Whitney, and probably Wither,' he is aware of parallel traditions which may overlap, and he warns that 'we must beware lest we assign to literature what is also the property of the popular sermon and the proverbial wisdom of the countryside' (p 107).

Sharrock finds a 'superficial resemblance' between the picture of Evangelist and Quarles's frontispiece to the first edition of the *Emblems*, but 'the most striking parallel is with one of Whitney's emblems, Book II, p. 225' (p 107), which shows a pilgrim turning his back on a globe of the world. Sharrock takes issue with an earlier critic who holds that this particular emblem contains the germ of *The Pilgrim's Progress*; the figure of the pilgrim was 'firmly fixed on the popular mind' (p 108), and the pilgrim metaphor was extremely common in the Christian tradition.

The dusty room, the room with two children representing Patience and Passion, and the man in the iron cage are all convincingly compared with emblems. The room in which a man is trying to put out with water a fire which is burning against a wall is 'another of those elaborate theological emblems, in which we admire the mechanical exactness of the imagery' (p 110). The passage in *The Pilgrim's Progress* reads as follows:

> This Fire is the Work of Grace that is wrought in the Heart; he that casts Water upon it, to extinguish and put it out, is the Devil: but in that thou seest the Fire notwithstanding burn higher and hotter, thou shalt also see the reason of that: So he had him about to the backside of the Wall, where he saw a man with a Vessel of Oyl in his hand, of which he did also continually cast (but secretly) into the Fire.

Sharrock stresses that it is pointless to seek 'precise originals' for some of Bunyan's universal and general symbols, such as the city of righteousness and the warrior of faith. The essay concludes with a discussion of some apparently original emblems. The man with the muck-rake is 'emblematic to the finger-tips,' but the author confesses that 'after ransacking Whitney, Quarles and Wither we find none to correspond' (p 112). The venomous spider (p 114) and the robin with a large spider in its mouth (p 115) seem, according to Sharrock, to be original.[21] Other scenes, such as those which depict chickens looking up to heaven as they drink and the bath of sanctification, are too general to warrant being called emblems. 'True emblems,' according to Sharrock, are 'endowed with arbitrariness and particularity' (p 115). A certain inconsistency may be detected in Sharrock's essay, since on the one hand he draws attention to the emblematic attitude to the universe (p 107) in which all creatures are held to carry the meanings imprinted on them by their Creator, and on the other hand the true emblem is supposed to be arbitrary.

On the whole, critics have been more successful when they interpret literature against the general background of emblem-books, using them not as sources but as parallels, or keys, to the understanding of literature. In this perspective the emblem-books are viewed as repositories of visual motifs and their attendant meanings. Dennis Biggins, for example, discusses the scene in *The Winter's Tale* where Antigonus is killed by a bear during a storm on the seashore.[22] After reviewing some opinions on the function of the scene he concludes that the bear itself is a symbol, and Antigonus's taking off is a 'complex function of symbolic, tonal, and structural movements in the play' (p 8). At the beginning of the scene Antigonus is already 'an emblem of broken integrity' (p 8; 'emblem' is not further defined). Biggins interprets Shakespeare's bear in the tradition of those carnivorous wild beasts that 'figure constantly in Shakespearian imagery as types of hideousness, ferocity and savage, remorseless cruelty' (p 10). Moreover, bears appear frequently in Elizabethan literature, proverbial wisdom, and the emblem-books to exemplify these qualities. Like the storm itself, which signifies destruction and moral disorder, the bear is 'the instrument of divine wrath, sparing the helpless and innocent infant, but hunting down the guilty agent of tyranny' (p 12). Biggins speculates that this aspect may have been emphasized by some dumb show in the original performances. 'The emblematic qualities of certain animals are emphasized in the Elizabethan emblem-books, which utilize them for moral *exempla* somewhat in the manner of the medieval bestiary tradition' (p 12). Biggins refers particularly to the popular belief that bears do not touch dead bodies, which appears in plate 11 of Henry Peacham's *Minerva Britanna* (London, 1612). This may be taken as a clue to the way Shakespeare's bear acted, and suggests how the scene should be understood. The infant Perdita, tightly swaddled, would lie motionless, apparently dead, so that the bear would perhaps sniff at her before pursuing Antigonus. The bear scene thus underlines in dramatic terms the play's movement from destruction to re-birth. As Biggins observes, the anomalies in the symbolism are only apparent; Shakespeare's symbols often 'operate in several different directions at once, so that the bear here is, like Antigonus, at once an emblem of divine retribution and an embodiment of Leontes' savage cruelty' (p 13). Perhaps it might be stressed that popular beliefs about the nature and habits of bears are the basis for this symbolic operation in different directions.

Eric Jacobsen's book *Die Metamorphosen der Liebe und Friedrich Spees 'Trutznachtigall'* (Copenhagen, 1954) contains one of the most thorough treatments of emblematic parallels to a particular literary work. Chapter 5 (pp 70–144) deals with the central question of Spee's love metaphors. After some introductory pages on Petrarchism and the pastoral Jacobsen makes a systematic investigation of the motifs, metaphors, and themes of love in Spee's *Trutznachtigall*, relating them to European Petrarchism by quotations from German, French, English, and Neo-Latin poets, and also to older traditions reaching back to the classics. At the end of each discussion Jacobsen cites parallels in the emblem-books, many of which are reproduced in this richly illustrated work.

One example from this long chapter must suffice. The motif of the name written in a heart is a variation on the theme of the picture of the beloved

painted in the lover's heart. Jacobsen first quotes a secular love poem by
Zesen:

Lisander's name would one read
printed in his beloved's heart.

Lisander's nahmen wuerd' man lesen
in seiner Liebsten Hertz getrükt.   (Jacobsen, p 114)

then he cites religious poems by Zesen and Balde which employ the same
motifs. Among the several quotations from Spee is the following:

O Jesu, Jesu wondrous name
How you burn in my heart.

O Jesu, Jesu, Wundernam',
Wie brennest mir im Herzen!   (Jacobsen, p 115)

The paragraph ends with a reference to the visual treatment of this motif by the
emblematist Daniel Cramer, *Emblemata sacra* (Frankfurt, 1624), p 103, and
François Berthod, *Emblesmes sacrez* (Paris, 1665), p 328, which is reproduced
in Jacobsen's book.

In a number of articles using emblem-books to support his interpretations of
literature, John M. Steadman stresses that the emblem-books are the transmit-
ters of tradition, not necessarily unique sources for ideas. In his short essay on
Una and the ass in *The Faerie Queene* (book I)[23] Steadman offers a new and
more plausible explanation of the significance of Una's riding on a 'lowly asse.'
In Steadman's view the ass symbolizes the ministry. Both Alciatus and Whitney have emblems in which worshippers kneel before a statue of Isis carried on
the back of an ass, which foolishly imagines itself to be the object of adoration.
Whitney and Alciatus's editor and commentator Claude Mignault interpreted
the emblem as a warning to the clergy. Spenser treated the fable with considerable freedom, shifting emphasis to the ignorant worshippers with their exaggerated reverence for their ministers, leading to a neglect of the Scriptures. As
Steadman notes, Spenser suggests that Una 'the orthodox doctrine' be 'carried
by her proper vehicle, the ministry of the word' (p 135).

Some critics compare literature with emblem-books, not only to uncover
hitherto unrecognized meaning, but also to enhance our understanding of the
structure and aesthetic values of the literary work. Marc F. Bertonasco in
Crashaw and the Baroque has made a concerted effort to correct the serious
misreadings of Crashaw's poetry by modern critics who have been unable or

unwilling to set aside private taste and expand their sensibilities to embrace the aesthetic of an earlier period. He argues that those conceits that have been attacked as 'merely ingenious, purely decorative, grotesque or perverse, are in fact emblems ... Failure to perceive this fact is perhaps the factor chiefly responsible for those numerous and gross misapprehensions which abound in critical studies' (p 8). He makes valuable comparisons with the emblem-books in order to show how usual, how normal, and, in fact, how English Crashaw's imagery was; how acceptable it was to the contemporary English reader; and just how plainly it stood in the mainstream of emblematic tradition. And this of the religious poetry of blood and wounds, breasts and suckling, cupid and anima, cardiomorphoses and animal lore (cf pp 27–39). Bertonasco's concern is not to uncover actual sources, but rather to reveal 'the emblematic mode of expression,' which 'more than individual plates ... affected his poetic utterance' (p 38). A number of studies which establish parallels between emblem-books and literary works are listed on pp 204–6.[24]

TOWARDS A PHENOMENOLOGY AND TYPOLOGY
OF THE WORD-EMBLEM

A number of related but different terms have been used to denote emblematic imagery in literature: they include 'emblem,' 'device,' and 'icon.' Of these 'icon' has enjoyed a greater vogue in English scholarship than in German, perhaps under the influence of Panofsky[25] and W.K. Wimsatt's collection of essays *The Verbal Icon* (Lexington, 1954). Wimsatt's definition and occasional use of the term overlap in certain particulars with the account of the word-emblem offered in this chapter. Wimsatt provides the following explanatory note on 'verbal icon':

> The term icon is used today by semeiotic writers to refer to a verbal sign which somehow shares the properties of, or resembles, the objects which it denotes. The same term in its more usual meaning refers to a visual image and especially to one which is a religious symbol. The verbal image which most fully realizes its verbal capacities is that which is not merely a bright picture (in the usual modern meaning of the term image) but also an interpretation of reality in its metaphoric and symbolic dimensions. (P x)

Wimsatt applies this definition to romantic imagery: Comparing William Lisle Bowles's sonnet 'To the River Itchin' with Coleridge's 'To the River Otter,' Wimsatt writes: 'The picture is more vivid ... also ... certain ideas, latent or involved in the description, have much to do with its vividness' (p 108; cf also p 109). 'Iconic or directly imitative powers of language' (p 115) are important in poetic structure, which Wimsatt defines as 'a fusion of ideas with material, a statement in which the solidity of symbol and the sensory verbal qualities are somehow not washed out by the abstraction' (p 115). Wimsatt briefly characterizes three kinds of iconicity. The metaphysical variety: 'The "stiff twin compasses" of Donne have a kind of iconicity in the very stiffness and odd emphasis of the metrical situation' (p 115); the neoclassical kind, which is 'of a highly ordered, formal or intellectual sort' (p 115); finally, the romantic form: 'romantic nature poetry tends to achieve iconicity by a more direct sensory imitation of something headlong and impassioned, less ordered, nearer perhaps to the subrational' (p 115).

'Iconic' is used by Jane Aptekar, and by Geoffrey Durant in an article on Wordsworth (*Mosaic*, 5 [1971], 107–19), among others. However, it would be wrong to assume that all English critics understand and use the term in the same manner. Peter Fingesten, for example, has some very definite views on the nature of iconic and non-iconic imagery:

> A so-called iconic symbol (identity between form and idea) requires no intuition or leap of imagination from the symbol to the concept because one sees, feels or experiences that the flame is heat, blood is life, wheel is motion, skull is death, hammer is power, phallus is procreation and so forth. A non-iconic symbol (no identity between form and idea) requires one leap – from the symbol to the concept: the wheelcross for a member of the Trinity, the anchor for salvation, the fish for Christ, seven golden rays for seven gifts of the Holy Spirit, the enclosed garden for the Virgin Mary, among others. [26]

The basis of the distinction advanced by Fingesten lies in the 'identity between form and idea.' This simple affirmation, however, fairly bristles with problems. Does Fingesten mean the identity of whole thing with a single meaning? with a meaning which is fixed and invariable? And is there not more than a hint of the fallacy of universal accessibility of meaning? The postulated inherence of significance is understood here in the most simplistic sense. Any attempt to classify verbal images by means of this definition leads inevitably to the rejection of many genuine word-emblems as non-iconic.

The term 'Ikon' is sometimes applied by German scholars to a particular kind of poem, in which the theme is stated in the title or opening line and then varied by means of a series of images, each separate and self-contained and usually encapsulated in a line of verse. The *Ikon-Gedicht* is usually associated with the name of Christian Hofmann von Hofmannswaldau.

If Sulzer is right when he asserts: 'Success has never attended the attempt ...

to establish the emblem as a form in its own right between allegory and symbol'
(p 39),[27] then the parallel phenomenon, the word-emblem, is likely to prove
equally difficult to define. Most critics have pursued emblematic motifs in
literature without adequately describing their quarry. Mere surface similarities
in picture content or parallels in wording between a poem and the *scriptura* of an
emblem are not enough. It is the manner in which the poet handles his visual
motif that determines whether or not it is an emblem. The verbal image must be
capable of translation into an emblem; it must have the qualities of an emblem.
This has little to do with the actual motif used.[28]

The visual quality of the word-emblem

To insist that the word-emblem must be a visual image may sound uncomplicated, but such an assertion is not without its problems. Visualization is not a
constant. If from the pulpit today we hear the words, 'Each must bear his cross,'
or when the song asserts that 'When your heart is on fire, smoke gets in your
eyes,'[29] I doubt whether we pay much attention to the metaphors 'cross' and
'fire.' We probably hear only the abstract meanings 'hardship' (cross) and
'passion' (fire). Today many readers are inclined to read similar passages of
poetry abstractly. The mixed metaphors of the Elizabethan poets and the
baroque imagery of many German poets of the seventeenth century startle
some modern readers, who frequently resolve their difficulties by reading such
imagery abstractly. That is, they either reduce the startling passage to a
denotational statement, or they interpret the key images in terms of abstract
notions. At the opposite end of the scale we find commonplace statements in
baroque literature which none the less depend on a figurative rather than literal
use of words. As I see it, the emblematist, the poet, and the reader in the
seventeenth century could experience both the startling and the commonplace
passages *visually*. Some evidence to support this view may be gathered from the
emblem-books themselves. For example, Georgette de Montenay illustrates the
notion that the king's heart is in the hand of God by a picture in which a hand
appears from a cloud holding a human heart that wears a crown (see illustration
14). The motto reads 'Dominus Custodiat Introitum tuum'; the poem beneath
the picture, which functions as a *subscriptio*, begins with the statement, 'le
coeur du roy est en la main de Dieu.'[30] The emblematist can render visual many
familiary sayings, such as 'where your treasure is there your heart is.' B. van
Haeften,[31] J. Mannich,[32] and D. Cramer[33] illustrate this idea with a picture of a
human being standing before a sack of money, or treasure chest, in which a
human heart sits upon a pile of gold. The modern reader is inclined to read these
commonplace statements abstractly, whereas the seventeenth-century poet,
emblematist, and reader frequently took them literally and visually.

DOMINVS CVSTODIAT.
INTROITVM TVVM

Le cœur du Roy eſt en la main de Dieu,
Qui le conduit ſelon ſon bon plaiſir.
Se plaindre donc du Roy, n'a point de lieu.
La cauſe en nous pluſtoſt deuons choiſir,
Quand ne l'auons ſelon noſtre deſir.
France, à ton Roy vieil de ſens, ieune d'aage,
Un regne heureux Chriſt donne & le loiſir
De ſe monſtrer treſchreſtien preux & ſage.

Je

Illustration 14
From Georgette de Montenay, *Emblemes ov devises chrestiennes* (Lyon, 1571)

Bertonasco draws attention to the danger of an incomplete response on the part of the modern reader, who may remain only half aware of the thought contained in a passage like the following from Crashaw's 'A Hymn of the Nativity':

We saw Thee in Thy balmy nest,
Young dawn of our eternal day;
We saw thine eyes break from the East,
And chase the trembling shades away.[34]

He also points to a stumbling-block of a different, in fact, opposite, kind: a too vivid visualization. 'Where the poet expects them [readers] to meditate or at least to grasp a concept, they remain immersed in sensuous particulars' (p 16). Kingsley Widmer attempts to resolve some of the difficulties in appreciating the similes for Satan and Christ in Milton's longer poems by seeking an intellectual coherence beneath the visual particulars, which have encouraged critics to apply the wrong aesthetic to such poetry. Too great an emphasis on visualization and the desire to relate organically the visual details of imagery only draw attention away from the poems' conceptual framework.[35]

The poet and the emblematist combine visual motifs in such a way as to produce quite unusual results, that is to say combinations unfamiliar to twentieth-century readers. At one time it was common to dismiss them as bad taste; now they are often simplified in reading and made abstract. I am suggesting that they should be read *literally and visually*, and interpreted according to emblematic tradition. But how can one in fact prove that the startling, combined image was intended to be taken visually; can it be shown that the contemporary reader experienced it visually? In sonnet 42 C.R. von Greiffenberg writes:

God tests the gold of faith, in the crucible, our body;
and knows how to control the fire of the cross
that both gold and crucible remain intact.

Gott probt des Glaubens Gold / im Tiegel unsrem Leib: /
und weiß des Creutzes Feur doch also zu regiren /
daß beedes unverseert / das Gold und Tiegel / bleib.[36]

Is 'the fire of the cross' an abstract phrase or an image? More specifically, is 'cross' an abstract term meaning 'trial,' 'tribulation,' and 'misfortune,' or does it denote the object cross, and embody those meanings, thus preserving the visual quality of the strange combination? In my view the object cross was intended and was read visually and emblematically. Lexicographers like Grimm, literary purists, and those who apply organic principles of literature indiscriminately might argue that the word 'cross' has lost its metaphoric meaning and become an abstraction, which alone makes possible such combinations as 'fire of the cross,' 'stone of the cross,' and 'steel of the cross.'[37] This is improper argumentation, since it proceeds in a circle to conclusions that are identical with initial propositions, the rightness of which was never demonstrated. One could point to cross imagery in emblem-books which exactly parallels the poetic images quoted above. For example, van Haeften has wine presses, coaches, ship's masts and rudders in the shape of a cross.[38] J.W. von Stubenberg's translation of Bacon's speeches[39] is introduced with an emblematic picture in which thorn bushes grow from the ground on which is placed a cross; a leafy plant pushes up through the thorns towards the sun which is encircled with thunder clouds. The accompanying poem speaks of 'misfortune's earth' ('Unglücks-Erd'), 'clouds of misfortune' ('unglückvolle Wolken'), and 'misfortune's thorny ground' ('Unglückdornengrund'), but no mention is made of the cross, although it appears in the picture. The pictorial presence of the cross and the absence of the word 'cross' demonstrate that the cross can function, visually, figuratively, and in a variety of combinations.

The emblem-books, then, contain many examples of things familiar and startling in picture form. The poetry of the period likewise brings us words describing similar objects and their combinations which produce visual impressions that the reader must interpret intellectually. Were this not so, no poet could write the following:

Oh that my breath were a praise-sweetened wind,
and blew to the stars the flames of my love!
Oh, that I cannot like phoenix ignite with love
and be consumed joyfully in so highly noble a desire.

Ach daß mein Athem wär ein lob=durchsüsster Wind /
und Sternen=werts aufführt die Flammen meiner Liebe!
ach daß ich mich vor Lieb wie Fönix nicht entzünd' /
und ganz beglückt vergeh in so hoch edlem triebe.   (Greiffenberg, sonnet 25)

The imagistic use of 'phoenix' depends on the literal and visual meaning of 'flame'; were the latter abstract there would have been no basis for the association with 'phoenix.'

Assuming that much baroque imagery is visual and that the basis of the word-emblem is a picture, we are led to the question: how does the word-emblem differ from the ordinary visual image? We may feel that the uncomplicated pictorial image with any accompanying explanation is too simple and obvious to be an emblem. An image such as 'Misfortune's wave breaks on the rock of virtue' ('Die Unglücks-Welle bricht am Tugend-Fels entzwey') might come to mind, since 'misfortune's wave' and the 'rock of virtue' are visual and their meanings are also obvious.[40] However, 'obviousness' is hardly a satisfactory criterion. To whom are these images obvious? And by the same token one might also ask: to whom is the sense of the complicated image not obvious? The twentieth-century reader may be perplexed by an emblematic image in a poem, assuming a protective rather than predatory role for the eagle in its relationship to the mole:

> To reach the eagles
> I act as a mole.

> Zu denn Adlern zu gelangen
> gieb Ich Einen Maulwurff Ab![41]

He may also ponder over the relationship of amber to a powerful prayer to God:

> [the sea of tears] holds the oyster-pearl in its womb
> which is joined by the amber, the call-prayer.

> Der Buße Muschel Perl in seinem [=Meer] schoß es hält /
> zu dem die Amber sich / das Ruf=Gebet / gesellt.   (Greiffenberg, sonnet 55)

Some readers will doubtless feel that these images are anything but obvious, and even judge them arbitrary. The fact is that, although they are allusive (and for the modern reader even elusive), they are not arbitrary; they were understood by the writer and the contemporary educated reader for whom the poem was intended. Eagle, mole, and ambergris together with their inherent meanings are embedded in the scientific lore of this period. To return to the simple images of 'misfortune's wave' and 'the rock of virtue,' these are emblematic in form and structure, providing at one glance the object, or rather its picture, and its abstract meaning, and furthermore in a manner peculiar to the emblem with its picture and motto.[42]

In the poetry of later periods images such as 'sceptre,' 'laurel,' and 'palm' can function as simple metonyms, but in the poetry of the sixteenth and seventeenth centuries many of these objects are associated with so many distinct objective meanings that they can stand alone without explanation, and function as emblems on an understood basis (cf Schöne, p 130). Freeman calls them 'abstract symbols' (pp 22–3), which she defines as images, concrete and complete, standing for an idea. They are, however, not simply abstract, since the word means literally the object referred to, and at the same time embodies meanings associated with the object.[43] They are *emblems*; the term is preferable, because it is more restrictive.

What is it, then, that makes a visual image emblematic? We could perhaps ask whether the motif itself is emblematic. But what does that mean precisely? If we are asking whether the poetic motif also occurs in an emblem-book, then, as was indicated earlier, we may be led to false conclusions. The truth is that in the seventeenth century any object or motif could be used emblematically. Harsdörffer frequently discusses the nature, form, and use of emblems in the *Frauenzimmer Gesprächspiele*. On one occasion the question is asked, whether anything and everything can be employed in emblems. The affirmative answer is: 'All that is visible painting undertakes to represent; that which is invisible can be understood through the art of the emblem by means of the motto' (*FG*, IV, 169; cf also p 176).[44]

The characteristics of the word-emblem

By comparing emblems with similar passages of poetry we may arrive at a description of the characteristics of the word-emblem which will pinpoint the differences between the emblem and other visual images in poetry.

Let us begin with an example compared by its author with an emblem-book, for then we know that the poet was conscious of the similarities between his image and the emblem. (This, incidentally, lends further support to the view that such images were visually intended). In one of the most influential of all collections of *impresa*, the *Symbola divina et humana* ... (Prague, 1601–3), Typotius has a picture of a heart sitting in a nest of thorns.[45] Andreas Gryphius refers to the Typotius source when he writes: 'Does not her heart now tremble in nothing but thorns?' ('Zittert nicht anitzt ihr Herz in lauter Dornen?').[46] The poetic image and the emblem are simple in so far as both feature only two motifs, a heart in thorns. The meaning is clear: the heart trembles in adversity. The structure of the image (in terms of picture and meaning) is characteristically emblematic. The picture presents objects, which are visual and concrete ('dinglich'), qualities described by Warren as 'hardness' and 'palpability' (p 74). For Bertonasco the word-emblem is characterized by 'a peculiar, often gross, quite unmistakable visual and tactile vividness' (p 38). Furthermore, these objects tend to be static. As Beachcroft observes: 'The true emblematic image stands motionless.'[47] The natural objects are combined unorganically in one picture; that is, the relationship between the objects is not given in nature. However, that is no reason to call the emblem 'contrived,' 'capricious,' or 'arbitrary.' Finally, there is often a 'dwelling on concrete detail, or sensuous particulars, which are directly related to clear concepts, religious or moralistic' (Bertonasco, p 38).

The meaning of the emblem is unambiguous. It is in fact univalent; that is, the context calls for only one of the several meanings which could be associated with the natural object. And, furthermore, part of the meaning is assumed rather than stated.

The *object* and its *meaning*, wherever stated, remain *distinct* and *separate*; there is no rich interaction of vehicle and tenor, picture and meaning, as in the more modern poetic symbol.[48] Since the structure of the emblem is such as to keep 'thing' and 'meaning' separate, there is little point in discussing the grammatical form of the word-emblem in terms of simile and metaphor. The distancing factor of words like 'such' and 'like,' which indicate, at least grammatically, a simile, is of little relevance to the understanding of the emblem, since it says nothing about the semantics or ontology of the motif. A word-emblem can have the grammatical form of a simile. To sum up: the treatment of the motif of 'a heart in thorns' is emblematic in that it presents visual and concrete objects, which convey a clear, objective meaning.[49]

It is instructive to follow the mutations of a simple device like the 'heart in thorns,' which illustrate how both the emblem and the word-emblem can become complicated structures. Greiffenberg provides another simple example:

My God, think how long
In this way of thorns
I have torn my heart with pain.

Mein Gott denke nur wie lange
Jch in diesem dörner gange
hab das herz mitt schmerz geritzt.[50]

In many emblem-books further motifs are added to the picture of the heart in thorns. Van Haeften includes lilies.[51] Cramer has roses grow out of a heart in a nest of thorns (emblem XXII), and in another picture three ears of grain grow out of a heart towards the bright sun (emblem II), illustrating the notion of 'Frucht in Geduld.' A strikingly similar image is used by Greiffenberg:

Out of the heart grows the fruit
which heaven in us seeks.

Aus dem Herzen wächst die Frucht
die der Himmel bei uns sucht.[52]

This is likewise an unorganic, visual combination of concrete objects. A seventeenth-century reader would immediately recognize the meaning, familiar as he was with the Bible (here Luke 8:15) and the extensive, if loose network of emblematic meanings understood at the time. On this basis van Haeften can add a palm tree to one of his 'heart in thorns' emblems with the understood sense of 'constancy in adversity.'[53]

Another of Cramer's complicated heart emblems finds a structural parallel in Greiffenberg's poetry. Cramer's thirtieth emblem depicts a heart, from which grows a branch; a dove sits on the branch with an olive twig in its beak; in the background stands Noah's ark. The motto is Genesis 8:10. Greiffenberg's sonnet 187, addressed to the dove of the Holy Spirit, begins:

Oh dove, that brings peace from Christ's wounds,
bring into the ark of my heart a little branch
while I am in the sin-flood of vanity.

Ach Taube / die den Fried' aus Christi Wunden bringet!
führ 'in mein' Herzens Arch ein kleines Zweiglein hin /
weil in der Sünden=Flut der Eitelkeit ich bin / .

To the emblematic image of the 'ark of the heart' she adds an allusion to Christ's sufferings and wounds, which are the source of redemptive peace. The little twig, presumably the olive, is here associated with 'peace' that flows with Christ's blood.

Not aiming at the rich interaction of meaning and feeling characteristic of the modern poetic symbol,[54] the emblematic poet combines motifs (which convey definite and recognizable meanings) in order to prove a point, or to persuade the reader of a truth, and, what is more, in such a way as to fulfil the requirements of *prodesse et delectare*. Opitz writes of 'Glück und Unglück' in the following words:

misfortune however watches
Before good fortune sleeps; the creature that makes honey
is for all its sweetness never free of its sting;
Where a rose blooms, a thorn stands nearby.

das Unglück aber wachet
Ehe als das Glücke schlafft; das Thier so Honig machet
Ist bey der Süssigkeit deß Stachels nimmer frey;
Wo eine Rose blüht / da steht ein Dorn darbey.[55]

It is a fact that the bee makes sweet honey, but stings sharply, and that the rose is inseparable from the thorn. These two things of nature, presented concretely and visually, are real, and at the same time they point to a general idea or embody a general meaning, and these meanings embody the truth of Opitz's general and literal statement about fortune and misfortune. Needless to say, the emblem-books have many examples of the 'bee' and 'rose' used in this way and carrying these meanings.[56]

Perhaps on the basis of these comparisons between emblems and poetry, it is possible to offer a description of the word-emblem. As mentioned earlier,[57] we can, and do, look at metaphor, simile, allegory, and symbol from different points of view. The difficulty arises when one and the same term is used for different descriptions and expectations. A satisfactory description of the word-emblem should take into account its ontology, semantic nature, structure, and purpose.

The ontology of the word-emblem
As we have seen, the word-emblem is a verbal structure in which words convey both pictures and meanings. The picture may be regarded as real, in the sense that it represents directly and concretely objects which for the most part are meant to be visualized, and believed in as facts. This is still true when objects are strangely combined, and when the effect of the combination seems unreal because objects cannot be found in such combinations in nature or man's world. Be that as it may, the individual object in the picture is real, concrete, visual, and believed. Fantastic creatures, hieroglyphic signs, and the superstitions surrounding certain natural phenomena were accepted as true on the authority of earlier writers. For example, the hieroglyphics of Horapollo were believed, in so far as scholars accepted the hieroglyphics as a secret sign language holding the key to the wisdom of ancient Egypt.

I have been stressing the non-organic combinations rather than such natural groupings of motifs as rose and thorn, ivy and tree, pearl and oyster, because the unusual combination is so characteristic of the baroque and also so foreign to the modern reader.

The relationship of the thing depicted by the picture-word to the outer world of objects is for the most part a real one, and not, fantastic or arbitrary. Albrecht Schöne speaks of the 'potential facticity' ('potentielle Faktizität, pp 27–8) of myth and legend, which accounts for their presence in emblems; they were believed in, since they were part of a long tradition, and were just as open to interpretation as were the facts of nature. This does not preclude the possibility of the writer using the 'fact' and its meaning ironically, although this may give the impression that he doubts the validity of the meaning. But when a poet shows laurel struck by lightning, he is usually signalling disorder in nature, the supreme power of God, and so on, and for its effect the image still presupposes the fire-resistance of the laurel. Similarly if a poet bases an argument on the blindness of the eagle and the sight of the mole, this does not indicate that he rejects the traditional meanings, but rather shows him playing with them paradoxically and ironically.[58] However, it seems that motifs and their meaning generally are *not* used emblematically by a writer who no longer believes in them.[59]

It is true that there are some extreme emblem-books which are based on puns, riddles, and games with hieroglyphics, and the 'potential facticity' of these remains in doubt. Mario Praz draws attention to certain Spanish and Italian examples[60] where, for example, a split pomegranate is used as a hiero-glyph of the emblem of the crown of thorns, which is itself emblematic of Christ's suffering and redemption: 'A fruit which breaks open its breast and offers its entrails deserves to be crowned.'[61] In itself the pomegranate might well function as an emblem, since the meaning of 'sacrifice' can be read out of certain facts concerning the form and quality of the fruit. But the emblematist, Alonso de Ledesma, uses it as an emblem of an emblem, and is evidently indulging in a kind of intellectual game whereby he introduces a further dimension between thing and meaning. Some later baroque writers are inclined to indulge in the more enigmatic possibilities of the emblem, and in such instances the distance between picture and meaning can be sufficiently great to warrant describing the word-component as the key to the meaning of the almost unintelligible picture. However, the fact remains that the majority of emblem-books and most emblematic poetry are not enigmatic to the point of obscurity. Harsdörffer, who represents informed and influential opinion, argues for the middle way between obviousness and obscurity when he writes: 'It cannot be denied that one emblem is easy, another difficult; one good and penetrating, the other bad and simple; one to be interpreted as one thing, another as pointing to many different matters. The best are, in my opinion, those in the middle that are neither much too high, nor much too low; that can certainly be understood, but do not immediately lie open to all and sundry' (FG, IV, 170).[62]

Although the emblematic literature of the age – and here the phrase includes emblem-books, literature, and religious writings – was not generally as obscure as it may frequently appear to the uninitiated modern reader, there are, none the less, levels of difficulty and sophistication. When attempting to assess the difficulty or obscurity of an emblematic passage, we must always bear in mind the intended audience. On the simplest level there is the uncomplicated emblem that reproduces an object of nature with a meaning easily recognizable by virtue of its closeness to experience or because it belongs to proverbial lore or Christian tradition. An instance of commonplace knowledge is the fact that the frog, known to be a noisy creature, can be silenced at night by placing at light near it. Sambucus uses this as illustrative of the way truth overcomes sophistry, Camerarius for truth conquering lies.[63] In his emblem-book originally titled *A Book for Boys and Girls* (1686) John Bunyan directs his attention to the obvious physical attributes of the frog, its croaking mouth, large belly, and generally damp and cold nature.

> The Frog by Nature is both damp and cold
> Her Mouth is large, her Belly much will hold:
> She sits somewhat ascending, loves to be
> Croaking in Gardens, tho unpleasently.
> (Emblem 31, from *Divine Emblems: or Temporal Things Spiritualized. Fitted for Boys and Girls* [New York, 1794], pp 57–8)

Bunyan then compares the frog, as described, with the hypocrite.

> The Hypocrite is like unto this Frog.

Similar to these emblems are the occasional meditations of the period, in which some object or activity encountered in everyday life becomes the focus of a simple meditation. Bishop Joseph Hall published in 1630 a collection of *Occasional Meditations* that was to become important in its own right and influential in translation. Both Harsdörffer and the poetess Margaretha Maria von Buwinghausen und Walmerode translated Hall into German. It was, however, Johann Scriver who took up the initiative and wrote a collection entitled *Gottholds Zufällige Andachten / Bey Betrachtung mancherley Dinge der Kunst und Natur* (Leipzig, 1667), which was to run through about thirty editions and be translated into English. Hall tended merely to name the object or describe it very briefly, e.g., 'Upon the sight of a pitcher'; then he would add a 'moralisation.' The purpose was to provide the Christian with training in a simple form of meditation that could enrich his spiritual life while he was still engaged in the business of the world. The objects and activities he observed were to become the springboards for spiritual contemplation. They are 'occasional' meditations, in so far as they are not planned, or formally and thematically arranged, but derive from accidental, yet spiritually meaningful, encounters with life.

Emblematic and meditative modes are clearly related. We noted earlier that, walking through a field of corn, Taurellus 'discovered' the moral meaning in the growing corn. Greiffenberg was reminded of the Crucifixion when the eggs she was preparing separated out into the form of a cross. This event happened on the eve of Ephiphany. It is not without its significance that the sonnet she wrote to record and interpret this event seems to divide naturally into three crosses. Greiffenberg's experience fell upon Ephiphany, the feast that celebrates Christ's appearance to the three Kings.[64] It seems to me that in this sonnet we find the convergence of three modes: occasional meditation, the emblem, and the pattern poem. The action of preparing food in a kitchen produced an unexpected, yet significant, experience: the cross. The meaning of the event is expounded in the pattern poem, which reproduces the shape of the cross and in a sense replaces the *pictura* of an emblem.

One of the most thorough discussions of emblems in German literature is found in Harsdörffer's *Frauenzimmer Gesprächspiele* and his *Bericht von den Sinnbildern*, published as an appendix to the *Großer Schau=Platz jämmerlicher Mord-Geschichte* (Hamburg, 1666). As well as offering many theoretical elucidations Harsdörffer also provides emblem games, which shed some light on the 'do-it-yourself' aspect of emblem writing. In volume I of *FG* Vespasian, an old courtier, suggests six different ways of organizing a 'conversation-game of emblems.' They are:

1 by naming a thing as the basis for an emblem;
2 by choosing a picture and inventing a motto;
3 by choosing a motto and inventing a picture;
4 by illustrating chapters of the Bible;
5 by going through nature and making emblems as Camerarius did of animals;
6 by choosing suitable sayings from the poets as mottoes.

These represent different approaches to the making of an emblem, here converted into an entertaining and educational game. Among the many mottoes discussed by the conversation group is the following: 'A Happy End to the Misery of War' ('Der Waffen Elend / frölich End,' *FG*, I, 66). Various pictures are suggested to embody this motto: a dove with an olive branch flying over a calm sea; a garden in which the 'Eisenkraut' (literally, 'iron plant') has withered and a central 'Friedelar' (from the root 'Friede,' meaning 'peace') flourishes; the temple of peace at Rome; a hieroglyphic combination of a crown hovering in the air above a flourishing olive tree at the base of which are scattered broken weapons of war. Thus motifs from classical and biblical tradition, nature lore, and simple metonymic symbols provide the graphic details in these *picturae*. They are not particularly intellectually demanding. However, Harsdörffer also describes some Italian *imprese* that are more esoteric, such as that of a religious society dedicated to the Virgin Mary which features a chain made up of individual, separate links held together by magnetism. The motto is 'In unknown manner ('Auff unbekannte Weiß,' *FG*, II, 7). Harsdörffer adapts this motif and adds a punning dimension to it in his emblem for the Fruchtbringende Gesellschat ('Fruitbringing Society'), which had been founded by Duke Ludwig von Anhalt-Köthen. A portion of the Duke's name, 'Anhalt,' becomes the occasion for the pun, 'anhalten' meaning to 'hold on' or 'maintain.' The emblem-picture depicts two eagles holding a chain to which a lodestone is attached; the magnetic power of the lodestone holds together the separate links of a chain. The motto reads 'Useful to all' ('Allen zu Nutzen'). In his explanation Harsdörffer says that 'maintaining virtue' ('Anhaltende Tugend') holds the individual members ('Gelieder') together. The final lines of his *subscriptio* read:

> From the praiseworthy tree of maintaining virtue
> The Fruitbearers find their root power
> protect our splendid German tongue
> and hold together through princely grace
> bringing varied fruits useful to all.

> Von Anhaltischer Tugend löblichem Stammen /
> Die Fruchtbringenden ihre Wurzelkraft finden!
> unsre herrliche Teutsche Zunge beschutzen /
>   und mit Fürstlichem Gnaden halten zusammen /
> bringt vielfältige Frücht' uns allen zu Nutzen.   (*FG*, IV, 227)

Although this emblem is more difficult than the others discussed thus far, it must be borne in mind that it was intended for the cultural, intellectual elite who made up the membership of the Fruchtbringende Gesellschaft. A challenge to the common man, it was not likely to have been a burden on the intelligence of the members of the society. An even more esoteric treatment of basically the same motif is found in an *emblemata nuda* of Greiffenberg. One of the 'shepherdesses' in a kind of conversation game entitled *Tugend-Ubung Sieben Lustwehlender Schäferinnen* (1675) chooses to demonstrate her ideal of love by means of a chain, the links of which are not forged, but held together by magnetism. The chain has alternate links of bronze and iron; the bronze links have magnets on both sides. The motto reads:

> The power of virtue
> creates something special.

Der Tugend Krafft
was sonders schafft.   (*Tugend-Übung*, p 336)

The poetess celebrates the theme of 'virtuous love' in a series of Petrarchistic antitheses and statements, such as:

The Love-Power of Virtue holds forever in freedom.
Of magnetic power are already the works of the virtues
which even make the iron senses run after them.
Virtue is so strong that everything is attracted to her.

Der Tugend Liebes-krafft in Freyheit hält allzeit.
Von Ziehstein sind die Werk der Tugenden bereit /
die auch die Eisnen Sinn nach ihnen machen rennen.
Die Tugend ist so stark / daß alles ihr anhängt.   (P 336)

Estienne gives a clear indication of what the well-read gentleman would consider too simple to deserve treatment in an *impresa*. He censures the combination of dolphin and anchor with the motto 'Festina lente' as being too commonplace: 'Besides, those words are too common, and have been so familiar in the mouth of *Augustus Cesar*, that at this day they deserve not to be made use of in *Devises*.'[65] On the other hand, as an example of obscurity Giovio cites the *impresa* of Pope Clement which was 'a round peece of Cristall, the Sunne with his beames passing through the flame proued by them, all set in a white hood, with this mot, *Candor illesus*.'[66] Giovio admits that the *impresa* was 'very obscure to those which knowe not the propertie' alluded to, which was the 'secret of nature' according to which the rays of the sun passing through the crystal 'burne euery object, sauing only things passing white.'[67] Giovio does not fault the reader who may be assumed to be a man of culture and learning for not understanding the *impresa*, nor does he question the facticity of the motif, but he does roundly criticize such 'obscurities [which] ought to be shunned in an *Imprese*.'

It is not easy to find a definition of the emblem which can cover the many relationships of word to picture, thing to meaning, or the various forms and functions of those illustrated books calling themselves emblem-books. However, by taking a central and representative group of emblem-books Schöne has arrived at a description of the nature and structure of the emblem. And so it is with the word-emblem. We must concentrate, for clarity of description, if at the cost of completeness, on some basic and representative examples.

The semantics of the word-emblem
What is the relationship of meaning to the object or its picture? Is it real or imagined? Inherent or contrived? For a good many years the relationship was deemed to be capricious and arbitrary; in many writers this judgment amounted to a sentence of death, which allowed of no reprieve for the emblem.

In an essay on mysticism Erich Seeberg[68] touches briefly on the subject of emblematics and its relationship to both poetry and mysticism. He draws attention to the relationship between emblematic thinking and the 'galante Lyrik' of the later Silesian poets (p 9). Like most English critics, Seeberg seizes upon the presumed 'contrived' and 'capricious' relationship between thing and meaning, probably because he holds a view of emblematics that overstresses the role of hieroglyphics, without recognizing their deeper justification as a mode of thought and vehicle of wisdom. Seeberg states: 'Here any and every object becomes a simile or symbol; everything acquires significance and is intensified by heated imagination in an artificially sublimated sense' (p 8).[69] He continues in similar vein: 'thus in emblematic mysticism and poetry an experience is, to a certain extent, artificially produced, in that from something already existing and external accidental, inward relationships and thoughts are derived, which develop and ultimately lose completely their connection with reality and their point of departure' (p 10).[70] He also speaks of emblematic mysticism as 'interpretations of an arbitrary object' (p 10).[71] Seeberg was writing at a time when 'experience,' usually understood in the biographical and anecdotal sense, was the criterion of value, and organic art was its natural corollary.

In 1926 Else Eichler produced a study of Scriver's 'occasional meditations,'[72] a form not unrelated to the religious emblem-books, as was noted earlier. Her brief account of the origins of the emblem makes reference to the hieroglyphics as the source of renaissance emblems, but, as in Seeberg's case, without recognizing the typological and also neoplatonic basis of the humanist's interest in hieroglyphics as a kind of prefiguration of Christian wisdom. Eichler makes no mention of the tradition of medieval symbolism, which provides the intellectual foundation of the emblematic mode of thought. Thus she can condemn the emblem as 'a degenerate form of allegory' (p 11). The framework of her set of values is sketched in by such terms as 'experience' ('Erlebnis'), 'reality' ('Wirklichkeit'), and 'living nature' ('lebendige Natur'; cf pp 18–19).

In 1927 Hermann Pongs spoke of the 'superficiality' ('Äußerlichkeit') and the 'degeneration' ('Entartung') of the baroque emblem, and he concluded: 'It had a paralysing effect on German life.'[73] With the weight of Pongs's authority behind such a judgment, its effect was serious and long-lasting. As Penkert observes, it blocked German research into emblematics for decades (cf p 114).

In his important study of Gryphius's imagery Gerhard Fricke[74] has a number of comments on the emblem which deserve mention in this survey by virtue of the influence they seem to have exercised on succeeding German scholars. Fricke writes: 'The emblem satisfied the tendency to find two or more meanings in all things; it represents the overly ingenious search through and beyond the visible world for a significance behind things, for a "that means," the need to take each thing not primarily as it is, but metaphorically, as the bearer and herald of mysteries, as the embodiment of meaning and spirit, as visual enigma' (p 29).[75] In some respects this is an acceptable statement, although I would quarrel with the implications of 'overly ingenious search,' as well as the use of the vague terms 'primary' and 'metaphorical,' since the emblematic attitude is one which sees the objects of nature as 'seiend' and 'bedeutend.' In fact, Fricke refers to the medieval belief that everything that exists is also significant ('alles Seiende [ist] auch ein Bedeutendes,' p 29). Like Seeberg, Fricke distinguishes between genuine mysticism and what he calls 'a kind of intellectual sport, the capricious, playful combination of unrelated "things" as an emblematic exercise for the mind and allegorical puzzle, or the veiling of chosen devices and maxims in an initially scarcely penetrable combination of individual objects' (p 31).[76] With his assumption of a specifically baroque spirit with an antithetical 'Weltgefühl' (p 32), Fricke postulates both a serious and a playful use of the emblem, which he labels as capricious. In his view this spirit '[treats] image and emblem now with mystic solemnity and now with playful caprice' (p 32).[77]

Ernst Friedrich von Monroy also sees obscurity, caprice, and ingenuity in the emblem, but for him these are aspects of the main virtues of the emblem, 'obscuritas' and 'novitas.' The hieroglyphic studies of Giehlow and Volkmann set the direction of Monroy's studies of art history in the latter part of the 1930s. His doctoral dissertation on the emblems of the Netherlands, 1560–1630, remains unfinished, because Monroy was killed during the Second World War.[78]

Monroy regards the emblem as a construction in which verbal and pictorial components have a distinct and separate existence: 'the attraction of the emblem consists in the tension between the two forms of expression [word and picture], which are juxtaposed as closed spheres, as the direct utterance and pictorial concealment of a concept' (p 16).[79] He argues that meaning is not inherent in the object pictured in the emblem, but 'is artificially derived from it, imposed on it. It [the meaning] does not lie in the object, is not discovered, but rather invented. The emblem has an inventor; it is the personal, ingenious ['unverbindlich'] aperçu of an author' (p 16).[80]

In 1940 Anna H. Kiel[81] published her Amsterdam dissertation on Rompler von Löwenhalt in which she devotes a short chapter to the relationship of Rompler's *Lehrgedichte* to emblematics. The date of publication presumably precludes the possibility of Kiel's having read Praz's book, which was published originally in Italian in 1934 and in English translation in 1939. The only critics that she refers to are Gerhard Fricke and Henry Green; the latter's important pioneering work was none the less marred by inaccuracies and a certain dilettantism. Kiel regards the characteristically baroque form of the emblem as reaching its zenith with Harsdörffer and the Nürnberg poets. She offers a neutral and quite accurate description of baroque emblems in the following words: 'the same picture receives the most divergent of interpretations; each individual picture is firstly divided into its elements and the allegorical explanation is attached to the individual parts (p 27).[82] Unfortunately she then proceeds to discuss Harsdörffer's 'Andachtsgemähl' ('devotional picture'), calling it 'the characteristically Harsdörffer emblem' (p 27). This is precisely the kind of unhappy extension of the term 'emblematic' that must be avoided if the term is to have a usefully circumscribed application. Kiel's account of the 'Andachtsgemähl' is perceptive, but misleading if taken as descriptive of the emblem. Squarely in the tradition of Seeberg and Fricke, she observes: 'the image in its intrinsic meaning recedes more and more and makes way for the overly ingenious combination of thoughts. Detail is set against detail, each brought to bear on the other' (p 28).[83] None of these critics seems willing to tell us wherein the 'intrinsic meaning of the image' ('eigentliche Bedeutung des Bildes') resides, although this is the basis upon which all such judgments are made. On the nature of this 'eigentliche Bedeutung' Jöns observes: 'the obscure criterion of the "intrinsic essence" of nature [derives] from the secular conception of nature that has become an absolute' (p 99).[84] Kiel's discussion of Rompler's emblematic *Lehrgedichte* ends with the following statement: 'the image in its intrinsic meaning, as in the emblematics of the Nürnberg writers, has disappeared to make way for overly ingenious association' (p 37).[85] Such basic misconceptions are frequently found side by side with valid and useful description of emblematic practice. Kiel, for example, observes that, whereas Rompler's poem 'unser Wandel ist in Himmel' presents the picture in the first eight lines, followed by an explanation in the final tercets, a sonnet like 'Gaistliche Spiegelberaitung' presents the individual picture element and its accompanying spiritual interpretation piece by piece. Both these poems are emblematic in the structural sense advanced by Kiel. However, she can also offer descriptions of emblematics so broad as to be meaningless: 'A second group in Rompler's exemplum poetry are the emblem-like poems composed of eight-line Alexandrines; in so far as they are connected with a New Testament parable or any mystic conception, they belong to the tradition of the

Emblemata sacra, as represented by the collections of Sudermann and Gloner'
(p 33).[86] A similarly sweeping definition, this time based on mythological
figures, has been noted in Goldman's essay on Daniel's *Delia* sonnets. These
examples must suffice to demonstrate the extent to which there was a tradition
in German studies that equated the emblem with arbitrariness: however, this
line of thought more or less ends with the publication of Schöne's theory of the
emblem in 1963. Peter Vodosek's somewhat pretentious essay 'Das Emblem in
der deutschen Literatur der Renaissance und des Barock,' in *Jahrbuch des
Wiener Goethe-Vereins* (Vienna, 1964), repeats the old criticism of 'Spitz-
findigkeit' (pp 29, 36); and in its mention of 'Entartung' and in quoting Pongs's
strictures, cited earlier, it sounds more like a product of the thirties than of the
sixties.[87] Admittedly, Vodosek may not have known of Schöne's researches,
but there is no hint of the far-reaching work of Praz and Freeman, nor is there
any indication that W. Kayser's *Das sprachliche Kunstwerk*[88] had much effect.

Virtually all the research into baroque imagery, and, indeed, into baroque
literature of any and every genre, had been influenced by the findings of Schöne
and Jöns, and scholarship has profited immeasurably from the publication of the
Emblemata. Thus, with but a few exceptions, the notion that emblems are
necessarily 'arbitrary' ends in 1963, as far as German studies go.[89]

In English studies the situation is rather different. On the one hand, some
sensitive critics, like Austin Warren and Ruth Wallerstein, writing in the
thirties, had already abandoned notions of caprice and arbitrariness. On the
other hand, some critics subscribed to the view that the emblem is arbitrary
without this conviction adversely affecting their interpretations – Beachcroft,
Freeman, and Sharrock might be cited as examples. The notion of 'arbitrariness'
may still occasionally be heard in English scholarship – Lederer (1946), Hough
(1961),[90] Goldman (1968).[91]

The seventeenth-century mind still has a medieval temper; its basic tendency is to think in analogies and allegories. Both the poet and the emblematist
look upon nature as God's second book, a revelation of his intentions for man.
Contemporary events and history, mythology and legend also carry distinct
meanings. The basis of this attitude is the typological thinking of the Middle
Ages, and the Neoplatonism of the Renaissance. Not that the theoreticians and
emblematists were aware of their debt to the Middle Ages, which is hardly
surprising since the renaissance humanists were more interested in classical
antiquity and the European present than in their own medieval past.

Since the emblematic image in literature is essentially a verbal emblem,
lacking only the visual *pictura* to be a *bona fide* emblem, it follows that it must
function semantically in an analogous fashion. What was said earlier of the
semantics of the emblem[92] must *per definitionem* also apply to the word-

emblem. The significance conveyed by the word-emblem derives from the form or from some quality of the creature or object named. Indeed, a factual or 'true' relationship between abstract meaning and the quality, whether named or assumed, is taken for granted. For instance, it was believed that the unicorn could purify a poisoned pond by dipping its horn into the water; and that no hunter could catch the unicorn, which, however, would tamely approach a pure virgin – these 'facts' of nature were frequently transferred to the immaculate conception.

As was stated earlier,[93] the erroneous view that emblematic images are arbitrary and necessarily obscure derives in part from the modern reader's confusion when he meets one image with many different, at times contradictory, meanings. The lion can denote Christ, the devil, the just Christian, or the heretic, because the lion can carry positive and negative meanings.[94] As Harsdörffer noted, recognition of meaning depends on a knowledge of the thing depicted by the emblem, or emblematic image.[95] Speaking as theorist, practising poet, and emblem writer, Harsdörffer suggests that comparison be drawn 'not from accidental but rather from essential qualities of a thing.'[96] Elsewhere he recommends that the emblem draw upon the 'most well-known and basic quality of the picture.'[97]

It would follow, then, that the concept of *similitudo* can only be advanced with reservations and applied with broad-minded flexibility. Some earlier essays on emblematic poetry are occasionally marred by too narrow and superficial an application of *similitudo*. Of Herbert's emblematic poetry Freeman comments: 'There is no necessary likeness between the church floor and the human heart, between stained glass windows and preachers,[98] or between two rare cabinets filled with treasures and the Trinity and the Incarnation. His method is always to evolve meaning by creating likenesses; the likenesses are rarely inherent or to be seen from the outset.'[99] Freeman insists that in the poetry of Quarles and Herbert 'there was never any essential likeness between the picture and its meaning,'[100] but she does not state what this 'necessary essential likeness' might be, or what its limits are.

The renaissance poet and reader gave credence to many things that we no longer regard as true. As the frame of reference for truth changes, so the beliefs of one age become the superstitions of another. Our modern ways of verifying truth and validating statements no longer include that respect for tradition and authority that had characterized the Renaissance – unless as individuals we subscribe to some rigid faith or ideology which provides us with unquestionable premises. A combination of disbelief and ignorance helped to produce the view that emblematic images are arbitrary. Although it is safe to say that the informed modern reader no longer regards the emblem as necessarily contrived and obscure, the question of the belief of the poet and emblematist remains unanswered, and in most cases unanswerable. We can show that ideas concerning frogs and crocodile's teeth, for example, have a long tradition, and were current during the sixteenth and seventeenth centuries, which demonstrates that they were not the capricious invention of the renaissance writer. Their 'truth' was established by reference to Pliny, Horapollo, *Physiologus*, the Bible, the Church Fathers, and so on. Generally we shall not be wrong in assuming that usage virtually equals belief. The proof is, however, usually not available. But there are a few instances of the writer admitting to his disbelief. Estienne, quoted earlier,[101] resolved the question of truth versus usage in favour of usage, by which he meant that the writer may and should employ the phoenix as a symbol of Christ's resurrection, even though the fact of the phoenix may no longer be believed by the educated minority. The majority did believe, and the Church Fathers had sanctioned the symbol. The symbolic value of the phoenix transcended the importance of the 'facts' of the case.

Critics who make sweeping statements about symbolism and the relationship of object and meaning rarely define their terms adequately or specify any temporal limitations to their application. It should be obvious that notions of 'necessary likeness' are highly relative and need to be approached with caution and historical tact. Freeman's criticism of the emblem stems from value assumptions which need to be more closely examined. In appreciation of her work it should be said that, unlike many critics, she is prepared to state clearly the basis upon which she makes her value judgments. Comparing the 'intrinsic symbol' with the 'arbitrary type,' that is, the emblem, she observes: 'inasmuch as it [the intrinsic symbol] has a significance outside its context and is part of general human experience, it is more accessible and more immediately productive of emotional response' (*English Emblem Books*, p 30). Her criteria of poetic value are, then, intrinsicality of meaning, universal appeal, and feeling.[102] Her reservations about the emblem stem from its failure to live up to these expectations. Universality might appear to be a valid criterion, but in the last analysis it also is relative, since different cultures and generations respond to different aspects of the so-called universal work, as a glance at the history of Shakespeare criticism will demonstrate. The argument of intrinsicality is equally relative: what is deemed intrinsic in one world-view may not be so in another. Set in the context of an exegetical tradition with its symbolism in which things are dissected into their constituent parts and attributes with assumed meanings, the emblematic interpretation of reality is a discovery of inherent or intrinsic meaning. The baroque emblem is, then, not necessarily arbitrary, but in a real sense it too can be an intrinsic symbol.

If God endowed the world with meaning, which man should seek to understand, then each individual may discover for himself new meanings in nature. Greiffenberg insists that nature is meaningful to all men, if only they will lift the curtain of laziness. [103] Discovering emblematic meanings in nature was not simply the intellectual hobby of the scholar. The self-taught Grimmelshausen has his Simplicissimus meditate on the emblematic meanings of his desert island: Simplicissimus is reminded of Christ's passion when he sees thorns, of the fall of man when he sees an apple or pomegranate, and so on. [104] This is not obscure erudition, but mainstream emblematic interpretation.

Most of the meanings read out of nature's phenomena were part of a widely held system of knowledge in which the meanings were general, objective, and largely divorced from the inner life of the poet. Jöns expresses it thus: 'The emblematic quality of a thing is not to be interpreted as being the result of a subjective assumption, but rather depends on its "representing" something that transcends the physical and factual domain of its reality' (p 79). [105] This is still the case where the individual discovers individual meanings; he is not using the natural object as an objective correlative of inner states of feeling; he is, rather, finding external relationships between a thing and a meaning. These general meanings, however, can be re-interpreted. As the seventeenth century progresses we find increasing specialization in the emblem-books, with the emergence of religious, moral, political, erotic, and scientific emblem-books.

From the foregoing discussion it should be clear that the word-emblem conveys important, conceptual meanings, and any decorative image that is merely a 'figurative form' [106] is not an emblem. Beachcroft is right in observing that richness of detail is not there for its own sake as superimposed decoration', but for the meaning that the detail supplies. [107]

The emblem tends to be univalent in meaning, that is to say, in any one context only one level of meaning is relevant. Again Harsdörffer represents informed seventeenth-century opinion when he writes that 'in an emblem only one comparison should be sought and intended.' [108] As an example one might consider Greiffenberg's sonnet 28, which deals with, among other things, the relation of faith to reason. The traditional image of a voyage is the basis of an extended word-emblem in which each interpreted detail plays a conceptual role. The danger inherent in reason is expressed through the image of the 'salt of unbelief' ('Unglaubens Salz'), which attacks the eyes of the diver after spiritual pearls:

> The eyes of reason, when one wishes to raise
> Treasures of coral and pearls – when one dives –
> Must be covered, lest the salt of unbelief penetrate.

Die Augen der Vernunfft / wann man da auf will heben
Corall= und Perlen=Schätz / wann man hinab vertiefft /
muß man verbinden / daß Unglaubens Salz nicht trifft.

This is characteristic of the emblematic image in which a single, clearly definable meaning is given: salt equals unbelief. The reader has no freedom to
interpret salt in any other way. Without the explicatory 'Unglaube' the reader
might have been tempted to interpret salt as Roman Catholicism, Calvinism, or
the New Science for that matter, but the line of understanding is firmly laid
down: the sonnet praises blind faith, secure from the threat of unbelief when
the eyes of reason are bound. The only latitude which remains is the extent to
which the reader may follow the predetermined line of meaning. May we go so
far as to impute to Greiffenberg a total rejection of reason? I do not believe so;
the image context is precise, and it concerns the relationship of faith to the
revelations in the Scriptures, where human reason is of little help and may even
be a liability in that it is susceptible to the influence of unbelief. However, to
extend the context further: just as the diver will use his eyes to examine the
pearl he has discovered, so the believer will apply his reason to an understanding
of the scriptural truth in which he believes.

By way of contrast one might consider Goethe's 'Gesang der Geister über
den Wassern,' which has interpretative hints in the initial and closing lines. The
main body of the poem, however, is a poetic description of a waterfall, which
becomes a river, flowing into a lake. At no point in the description of nature does
Goethe set down the lines of interpretation; thus the reader is free to understand the poem as a whole in different ways and on several different levels, as a
symbol of man's journey through life, or of the relationship of mature man to
his material and spiritual environment, or of the relationship of his soul to
existence.

Where the word-emblem does convey a plurality of meanings, these do not
interweave, as in the modern poetic symbol, but rather form a list of distinct and
separate meanings, deriving from different qualities of the pictured object.
When in sonnet 227 Greiffenberg meditates emblematically upon the forget-
me-not, she isolates four distinct meanings which derive from various attributes of the flower and point to a higher Christian truth. She treats these
meanings separately, and they remain distinct. The colour blue is indicative of
heaven and God; the colour green in German is still proverbial for hope; the five
petals remind the poet of Christ's five wounds and also focus man's five physical
senses on the suffering of Christ; finally the name 'forget-me-not' call to
mind God's promise that he will not forget man. These meanings do not

interfuse and interact, as they would in the modern poetic symbol, but are individual steps in a Christian meditation.[109]

Although the word-emblem tends to convey a single meaning, on occasions the motif stands in such a rich tradition that other meanings associated with it may be suggested to the reader by the context. However, the context of the meaning – and therefore the scope for interpretation – is determined by the dominant meaning of the word-emblem, whether it be assumed or stated. Emblematic thinking is controlled associative thinking; within a poetic context an emblem can lay down a line of meaning along which several associations may be plotted. Vaughan's poem 'The Palm-Tree' is a case in point. The central image is of a palm-tree, which is bent under heavy weights, but none the less flourishes. Vaughan explains the weights as sin, and the striving as:

> Celestial natures still
> Aspire for home ...

Vaughan does not stay with the burdened palm-tree, but moves on to other associations. As a tree the palm is related to the Tree of Life, 'whose fruit is immortality.' This in turn leads the poet to consider the 'Spirits that have run this race,' fought the fight, and achieved after earthly life their 'Crown,' possibly palm wreaths. Finally, the poet will 'pluck a Garland' from the palm-tree, the sign of victory. Unlike Freeman, I do not regard this poem as having outgrown its emblematic basis;[110] in my view it remains very much within the broad traditions of emblematic writing. Freeman reaches her conclusion because of a narrow and restrictive conception of the emblem expressed in such phrases as 'the unwinking concentration upon one image' and 'the emblem method ... required ... simple ... equation between image and its meaning.'[111] What this amounts to is the equation of a single motif with a single significance; this describes one form of the word-emblem, but one form only.

The word-emblem in its semantics differs essentially from the more modern poetic symbol which is characterized by rich plurisignation. As an illustration, consider Marvell's 'desarts of vaste eternity,' which the poet sees before him in the poem 'To His Coy Mistress.' In this symbol the known quantity 'desert,' a concept deriving from human experience, is made the measure of an unknown quantity 'eternity,' a concept beyond human verification. Marvell is telling us what he fears eternity may be like, and he does so by means of a comparison which invites exploration, in terms of both the ideas and the feelings which it generates. Some of the ideas engendered by the marriage of desert and eternity are: the endlessness, sameness, emptiness, deadness, and coldness (since, for me at least, the context suggests the cold night sky over the desert, rather than the blistering heat of a desert day). This last association indicates the manner in which the abstract tenor 'eternity' modifies the concrete vehicle 'desert,' limiting the field of relevant association – camels and dancing girls do not fit in here. The ideas, however, are not divorced abstractions: they in turn generate emotional responses to the intellectual significance discovered in the image. These 'feelings' might be described as insignificance, loneliness, fear, and desolation. Desert + eternity = despair, a knowledge which is only hinted at in this discussion. The poetic symbol, unlike the explicit emblem, implies a rich significance, because it is a focus of feeling and attitude, as well as conceptual meaning.

The emotional and intuitional content of symbol and word-emblem
Emotional content ('Gefühlsgehalt') is one of the elements which differentiates symbol from emblem. The symbol can conjure up an interplay of meanings which invites exploration and personal interpretation, but it is not exclusively, nor indeed primarily, an intellectual vehicle for the transmission of abstract meaning.[112] It generates ideas and feelings which interact and ultimately defy logical analysis. It is the emotional and intuitional content of symbol that sets it apart from emblematic imagery. As Freeman puts it: 'no emblem ever achieved the fullness and richness of the emotional content of one of Blake's symbols' (*English Emblem Books*, p 24). Essentially the word-emblem is a visual image conveying an intellectual meaning; any emotional reverberations are secondary. This is not to imply that the emblem is necessarily unpoetic or unaesthetic. On the contrary, the emblem can fully satisfy the baroque requirements of high rhetorical style and also the aesthetic expectation of 'ut pictura poesis.'

If we compare the way in which a baroque and a romantic poet use the motif 'gold' the difference in emotional content between symbol and word-emblem may emerge more clearly. In his poem 'Abendständchen' Clemens Brentano writes:

Listen, the flute laments once more,
And the cool fountains play,
The tones waft golden down,
Peace, be still, let us listen.

Hör, es klagt die Flöte wieder,
Und die kühlen Brunnen rauschen.
Golden wehn die Töne nieder –
Stille, stille, laß uns lauschen.

Brentano's use of 'golden' to describe the sound of the flute and fountains is not only symbolic but also synaesthetic, in that the poet transfers the warmth of the sunset to the sounds he hears. He is not conveying such clearly definable ideas as the colour or value of the object (here a sound); he is expressing the way he *feels* about the sound of the flute and the fountains. He is re-creating their effect upon his consciousness, and this is not intellectual at all. The 'lamenting flute' and 'cool fountains' strike me personally as cool, and, if anything, blue sounds. Brentano seems to take pleasure from the sadness of these sounds, since he uses the richness and warmth associated with 'golden' to qualify the impressions of 'lament,' 'cool,' and 'flute.' A consummate word artist like Brentano cannot have been unaware of the slight and untranslatable ambiguity in 'wehn' ('we-hen' = waft, 'Weh' = pain, sorrow) which lightly reinforces the impression of the lamenting flute. Brentano's use of 'golden' is private and emotional, rather than public and intellectual.

Greiffenberg and Gryphius use the gold image quite differently in the following poems:

> God tests the gold of faith, in the crucible, our body;
> and knows how to control the fire of the cross
> that both gold and crucible remain intact.   (Original quoted on p 68)

> The man whom God has tested, as gold thrice through fire,
> Through misery, sword and pestilence, who believes undaunted ...
>
> Der Mann den Gott als Goldt dreymall durch Glutt bewehret.
> Durch Elendt Schwerdt / und Pest / der unverzagt geglaubet ...
> (Gryphius, sonnet i, 50)

> One must put gold to the test,
> The loyal mind
> nor fire
> nor torment will turn from God ...
>
> Man muß das Gold bewehren /
> Den treuen Muth
> wird keine Gluth
> Noch Quaal von Gott abkehren.   (Gryphius, Geistliche Lieder 10)

You [Christ] purify this gold [faith] in love / let in pain
Patience be incense, let me be your censer ...

Du [Christ] läutere diß Gold [faith] in Liebe / laß in Pein
Für Weyrauch die Gadult / ja mich dein Räucherwerck seyn ...
(Gryphius, sonnet III, 10)

Faith and loyalty are identified with gold to bring out the distinct and clear meanings of 'value' and 'permanence,' and the testing function of misfortune with reference to faith and loyalty. Such meanings or feelings associated with gold as colour, texture, beauty, warmth are irrelevant, and, although potential in the motif, are not realized in this context. The most important idea conveyed by the gold image is that valuable faith is tested by the fire of tribulation. Here is a direct intellectual equation of gold with faith.

Lest it be thought that seventeenth-century metaphor necessarily lacks the imaginative and connotative richness that we have postulated as a criterion of symbol *per se* – a misconception that might arise from the choice of a Brentano poem as an instance of such symbolic richness – consider these baroque examples of the metaphoric use of a concrete image. John Donne writes in his 'Valediction: forbidding mourning:'

Our two soules therefore, which are one,
Though I must goe, endure not yet
    A breach, but an expansion,
    Like gold to ayery thinnesse beate.

The tenor of the image might be stated as the indivisible unity of two souls in love, even though one lover is physically absent. This abstract statement of meaning is enriched, however, by the concrete vehicle of its poetic expression. The point of the analogy is the malleability of gold, which is here used hyperbolically in conjunction with the superb exaggeration of 'ayery thinnesse.' We might note in passing that 'ayery' is a particularly appropriate adjective for 'soules.' Other associations of gold, which are relevant and interact with this dominant meaning, are warmth and beauty, and richness, which is a guarantee of permanence.

Greiffenberg condenses much of the mystery of Christ's birth into the following image: 'Into the glass of a weak body the ocean of the divinity is poured' ('In das Glas des schwachen Leibes wird der Gottheit Meer gethan,' sonnet 8). The image contrasts the great and small, immense power and fragile weakness; it captures the paradox of the limitation of the unlimitable. Yet such abstract statements hardly re-create the depth of meaning of such an image, which also draws on interacting associations. 'Glass' calls to mind purity and fragility, and, in the context, a certain passivity, since it is the receptacle into which the 'ocean of divinity' is poured. These associational meanings are relevant and were frequently used in the period. 'Ocean' not only denotes size, but, just as important, connotes a life-giving, yet also potentially destructive, force, and as such it is a valid metaphor for God. These are but some of the meanings caught up in an imaginative interaction, which invites the reader to explore and interpret.

According to rhetorical definitions a word-emblem is frequently a metaphor, since it presents an identification or equation of thing and meaning, vehicle and tenor, and usually lacks the distancing link-word characteristic of the simile. From the semantic view, however, the word-emblem is a simile, since it is simple and frequently univalent in meaning.[113] Furthermore, its emotional content is secondary, and often incidental; it lacks the imaginative, intuitional quality which has led one critic to describe metaphor as a 'Gefühlseinsicht,'[114] the insight of feeling.

The structure of the word-emblem
By structure I mean the verbal interrelationship between the objects in the image and their meanings as they combine in a larger pattern. The baroque word-emblem frequently combines visual images either with no explanation at all, or with a precise explanation; the meaning of the whole structure may be given either immediately before or after the *pictura* in a valid, objective statement. Just as the verbal picture depicts things that are for the most part real, concrete, static, and not caught up in flux or movement, so the statement of meaning tends to keep the picture and concept separate though related. Thing and meaning are placed side by side; this has the effect of preventing any dynamic interaction or fusion of object and concept. Where several things and concepts are combined, the relationship is not organic, that is to say, the part is not perceptibly modified by the whole, as in much modern poetry, written roughly from the mid-eighteenth century up to the symbolists, of whom often the reverse is true. Each part in the emblematic combination is complete and usually univalent, a contribution to the total mosaic. The relationships are primarily intellectual. In one of the *Gesprächspiele* Harsdörffer offers the following summary description of the emblem stressing the intellectual aspect: 'The art of the emblem is the thoughtful expression of special reflection by means of an appropriate simile which is introduced by natural or artificial objects and interpreted in a few thought-provoking words' (*FG*, IV, 176–7).[115]

The intellectual nature of baroque imagery and emblem is noted by Beachcroft in his article on Crashaw: 'Partly from the Emblem habit of mind comes the taste of the seventeenth century for choosing poetic similes in general, not for their sensuous beauty nor emotional propriety, but for an esoteric intellectual application, which is not fully seen till the poet exploits it' (p 421). One might dispute the extent to which 'esoteric' is an appropriate epithet,[116] but by and large Beachcroft is right. More recently Bertonasco has stressed the importance of recognizing and respecting the conceptual foundation of emblematic imagery (cf pp 9ff).

The function of the word-emblem

Basically the word-emblem serves a conceptual function; it is primarily a vehicle of meaning, not a means of decoration. In some literary works it can have a structurally unifying function. Of Spenser's *The Faerie Queene* A.D.S. Fowler[117] makes the following remark: 'In Book II, where emblems are heavily relied on for structure as well as for imagery, either their existence is now not even noticed, or else they are treated as mere surface decoration' (p 143).

In the third chapter of *Emblematik und Drama im Zeitalter des Barock* Schöne establishes seven functions for the word-emblem in its role of *argumentum emblematicum* in German baroque drama. These are:

1 Proof of the truth of a fact doubted by the character addressed ...
2 Basis of teleological interpretation of present events and of prophetic exhortation ...
3 Instrument of knowledge of a situation ... Rule for the behaviour of the speaker ...
4 Basis for the challenge to the speaker addressed to perform certain acts ...
5 Standard of judgment of negative conduct, argument of condemnation ...
6 Self-confirmation of the speaker in correct conduct ...
7 Laudatory confirmation of an exemplary act.   (P 89)[118]

These brief descriptions of the functions of *argumenta emblematica* in the dramatic text are taken from Schöne's summary, which is preceded by some twenty pages in which he analyses characteristic examples of each group. Schöne stresses that this list is not complete and could be extended. In my view some of the differentiations are already unnecessarily precise, and probably little would be gained by a further breakdown into smaller groups. I fully concur, however, in Schöne's concluding remarks that, more important than this list, is the insight that dramatic texts are 'threaded through with emblems whose meaning is often accessible only through the emblem-books' (p 89).[119] The characters use: 'emblematic symbols, their meaning and teachings, as an instrument of knowledge and interpretation, to determine the truth and arrive at a judgment, to persuade, to confirm and justify self, to provide a foundation for relating the immediate situation to that which is typical and normative, for orienting the particular to the basic, for raising the isolated to the general and eternally valid' (p 90). [120]

THE FORMS OF THE WORD-EMBLEM

The tendency to emblematize manifests itself in various ways in poetic imagery; however, the complete word-emblem will contain both a pictorial and an interpretative element. The simplest forms of emblems are compound nouns and genitive noun constructions. [121] The following examples are taken from the religious poetry of Greiffenberg:

> That my rock of faith were a clear stream of joy.

> Mein Glaubens=Felse werd' ein klarer freuden=bach.   (Sonnet 34)

> Oh, but hold, my faith, to the blood of Christ's wounds:
> In the rock of his heart you are unconquerable.

> Ach halt dich nur / mein Glaub / zu Christus Wunden=Blut:
> in seinem Herzen=Felß bistu unüberwindlich.   (Sonnet 98)

> You will yet drink the water of salvation from this rock.

> Du wirst nach Heiles=Safft aus diesem Felsen trinken.   (Sonnet 125)

In each instance the old testament story of Moses and the rock is emblematized, and the image interpreted in different ways: in the first example the poetess applies the image to the relationship of faith to joy; in the second and third to Christ and his redeeming blood.

From such compound nouns it is but a short step to those emblematic structures in which image and meaning stand in an appositional relationship to each other. Praying for divine inspiration, Greiffenberg writes:

> That the flame-river, God's wisdom, would give me drink.

> mich woll der Flammen-Fluß / die Gottes weisheit / tränken.   (Sonnet 8)

The single motif 'Flammen=Fluß' is interpreted by the words 'die Gottes weißheit,' which follow immediately after the image. Longer and more complex images are treated in the same way:

> The laurel withstands fire and thunderbolt.
> Virtue does not allow itself to be harmed by evil.

> Der Lorbeer widersteht dem Feur und Donnerstein.
> Die Tugend lässet sich von Boßheit nicht verletzen.   (Sonnet 83)

Although I am not trying to establish rigid categories, the following forms represent different ways in which the emblematic process was realized in verbal imagery:

1 the contracted word-emblem;
2 the extended word-emblem;
3 the complex word-emblem. [122]

The contracted word-emblem

A form of verbalized emblem that has caused modern readers much offence – only to be abused in return – is the contracted word-emblem. One of the few critics to face up to this problem is Bertonasco. In his book on Crashaw he singles out examples of the contracted emblem which have been attacked by other scholars. Crashaw's meditative poem 'On the Bleeding Wounds of Our Crucified Lord' contains the following image condemned by Odette de Mor-gues:

> But o thy side! thy deepe dig'd side
> That hath a double Nilus going.

Bertonasco interprets this contracted emblem as follows: 'Just as the Nile, by overflowing its banks, enriches the arid land, bringing forth crops and fruits, so the precious blood of Christ sanctifies, making possible the life of grace. In short, the doctrine of mankind's redemption through Christ's passion and death has been compressed into this image' (p 8). Presumably what shocks a-historical modern taste is the juxtaposition of *two* visual images: the literal image of the suffering and bleeding Christ and the figurative visual image of the 'double Nilus'; this shock is intensified by the lack of explicit and interpretative connection between the two. In other words, the full emblem is contracted by the omission of explicit interpretation. The relationship is assumed. Bertonasco points out that 'a Christian doctrine has been embodied in the *Nilus* image: the image is the sign of a concept' (p 9). He then offers a second valuable observation, which he admits is less susceptible to proof, namely, the qualification that the *Nilus* image was 'probably not intended to be visualized in all its particulars' (p 9.).

Bertonasco's insistence on the 'conceptual basis' of such emblematic imagery is a welcome correction to modern reading habits, which became derailed on the narrower gauge of emblematic thinking. Nowhere is this advice more essential than in the context of such religious poetry as Crashaw's 'Blessed Be the Paps which Thou Hast Sucked':

> Suppose He had been tabled at thy teats,
> Thy hunger feels not what He eats:
> He'll have His teat ere long, a bloody one –
> The mother then must suck the Son.

For one critic this comes close to being a 'revolting joke on Jesus and Mary,' with horrible suggestions of 'incest and perversion' (cf Bertonasco, p 10). Bertonasco argues that the basis of the poem is conceptual and doctrinal and that this knowledge should control our response to the imagery. 'The prose "meaning" of the poem is that although during His infancy Christ was dependent upon His mother for food (physical sustenance), she, to be redeemed, depended upon the shedding of His precious blood during the Crucifixion (spiritual sustenance)' (p 10).

Not all contracted emblems offend modern taste, or baffle the modern mind. The pages of the emblem-books are filled with pictures of objects from the world of man and nature which convey directly and unambiguously certain abstract meanings: the insignia of power, the tools of labour, birds, trees, and animals are all capable of conveying simple meaning directly and without explanation. Many live on as metonyms in the poetry of later periods. Greiffenberg employs the cedar tree as an emblem to convince the reader of the truth that even great strength is overcome by perseverance:

> constant effort
> relaxes never,
> even bends the cedars.

state Müh
feyret nie /
gar die Cedern beuget.   (P 371)

The extended word-emblem

In Bertonasco's opinion the extended word-emblems in poetry are far 'more formidable stumbling blocks' (p 16) than the contracted forms, largely because they have been wrongly regarded as merely superimposed ornamentation. As an example he quotes and analyses a stanza from 'On the Bleeding Wounds of Our Crucified Lord':

Water'd by the showres they bring,
The thornes that thy blest browes encloses
(A cruel and costly spring)
Conceive proud hopes of proving roses.

Far from seeing in these lines, as one critic does, a 'Perverse logic of ornamentation' (cited on p 18), Bertonasco argues that the image is there because of the 'conceptual exigencies' of the poem (p 19). The preceding stanza has announced the redemptive power of the passion. 'Logically following from this dogma (logic of *thought*, not image) is the *preciousness* of Christ's blood' (p 19). This though is embodied in Crashaw's sensuous emblem.

The emblem of the thorn and roses, lightly extended in Crashaw's poem, occurs in many German poems on Christ's passion. In a sonnet placed among the meditations on the *Leiden und Sterben Christi* Greiffenberg speaks of 'The roses of praise on the thorns of His shame' ('[die] Lobes Rosen auf den Dornen [seiner] schmach,' p 68). The higher degree of compression in this emblem results from the tendency of the baroque poet to sharpen antitheses, and is also in no small measure attributable to the fact that the German language, especially in the seventeenth century, is dominated by the noun and nominal constructions.

Bertonasco draws attention to another form of the extended word-emblem, in which a series of images passes in swift succession to illustrate a concept. A particularly lavish example is a twenty-five line passage from Crashaw's 'To the Name Above Every Name, the Name of Jesus. A Hymn.' Images such as 'Arabias,' 'frankincense,' and 'myrrh' express the richness of the name Jesus. Crashaw is not only conveying 'the *infinite extent* of the sweetness and goodness ... each iterative image subtly advances the thought' (p 23). In other words this is not redundant repetition, but amplification and variation.

I have drawn attention to similar examples in the poetry of Greiffenberg.[123] In a sonnet addressed to the Canaanite woman who 'forced' a miracle from Christ, the poetess offers the following words of encouragement:

You bold fighter! do not lose courage,
hold on, praying and urging! knock hard on this stone:
a spark of grace will surely be found there,
which, after a hard blow, will flash with joy from it.
You will yet drink the water of healing from this rock.
The tiger will soon be a pelican to you:
Mars, a star of Venus; thunder and lightning, sunshine.

Du kühne Kämpferin! laß nur den Muht nicht sinken /
halt bet= und nötend' an! klopf' hart an diesen Stein:
ein Gnaden=fünklein wird unfehlbar seyn darein /
das wird / nach starken stoß / mit Freuden aus ihm blinken.
Du wirst nach Heiles=Safft aus diesem Felsen trinken.
Das Tieger / wird gar bald ein Pelican dir seyn:
der Mars / ein Venus Stern; Blitz=Donner / Sonnenschein.   (Sonnet 125)

Characteristically emblematic is the structure of the image: Christ, because of his apparently hard-hearted neglect of the woman, is a stone; the woman is told to strike the stone, which leads to two associations: that of the spark of grace and the 'water' of healing. Typically, Christ the stone becomes Christ the rock, with obvious Old Testament echoes. The row of images that concludes the sonnet is not superfluous repetition, but rather a listing of the divine attributes which are about to be showered upon the woman. In spite of appearances to the contrary, the remorseless tiger will become her pelican (= self-sacrificing grace), fierce Mars will become a star of Venus (= love), and finally the thunderstorm, connoting divine wrath and perhaps punishment, will turn to sunshine (= grace and illumination).

It is tempting to see a connection – at least in terms of formal composition – between the extended word-emblem and the 'mehrständige Sinnbilder,' or multiple emblems, of the later seventeenth century. Harsdörffer's *Frauenzimmer Gesprächspiele* contain a number of examples. For instance, in book VIII Julia is given six wineglasses upon each of which three emblems are engraved. She asks the giver, Herr Reymund, to explain the emblems, which are in fact *impresa*. The emblems describe the causes, beginning, and end of war, a subject very close to the experience of most Germans living at the time the *Gesprächspiele* were written. The first glass has the following devices engraved upon it: a rhinoceros, with the motto 'Per arma quiesco'; a lion and dog, with the motto 'me haud impune lacessis'; and finally, a porcupine, with the motto 'repellere fas est.' Each of the emblems is explained in a five-line epigram. Taken together, this set of 'multiple emblems' makes a composite statement on different aspects of war. [124]

There is ample evidence among the Nürnberg group of poets alone to indicate that what Harsdörffer describes was in fact a fairly common practice. From a letter of Greiffenberg's it is clear that her friend Sigmund von Birken presented her with a wine goblet as a kind of cup of reconciliation after a period of prolonged estrangement. The goblet was engraved with sunflowers and the motto 'jetzt aufgegange.' [125]

The complex word-emblem

The complex word-emblem is the richly extended emblem, which contains a number of individual motifs related in different ways to the thought or concept at the basis of the poem. Southwell's 'The Burning Babe' provides a famous example:

My faultlesse breast the furnace is,
    The fuell wounding thornes:
Love is the fire, and sighs the smoake,
    The ashes, shame and scornes;

The fewale Justice layeth on,
    And Mercie blowes the coales,
The metall in this furnace wrought,
    Are mens defiled soules. [126]

A less ambitious complex emblem may be found in Greiffenberg's sonnet 'Über des Creutzes Nutzbarkeit'; the title names the theme, somewhat in the manner of an *inscriptio*. The first six lines of the octave present six visual demonstrations of the basic notion expressed by the title:

A fine thing to bring fruit in suffering!
The precious stone is produced by the salty flood.
Gold becomes perfect in the fire.
From hard rocks the sweet fountains spring.
The rose must push through the thorns.
The martyr's crown grows out of shed blood.

EIn schöne Sach / im Leiden Früchte bringen /
die Edlen Stein / zeugt die gesalzne Flut.
Es wird das Gold vollkommen in der Glut.
Aus hartem Felß die süssen Brunnen springen.
Die Rose muß her durch die Dörner dringen.
Die Martyr=Kron / wächst aus vergossnem Blut /   (Sonnet 82)

The general sense of the images is clear; however, the final lines of the octave bring a more precise interpretation:

out of torment and struggle grows christian heroism.
He who will be high, must struggle after greatness.

aus Plag' und Streit der Christlich Helden=muht.
Wer hoch will seyn / muß nach der Hoheit ringen.

Bertonasco finds that Crashaw demonstrates a 'remarkable skill in matching imagistic and logical relationships' (p 27) in the following complex emblem contained in the poem 'A Hymn to the Name and Honour of the Admirable Saint Theresa.' In death the saint's soul is:

Like a soft lump of incense, hasted
By too hot a fire, and wasted
Into perfuming clouds, so fast
Shalt thou exhale to heaven at last
In a resolving sigh.

The traditional symbols of incense for consecration, fire for ardour, and perfume for acceptability are here moulded into one emblematic picture.

A veritable *tour de force* of emblematic extension is provided by a passage in one of Greiffenberg's meditations on the sacrament. Of Christ's blood, which she receives in the sacrament, she writes:

how sweet you are to my soul and throat in the holy sacrament! I will be a bee and fly to this honey hill and red clover, and take away this purple booty. I will carry it into the cell of my memory: I will build a house of honour and praise to God. Wax of illumination shall grow from it: candle lamps which can withstand all the winds of storm and opposition; church candles to illuminate the altar and sacrament; bridal torches for the heavenly marriage of the lamb; table lights for the holy sacrament;

and finally, funeral torches for my grave, which will also make the grave light and lovely.

wie süß bist du meiner seele und kehle im heiligen Abendmal! Jch will ein Bienlein seyn / auf diesen honig hügel und roten klee zufliegen / und diesen purpur=raub hinwegführen. Jch will ihn eintragen / in die Zelle meiner gedächtnus: ich will ein gebäu der ehre / lob / und preises Gottes daraus bauen und aufführen. Es soll wachs der erleuchtung daraus werden; windlichter / die in allen winden der stürme und anfechtungen bestehen können; Kirchen=kerzen / Altar und heiligtum zu er-leuchten; Brautfackeln zu der himmlischen Hochzeit des Lam͂s; Tafel-lichter / zu dem heiligen Abendmal; und endlich leichfackeln / zu meiner begräbnus / die auch das Grab licht und lieblich zu machen.   (*Leiden und Sterben* CHRISTI, p 121)

Far from being mere empty repetition, the extension of imagery is controlled by a progression in thought from the candle of illumination through the bridal torch to the funeral torch.

The verbal 'impresa'

One might wonder whether there is anything to be gained by differentiating terminologically between the word-emblem and the verbal *impresa*. The criteria for the verbal *impresa* are basically Giovio's: namely that the pictorial elements shall contain no more than three motifs, and that the interpretation, where actually stated in words, shall be short, consisting either of a few words or a line of verse; furthermore, it shall represent a maxim, a line of conduct, a 'personal aim' ('eine persönliche Zielsetzung,' Schöne, p 43). It is certainly possible to find examples of poetic motifs that fulfil all these criteria. For instance, Günther has a perfect example of the poetic *impresa* in his poem 'An seine Leonora die immer grünende Hofnung.' In the first two stanzas the poet laments his misfortune, but determines to remain stoic and strong. Stanza 3 treats of his love, which is a source of strength and consolation to him.

Love pours from golden bowls
For me wine to bravery,
She promises to pay me a good reward,
And sends me into misfortune's fight.
   Here will I do battle,
   Here will I conquer;
   A green field
   Serves my shield
   As coat of arms
By which a palm-tree holds two anchors.

Die Liebe schenkt aus göldnen Schaalen
Mir einen Wein zur Tapferkeit,
Sie spricht, mir guten Sold zu zahlen,
Und schickt mich in den Unglücksstreit.
   Hier will ich kriegen,
   Hier will ich siegen;
   Ein grünes Feld
   Dient meinem Schilde
   Zum Wappenbilde,
Bey dem ein Palmenbaum zwey Anker hält. [127]

In the context of chivalrous love the lover is to do battle for his lady, who pours him wine before the contest and promises him a reward, presumably her love. He carries into the contest a coat of arms which is a 'Wahlwappen,' as opposed to the 'Erbwappen.' Against the green field, signifying hope, three motifs stand out: the palm-tree, signifying constancy, and two anchors, representing the hope that each has in the love of the other. It is a perfect *impresa* in form, content, and purpose.

In *Richard Crashaw. A Study in Style and Poetic Development* (Madison, 1935) Ruth Wallerstein has argued that many of Crashaw's images can be called *impresa* or heroic symbols rather than emblems. In addition to the five rules of Giovio, she describes the *impresa* as being 'more concentrated and more abstract even than the emblem' (p 124). However, as was stated earlier (chap 1, pp 23–5), the dividing line between the emblem and the *impresa* was a shifting one; what Wallerstein describes could equally well be a simple emblem, simple in that it contains a limited number of motifs and excludes the human form. The passage she quotes in support of her contention does not adequately illustrate the verbal *impresa*, since its function can hardly be regarded as representing a maxim or 'personal aim' (Schöne, p 43). The passsage reads:

Euen ballance of both worlds! our world of sin,
And that of grace heaun way's in HIM,
   Vs with our price thou weighed'st;
   Our price for vs thou payed'st;
Soon as the right hand scale reioyc't to proue
How much Death weigh'd more light than loue.

This may be emblematic, but to call it a verbal *impresa* only dilutes the concept of *impresa*. Critics who limit their pursuit of *impresa* to chivalric contexts are more likely to be successful. The works of Sidney, Nashe, and Marlowe – to name but three – have produced good examples. [128]

3

Emblematic Poetry

The most easily recognizable examples of emblematic structures in poetry may be found in those poems in which the writer appears to copy emblems, or at least produces exact verbal equivalents which he names emblems. Rosemary Freeman draws attention to the following 'unmistakable emblems' in Henry Vaughan's poem 'Les Amours':

... And on each leafe by Heavens command,
   These Emblemes to the life shall stand:
      Two Hearts, the first a shaft withstood;
... The second, shot, and washt in bloud;
   And on this heart a dew shall stay,
   Which no heate can court away;
   But fixt for ever witnesse beares,
   That hearty sorrow feeds on teares.
      Thus Heaven can make it knowne, and true,
      That you kill'd me 'cause I lov'd you.[1]

In *Richard Crashaw. A Study in Style and Poetic Development* Ruth Wallerstein has noted in the lyrics of Crashaw a 'transfer of the emblem into the actual texture of the verse' (p 120), by which she means the mixture of 'literal terms and ingenious figures' (p 120). For instance, Crashaw's 'Sancta Maria Dolorum' may owe much to Marino's 'Stabat mater,' but, she argues, the 'figurative method, whereby Crashaw strives to realize the idea as sensuous-emotional perception, is emblematic' (p 121). The following passage is offered as representative:

> O Mother turtle-doue!
> Soft sourse of loue
> That these dry lidds might borrow
> Something from thy full Seas of Sorrow!
> O in that brest
> Of thine (the noblest nest
> Both of loue's fires & flouds) might I recline
> This hard, cold, Heart of mine!

In its combination of concrete and visual imagery with religious fervour and controlled intellectual movement, this poem is of a kind with Southwell's 'Burning Babe.'[2] Wallerstein describes as emblematic another feature of Crashaw's poetry: the 'quaint blending of literal and figurative, of minute detail of resemblance with larger suggestive elements' (p 121). She notes that the combination of realism and symbolism[3] found in several emblem-books may also be discovered in Crashaw's verse. There is, for example, Cramer's emblem xxx, which shows a woman with padlocked lips standing before an anvil about to strike a heart with a hammer. The tools, the scene, and the background are all realistically drawn. 'The startling juxtaposition of highly symbolic design and homely realism of execution is, in technique and imaginative effect, very like Crashaw's "In this sad House of slow Destruction / (His shop of flames) hee fryes himselfe"' (p 122).

THE WORD-EMBLEM AS THE FOUNDATION OF A POEM

On occasions an emblem may be the inspiration for a whole poem, or at least its underlying foundation. When this is recognized, the emblem provides a key to the proper understanding of the poem, although the emblem itself may remain implicit.

In a brief note on Shakespeare's sonnet 116 'Let me not to the marriage of true mindes' John Doebler[4] suggests that the first quatrain implies the compass emblem, a common symbol for constancy. This supplies a better reading than the traditional view that Shakespeare means by 'alteration' the betrayal or indifference of the beloved, which none the less does not affect the constancy of the poet's love. Doebler points out that this interpretation is at variance with the famous statement in the opening line about 'the marriage of true mindes.' A love that does not change 'when it alteration findes' suggests to him the fixed foot of a pair of compasses, whereas the physical alteration of the lovers (cf 'rosie lips and cheeks') implies the spreading foot. Caught up in physical change, the lovers are stabilized by spiritual love. Doebler notes that the 'stable foot of ideal love' (p 110) merges with the Petrarchistic conceit of the star and the ship; both the compass and the star are 'an ever fixed marke.' This leads him to find in line 8 the suggestion of the navigator's sextant, itself a special form of the compass. The author concludes that this allusion and the reference to 'the "compasse" of Time's sickle in line ten both echo the emblem Shakespeare had in the back of his mind when he wrote the first quatrain' (p 110).

Doebler's is a useful contribution, not only because it enhances our understanding of Shakespeare's sonnet, but also because it indicates how emblematic structures may lie at the very foundation of a poem. I would only draw attention to a small homographic matter which seems to have escaped Doebler's notice. The word 'compass,' in its various spellings, is used by Shakespeare and his contemporaries for both the geometer's instrument (the pair of compasses) and the mariner's aid (the magnetic compass). However, the magnetic compass, like the pair of compasses, was a common emblem of constancy; it too belongs to the context of ships, stars, and 'ever fixed marks,' and, what is more, it could also connote constancy in the service of higher, immutable values. I would suggest that Shakespeare has woven three separate meanings of 'compass' into his sonnet: the pair of compasses, the magnetic compass, and 'compasse' in the sense of the scope or sweep of Time's sickle. The first two are emblems of constancy, the third an accidental verbal echo. The homographic association was possibly only because of the emblematic tradition of which these two objects were an important part.[5]

In the case of Shakespeare's sonnet 116 the compass emblems were submerged beneath the surface of the words, and their discovery provided a better reading of the whole poem. Höltgen presents good evidence of a series of emblems implied by the first quatrain of Donne's Holy Sonnet XIV, 'Batter my heart ...'[6] He seeks to establish parallels between emblem-books and the verbal metaphors 'knocke, breathe, shine and seeke to mend,' and 'breake, blowe, burn and make me new,' in order to suggest a more satisfactory interpretation to replace the older view that these images refer to God (power), the Holy Ghost (breath), and Christ (light).

Noting that an 'emblematic principle of composition and interpretation' (p 348)[7] can be assumed for both authors and readers of the period, Höltgen proceeds to describe the emblematic qualities of the images in question: 'They reveal a sharply defined, visually highly concrete image process in a gross immediacy, indeed almost unpleasant concreteness, the individual details of which require exact, quasi-logical allegorical interpretation' (p 348).[8] He compares Donne's images with various heart emblems of Quarles and van Haeften, and produces the following tabulated results (p 351):

knocke	*breathe*	*shine*	*seeke to mend*
Durities	Quarles	Illuminatio	Rectificatio
Cordis (II, 5)	Emblem v, 5	Cordis (III, 2)	Cordis (II, 20)
hammer and	flaming	lighted	levelling
anvil	breath	candle	instrument

breake	*blowe*	*burn*	*make me new*
Contritio	Hatfield	Inflammatio	Renovatio
Cordis (II, 11)	Tapestry	Cordis (III, 15)	Cordis (III, 1)
mortar and	bellows	lighted	new heart
rammer		torch	

Höltgen resists the temptation to press the intensification of Donne's imagery into the mystic framework of *via purgativa, illuminativa et unitiva*, which it does not quite fit, but he rightly observes that there is 'a certain intensification to the point of renewal of the heart' (p 351).[9]

A much more ambitious attempt to read poetry emblematically has been made by Frances Yates in an essay on Giordano Bruno and the Elizabethan sonneteers, published in 1943.[10] Basing her argument on parallels between the emblems of Bruno's *De Gli Eroici Furori* and the Petrarchistic conceits of Sidney's Stella cycle, Yates argues that Sidney's sonnets, and even Drayton's, should be read 'anti-petrarchistically' and spiritually. The discussion of Bruno's 'unillustrated emblem-book' (p 105) is illuminating. The work contains, first, an emblem or device, described in words; secondly, a poem in which the emblematic motifs reappear as verbal conceits; and thirdly, a commentary, bringing out the spiritual or philosophical meaning latent in the imagery. The book only lacks illustrations to be an emblem-book proper. The themes, attitudes, and *topoi* of the *De Gli Eroici Furori* are all Petrarchistic; the expressed purpose of the author is, however, anti-Petrarchistic, indeed intensely religious. His emblems are to be interpreted as representing the soul seeking God; and Bruno himself compares his intention to that of the Song of Solomon. After comparing Bruno's verbal conceits with his emblems, Yates, finding support in Mario Praz, concludes that 'the conceit is an emblem' (p 102). 'A large number of conventional sonnet images are used by Bruno in this way, that is to say, as emblems of mystical experience' (p 103). It is, then, Bruno's use and interpretation of motif, not the motif itself, which the author terms emblematic: 'to use the ordinary conceit with the other (spiritual) meaning, as Bruno does, is to use it as a genuine emblem – that is to say, as a picture which secretly refers to something other than that which it appears on the surface to represent' (p 107).

Because we are dealing with a 'naked' emblem-book, which the author expressly intends to be read as an emblem-book of sacred love, Yates is correct. But the statement quoted above is too general to serve as a description of emblematic structures in poetry. Both in theory and in practice, what Yates describes could as well be called a contra-fact. Any attempt to apply such a definition to poetry is likely to lead to difficulties. In moving from an emblem-book with expressed spiritual intentions to a Petrarchistic sonnet cycle Yates makes a leap – and falls on the other side of the emblem.

Let it be said at once that there may well be a connection between the Italian philosopher and the English sonneteer; it must also be conceded that there are similarities in theme, motif, and attitude between Bruno's emblems and Sidney's conceits. However, that similarity is more likely to have resulted from the two poets drawing on the common tradition of Petrarchism than to have been the outcome of Bruno's influence on Sidney. Furthermore, one misses any effort to describe the specific qualities of the word-emblem (formal, phenomenological, or semantic). Consequently, it is difficult to accept Yates's conclusions: 'Read in the light of the *Eroici Furori* Sidney's sonnets are seen to be, like Bruno's, a spiritual autobiography, reflecting in terms of Petrarchan emblems, the moods of a soul seeking God' (p 114). There is nothing in any of the sonnets quoted to suggest that Sidney intended his *Stella* to be a spiritual biography. Yates admits that there are problems in her thesis, acknowledging that it is difficult to reconcile her interpretation with the poet's reproaching himself for loving Stella, and furthermore with the fact that Stella herself is something less than perfect.

THE WORD-EMBLEM AS A CONTROLLING OR UNIFYING
ELEMENT IN POETRY

A number of critics have advanced interpretations of individual poems based on the notion that emblems, in addition to being important in terms of meaning, can also be structurally significant. Lloyd Goldman[11] believes that the word-emblem may structurally control or unify a poem. He discusses Daniel's fifteenth Delia sonnet in the light of its emblematic forerunners, especially as they bear on the image 'my Vultur-gnawne hart.' He writes: 'The most obvious indication of the controlling conceit in the sonnet occurs in line 8, an allusion to the Prometheus of Aeschylus' *Prometheus Bound*; but the use of the conceit seems to be based ultimately on the way the figure of Prometheus is employed in an emblem of Alciat's' (p 55). Although the notion that the vulture-heart image is a 'controlling conceit' may be attractive, there is little evidence either in Goldman's article or in the poem to support it. It is not clear what is supposed to be organized by the image; I can discover no related images, which, by a stretch of the argument, may be described as being controlled by the Promethean allusion. If any pattern at all develops, it is perhaps a religious one: 'smoake' and 'fire' possibly connote incense and adoration, and lead to the 'Temple sainted' mistress to whom 'homage is done.' If this be a pattern, it has little to do with the crime and punishment of Prometheus. According to Goldman, however, the Elizabethan poet 'wanted the idea of a complete emblem to be the inspiration that controlled the conceits in his sonnet sequence' (p 57). Is there a hint of the intentional fallacy here? Goldman may be right, both about Daniel's 'intention' and the resulting poem, but he nowhere demonstrates the correctness of these assertions. Sonnet 15 should prove the point, but it is not a convincing example. Goldman argues that 'Daniel places the idea of Prometheus' suffering in the background of the sonnet, in order to direct the moral import of that suffering to an end different from that of the emblematists' (p 57). We can at best infer intention from the effects we read out of the interrelationships between the individual structures which go to make up the poem as a whole. The point I am belabouring is more than a quibble about Goldman's phraseology; it concerns interpretational methods and assumptions. Daniel's sonnet does contain a Promethean allusion in the image quoted, and it may be in the form of a word-emblem; however, I search in vain for any relationship between this isolated image and the rest of the poem that would justify calling it the 'inspiration that controlled the conceits.' It is not 'in the background of the sonnet,' but rather in the foreground of line 8, expressing dramatically and visually the poet's suffering (not his punishment and implied crime), which is the theme of the sonnet.

Roger B. Wilkenfield is more successful in demonstrating the thematic function of the complex phoenix emblem which concludes Milton's *Samson Agonistes*.[12] In this dramatic poem where words replace stage actions the central theme is transcendent freedom which can result only from individual transformation. Blinded and in chains, Samson remembers his former greatness and betrayal through Delila, but, when summoned to amuse the Philistines in their games, he refuses. This marks the turning-point in his movement from passive slavery to an active decision to destroy his enemies and their temple. The great emblem of the phoenix not only draws together many fragmentary motifs such as 'fire,' but also 'resolves the poem's structural patterns' (p 160) and establishes for the last time 'the basic themes of freedom and transformation' (p 166).

In some poems word-emblems reappear from time to time, lending a certain thematic continuity to the piece; in larger works they can function almost as leitmotifs. In Spenser's *The Faerie Queene* Guyon has a horse called Brigador (v.ii.34), which means 'golden bridle' (brigilia d'oro). A.D.S. Fowler[13] shows that, like the golden set-square in the same book, the bridle is an emblem of temperance, a commonplace in books of emblems and *impresa*. Fowler demonstrates that this emblem is functional, 'for it is Braggadocchio's theft of Brigador which precipitates Guyon into the pedestrian adventures which follow; that is to say, it is originally through pride (Braggadocchio) that the Platonic horse of man's desires ceases to be bridled by temperance' (pp 143–4). In a brief footnote Fowler refers to other instances of this horse and bridle pattern. Guyon is described as being able to 'menage ... his pride' (II.iv.2), and later we find him 'Bridling his will' (II.xii.53). Fowler's references to Ripa and Valerianus's *Hieroglyphica* (Lyons, 1611), where the horse is a symbol of wilful passion, indicate that Spenser is emblematically drawing upon renaissance tradition.

The main body of Fowler's essay deals with a third emblem of temperance, namely the pouring of water into wine. 'This emblem makes the least obvious appearance, but only because it is developed on a scale we do not expect; it is hidden, only because most deeply structural' (p 144). Fowler interprets the nymph's fountain as the emblematic fusion of the three fountains of repentance, regeneration, and life, with Christ-Eros as the fountain figure. The principle water-image Guyon, whose name patristic tradition associated with the river of temperance which flowed through paradise, comes into contact with the wine images which are connected with the temptations of the Bower of Bliss. 'Since Guyon's entry into the Bower of Bliss brings images of water and wine together, the missing emblem of temperance has been found' (p 147).

Jane Aptekar has devoted a book-length study to an investigation of the iconographical presentation of themes of justice in book v of Spenser's *The Faerie Queene*.[14] There are three threads of thematic imagery – imagery that works by direct statement, by allusion, or by association – woven through book v (cf p 6). The first pattern is an orthodox Elizabethan presentation of justice: the good king imitates God in his execution of justice through the exercise of power and law, reconciling mercy and justice. Artegall's career illustrates this. However, there is ambivalence here, since the agents of justice, like good Machiavellian princes, employ force and fraud in combating those very evils of force and fraud. Furthermore, Spenser ironically undercuts the character of Artegall by associating him with the cruel and concupiscent Hercules, a classical champion of justice, but no paragon (cf p 7). The three iconic themes are, then, divine justice, force and fraud, and Hercules.

In part 1 of her study, 'God's Justice,' Aptekar shows how the agents of justice, the monarchs and judges Gloriana, Mercilla, Britomart, Artegall, and Arthur, are portrayed with the divine and kingly qualities and associates of Jove (pp 13–26) and the attributes of the sun (pp 70–83). Whereas Mercilla embodies merciful justice, Artegall and Arthur represent the wrathful justice more characteristic of Jove. These characters are provided, literally or figuratively, with the lion (pp 58–69), the sword (pp 39–40), the sun's rays (pp 70–83), thunderbolts (pp 75–6), and the brazen man (pp 41–54) to uphold justice and order on earth. Throughout this and the other sections of book v the author makes frequent comparison with emblem-books in order to uncover parallels in pictures and meaning.

Aptekar shows that Spenser's is no simple or straightforward treatment of the theme of justice. A careful analysis of Mercilla's lion (pp 61–9) reveals the complexity and ambiguity of Spenser's treatment of merciful justice. She concludes: 'The poet calls upon every available tradition to deepen his effect. He does not, however, do this in a doctrinaire manner: he merely hints at images which the reader should then create, in full for himself, and afterwards apply back to the poem as explicatory emblems. Because Mercilla's lion is chained, royning, and rebellious, it cannot be *only* the lion of England, or of magnanimity, or of clemency, or of force; it must suggest also various complex psychological and political truths' (p 69). Part II deals with the dubiety of justice, tracing the two emblematic patterns of force and fraud and Hercules. Virtually all the enemies of justice in book v employ guile; Geryoneo and his monster embody force and fraud, but iconographical parallels reveal that the knights who espouse the cause of justice also resort to the use of force and fraud.

It would take me beyond the scope and purpose of my investigation into emblematic literature and deep into Spenser studies were I to attempt to do justice to Aptekar's book. It must therefore suffice to offer as a sample of her research a résumé of her chapter on the crocodile. I choose it because it reveals 'Spenser's complex view of justice' (p 88). At the temple of Isis, where Britomart spends the night on her mission to rescue Artegall from Radigund, Britomart has a strange dream. She dreams that she becomes a queen-like figure (like Isis), threatened by a fire that erupts in the temple. The crocodile, sleeping at the feet of the idol Isis, awakens, devours 'Both flames and tempest' (vii.12), and then turns on Britomart-Isis 'to threaten her likewise to eat' (vii.14). Aptekar interprets the crocodile's attempted attack on Britomart as a would-be sexual assault. Britomart beats the creature into submission with a rod. The priest explains that the crocodile represents her 'faithful lover' (vii.22), who is 'like to Osyris' (vii.22). The apparently odd situation of Artegall = Osiris = justice, embodied in a crocodile at the feet of a victorious mistress, is explained by reference to two different renaissance traditions. Crocodiles were associated through Egyptian tradition *via* the hieroglyphics with Osiris, the sun, god, and justice. Set against this positive tradition was the negative one: since Osiris is a heathen god associated with hermetic magic, the crocodile is also an evil beast characterized by greed, guile, and lust (cf p 94). Spenser explains the meaning of the idol of Isis standing with one foot on a crocodile in orthodox terms: 'to suppress both forged guile, and open force' (vii.7). Traditionally the crocodile has the evil qualities of greed, brute force, deception, and lust; in submitting to Isis, i.e., Britomart, the crocodile 'embodies the whole significance of the Legend of Justice' (p 96). On a primary plane this episode signifies the proper submission of the god to the goddess, i.e., one aspect of justice to another, rigour to clemency; on a secondary plane it suggests an evil side of justice; on a third plane there is a pattern of love and marriage (cf p 97). Since the crocodile is at various times Britomart's assailant, saviour, and slave, the emblem contributes to the discussions of lust, marriage, and adultery, which fall within Aristotle's concept of justice. Aptekar concludes her analysis of this theme with the following statement: 'Isis's crocodile simultaneously manifests the energy that is creative concupiscence and the energy that is destructive lust; in synthesis, it manifests, too, the sexuality and uxoriousness which must be rationally restrained in right marriage' (p 107). These are regarded as 'metaphorical parallels' (p 107) to the central theme of justice, which is as ambivalent as that of sexual energy.

The third area of emblematic allusion is to Hercules, whose greatest trial was the temptation of Pleasure over Wisdom. The author notes that Artegall's sojourn with Radigund and the intervention of Britomart are reminiscent of the Choice of Hercules. Just as Hercules was unable to defeat Envy and her dog, so Artegall is vanquished finally by Envy and the Blatant Beast. Aptekar concludes that, although divine and heroic, justice is at times not only dependent on guile and force, but also subject to excesses of passion and even powerless in the face of envy and fame.

It is only natural that the *Delie* of Maurice Scève should have attracted a good deal of critical attention. Ruth Mulhauser[15] discusses the poetic function of the emblems in *Delie*, agreeing with other Scève scholars that the emblems are indeed 'symbolic visual equivalents, which often show a complexity of content that the simplicity of craftsmanship conceals' (pp 80–1). She finds that the 'visual concept becomes a verbal theme not only in the gloss *dizain* but in various forms throughout the group and may even help to provide a meaningful thematic organization or aesthetic structure to the entire work' (p 81). It is this feature of the recurrence of an emblem serving as a structural principle that Mulhauser deals with, taking as an example the emblem of a sawn-off tree trunk which has one or more leafing branches. This motif occurs in seven different emblems almost entirely in the first half of the series of fifty emblems. She finds it difficult to believe that this pattern is the result of mere chance. She examines closely the seven emblems as graphic picturizations, and then looks at the poetry with these in mind, discovering 'new richness of meaning' (p 83). These seven emblems create tension with the poems whose imagery is straight-forwardly sensual. In the second series the snow-laden tree recalls Delie's frigid purity. In the third group there are two trees signifying life and self-knowledge. And so on.

This careful and sensitive interpretation brings to the surface a 'subtle interplay between visual and poetic symbol' (p 89). Mulhauser is, however, careful to observe that it would be premature to conclude on the basis of this study of one symbol that the 'aesthetic structure of the total work derives from the subtle interplay between visual and poetic symbol. The evidence from this one group is too strong, nevertheless, to dismiss this meaningful aesthetic structure as coincidental or chance in the work of a poet like Scève who is at his best in the dense, multi-suggestive expression of his inner torment and strug-gle' (p 89).

One of the few literary works in the German language to combine a series of pictures with poetry is Sebastian Brant's verse satire the *Narrenschiff* (1494). Opinions have differed on the questions of whether, or to what extent, this work is an emblem-book. In a methodologically sound article Holger Homann[16] has investigated the nature and function of the pictures in the *Narrenschiff*. Basing his analysis on Schöne's structural definition of the emblem, Homann concludes that Brant's introductory remarks to the effect that the pictures are additional material for the illiterate holds true for the majority of the illustra-tions. Thus, the *Narrenschiff* is neither an emblem-book, nor emblematic. However, Homann shows that Brant's method of composition occasionally borders on the emblematic, where the *picturae* allow of several interpretations, one of which is seized upon by the poet (cf p 475). Even though this may be so, there remain important differences between Brant's illustrations and the characteristic emblem: 'The subjects represented in them are, however, used in the text as exempla, as demonstrations of explicit teaching, not as sources of knowledge; in no case does the text show that it has its point of departure in the *pictura*' (p 475). Brant's pictures are not 'functioning parts of a whole,' but merely an 'addition.'[17]

In the majority of the examples discussed above it is the picture or object that lends emblematic significance, be it structural or semantic, to the poem. How-ever, the reverse may also be true: the relation of the meaning of images to the underlying theme of a poem may provide the coherence missed in the *picturae* of the images themselves. The implied *subscriptio* thus constitutes a link between image and theme. Kingsley Widmer's essay 'The Iconography of Renunciation: The Miltonic Simile'[18] is primarily concerned with the theme of

Christian renunciation as the 'greatest heroism' (p 259) in Milton's longer poems. The author chooses Milton's similes to illustrate the polarity between good and evil in Milton's work. In the course of his interpretation Widmer finds it necessary to defend Milton's similes for Satan, which include flies and waves, and those for Christ, among them the wine-press and the rock. The close juxtaposition of these similes has offended the modern sensibilities of many critics. Widmer comments that the 'deeper coherence' of Milton's poetic comparisons has not always been recognized because of a 'misapplied aesthetic' (p 263). What he in fact describes is a conceptual emblematic structure; although the word 'emblematic' nowhere appears, the title 'The Iconography of Renunciation ...' indicates the direction Widmer is taking. In answer to the frequent criticism that Milton's similes are visually and logically inconsistent Widmer writes: 'The hyper-logical critic ... might ask ... how ... puny flies can be powerful waves, how a wine-press can also be a rock, how buzzing can also be battery, and how the single person of Satan can reasonably be compared to a swarm of flies and a series of waves ... Milton's similes, however, do not attempt to elaborate the visual logic of a scene or character. The coherence of the Miltonic texture requires the application of a dialectical rather than a visual principle' (p 262). The images are, then, justified by the vertical connection with the underlying conceptual themes, rather than by any horizontal, organic, or associative relationship with each other, and this is an emblematic structural principle. 'Puzzling qualities of Milton's poetic texture frequently receive a deeper coherence if read as part of Milton's theological polarity between a dynamic and plentitudinous evil and an unchanging and absolute good' (p 263). Widmer's comment on the function of detail in baroque style is one that has been with much justification applied to baroque architecture and music: 'the apparent disparity and flourish of detail re-enforces rather than dissolves the underlying equilibrium and logic of the art work' (p 263).

THE EMBLEMATIC POEM

Until now we have been concerned with poetry containing examples of the word-emblem, singly or in groups; there are, however, also emblematic poems, which dispense with the printed picture altogether, creating through words a structure which parallels the emblem at all points, providing both the picture and its interpretation or application. Some seventeenth-century theoreticians such as Jacob Friedrich Reimann go so far as to argue that there is a genre of emblematic verses which imitates the threefold pattern of the emblem in individual stanzas or as whole poems (cf Manfred Windfuhr, p 96). Windfuhr is certainly right when he suggests: 'It would be rewarding to investigate more closely baroque lyric poetry from this angle' (p 96).[19]

A number of English critics have made reference to the emblematic poem. Samuel Chew finds that Verstegen's poem 'A resemblence of Martyrs' is 'a naked emblem ... an emblematic poem without any accompanying design, the design being left to the reader's imagination. The theme is that, as from the meeting of flint with steel comes the spark, so from the meeting of "resolved minds" comes the "fire of sacred love".'[20] In *The Sister Arts* Jean Hagstrum observes that 'when not accompanied by a design ... [poetry] then verbally creates or implies its own design. The title or the metaphorical words of its text bring an image to mind, which then becomes the emblem of the poem, the "visual" embodiment of its abstract meaning' (p 98). Herbert's poems 'The Collar,' 'The Pully,' and 'Windows' are frequently cited as examples. Rosemary Freeman finds that in these poems 'visual images are certainly present – they form, in fact, the basis of the poem' (*English Emblem Books*, p 154). According to T.O. Beachcroft: 'Poems which need only the picture to make them acknowledged emblems are frequent, and among the most characteristic of the [Jacobean] age.'[21]

It seems to me that there are, broadly speaking, three kinds of emblematic poem. In one arrangement the picture is broken down into a series of related images, or image details, each self-contained and supplied with its interpretation. Anna H. Kiel[22] has drawn attention to examples in the writing of Rompler von Löwenhalt. As in Rompler's sonnet 'Kirch-schiff,' the pattern of parallel image and interpretation may actually begin in the title:

CHURCH-SHIP

The Holy Church of God may be compared with a ship,
Which travels through the sea of the world, voyaging through the flood of time,
Until it can land, attain salvation.
If it is not to founder, not to be driven off course,
When the storms of misfortune come, the winds blow cross-ways,
Then God himself must be the captain, good spirits the helmsmen;
Faith a strong mast, on which long and wide
The sails of prayer reach even to the clouds.
From the front this ship is very narrow in shape,
For from Adam the number of Christians
increases towards the middle, then declines again,
Gradually closing to a point behind.
Oh, Captain, help us soon to reach the longed-for peace,
That we, full of joy, may reach the Kingdom of Heaven.

KIRCH-SCHIFF

Die frome Gottes-kirch ist einem schiff zugleichen /
So durch das Wält-mér-fährt / reisst durch die flutt der Zeit /
Bis daß es länden kan / erlangt die Séligkeit.
Soll es nicht untergehn / nicht abwegs etwan weichen /
5 Wan Unglücks-wetter komt / die Wind auch kreützweis streichen /
Mus Got selbs schiff-herr seyn; fron-gaister steüer-leüth;
Der Glaub ein starcker mast / an welchem lang und breit
Die ségel des Gebäts bis an die wolcken reychen.
Diß schiff gestaltet sich von vornenher gar schmal /
10 Dan von dem Adam an hat sich der Christen zahl
Dem mittelzu vermehrt; bald wider abgenomnen /
Es spitzt sich nach-und-nach von hinden endlich zu.
Ach / Schiff-herr / hilf uns bald in die gewünschte ruh /
Aufdaß wir voller freüd im Himelreich ankommen!

The image of a voyage is divided into its constituent components, sea, ship, landing, storm, anchor, and so on, and each visual detail is interpreted with reference to the spiritual life. Rompler's 'Öl-liecht der glaubigen Sel' and 'Gaistliche Spiegelberaitung' reveal a similar structure: the central motif is analysed through a series of individual images each of which is named and interpreted.

Comparison with the tripartite emblem produces the following scheme:

1 Poem title naming the theme: *inscriptio*
2 Poem with images and interpretation: *pictura* and *subscriptio*[23]

A second group of emblematic poems presents a fuller and more detailed picture first, and gives the interpretation afterwards. Kiel cites Rompler's 'Unser wandel ist im Himel' as representative of this form:

WE ARE CITIZENS OF HEAVEN
Phil. 3:20
He who travels in the Indes, he who finds himself in foreign lands,
Does he not long for home and his own people,
Almost like a little child, weaned from the breast, who
Does not want to be weaned? If one thinks of relatives,
Wife, child, home and hearth, companions and acquaintances,
If elsewhere his head were even crowned with gold,
Home would still hold his heart in strong bonds,

Would still remain a magnet. What are we Christians doing
Here in this alien world, but gradually falling in love
With vanity and dallying with danger?
Oh, do not delay too long, think on eternity!
We are from Heaven and have but little time here:
Let us hurry, like travellers, towards our home.

UNSER WANDEL IST IM HIMEL
Phil. 3/20

1   Wer raist in Indien / wer ist in frömden landen /
   Der sich nicht wider heym und zu den seinen söhnt /
   Fals als ein kleines kind / daß von der brust entwöhnt /
   Nicht wil entwöhnet seyn? Denckt einer an verwandten /
5   An weib / kind / haus und hof / gesellen und bekanten /
   So ist er / wa er ist / nur halb / und als entlöhnt;
   Würd' anderst-wa sein haupt schon gar mit gold gekrönt /
   So hielt' die heymat doch sein härtz in starcken banden /
   Blib immer sein magnet. Waß thun wir Christen hie
10 In diser frömden Walt / als daß wir / ie-und-ie
   In eütelkeit verliebt / uns mit gefahr verweilen?
   Ach saumt euch nicht zuvil / denckt an die éwigkeit!
   Wir seyn von Himelher / und haben kurtze zeit:
   Lasst uns der heymatzu / als wandersleüthlein / eillen!

Basically the octave presents the picture of the traveller longing for home, which the sestet then applies to the situation of the Christian in the world.

Rosemary Freeman observes that the structure of Vaughan's poem 'The Waterfall' follows that of an emblem exactly: 'It is divided into three sharply distinguished sections, each marked by a change in form and rhythm. In the first the waterfall is described ... Then it is interpreted, and the meaning ... in the vocabulary of the second half of the description, is made explicit' (*English Emblem Books*, pp 151–2).

However, there are times when Freeman's somewhat negative view of the emblem (as an arbitrary symbol) clouds her appreciation of the poetry of emblematic meditation. A case in point is the relatively pedestrian poem by George Wither entitled 'Marigold,' which Freeman criticizes as an arbitrary emblem.

When, with a serious musing, I behold
The gratefull, and obsequious *Marigold*,

How duely, ev'ry morning, she displayes
Her open brest, when *Titan* spreads his Rayes;
How she observes him in his daily walke,
Still bending towards him, her tender stalke;
How, when he downe declines, she droopes and mournes,
Bedew'd (as 'twere) with teares, till he returnes;
And, how she vailes her *Flow'rs*, when he is gone,
As if scorned to be looked on
By an inferiour *Eye*; or, did contemne
To wayt upon a meaner *Light*, then Him.
When this I meditate, methinkes, the Flowers
Have *spirits*, farre more generous, then ours;
And, give us faire Examples, to despise
The servile Fawnings, and Idolatries,
Wherewith, we court these earthly things below,
Which merit not the service we bestow.
   But, oh my God! though groveling I appeare
Vpon the Ground, (and have a rooting here,
Which hales me downward) yet in my desire,
To that, which is above mee, I aspire:
And, all my best *Affections* I professe
To *Him*, that is the *Sunne of Righteousnesse*.
Oh! keepe the *Morning* of his *Incarnation*,
The burning *Noone tide* of his bitter *Passion*,
The *Night* of his *Descending* and the *Height*
Of his *Ascension*, ever in my sight:
   That imitating him, in what I may
   I never follow an inferiour *Way*.[24]

The poem opens with a twelve-line description of the marigold and sun; line 13 represents the point at which the 'representational,' or pictorial, part is complete, and the application begins. Wither is explicit: the 'serious musing' of line 1 becomes 'When this I meditate ...' There follows a passage, equal in length, which interprets the meaning of the flower in terms of the soul's relation to God, and, as with all meditation, the poem concludes in a colloquy, which itself is a miniature meditation on the significance of the times of the day. Freeman disapproves of the explicit working out of parallels. She writes: 'In spite of the accumulation of parallels which he can produce, the emblem writer fails in the end to provide any convincing reason for his choice of that particular image. It remains arbitrary. Wither, for instance, takes the symbol of the Marigold and gives it a religious significance ... There are plenty of likenesses yet the Marigold carries no conviction as a symbol of religious life in the poem, and Wither might multiply his points of resemblance indefinitely without ever being able to persuade the reader that they are anything more than accidental' (pp 26–7). She prefers Blake's poem on the same flower, which does not draw 'explicit comparisons' (p 27). This is, of course, circular argumentation, proceeding from an unproven contention that *per definitionem* the emblem is arbitrary. At best such literary criticism is an exercise in private taste.

An interesting variation of this emblematic structure is found in Greiffenberg's sonnet 57 on tears. The function of tears is demonstrated by reference to visually perceived facts of nature: the action of the sun on the dampness of the earth. The sun draws off the damp vapours, bringing warmth and fine weather, and banishing storms and rain. This description is presented in the two quatrains without any interpretation, as is always the case in the *picturae* of the emblem-books. The interpretation follows in the first five lines of the sestet, in which the individual images are repeated and supplied with an explanatory word ('Geistes freud,' spiritual joy; 'trübsal dieser zeit,' affliction of this time); in itself, this is reminiscent of the explanatory poem frequently added to the tripartite emblem in the vernacular tongue of the emblematist. The final line sums up the meaning of the poem in a general and abstract statement, which functions as a kind of *subscriptio*:

Thus God's mercy must unite with our distress.

So muß sich GOttes gnad mit unser Noht vereinen.[25]

The overall pattern might be stated as follows:

1 Poem title naming theme: *inscriptio*
2 Poem with
   (a) pictorial representation: *pictura*
   (b) pictorial interpretation: explanatory poem
   (c) verbal interpretation: *subscriptio*[26]

Windfuhr notes a similar structure in a number of Gryphius's sonnets. After comparing Gryphius's 'An die Welt' with Goethe's 'Seefahrt' to demonstrate some differences between allegorical and symbolical methods of composition, Windfuhr makes a general observation which applies to Gryphius and to a host of other baroque poets: 'The positioning of the interpretative comments shows that Gryphius usually placed his explanations above or beneath the image section, in the title or tercets. His sonnet thus approaches the three-part structure of the emblem.'[27]

Jöns finds that in its two-part structure Gryphius's sonnet to morning 'Die ewig helle Schaar ...' is an exemplary instance of the kind of emblematic poem he frequently wrote (p 102). 'Composition and content of this sonnet are straightforward: after the description of the sunrise there follows the plea for illumination of the soul and the attainment of eternal salvation' (ibid, p 91).[28] Jöns points out that the very symmetry and parallelism in this poem – and the observation could be extended to all poetry of this emblematic meditative kind – has been an obstacle to its understanding and appreciation. He quotes passages from Ziemendorff, Fricke, and Herbert Cysarz to demonstrate how often such poetry has been criticized for its lack of 'mood' and misuse of nature, or for the faulty combination of 'purpose-free creation' and 'nature mood' with religious and moral didacticism, which destroys the organic unity of the poem. The most frequent objection is that a didactic moral is tacked on to a nature poem. Jöns summarizes: 'In this view, which wants to see its concepts of purpose-free creation, basic feeling for nature, and unity of mood fulfilled in Gryphius's sonnet, all of which was only to be fulfilled through the release of subjectivity in the lyrical poetry of Storm and Stress, the second part must needs appear to be an appended religious thought, and at the same time an aesthetically disruptive addition that breaks the unity of the poem' (ibid., p 92).[29]

Unlike Ziemendorff, Cysarz, and to some extent Fricke, who all in varying degrees approach baroque poetry with preconceptions from the age of Goethe, Jöns takes a different tack: he follows up the older tradition of *Dingsymbolik* with the intention of showing that the nature motifs in Gryphius's sonnet are determined by an older and firmly established tradition of symbolism (cf ibid, p 94). This tradition culminates in the emblematic lexica, meditative books, and religious poetry of the seventeenth century (cf ibid, pp 94–8). For example, in Arndt's *Wahres Christentum* the different qualities of the sun are not only interpreted but assigned corresponding biblical passages, producing a veritable concordance. Under the influence of rhetoric this interpretational practice becomes an art (ibid, p 98). Jöns concludes his discussion of this sonnet and its allegorical precursors with the statement: 'For a judgment of the poem it follows that ... it is the expression of an old, firmly traditional motif of Christian nature interpretation, and that its two-part structure is already determined by the form of allegory as an analogy between concrete reality and spiritual significance' (ibid, p 99).[30] The first half of the poem contains the poetic description of nature which corresponds to the *pictura* of an emblem. Jöns's interpretation establishes convincingly that this poem – and others like it – are emblematic, in the sense of emblem both as 'art form' and as 'mode of thought.'

Finally, there are those emblematic poems in which a single theme or concept is expressed through a series of image variations, each complete in itself and different from the next, linked to its neighbour by the basic theme, rather than by continuity or kinship of imagery. Crashaw's 'The Weeper' – so frequently criticized for its faulty construction – is, as Beachcroft points out, 'an Emblem poem.' He observes: 'it could not have been constructed in any other way. It is simply a series of descants upon a central theme: when one verse is closed there is nothing to do save to begin another: and Crashaw over a number of years continued to add verses to his collection of conceits on the 'Weeping Magdalen,' which are not intended to develop one from the other any more than are the beads of a rosary.'[31]

Some so-called icon poems reveal on occasions an emblematic structure.[32] In the icon poem a theme, always stated in the title or initial lines, is expressed through a series of imagistic variations, each complete and self-contained and usually limited to a single line of verse. Hofmannswaldau is perhaps the best-known German poet to make fairly extensive use of this form in both a light-hearted and serious vein. Poems such as 'Der Todt' show certain structural similarities with the kind of emblematic poem we have been considering above.

DEATH
What is death to the pious?
A key to life,
A boundary stone to evil times,
A sleep potion of old grapes,
Peace after war and struggle,
A guide to the sun,
A path to the fatherland,
A sunrise of all joy,
An impetus from a great hand,
A tinder to the light,
A flight into the other world,
A meal of paradise,
A blow that brings all down,
A departure of all sufferings,
A tree against all misery,
What should I say more?
All this is death.

DER TODT
WAs ist der Todt der Frommen?
Ein Schlüssel zu dem Leben,

Ein Gräntzstein böser Zeit,
Ein Schlafftrunk alter Reben,
Ein Fried auf Krieg und Streit,
Ein Führer zu der Sonne,
Ein Steg ins Vaterland,
Ein Auffgang aller Wonne,
Ein Trieb von grosser Hand,
Ein Zunder zu dem Lichte,
Ein Flug in jene Welt,
Ein Paradiesgerichte,
Ein Schlag, der alles fällt.
Ein Abtritt aller Plagen,
Ein Baum vor alle Noth,
Was soll ich ferner sagen?
Diß alles ist der Todt.
(*Deutsche Nationallitteratur*, XXXVI, 86–7)

In poems such as 'Die Welt' the imagistic variations on the theme, so charac-teristic of the icon poem, finally make way for a meditation[33] on the significance of the subject, which, in this instance, amounts to the religious decision to turn away from vain worldly affairs:

THE WORLD
What is the world and its famed splendour?
What is the world and all its show?
A vile light set in narrow limits,
A sudden lightning in a black-clouded night;
A colourful field where thorns of care grow;
A beautiful hospital, full of sickness.
A house of slavery, where all men serve,
A foul grave, covered with alabaster.
That is the foundation upon which we men build,
And what flesh considers an idol,
Come, soul, come and learn to look further,
Than the compass of this world stretches.
Cast aside its short-lived glory,
Consider its joy a heavy burden.
Thus you will easily enter into this port,
Where eternity and beauty will enclose you.

DIE WELT

WAs ist die Welt und ihr berühmtes gläntzen?
Was ist die Welt und ihre gantze Pracht?
Ein schnöder Schein in kurtzgefaßten Gräntzen,
Ein schneller Blitz, bei schwargewölkter Nacht;
Ein bundtes Feld, da Kummerdisteln grünen;
Ein schön Spital, so voller Kranckheit steckt.
Ein Sclavenhauß, da alle Menschen dienen,
Ein faules Grab, so Alabaster deckt.
Das ist der Grund, darauff wir Menschen bauen,
Und was das Fleisch für einen abgott hält,
Komm Seele, Komm, und lerne weiter schauen,
Als sich erstreckt der Zirkel dieser Welt.
Streich ab von dir derselben kurtzes Prangen,
Halt ihre Lust für eine schwere Last.
So wirst du leicht in diesen Port gelangen,
Da Ewigkeit und Schönheit sich umbfast.
(*Deutsche Nationallitteratur*, XXXVI, 87–8)

These three forms of the emblematic poem are provisional models that may make it easier for the modern reader to approach emblematic poetry; they are not to be taken as watertight compartments into which all poems of this kind must be fitted. They are more like crutches to be cast aside when their purpose is served. There are other ways in which poetry of this period reveals an emblematic structure.[34]

Most of the examples of emblematic poetry quoted in this chapter have been sonnets, with the exception of the last two icon poems. That is perhaps not a coincidence. The sonnet form, with its strict division into quatrains and tercets, not only allows, but also encourages, a division into pictorial and interpretational sections. However, the sonnet is not the only form of emblematic poetry; epigrams of various length are equally suited to the emblematic purpose, as the following examples, chosen at random from Silesius's *Der Cherubinische Wandersmann* (1657, expanded ed 1674), may demonstrate:

THE MAKING OF SPIRITUAL GOLD

Lead turns to gold, and accident falls away,
When I with God, through God, am turned into God.

DIE GEISTLICHE GOLDMACHUNG

Dann wird das Blei zu Gold, dann fällt der Zufall hin,
Wenn ich mit Gott durch Gott in Gott verwandelt bin.   (1.102)

ETERNAL LIGHT
I am an eternal light, I burn without ceasing:
My wick and oil is God, my spirit is the vessel.

DAS EWIGE LICHT
Ich bin ein ewig Licht, ich brenn ohn Unterlaß:
Mein Docht und Öl ist Gott, mein Geist, der ist das Faß.   (1.161)

THE BIRTH OF THE PEARL
The pearl is conceived of the dew and born
In an oyster, and this is soon proven
If you do not believe it: the dew is God's Spirit,
The Pearl Jesus Christ, the oyster my soul.

DIE PERLENGEBURT
Die Perle wird vom Tau in einer Muschelhöhle
Gezeuget und geborn und dies ist bald beweist,
Wo dus nicht glauben willst: der Tau ist Gottes Geist,
Die Perle Jesus Christ, die Muschel meine Seele.   (III.248)

THE PATTERN POEM

In the pattern poem, *Bildgedicht* or *Figurengedicht*, the lines of verse vary in length to produce an outline of the object described or referred to by the poem. Occasionally other typographical means are employed to create or enhance the visual impression. The pattern poem may be regarded as the pinnacle of *ut pictura poesis* poetry; in some instances it represents the ultimate triumph – or ultimate degradation, depending on taste and point of view – of the emblematic tradition in poetry. Given the ancient origins of the pattern poem in Greek and oriental literature,[35] doubts may arise whether it can be properly regarded as emblematic at all. The earliest examples of pattern poetry are contained in the *Greek Anthology*, where we find six simple shapes: two altars, an axe, an egg, shepherd's pipes, and a pair of wings. The rediscovery of this poetic form is the work of renaissance humanists, who were responsible for popularizing the *Greek Anthology* in the sixteenth century.

Even during its heyday the pattern poem was the subject of widely differing opinions, and those who composed them occasionally felt it necessary to justify them. Modern scholars by and large view the pattern poem as an eccentric exercise, at best ingenious, at worst puerile. The history of its reception is more chequered even than that of the emblem, which during the seventeenth century seems to have had fewer detractors.

Perhaps it would be well to begin with E.R. Curtius who ascribes to the pattern poem a place in the development of mannerism, that much used and ill-defined label for what many critics appear to dislike. It seems necessary to begin here, since both Curtius's description of mannerism and his critical attitude to it have coloured the response of most scholars to both mannerism and the pattern poem, since the publication of his monumental *European Literature and the Latin Middle Ages* in 1948. Curtius describes mannerism as 'a decadent form of Classicism' (p 273), and the latter as 'Nature raised to the Ideal' (p 273). Curtius regards mannerism as a 'constant in European literature' (p 273), and the complementary or polar opposite of classicism. His 'litmus test' is the application of the concepts *aptum*, *perspicuitas*, and *ornatus*. The mannerist piles on ornamentation without respect for the subject of his composition: the style is the thing, the more ingenious, the more 'unnatural' and 'abnormal' (cf Curtius, p 282), the better. Or so the argument goes. Put less contentiously, in mannerist poetry there is an alleged discrepancy between 'content' and 'form.' Of the pattern poem Curtius writes: 'Manneristic virtuosity celebrates its greatest triumphs when it combines grammatical with metrical trifling' (p 284).

In a somewhat similar vein Margaret Church refers to pattern poetry as 'Grecian pedantries' (p 646) and an 'intellectual game' (p 646). In their article on the German pattern poem Roger G. Warnock and Roland Folter[36] refer to pattern poems as 'manneristic oddities' (p 42), and a 'manifestation of the ornamental' (p 40), a statement which follows a quotation from Curtius in which he says: 'in manneritistic epochs, the *ornatus* is piled on indiscriminately and meaninglessly.' On the other hand, Warnock and Folter recognize the serious religious use made of the pattern poem and themselves refer to its connections with the emblem tradition, a connection they do not, however, fully investigate. Conrad Wiedemann has a less negative view of mannerism; in his study of Klaj he advances the view that the roots of mannerism lie in the mysteries of religion.[37]

Although I must resist the temptation to enter the labyrinth of mannerism, it is necessary for my purposes to make a couple of obvious points: if mannerism can be usefully defined as empty formalism (much in the Curtius sense), and properly applied to much religious poetry of the Baroque, and religious pattern poetry in particular, then the latter must be written off as empty exercises. If, on the other hand, such poetry can be shown to convey meaningful statements, and its *ornatus* can be demonstrated to make a functional contribution, then the term 'mannerism' (in the above sense) is out of place.

Just as some emblems are serious and others may be merely frivolous trifles, so too there are serious and playful pattern poems, and there are good and bad ones in each group. Herbert's 'Altar' and 'Easter-Wings' are certainly not mere 'intellectual games,' 'manneristic oddities,' or 'Spielereien.'

'Easter-Wings' (see illustration 15) is a 'visual hieroglyph,'[38] but not in the sense of a contrived or enigmatic sign. C.C. Brown and W.P. Ingoldsby[39] insist that the winged shape 'was not used arbitrarily by the poet' (p 131) and argue that 'the poem will not yield its meaning unless one reads the visual shape as part of its carefully controlled symbolic language' (p 131). They show how the shortening of the lines of verse figures 'fall and decay' (p 134), while the lengthening of the lines figures 'redemptive arising, spiritual growth' (p 134). As far as the pattern is concerned, 'the general shape of [Herbert's] stanzas is Greek; the precise dimensions Hebrew' (p 131). Brown and Ingoldsby observe that whereas the Simmias stanza had six lines, Herbert's poem has five lines in each wing, which compares exactly with the description of two cherubim in the temple of Solomon, whose wings were five cubits high. Hence, perhaps, the pair of double wings in Herbert's poem. They go on to enumerate instances of winged angels in the Old and New Testament, and the fact that Christ himself is depicted as winged, indeed 'bearing healing in his wings.' All this merges in the poet's desire to arise with Christ at Easter. One can but agree with Brown and Ingoldsby that in the past readers have over-emphasized the childlike qualities of Herbert's verse in general, and this poem in particular; their interpretation does much to demonstrate the 'intellectual rigor' and 'sophisticated awareness' (p 142) of the poet.

Rosemary Freeman recognizes the 'emblematic quality' (*English Emblem Books*, p 155) of poetry such as this, which reflects 'an habitual cast of mind, a constant readiness to see a relation between simple, concrete, visible things and moral ideas' (ibid, p 155). In a century which used emblematic syntheses seriously in all the arts, it is only natural that the pattern poem should take on an emblematic function, the visual outline replacing an actual illustration of the object under consideration. What could be more natural than to transform the emblematic poem with its serious conceptual foundation into a pattern poem by condensing the *pictura* of an emblem into the shape of the verbal work? In such a synthesis the outline visually introduces the object of thought or meditation and constantly reinforces the meaning by appealing to the sense of sight and fixing attention on the concrete basis of thought. Such poetry appeals simultaneously to the senses and the intellect, as does the emblem.

Warnock and Folter draw attention to 'close parallels' (p 50) between some pattern poems and emblems; it is, however, source relationships that they are primarily interested in, although they recognize the 'possibility of a common

EASTER WINGS

Lord, who createdst man in wealth and store,
Though foolishly he lost the same,
Decaying more and more,
Till he became
Most poor:
With thee
Oh let me rise
As larks, harmoniously,
And sing this day thy victories:
Then shall the fall further the flight in me.

My tender age in sorrow did begin:
And still with sicknesses and shame
Thou did'st so punish sin,
That I became
Most thin.
With thee
Let me combine,
And feel this day thy victory,
For, if I imp my wing on thine,
Affliction shall advance the flight in me.

Illustration 15
George Herbert's *Easter Wings*, from *The Temple* (1633)

cultural heritage serving as an independent source for both forms' (p 50). This primary concern with sources leads the authors to underestimate the importance of seeing in the pattern poem a structural parallel to the emblem. They write: 'It is perhaps not too important for the patterns of Helwig and Kornfeld that the hourglass was a frequent emblematic device of death and the transitoriness of life, nor for the eulogistic palm-tree poems of Zesen and Männling to know that the figure, like the goblet, was an emblematic symbol of virtue' (p 50). I believe that the opposite is true, if by 'emblematic' we understand that form of thought and expression established by Schöne and Jöns. If the pattern poem can exhibit qualities which connect it structurally and conceptually with the emblem, then the discovery of such a parallel is significant and must lead to revaluation of the genre and its potentialities. The point is that, if certain pattern poems are emblematic, then they should not be judged to be 'mannerist' in the sense of marked by empty formalism and redundant ornamentation.

Warnock and Folter have discovered in Alciatus a 'precise parallel' (p 51) to the pattern of a nut-tree in Helwig's *Nymphe Noris*. Alciatus's emblem, which shows two peasant boys bringing down nuts by throwing sticks and stones at the tree, illustrates the them of ingratitude and abundance causing its own misfortune. In the version of Geoffrey Whitney, *A Choice of Emblemes* (Leiden, 1586), the *subscriptio* reads:

If sence I had, my owne estate to knowe,
Before all trees, my selfe hath cause to crie:
In euerie hedge, and common waye, I growe,
Where, I am made a praye, to passers by:
    And when, they see my nuttes are ripe, and broune,
    My bowghes are broke, my leaues are beaten doune.

Thus euerie yeare, when I doe yeelde increase,
My proper fruicte, my ruine doth procure:
If fruictlesse I, then had I growen in peace,
Oh barrennes, of all most happie, sure
    Which wordes with griefe, did AGRIPPINA grone,
    And mothers more, whose children made them mone.[40]   (P 174)

Helwig's pattern poem on the same subject (see illustration 16)[41] is structurally more emblematic than the explanatory emblem poem in Alciatus's *Emblematum liber*. This example is particularly interesting, in that it reveals the bipartite structure characterisitc of the word-emblem. In the first part of the

Nußbaum

Ach!
ohn Schuld'
hier leid' ich
williglich /
und ertrage mit Gedult
den/d'quälet mich.
Soll dann das lieben seyn.
bittre schwere Pein!
So man meiner Früchten wil/
schau/geniessen schlecht/
werd' ich meiner Zier beraubt mit Unbill/
Bauren Kinder/Mägd' und Knecht/
schenken mir an stat eines Dankeskuß/
Stein' und Stekken mit Verdruß/
so   alhier
für   und   für
ist der Lauff/,
ist der Kauff;
Hass für Ehr
itzt   vielmehr
hier   regirt/
Und   verführt
ieden   Stand.
Sonder Schand
fremd Gut nemen mit Gewalt/
macht / daß alle Lieb' erkalt.

Illustration 16
Johann Helwig's poem 'Nußbaum,'
from his *Die Nymphe Noris in Zweien Tagzeiten vorgestellet*
(Nürnberg, 1650), p 85
OPPOSITE English translation by PMD

NUT-TREE

Oh!
Without guilt
I suffer here
willingly,
I bear with patience
him, who torments me.
Is that then love?
bitter, heavy pain!
When they want simply to
enjoy my fruit, look,
I am unjustly robbed of my ornament,
Peasant children, girls and servants
peevishly bestow on me sticks and stones
instead of a kiss of thanks.
So is the course,
so is the purchase
here with us
through & through.
Hate, not honour,
it is that
rules here,
And seduces
each station.
Without disgrace
taking another's property with force,
makes all love turn cold.

Uber den gekreutzigten
JESUS.

Seht der König König hängen/
und uns all mit Blut besprengen.
Seine Wunden seyn die Bruñen/
draus all unser Heil gerunnen.
Seht/Er strecket seine Händ aus / uns alle zu umfangen:
hat/an sein liebheisses Hertz uns zu drucken/Lust verlangen.
Ja er neigt sein liebstes Haubt/ uns begierig mit zu küssen.
Seine Sißen und Gebärden/sind auf unser Heil geflossen.
Seiner Seiten offen = stehen /
macht sein gnädigs Herz uns seh:
wañ wir schauen mit den Siñen/
sehen wir uns selbst darinnen.
So viel Strieme/so viel Wundẽ/
als an seinen Leib gefunden/
so viel Sieg=und Segens=Quellen
wolt Er unsrer Seel bestellen.
zwischen Himmel und der Erden
wolt Er aufgeopffert werden :
daß Er GOtt und uns vergliche/
uns zu stärken / Er verbliche:
Ja sein Sterben/ hat das Leben
mir und aller Welt gegeben.
Jesu Christ ! dein Tod und Schmerzen
leb' und schweb mir stets im Herzen!

Spruch=

Illustration 17
Catharina Regina von Greiffenberg's poem 'Uber den gekreutzigten JESUS,'
from her *Sonnette, Lieder und Gedichte* (Nürnberg, 1662), p 403
OPPOSITE English translation by PMD

ON THE CRUCIFIED
CHRIST

See the King of Kings hanging,
bespattering us all with blood.
His wounds are the fountains,
whence all our salvation runs.

See, he stretches out his hands to embrace all of us; joyously desires to press
us to his heart, ardent with love. Indeed, he inclines his lovely head long-
ingly to kiss us. His thoughts and gestures are all directed to our salvation.

The opening in his side
lets us see his merciful heart:
when we see with our minds
we see ourselves therein. As
many weals, as many wounds
as there are found on his body,
so many springs of blessing
appointed he for our soul.
Between heaven and earth
he wanted to be sacrificed:
to reconcile God with us.
To strengthen us, he died.

Yes, his death has given
me and all the world life.
Jesus Christ! your death and suffering
live and stay always in my heart!

poem there is described the situation of the nut-tree, abused, robbed of its fruit, and denied gratitude for its bountifulness; the second half of the poem applies this example to human life, where 'hate' replaces 'honour,' and where 'force' and robbery are widespread. In every respect this pattern poem is an emblematic poem: the title names the object, which embodies the moral meaning explained in the last lines; the verse is arranged so as to produce the outline of the tree, as a *pictura*: the first half of the poem is pictorial, the second half interpretative.

There are many moral and religious reflections cast in the shape of concrete objects which body forth meaning. As such, pattern poems are short, visual-verbal statements.

Harsdörffer was well aware of the connection between pattern poetry and emblems; he felt the latter supported the former: 'One considers these inventions poetic fencing-leaps, and if they are not quite natural, or connected with a picture and emblems, they will not find favour among discriminating readers' (*FG*, v, 23).[42] In fact Nürnberg became a centre for the writing of pattern poetry, both of the frivolous and occasional kind, as well as of the more serious variety. Birken certainly considered pattern poetry suitable for religious themes; in his *Teutsche Rede-bind- und Dicht-Kunst* (Nürnberg, 1679) he writes: 'He who knows and loves his Jesus will make many more imitations of the cross opposite; also he will be able to invent similar things with the crown of thorns, the scourging post, and other instruments of our Saviour's precious passion' (p 144).[43] Nearly half of Theodor Kornfeld's pattern poems are on religious subjects, as Warnock and Folter point out (p 49).

I will conclude with a cross poem by Greiffenberg[44] not mentioned in Warnock's and Folter's bibliography (see illustration 17). The poem bears witness to the control exercised by this religious poetess over both the form of her poem and the meditational thought it expresses. Reading from top to bottom we note the progression from 'the King of Kings' in line 1 to the final mention of 'death and suffering' in the penultimate line at the foot of the cross. As we read down, we see the figure of Christ hanging on the cross: his arms are mentioned in the lines forming the horizontal bar; just beneath this his heart and wounded side are described. The attention to visual detail is even more evident in the manuscript version of the poem. Whereas the printed poem makes general reference to 'wounds,' the manuscript specifies 'the fountains of the thorn wounds,' which draws attention to the crown of thorns of the 'King of Kings'; two lines describing the closing of Christ's eyes in death are omitted from the printed version.

This cross poem is meditative, almost in an Ignatian sense. It opens graphically, dramatically, *in medias res*: the reader is twice exhorted to behold the crucifixion scene before him. Through the exercise of his imagination and

physical senses the reader takes part in an experience which the poetess interprets as she creates it. Thus the first three lines describe the bleeding Christ on
the cross, whereas the fourth line gives the interpretation, 'whence all our
salvation runs.' In a certain way meditation is also an exercise in 'representation
and interpretation' (Schöne's characterization of the dual function of the
emblem).

Having confronted the reader with the suffering Christ, and having led him
through an imaginative experience of the pain to an understanding of the love
and forgiveness inherent in Christ's sacrifice, Greiffenberg closes this pattern
poem of emblematic meditation with a prayer, the traditional conclusion to any
meditation.

4

Emblematic Drama

During the sixteenth and seventeenth centuries drama in its various forms was the most emblematic of all the literary arts, combining as it does a visual experience of character and gesture, silent *tableau* and active scene, with a verbal experience of the spoken and occasionally the written word.

The emblematic quality of Shakespeare's plays was early noted by Henry Green,[1] today more maligned than read; however, it is true that he concentrated almost exclusively on imagery. More recently Glynne Wickham[2] has commented upon the emblematic quality of the Elizabethan stage and contrasted it with the attempt of the modern stage to produce the illusion of photographic reality. In German scholarship Walter Benjamin[3] and Albrecht Schöne[4] have produced the basic studies of the emblematic form of baroque drama, viewed both as literature and theatre. In 1969 Dieter Mehl[5] could write that, although there are a number of studies that examine the relation of emblematics to literature, the emblem in Elizabethan drama has been strangely neglected.[6] He notes that no comprehensive study of the emblematic character of Elizabethan drama exists. But, to my knowledge, no comprehensive study exists, in any language, of the emblematic characteristics of any genre, in the broad sense of poetry, drama, and prose fiction. This is hardly surprising, since the study of emblematic literature has only now come of age.

The emblematic image
As was noted earlier, the word-emblem is found in every literary genre and form. In German the most commonly encountered form is the compound noun or genitive-noun construction, which perfectly recreates in encapsulated form the emblem with its *pictura* and *subscriptio*. Schöne puts it as follows: '*Misfor-*

tune's wave, Virtue's rock, Arrogance's wings, Envy's snakes [in German all compound nouns] are each compounded of a concrete and abstract noun – corresponding to the representational and interpretative functions of the emblem with its picture and text' (p 142).[7] German baroque drama is filled with such emblematic compound nouns; according to one critic they account for some 27.3 per cent of all compound nouns in a representative sample taken from Lohenstein's dramas (cited in Schöne, p 142, n 3).

The genitive case is also capable of linking two nouns in an emblematic structure. Examples such as 'Fortune's glass ball' ('des Glückes gläsern Ball'), 'Virtue's compasses' ('der Kompaß der Tugend'), 'the sun of York,' and 'the winter of our discontent' reveal a structure that is essentially the same as the compound noun: the pictorial component is the basic element in the genitive phrase (cf Schöne, p 147). The interpretative and usually abstract noun is linked by means of the genitive case to the image noun and is dependent upon it. 'The concrete object (picture word), conceived of as the determining word, to which belongs conceptual priority in the emblematic structure, is interpreted, "explained," by the addition of an abstract term (meaning word) which is connected by the genitive case' (Schöne, p. 147).[8] As the seventeenth century progressed this structure was used with greater frequency by German dramatists, as Schöne's statistics indicate: in 11,537 verses Gryphius used 18 genitive compound nouns and 150 genitive phrases; in 16,758 verses Lohenstein employed 239 compound nouns and 509 genitive phrases, and finally in 13,775 verses Hallmann used 397 compound nouns and 521 genitive phrases (cf Schöne, p 146).

As soon as one moves away from the characteristic structure of the word-emblem, which explicitly unites picture and meaning, to the emblematic image in its contracted form problems of identification set in. We are left with the motif and its contextual role as the sole means of identification. As a number of studies have shown, the emblem gave new pictorial and intellectual life to older literary *topoi*, which, however, continued to live on as verbal images long after emblems ceased to play any serious part in art and thought. And this applies to mythological and biblical materials in addition to literary *topoi* deriving from nature and the various cultural traditions of men. We are, then, justified in labelling images in dramatic texts 'emblematic' only if their formal and structural qualities, or their meaning, actively invite comparison with emblems, in other words, only if the dramatic image could be translated into the emblem of an emblem-book. Those unfamiliar with emblem-books frequently overlook important emblematic structures in literature; but the reverse is also true: those acquainted with the theory and practice of emblems occasionally discover emblems in passages of imagery that have but the most tenuous links with the emblem tradition. Mehl[9] is right in observing that German baroque dramatists were more inclined to name emblem-book sources for certain of their word-emblems than were their Elizabethan or Jacobean counterparts in England. However, whether he is correct in asserting that Elizabethan drama contains emblematic images that are 'so closely integrated in the dramatic movement of the scene that they lose their static and pictorial character and are hardly recognizable as emblems at first sight' (p 43)[10] is quite another matter. If such images have lost their 'static and pictorial' quality, then it is only the meaning that they convey which can justify their being called emblems. Mehl's example of a 'veiled emblem' (p 43) in *Twelfth Night* is not convincing, because it depends solely upon the recognition of a common classical allusion to Actaeon (cf p 44). The love-sick Orsino says:

> O, when mine eyes did see Olivia first,
> Methought she purg'd the air of pestilence!
> That instant was I turn'd into a hart,
> And my desires, like fell and cruel hounds,
> E'er since pursue me.   (I.i.19–23)

Mehl's account of the emblematic quality of this passage is somewhat contradictory. He begins by calling it a 'veiled emblem' and ends the same paragraph by admitting that 'little is gained by a reference to emblem-books because neither is the use of the Actaeon story confined to them nor is there anything distinctly emblematic in the way it is employed here' (p 44). Two sentences later the Actaeon passage has become an emblem again, 'a typical instance' of the way 'the quoting of emblems can often serve to characterize a certain situation or an individual speaker' (p 45). Mehl's interpretation of the supposed emblem is hardly more illuminating: we are told that the image 'is more than a picturesque metaphor and that its full meaning is only intelligible if we see the allusion to the unhappy Actaeon' (p 44). Unfortunately, we are left with three suggestions about that 'full meaning': these are 'blind desire,' 'foolish curiosity,' and 'man's innate desire for the [sic] divine beauty' (p 44), all adduced from the tradition of the emblem-books. Mehl may be right that the allusion to Actaeon 'adds a new dimension,' but the reader wishes that Mehl had decided precisely which dimension had been added.

John M. Steadman is evidently aware of the pitfalls that must be circumvented in the pursuit of the emblematic quarry. His equation of Falstaff and Actaeon in *The Merry Wives of Windsor*[11] is convincing, because it is based on more than mere similarities in motif. Although the dramatic situation he describes goes beyond the purely verbal, which is the subject of this sub-chapter (and includes word, mime, costume, and action), this seems an appropriate place to mention his account. Steadman argues that the scenes in *The Merry Wives of Windsor* in which Falstaff impersonates Actaeon are an 'obvious burlesque of the Actaeon myth' (p 231); the parallel between Falstaff and Actaeon reveals 'marked affinities with the representation of the myth in Renaissance iconography and mythography' (p 231). The knight's disguise of a stag's head and hunter's clothing is virtually identical with the pictures in Whitney; Actaeon is depicted in the emblem-books of Alciatus, Sambucus, Aneau, and Whitney as a figure with a human body, stag's head, and hunter's apparel. Furthermore, the resemblance is strengthened by a similarity in posture: Falstaff decides to 'winke, and couche,' while Sambucus and Whitney show Actaeon in a prostrate postion. Just as important is the overlap in interpretation. In Whitney Actaeon is an emblem of the 'ravages of desire' (p 234). Falstaff is an 'emblematic expression of lust and its chastisement' (p 234). The fat knight compares himself jestingly with Jove and observes that love can make a beast of a man; he comments on his own 'beastly fault' and 'foul fault.' The theme of the Fairies' song is lust, 'unchaste desire,' and 'luxury.' The central theme of Falstaff's impersonation of Actaeon is, then, the 'exposure and humiliation of lechery' (p 234). As Steadman observes, the emblematic value of any scene or character depends upon its visual impact and the facility with which the audience can interpret the meaning of the visual experience (cf p 244).

Horst Oppel includes in his book on *Titus Adronicus*[12] a discussion of Shakespeare's use of emblematic imagery, which is characterized by perceptive comment but the doubtful generalization that is inescapable where a firm basis in emblem theory is lacking. One passage may serve to illustrate this insecurity in identifying emblematic imagery. In *Titus Andronicus* the sight of the raped and mutilated Lavinia, whose hands had been cut off by her assailants, calls forth from Marcus the following response:

Speak gentle niece, what stern, ungentle hands
Have lopp'd and hew'd and made thy body bare
Of her two branches ... (ii.iv.16–18)

In this image Lavinia's body has become by implication a tree that has lost two branches (i.e., her hands). For Oppel this is an emblem (cf pp 76–7). As far as I can see, however, the image remains a concrete metaphor, or as Schöne puts it a 'bildliche Einkleidung' (p 91). It has little in common with the emblematic 'art form,' nor can I find a specific significance in the equation of body with tree that would enrich the meaning of the image and thereby raise it to the level of an emblematic 'mode of thought.' Oppel indicates no such dimension of significance either.

A related motif is also found in *Cymbeline*, which is, as Oppel suggests, emblematic by virtue of its function and interpretation. In prison awaiting death, and separated from his wife Imogen, daughter of Cymbeline, King of Britain, Posthumus Leonatus has a strange dream in which the ghosts of his parents and brothers beg for justice from Jupiter. The god appears, promises a happy resolution to the situation, and disappears. On awaking Posthumus finds a book containing as ambiguous an oracle as ever came out of Delphi:

> Whenas a lion's whelp shall, to himself unknown, without seeking find, and be
> embraced by a piece of tender air; and when from a stately cedar shall be lopped
> branches which, being dead many years, shall after revive, be jointed to the old stock,
> and freshly grow, then shall Posthumus end his miseries, Britain be fortunate, and
> flourish in peace and plenty.   (v.iv.137–95)

In the final scene of recognition and reconciliation Imogen appears, Posthumus is released from prison and re-united with her, and the long-lost sons of Cymbeline are returned to their father. The cedar and its severed branches, which are grafted back onto the original tree, is the basis for the prophecy and, as a 'fact of nature,' it is used somewhat like an *argumentum emblematicum* which consequent events prove true. The motif of regrafting branches onto the original tree is not to be found in the emblem-books in Henkel and Schöne's *Emblemata*, but that is far from conclusive; in addition, the motif of grafting is not uncommon (cf *Emblemata*, cols 165–6). More important than the presence or absence of the motif in the emblem-books is the recognition that in function and meaning the image is emblematic.

Evidently Oppel, like Jean Hagstrum,[13] has so broad a conception of the emblem as to embrace the 'iconic' themes of painters and their subjects. Oppel writes: 'It is certainly no coincidence that Shakespeare's image-language always becomes emblematic where the theme itself takes up the question of the nature of art or touches upon the rivalry between the arts' (p 78).[14] The examples cited[15] are certainly iconic in the general sense of having to do with painters, their art, and their subjects, but I can find nothing emblematic in them in terms of significance or structure.

In spite of difficulties of identification the drama of the period does give evidence of the popularity of both the contracted word-emblem[16] and also the complete emblem *in nuce* described at the beginning of this chapter. In the contracted word-emblem the explanatory element is omitted and the meaning of the image is assumed on the basis of traditional interpretation and the controlling dramatic context. Much of Shakespeare's emblematic imagery is of this kind, depending for its full understanding on the emblematic meanings of certain natural phenomena and a knowledge of royal heraldry and devices. James Hoyle[17] has shown in an essay on the *Henry IV* plays that the moon and hare, applied to Falstaff by others and the fat knight himself, are particularly fitting emblems (cf pp 518–20). Falstaff wants Hal to be, like himself, a 'minion of the moon,' which is a suitable device for his inconstant, changeable, and nocturnal habits. The reference to the moon governing the ebb and flow of the sea is a fitting image for Falstaff's death 'at the turning of the tide.' The moon was also a well-known emblem of folly; for example, it was featured on the flag at the masthead of Bosch's 'Ship of Fools.' Hal compares his corpulent friend ironically with an old lion and then more contemptuously with a hare, and thereby alludes to both the proverbial melancholy and cowardice of the hare. The hare-lion emblem is also the basis of two incidents: in the first Falstaff in cowardly fashion runs away from Hal in a fight, and afterwards offers the ironic justification that 'the lion will not touch the true Prince' (II.iv.290–302); and in the second Falstaff wounds the dead Hotspur, a brave prince and a lion of a man. It was common knowledge that the cowardly hare would bite a dead lion, a motif used by Whitney, Alciatus, and Reusner, and by Shakespeare himself in *King John* (II.i.137–8). Furthermore, the hare was known for its lechery. The emblems of the moon and hare are then minor emblematic threads in the characterization of Falstaff.

Some of the sun imagery in Shakespeare's historical plays should be read in the light of heraldic devices. The heraldic badges of Richard II and Henry IV include the sun in splendour, the sunburst, the sun clouded, and the rose *en soleil*. The sun clouded is the background for Hal's famous monologue at the beginning of *Henry IV, Part I*:

> I know you all, and will awhile uphold
> The unyok'd humour of your idleness:
> Yet herein will I imitate the sun,
> Who doth permit the base contagious clouds
> To smother up his beauty from the world,
> That, when he please again to be himself,
> Being wanted he may be more wonder'd at,
> By breaking through the foul and ugly mists
> Of vapours that did seem to strangle him.   (I.ii.188–96)

Saxon Walker[18] suggests that in the production of *Henry IV, Part I* this heraldic background should be taken into account by having 'as a backcloth to the Palace scenes, a royal red arras figured with this [sun clouded] and other badges, at which the Prince might glance in the course of this speech, and later when the King inverts the same simile in his rebuke in the third act' (p 96).

The 'argumentum emblematicum'

Schöne devotes a chapter of his study *Emblematik und Drama im Zeitalter des Barock* to a specific form and function of the emblematic image in baroque drama that he calls the *argumentum emblematicum*. One of the many examples that he discusses comes from Gryphius's tragedy *Papinianus*. The lawyer Papinianus refuses to go against law and conscience and pronounce a public justification of Emperor Bassianus's murder of his own brother. The Emperor tries to pressure Papinianus by threatening his life and that of his son, which elicits from his wife Plautia the fearful comment:

We fight / but oh! the enemy presses too hard.

Wir kämpffen / aber ach! der Feind drückt was zu sehr.

Papinianus counters this with the emblematic argument:

The noble palm grows the more one weights it down.

Die edle Palme wächst je mehr man sie beschweret.

Alciatus had already used the image of the weighted palm-tree to signify the constancy of virtue in adversity, and, picking up the key word 'drücken' ('press') in Plautia's speech, Papinianus translates it into the visual image of the burdened palm-tree. This not only signals his decision to be true to the virtue of truth, law, and conscience, but anticipates his own martyr's death at the end of the play (cf Schöne, pp 68–9).

An example of the emblematic argument used to condemn the action of a character in a play is found in Lohenstein's *Agrippina*. In the final act there appears to Emperor Nero the spirit of his mother Agrippina, whose murder Nero had ordered. As the terrified Nero falls to the floor, the spirit Agrippina observes that while she lived 'she was not able to tame him.' Recalling his earlier cruel and murderous acts she comments:

A tiger must have paired with me:
That this body should have born such a snake.

Ein Tiger hat sich mit mir müssen gatten
Daß dieser Leib solch einen Wurm gebahr.

This is still metaphor, but the image association leads on to emblematic argumentation:

The adder does not tear the mother's
vitals apart, except in birth:
As I now suffer this in death from you,
I see: that Nero is more than a snake and adder.

Die Natter reist' der Mutter Eingeweide
Nicht außer der Geburth enttzwey:
Weil ich von dir dis auch nun sterbend leide /
Seh' ich: Daß Nero mehr als Schlang' und Natter sey.

Agrippina's condemnation of her murderous son is based on a 'fact of nature,'
the belief that the adder bites through the body of the mother snake at birth, a
notion also found in the *Physiologus* and the emblem-books of Théodore de
Bèze, Camerarius, and Schoonhovius with different applications. In the context
of the play the adder emblem is used to condemn Nero, who is worse than the
adder, which only turns on its mother at birth (cf Schöne, pp 87–8). The adder
emblem as used by Lohenstein's Agrippina is prepared for earlier in the play,
when Agrippina is murdered; she cries:

Stab through the naked belly that produced a snake,

Stoß durch den nackten Bauch / der einen Wurm gezeuget,

and one of the murderers retorts:

The snake still turns / it is not dead yet.

Die Schlange dreht sich noch / sie ist noch nicht gestorben.

Emblematic argumentation is used by many different characters in the most
diverse of situations; Schöne concludes his analysis with a résumé of the main
functions of the *argumentum emblematicum*. [19] He observes that more important than a catalogue of functions is the recognition that the drama of the period
is interspersed with images whose meaning is often accessible only through the

emblem-books. In the plays the emblems are important 'as a foundation for relating the immediate situation to that which is typical and normative, for orientating the particular to the basic, for raising the individual and the isolated to the general and eternally valid' (Schöne, p 90).[20]

Sententiae and stichomythia

It has been a commonplace among literary critics of the sixteenth and seventeenth centuries to observe that maxims or *sententiae* were the very pillars of drama (cf Schöne, p 151). Like the supporting columns of a great building, the maxim can stand isolated from its surroundings or in groups; nowhere is the cluster of maxims more dramatically effective than in stichomythia, that most epigrammatic and rhetorically balanced form of verbal duelling.

Schöne has shown how structurally effective the maxim could be in German baroque drama, where the epigrammatic and generalizing statement frequently functions as a kind of interpretative comment on the action of the play. In Gryphius's *Leo Armenius* the Emperor is murdered in church before the altar during the celebration of Christ's birth; Leo's murder is reported to his Queen by an eyewitness, and shortly afterwards a group of the conspirators breaks into her room. One of the murderers describes the murder as the assassination of a tyrant, the removal of the 'diamond-firm yoke of tyranny,' and exhorts the Empress to learn now to obey, and to understand:

That often there is but a night between fall and height.

Daß offt nur eine nacht sey zwischen fall vnd höh.

The significance of this concluding maxim, which sums up the transience and unpredictability of life, extends far beyond the immediate situation of the dead Leo Armenius, or his Queen: its applicability to all human life and experience is evident. The dramatic portrayal of the fate of one ruler is the *pictura*, which receives its *subscriptio* in the generalizing and interpretative maxim of the murderer (cf Schöne, pp 154–5).

Robert B. Heilman[21] has recognized the function and importance of such pithy sayings, which he calls 'choral comment,' in Shakespearean drama. Just as the Greek Chorus expounds on the significance of the events presented on stage, so certain characters in a Shakespearean play offer interpretative and generalizing statements which have a validity that extends beyond the immediate situation. Heilman finds that in *King Lear* Kent's comment on Lear's ironic fate has a 'choral value' (p 62):

> Good King, that must approve the common saw,
> Thou out of heaven's benediction com'st
> To the warm sun!   (II.ii.167–9).

This is part of the *seeing* pattern, in which various images for light carry forward the theme of understanding and suffering. Of such 'choral comment' Heilman observes: 'It needs to be integral with the design, and ... transcends the context and becomes an imaginative commentary upon the whole world of the drama' (pp 62–3). The Fool has the imaginative power which ultimately the mad Lear achieves, the ability 'to leap from the concrete manifestation to the meaning, to the values implied' (p 182).

However, it seems that Benjamin[22] was one of the first to recognize the emblematic quality of the 'choral comment' or maxim. He writes: 'Speech in the dialogues is not infrequently only the *subscriptio*, conjured up for the allegorical constellation in which the figures find their way to each other. In short, the maxim as *subscriptio* pronounces the scene allegorical ... However, not only actual emblematic sayings, but also whole speeches sound now and then as though it were natural for them to stand beneath an allegorical plate' (p 220).'[23] In baroque drama interpretative maxims are interwoven with mimetic and visual passages of action and word to produce a constant interplay of representation and interpretation. In many instances the maxim preceeds as a kind of *inscriptio*; in others it follows as a kind of *subscriptio* (cf Schöne, p 156). Schöne writes: 'The "emblematic" maxims are bearing elements in the construction of tragedy: pillars between which the scenic pictures are stretched, columns upon which the stage action is founded as exemplary action' (p 159).[24]

The presence of the emblematic maxim is occasionally signalled in the German printed text by quotation marks, but more often by the colon, or semicolon, with the same function. The attention of the reader and spectator is drawn to maxims by the use of such deictic formulae as 'Look' ('Schaut') or 'Look here' ('Seht her'), or by other imperatives, such as 'Mark' ('Merkt'), 'Learn' ('Lernt'), 'Think' ('Denkt'), and 'Believe' ('Glaubt'), or by a change from a personal pronoun to one with a more generalizing function (cf Schöne, pp 161–2 and 219–20).

THE EMBLEMATIC CHARACTER

Personifications in masques and pageants
Renaissance and baroque drama abounds in characters who owe something, if not all, of their very existence to the emblematic tradition. This holds true in varying degrees of both the uncomplicated representation of virtues and vices in

a pageant or masque and of the more complex characters in Shakespeare's mature plays.

The emblematic character is seen very clearly in the learned masques that Ben Jonson produced for the English court, which were intended to be something more than ephemeral entertainment. Jonson described his *Hymenaei* as being 'grounded vpon *antiquitie* and solide *learnings*,' and the 'sense' of the masque was 'to lay hold on more remou'd mysteries.'[25] Gordon has shown that both *The Masque of Blacknesse* and *The Masque of Beautie* are steeped in neoplatonic doctrines of Beauty and Love. It would follow that the use of emblematic details in the presentation of character and action to embody such philosophical themes is not dictated primarily by the desire to embellish but rather employed to express significance.[26]

Two examples from the masques must suffice as illustration. It is Johnson's practice to describe in detail the garments, ensigns, and attributes of the emblematic characters in his masques, but he frequently does more than merely describe them; he includes an interpretation of the visual accountrements. A case in point is Eschyia, or Quiet, who appears in the *Kings Entertainment*, II, and is portrayed as being 'attired in black, upon her head an artificial nest, out of which appeared stork's heads, to manifest a sweet repose. Her feet were placed on a cube, to shew stability, and in her lap she held a perpendicular or level, as an ensign of evenness or rest; on the top of it sat an halcyon, or kings-fisher.[27] Allen has compared this figure with Ripa's *Iconologia* and found that the portrayal tallies with two descriptions of Quiet by Ripa that contain all the details with the exception of the halcyon, which elsewhere in Ripa is used to denote quiet.

In Jonson's *Hymenaei* Reason appears as a venerable woman with white hair to suggest sagacity and dignity. She is 'crowned with lights, her garments blue, and semined with starres, girded vnto her with a white bend, fill'd with *Arithmeticall* figures, in one hand bearing a Lampe, in the other a bright sword.'[28] In this instance Jonson does not interpret the meaning of the visual details, which would probably have been evident to the educated and judicious spectator at court. Gordon has compared this figure with Ripa and discovered that, but for the lamp, all the details derive from several descriptions of Reason in Ripa's iconographical lexicon. Reason's blue garments are the colour of the sky and heaven, suggesting that reason is divine in origin and aspiration. Her white belt covered with arithmetical signs comes from Ripa's second description of Reason, and Ripa's explanatory comment is, 'because it is by the use of such figures that Arithmetic provides proofs of the reality of things, just as Reason which lodges in our soul tests and recognizes all that pertains to our good' (cited in Gordon, 'Hymenaei ... ,' p 111). Of Reason's sword Ripa writes that its function is 'to keep the field of the virtues free from the vices which prey on the good of the soul' (cited in Gordon, 'Hymenaei ... ,' p 111). Finally the lamp is clearly enough the source of Reason's light.

These characters from Jonson's masques are personifications of abstractions which rely heavily upon emblematic attributes, expressed by stage properties, for their identification. The visual details constantly remind the audience of the nature of the character before them. An investigation of characteristic pageants reveals a similar convention. Thomas Dekker's *London's Tempe* (1629) contains a palace of Apollo where there are enthroned seven persons representing the seven liberal sciences. The dramatist's direction is as follows: 'Those seven are in loose roabes of severall cullors, with mantles according, and holding in their hands Escutcheons, with Emblemes in them proper to every one quality.'[29] In Wickham's view 'the devisers of the pageants made sweeping assumptions about the ability of the beholders to interpret this symbolism for themselves. Personifications ... were so commonplace that writers often felt able to dispense with detailed description of their costumes in an otherwise full account' (II, i, 227).

The emblematic function of more complex characters

Certain early plays of Shakespeare are reminiscent of the pageant in the way both characters and visual impressions are handled. Muriel Bradbrook draws attention to the 'emblematic or heraldic quality about all the characters of *Titus Andronicus*.'[30] Aaron is a mixture of medieval devil, Machiavellian schemer, and atheist, whose blackness is emblematic of his diabolic nature, and he is recognized by all the characters in the drama as such. Tamora's passion for Aaron, 'her raven colour'd love' (II.iii.83), discolours her honour, and this is emphasized in visual and dramatic terms by her child, which is as black as its father. The nurse apostrophizes the baby as a symbol of their union:

A joyless, dismal, black and sorrowful issue!
Here is the babe, as loathsome as a toad.   (IV.ii.67–8)

Tamora's son Demetrius follows in like vein:

Woe to her [Tamora's] chance, and damn'd her loathèd choice!
Accurs'd the offspring of so foul a fiend!   (IV.ii.79–80)

Titus Andronicus is rich in emblematic and visual effects. Mehl writes: 'He [Shakespeare] creates living pictures, which are interpreted through the rhetorical language of imagery. Visual and verbal rhetoric are here inextricably combined.'[31] The ravished and mutilated Lavinia, whose hands were cut off and tongue torn out, stands silently on stage through several scenes. Incapable of utterance, she is an eloquent monument to the crimes committed, an emblem of 'ravished nature' (Mehl, 'Schaubild und Sprachfigur in Shakespeare's Dramen,' p 19), of moral and political disorder, constantly drawn into the speeches of the other characters, who offer descriptions and commentaries on her condition somewhat in the manner of the emblematic *subscriptio*. A striking instance is Titus's formal moralizing on his daughter's condition: 'Thou map of woe,' he calls her, 'that dost talk in sign' (III.ii.11–12). In his madness Titus shoots up to the gods arrows bearing messages invoking vengeance for the savage injustice meted out to his family.

The closeness of *Titus Andronicus* to pageant is shown in the nature of the characters, who tend to typify attitudes and moral qualities; they lack the ambivalence and shifting complexity of Shakespeare's great tragic heroes. Bradbrook calls Aaron 'half-symbol, half stage-formula' (p 107). In a play in which many of the protagonists are driven by lust, treachery, and revenge it is particularly fitting that three of the evil characters, Tamora and her sons, who in their actions embody lust, murder, rape, and revenge, should disguise themselves as Revenge, Murder, and Rape in an attempt to influence the half-demented Titus. It is quite likely that the figures of Revenge, Murder, and Rape would have been appropriately clothed and provided with insignias to reveal their nature. The visual and dramatic irony of characters who reveal their true selves through a disguise is an indication that emblematic stage techniques, like any other convention, are a limitation only to the hack-writer; the talented dramatist can turn them to good account. The characters in *Titus Andronicus* are, in general, closer to the figures of the masque, pageant, and emblem-book, which distances them somewhat from our sympathies; that is just as it should be in a play of blood and mutilated flesh. Bradbrook puts it well: 'Throughout the play the murders, rapes, mutilations and other atrocities remain mere moral heraldry, with no more sense of physical embodiment than if all the characters had been given such names' (p 108).

Not only the uncomplicated protagonist driven by an all-consuming passion or committed totally to a particular virtue can function as a dramatic emblem; at certain junctures Shakespeare's more complex characters are temporarily frozen into a static posture to become emblems pointing to a meaning that transcends the particularity of their situation. For Mehl the suicide of Brutus is just such an instance; it carries the overriding, general significance of 'Fortuna virtutem superans,' as the emblem-book puts it.[32] One may not agree with Mehl's interpretation of the emblematic meaning which emerges from Brutus's suicide,[33] but there is little doubt that the dead Ceasar becomes, as Mehl says, a 'symbol of the destroyed order of the commonwealth' ('Symbol der zerstörten

Ordnung des Gemeinwesens,' p 14). In *Macbeth* the situation is even clearer: Duncan embodies the virtues of the good ruler and the health of the nation, both of which are destroyed by the ambitious Macbeth. As the play progresses Macbeth himself becomes increasingly a representation of general tyranny, as he subdues, or ignores, his own conscience. Macbeth's function as an emblem of tyranny is clearly illustrated by the challenge hurled at him by Macduff: to fight or surrender to become, 'as our rarer monsters are,' a sideshow, whose cage would bear the inscription 'Here may you see the tyrant' (v.viii.25–7).[34]

In the view of Benjamin the corpse is the highest emblem in seventeenth-century tragedy: 'For the tragedy of the seventeenth century the corpse becomes the highest emblematic property bar none' (cited in Schöne, p 218).[35] Stripped of all that is private and individual, the corpse is not simply a dead character, but a warning to others to learn certain truths from his death; the corpse is an emblem that instructs. Lohenstein's Kleopatra offers the following elucidation over Antony's corpse:

He who trusts in the light wheel of blind fortune,
Does not build simple towers on the foundation of his virtue;
Calls the princes of this world gods of the earth,
He who knows much, but does not know himself,
He who leans on the sceptre's glass, the ground-ice of the throne;
Let him come and learn here, how uncertain he sits,
Who stands on the peak.

WEr auf das leichte Rad des blinden Glückes traut /
Auf seiner Tugend Grund nicht schlechte Thürme baut /
Die Fürsten dieser Welt der Erde Götter nennet /
Wer viel weiß ausser sich / sich in sich selbst nicht kennet /
Wer sich aufs Zepters Glas / des Thrones Grund-Eiß stützt;
Der komm und lern allhier / wie der so schwanckend sitzt /
Der auf dem Gipffel steht.   (III.485–91)

The emblematic status of the corpse results from what Schöne has called 'The overcoming of the barrier of personality' and its 'pictorial rigidity' (p 219).[36]

The dramatist employs many devices to underscore the emblematic and generalizing function of a character in a particular situation. He can allow one character to point an interpretative finger at the emblematic figure, as does Macduff; he can also have the emblematic figure point to himself. The deictic formula 'look at me,' in its many variations, accomplishes this purpose. In *The*

Winter's Tale Hermione stands falsely accused of adultery, and in the trial scene she becomes a symbol of 'persecuted innocence' (Mehl, 'Schaubild und Sprachfigur in Shakespeare's Dramen,' p 18). After pleading 'not guilty' to the charge Hermione expresses her faith that 'innocence shall make / False accusation blush, and tyranny / Tremble at Patience.' From these generalizations and abstractions, which the reader or spectator can hardly avoid associating directly with the characters of Leontes and Hermione, the Queen moves on to point to her own case with the words 'For behold me ... here standing' (iii.ii.38–45).[37]

The dramatist does not always need to use the explicit deictic formula to spotlight the temporary emblematic function of his characters. On occasions the combination of visual effect and spoken word is sufficient in itself. Hoyle draws attention to such an emblematic cameo in *Henry iv, Part ii*, where the young whore Doll Tearsheet sits on Falstaff's knee and reminds him of his mortality:

DOLL ... Thou whoreson little tidy Bartholomew boar-pig, when wilt thou leave fighting o'days, and foining o'nights, and begin to patch up thine old body for heaven? ·

FALSTAFF Peace, good Doll! do not speak like a death's head: do not bid me remember mine end. (ii.iv.213–18)

In the theatre this little scene is most effective: the old man and his young whore in a static pose discoursing upon death is a veritable dramatic emblem of 'memento mori' and 'vanitas.' The emblematic stage property of the skull, so frequently the occasion of thoughts on transcience and death, is woven into the conversation, and adds a further motif to the emblematic structure.[38]

The emblematic function of an individual figure in a play is frequently emphasized by the momentary use of emblematic signs and symbols provided by the stage manager. Mehl sees Shylock in this light: 'When, for example, in the fourth act of *The Merchant of Venice* Shylock waits with whetted knife and scales ready for the announcement of judgment against Antonio, he must appear to the spectator as a personification of immovable, perverted justice; for the scales as an attribute of justice were an iconographical commonplace' ('Schaubild und Sprachfigur in Shakespeares Dramen,' p 16).[39] Falstaff likewise finds himself in a situation where he needs an emblematic stage property for a bit of dramatic fun in the tavern. He will play the part of Hal's father, King Henry iv, in order to prepare the young prince for the impending encounter with his father. Lacking a crown Falstaff uses a cushion. This is a telling substitute, revealing in visual terms both the nature of Falstaff's influence (even if unsuccessful) and an aspect of his character. Mehl writes: 'The cushion as an attribute of laziness and lust is an unequivocal demonstration in image terms of the kind of rule which would replace just kingship under Falstaff's influence, and here in playful reversal for a moment does replace it' (ibid).[40]

From these visual emblems in the form of stage properties woven into the action and dialogue of the drama it is but a short step to the verbal emblem itself. Thus we come full circle and return to the subject of the first part of this chapter.

THE EMBLEMATIC STAGE

The emblematic backcloth

The simplest and yet most obviously emblematic of stage devices is the use of a painted canvas, set up at the rear of the stage, portraying a scene or figure which has some connection with the play being acted out on the main stage. For want of a better term we might call this device the emblematic backcloth. Schöne discusses the emblematic backcloth and dumb-show under the heading 'Stille Vorstellungen' (pp 185–93), the German dramatist Hallmann's terms for silent scenes. Evidence for the actual use of an emblematic backcloth is largely inferential, but quite plausible. For instance, the third act of Lohenstein's *Agrippina* ends with Nero's departure from his mother, who is to undertake a voyage that is intended to end in her death. Nero has arranged that the ship will break in half on the high seas. This part of the action is described by the Chorus of the Goddesses of the Mountains and the Sea, whose words depict both the shipwreck and Agrippina's miraculous escape. However, there is more than verbal description; the stage directions read: 'The stage represents Agrippina's shipwreck on a still sea under a starry sky.'[41] As Schöne observes, this could not have been realized except by means of a visual portrayal ('bildliche Vorstellung,' p 186). Comparing this scene and its stage direction with the emblematic frontispiece to the play, Schöne concludes: 'The representation is evidently to be conceived in the manner of this picture section which – probably painted on canvas and stretched over a wooden frame – was visible during the third Chorus on the rear stage: a *pictura*, which the Chorus of Goddesses of the Mountains and Sea transform into action by their lively description of the event and through their agitated sympathy for the happening' (p 186).[42] The ship breaks, and Agrippina is cast into the sea and rescued by dolphins. The chorus's comment has the generalizing function of a *subscriptio*:

That all the world may judge:
An evil child is wilder than the waves.

Daß alle Welt ein Urtheil könne fällen:
Ein böses Kind sey wilder als die Wellen.

Many of Hallmann's plays require the 'stille Vorstellung' to be enacted by the players in a kind of dumb-show. But there are also 'silent scenes' which, by virtue of the motifs described in the stage directions, could only have been painted on canvas. The final scene of Hallmann's *Catharina* requires the following 'stille Vorstellung': 'Twenty-seven thousand souls of those who were martyred under Henrico for the Catholic faith accuse the soul of Henrico before Christ's judgment seat.'[43] While twenty-seven thousand souls could not have mimed this accusation of Henrici on stage, a painted canvas could convey the impression of a multitude of martyrs. According to Schöne there are no less than 65 examples of the 'stille Vorstellung,' including dumb-shows and the emblematic backcloth, in Hallmann's plays (cf Schöne, pp 187–8).

The emblematic dumb-show

From the emblematic scene painted on a backcloth it is but a short step to the *tableaux vivants* and dumb-shows[44] so popular in the drama of the period. In the dumb-show the actors demonstrate silently, by means of costume, mime, and stage properties, what was also capable of representation in the painted 'stille Vorstellung.' The verbal interpretation of both the painted backcloth and the dumb-show is sometimes provided by a character in the drama, or more usually by a kind of Chorus or 'Presenter.'

Rosemary Freeman was among the first to draw attention to the similarity that exists between the emblem and the dumb-show; she writes: 'Indeed the dumb show of the stage is in both form and function only a more elaborate version of the pictures in an emblem book' (*English Emblem Books*, p 15). More recently Mehl has taken up this lead in his study *The Elizabethan Dumb Show*. In this book Mehl's conception of the emblem derives largely from the theories of Praz and Freeman, which is understandable, since its date of publication precludes the possibility of Mehl having become acquainted with Schöne's theory. Mehl's point of departure and reference – as far as emblematics are concerned – is, then, rather narrow, as the following generalization demonstrates: '[the emblem's] technique is remarkably similar to that of early dumb shows and reveals the same liking for puzzles and allegories as do the pantomimes and pageants. They were used to illustrate an abstract idea or moral lesson in the form of a mythological or allegorical scene accompanied by a short motto' (pp 13–14). Indeed, a little later we find the statement: 'They have in common the fact that they both, because of their abstract representation and stylization, are somewhat removed from reality and that the visible scene is only a vehicle for some deeper meaning' (pp 14–15). Mehl's choice of 'only' seems to indicate that he regrets, or finds fault with, what is an essential function of the dumb-show, and one which it shares with the emblem, namely, the function of raising the action or problem of the play to a different plane, of distilling a timeless truth from the particular, time-bound, and localized action of the main plot.[45]

In its simplest form the dumb-show tells a moral tale as a brief prelude to the action which is about to unfold. For instance, *Gorboduc* (London, 1561) contains the following account of the dumb-show performed before the first act, and also provides an explanation of its significance:

> Firste the Musicke of violenze began to play, durynge whiche came vppon Stage sixe wilde men clothed in leaues. Of whom the first bare in his necke a Fagot of smal stickes, whiche thei all, both suerallie and togither, assaied with all their strengthes to brake, but it could not be broken by them. At the length one of them plucked out one of the stickes and brake it: And the rest, pluckinge oute all the other stickes one after an other, did easilie breake, the same beynge severed; which beyong conioyned they had before attempted in vayne. After they had this done, they departed the Stage, and the Musicke ceased. Herby was signified, that a state knit in vnitie doth continue stronge against all force. But beynge deuyded, is easely destroied. As befell upon Duke *Gorboduc* deuidinge his Lande to his two Sonnes, which he before held in Monarchie. And vpon the discention of the Brethrene to whome it was deuided.[46]

This account of the action and meaning of the dumb-show is, in fact, a stage-direction, and there is no indication that this explanation was actually given from the stage for the benefit of the audience. Mehl's comment on this dumb-show reveals a certain insensitivity to the value of the emblematic structure in general; he observes: 'The whole pantomime, in spite of its liveliness, is abstract and there is no indication of place and time' (p 32). This is to miss the emblematic point completely: just as the emblem makes generally valid statements, so this dumb-show introduces the play with a visual statement, timeless and general, which will be made particular by the play about to unfold. In a sense the dumb-show is the *inscriptio* to the *pictura* of the whole play. Mehl is correct in noting that 'It is not so much a preview of what is to come as a moral that applies to the whole play' (p 32). Just as the emblem's *inscriptio* and *pictura* are often almost incomprehensible when taken in isolation, but together are mutually explanatory, so the meaning and function of the dumb-show emerge only as the action of the play progresses. In fairness to Mehl it should be noted that he himself has commented on the fact that he 'paid too little attention to the emblematic aspect of the dumb-show tradition' (p 47, n 26). In the same essay, however, he refers to the use of the bundle of sticks as a motif in the emblem-books of Paradin and Whitney (cf pp 47–8, p 48, n 28).

The anonymous Elizabethan play *Locrine* employs dumb-shows that are even more closely related to the emblem than was the case in *Gorboduc*. In *Locrine* the figure of Ate performs the function of a Chorus, recounting the action mimed by the players and interpreting its meaning, showing its relevance to the play. What is more, Ate prefaces all of her explanations with a Latin motto, which, like the *inscriptio* of the emblem, captures the essential meaning of the visual scene and expresses it in general terms. The act that follows plays out the meaning of the dumb-show; 'each act forms a complete emblem, with its picture and its interpretation visibly enacted on the stage' (Mehl, *The Elizabethan Dumb Show*, p 48). The dumb-show before the fourth act is described as follows:

> Enter Ate as before. Then let ther follow Omphale daughter to the king of Lydia, hauing a club in her hand, and a lion's skinne on her back. Hercules following with a distaffe. Then let Omphale turn about, and taking off her pantofle, strike Hercules on the head, then let them depart. Ate remaining, saying:
>> Quem non Argolici mandata severa Tyranni,
>> No potuit Iuno vincere, vicit amor.

After describing the action just mimed, Ate applies the incident to the plot of the fourth act:

> So martiall Locrine cheerd with victorie,
> Falleth in loue with Humbers concubine,
> And so forgetteth peerlesse Guendoline.[47]

Locrine's dumb-shows are not restricted to mythological and allegorical persons and situations. There appear a number of animals that are also found as motifs in the emblem-books. Before the third act the audience sees a crocodile bitten by a snake, both of which then fall into the water; the motto 'Scelera in authorem cadunt' is spoken by Ate.

Thomas Hughes's *The Misfortunes of Arthur* provides an even 'more elaborate and sophisticated use of emblematic dumb-shows.'[48] One of the many 'living emblems' (Mehl, 'Emblems in English Renaissance Drama,' p 48) in the dumb-shows before the final act features a pelican pecking open its own breast; the motto reads 'Qua foui perii,' and the stage-direction informs the reader that it signifies '*Arthurs* too much indulgencie of *Modred*, the cause of his death.' Again, as this interpretation of the emblematic dumb-show is not expressly addressed to the audience, the assumption is that drama and dumb-show explain each other: 'the action of the play serves as an illustration of the general truths presented in the allegorical tableaux, and these, in turn, can be said to add a timeless meaning to the history of Arthur which is the subject of the play' (Mehl, ibid, p 49).[49]

The emblem as an element in the dramatic action
On occasions the emblem may also be found as a functional element in the main dramatic action of a play. At a time when the emblem was extremely fashionable it evidently did not stretch the imagination of a Jacobean audience too far when a dramatist used an emblem to replace the anonymous letter as a device to inform a man that he has been cuckolded. John Webster does this in *The White Devil*; Monticelso brings Camillo an emblem that had been thrown through his window. The *pictura* is of a stag that weeps for the loss of its horns, and the motto reads 'Inopem me copia fecit' (ii.ii.5). Monticelso translates the Latin as follows: 'Plenty of horns hath made him poor of horns' (ii.ii.6); he also explains the reference to cuckoldry.

A more complicated example is found in Cyril Tourneur's play *The Atheist's Tragedy*, where in the house of Cataplasma the bawd a lengthy discussion develops on the subject of Soquette's embroidery. The work depicts 'a medlar with a Plumb-tree growing hard by it; the leaues o' the Plumb-tree falling off; the gumme issuing out o' the perish'd joynts; and the branches some of 'em dead, and some rotten; and yet but a young Plumb-tree' (iv.i.2–5). Soquette explains that the plum tree grows too near the medlar, which 'sucks and drawes all the sap from it' (iv.i.8). These ladies of doubtful virtue are joined by the profligate Sebastian who adds to the 'moralizing vpon this Gentlewoman's needlework' (iv.i.21), in which the licentiousness and corruption of a sophisticated society are obliquely read out of the elaborate pattern of embroidery, depicting trees, plant, and a 'wanton Streame,' compared with a 'Strumpet.'

It is, however, to Christopher Marlowe's *Edward II* that we must look for a truly dramatic and highly developed use of the emblem as a functional element in the action of a play. In the second act King Edward awaits the return of his favourite Gaveston and asks the latter's enemy Mortimer what 'device' he has for the 'stately triumph we decreed' (ii.ii.11–12). For this special occasion Mortimer suggests the following ominous *impresa*:

A lofty cedar-tree, fair flourishing,
On whose top-branches kingly eagles perch,
And by the bark a canker creeps me up,
And gets into the highest bough of all:
The motto, *Æque tandem*. (ii.ii.16–20)

The King then turns to Lancaster, who is no better disposed towards Gaveston, and asks for his device. Lancaster's *impresa* is no less threatening:

Pliny reports there is a flying fish
Which all the other fishes deadly hate,
And therefore, being pursued, it takes the air:
No sooner is it up, but there's a foul
That seizes it; this fish, my lord, I bear,
The motto this: *Undique mors est.* (II.ii.23–8)

Kent is the first to comment on the 'show of amity' which is belied by the shields which display 'rancorous minds' (II.ii.32–3). The King is also quite aware of the intentions of Mortimer and Lancaster, whose choice of *impresa* reveals their attitude to Gaveston and their intention to remove him. King Edward's interpretation is unequivocal:

I am that cedar, shake me not too much;
And you eagles; soar ye ne'er so high,
I have the jesses that will pull you down;
And *Æque tandem* shall that canker cry
Unto the proudest peer of Britainy.
Though thou compar'st him to a flying fish
And threatenest death whether he rise or fall,
'Tis not the hugest monster of the sea,
Nor the foulest harpy that shall swallow him. (II.ii.38–45)

These *impresa* are not mere verbal conceits; Kent's words make it clear that the device and its motto were painted on a shield for the King and his retinue to see. The two *impresa* are thus woven into the main action, and, as Oppel suggests, they are fully integrated in the 'forcefield of tensions' ('Kraftfeld der Spannungen,' p 71), which works itself out as the play progresses.[50]

A similar situation will be encountered in Shakespeare's *Pericles*. In act II, scene ii, six knights express their love for Princess Thaisa by displaying on a shield a visual device which is interpreted by a brief motto in a foreign tongue. The *impresa* is thus drawn into the dramatic action of the play.

In passing it might be noted that Marlowe's use of the *impresa* is in complete accordance with Giovio's five rules with regard to the number of motifs in the *pictura* (as well as the absence of the human form) and the number of words in the motto. Furthermore, Marlowe's devices fulfil the function of the *impresa*, which was to reveal through a slightly enigmatic combination of picture and motto a 'personal objective' or a line of conduct relating to a specific occasion.

Emblematic stage properties as scenic elements

Glynne Wickham has probably done more than any other scholar to redirect attention to the emblematic nature of the Elizabethan stage.[51] In his view the English theatre of the period is the outcome of 'a head-on collision of two fundamentally opposed attitudes to art: the typically mediaeval contentment with emblematic comment on the significance of the visual world versus a new, scientific questing for the photographic image.'[52] Some of the best examples of emblematic stagecraft are contained in the pageants of the time. 'Pageantry,' writes Wickham, 'is itself the quintessence of emblematic art.'[53]

Among the many major scenic devices Wickham discusses is the mountain, which was very popular with dramatists during the Elizabethan and Jacobean era. Particularly interesting is the 'differentiation between green hill and barren rock [that] allowed too of emblematic contrast between one part of the world and another, and between desirable and undesirable states of being' (II, i, 213). In the pageant celebrating Elizabeth's coronation in 1559 there were two hills representing the decayed and the flourishing commonwealth, the 'ruinose Respublica' and the 'Respublica bene instituta.'[54] This image is truly emblematic in that the general scenic device takes on a specific and abstract meaning which transcends the nature of the object represented on the stage. Only where a scenic element points to a significance beyond itself may it be considered emblematic. To what extent the metonymic use of stage properties may be regarded as emblematic is another question. The use of the crocodile to signify Egypt and the Nile results from metonymic association rather than from emblematic modes of thought.[55] In fact, when one reads Wickham's highly informative study of early English stages it is difficult not to suspect that he has stretched the concept of the emblem by applying it to such major scenic devices as arbour, tree, castle, cave, fountain, mountain, pavilion, ship, and tomb, many of which do not appear, from his account, to point to meanings beyond themselves. In many instances they are used instead to localize action in a very concrete sense, as is the case with the tree standing for the forest of Arden in *As You Like It*.[56]

In 'Becketts Baum und Shakespeares Wälder' Werner Habicht comments on the fact that Shakespeare's trees are seldom mere decoration, but serve to localize the action (cf p 87). The undifferentiated stage tree may become 'the elder tree' in *Titus Andronicus* (II.ii.272), 'Herne's oak' in *The Merry Wives of Windsor* (v.iv.3), and the 'Duke's oak' in *A Midsummer Night's Dream* (I.ii.97). This is certainly the case, but this particularizing is not emblematic.

However, the elder-tree and yew do become charged with several emblematic meanings in *Titus Andronicus*. Habicht writes: 'Traditionally elder and yew were associated with death, despair, and magic. In addition, folk superstition knows the elder as the tree of love. The forest, at first a place of pleasure, is turned by Tamora when she names the yew – emblem of death – into a place of crime and death. Furthermore, the elder is traditionally considered the tree on which Judas hanged himself: the stage tree, which here indicates the place of Aaron's treachery, is used in a later scene as Aaron's gallows ('A halter, soldiers! Hang him on this tree!' v.i.47)' [pp 88–9].[57]

A critic who knows the emblem-books may discover emblematic meanings where none is present. Habicht believes that the oak in *As You Like It*, if considered together with the 'palme' (iii.ii.163), indicates the 'impossibility of hope for a Golden Age on earth,' a motif found in Camerarius. As Habicht puts it: 'the combination [of oak and palm] ... points expressly in Camerarius to the impossibility of hope for a Golden Age on earth ("Aurea in hoc frustra speramus saecula mundo, / Alterius saeculi quae dabit ille Pater"); this could not catch more pregnantly the meaning of the scenes in the forest of Arden, in which an apparently paradise-like world is constantly treated relatively and called into question' (p 89).[58] The emblematic meaning latent in the combination of oak and palm is only realized in a situation where the two trees appear together – verbally or visually; in Shakespeare's play the two trees are separated by whole scenes. Habicht's interpretation makes too great a demand on the memory and mental process of emblematic association on the part of the audience. However, in its own context each tree is significant: the royal oak is the appropriate tree for the Duke, and the palm tree, an emblem of constancy, a fitting choice for a lover.

Emblematic stage properties as elements in the dramatic action
In addition to their function as major scenic units emblematic stage properties can also play a significant role in the dramatic action. As hand properties they frequently give visual emphasis to an aspect of the action, or a theme, in a given scene. Torches, candles, and tapers are found as motifs in emblem-books and poetry, where they connote life and death, wisdom and love, but they are also often carried as hand properties by actors in renaissance drama. In George Chapman's *Bussy D'Ambois* Montsurry explains to his adulterous wife how his love for her has died. The verbal image of the self-consuming taper becomes a stage emblem, as Montsurry's speech becomes a visual demonstration, which he interprets much in the manner of a *subscriptio*:

> And as this Taper, though it upwards look,
> Downwards must needs consume, so let our love;

As having lost his honey, the sweet taste
Runs into savour, and will needs retain
A spice of his first parents, till (like life)
It sees and dies; so let our love: and lastly,
As when the flame is suffer'd to look up
It keeps his lustre: but, being thus turn'd down
(His natural course of useful light inverted)
His own stuff puts it out: so let our love
Now turn from me, as here I turn from thee ... (v.iii.252–62)

As Mehl observes: 'The taper in front of him is turned into an emblem, illustrating and generalizing what is going on in the scene.'[59]

Jonson's masque *Hymenaei* reaches its climax at the appearance of the goddess Juno, revealed in the highest region of the air. From her throne a golden chain is let down to the stage, which represents the earth. The golden chain is here a stage property that embodies the meaning inherent in the ancient verbal symbol of the unbroken chain of being.[60]

Some German baroque dramas are so rich in emblematic stage properties that they remind us of the heaping up of imagery in baroque poetry. Lohenstein's *Ibrahim Bassa* contains a scene in which Desire and Reason argue over their respective powers and strengths. The use of demonstrative adjectives in the text makes it clear that the arrow and candle, bridle and syringe mentioned in the speeches are not verbal images but emblematic stage properties carried by Desire and Reason. Desire says:

This is the arrow, and this the candle
Which with flames of desire can
Bewitch man's limbs, mind and heart,
And enflame them.

Dis ist der Pfeil / und dis die Kertze
    Die mit begihrgen Flammen kan
Des Menschen Glider Sinn und Hertze
    Verzaubern und sie zünden an.

Reason replies:

This is the bridle, and this the syringe
Which fight against your arrows,
Which extinguish, blow out, and quench,
The flame and heat of desire.

Dis ist der Zaum / und dies die Spritze
    Der wider deine Pfeile kämpfft /
Die der Begihrde Flamm und Hitze
    Verläschet / bläset auf und dämpfft.   (Cited in Schöne, p 215)

Heraldic motifs can also become emblematic stage properties. Early in Shakespeare's *Henry VI, Part I* there is a scene in a Temple garden, where the legal and political arguments of the Temple-hall are translated into visual terms as the supporters of York and Lancaster pick white and red roses to demonstrate their allegiance to the respective houses. The rose bushes of the Temple garden become the emblems of the rival houses. The emblematic play with roses, which presages the coming civil strife, is both tersely dramatic and highly emblematic, in that several speakers base their comments and arguments upon some natural quality of the rose, which is interpreted in a general and abstract manner. Thus for Vernon the white rose, 'this pale and maiden blossom,' stands for 'the truth and plainness of the case' (II.iv.46, 47). Tauntingly Plantagenet says that the colour of Somerset's cheeks counterfeit the white rose of York, 'For pale they look with fear, as witnessing / The truth on our side' (II.iv.63–4). Not to be outdone Somerset replies:

'Tis not for fear, but anger that thy cheeks
Blush for pure shame to conterfeit our roses,
And yet thy tongue will not confess thy error.   (II.iv.65–7)

Further allusion is made to the thorn and canker in the verbal duel. The coming Wars of the Roses is emblematically presaged in Somerset's answer to the question 'where is your argument?':

Here in my scabbard; meditating that
Shall dye your white rose in a bloody red.   (II.iv.60–1)

Towards the end of the scene Warwick makes the following prophecy:

This brawl to-day
Grown to this faction, in the Temple-garden,
Shall send, between the red rose and the white,
A thousand souls to death and deadly night.   (II.iv.124–7)

Almost without exception Elizabethan revenge plays make provision for at least a skull, if not a full graveyard or charnel house. Yorick's skull, as highlighted in Hamlet's conversations with the gravediggers, is probably the most famous example of the skull as an emblematic stage property embodying notions of 'memento mori' and 'vanitas.' Somewhat more ambitious use is made of the skull by Tourneur in *The Revenger's Tragedy* where Vindice appears with the skull of his former mistress, a victim of the Duke's seduction. Later, the skull provokes a speech on the vanity of the world, and finally, dressed up as a living woman, it is presented to her seducer. As Mehl has noted: 'this has nothing to do with any kind of sensational and macabre realism, as is often suggested, but implies a concept of dramatic representation ... for which 'emblematic' is perhaps the most accurate term. Again it is the concrete visualization of a spiritual and moral experience that the dramatist is striving for, not a realistic imitation of actual events and characters.'[61] This is a fair enough comment, and one which might be applied to other dramas of the period.[62]

Stage properties were not only used to underline the meaning of certain scenes or pieces of action, but were also drawn into the presentation of character. Some instances of this are described above.[63]

There is no doubt that many of the stage properties used in the drama of the sixteenth and seventeenth centuries have a truly emblematic function, pointing to meanings beyond themselves. However, not all the visually striking and dramatically used properties are emblematic in the strict sense. I feel that Mehl, for example, has allowed his enthusiasm to run away with him, when he writes: 'A closer examination of the stage properties used by Shakespeare would show time and again how Shakespeare draws into the action the iconographical associations of certain objects and thereby indicates deeper possibilities of interpretation, from the picture of the dagger in *Macbeth* to the snakes Cleopatra puts to her breast, from the ruler's insignia, drawn so demonstratively into the history plays to the fool's cap in *King Lear*' ('Schaubild und Sprachfigar in Shakespeares Dramen,' p 16).[64]

Act and chorus

German tragedy of the seventeenth century has a specific and well-defined form; the action is divided into five acts, each of which, with the exception of the last act, is followed by a Chorus, called by Gryphius 'Reyen' in imitation of the Dutch. Schöne begins his discussion of the emblematic quality of this dramatic form with an analysis of Gryphius's *Leo Armenius*, the first German tragedy in the age of the Baroque. (cf pp 162–70). The first act introduces the audience to Michael Balbus, highest ranking commander of the Byzantine armies, who is critical of his Emperor Leo Armenius. His fiery speeches against Leo loosen the tongues of other malcontents who form a conspiracy to overthrow Leo, in their eyes a tyrant. Informed of the growing opposition of Balbus and his friends, Leo feels concern, but is none the less reluctant to have his adversary quietly assassinated, as his counsellors advise. Leo instructs his advisers to try to persuade Balbus to mend his ways and render to the Emperor loyalty and obedience; should words have no effect, then he is to be arrested and condemned to death. The attempt fails, Balbus is thrown into chains, and his death seems certain.

The theme of the first act is 'the ambivalent faculty of human speech' (Schöne, p 164).[65] The action has demonstrated the salutary and destructive effects of speech, which can bring good and evil, life and death, to the speaker.

What follows the dramatic action is a Chorus of Courtiers, who deliver three speeches: the 'Satz' ('thesis'), 'Gegensatz' ('antithesis'), and 'Zusatz' ('supplement'). These courtiers had not been present, either as participants or spectators, in the action of the first act; their songs are not brought into any direct relationship with that action, in so far as the songs mention neither characters nor events by name. The first song praising the power of human speech begins:

> The wonder of nature, the more than wise animal,
> has nothing to compare with his tongue.

> Das Wunder der Natur / das überweise Thier
> Hat nichts das seiner zungen sey zugleichen

The chorus continues to praise language as the means by which man has made progress in all fields of human endeavour and concludes:

> Man's life itself rests on his tongue.

> Deß Menschen leben selbst; beruht auf seiner zungen.

The second song, 'Gegensatz,' takes the opposing view:

> Yet there is nothing so sharp as a tongue!
> Nothing that can bring us poor ones so low.

> Doch / nichts ist das so scharff / als eine zunge sey!
> Nichts das so tief vns arme stürtzen könne.

The Chorus then lists the catastrophes which the power of speech can produce: bloody crimes, witchcraft, heresy, war, religious dissention, and vice. The conclusion reached in 'Gegensatz' contradicts that of the first song:

Man's death rests on each man's tongue.

Deß Menschen Todt beruht auff jedes Menschen zungen.

The 'Zusatz' begins with a warning:

Learn, you that live, to put a bridle on your lips
In which prosperity and mischief live,
And what damns and what rewards.

Lernt / die jhr lebt / den zaum in ewre Lippen legen!
In welchen heil vnd schaden wohnet /
Vnd was verdammt / vnd was belohnet.

The opposing views of the first two songs are mirrored in the antithesis of the third:

The tongue is this sword
That protects and injures.
The flame that destroys
And also pleases well.
A hammer that builds and breaks,
A rose branch that smells and pricks.

Die Zung ist dieses Schwerdt
So schützet vnd verletzt.
Die flamme so verzehrt
Und ebenwol ergetzt.
Ein Hammer welcher bawt vnd bricht /
Ein Rosenzweig / der reucht und sticht /.

The conclusions of the first two songs are likewise brought together in the third:

Your life, man, and death is always on your tongue.

Dein Leben / Mensch / vnd todt hält stets auf deiner Zungen.

Schöne compares this theme with an emblem of Camerarius (pp 167–8) which also demonstrates that the life and death of man are dependent upon his tongue. More important than the possible indebtedness of Gryphius to Camerarius, which cannot be ruled out, is the structural analogy. The Chorus corresponds to the *subscriptio* of an emblem. Schöne writes: 'What Camerarius derives from the *res significans*, the silent, static picture of oyster-catching, and communicates in the *subscriptio* is – to use Harsdörffer's definition of a play – is developed here out of the *essential* (i.e., significant) *living and speaking picture* of the dramatic incidents between Michael Balbus and Emperor Leo Armenius, and is announced by the Chorus' (p 169).[66]

Act and Chorus are interrelated in accordance with the emblematic structural principle ('Formprinzip,' Schöne, p 170): 'representation and interpretation, the particular and the general, picture and meaning only together [make up] as complementary parts the characteristic whole' (p 169).[67]

DRAMA AS EXTENDED EMBLEM

Pageants and processions[68]

Pageant-theatre and processions of various kinds, both secular and religious, through the streets of towns and cities, existed long before the establishment of public theatres. In its organization of visual impressions (vignettes, static figures, stage properties) and verbal explanation (written on shields and placards, spoken by actors) the pageant is often emblematic. For Wickham the pageant is 'the quintessence of emblematic art,'[69] a judgment that has the approval of David Bergeron, whose studies of English civic pageantry culminated in the publication of his book of that title (London, 1971). An example from his account of Elizabeth's coronation entry into London in 1559 will suffice to illustrate the emblematic method in creating and staging pageants. *The Quenes Majesties Passage through the Citie of London* made provision for a number of tableaux; at Soper Lane 'on a scaffold arrangement were eight children representing the eight Beatitudes "eche having the proper name of the blessing, that they did represent, written in a table and placed above their heades." In addition, "Everie of the children wer appointed and apparelled according unto the blessing which he did represent"' (cited in Bergeron, p 275). This combination of personification and identifying inscription corresponds to the *pictura* and *scriptura* of the emblem. What is more, we read: 'And all voide places in the pageant wer furnished with prety sayings, commending and touching the meaning of the said pageant, which was the promises and blessing of almightie god made to his people' (cited in Bergeron, p 275).

The characters portrayed in the pageants often uttered speeches that explained and applied the concepts they represented. Thus one of the beatitudes in the coronation pageant spoke the following lines of verse upon the arrival of Elizabeth at the tableau:

> Thou has been .viii. times blest, o quene of worthy fame
> By mekenes of thy spirite, when care did thee besette
> By mourning in thy grief, by mildnes in thy blame
> By hunger and by thyrst, and justice couldst none gette.
> By mercy shewed, not felt, by cleanes of thyne harte
> By seking peace alwayes, by persecucion wrong.
> Therfore trust thou in god, since he hath helpt thy smart
> That as his promis is, so he will make thee strong.   (Cited in Bergeron, p 275)

As Bergeron observes: 'The pageant-emblem is thus complete and the observer has been duly instructed. From this pageant one could easily construct a corresponding emblem' (p 276). Bergeron proceeds to enumerate 'parallels between specific emblems and specific pageants without worrying over the problem of possible indebtedness' (p 276). Particularly interesting is his investigation of the theme of Time and Fortune in the emblem-books of Whitney and Peacham and a number of civic pageants (cf pp 276–81).

The close affinities between pageant and theatre are probably nowhere more clearly seen than in Schöne's account of the procession invented by the headmaster of the *Gymnasium* at Görlitz in the year 1699. The printed programme explains that the purpose of the pageant was to show 'The weight of war withstood during the latter years of this century and the joys of peace now blossoming again' (cited in Schöne, p 209).[70] The procession included such allegorical figures as Eris, Europa, Envy, Greed, Hypocrisy, Peace, Justice, and representatives of the various levels of society. The meaning of a given figure was written on emblematic insignias or on placards which were carried in the procession. Schöne comments: 'If in this way the connection with the *pictura* and *scriptura* of the emblem is revealed, then at the same time the affinity of the allegorical-emblematic procession to the stage play is also indicated' (p 209).[71] In fact a play on the same subject was performed in Görlitz in the same year (cf Schöne, p 210).

The masque[72]

Clearly the most emblematic of all the forms of drama intended for performance indoors is the masque; here the graphic artist and the poet collaborate to produce an entertainment in which the visual element is more symbolically significant than in any other form of theatre. Masques are for the most part occasional pieces, in the sense that they were commissioned for a specific occasion. However, like the occasional poem of the same period, the masque frequently transcended its time-bound occasion to embody more timeless concerns and to make valid statements of a general nature on the themes deriving from the specific occasion. A good example is Ben Jonson's masque *Hymenaei*, written to celebrate the marriage of the young Earl of Essex to Frances Howard, younger daughter of the Earl of Sussex, in 1606. My account of this masque follows closely Gordon's essay '*Hymenaei*: Ben Jonson's Masque of Union.'

I shall begin with the emblematic qualities of the piece before proceeding to a consideration of the masque as occasional literature. When the curtain rises the first thing the audience sees is an altar in the centre of the stage bearing the following inscription in gold:

Ioni.   Oimae.   Mimae.
        VNIONI
        SACR.

The altar is the focus of all the dramatic and intellectual action of the masque, which develops the themes contained in the different meaning of *Vnio*. As in the emblem the spectator is first introduced to a visual experience of an object, which signifies more than it is; we have, in Schöne's terms, the priority of picture. At this altar there will be performed a highly allegorical wedding according to Roman nuptial rites, a fitting entertainment for the wedding celebrations of the Earl of Essex. We are told that the altar is 'sacred to *marriage*, or Vnion; over which Iuni was President' (cited in Gordon, p 108). By a fortunate anagram – IVNO/VNIO – Juno becomes the patroness of marriage. Two wedding parties appear and process to the altar, but the wedding rites are disrupted by eight men, who appear from a globe representing the 'little world of man,' and who dance, brandishing swords, to contentious music. This dumb-show signifies man in chaos, and Jonson gives to the four Humours and four Affections ensigns and colours symbolic of their meaning. Reason appears, summoned by Hymen from the microcosm, to tame them. She is an allegorical figure taken from Ripa's *Iconologia*, a venerable woman with white hair, 'crowned with lights, her garments blue, and semined with starres, girded vnto her with a white bend, fill'd with *Arithmeticall* figures, in one hand bearing a Lampe, in the other a bright sword' (cited in Gordon, p 111). The symbolism of her clothing and attributes is all traditional and emblematic. Reason rebukes the Affections and Humours, and from this point on assumes the role of Chorus, whose words interpret the meaning of the ceremonies, dresses, and ritual objects. Again the symbolism is apt: Reason is the guide and interpreter; the function is also emblematic: Reason becomes the speaking *scriptura* to the various *picturae* of the masque. Reason expostulates on the correspondences between microcosm and macrocosm; the rebellion of the passions against reason is held up as the image of civil insurrection against the king; and harmonious man and the harmonious state are figured in the mystical body of marriage.

The most dramatic moment of the whole masque is the appearance of Juno: a curtain opens to reveal three regions of Air, with Juno enthroned in the highest region, and above her a statue of Jupiter. On stage now the spectator sees various groupings that represent the correspondence between microcosm and macrocosm, a visible counterpart to the earlier verbal statement. A golden chain is let down from heaven, a stage property which embodies the meaning of the unbroken chain of being, that age-old symbol for the hierarchical ordering of creation. The rites are consummated in a dance which takes the shape of a circle, the symbol of God, eternity, and perfection. The grouping is carefully arranged and symbolic: Reason is in the centre, surrounded by the bridal party, which in turn is surrounded by the Affections and Humours and the eight powers of Juno. This is, then, the final visual statement of the great union of which the masque is the expression.

Reason's final remarks on union are a reference to the union of the kingdoms of England and Scotland under James I, who liked to think of himself as the husband and the United Kingdom as his wife.[73] Gordon concludes: 'in effect *Hymenaei* is not only a formal wedding masque; *Hymenaei* is a dramatic and symbolic representation of the Union of the Kingdoms as it was conceived in the propaganda issued by men who had the approval of the King himself' (p 127).

From this it may already be seen to what extent *Hymenaei* transcends the immediate occasion of the marriage of Essex to Frances Howard. But Jonson has yet other things in mind. Quite early on in the masque King James's marriage had been celebrated as an instance of 'the union wrought in the world by the power of love' (cited in Gordon, p 109), a universal union, in fact, 'which includes both man and the elements in an order figured by the concord of music' (p 109). But Juno is not only the patroness of marriage; she is also Union, Unity, and *Unitas*. Steeped in the traditions of renaissance neoplatonism, Jonson sees Juno as the indivisible One, and One represents God, mysterious, irreducible source of all things. The wedding rites at Juno's altar now celebrate the actual marriage of Essex; the marriage of James; the unity of man and nature; the unity of the whole universe, honouring James I and God himself; the unity of the kingdoms of England and Scotland with James at its head. Gordon's summary makes the point clearly: 'To relate present occasions to sublime and removed mysteries (Jonson's phrase), to link Whitehall, the marriage of the Earl of Essex with Frances Howard, James and his cherished plan to the union of man, the universe and God: this for Jonson was the art of the Masque. Rarely has it been so ingeniously exemplified as in *Hymenaei*, where the altar that meets the curious eyes of the spectators becomes the nodal point on which the lines that connect the universe converge' (pp 127–8).

In his book on Stuart masques Nicoll observes: 'It were by no means too much to say that in the masque the fashion for the courtly *impresa* and for the emblem-book reached its completest expression' (p 154). No scholar would seriously challenge that judgment, but its application has led to basic disagreements about the relationship of word to spectacle in the masque that date back to the famous dispute between Inigo Jones and Ben Jonson in the early seventeenth century.[74] In the body-soul debate poets such as Daniel, Jonson, and Dekker had no doubt that poetry was the soul of the masque, which found its substance in the visual embodiment that they, the poets, 'invented' and craftsmen executed under their direction. Apart from an understandable jealousy of Jones's popularity with the audiences – a popularity achieved through the brilliance of his spectacular sets – Jonson's disagreement with Jones had a serious basis: Jones's creations often departed from the details of theme, figure, and attribute that Jonson had invented. For instance, Jones would choose colours and symbols – originally the province of the poet, and part of his invention – according to their aesthetic effect and for their meaning. Thus alteration of the 'body' changed some aspects of the 'soul' of the masque. Nicoll comments that, 'as in the popular emblem literature of the age, the visual and auditory have to meet in harmony if complete expression is to be secured' (p 25).

As time went on the poet lost control over the invention of the masque. In so far as the artist devised the theme and its visual details, and the poet provided an explanatory commentary, the visual spectacle might be said to have become the 'soul' and the verbal part merely the 'body.' However, that was not the intention of the poet-creators of the masques, nor does it describe the nature of the best masques of Jonson. For this reason I cannot agree with Hagstrum that 'The picture is substantive and essential, the word adjectival and ancillary' (p 89). Hagstrum also asserts: 'It is not true that the soul of the masque was verbal, even when the words were as eloquent as the art of Ben Jonson at its best could make them ... Words are unmistakably the pendants of the visual scene' (pp 90–1). This merely confuses the impression on the audience, which sees a spectacle and hears its interpretation, in that order, with the methods of composition; it completely overlooks the fixed meanings traditionally associated with certain colours, symbols, and myths.

But historians of literature and art tend to overstress the role of poetry and visual effects respectively, and both are inclined to forget that the purpose of the masque was primarily to entertain. Nicoll reminds us of its connection with feasting and music (pp 30–1); he shows how the masque grew out of an 'elaborate charade' performed by disguised dancers, who moved among the audience and invited individuals to join them in the 'dancing place' situated between the stage and the feast table (cf pp 35–6).

5

Emblematic Narrative Prose

It would be surprising if the great narrative prose works of the sixteenth and seventeenth centuries did not reveal something of the emblematic world-view of their authors. This emblematic world-view is, of course, based on the emblematic mode of thought, which sees inherent meaning in the objects of nature and human history.[1] The attitude of Bunyan,[2] Grimmelshausen,[3] and Defoe[4] – to name but three novelists – is fundamentally emblematic in that they regard the world and nature as 'a gigantic canvas upon which God has stroken in a wealth of moral meaning.'[5] In a variety of ways *The Pilgrim's Progress*, *Simplicissimus*, and *Robinson Crusoe* reveal a coincidence of the emblematic mode of thought and the emblematic form of expression. We know that Bunyan was interested in emblems because towards the end of his life he wrote an emblem-book for children.[6] There are also many explicit expressions of an emblematic world-view scattered through his works, such as the following from his *Solomon's Temple Spiritualized* (1688): 'Since it is the wisdom of God to speak to us oftimes by trees, gold, silver, stones, beasts, fowls, fishes, spiders, ants, frogs, flies, lice, dust etc., and here by wood; how should we by them understand his voice, if we count there is no meaning in them?'[7]

For the seventeenth-century Puritans the emblems depicted objects from the natural world which embody spiritual significance. As Hunter puts it: 'For Puritans emblems become substitutes for icons. Unable to create objects to symbolize spiritual truths (because such action would usurp a divinely reserved prerogative), they permit themselves to isolate and interpret objects and events created by God' (p 29, n 10). The Puritans especially held to the old notion of correspondences between physical reality and spiritual truth. Even when empirical observation cast doubt on the precision of correspondences, the puritan mind remained committed to pictorialism, substituting for analogy the less precise mode of visual metaphor. Thus the Book of Nature became an imperfect emblem of the spiritual world, needing careful interpretation, if it were to lead to truth (cf Hunter, pp 95–6). Hunter describes the emblematic world-view of Defoe, as it informs the pages of his novel *Robinson Crusoe*, in the following words:

> The physical world was a series of emblems, symbols made by God to clarify to men great spiritual truths: each thing and event contained a meaning which might be discovered by men who studied all aspects of that thing or event. Typology, as the Puritans practiced it, was the particular device by which time was comprehended into their emblematic scheme. Metaphor was to words what emblem was to physical objects: just as God informed the objects in his book of nature with discoverable spiritual significance, so his amaneunses in his book of revelation infused words with a significance that extended to later ages within the same divinely controlled cycle. Interpreters of Defoe's day might use this metaphorical biblical language to express patterns of thought deriving from an emblematic understanding of the world of thing and event, but metaphor was to be understood as approximate, for the precise system of analogies no longer applied, and man's understanding was now partial. When an interpreter imposed a total system on his metaphor (a system which he hoped would approximate the spiritual reality), he constructed an allegory, suggesting the comprehensive emblematic significance of each thing and event he portrayed.   (P 122)

EMBLEMATIC IMAGERY

Emblematic imagery is used in figurative language by narrators and characters alike in Grimmelshausen's novels. In the *Vogelnest* we find the following comment on books: 'Just as bees suck honey and spiders poison from flowers, so good men draw good and evil men draw evil from books' ('Gleichwie die Bienen Honig und die Spinnen Gift aus den Blumen saugen, also schöpfen die guten Menschen Guts und die schlimmen Böses aus den Büchern,' (Part II, chap 22).[8] In 'Emblematisches bei Grimmelshausen' Jöns points to a close parallel between this passage and the emblem-book *Emblemata moralia* (1615) of Jakob von Bruck (p 386). The action of bees and spider, which draw from the same flowers respectively honey and poison, is not merely an illustration of a concept, not just an exemplum, i.e., an individual instance proving a rule, but a 'fact of nature' with a broad and general validity which becomes a 'mirror of a generally valid truth' (Jöns, p 388).

In Simplicissimus's satirical dream allegory there is a discussion between an old sergeant-major – a commoner who has come up through the ranks – and a young officer – who owes his commission to his privileged position as an aristocrat. The sergeant-major argues against the injustice inherent in a system that favours aristocratic birth over experience, when it is the experience of a commoner. Both characters use emblematic arguments to support their points of view, and, as in the emblematic stichomythia of contemporary drama, neither actually takes issue directly with the point made by the other, but rather seeks to counter it with an equally strong argument. In order to prove his point that youth should lead in war, the youthful officer uses the emblem of a young bull leading the herd:

> A young bull is put at the head of
> the herd as experienced,
> which he keeps prettily together,
> over another of greater years:
> The herdsman can trust him too
> in spite of his youth.
> It is a bad custom which
> judges virtue by age.

> Ein junger Stier wird vorgestellt
>   Dem Hauffen / als erfahren /
> Den er auch hübsch beysammen hält /
>   Trutz dem von vielen Jahren;
> Der Hirt darff ihm vertrauen auch /
>   Ohn Anseh'n seiner Jugend /
> Man judicirt nach bösem Brauch
>   Auß Alterthum die Tugend.
> (*Simplicissimus Teutsch*, ed. J.H. Scholte [Halle, 1949], p 47)

The sergeant-major is not convinced by this example, and later on introduces the notion of just reward into the discussion: the commoner who fights loyally and bravely should be rewarded with promotion and payment. The truth of this argument is reinforced by comparison with the oil lamp, which must be given oil if it is to shine and fulfil its function:

> The lamp shines well, but you must often replenish it
> With the fat oil of olives, lest the flame soon die;
> Loyal service is increased by reward and refreshed;
> Soldiers' bravery will have its maintenance.

DIe Lampe leucht dir fein / doch mustu sie offt Laben
Mit fett Oliuen safft / die Flam sonst bald verlischt /
Getreuer Dienst durch Lohn gemehrt wird / und erfrischt;
Soldaten Dapfferkeit will Unterhaltung haben
(*Simplicissimus Teutsch*, p 49)

Jöns has discovered an exact source for both these emblematic arguments in Zincgref's *Sapientia picta* (cf Jöns, pp 388–90).

Jöns also considers emblematic the commonplace comparison of pleasure to a rose surrounded by thorns. In his conversation with Simplicissimus the Prince of the Mummelsee characterizes worldly pleasure as 'as little without aversion and pain, as roses are without thorns' ('so wenig ohne Unlust und Schmertzen / als die Rosen ohne Dörner sind / ,' *Simplicissimus Teutsch*, pp 422–3).[9] This is a further instance of the 'coincidence in thought of the facts of nature and Christian teaching' (Jöns, p 385).[10] A precise parallel may be found in de la Perrière (cf *Emblemata*, col 298).[11]

THE EMBLEMATIC EPISODE

In poetry the emblematic motif usually takes the form of a word-emblem, but in narrative verse, prose fiction, and drama the emblematic motif can also become part of the action. We have already noted (pp 61–2) that a full understanding of the bear and storm scene in *The Winter's Tale* requires us to see the motifs of the bear and storm from the vantage-point of the emblem-books, which also provide a clue as to how the scene might actually have been staged.[12]

Emblematic knowledge about trees has shaped Grimmelshausen's treatment of Simplicissimus's dream allegory of the holm-oak, which is itself an extended emblem.[13] In his dream Simplicissimus finally sees the forest become one great oak tree overshadowing the whole of Europe, only to be attacked by strong north winds, whereupon it breaks its own branches. On the trunk of the tree Simplicissimus reads the following inscription:

The evergreen oak tree, driven and damaged by the wind,
Breaks its own branches and plunges itself into ruin:
Through internal war and civil dissension,
Everything is thrown into disorder, and only misery follows.

Die Stein-Eych durch den Wind getrieben und verletzet /
Ihr eigen Aest abbricht / sich ins Verderben setzet:

Durch innerliche Krieg / und brüderlichen Streit /
Wird alles umbgekehrt / und folget lauter Leid
(*Simplicissimus Teutsch*, p 51)

Jöns has not only found the actual source of this motif in Zincgref's *Sapientia picta*, but also noted that this is an instance of the emblematization of nature (cf p 390). The example shows further the kinship of the emblem with the original form and purpose of epigrammatic writing: the placing of inscriptions on significant objects.

A further instance of the way in which an emblematic motif may become the centre of a little episode, an event in the action of a novel, is found in Grimmelshausen's *Vogelnest*, where the impoverished hero comes across flower bulbs in a garden. He contemplates how these ugly and dead-looking bulbs will come to life and produce flowers of great beauty. The flower bulb is an emblem of hope, and from these silent plants ('stummen Gewächsen') the hero derives the faith and hope that God will bless him with success and riches. Jöns argues that through this emblem Grimmelshausen has provided the reader with a touchstone with which to measure the hero's motives and actions; the emblem here implies criticism of the character. 'It can certainly be assumed that Grimmelshausen knew of the Christian meaning of this emblem, and that he consciously gave it a worldly twist in order to characterize the worldly attitude, the foolishness of his hero by making him interpret secularly something intended spiritually' (p 386).[14] Since the emblem allows of so varied an application it is difficult to prove in a particular instance that the profane use of an emblematic motif is intended to imply a religious criticism. None the less, in general terms a strong case can be made for assuming that the seventeenth-century reader would find moral or religious criticism where we see none. In *Literature and the Delinquent: The Picaresque Novel in Spain and Europe, 1599–1753* (Edinburgh, 1967) Alexander A. Parker argues that there is an implied religious basis for the evaluation of character and incident which escapes the modern reader not accustomed to seventeenth-century ways of thinking.

The Pilgrim's Progress abounds in emblematic episodes;[15] indeed, Christian's path to the Celestial City is the thread upon which Bunyan has arranged a series of emblematic events that test and prepare the pilgrim. On one occasion Christian and Hopeful come upon a strange monument in a desert, which looks as though it had been a woman transformed into a pillar. They study it for some time, but can make nothing of it, until Hopeful draws Christian's attention to an inscription on the pillar; the meaning, which Christian pieces together, is 'Remember Lot's wife.' As Alpaugh points out, their interpretation is 'solidly grounded in an empirical experience' (p 302). The pilgrims then discourse at length upon the meaning of the event, and its application to their lives.

On occasions the substance of the emblematic episode is material well-known from the popular emblem-books. Among the visions revealed to the pilgrims on the top of the Delectable Mountains is the washing of the Ethiopian. Christiana and Mercy see 'one *Fool* and one *Want-Wit* washing of an *Ethiopian* with the intention to make him white, but the more they washed him, the blacker he was.' The meaning is expounded as follows: 'Thus shall it be with the vile Person: all means used to get such one a good Name, shall in conclusion tend to make him more abominable. Thus it was with the *Pharisees*, and so shall it be with all Hypocrites' (cited in Freeman, *English Emblem Books*, p 216). In the emblem-books the picture of the washing of a black man usually has the more general meaning of 'impossible' (cf *Emblemata*, cols 1087–8).

In *The Pilgrim's Progress*, as in the contemporary drama, there are many instances of the emblematic object becoming involved directly in the action. Before beginning her journey through the Valley of the Shadow of Death Christiana is given the Golden Anchor that hung on a wall in the Palace Beautiful, 'in case [she] meet with turbulent weather.' The anchor which she receives is clearly an emblem of hope that, only by a considerable stretch of the imagination, may preserve her on land against the physical storms of the Valley; it will certainly provide her with the spiritual strength to withstand the fear of death.

Thus far we have been concerned with establishing the emblematic character of the individual, isolated episode; but there are also whole series of episodes containing emblematic characters, actions, and objects in many novels of the period. Probably the most famous example is contained in *The Pilgrim's Progress*, where Christian is introduced to the Interpreter's House. What Christian finds in the Interpreter's House is virtually an emblem theatre (cf Sharrock, p 107). In each room the hero is confronted with a visual and silent experience, the meaning of which is expounded by the Interpreter. The dusty room which a girl sprinkles with water before a man with a broom brushes it clean represents the cleansing of the unregenerate heart by means of the Law under the influence of the Gospel; the room with the two children Patience and Passion may be understood in the emblematic context of the profane and sacred cupids (cf Sharrock, p 110); the room in which a man seeks to extinguish with water a fire burning against a wall, secretly fed with oil by a hand behind the wall, signifies the secret work of grace, which the devil attempts to frustrate;[16] the dark room containing a man in an iron cage represents despair. There are also the man with the muck-rake; the venomous spider living in a fine room; the room with chickens that look up to heaven as they drink; the garden where all the flowers, no matter how different, live in harmony; and the fair tree, rotten at the heart. As all of these visual scenes pass before the eyes of Christian, they are interpreted and their meaning applied to the Christian life by the Interpreter. Had Bunyan been a dramatist and cast his *Pilgrim's Progress* in the form of a morality play, these silent scenes would most likely have taken the form of dumb-shows, or silent *tableaux*.

In Alpaugh's view the full significance of Christian's experiences at the House of the Interpreter has not been recognized: 'the art of emblem interpretation that Christian learns, as the Interpreter explains the significance of a number of emblems by the light of a figure called Illumination, is in a larger sense the art that all aspiring pilgrims must learn before they can enter the Celestial City' (p 301). Alpaugh has discovered a pattern of thematic continuity in the emblems that fill the pages of *The Pilgrim's Progress*: broadly speaking there are two groups of emblems that Christian encounters on his way, those of darkness and those of light. Gold and light are the primary symbols of the Celestial City, God, truth, and reality. The darkness of the Valley of the Shadow of Death, Doubting Castle, the black-skinned Flatterer, and the cave in the hillside signifies sin, despair, and damnation. 'Light is creation and therefore reality; darkness is merely the chaotic illusion that the light of creation dispels. In human terms light corresponds to faith and hope, darkness to doubt and despair' (Alpaugh, p 304). The episode of Christian in Doubting Castle illustrates the point: the pilgrim is locked in Doubting Castle only because he has forgotten that he possesses the key called promise.

Christian is not the only character in *The Pilgrim's Progress* to find himself confronted with the emblem, although it is true that, as he accumulates experience, he becomes the most reliable interpreter (cf Alpaugh, p 309). Many other characters either avoid experience, or, as in the case of divisive figures in the novel, 'ignore or misinterpret the emblems of salvation and damnation that surround them' (pp 304–5). For instance, Mr Hold-the-world uses language to distort experience, refusing anything that might be unpleasant or make moral demands of him.

One of Hunter's principal aims in his study of *Robinson Crusoe* is to suggest that there exists a 'relationship between characteristic Puritan ways of thinking in the seventeenth century and the new prose fiction of the eighteenth' (preface, p xii). In pursuit of this aim Hunter examines the Crusoe story as one man's journey through life from rebellion to repentance, a journey which reveals a pattern of progression from divine judgment to divine mercy. Crusoe is something of an Everyman, whose conflict between reason and natural desire is a basic human experience shared by all readers. Crusoe's sin is having a restless mind and body, which leads him to be discontented with his station in life and to pursue a wandering existence. The desert island resolves Crusoe's conflicts.

'What Defoe distills from desert island experience is ... a rigorous multilevel moral examination of life, for the narrative is structured to render dimensions which are absent in stories of similar plot' (Hunter, p 126).

The realism in the depiction of the desert island narrative has obscured the emblematic quality of many of the episodes, and an understanding of events as a 'potential means of communication between man and God' (Hunter, p 154). The thunder-lightning episode and the earthquake are rooted in the ancient tradition of God speaking through awe-inspiring natural events. Hunter points to parallels in contemporary providence books, where such natural phenomena are seen as warnings and punishments (cf p 154).[17] In fact, quite generally, physical events in *Robinson Crusoe* reflect the hero's spiritual state: 'his efforts to come to terms with his physical environment parallel his efforts to find a proper relationship with his God' (Hunter, p 189). Tracing the main outlines of this dual concern, Hunter writes:

> Crusoe's erratic straying from his course at sea, his Turkish slavery, and his ship-wreck upon the rocks parallel his spiritual drift, his bondage to sin, and the 'spiritual shipwreck' (to use the standard term of the guide tradition) of his soul, just as his island deliverance presages his being set apart and his relief from sickness parallels the cure of his soul. Similarly, his efforts to convert the island wilderness into a garden parallel his efforts to cultivate his spiritual self, weeding out the wild undergrowth of desires which, since man's fall, 'naturally' choke the life of the soul. (Pp 189–90)

Seen from an emblematic perspective even the final episode of the battle with the wolves in the Pyrenees is a justifiable event, which, modern critical disapproval notwithstanding, 'provides a dramatic climax to the previous physical and spiritual adventures' (Hunter, p 191).[18]

Grimmelshausen's hero Simplicissimus also becomes a meditating hermit on a desert island, which assumes for him the function of a great religious emblem-book. Deprived of both human friendship and the companionship of books, Simplicissimus recalls the example of a holy man to whom the whole world was a book. Because of their inherent qualities the things of nature become for Simplicissimus 'emblems of salvation' (Jöns, p 385). The thorny bush reminds the castaway of Christ's crown of thorns; at the sight of an apple or pomegranate he thinks of the Fall of Adam and Eve; when he drinks palm wine from the tree, Simplicissimus remembers how Christ gave his blood on the tree of the cross; the sea and mountains remind him of certain of Christ's miracles or parables; stones bring to mind how the Jews stoned Christ; in his garden Simplicissimus thinks of Christ in the garden of Gethsemane; when he eats, he thinks of the sacrament; the cooking-fire raises images of hell-fire in his mind (cf *Simplicissimus*, book 6, pp 102–3).

We see from these examples how closely related is the religious practice of meditation to the emblem. Indeed, what Simplicissimus and Crusoe do on their desert island is essentially what Herbert was doing at Little Gidding and Greiffenberg on her estate in Lower Austria; they are all applying the methods of occasional meditation in their everyday lives. No matter how dissimilar their national and geographical situations, no matter how divergent their political and theological convictions, no matter how different their personal positions, the fact remains that for a variety of reasons English Anglicans and Puritans, German Lutherans, and Continental Catholics were united in their practice of various kinds of meditation, both formal and occasional. And wherever meditation was practised the emblem was close at hand.[19]

EMBLEMATIC NARRATIVE STRUCTURE

To what extent, if any, do seventeenth-century novels reveal an emblematic structure? Without doubt many of these narrative works contain images, maxims, episodes, and characters that owe much to the emblem-books and to emblematic modes of thought and composition. Furthermore, patterns of recurring images and episodes have been discovered, which lend a certain thematic continuity. But what evidence is there that formal emblematic principles have shaped the organization of a whole novel? Sibylle Penkert appears to believe that emblematic structure may inform the baroque novel as a 'Ferment' (leaven), although how or why this should be so is a question that awaits further investigation.[20] Since critics have in general thus far shown reluctance to study the relationship between narrative prose and the emblem, it is not surprising that virtually no work has been done on the emblematic structure of the novel. A partial reason for this may lie in the inadequacy of theories of the emblem, a situation remedied only during the last decade. However, another reason may perhaps be found in the genre itself. On the whole, structuralist critics have tended to avoid longer novels, probably because of difficulties inherent in their approach: it must be well-nigh impossible to discuss *The Brothers Karamazov*, for instance, in the detailed way one might interpret a short lyric poem; the sheer bulk and complexity of the novel make it difficult to hold clearly in mind the web and weft of theme and character, action and symbolic language. The mind boggles at the thought of doing a structural interpretation of *Simplicissimus* or *Aramena*!

In my view the problem lies in the fact that an emblematic structure must be concrete, visual, and bear a clearly definable, though not necessarily stated, meaning. To get the structure of a novel into focus, on the other hand, one must describe the organization and interaction of the language, characters, and action of the novel, and only these constituent parts of the whole may be concrete, visual, and symbolic. The relationship between these constituents is susceptible to an analysis, which will abstract form and meaning out of the concrete particulars. To compare narrative structure with the structure of an emblem is to compare two constructs, two sets of perhaps irreconcilable abstractions.

In one of the very few attempts to analyse the underlying structure of a baroque novel John Heckman has noted an emblematic compositional principle in *Simplicissimus Teutsch*.[21] It is Heckman's hope that the essential character and structure of the emblem will be helpful in illuminating certain problems at the centre of Grimmelshausen's novel (cf p 876). The basic questions for Heckman are how emblematic elements as 'particular instances and as a structural principle' are to be interpreted, and 'whether a moral/religious interpretation is sufficient' (p 877). The essay has, then, two central concerns: the first is structural – and this is where the emblem plays a part; the other is thematic, and relates to the overall interpretation of the novel's meaning. Although the two problems are interrelated, I shall limit my discussion of Heckman's findings to the former. Thus, I shall not in this study get embroiled in the controversy over just what constitutes the *Simplicissimus* novel – the original five books of the *Simplicissimus Teutsch*, the *Continuatio* and the five books as a single, integrated whole, or the continuous serial novel consisting of all the Simplicianic writings.[22]

It is necessary to begin with Heckman's view of the emblem, since this is the foundation upon which he builds his interpretation of Grimmelshausen's novel. The value of his analysis and the validity of his conclusions will depend upon the reliability of his definition of the emblem. Heckman's conception of the emblem is an uncomfortable mixture of Schöne and Benjamin, and the weaknesses in his theory concerning the structure of *Simplicissimus* derive from his failure to make a critical comparison of the two views, which in certain essential respects are incompatible. It would appear that Heckman has taken over some of Schöne's structural findings, while retaining Benjamin's philosophy of the emblem. As a mode of perception the emblem, according to Benjamin in *Ursprung des deutschen Trauerspiels* is characterized by 'discontinuity' and 'disintegration' (cited in Heckman, p 879); it possesses only the 'false appearance of a totality' (p 879). For Heckman the emblem centres on the relationship between spirit and nature, rather than on either pole (cf p 878). 'It is therefore essential to the emblem that it be discontinuous in form' (p 879). Heckman argues that the formal discontinuity of the emblem derives from the difference between the *pictura* and its written explanation, which frequently have no clear relationship with each other. His reference to the snake, which can connote sin and evil as well as such positive values as friendship, art, and fame, places the discussion in the older context of the quarrel over the 'arbitrariness' of the emblem, although the word 'arbitrary' is nowhere used. Heckman appears to have either ignored, or by implication rejected, the semantic and ontological findings of Schöne in *Emblematik und Drama in Zeitalten der Barock*, which place the emblem in the tradition of *Bild-* and *Dingsymbolik*.[23] Notions of discontinuity are central to Heckman's conception of the emblem: 'The fundamental discontinuity of the emblems means, according to Benjamin, that the *devenir* of the emblem is that of disintegration, and that a group of emblems is necessarily the story of a disintegration, of a fall away from some original, but never graspable unity' (p 879). The reference to unity would suggest that Heckman has in the back of his mind the more modern poetic symbol, an impression reinforced by his remark that 'the emblem never took on the necessity of an "organic totality" which he [Benjamin] sees as characteristic of the symbol, but rather possesses merely "the false appearance of a totality". Thus the interpretation of a given emblem centers around the difference between the pictura and the subscriptio, between the *signifié* and the *significant*, but never exclusively on either pole' (p 879). I would suggest that any attempt to measure the purpose and performance of the emblem by comparing it to the symbol (in its complex and honorific sense) is a-historical and can only lead to an unnecessary disparagement of the emblem.

The fact that a single motif allows of a variety of interpretations leads Heckman to conclude: 'Thus by its nature the emblem does not present a finished form' (p 879); this, he says, is true even though each individual emblem may lay claim to indisputable authority. It seems to me that this is not a valid argument: an emblem must be judged on its own terms, as a complete verbal-visual statement, and not set in a context of all the possible uses and interpretations of the motif. We do not pass judgment on Goethe's poem 'Selige Sehnsucht' by setting it against the history of the motif of the moth and flame, and conclude that the poem is an incomplete, unfinished, or relative statement. This issue is not a minor one, because Heckman applies his theory of the emblem to the novel as a whole: 'The gap between the absolute truth claims of any single emblem and the radical contingency of that claim in the light of emblems taken as a whole is at the base of difficulties in interpreting Grimmelshausen's novel' (p 879).

Heckman regards *Simplicissimus* as a novel with two centres of interest, the one religious, and the other personal, which he describes as a 'voyage to self-realization ... [as] author' (p 881). This duality is regarded as constituting a shift of the centre of the novel which undercuts the validity of the religious theme and provides a key to many of the confusing episodes. Heckman doubts the conclusiveness of the religious interpretation, since Grimmelshausen takes his hero off the island and plunges him into a series of further adventures. He finds that this has the effect of undermining both Simplicissimus's religious intent and the viability of authorship as an alternative (cf p 889). This is, unfortunately, not the place to offer a critique of the interpretation of the novel advanced by Heckman. In resisting the temptation I note only that my reservations stem from the feeling that Heckman is imposing, no matter how subtly and implicitly, an anachronistic psychological pattern on the novel by setting up the theme of 'self-realization,' albeit as an author, as the focal centre of the novel, to which all the other themes are relegated, or at least related.

Heckman's conclusion that the structure of *Simplicissimus* corresponds to that of the popular emblem in that there is a discontinuous relationship between an event and its interpretation is neither very illuminating, nor accurate. It does not concur with the theory of the emblem as established by Schöne, and as a structural description of *Simplicissimus* it is too wide and unfocused to be useful. Heckman goes on to write that the 'main focus [is] on the relation between the two ... rather than on any single conclusion' (p 889). As far as the emblem is concerned, I would suggest that the reader is interested in the *combination* of picture and word, material object and meaning, not merely in their *relationship* as separate and distinct entities. Heckman's final statement reads: 'The emblematic relation between the realistic episodes and the non-realistic episodes which stand in an interpretative relation to them is the background against which the problem of the interpretation of the self emerges ... [this] allows the new center of the novel to be perceived more clearly' (p 890).

Although I find myself in disagreement with Heckman's concept of the emblem and his overall interpretation of *Simplicissimus*, I must acknowledge that he has made a number of stimulating suggestions about smaller emblematic structures in the novel. He terms emblematic the relationship between realistic and non-realistic episodes which interpret each other (cf p 877). Furthermore, several episodes 'reflect on each other' (p 877): for instance, the Witches' Sabbath is a 'reverse parallel' to the Mummelsee. Heckman is right in observing that the emblematic motifs of the frontispiece are also present as 'a structural principle' in the novel (cf p 877). Equally valid are his remarks concerning the function of certain chapter headings, which go beyond the merely descriptive. Chapter 9 of book 1 is entitled 'Simplicius wird aus einer Bestia zu einem Christenmenschen' ('Simplicius develops from a beast into a Christian'), and this title functions as an *inscriptio* to the action of the chapter. One could wish that Heckman had followed up his own lead and investigated some of these examples more closely, because this might have uncovered something like a structural organization showing affinities with the emblem.

The single most important development in Grimmelshausen scholarship in recent years is doubtless the work of Günther Weydt[24] and some of his students[25] who have provided new insights into the structure and meaning of the novel. Weydt's elaborate astrological reading of *Simplicissimus* provides a pattern of coherence that transcends details of plot, character, and 'idea.' In so far as the astrological symphonic plan of the novel is based on correspondence-thinking, the great chain of being, and nature as God's Second Book, the mode of thought underlying the discovered unity and coherence is emblematic.

THE EMBLEMATIC FRONTISPIECE

It was a common practice during the seventeenth century for an author to design, or cause to be designed, an emblematic frontispiece for his book, whether it was a work of prose fiction, a collection of poetry, or a meditational work. As Harsdörffer observed: 'In these days almost no book can be sold without an engraved frontispiece, which presents to the reader its content not only through words but also through a picture' (*FG*, VI, Vorrede, para 10, p 109, of newly paginated facsimile edition).[26] Harsdorffer then proceeds to discuss the use of emblems in these illustrated frontispieces. The intention was to capture the essential purpose of the book in visual form. In some instances the overall meaning of a complex frontispiece is readily understandable to those with a little knowledge of the traditions behind the picture.[27]

Perhaps the most famous, even infamous, of all emblematic frontispieces in German literature is that which introduces Grimmelshausen's *Simplicissimus*. It is still a matter of dispute, and will remain so, as long as the novel itself continues to be a subject of controversy. Since the frontispiece, by general consent, stands in direct relation to the central character, action, and purpose of the novel, critics have necessarily moved from their understanding of the novel as a whole to the illustration. There is general agreement that *Simplicissimus* is in part a *Zeitroman* with decidedly picaresque qualities, but whether, or to what extent, the novel is an *Entwicklungsroman* (a novel of development) is still a debated question.

It would take me beyond the scope of my investigation to review all the interpretations of the *Simplicissimus* frontispiece, since this would involve first establishing a comprehensive reading of the novel. Such an attempt would probably overlap in part with, and possibly merely duplicate, the study of the relationship between Grimmelshausen's Simplicianic novels and their emblematic frontispieces that we may shortly expect from Sibylle Penkert.[28] I intend therefore to take some representative interpretations to illustrate the problem.

The first question concerns the choice of frontispiece to interpret, since in the

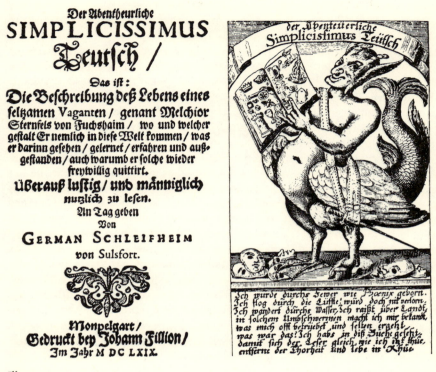

Der Abentheurliche
SIMPLICISSIMUS
Teutsch /
Das ist:
Die Beschreibung deß Lebens eines
seltzamen Vaganten / genant Melchior
Sternfels von Fuchshaim / wo und welcher
gestalt Er nemlich in diese Welt kommen / was
er darinn gesehen / gelernet / erfahren und auß-
gestanden / auch warumb er solche wieder
freywillig quittirt.
Überauß lustig / und männiglich
nutzlich zu lesen.
An Tag geben
Von
GERMAN SCHLEIFHEIM
von Sulsfort.

Monpelgart /
Gedruckt bey Johann Fillion /
Im Jahr M DC LXIX.

Illustration 18
Frontispiece to the first edition of Grimmelshausen's *Simplicissimus Teutsch*

different editions of *Simplicissimus* there are significant variations in the pictorial motif. We should know precisely which frontispiece Grimmelshausen was responsible for if we are to infer his intentions. Although there is no firm evidence upon which to make an absolute decision, Penkert advances plausible reasons for assuming that Grimmelshausen drafted the frontispiece to the first edition.[29] Before considering any specific interpretation it would be as well to attempt to identify the various motifs in it (see illustration 18). The frontispiece has the tripartite structure reminiscent of the emblem: the banderole 'der abendteüerliche Simplicissimus Teütsch' stands in place of an *inscriptio*; the 'symbolic' picture, a conglomerate of organically unrelated motifs, functions as the *pictura*; the printed poem beneath, which is a partial explanation of the picture, assumes the role of the *subscriptio*. However, as soon as we look more closely at the fabulous creature in the centre, the difficulties begin. The creature is composed of elements of man, bird, fish, and animal, but precisely which? Is the bird a phoenix or an eagle? Does the webbed foot belong to a duck or a swan? Are the horns and hoof a goat's or a satyr's? And then, after deciding what the elements are, we are still left with the question of what they represent. What is meant by the sword and by the masks? Are we intended to read the open book carefully enough to identify the objects depicted there? And do they produce some meaningful pattern? Do the fingers point to any particular motif? Is the gesture of the hand significant.

Many critics are agreed that the fabulous creature represents Simplicissimus, who is at home in the four elements that make up the world; he has experienced what the world has to offer, as depicted in the open book, and he has played the many roles that life has offered him, as shown in the abandoned masks. The verse makes it clear that it is a world of *vanitas*; man's goal is, or should be, to turn aside from worldly folly and seek inner peace. But such a description is too general to do justice to the frontispiece or the novel. Critical opinion differs on the question of whether the illustration is to be related to the titular hero, whose ups and downs we follow in the novel, or to the more complex relationship of the narrator to his narration of the hero's path through life. Then again, if one decides that the frontispiece represents Simplicissimus the hero, do we regard the hero as an individual developing into some sort of consistent personality (*Entwicklungsroman*), or do we view Simplicissimus as a thematic device incorporating a number of different roles, which represent divergent, indeed incompatible, ways of life? Is Simplicissimus a character or a series of *figurae*?

Hellmut Rosenfeld regards the fabulous beast as a hieroglyphic representation of man, the wanderer through the four elements. Only the sword makes this general image into the special symbol of the poet. The horns and hoof indicate the satyr, an ancient embodiment of wisdom and insight. The masks denote the different stages in Simplicissimus's development to wisdom; they are, in Rosenfeld's words 'various developmental stages of Simplicissimus's struggle for self-knowledge, the masks of foolishness which he had to abandon before the true face of the wise man, who had turned away from the world and attained peace could emerge' (*Das deutsche Bildgedicht*, p 65).[30] This view, also adopted by Jan Hendrik Scholte,[31] is based on the theory that Grimmelshausen's novel is a novel of development. But even with a careful redefinition of the terms 'self,' 'self-realization,' and 'self-knowledge,' so as to remove the more glaring anachronisms inherent in such a psychological reading, the underlying assumption seems dubious to me.

Scholte extends this interpretation by insisting that the wings of the bird are those of a phoenix, which he relates to Simplicissimus's description of his condition at Hanau, where he was born, 'like a phoenix from ignorance to understanding' ('gleich dem Phönix vom Unverstand zum Verstand,' book 2, chap 8).[32] Both the open book and the poem refer to the hero's experiences in the world.

In a penetrating article entitled 'Die Personalität des Simplicissimus'[33] Gerhart Mayer joins the ranks of those who reject the idea that *Simplicissimus* is a baroque form of the novel of development. His reading of the novel leads him to see in the frontispiece 'the narrator's spiritual portrait' (p 516).[34] Mayer adduces some evidence for this view from the banderole, which names the title of the novel, rather than the hero directly: 'the banderole ... indicates that it is not the story-teller as an isolated person that is meant, but the work – the narrative attitude, complex and fraught with tensions, realized in the work' (p 516).[35] Stressing the religious and moral intentions of the novel, Mayer interprets the wings as those of faith. The wings of the phoenix were a religious emblem of simplicity of faith, while the eagle's wings could also connote trust in God. The ears of the ass represent the sly fool ('schalkhafter Narr') with his 'pleasure in the ironic game of mutually relativizing roles' (p 516).[36] Like earlier critics, Mayer also regards the creature as being at home in the four elements, indicating a certain 'Weltverbundenheit' (p 516). The webbed foot, which Scholte thought to be a duck's with possible devilish connotations, is, in Mayer's view, a swan's foot; the swan is the common emblem of the poem. The horned head and hoof indicate also for Mayer the satyr, the concerned admonisher ('der besorgte Warner'), with its 'incorruptible x-ray vision of the inner truth of man' (pp 516–17).[37] The creature treads on masks 'because he has seen through the deceptive illusion of the worldly way of life' (p 517).[38] The sword represents the punishment which is meted out to the guilty. With this overall religious interpretation Mayer sees the words 'not lost' ('nit verlorn') of the poem beneath as meaning 'not damned.'

Most recent studies of *Simplicissimus*[39] have continued in the direction taken by Mayer, and the frontispiece is seen as referring to the attitude of the novelist to his story, rather than representing the hero himself. Penkert stresses the relation between *res* and *figura* in the picture, suggesting that the motifs of child and tree are 'decisively involved' in the pattern of relationships ('Grimmelshausens Titelkupfer-Fiktionen,' p 66).[40] The tree assumes a position of central importance in book 6, where on a desert island Simplicissimus finds his way to God, self-knowledge (in the spiritual rather than psychological sense), and constancy in the religious life. Writing his life-story on palm leaves, Simplicissimus reports that 'everything, indeed each tree [was] an impulse to religious experience' ('ein jedes Ding / ja ein jeder Baum [sic] ein Antriebe zur Gottseligkeit') ;[41] palm wine, for example, calls to mind Christ's blood. Penkert also sketches in the traditional relevance of the tree as 'tree of sin,' 'tree of life and peace,' and the eschatological tree (cf p 68).

Leaving aside their differences, both Penkert and Gersch recognize in the satyr's gesture a sign connoting both the derision of satire and the prophecy of Christian tradition. This motif thus indicates a moral and spiritual dimension in both frontispiece and novel. Gersch has studied this aspect of the frontispiece closely.[42] He is doubtless correct in noting that the body of the satyr has until now not been 'icologically identified' (p 77), if one regards the figure as something more than a mere figural representation of the titular hero. Gersch sees in the figure a poetological motif going back to Plato and Aristotle, who compared the integrated work of literature with the harmoniously co-ordinated body. The opposite image of the monster caricatured the literary work which lacked classical harmony. It can be shown that Grimmelshausen was aware of this tradition (cf Gersch, pp 77–8). Gersch comments: 'Thereby the *Simplicissimus*-novel is presented as a *mixtum compositum* of different materials, forms, genre elements, and organizational principles, as criticized by classical tradition. Yet with the original addition of the satyr's head Grimmelshausen places his monster and therefore *Simplicissimus* under the law and freedom of satire' (p 78).[43] Both the open book and the gesture of the finger may be associated with prophecy, indicating an 'allegorical-mystical' (p 79) dimension in the novel.

The purpose of this brief excursus into the literature on Grimmelshausen's frontispiece has been to demonstrate that the frontispiece is emblematic in composition and function. Although critics may disagree on the interpretation of detail – and indeed on the overall conception – there is little doubt that the complex relationship of frontispiece to novel is emblematic.

6

Conclusion

In light of the fact that over six hundred writers produced over two thousand emblem-books during the sixteenth and seventeenth centuries, it is evident that the emblem is more than a 'fad'[1] or a 'strange fashion'[2] or a 'secondary cultural phenomenon.'[3] The emblem in art and literature does, however, present certain aesthetic problems for the post-Shaftesbury and post-Herder reader, which can only be resolved by a historical and flexible aesthetic. T.S. Eliot observed that we need to enjoy for the right reasons. Reversing that coin, it seems to me equally important not to criticize for the wrong reasons. One is occasionally still disturbed by the terms plagiarism,[4] baroque license,[5] and arbitrariness,[6] which stem from inappropriate assumptions. In some critics these may be but lapses, but they illustrate, none the less, the tenacity with which modern notions of originality hang on, even though the less personal quality of much renaissance and baroque art has been firmly established. Muriel Bradbrook puts her finger on the problem when she observes that today we 'accept the pansy on its own merits,' but for the people of the baroque age to do so was 'almost unthinkable.'[7] Jewels, costumes, colours, flowers, in short all things, were charged with significant meaning.

Half-submerged value judgments and prejudices about form come to the surface every time a reader complains about the arbitrariness of a poet; and to find that didacticism or formal virtuosity has smothered the personal and confessional quality of a poem,[8] presupposes that subjectivity and confession are the intention. In most Elizabethan and in German baroque poetry the writer seeks to make valid statements about the themes of his poetry. Following Horace's precept of *labor limae*, he files and polishes his poem until it is a valid, i.e., generalized, poetic statement, from which he has removed the imperfections and irrelevances of the too-personal. His poem is beautiful and persuasive according to his canons of aesthetics and rhetoric. As we know, the function of the emblem is both aesthetic and didactic, and these qualities often merge so inextricably that it is impossible to separate them.

The emblem-books provide an important cross-reference for the meaning of motifs in poetry. The compilers of emblem-books were frequently poets themselves, and when that was not the case, they shared the same kind of education and world-picture. The emblem-books indicate what educated readers knew about nature, history, and mythology, and furthermore how they interpreted this knowledge. This does not mean that the emblem-book is necessarily the original or sole source for information, say about the eagle, which derives primarily from bestiaries, *Physiologus*, and biblical and classical literature. The emblem-books are, however, a reservoir of such information and its interpretation, and, as they were to be found in every public and private library, they were accessible to all who could read. The illiterate were also made aware of emblems by the preacher in his sermons; they saw and heard emblems on the stage and in pageants and processions; they were surrounded by emblematic motifs in the visual arts: in church windows, coats-of-arms, paintings, and decorations. By comparing literature with emblem-books we may determine which words and objects were capable of visualization, and establish the basic meanings associated with those objects, all of which can increase our understanding of sixteenth- and seventeenth-century literature.

The discovery of emblematic sources and parallels may illuminate individual passages of literature, or indeed, whole poems, but the importance of such discoveries should not be overemphasized. Of George Herbert's poetry Rosemary Freeman observes that occasional connections with specific emblem-books can be found, 'and while they do establish incontrovertibly Herbert's closeness to the form, scattered parallels are never a very fruitful method of comment' (*English Emblem Books*, p 167). She stresses that the emblematic mode has a wider application in Herbert's poetry. 'What is displayed in every poem is the habitual formulation of ideas in images, each brief and completed yet fully investigated.'[9] The emblematic way of thinking and the emblematic method of composition are undoubtedly more important and more pervasive than the instances of exact parallels with emblem-books.

It is not only as a mode of thought, but also as an art form, that the emblem offers such a valuable perspective on the purely verbal art of literature, in all its genres and forms. As a formal, shaping principle emblematic structures are discovered in poetry in many ways. An actual emblem, or an emblematic image, may be the foundation of a whole poem; the emblematic motif may be visibly or tangibly present or submerged beneath the surface of the words. An emblematic theme or a sequence of separate but related emblems can also function as a controlling or unifying element in both the short poem and the longer epic. Many short poems, of roughly the length of a sonnet, reveal a totally emblematic structure in the organization of abstract, interpretative statements and pictorial representation. From here it is but a short step to the emblematic pattern poem, where the visual outline of the poem reproduces the silhouette of the subject of the poem – shape replaces *pictura*. In narrative prose and drama we shall discover emblematic images, arguments, characters, and episodes. The stage is perhaps the ultimate emblematic form with its stage properties, static scenes ('silent scenes' and dumb-shows), use of gesture, and character grouping, in addition to the spoken word and individual character.

My chief interest in this book has been structural, though not a-historically so. I have directed attention to the historical emergence of the emblem, and stressed the need for a historical approach to the meaning and form of emblematic structures. However, I have not attempted to write a history of the emergence and development of any single emblematic literary genre. Given a more complete and sophisticated theory of the emblem and an account of the structural possibilities of the emblematic stage, it would be possible to undertake a history of emblematic drama. I believe a similar historical account of emblematic poetry would be feasible and rewarding. The word-emblem is a functional, not merely decorative, piece of imagery, and it has been employed in all poetic forms, from the epigram through the song to the sonnet and ode; emblematic structures are encountered in love poetry, didactic, occasional, religious, and political poetry. It would be fascinating to ascertain which verse forms (e.g., the sonnet) and which kinds of poem (e.g., the love song) were best served by the emblem. However, such large-scale historical investigations need as a foundation an adequate theory of the emblem (which, I believe, we now have); an account of the structural possibilities within the genre of poetry (a modest beginning is offered here); and also detailed analyses of the use of emblematic structures by individual poets. There is no reason to suppose that all poets employed emblematic structures to the same extent and in the same manner. For instance, it is my impression that Paul Fleming uses emblematic imagery more in his love sonnets than in his odes, and that in general Fleming utilizes the emblem more than did Georg Weckherlin, although in their love poetry both poets draw heavily on the same international storehouse of Petrarchistic conceits and attitudes. Greiffenberg made extensive use of emblematic images, arguments, and structures in her religious lyrics and meditations. It would also appear that the use of emblematic structures underwent a historical development. Writing during the first half of the seventeenth century, Martin Opitz shows greater reserve in his use of emblematic devices: his images are less compressed, simpler, and not 'piled up' ('gehäuft'), as they are in the work of some of the later Nürnberg and Silesian poets.

Finally, leaving literature in the sense of 'belles lettres' aside, there is a vast field of utilitarian writing ('Gebrauchsliteratur') – religious, didactic, social, and political – which draws upon the same emblematic modes, for example, the sermon[10] and the meditation. It is unfortunate that recent books on John Donne[11] and Andreas Gryphius[12] have not considered this question.

Notes

NOTES TO PREFACE

1 Robert J. Clements, *Picta Poesis. Literary and Humanistic Theory in Renaissance Emblem Books* (Rome, 1960).
2 Recent work published by Wolfgang Harms has demonstrated the extent to which emblematic attitudes and relics of emblematic 'knowledge' may be discovered in didactic and also in scientific writings from the seventeenth to the nineteenth centuries. See Wolfgang Harms, 'Wörter, Sachen und emblematische "res" im "Orbis sensualium pictus" des Comenius,' in *Gedenkschrift für W. Foerste* (Cologne/Vienna, 1970), pp 531–42; 'Diskrepanzen zwischen Titel und Inhalt der "Explicatio oder Außlegung über die Wohrten Salomonis ..." (1663) des Chemikers Johann Rudolf Glauber,' in *Rezeption und Produktion in Renaissance und Barock. Festschrift für G. Weydt* (Bern/Munich, 1972), pp 155–67; 'Der Eisvogel und die halkyonischen Tage. Zum Verhältnis von naturkundlicher Beschreibung und allegorischer Naturdeutung,' *Verbum et Signum. Festschrift für Friedrich Ohly* (Munich, 1975), I, 477–515.
3 Cf Peter M. Daly, 'Goethe and the Emblem Tradition,' *JEGP*, 74 (1975), 388–412.

NOTES TO CHAPTER 1

1 Henri Stegemeier, 'Problems in Emblem Literature,' *JEGP*, 45 (1946), 27.
2 The most thoroughly researched investigation of the origin of the term 'emblem,' and its use in the earliest editions of Alciatus's *Emblematum liber*, is to be found in Hessel Miedema, 'The term *Emblema* in Alciati,' *JWCI*, 31 (1968), 234–50.
3 '... eine Abart der Allegorie': Else Eichler, 'Christian Scrivers "Zufällige An-

dachten,'' ein Beitrag zur Geistes- und Formgeschichte des 17. Jhs. (Diss. Halle, 1926), p 11.

4 Charles Hayes, 'Symbol and Allegory: A Problem in Literary Theory,' *GR*, 44 (1969), 283. For Odette de Mourgues the emblem is 'objectionable' as a substitute for another art *Metaphysical, Baroque, and Precieux Poetry* (Oxford, 1953), p 79.

5 Marc F. Bertonasco, *Crashaw and the Baroque* (University, Alabama, 1971), p 22.

6 Peter M. Daly, 'The Poetic Emblem,' *Neoph*, 54 (1970), 381–97.

7 Heinrich Lausberg, *Handbuch der literarischen Rhetorik* (Munich, 1960).

8 Philip Wheelwright, *The Burning Fountain* (Bloomington, Indiana, 1954), pp 93–123. An instance of yet a different set of values and expectations is contained in Martin Foss's *Symbol and Metaphor in Human Experience* (Princeton, 1949). For Foss a symbol is any sign whose meaning is limited, even to the point of falsification, whereas metaphor denotes broad and true meaning approaching the ideal.

9 Mario Praz, *Studies in Seventeenth-Century Imagery*, 2nd ed considerably increased (Rome, 1964).

10 Cf William S. Heckscher and Karl-August Wirth, 'Emblem, Emblembuch,' in *Reallexikon zur Deutschen Kunstgeschichte* (Stuttgart, 1959), vol v, cols 85–228; Dieter Sulzer, 'Zu einer Geschichte der Emblemtheorien,' *Euph*, 44 (1970), 48; Holger Homann, 'Prologomena zu einer Geschichte der Emblematik,' *CG*, 3 (1968), 253ff.

11 The connection between illustrated broadsheets and emblem-books invites closer investigation. In his book *The German Illustrated Broadsheet in the Seventeenth Century*, 2 vols (Baden-Baden, 1966) William A. Coupe has assembled and described a large number of German broadsheets; he makes occasional reference to emblematic parallels and in one instance observes that 'broadsheet publishers evidently regarded the *Emblemata* [of de Bry] as a sort of quarry from which they could extract suitable material' (p 179). Many of the broadsheets Coupe reproduces bear a striking resemblance to the *picturae* of emblem-books. The fact that such poets-cum-emblematists as Johann Klaj and Daniel Sudermann also produced broadsheets lends credence to the suspicion that some broadsheets actually utilize plates of earlier emblem-books.

12 Cf Barbara Tiemann, 'Sebastian Brant und das frühe Emblem in Frankreich,' *DVJs*, 47 (1973), 598–644; Barbara Tiemann, *Fabel und Emblem. Gilles Corrozet und die französische Renaissance-Fabel* (Munich, 1974); and Monika Hueck, *Textstruktur und Gattungssystem. Studien zum Verhältnis von Emblem und Fabel im 16. und 17. Jahrhundert* (Kronberg/Ts., 1975).

13 '... offenbart die Unsicherheit, die über die Herkunft und den Sinn der Emblematik zu dieser Zeit noch bestand und die der Grund dafür war, daß sich diese Gattung in unterschiedlichsten Varianten ausbreiten konnte.' This is the view of the editors

Peter von Düffel and Klaus Schmidt of Holtzwart's *Emblematum Tyrocinia* (Stuttgart, 1968), p 214.

14 E.N.S. Thompson, *Literary Bypaths of the Renaissance* (New Haven, 1924).

15 Rosemary Freeman, *English Emblem Books* (London, 1948; repr 1967).

16 Cf n 10.

17 Albrecht Schöne, *Emblematik und Drama im Zeitalter des Barock*, 2nd rev. ed (Munich, 1968).

18 Dietrich Jöns, *Das 'Sinnen-Bild'. Studien zur allegorischen Bildlichkeit bei Andreas Gryphius* (Stuttgart, 1966).

19 Cf n 10.

20 Cf n 2.

21 Cf n 10.

22 Wolfgang Harms, '*Mundus imago Dei est.* Zum Entstehungsprozeß zweier Emblembücher Jean Jacques Boissards,' *DVJs*, 47 (1973), 223–44; Wolfgang Harms, 'Der Fragmentcharaketer emblematischer Auslegungen und die Rolle des Lesers. Gabriel Rollenhagens Epigramme,' *Deutsche Barocklyrik. Gedichtinterpretationen von Spee bis Haller*, ed Martin Bircher and Alois M. Haas (Bern/Munich, 1973), pp 49–64.

23 Sibylle Penkert, 'Zur Emblemforschung,' *GgA*, 224. Jahrgang (1972), Heft 1/2, 100–20.

24 Ludwig Volkmann, *Bilderschriften der Renaissance, Hieroglyphik und Emblematik in ihren Beziehungen und Fortwirkungen* (Leipzig, 1923).

25 Karl Giehlow, *Die Hieroglyphenkunde des Humanismus in der Allegorie der Renaissance, besonders der Ehrenpforte Kaisers Maximilian I*, Jahrbuch der Kunsthistorischen Sammlungen des allerhöchsten Kaiserhauses, XXXII, Heft I, (Vienna/Leipzig, 1915).

26 Gustav René Hocke, *Die Welt als Labyrinth. Manier und Manie in der europäischen Kunst*, rde, L/LI (Hamburg, 1957); and *Manierismus in der Literatur. Sprach-Alchemie und esoterische Kombinationskunst*, rde, LXXXII/LXXXIII (Hamburg, 1959). William S. Heckscher and Cameron F. Bunker in their review of Arthur Henkel and Albrecht Schöne, *Emblemata, Handbuch zur Sinnbildkunst des XVI. und XVII. Jahrhunderts* (Stuttgart, 1967) [subsequently referred to as *Emblemata*] express uncompromisingly their rejection of Hocke in a footnote: 'Hocke (for reasons unknown the darling of German scholars) should be omitted from scholarly publications once and for all': *RQ*, 23 (1970), 60. For a critical discussion of Hocke's views on mannerism, see Reinhold Grimm, 'Bild und Bildlichkeit im Barock. Zu einigen neueren Arbeiten,' *GRM*, 19 (1969), 396ff.

27 Cf 'Man hat es beim Emblem demnach mit einer Vereinigung vom Wort des Lemma mit dem Bild der Icon zu einem Rätsel zu tun, dessen Auflösung durch das Epigram ermöglicht wird' ('In the emblem one is dealing with the combination of

the word of the lemma with the picture of the icon which produces an enigma, the resolution of which is made possible by the epigram'), col 95.

28 Erwin Panofsky, *Studies in Iconology. Humanistic Themes in the Art of the Renaissance* (New York, 1962).

29 Cf Panofsky, p 123, n 73. Elsewhere Panofsky quotes Claudius Minos's characterization of the emblem, which is printed in the preface to Alciatus's *Emblemata* (Lyons, 1571). The description, accurate though it may be with respect to certain characteristics of some emblems, is inadequate as a definition of the genre: the emblem 'partakes of the nature of the symbol (only that it is particular rather than universal), the puzzle (only that it is not quite so difficult), the apophthegm (only that it is visual rather than verbal), and the proverb (only that it is erudite rather than commonplace). 'Cited in *Meaning in the Visual Arts* (Harmondsworth, 1970; first published 1955), p 183.

30 Anne Gerard Christiaan de Vries, *De Nederlandsche Emblemata. Geschiedenis en Bibliographie tot de 18ᵉ eeuw* (Amsterdam, 1899).

31 Schöne's terminology, although generally adopted by German scholars, is judged by Heckscher and Bunker in their review of *Emblemata* to be a 'half-hearted attempt ... to introduce new *ad hoc* terminology by speaking of *pictura* (instead of *Bild* or *icon*), of *inscriptio* (instead of motto or lemma) and of *subscriptio* (instead of epigram)': p 61, n 5. On the other hand, Sulzer finds Heckscher's and Wirth's terminology *Lemma, Ikon, Epigramm* 'ist nur für die frühe Emblematik geeignet, die eine Dreiteilung in dieser Form vornimmt, die spätere verfährt oft anders, deshalb ist die lateinische Terminologie vorzuziehen' ('is only suited to early emblem-books, which undertake a tripartite structure in this form; later emblem-books often proceed differently, consequently the Latin terminology is preferable'), p 23, For Heckscher's and Wirth's use of terms, see cols 88–95. Those interested in the interminable wrangle over terminology should also consult Miedema.

32 Homann informs us in a footnote to his article 'Prologomena zu einer Geschichte der Emblematik' that 'Eine kritische Gegenüberstellung der verschiedenen Definitionsversuche soll an anderer Stelle in größerem Zusammenhang erfolgen' ('A critical juxtaposition of the various attempts at a definition will follow elsewhere in a larger context'), p 244.

33 The reference is to Hessel Miedema, author of the article 'The term *Emblema* in Alciati.'

34 Heckscher and Bunker, review of *Emblemata*, p 65.

35 I am working towards a critical theory of the emblem genre, which is based on a critical comparison of modern theories, especially those of Schöne and Jöns.

36 Cf Homann, *Studien zur Emblematik des 16. Jahrhunderts* (Utrecht, 1971), p 51.

37 Cf Sulzer, p 24, and n 3.

38 In discussing the primacy of the verbal or pictorial component we should perhaps

distinguish between the reader's perception of the emblem as a whole and the author's process of composition. Freeman's balanced view is that: 'From the very beginning it had been uncertain whether the form derived from Egyptian hieroglyphics or from the Greek anthology, whether, that is, its pictorial or its rhetorical side was of prime importance' (pp 85–6). A somewhat similar view if to be found in Austin Warren, *Richard Crashaw. A Study in Baroque Sensibility* (Baton Rouge, 1939), pp 73–4. Schöne is convinced of the primacy of the picture (pp 26, 28), an opinion shared by virtually all Germanist critics writing since 1963. Cf Daly, 'The Semantics of the Emblem – Recent Developments in Emblem Theory,' *WascR*, 9 (1974), 199–212.
On the other hand, Miedema has shown that Alciatus himself was not responsible for the illustrations in the first edition – they were added by the publisher; furthermore the editions of 1547 and 1548, which he produced, are also without illustrations. Consequently, Miedema argues for the primacy of the words (cf p 237), as do Heckscher and Wirth (col 95). English critics, unaware of Schöne's work, follow in the tradition of Praz and to some extent Freeman in this matter, either regarding the words as of primary importance, or remaining undecided.
We are obviously on shaky ground here. In speaking of the primacy of the picture, Schöne's perspective is phenomenological and typological, whereas Miedema and Heckscher and Wirth would appear to be looking at the emblem more pragmatically, attempting to infer something from the absence of illustrations on the one hand, and from actual methods of composition on the other. Robert J. Clements notes that some emblematists (e.g., Peacham and Van Veen) did design their own *picturae*, while there are also examples of artists being given the *subscriptio* to illustrate (Clements, *Picta Poesis*, p 24). We are on the thin ice of intentional and compositional fallacies. The absence of an illustration is no evidence that the words (i.e., abstract thought) were primary, since the visual object or scene conveyed by a word and bearing abstract significance may have been uppermost in the poet's mind. And the reverse may also be true.

39 Cf Stegemeier, p 33; *Emblemata* with its invaluable list of pictures (*Bild-Register*) and meanings according to key words (*Bedeutungs-Register*).
40 Cf Praz, pp 22, 25–34; Schöne, pp 24–6; Jöns, pp 14–16.
41 'Die Verwendung für emblematische Zwecke war gleichwohl ein Unding, da die Deutungen an die Bildwerke herangetragen wurden, Emblematik aber die Deutung unmittelbar aus dem Bild herauslesen will': Helmut Rosenfeld, *Das deutsche Bildgedicht*, Palaestra, CIC (Leipzig, 1935), p 54.
42 Cf Henry Green, *A. Alciati and His Books of Emblems. A Biographical and Bibliographical Study* (London, 1872), reprinted in Burt Franklin Bibliography and Reference Series 131 (New York, n.d.), pp 7–9, 38–9.
43 Virginia Woods Callahan, 'The Erasmus-Alciati Friendship,' *Acta Conventus*

Neo-Latini Lovaniensis, Proceedings of the First International Congress of Neo-Latin Studies, Louvain, 23–8 August 1971 (Leuven University Press/Munich: Wilhelm Fink Verlag, 1973), pp 133–41.

44 Cf Callahan, p 133.

45 Cf Giehlow; Volkmann; Praz, pp 23ff, 59, 79–80; Schöne, pp 34–42; Heckscher and Wirth, cols 122–3, 137–44; Jöns, pp 1–14; Erik Iversen, *The Myth of Egypt and Its Hieroglyphics in European Tradition* (Copenhagen, 1961); Sulzer, pp 42, 27–30, 37; Liselotte Dieckmann, *Hieroglyphics. The History of a Literary Symbol* (St Louis, Missouri, 1970), pp 26–30; Rudolf Wittkower, 'Hieroglyphics in the Early Renaissance,' *Developments in the Early Renaissance*, ed Bernard S. Levy (Albany, 1972), pp 58–97.

46 '... eine aus hellenistischer Zeit stammende Geheimschrift ... die keineswegs zum Verständnis der eigentlichen ägyptischen Hieroglyphenschriften führen konnte.'

47 Cited in Wittkower, pp 69–70.

48 Cf Dieckmann, pp 33–4.

49 Cf Wittkower, pp 71 ff.

50 Cf p 25.

51 Although the *Poliphili* was influential, there is little reason to assume that 'the emblem-books are the indirect and certainly unintended result of the *Hypnerotomachia*,' as Dieckmann suggests (p 46).

52 Cf pp 16–17 above.

53 Cited in Wittkower, pp 84–5.

54 The relationship should, however, not be overrated. As early as 1934 Praz described Volkmann's point of view as 'one-sided'; cf 'The English Emblem Literature,' *ES*, 16 (1934), a judgment echoed by Eric Jacobsen, *Die Metamorphose der Liebe in Friedrich Spees 'Trutznachtigall'* (Copenhagen, 1954). See also Sulzer, p 37.

55 Cf Praz, *Studies in Seventeenth-Century Imagery*, chap 2; Schöne, pp 42–5; Heckscher and Wirth, cols 98 ff; Jöns, pp 18–22; Sulzer, pp 24–7.

56 For example, the employment of the human form in the *impresa* was a matter of continual disagreement. Estienne, Ruscelli, and Palazzi held that it could be used, whereas Bargagli and Giovio insisted that the human form had no place in the *impresa*.

57 Cf Praz, *Studies in Seventeenth-Century Imagery*, p 63; Giovio's rules are quoted in Italian and in German translation by Schöne, p 44.

58 '[Harsdörffers] ... Formulierung ... legt es nahe, res significans und significatio in jener festen Beziehung zu einander zu denken, die zwischen Leib und Seele herrscht ...'

59 '... ganz formaler Natur ... Von einer objektiv gültigen Beziehung zwischen Bild und Motto im Sinne einer analogia entis zwischen Ding und Bedeutung ist bei diesem Vergleich keine Rede.'

60 'Eine feste Beziehung zwischen res significans und significatio besagt diese Terminologie nicht.'

61 Jean Hagstrum, *The Sister Arts. The Tradition of Literary Pictorialism and English Poetry from Dryden to Gray* (Chicago, 1958), p 95.

62 This was the standard etymology. Cf Estienne, *The Arte of Making Devises* ... trans Theodore Blount (London, 1646); and *The Worthy tract of Paulus Iouius, contayning a discourse of rare inuentions, both Militarie and Amorous called Imprese* ..., trans Samuel Daniel (London, 1585), p 8.

63 Cf Heinrich Wölfflin, *Renaissance and Baroque*, trans Kathrin Simon (Fontana/Collins, 1964) and *Kunstgeschichtliche Grundbegriffe* (1915).

64 Or as Daniel's friend N.W. expresses it: 'In Emblems is more libertie and fewer lawes': *The Worthy tract of Paulus Iouius*, p 8.

65 Wittkower, pp 58–97.

66 Cf p 17.

67 Cf Wittkower, pp 74 ff. The author discusses other medals on pp 76–83.

68 Cf Anneliese Stemper, *Die Medaillen des Herzogs Heinrich Julius von Braunschweig-Wolfenbüttel und ihre Beziehungen zu den Emblemata des Joachim Camerarius*, Arbeitsbericht aus dem Städtischen Museum Braunschweig, no. 8 (Brunswick, 1955).

69 'EIN PROPFREIS THVT GAR BALD BEKOMN WAN ES HAT REGEN WIND VND SONN ALSO WEM GOTT VNDS GLÜCK WOL PÜGT WIRD GROSS VND WECHST DAS IM GENÜGT. H.R.'

70 Cf Heckscher and Wirth, cols 133 ff; C. Wilfred Scott-Giles, *Shakespeare's Heraldry* (London, 1950); William L. Goldsworthy, *Shakespeare's Heraldic Emblems: Their Origin and Meaning* (London, 1928); Muriel Bradbrook, *Shakespeare and Elizabethan Poetry* (Harmondsworth, 1964), pp 105 ff; Saxon Walker, 'Mime and Heraldry in *Henry IV, Part I*,' *E*, 11 (1956), 91–6; H.L. Savage, 'Heraldry in Shakespeare,' *SQ*, 1 (1950), 286–91.

71 Cf col 133 ff.

72 N.J.R. Crompton, 'Sidney and Symbolic Heraldry,' *CA*, 8 (1965), 244.

73 Cf Grete Lesky, *Schloß Eggenberg. Das Programm für den Bildschmuck* (Graz/Vienna/Cologne, 1970).

74 'Die Emblematik erfüllt in solchem Fall ähnliche Funktionen wie in einem Anspruchswappen das heraldische Zeichen für einen gewünschten Besitz': Wolfgang Harms and Hartmut Freytag, *Außerliterarische Wirkungen barocker Emblembücher. Emblematik in Ludwigsburg, Gaarz und Pommersfelden* (Munich, 1975), p 138.

75 Harms and Freytag, *Außerliterarische Wirkungen barocker Emblembücher*, pp 135–54.

76 '... eine Annäherung an die eher heraldische Identifizierung von "Ding" und gemeinter Person, zugleich aber eine Aufrechterhaltung der nicht-heraldischen allegorischen Bedeutungsdimension des emblematischen "Dinges"' (p 139).

77 'Die Grenzen zwischen Emblematik, Devisenkunst und Heraldik und damit auch zwischen objektiver und subjektiver bildgebundener Aussage sind bei dieser Selbstdarstellung des Auftraggebers durchlässig.'

78 Harsdörffer, *Frauenzimmer Gesprächspiele*, ed Irmgard Bottcher (Tübingen, 1968–9), subsequently referred to as *FG*.

79 Cf Peacham, emblems 11, 90, 101, 102.

80 Blue generally connotes high and heavenly matters in the European literature of the period. Cf the blue gown of many a madonna in her role as queen of heaven; Greiffenberg speaks of blue as indicating God's majesty ('Hoheit') in *Sonnette, Lieder und Gedichte* (Nürnberg, 1662), p 238. Similarly Rabelais admits that 'blue doth certainly signify heaven and heavenly things, by the very same tokens and symbols, that white signifieth joy and pleasure' (*Gargantua*, bk 1, chap 8), although in the previous chapter he had made fun of the idea that the combination of blue and white signified 'heavenly joy.'

81 Blue also connotes generally lofty thought. Cf Martin Opitz: 'And skyblue / very lofty thoughts' ('Vnd Himmelblo / sehr hohe sinnen') in the poem 'Bedeutung der Farben'; also Paul Fleming:

> Blue ... those, full of devotion,
> who constantly long for heaven that God shall hear them.

> Blau ... die, der Andacht voll,
> gen Himmel stetigs sehn, daß sie Gott hören soll.

in the poem 'Aus dem Alziat über die Farben,' which, as the title suggests, is based on Alciatus's emblem LXI (edition published in Frankfurt am Main, 1556). Fleming's poem is in fact a free translation of Alciatus's *subscriptio*.

82 '... kein innerer Zusammenhang zwischen Wappenbild und Wappenspruch bestand ... Zu einer solchen kam es erst, nachdem eine gewisse Auflockerung der heraldischen Form ... die Verarbeitung von Anregungen der Devisenkunst ... erlaubte.'

83 Cf 'Welche Rückwirkungen die Aufnahme heraldischer Elemente auf den Objektivitätsanspruch der Emblematik hat, wäre noch zu untersuchen aufgrund breiteren Materials, wozu etwa auch die Embleme Zincgrefs und emblematisch strukturierte Einblattdrucke aus dem Dreißigjährigen Krieg heranzuziehen wären' (Harms and Freytag, *Außerliterarische Wirkungen barocker Emblembücher*, p 144, n 30).

84 Cf Praz, *Studies in Seventeenth-Century Imagery*, pp 12–13, 24; Gerhard Fricke, *Die Bildlichkeit in der Dichtung des A. Gryphius* (Berlin, 1933), pp. 29–30; Heckscher and Wirth, cols 125–8; David Greene, 'Medieval Backgrounds of the Elizabethan Emblem Books (Diss. Berkely, 1958); Schöne, pp 43–8; Jöns, pp 29–45.

85 '... das Seiende als ein zugleich Bedeutendes.'

86 Cf Friedrich Ohly, 'Vom geistigen Sinn des Wortes im Mittelalter,' *ZfdAdL*, 89

(1958–9), 1–21. On the role of neo-platonism in renaissance exegesis see E.H. Gombrich, 'Icones Symbolicae. The Visual Image in Neo-Platonic Thought,' *JWCI*, 11 (1948), 163–88.

87 '... einem wahrhaft weltumspannenden Bezugs- und Bedeutungsgewebe.'

88 'Nun sind im Barock Moral und Seelenheil immer noch mit einander verknüpft ...'

89 '... die Zeugnisse ma.-*typologischen* Denkens ... [haben] das Schaffen der Emblematiker wesentlich befruchtet.'

90 The passage reads 'von einer direkten Auswertung ['ma.-*typologischen* Denkens'] kann allerdings nicht gesprochen werden, denn jede Auswertung typologischer Vorstellungen setzte eine entscheidende Umdeutung voraus: das argumentum per analogiam der Typologie hatte im wissenschaftlichen Denken zu Beginn der Neuzeit keinen rechten Platz mehr und seine Beweiskraft weithin verloren' ('there can be no suggestion of a direct evaluation of medieval-typological thinking, for any evaluation of typological conceptions presupposes a decisive re-interpretation: in the scientific thinking of the modern period argumentation by analogy with typology no longer had a proper place and it had largely lost its power of proof'), col 127.

91 Cf preface, n 1.

92 Cf Wolfgang Harms, 'Diskrepanz zwischen Titel und Inhalt der *Explicatio oder Auslegung über die Wohrten Salomonis* ... (1663) des Chemikers Johann Rudolf Glauber,' *Rezeption und Produktion zwischen 1570 und 1730*, ed W. Rasch, et al (Bern/Munich, 1972), pp 169–82.

93 Cf Erasmus Franciscus, *Das Unfehlbare Weh der Ewigkeit* ... (Nürnberg, 1682), unpaged foreword, p 4: 'Krokodil-Zähne des ewigen Todes,' 'Seelen-fieber,' and 'Weihrauch des Gebets.'

94 Cf Schöne, pp 47–8; Jöns, pp 29–40.

95 Cf also Karl Josef Höltgen, 'Arbor, Scala und Fons vitae. Vorformen devotionaler Embleme in einer mittelenglischen Handschrift,' *Chaucer und seine Zeit*, Symbosium für Walter F. Schirmer, Buchreihe der *Anglia*, vol 14 (Tübingen, 1968).

96 Cf Schöne, pp 29–30.

97 '... wird das Emblem in seiner strengen Form aufgehoben und eine allegorische Spielart ausgebildet.'

98 Published in *DVJs*, 37 (1963), 197–321.

99 For instance, Jane Aptekar's book *Icons of Justice, Iconography and Thematic Imagery in Book V of 'The Faerie Queene'* (New York, 1969) contains a brief bibliographical footnote in which she refers to Praz and the German article by Heckscher and Wirth, but makes no mention of Schöne (p 244, n 14). Neither does Bertonasco in his *Crashaw and the Baroque.*

100 Cf n 77.

101 Cf n 25.

102 'Man wird der Fülle der Erscheinungen offenbar eher gerecht, wenn man das

Emblem dahingehend bestimmt, daß seiner dreiteiligen Bauform eine Doppelfunktion des Abbildens and Auslegens oder des Darstellens und Deutens entspricht. An
der abbildenden Leistung der pictura kann sich aber sowohl die inscriptio beteiligen,
sofern sie nämlich nur als gegenstandsbezogene Bildüberschrift erscheint, wie auch
die subscriptio – dann, wenn ein Teil des Epigramms bloße Bildbeschreibung oder
eine eingehendere Darstellung des von der pictura Gezeigten gibt. Andererseits
vermag an der auslegenden Leistung der subscriptio (oder jedenfalls ihres der
eigentlichen Deutung zugewandten Teils) auch die inscriptio teilzunehmen ; durch
ihre sentenzhafte Kurzfassung kann sie dabei im Verhältnis zur pictura jenen
Rätselcharakter gewinnen, der einer Auflösung durch die subscriptio bedarf.
Schließlich beteiligt sich an der Deutung des Dargestellten durch das Epigramm in
vereinzelten Fällen schon die pictura selbst, wenn etwa ein im Bildhintergrund
dargestellter gleichbedeutender Vorgang den Sinn des Vordergrundgeschehens
erklären hilft.'

103 'Die Doppelfunktion des Abbildens und Auslegens, Darstellens und Deutens,
welche die dreiteilige Bauform des Emblems übernimmt, beruht darauf, daß das
Abgebildete mahr bedeutet, als es darstellt. Die res picta des Emblems besitzt
verweisende Kraft, ist res significans.'

104 de la Perrière, *Le Theatre des bons engins* (Paris, 1539), no. 52.

105 Ibid, no 82.

106 Camerarius, *Symbolorvm et emblematvm ex re herbaria desvmtorvm centvria
vna* (Nürnberg, 1595), no. 26.

107 Rosemary Freeman, 'George Herbert and the Emblem Books,' *RES*, 17 (1941), 154.

108 'Den die res picta übersteigenden Sachverhalt aber, auf den das Bild hindeuten und
den die das Bild auslegende subscriptio in Worte fassen will, nannte Harsdörffer,
(der für die Bezeichnung Emblem 'das unbekante Wort der Sinnbilder' wählte) 'die
Seele des Sinnbildes / dessen Dolmetscher die Obschrift [Motto und Epigramm] /
und der Leib ist das Bild oder die Figure [pictura] an sich selbsten'. Seine Formulierung, die sich von Paolo Giovios Bestimmungen der Imprese herleitet, legt es
nahe, res significans und significatio in jener festen Beziehung zueinander zu
denken, die zwischen Leib und Seele herrscht, alle Deutung durch inscriptio und
subscriptio entsprechend als Erfassung eines vorgegebenen und unauswechselbaren
Sinngehalts zu verstehen.'

109 '... sie und erst sie repräsentiert ganz unmittelbar, nämlich auf anschaubare Weise,
was durch die emblematische subscriptio dann ausgelegt wird, indem diese die in
der pictura beschlossene, über die res picta hinausweisende significatio offenbar
macht. Jedes Emblem ist insofern ein Beitrag zur Erhellung, Deutung und Auslegung der Wirklichkeit.'

110 'Gleichgültig deshalb, ob zunächst die subscriptio da war, hier bei Alciati als
griechisches Epigramm, oder ob andere, spätere Emblematiker von der pictura

ausgehen und ihr das Epigramm dann hinzufügen: das Emblem setzt die zu
deutende pictura der Deutung durch die subscriptio voran und nötigt seinen Bet-
rachter und Leser, die Priorität des Bildes anzunehmen.'

111 Cited in Schöne, p 26.

112 'So stellen die pictura und die an ihrer abbildenden Leistung mitwirkenden Textteile
des Emblems dar, was tatsächlich oder doch der Möglichkeit nach existiert, was
zwar nicht immer oder noch nicht vor Augen stehen muß, aber jederzeit doch in den
Gesichts- und Erfahrungskreis des Menschen treten könnte. Neben der ideellen
Priorität der emblematischen pictura (gegenüber der subscriptio), ja als Vorausset-
zung solcher Priorität bestimmt eine potentielle Faktizität seines Bildinhaltes das
Emblem.'

113 'Wenn es richtig ist, daß das emblematische Bild eine potentielle Faktizität besitzt
und eine ideelle Priorität gegenüber dem aus legenden Text, der einen höheren Sinn
in ihm entdeckt, eine in ihm gleichsam angelegte Bedeutung aufschließt, so wird
man das zurückbeziehen müssen auf die typologische Exegese und das allegorische
Verfahren der mittelalterlichen Theologie, die alles Geschaffene als Hinweis auf
den Schöpfer verstand und die von Gott in die Dinge gelegte Bedeutung, ihren auf
die göttliche Sinnmitte hingeordneten heilsgeschichtlichen Bezug aufzudecken
suchte. ''Omnis mundi creatura, / Quasi liber, et picture / Nobis est, et speculum'',
schrieb im 12. Jahrhundert Alanus ab Insulis.'

114 'Nach der patristisch-scholastischen Lehre vom vierfachen Sinn der Schrift hatte die
mittelalterliche Exegese eine buchstäbliche, wörtliche und eine geistliche Bedeutung: einen sensus litteralis seu historicus und einen sensus spiritualis un-
terschieden, den spirituellen Schriftsinn dabei in einen sensus allegoricus, einen
sensus tropologicus und einen sensus anagogicus untergliedert. Vor allem das
Interesse am sensus tropologicus scheint in der Weltauffassung und Weltauslegung
der Emblematiker fortzuleben. Er meint die Bedeutung der Realien für den einzelnen Menschen und seine Bestimmung, für seinen Weg zum Heil und sein Verhalten in der Welt. In solchem Sinne versteht die Emblematik noch immer das Seiende
als ein zugleich Bedeutendes. Alles in der historia naturalis vel artificialis Exis-
tierende, das die riesenhafte Bilderenzyklopädie der emblematischen Bücher aufnimmt und widerspiegelt in den res pictae, weist so als res significans über sich
hinaus und wird in dieser verweisenden Bedeutung, in seinem tropologischen Sinn
durch die subscriptio bestimmt.

115 Cf Physiologus, chap 32.

116 'Die Deutung ist auch mehrmals als zweiffelhafftig / und kan / wie vor von den
Löwen gesagt worden / gut und boß seyn. Die Schlange ist ein Bild der Klugheit /
der gifftigen Verleumdung / und wann sie den Schwantz in dem Mund hat / eine
Abbildung der Ewigkeit.'

117 '... daß man von keinem Sinnbilde urtheilen kan / man habe dann zuvor der Figuren

Natur und Eigenschaften gründlich erlernet / welche vielmals verborgen ist / und nicht ausgemahlet werden kan / daher dann des Sinnbildes Verstand schwer und tunkel wird.'

118 Cf Edgar Wind, *Pagan Mysteries in the Renaissance* (Harmondsworth, 1967) p 208.

119 'Diese Gleichniß ... muß nicht von zufälligen / sondern wesentlichen Eigenschaften eines Dings hergenommen seyn.'

120 Estienne, trans Blount, p 45.

121 Ibid, p 46. For a fuller discussion of Estienne's conception of truth in the emblem, see pp 34–5.

122 Camerarius, no. 73.

123 de la Perrière, no. 61.

124 T.O. Beachcroft, 'Crashaw – and the Baroque Style,' *Cri*, 23 (1934), 407–25. Cf also Beachcroft, 'Quarles – and the Emblem Habit,' *DubR*, 187 (1931), 95.

125 Reinhold Grimm, 'Bild und Bildlichkeit im Barock,' *GRM*, 19 (1969), 379–412. Since I completed work on this study some articles and reviews have appeared that are critical of certain aspects of Schöne's emblem theory. Apart from the slight reservations expressed by Barbara Tiemann in her article on Sebastian Frank pp 598–644, the only attack on Schöne's theory is to be found in Dieter Sulzer's recently published review of Holger Homann's *Studien zur Emblematik des 16. Jahrhunderts* in which he opposes Schöne's theory of the emblem. Sulzer's perspective on the genre is slightly different in that he regards the emblem as a 'hybrid genre' since two arts are equally involved. Schöne's view (which I tend to share) is that the emblem in a general sense is a 'symbolic' mode, essentially literary in so far as its mode of thought is determined by the manner in which things are associated with concepts. Sulzer is also critical of Schöne's concept of 'potential facticity.' It seems to me that some such term as 'credibility' or 'assumed facticity' would probably suffice. See Sulzer's review in *Daphnis*, 4 (1975), 99–104. As we are still waiting for Sulzer's dissertation to appear in print, it is not yet completely clear what alternative theory of the emblem Sulzer has to offer (cf n 10).

126 'In manchen Fällen nähert sich die emblematische subscriptio ... der Figur des Concetto, das mit Hilfe einfallsreicher, scharfsinniger Trugschlüsse weit auseinander liegende oder gar einander ausschließende Bilder und Begriffe zu überraschended, geistreich zugespitzten Vergleichen, Korrespondenzen oder Konfrontationen verbindet.'

127 'Embleme, so bestimmt der Verfasser, sind ingeniöse Schlußfiguren, "però che la simiglianza della proprietà significante, con la proprietà significata ha una tacita virtù entimematica". Damit ordnen sie sich auch dem Bereich der Acutezza oder Argutezza, "gran madre d'ogni ingegnoso concetto" ein.'

128 On the relation of emblem to truth and Neo-Platonism, Gombrich writes: 'The

gravity with which the casuistry of the emblem and device was discussed by otherwise perfectly sane and intelligent people remains an inexplicable freak of fashion unless we understand that for them a truth condensed into a visual image was somehow nearer the realm of absolute truth than one explained in words' (p 173).

129 'Die bewußte Täuschung, soweit von ihr überhaupt die Rede sein kann, steht also eindeutig im Dienste der Wahrheit und hat an denselben "metaphysischen Zusammenhängen" [Jöns, p 49] teil, die auch die Emblematik durchwalten. Emblem wie Concetto, ja die gesamte Bild-Kunst des Barock münden in Tesauros Worte:

Quanto ha il mondo d'ingegnoso, o è Iddio o è da Dio.   [Trattatisti, p 24]
Wenn man daher, ohne genauer zu differenzieren, von "Trugschlüssen," "Fehlschlüssen," "Paralogien" und "Sophismen" redet, so erweckt man Vorstellungen, die, gelinde gesagt, schief sind und im Fall Hockes bis zur völligen Verzerrungen führen.'

130 Joseph Mazzeo, 'Metaphysical Poetry and the Poetic of Correspondencies,' *JHI*, 14 (1953), 221–34.

131 Joseph Mazzeo, 'A Critique of Some Modern Theories of Metaphysical Poetry,' *MP*, 50 (1952), 88–96.

132 Especially the theory of Austin Warren, as expressed in *Richard Crashaw. A Study in Baroque Sensibility*, pp 74–6.

133 A distinction made by Beachcroft earlier, who uses the phrases 'mode of thought' and 'means of expression' in the article 'Quarles – and the Emblem Habit,' p 84.

134 'Zwischen der Überschrift und dem Bild bestand ein mehr oder weniger verborgener Sinnzusammenhang, den das Epigramm erhellte.'

135 '... ein durch Verrätselung gewonnenes Spannungsverhältnis von Bild und Bedeutung.'

136 '... ohne daß eine verbindliche Beziehung von Bild und Bedeutung, die über das Ästhetische hinausreicht, behauptet wird.'

137 Cf 'Die sinnbildliche Qualität eines Dinges ist nicht als das Resultat einer subjektiven Setzung zu interpretieren, sondern beruht darauf, daß es als soches etwas "abbildet", das den physischen oder faktischen Bereich seiner Wirklichkeit übersteigt' ('The emblematic quality of a thing is not to be interpreted as the result of a subjective assumption, but rather depends on its "representing" something that transcends the physical and factual domain of its reality'), p 79.

138 '... verschlüsselt wird um des Reizes der Entschlüsselung willen.'

139 '... letzte Verwirklichung eines in der christlichen Allegorese begründeten spirituellen Weltverständnisses.'

140 'Und wenn sich dies allegorische Denken der von Alciatus geprägten Kunstform des Emblems bedient, dann als Mittel zur Verdeutlichung und größeren Wirkung.'

141 '... ein innerer Widerspruch zwischen Inhalt und Form, zwischen geistlichen und weltlichen, historischen und theoretischen Befunden und Thesen.'
142 Further doubts about Jöns's application of the concept of allegory and 'Verbildlichung' are noted in Penkert's article 'Zur Emblemforschung,' n 48.

NOTES TO CHAPTER 2

1 Dieter Mehl, 'Emblems in English Renaissance Drama,' RD, n.s. 2 (1969), 44. This essay appeared also in German, entitled 'Emblematik im englischen Drama der Shakespearezeit,' A, 87 (1969), 126–46.
2 'Dabei wird nicht bedacht, ob es überhaupt sinnvoll ist, bei Texten von Emblemen zu sprechen, da doch vergleichbaren literarischen Topoi das Konstituens fehlt, das die Sprache erst nachbilden muß: die Pictura' ('Zu einer Geschichte der Emblemtheorien').
3 'Emblem hat, wie Symbol, die allgemeine Bedeutung von *Sinnbild* bekommen. Nach unserer Auffassung ist es ... kein Bild, sondern ein Gegenstand' (André Jolles, *Einfache Formen*, 4th ed [Darmstadt, 1968], p 170).
4 John Shearman, *Mannerism* (Harmondsworth, 1967), p 16.
5 Cf Rosemary Freeman, *English Emblem Books*, p 30. If there were any doubt about it, a glance at Mario Praz's appendix 'Emblems and Devices in Literature' (pp 205–31) in *Studies in Seventeenth-Century Imagery* would satisfy the unconvinced. Praz cites scores of examples of poets using both the words 'emblem' and 'device,' as well as instances of the word-emblem in dozens of poets. See also Freeman, chap 4, 'Emblems in Elizabethan Literature' (pp 85–113).
6 Cf Martin Opitz, 'Trostgedicht in Widerwertigkeit Deß Kriegs' *Geistliche Poemata*, ed E. Trunz (Tübingen, 1966), p 348.
7 Peter Demetz, 'The Elm and the Vine: Notes towards the History of a Marriage Topos,' *PMLA*, 73 (1958), 521–32.
8 A.H.R. Fairchild, 'A Note on *Macbeth*,' *PQ*, 4 (1925), 348–50.
9 Fairchild's essay on Shakespeare's 'The Phoenix and Turtle' is a much more substantial piece. He establishes the meanings of many of the key symbols by reference to the tradition of the Court of Love and parallels in the emblem tradition. See A.H.R. Fairchild, '*The Phoenix and Turtle*. A Critical and Historical Interpretation,' *ESt*, 33 (1904), 337–84.
10 Edward D. Johnson, 'Some Examples of Shakespeare's Use of the Emblem Books,' *B*, 29 (1945), 1956, and 30 (1946), 65–8.
11 There is no Constau listed in Praz's bibliography; a misprint for Pierre Coustau perhaps? Cf Praz, *Studies in Seventeenth-Century Imagery*, p 309.
12 W.S. Hoole, 'Thomas Middleton's Use of "Imprese" in "Your Five Gallants",' *SP*, 31 (1934), 215–23.

13 Lloyd Goldman, 'Samuel Daniel's *Delia* and the Emblem Tradition,' *JEGP*, 67 (1968), 45–59.
14 Goldman cites Freeman (p 33) in support of this statement.
15 Goldman is occasionally inaccurate in his general statements on the presence or absence of certain classical motifs in emblem-books. He suggests that Helen of Troy 'has not been made into a standard emblem' (p 59). A glance at the *Emblemata* reveals that both Sambucus (cf *Emblemata*, col 1679) and Rollenhagen (cf *Emblemata*, col 1320) employed this motif. As the *Emblemata* appeared in 1967 and Goldman's essay a year later, it is possible that he did not have access to this invaluable reference work. None the less, it shows the care that must be exercised in making statements about emblem-books. A more successful attempt to uncover sources is made by Joseph Kau, who traces four images in the Delia sonnets to specific *imprese* in Giovio's collection; see Joseph Kau, 'Daniel's *Delia* and the Imprese of Bishop Paolo Giovio: Some Iconographical Influences,' *JWCI*, 33 (1970), 325–8.
16 Dietrich Jöns, 'Emblematisches bei Grimmelshausen,' *Euph*, 62 (1968), 385–91. Following Jöns's lead, Jeffrey Ashcroft has established Zincgref's *Sapientia picta* (Frankfurt, 1624) as the source for the rue-fern image in Grimmelshausen's *Simplicissimus* novel; cf Ashcroft, 'Ad Astra Volandum: Emblems and Imagery in Grimmelshausen's "Simplicissimus",' *MLR*, 67 (1973), 843–62.
17 '... die Kriterien für die Identifizierung einer emblematischen Vorlage sehr oft unzureichend [sind].'
18 Don C. Allen, 'Ben Jonson and the Hieroglyphics,' *PQ*, 18 (1939), 290–300.
19 The following source studies identify with greater or lesser success emblem-book sources for poetic imagery:
Chew, Samuel, 'Spenser's Pageant of the Seven Deadly Sins,' *Studies in Art and Literature for Belle da Costa Greene*, ed D. Miner (Princeton, 1954), pp 37–54
Datta, Kitty Scoular, 'New Light on Marvell's "A Dialogue between the Soul and Body",' *RQ*, 22 (1969), 242–55
Gilbert, Allan H., 'Falstaff's *Impresa*,' *N&Q*, 154 (1933), 389
Goldman, Lloyd, 'Samuel Daniel's *Delia* and the Emblem Tradition,' *JEGP*, 67 (1968), 49–63
Gordon, D.J., 'The Imagery of Ben Jonson's *The Masque of Blacknesse* and *The Masque of Beautie*,' *JWCI*, 6 (1943), 122–41
Gordon, D.J., 'Hymenaei: Ben Jonson's Masque of Union,' *JWCI*, 8 (1945), 107–45
Graziani, René, 'Philip II's "Impresa" and Spenser's Souldan,' *JWCI*, 27 (1964), 322–4
Green, Henry, *Shakespeare and the Emblem Writers* (London, 1870)
Kau, Joseph, 'Daniel's *Delia* and the *Imprese* of Bishop Paolo Giovio: Some Iconographical Influences,' *JWCI*, 33 (1970), 325–8

Lederer, Josef, 'John Donne and the Emblematic Practice,' *RES*, 22 (1946), 182–200

McManaway, James G., '"Occasion," *Faerie Queene*, II, iv, 4–5,' *MLN*, 49 (1934), 391–3

Rusche, H.G., 'Two Proverbial Images in Whitney's "A Choice of Emblemes" and Marlowe's "The Jew of Malta",' *N&Q*, n.s. 11 (1964), 261;

Scott, W.O., 'Another "Heroical Devise" in *Pericles*,' *SQ*, 20 (1969), 91–4

Steadman, John M., '*Aeropagitica* and the *Hieroglyphica* of Goropius Becanus,' *N&Q*, n.s. 7 (1961), 181–2.

20 Roger Sharrock, 'Bunyan and the English Emblem Writers,' *RES*, 21 (1945), 105–16.

21 The venomous nature of the spider is, however, well-known to continental emblematists; cf. *Emblemata*, cols 302–3. The emblem of the rose and the venomous spider was also adopted by Whitney, p 51.

22 Dennis Biggins, '"Exit pursued by a Beare": A Problem in *The Winter's Tale*,' *SQ*, 13 (1962), 3–13.

23 John M. Steadman, 'Una and the Clergy: The Ass Symbol in *The Faerie Queene*,' *JWCI*, 21 (1958), 134–7.

24 The following establish parallels between emblem-books and literature:

Aptekar, Jane, *Icons of Justice, Iconography and Thematic Imagery in Book V of 'The Faerie Queene'* (New York, 1969)

Ashcroft, Jeffrey, 'Ad Astra Volandum: Emblems and Imagery in Grimmelshausen's "Simplicissimus",' *MLR*, 67 (1973), 843–62

Berthoff, Ann Evans, *The Resolved Soul. The Study of Marvell's Major Poems* (Princeton, 1970)

Bertonasco, Marc F., *Crashaw and the Baroque* (University, Alabama, 1971)

Braunmuller, A.R., 'The Natural Course of Light Inverted: an *Impresa* in Chapman's *Bussy D'Ambois*,' *JWCI*, 34 (1971), 356–60

Chew, Samuel C., 'Time and Fortune,' *ELH*, 6 (1939), 83–113

Chew, Samuel C., *The Pilgrimage of Life* (New Haven and London, 1962)

Clark, Ira, 'Samuel Daniel's "Complaint of Rosamond",' *RQ*, 23 (1970), 152–62

Daly, Peter M., 'Die Metaphorik in den Sonetten der Catharina Regina von Greiffenberg' (Diss. Zürich, 1964)

Daly, Peter M., 'Southwell's "Burning Babe" and the Emblematic Practice,' *WascR*, 3 (1968), 29–44, to be reprinted in *Emblemforschung*, ed S. Penkert (Darmstadt, forthcoming)

Daly, Peter M., 'Emblematic Poetry of Occasional Meditation,' *GLL*, 25 (1972), 126–39

Daly, Peter M., 'Emblematische Strukturen in der Dichtung der Catharina Regina von Greiffenberg,' *Europäische Tradition und deutscher Literatur-Barock*, Internationale Beiträge zum Problem von Überlieferung und Umgestaltung, ed G. Hoffmeister (Bern, 1973), pp 182–215

Daly, Peter M., 'Goethe and the Emblematic Tradition,' *JEGP*, 74 (1975), 388–412

Daly, Peter M., *Dichtung und Emblematik bei Catharina Regina von Greiffenberg* (Bonn, 1976)

Daly, Peter M., 'A Note on Shakespeare's Sonnet 116: A Case of Emblematic Association,' *SQ*, 28 (1977), 515–16

Doebler, John, 'A Submerged Emblem in Sonnet 116,' *SQ*, 15 (1964), 109–10

Fairchild, A.H.R., '*The Phoenix and Turtle*. A Critical and Historical Interpretation,' *ESt*, 33 (1904), 337–84

Fowler, A.D.S., 'Emblems of Temperance in *The Faerie Queene*, Book II,' *RES*, 11 (1960), 143–9

Freeman, Rosemary, 'George Herbert and the Emblem Books,' *RES*, 17 (1941), 150–65; see also *English Emblem Books* (London, 1948, repr 1967), pp 148–72

Gersch, Hubert, *Geheimpoetik. Die 'Continuatio des abentheuerlichen Simplicissimi' interpretiert als Grimmelshausens verschlüsselter Kommentar zu seinem Roman* (Tübingen, 1973)

Gilbert, Allan H., 'The Monarch's Crown of Thorns; (1) The Wreath of Thorns in Paradise Regained,' *JWCI*, 3 (1939–40), 156–60

Gilbert, Allan H., 'The Embleme for December in "The Shepheardes Calender",' *MLN*, 63 (1948), 181–2

Gordon, Donald, '"Veritas Filia Temporis": Hadrianus Junius and Geoffrey Whitney,' *JWCI*, 3 (1940), 228–40

Green, Henry, *Shakespeare and the Emblem Writers* (London, 1870);

Höltgen, K., 'Eine Emblemfolge in Donnes Holy Sonnet XIV,' *ASnS*, 200 (1963), 347–52

Hough, G., and Fowler, A., 'Spenser and Renaissance Iconography,' a critical forum of *Essays in Criticism*, 11 (1961), 233–8: it presents Fowler's answer to Hough's 'doubts on the claims of Renaissance iconography to provide a lexicon for Spenser's images' (p 233)

Reichenberger, Kurt, 'Das Schlangensymbol als Sinnbild von Zeit und Ewigkeit. Ein Beitrag zur Emblematik in der Literatur des 16. Jahrhunderts,' *ZRP*, 81 (1964), 346–51

Ross, Lawrence J., 'The Meaning of Strawberries in Shakespeare,' *SR*, 7 (1961), 225–40

Steadman, John M., 'Spenser's House of Care: A Reinterpretation,' *SR*, 7 (1960), 207–24

Steadman, John M., 'Spenser's "Errour" and Renaissance Allegorical Tradition,' *NM*, 62 (1961), 22–38

Steadman, John M., "Dalila, the Ulysses Myth, and the Renaissance Allegorical Tradition," *MLR*, 57 (1962), 560–5

Steadman, John M., 'Falstaff as Actaeon: A Dramatic Emblem,' *SQ*, 14 (1963), 230–44

Wallerstein, Ruth, *Richard Crashaw. A Study in Style and Poetic Development* (Madison, 1935)

Yates, Frances, 'The Emblematic Conceit in Giordano Bruno's *De Gli Eroici Furori* and in the Elizabethan Sonnet Sequences,' *JWCI*, 6 (1943), 101–21.

25 Cf Erwin Panofsky, *Studies in Iconology: Humanistic Themes in the Art of the Renaissance* (New York, 1962); *Meaning in the Visual Arts* (Harmondsworth, 1970; first published 1955).

26 Peter Fingesten, 'Symbolism and Allegory,' *Helen Adolf Festschrift*, ed Sheema Z. Buehne, et al (New York, 1968), pp 127–8.

27 'Es ist ... nie befriedigend gelungen, das Emblem zwischen Allegorie und Symbol als eigene Form zu etablieren' in 'Zur Geschichte der Emblemtheorien.'

28 Less concerned with actual sources, Dieter Mehl writes of the need to examine 'verwandte Züge' and 'Symptome einer Entwicklung' ('Emblematik im Englischen Drama der Shakespearezeit,' p 130). Mehl's translation of the German article ('Emblems in English Renaissance Drama') mentions only 'symptoms of a development' and omits the reference to 'related features' (p 43).

29 There is an interesting revitalization of such imagery in many modern rock songs and protest lyrics. In no small measure because of the interaction of verbal pattern with musical rhythm The Doors succeed in re-kindling the erotic power of Petrarchistic fire imagery in their song 'Baby Light My Fire.' Leonard Forster half-seriously draws attention to the presence of Petrarchistic conceits in contemporary advertising (*The Icy Fire* [Cambridge 1969], p 191). To what extent – if any – either The Doors or the London Gas Company were aware of the tradition within which they were working is, of course, another question.

30 Georgette de Montenay, *Emblèmes, ou Devises Chrestiennes* (1571), emblem 30.

31 B. van Haeften, *Schola cordis* (1629), lib. III, lect. iv.

32 J. Mannich, *Sacra emblemata* (1624), p 43 [*Emblemata*, col 1548].

33 D Cramer, *Decades quator emblematum sacrorum* (1617), emblem 32.

34 Cf Bertonasco, pp 12–13.

35 See pp 112–13; and Kingsley Widmer's essay, 'The Iconography of Renunciation: The Miltonic Simile,' *ELH*, 25 (1958), 258–69.

36 C.R. von Greiffenberg, *Geistliche Sonnette, Lieder und Gedichte* (Nürnberg, 1662).

37 Ibid, pp 42, 43; also pp 22, 93, 198.

38 van Haeften, *Schola cordis*, lib. III, lect. iv; *Regia via crucis* (1635), pp 314, 328, 370.

39 Cf M. Bircher and P. Daly, 'C.R.v. Greiffenberg und J.W.v. Stubenberg. Zur Frage der Autorschaft zweier anonymer Widmungsgedichte,' *Literaturewissenschaftliches Jahrbuch*, 7 (1966), 17–35.

40 Lohenstein, *Epicaris*, ii, 570; cf also Greiffenberg, sonnets 37 and 76.
41 The poem is reproduced with commentary in Ingrid Black and Peter Daly, *Gelegenheit und Geständnis. Unveröffentlichte Gelegenheitsgedichte als verschleierter Spiegel des Lebens und Wirkens der Catharina Regina von Greiffenberg*, vol. iii of 'Kanadische Studien zur deutschen Sprache und Literatur' (Bern, 1971). Joannes Sambucus also uses the eagle and mole in his *Emblemata* (1566), p 212 [*Emblemata*, col 489], which must have been an influential work if the two translations and six known editions are any indication (cf Praz, *Studies in Seventeenth-Century Poetry*, pp 486–7).
42 Cf Schöne, pp 133–4.
43 For an opposing view see Windfuhr, *Die barocke Bildlichkeit und ihre Kritiker. Stilhaltungen in der deutschen Literatur des 17. und 18. Jahrhunderts* (Stuttgart, 1966), p 95.
44 'Alles / was sichtbarlich ist / unterfangt die Mahlerey vorzustellen; was aber unsichbarlich ist / kan mit der Sinnbildkunst / vermittelst der Umschrift / verstanden werden.'
45 Typotius, *Symbola divina et humana* ... (Prague, 1601–3) part ii, p 78.
46 A. Gryphius, *Leichenabdankungen*, p 108. Gryphius also refers to Typotius when he speaks of an eagle flying upwards carrying a snake which bites him, causing his downward plunge to death (*Leichenabdankungen*, p 602).
47 Beachcroft, 'Quarles – and the Emblem Habit,' p 89.
48 Cf Philip Wheelwright, *The Burning Fountain*.
49 Cf Freeman, *English Emblem Books*, pp 103 ff.
50 Greiffenberg, unpublished ms poem 'Trauer Liedlein in unglükk und Wiederwerttigkeit,' reproduced and discussed in Peter M. Daly, 'Vom privaten Gelegenheitsgedicht zur öffentlichen Andachtsbetrachtung (zu C.R.v. Greiffenbergs *Trauer Liedlein*),' *Euph*, 66 (1972), 308–14.
51 Haeften, *Schola cordis* (1629), lib. iii, lect. v; cf also J. von Bruck, *Emblemata moralia et bellica* (1565), emblem 6 [*Emblemata*, col 1030].
52 *Des Allerheiligsten Lebens JESU Christi Ubrige Sechs Betrachtung* ... (Nürnberg, 1693), p 568.
53 Van Haeften, *Schola cordis* (1629), lib. iv, lect. v.
54 Freeman (*English Emblem Books*, p 28) notes this essential difference between emblematic and modern symbolic forms, and yet she still faults the emblematic structure for not fufilling a symbolic function, which it was never intended to do.
55 Opitz, 'Vesuvius,' in *Weltliche Poemata*, p 53.
56 Cf *Emblemata*, cols 921, 1758; 296, 298, 299.
57 See p 4.
58 See Greiffenberg 'An die Deogloria,' reproduced and discussed in Black and Daly, *Gelegenheit und Geständnis*, pp 46–53.

59 On the question of 'truth' in the emblem, see pp 34–5.

60 M. Praz, *Studies in Seventeenth-Century Imagery*, pp 138 ff.

61 Cited in Praz, ibid, p 141.

62 'Es ist nicht zu laugnen daß ein Sinnbild leicht / das andere schwer; eines gut und eingrifflich / das andere schlecht und einfältig; eines auf eine gewiese Sache / das andere auf viel unterschiedliche Händele zu deuten. Die besten aber sind meines Bedunkens / welche in dem Mittelstande nicht allzuhoch / nicht allzu nieder kommen; die wol verstanden werden können / aber nicht gleich einem jeden eröffnet darliegen.'

63 Cf *Emblemata*, cols 603–4.

64 Cf Greiffenberg, *Sonnette, Lieder und Gedichte*, p 210, and my discussion in Daly, *Dichtung und Emblematik bei Catharina Regina von Greiffenberg* (Bonn, 1976), pp 139–40.

65 Estienne, *The Art of Making Devises*, trans Blount p 45.

66 *The Worthy Tract of Paulus Iouius* ... trans Samuel Daniel, p Di.

67 Ibid, p Di.

68. Erich Seeberg, *Zur Frage der Mystik* (Leipzig, 1927), p 13.

69 'Hier wird jeder beliebige Gegenstand zum Gleichnis oder zum Symbol; alles gewinnt Bedeutung und wird von einer erhitzten Einbildungskraft in einem künstlich sublimierten Sinn hineingesteigert.'

70 '... so wird in der emblematischen Mystik und Poesie das Erlebnis gewissermaßen künstlich herbeigeführt, indem aus einem Gegebenen und Äußerlichen zufällige innere Beziehungen und Gedanken gewonnen und abgeleitet werden, die sich schließlich gegenseitig fortbilden und die Beziehung zur Wirklichkeit und zum Ausgangspunkt völlig verlieren.'

71 '... Ausdeutungen einer willkürlichen Gegebenheit.'

72 Else Eichler, 'Christian Scrivers "Zufällige Andachten", ein Beitrag zur Geistes- und Formgeschichte des 17. Jhs.' (Diss. Halle, 1926).

73 '... lähmend legte sie sich über das deutsche Leben': Hermann Pongs, *Das Bild in der Dichtung*, vol I (Marburg, 1927), p 14.

74 Gerhard Fricke, *Die Bildlichkeit in der Dichtung des A. Gryphius* (Berlin, 1933).

75 'Das Emblem befriedigt die Neigung nach der Zwei- und Mehrdeutbarkeit alles Vorhandenen; es enthält das Tüfteln über das Sichtbare hinaus und durch das Sichtbare hindurch nach einem Hintersinn, nach einem 'das bedeutet', das Bedürfnis, jedes Ding nicht zunächst eigentlich, sondern uneigentlich zu nehmen, als Träger und Künder von Geheimnissen, als Umhüllung von Sinn und Geist, als sichtbare Rätselaufgabe.'

76 '... eine Art intellektueller Sport, das willkürlich spielerische Komponieren beziehungsloser "Sachen" also emblematische Denkaufgabe und allegorisches Rätsel oder die Verkleidung beliebiger Devisen und Sentenzen in eine zunächst schwer durchschaubare Verbindung von Einzeldingen.'

77 '.. [behandelt] Bild und Emblem jetzt mit mystischer Feierlichkeit und dann wider mit spielerischer Willkür.'

78 Ernst Friedrich von Monroy, *Embleme und Emblembücher in den Niederlanden 1560–1630. Eine Geschichte der Wandlungen ihres Illustrationsstils*, ed Hans Martin von Erfa (Utrecht, 1964).

79 '.. der Reiz des Emblems besteht gerade in der Spannung zwischen beiden Ausdrucksweisen, die sich als geschlossene Bereiche, als unmittelbares Aussprechen und bildliches Verhüllen des Begriffes, gegenüberstehen.'

80 '... er [der Gehalt] muß künstlich aus ihm abgeleitet, ihm beigelegt werden. Er liegt nicht in der Sache, wird nicht entdeckt, sondern erfunden. Das Emblem hat einen Erfinder. Es ist der persönliche unverbildliche Einfall eines Autors.'

81 Anna H. Kiel, *Jesias Rompler von Löwenhalt. Ein Dichter des Frühbarock*, Diss. Amsterdam (Utrecht, 1940).

82 '... dasselbe Bild erfährt immer die verschiedensten Deutungen; jedes Einzelbild wird zunächst in seine Elemente zerlegt und an die einzelnen Teile knüpft sich die allegorische Erklärung.'

83 '... das Bild in seiner eigentlichen Bedeutung schwindet immer mehr und macht der ausgeklügelten Gedankenverbindung Platz. Einzelheit wird gegen Einzelheit gehalten und zu einander in Beziehung gebracht.'

84 '... das unklare Kriterium des 'eigenen Wesens' der Natur [entspringt] der Verabsolutierung eines profanen Naturbegriffs (*Das 'Sinnen-Bild.' Studien zur allegorischen Bildlichkeit bei Andreas Gryphius*).

85 '... das Bild in seiner eigentlichen Bedeutung ist, wie in der Emblematik der Nürnberger, geschwunden und hat der tüftelnden Assoziation Platz gemacht.'

86 'Eine zweite Schicht in Romplers Exempeldichtung sind die emblemartigen, achtzeiligen Alexandrinergedichte; insoweit sie an ein neutestamentliches Gleichnis oder irgendeine mystische Vorstellung anknüpfen, gehören sie noch zu der Tradition der *Emblemata sacra*, wie sie von den Sammlungen Sudermanns und Gloners vertreten wurde.'

87 The impression that Vodosek's essay belongs to the thirties in substance and attitude is further supported by the extensive, and largely unacknowledged, use he has made of Helmut Rosenfeld's *Das deutsche Bildgedicht* (1935). Vodosek's treatment of the Nürnberg poets, for instance, is heavily indebted to Rosenfeld's chapter on the same subject (pp 69–79). Sentence after sentence of Rosenfeld's book (cf pp 69–72) reappear in Vodosek's essay (cf pp 26–9), either as unacknowledged quotations or as slightly modified borrowings. The use of many Harsdörffer passages is identical in both, except for Vodosek's erroneous citation of *Trichter*, I, 51 ff, for *Gesprächsspiel*, I, 51 ff, an error which presumably crept in because Rosenfeld refers only to volume and page (cf Vodosek, n 55, and Rosenfeld, p 72). Vodosek mentions Rosenfeld only once in a footnote to the discussion, which hardly suffices!

88 Kayser, *Das sprachliche Kunstwerk*, 9th ed (Bern/Munich, 1963), pp 75–7, 316, 349, 404. Cf Penkert, p 114.

89 Although John Sullivan discusses the emblematic poetry of Greiffenberg, there is no indication that he is aware of Schöne's work; see 'The German Religious Sonnet of the Seventeenth Century (Diss. Berkeley, 1966), pp 22, 201, 206, 212–13, 220, 223. Ruth Angress also levels the old charge that the emblem is far-fetched in her study of the German baroque epigram, *The Early German Epigram. A Study in Baroque Poetry* (Lexington, 1971), p 107. Since neither Sullivan nor Angress is primarily concerned with emblematics, they can hardly be expected to be acquainted with the corpus of literature on the subject. However, failure to take Schöne's findings into account undermines some of their interpretations and conclusions.

90 G. Hough and A. Fowler. 'Spenser and Renaissance Iconography,' a critical forum in *Essays in Criticism*, 11 (1961), 233–8.

91 One of the very few critics of English literature who expressly rejects the idea that the emblem is necessarily arbitrary is Dieter Mehl; see his 'Emblems in English Renaissance Drama,' p 41 and n 9. Mehl is in fact a German and acquainted with Schöne's work.

92 Cf pp 21–7.

93 Cf p 43.

94 Cf Friedrich Ohly, 'Vom geistigen Sinn des Wortes im Mittelalter,' *ZfdAdL*, 89 (1958/9), 7.

95 Cf p 43.

96 Cf p 43.

97 'Es muß das meinste Absehen auff die bekantste und gemeinste Eigenschafft deß Bildes gerichtet werden': Lehrsatz 31 of Harsdörffer's introduction to his *Bericht von den Sinnbildern*.

98 I am not aware of any serious objection to Goethe's poem 'Gedichte sind gemalte Fensterscheiben' on the grounds that there is no necessary likeness between stained glass windows and poems.

99 Freeman, 'George Herbert and the Emblem Books,' p 159; also *English Emblem Books*, p 163.

100 Freeman, 'George Herbert and the Emblem Books,' p 154.

101 Cf pp 34–5.

102 Cf also Lederer, p 197, whose criteria are 'feeling' and 'spontaneity.'

103 Greiffenberg, sonnet 227.

104 Grimmelschausen, *Simplicissimus*, bk 6, chap 23, Cf Jöns, 'Emblematisches bei Gimmelshausen,' pp 385–91. See p 175.

105 'Die sinnbildliche Qualität eines Dinges ist nicht als das Resultat einer subjektiven Setzung zu interpretieren, sondern beruht darauf, daß es als solches etwas ''abbildet'', das den physischen oder faktischen Bereich seiner Wirklichkeit übersteigt' (*Das 'Sinnen-Bild. Studien zur allegorischen Bildlichkeit bei Andreas Gryphius*).

106 '... bildliche Einkleidung': Schöne, p 95.
107 Beachcroft, 'Quarles – and the Emblem Habit,' p 89.
108 'In dem Sinnbild sol nur eine Gleichniß gesucht und abgesehen werden': Lehrsatz 37 of Harsdörffer's introduction to his *Bericht von den Sinnbildern*.
109 For a fuller analysis of emblematic meditation which draws upon Catholic rules for meditation, see Daly, *Dichtung und Emblematik bei Catharina Regina von Greiffenberg*, pp 114–43. The standard work on the subject of meditational poetry is Louis Martz, *The Poetry of Meditation*, rev ed (New Haven, 1962).
110 Freeman, 'George Herbert and the Emblem Books,' pp 150–1.
111 Freeman, ibid, p 155.
112 Cf Kayser, *Das sprachliche Kunstwerk*, p 119.
113 Cf Wheelwright, *The Burning Fountain*.
114 I. Ziemendorff, *Die Metapher bei den weltlichen Lyrikern des deutschen Barock* (Berlin, 1931), p 8.
115 'Die Sinnbildkunst ist eine nachdenkliche Ausdruckung sonderlicher Gedanken / vermittelst einer schicklichen Gleichniß welche von natürlichen oder künstlichen Dingen an- und mit wenig nachsinnlichen Worten ausgeführt ist.'
116 Cf Praz, 'The English Emblem Literature,' p 131.
117 A.D.S. Fowler, 'Emblems of Temperance in *The Faerie Queene*, Book II,' *RES*, 11 (1960), 143–9.
118 1 'Beweismittel für die Wahrheit eines vom Angesprochenen bezweifelten Tatbestandes' ...
   2 'Grundlage für eine teleologische Deutung des gegenwärtigen Geschehens und für den vorausdeutenden Zuspruch' ...
   3 'Instrument der Erkenntnis einer Situation,' 'Regulativ für das Verhalten des Sprechers' ...
   4 'Begründung für eine Aufforderung des Angesprochenen zu bestimmten Handlungen' ...
   5 'Maßstab des Urteils über ein negatives Verhalten' ... 'Verdammungsargument' ...
   6 'Selbstbestätigung des Sprechers im rechten Verhalten' ...
   7 'preisende Bestätigung des beispielhaften Handelns.'
119 '... durchzogen von Sinnbildern, deren Bedeutung oft erst über die Emblematik zugänglich ist.'
120 '... emblematische Sinnbilder, ihre Bedeutung und Lehre als Instrument der Erkenntnis und Sinngebung, der Wahrheitsbestimmung und Urteilsfindung, der Überredung, Selbstbestätigung und Rechtfertigung, als Grundlage einer Beziehung des Aktuellen auf das Typische und Normative, einer Orientierung des Besonderen am Grundsätzlichen, einer Erhebung des Vereinzelten, Isolierten ins Allgemeine und Immergültige.'
121 Cf Schöne, pp 139–51.

122 Cf Bertonasco, *Crashaw and the Baroque.*
123 Cf Daly, 'Emblematische Strukturen in der Dichtung der Catharina Regina von Greiffenberg,' pp 203–5.
124 Cf also *FG*, VI, 230 ff.
125 Letter from Greiffenberg to Birken, 4 October 1672. Birken had a passion for devising emblematic gifts; his MSS include notes for 'Sinnbilder auf einem Hochzeit-Becher für einen Bedienten'; but in addition to such dedicatory emblems, there are also deprecatory multiple emblems, such as that addressed as follows: 'Auf einen faulen aber gut mütigen Arbeiter, Rab genannt.' Birken's diaries for the years 1667, 1668, and 1669 contain many entries noting his designs for emblems; see *Die Tagebücher des Sigmund von Birken*, ed Joachim Kröll (Würzburg, 1971), pp 283, 305, 319, 369, 413, and 436, n 86.
126 Cf Daly, 'Southwell's "Burning Babe" and the Emblem Tradition.'
127 *Johann Christian Günthers Sämtliche Werke*, ed W. Krämer, (Leipzig, 1930), I, 189.
128 Cf Werner von Koppenfels, 'Two Notes on *Imprese* in Elizabethan Literature: Daniel's Additions to *The Worthy Tract of Paulus Giovio*; Sidney's *Arcadia* and the Tournament Scene in *The Unfortunate Traveller*,' *RQ*, 24 (1971), 13–25; Frances Yates, 'The Emblematic Conceit in Giordano Bruno's *De Gli Eroici Furori* and in the Elizabethan Sonnet Sequences,' *JWCI*, 6 (1943), 101–21; N.J.R. Crompton, 'Sidney and Symbolic Heraldry.'

NOTES TO CHAPTER 3

1 Rosemary Freeman, 'George Herbert and the Emblem Books,' p 154; cf also *English Emblem Books*, p 149.
2 Cf Daly, 'Southwell's "Burning Babe" and the Emblematic Practice.'
3 Noted by Marc F. Bertonasco, *Crashaw and the Baroque*, p 11.
4 John Doebler, 'A Submerged Emblem in Sonnet 116,' *SQ*, 15 (1964), 109–10.
5 Cf Peter M. Daly, 'A Note on Shakespeare's Sonnet 116: A Case of Emblematic Association,' *SQ*, 28 (1977), 515–16.
6 Karl Josef Höltgen, 'Eine Emblemfolge in Donnes Holy Sonnet XIV,' *ASnS*, 200 (1963), 347–52.
7 '... [eine] emblematisches Kompositons- und Deutungsprinzip.'
8 'Sie zeigen einen scharf umrissenen, visuell höchst anschaulichen Bildvorgang in krasser Unmittelbarkeit, ja fast unangenehmer Körperlichkeit, dessen Einzelaspekte nach genauer, quasi-logischer allegorischer Auslegung verlangen.'
9 '... eine gewisse Steigerung bus hin zur "Erneuerung des Herzens".'

10 Frances Yates, 'The Emblematic Conceit in Giordano Bruno's *De Gli Eroici Furori* and in the Elizabethan Sonnet Sequences,' pp 101–21.

11 Lloyd Goldman, 'Samuel Daniel's "Delia" and the Emblem Tradition.'

12 Roger B. Wilkenfield, 'Act and Emblem: the Conclusion of *Samson Agonistes*,' *ELH*, 32 (1965), 160–8.

13 A.D.S. Fowler, 'Emblems of Temperance in *The Faerie Queene*, Book II,' pp 143–9. See also Sander Gilman, 'The Uncontrolled Stead: A Study of the Metamorphosis of a Literary Image,' *Euph*, 66 (1972), 32–54.

14 Jane Aptekar, *Icons of Justice. Iconography and Thematic Imagery in Book V of 'The Faerie Queene,'* Diss. Columbia, 1967 (New York, 1969).

15 Ruth Mulhauser, 'The Poetic Function of the Emblems in the *Delie*,' *L'EC*, 5 (1965), 80–9.

16 Holger Homann, 'Emblematisches in Sebastian Brants *Narrenschiff*?' *MLN*, 81 (1966), 463–75; reprinted in Holger Homann, *Studien zur Emblematik des 16. Jahrhunderts.*

17 'Die in ihnen dargestellten Sachverhalte werden jedoch im Text als Exempel, als Belege für die vorgetragene Lehre verwandt, nicht als Quellen der Erkenntnis: in keinem Fall zeigt der Text, daß er seinen Ausgang von der *pictura* genommen hätte … Funktionsglied eines Ganzen … eine Zugabe.'

18 Kingsley Widmer, 'The Iconography of Renunciation: The Miltonic Simile,' 258–69.

19 'Es würde sich lohnen, die barocke Lyrik unter diesem Gesichtspunkt genauer zu untersuchen.'

20 Samual Chew, 'Richard Verstegan and the "Amorum Emblemata" of Otho van Veen,' *HLQ*, 8 (1945), 197.

21 T.O. Beachcroft, 'Quarles – and the Emblem Habit,' p 83.

22 Anna H. Kiel, *Jesias Rompler von Löwenhalt. Ein Dichter des Frühbarock.*

23 Daly, 'Emblematische Strukturen in der Dichtung der Catharina Regina von Greif-fenberg,' pp 207–8.

24 Cited in Freeman, *English Emblem Books*, p 26.

25 Cf also sonnets 50 and 92.

26 Daly, 'Emblematische Strukturen in der Dichtung der Catharina Regina von Greif-fenberg,' pp 206–7.

27 'Bei den Positionen der auslegenden Hinweise fällt auf, daß Gryphius die Er-läuterungen vorwiegend über und unter den Bildbereich setzt, in die Überschrift und die Terzette. Sein Sonett nähert sich dadurch der Dreiteiligkeit des Emblems' (*Das 'Sinnen-Bild.' Studien zur allegorischen Bildlichkeit bei Andreas Gryphius*, p 92).

28 'Aufbau und Inhalt dieses Sonetts sind eindeutig: auf die Schilderung des Son-nenaufgangs folgt die Bitte um Erleuchtung der Seele und Erlangung des ewigen Heils.'

29 'Dieser Auffassung, die mit ihren Begriffen von zweckfreier Formung, ursprünglichem Naturfühlen und Einheit der Stimmung in Gryphius' Sonett erfüllt sehen will, was erst mit der Entbindung der Subjektivität in der Lyrik des Sturm und Drang erfüllt werden konnte, muß von diesen Kriterien her ... der zweite Teil zwangsläufig als angefügter religiöser Gedanke und damit zugleich als ästhetisch störende, die Ganzheit des Gedichts sprengende Zutat erscheinen,'

30 'Für die Beurteilung des Gedichts ergibt sich ... , daß es die Gestaltung eines alten, fest überlieferten Motivs christlicher Naturdeutung ist und daß seine Zweiteiligkeit mit der Form der Allegorie als einer Analogie zwischen dinglichem Sein und spiritueller Bedeutung gegeben ist.'

31 Beachcroft, 'Crashaw – and the Baroque Style,' p 423.

32 Cf Helmut Rosenfeld, *Das deutsche Bildgedicht*, p 88.

33 Johann Arndt, far from disdaining this 'manneristic' form, utilized it on several occasions in his *Vom Wahren Christentum*. Book 2 contains three examples, addressed to Christ (74 lines), to the cross (45 lines), and to prayer (62 lines), which indicates that the form could serve the purposes of meditation. See *Vom Wahren Christentum* (Riga, 1679), book 2 pp 11–13, 236–8, 308–9.

34 Cf M. Bircher, 'Unergründlichkeit. Catharina Regina von Greiffenbergs Gedicht über den Tod der Barbara Susanna Eleonora von Regal,' *Deutsche Barocklyrik. Gedichtinterpretationen von Spee bis Haller*, ed Martin Bircher and Alois M. Haas (Bern, 1973), pp 127–8..

35 Cf Rosenfeld, pp 87–92; Margaret Church, 'The First English Pattern Poems,' *PMLA*, 61 (1946), 636–50; A.L. Korn, 'Puttenham and the Oriental Pattern-Poem,' *CL* 6 (1954), 289–303.

36 Robert G. Warnock and Roland Folter, 'The German Pattern Poem: A Study in Mannerism of the Seventeenth Century, '*Festschrift für Detlev W. Schumann Zum 70. Geburtstag*, ed R. Schmitt (Munich, 1970), pp 40–73.

37 Conrad Wiedemann, *Johann Klaj und seine Redeorationen* (Nürnberg, 1966), p 134.

38 J.H. Summers, *George Herbert: His Religion and Art* (London, 1954), pp 134 ff.

39 C.C. Brown and W.P. Ingoldsby, 'George Herbert's "Easter-Wings",' *HLQ*, 35 (1972), 131–42.

40 The German translation of Alciatus, by Jeremias Held, and quoted by Warnock and Folter, is as follows:

VON DER FRUCHTBARKEIT SO JR SELBS SCHEDLICH
Der Bauwer hat mich arme nauß gsetzt
    An diese Wegscheid da ich stets
Von Buben wird geplagt ohn zal
    Die mit steinen mich werffen all
Mit benglen sie mir zwerffen dNest
    Zerreissen mir mein rinde fest

An allen orten vmb vnd vmb
    Wirt ich geplagt in einer sumb
Was kundt aber ergers geschehn
    Einem Baum der kein frucht thut gebn
Aber zu meinem größen schaden
    Gib vnd trag ich mein Frucht beladen.

41 Johann Helwig, *Die Nymphe Noris* (1650), cited from Warnock and Folter, p 68.

42 'Diese Erfindungen hält man für Poetische Fechtsprünge / und wann sie nicht gantz ungezwungen / oder mit dem Gemähl / und Sinnbilderen / verbunden sind / mögen sie bey den Verständigen schlechte Ehre erlangen.'

43 'Wer seinen JESUM recht kennet und liebet / wird neben-stehendem Creuz noch viele nachmachen / auch dergleichen mit der DornKrone der Geisel-Seule / und andrem unsers theuren Heilands Passion-Zeug / ersinnen können.'

44 I have discussed this poem more fully in *Emblematik und Dichtung bei C.R.v. Greiffenberg*, pp 125–8.

NOTES TO CHAPTER 4

1 Green, *Shakespeare and the Emblem Writers.*

2 Glynne Wickham, *Early English Stages* (London, 1959), esp II, 206–44.

3 Walter Benjamin, *Ursprung des deutschen Trauerspiels* (Berlin, 1928).

4 Albrecht Schöne, *Emblematik und Drama im Zeitalter des Barock*, 2nd ed (Munich, 1968).

5 Dieter Mehl, 'Emblematik im Englischen Drama der Shakespearezeit,' *A*, 87 (1969), 126–46, translated as 'Emblems in English Renaissance Drama,' *RD*, 2 (1969), 39–57.

6 A partial exception is the unpublished dissertation by Arthur O. Lewis, 'Emblem Books and English Drama: A Preliminary Survey, 1581–1600' (Diss. Pennsylvania State College, 1951), which, as Mehl suggests, is largely concerned with documenting instances of parallels between emblem-books and drama.

7 '*Unglucks-Welle, Tugend-Fels, Hochmuths-Flügel, NeidesSchlangen* werden aus je einem konkreten und einem abstrakten Substantiv zusammengesetzt, – so wie es der abbildenden und auslegenden, darstellenden und deutenden Funktionen des aus Bild und Text gefügten Emblems entspricht.'

8 'Das als regierendes Grundwort gefaßte Konkretum (Bildstichwort), dem in der emblematischen Struktur die ideelle Priorität zukommt, wird durch die Beigabe des genitivisch angeschlossenen Abstraktums (Bedeutungsstichwort) ausgelegt, gedeutet: "expliziert".'

9 Mehl, 'Emblems in English Renaissance Drama.'

10 The German version is somewhat more dogmatic, rendering 'at first sight' as 'nicht mehr' (p 130).

11 John M. Steadman, 'Falstaff as Actaeon: A Dramatic Emblem,' *SQ*, 14 (1963), 230–44.

12 Horst Oppel, *Titus Andronicus. Studien zur dramengeschichtlichen Stellung von Shakespeares früher Tragödie*, Schriftenreihe der deutschen Shakespeare-Gesellschaft, NF. IX (Heidelberg, 1961).

13 Jean Hagstrum, *The Sister Arts*, pp 70–81, 112–20.

14 'Es ist sicher kein zufall, daß Shakespeares Bildersprache stets dort am fühlbarsten ins Emblematische übergeht, wo das Thema von sich aus die Frage nach dem Wesen der Kunst aufnimmt oder den Rangstreit der Künste berührt.'

15 Oppel lists the following: *Titus Andronicus*, III.i.104–6; *Cymbeline*, III.iv.6–8; *Antony and Cleopatra*, II.ii.205–9; and *Timon of Athens*, I.i.85–93.

16 Cf pp 57–9.

17 James Hoyle, 'Some Emblems in Shakespeare's *Henry IV* Plays,' *ELH*, 37 (1971), 512–27.

18 Saxon Walker, 'Mime and Heraldry in *Henry IV, Part I*,' *E*, 11 (1956), 91–6.

19 Cf p 93.

20 … als Grundlage einer Beziehung des Aktuellen auf das Typische und Normative, einer Orientierung des Besonderen am Grundsätzlichen, einer Erhebung des Vereinzelten, Isolierten ins Allgemeine und Immergültige.'

21 Robert B. Heilman, *This Great Stage. Images and Structure in 'King Lear'* (Baton Rouge, 1948).

22 Benjamin, *Ursprung des deutschen Trauerspiels*.

23 'Nicht selten ist die Rede in den Dialogen nur die an allegorischen Konstellationen, in welchen die Figuren zueinander sich befinden, hervorgezauberte Unterschrift. Kurz: die Sentenz erklärt das Szenenbild als seine Unterschrift für allegorisch … Aber nicht nur eigentlich emblematische Aussprüche, sondern ganze Reden klingen hin und wieder, als stünden sie von Haus aus unter einem allegorischen Kupfer.'

24 'Die "emblematischen" Sentenzen sind tragende Elemente im Bau des Trauerspiels: Pfeiler, zwischen denen die szenischen Bilder sich spannen, und Säulen, auf die das Bühnengeschehen als ein exemplarisches Geschehen sich gründet.'

25 Cited in D.J. Gordon, 'The Imagery of Ben Jonson's *The Masque of Blacknesse* and *The Masque of Beautie*,' *JWCI*, 6 (1943), 122–41.

26 Cf A.H. Gilbert, *The Symbolic Persons in the Masques of Ben Jonson*, pp 15–16.

27 Cited in Don C. Allen, 'Ben Jonson and the Hieroglyphics,' p 297.

28 Cited in D.J. Gordon, '*Hymenaei*: Ben Jonson's Masque of Union,' *JWCI*, 8 (1945), 111.

29 Cited in Wickham, II, i, 223.

30 Muriel Bradbrook, *Shakespeare and Elizabethan Poetry* (London, 1961), p 105.

31 'Er [Shakespeare] schafft lebende Bilder, die durch die rhetorische Bildersprache ausgedeutet werden. Die visuelle Rhetorik ist hier untrennbar mit der sprachlichen verbunden.' Dieter Mehl, 'Schaubild und Sprachfigur in Shakespeares Dramen,' *Deutsche Shakespeare-Gesellschaft West. Jahrbuch*, 10 (1970), 19.

32 Mehl, 'Schaubild und Sprachfigur in Shakespeares Dramen,' p 14.

33 Mehl's interpretation of the emblematic significance of Brutus's suicide derives from a view of Brutus's character and motives which – to say the least – is open to discussion. It could be argued that Brutus, far from being an exemplar of virtue, has tarnished his virtue by turning his hand to the preventive assassination of a possibly would-be tyrant. Any assessment of Brutus depends partly on a decision about whether Caesar is a powerful ruler or a tyrant. That certain emblematists have used the motif of Brutus's suicide as Mehl suggests is true, but not necessarily relevant. My reservations were increased by the discovery that Brutus's suicide was not always given so positive an interpretation in the emblem-books. In Henkel and Schöne's *Emblemata*, immediately after the Alciatus source that Mehl uses, comes a quotation from Aneau's *Picta poesis*, in which Brutus's death exemplifies the power of a bad conscience. The *inscriptio* reads, 'Mens sibi bene conscia nescit timere' (*Emblemata*, col 1181). Mehl certainly overstates his case when he writes 'The most well-known emblem-books' (p 14) employ the suicide of Brutus to demonstrate the truth of the sentence 'Fortuna virtutem superans.' The only example of this interpretation cited in the *Emblemata* is from Alciatus – Green also mentions Whitney (cf p 517) – and if there are others Mehl does not identify them. Finally, it seems to me that Mehl is caught in a certain contradiction in his interpretation of character: on the one hand, Brutus is equated with virtue, and on the other, Caesar is the symbol of a 'destroyed order of the commonwealth.' If Caesar does represent order, then Brutus's act is one of disorder, no matter how nobly and selflessly it is intended.

34 Cf Mehl, 'Schaubild und Sprachfigur in Shakespeares Dramen,' pp 17–18.

35 'Fur das Trauerspiel des siebzehnten Jahrhunderts wird die Leiche oberstes emblematisches Requisit schlechthin.'

36 '... die Überwindung der Personalitätsschranke' and 'bildhafte Starre.'

37 Cf also Schöne, pp 219–20, and Mehl, 'Emblems in English Renaissance Drama,' p 55.

38 Cf Hoyle, p 513.

39 'Wenn etwa im vierten Akt des *Kaufmanns von Venedig* Shylock mit gewetztem Messer und bereitgehaltener Waage auf die Verkündung des Urteilsspruches gegen Antonio wartet, so muß er dem Zuschauer wie eine Personifizierung unnach-giebiger, ja pervertierter Gerechtigkeit erscheinen; denn die Waage als Attribut der *Justitia* war ja ein ikonographischer Gemeinplatz.'

40 'Das Kissen als Attribut der Faulheit und Lust läßt im Bild recht eindeutig erken-
nen, welche Art von Herrschaft mit Falstaffs Einfluß an die Stelle des rechmäßigen
Königtums treten würde und hier in spielerischer Verkehrung sogar für einen
Augenblick getreten ist.'

41 'Der Schauplatz stellet für auf der stillen See unter dem gestirnten Himmel den
Schiffbruch der Agrippinen.'

42 'In der Art dieses Bildausschnitts ist offenbar die Darstellung zu denken die –
vermutlich auf Leinwand gemalt und in einen Holzrahmen gespannt – während des
dritten Reyen auf der Hinterbühne zu sehen war: eine pictura, die der Chor der
Berg- und Meer-Göttinnen durch lebhafte Beschreibung des Vorgangs, durch
erregte Anteilnahme am Geschehen gleichsam in Handlung umsetzt.'

43 'Zwey und siebentzig tausend Seelen derer unter Henrico um deß Catholischen
Glaubens willen hingerichtete Märterer verklagen vor dem Richterstuhl Christi die
Seele Henrici.'

44 Cf Schöne, pp 185–93 ; Dieter Mehl, *The Elizabethan Dumb Show* (London, 1965),
a translation of *Die Pantomime im Drama der Shakespearezeit* (Heidelberg, 1964) ;
Wolfgang Clemen, *Die Tragödie vor Shakespeare, Ihre Entwicklung im Spiegel der
dramatischen Rede* (Heidelberg, 1955).

45 Cf Schöne, p 187: 'Emblematische Züge tragen diese *dumb shows* vor allem dort,
wo sie nicht nur als Ersatz für die in den Szenen ausgesparten Teile der Handlung
dienen, sondern eine moralisch-didaktische Quintessenz des nachfgolgenden
Geschehens geben' ('These dumbshows have emblematic characteristics especially
where they do not only serve to replace parts of the action omitted from the scenes,
but give the moral-didactic quintessence of the following action').

46 Thomas Sackville and Thomas Norton, *Gorboduc*, facsimile repr (Mentson, 1968),
p A.iij.

47 Cited in Mehl, *The Elizabethan Dumb Show*, p 74.

48 Mehl, 'Emblems in English Renaissance Drama,' p 48.

49 For German examples of the emblematic dumb-show see Schöne, pp 185–93.

50 For further examples see Schöne, pp 208–17.

51 Wickham, *Early English Stages*, vols I and II.

52 Wickham, II, i, p 209

53 II, i, 209. Cf also: 'With similar caution, I would attribute the emblematic nature of
the stage-directions in Elizabethan plays to a borrowing from the conventions of the
religious stage preserved, after the suppression of the latter, in all forms of
pageantry' (II, i, 267).

54 Cf Wickham, I, 91; and II, i, 213.

55 Cf Wickham, II, i, 216, 228–9.

56 Cf Wickham, II, i, 310–23, and Werner Habicht, 'Becketts Baum und Shakespeares
Wälder,' *Deutsche Shakespeare-Gesellschaft West. Jahrbuch*, 10 (1970), 84, 86.

57 'Sowohl Holunder als auch Eibe waren traditionellerweise mit Tod, Verzwei-
flung und Magie verbunden. Den Holunder kennt der Volksglaube überdies als
Liebesbaum. Der Wald, zunächst ein Lustort, wird von Tamora, als sie die Eibe –
das Todesemblem – nennt, in eine Stätte des Verbrechens, des Todes verkehrt.
Überdies gilt der Holunder herkömmlicherweise als der Baum, an dem sich Judas
erhängte: Der Bühnenbaum, der hier den Ort von Aarons Heimtücke bezeichnet,
wird in einer späteren Szene als Aarons Galgen benötigt ("A halter, soldiers! Hang
him on this tree!"; v, i, 47).'

58 '… die Kombination [von Eiche und Palme] … deutet bei Joachim Camerarius
ausdrücklich auf die Vergeblichkeit der Hoffnung auf ein Goldenes Zeitalter auf
Erden ('Aurea in hoc frustra speramus saecula mundo, / Alterius saeculi dabit ille
Pater'); dies aber könnte den Sinn der Ardennerwaldszenen, in denen eine schein-
bar paradiesische Welt beständig relativiert und in Frage gestellt ist, prägnanter
nicht treffen.'

59 Mehl, 'Emblems in English Renaissance Drama,' p 52.

60 Cf p 165.

61 Mehl, 'Emblems in English Renaissance Drama,' p 53.

62 Cf also Tourneur's *The Atheist's Tragedy*.

63 Cf pp 144–5, 148–9, 153–4.

64 'Eine genauere Betrachtung der bei Shakespeare verwendeten Requisiten würde
immer wieder zeigen können, wie Shakespeare die ikonographischen Assoziationen
bestimmter Gegenstände in das Geschehen einbezieht und dadurch tiefere Mög-
lichkeiten der Interpretation andeutet, von dem Bild des Dolches in *Macbeth* bis zu
den Schlangen, die Kleopatra an ihre Brust legt, von den so demonstrativ in den
Vorgang einbezogenen Herrscher insignien in den Königsdramen bis zu der Nar-
renkappe in *King Lear*.'

65 '… das ambivalente Vermögen menschlicher Sprache.'

66 'Was Camerarius aus der res significans, dem stummen, unbewegten Bilde des ·
Schneckenfangs ableitet und in der subscriptio mitteilt, das wird hier – um
Harsdörffers Schauspiel-Definition aufzunehmen – aus dem *wesentlichen* (nämlich
bedeutsamen) / *lebendigen und selbstredenden Gemähl* der dramatischen Vor-
gänge zwischen Michael Balbus und dem Kaiser Leo Armenius entwickelt und im
Reyen verkünde.'

67 '… Darstellung und Auslegung, Besonderes und Allgemeines, Bild und Bedeutung
[bilden doch] als Komplimentärerscheinungen erst miteinander das charakteris-
tische Ganze.'

68 Cf Schöne, pp 208–14; Wickham, *Early English Stages*.

69 Wickham, ii, i, 209.

70 'Die in den letzten Jahren ausgehenden Seculi überstandne Krieges=Last / und
wiederumb hervorblühende Friedens=Lust.'

71 'Wird auf solche Weise der Bezug zur pictura und scriptura der Emblembücher offenkundig, so deutet sich zugleich auch die Affinität des allegorisch-emble-matischen Umzugs zum Bühnenspiel an.'

72 Cf Wickham, *Early English Stages* and *Shakespeare's Dramatic Heritage*; Allar-dyce Nicoll, *Stuart Masques and the Renaissance Stage* (London, 1937); and *Renaissance Drama*, n.s. 1 (1969), which contains essays on masques and enter-tainments.

73 Cf Gordon's discussion of the 'intimate connection' (p 123) between the *Hymenaei* and two political tracts defending James I's assumption of the title King of Great Britain and the Union of the Kingdoms.

74 For an account of the quarrel between Ben Jonson and Inigo Jones, see Wickham, II, i, 271–4; and D.J. Gordon, 'Poet and Architect: The intellectual Setting of the Quarrel between Ben Jonson and Inigo Jones,' *JWCI*, 12 (1949), 152–78.

NOTES TO CHAPTER 5

1 Cf pp 32–5, 83–6.
2 Roger Sharrock, 'Bunyan and the English Emblem Writers,' pp 106–7.
3 Dietrich Jöns, 'Emblematisches bei Grimmelshausen,' pp 386 ff. Subsequent refer-ences to Jöns in this chapter are to this article.
4 J. Paul Hunter, *The Reluctant Pilgrim. Defoe's Emblematic Method and Quest for Form in 'Robinson Crusoe'* (Baltimore, 1966), pp 94 ff.
5 David J. Alpaugh, 'Emblem and Interpretation in *The Pilgrim's Progress*,' *ELH*, 33 (1966), 300.
6 Cf Rosemary Freeman, *English Emblem Books*, pp 209–15.
7 Cited in Sharrock, p 7.
8 Cited in *Simplicianische Schriften*, ed A. Kelletat (Darmstadt, 1958), p 507.
9 Cf Jöns, p 388, n 14.
10 '... Zusammendenken von Naturfaktum und christlicher Lehre.'
11 Further instances of emblematic imagery in prose fiction are noted in: J. Ashcroft, 'Ad astra volandum: Emblems and Imagery in Grimmelshausen's "Simplicis-simus",' *MLR*, 67 (1973), 843–62; H. Gersch, *Geheimpoetik. Die 'Continuatio desabentheurlichen Simplicissimi' interpretiert als Grimmelshausens verschlüssel-ter Kommentar zu seinem Roman* (Tübingen, 1973).
12 Cf Dennis Biggins, '"Exit Pursued by a Beare": A Problem in *The Winter's Tale*,' pp 3–13.
13 Support for the contention that such a tree allegory was fully visualizable to seventeenth-century writers and their readers may be found in the illustrated broadsheets. See William A. Coupe, *The German Illustrated Broadsheet in the Seventeenth Century*, pp 101–4, for examples of the tree emblems conveying social and political criticisms.

14 'Es ist mit Sicherheit anzunehmen, daß Grimmelshausen der christliche Sinn dieses Emblems bekannt gewesen ist, und daß er ihn bewußt ins Weltliche gewandt hat, um die weltliche Gesinnung, die Torheit seines Helden auf diese Weise zu charakterisieren, da er ihn geistlich Gemeintes weltlich deuten läßt.'
15 In addition to instances noted by Alpaugh and Sharrock, see Freeman, pp 204–28.
16 The passage is quoted on p 61.
17 For details of the sensational circumstances in which the virtuous and charitable Barbara Susanna Eleonora von Regal met her death in a house during an electrical storm, see Martin Bircher, 'Unergründlichkeit. Catharina Regina von Greiffenbergs Gedicht über den Tod der Barbara Susanna Eleonora von Regal.'
18 For an interpretation of the event see Hunter, pp 191, 199. See also Robert Ayres, 'Robinson Crusoe: "Allusive Allegorik History",' PMLA, 82 (1967), 399–407.
19 See Louis Martz, The Poetry of Meditation; Marvin Schindler, The Sonnets of Andreas Gryphius. Use of the Poetic Word in the Seventeenth Century (Gainesville, 1971); Daly, 'Southwell's "Burning Babe" and the Emblematic Practice'; Daly, 'Emblematische Meditation,' in Dichtung und Emblematik bei C.R.v. Greiffenberg, pp 114–43.
20 Cf Penkert, 'Zur Emblemforschung,' p 115.
21 John Heckman, 'Emblematic Structures in Simplicissimus Teutsch,' MLN, 84 (1969), 876–90.
22 For my part, I regard the Simplicissimus Teutsch together with the Continuatio as the Simplicissimus-novel. Cf my review of Kenneth Negus, Grimmelshausen (New York, 1974), in Seminar, 11 (1975), 170–2.
23 Cf p 32.
24 Günther Weydt, Nachahmung und Schöpfung im Barock. Studien um Grimmelshausen (Bern/Munich, 1968).
25 Cf Hubert Gersch, Geheimpoetik. Die 'Continuatio des abentheurlichen Simplicissimi' interpretiert als Grimmelshausens verschlüsselter Kommentar zu seinem Roman (Tübingen, 1973); also Klaus Haberkamm, 'Sensus astrologicus'. Zum Verhältnis von Literatur und Astrologie in Renaissance und Barock (Bonn, 1972).
26 'Bey dieser Zeit / ist fast kein Buch verkaufflich / ohne einen Kupfertitel / welcher dem Leser desselben Jnhalt nicht nur mit Worten / sondern auch mit einem Gemähl vorbildet.'
27 E.g., Friedrich Spee's Trutznachtigall, or Herbert Vaughan's Silex scintilans.
28 Cf Penkert, 'Zur Emblemforschung,' p 119, n 77; and 'Grimmelshausens Titelkupfer-Fiktionen. Zur Rolle der Emblematik-Rezeption in der Geschichte poetischer Subjektivität,' Dokumente des internationalen Arbeitskreises für deutsche Barockliteratur (Wolfenbüttel, 1973), I, 52–75.
29 Cf Penkert, 'Grimmelshausens Titelkupfer-Fiktionen,' pp 61f–2.
30 '… die verschiedenen Entwicklungsstufen des nach Selbsterkenntnis ringenden Simplizissimus, die Larven der Torheit, die er ablegen mußte, bis das wahre

Gesicht des weltabgewandten, zur Ruhe gekommenen Weisen emportauchen konnte.'

31 Jan Hendrik Scholte, *Der Simplicissimus und sein Dichter. Gesammelte Aufsätze* (Tübingen, 1950).

32 Scholte, p 254.

33 Gerhart Mayer, 'Die Personalität des Simplicissimus,' *ZdP*, 88 (1969), 497–521.

34 '... des Erzählers geistiges Konterfei.'

35 '... das ... Spruchband ... deutet daraufhin, daß hier nicht der Erzähler als isolierte Person gemeint ist, sondern das Werk – die in diesem realisierte spannungsvoll-komplexe Erzählhaltung.'

36 '... Freude am ironischen Spiel der sich gegenseitig relativierenden Rollen.'

37 '... unbestechlichen Röntgenblick für die innere Wahrheit des Menschen.'

38 '... weil er die trügerische "Wahn" der weltlichen Lebensformen durchschaut hat.'

39 Penkert, 'Grimmelshausens Titelkupfer-Fiktionen'; Hubert Gersch, 'Dreizehn Thesen zum Titelkupfer des Simplicissimus,' in *Dokumente des internationalen Arbeitskreises für deutsche Barockliteratur*, (Wolfenbüttel, 1973), I, 76–81. I am indebted to Hubert Gersch for sending me the manuscript of his lecture, which will be appearing in print in due course.

40 'Res und Figura stehen in der Pictura des *Simplicissimus* in einer Wechsel-beziehung, an der Kind und Baum entscheidend beteiligt sind.'

41 Cited in Penkert, 'Grimmelshausens Titelkupfer-Fiktionem,' p 67.

42 Cf Gersch, pp 77 ff.

43 'Damit wird der *Simplicissimus*-Roman als ein mixtum compositum aus sehr verschiedenartigen Stoffen und Formen, Gattungselementen und Ordnungsprinzi-pien zu erkennen gegeben, wie es von der klassizistischen Theorie kritisiert wird. Doch mit der eigenwilligen Hinzufügung des Satyrkopfs stells Grimmelshausen sein Monstrum und also den *Simplicissimus* unter die Gesetzlichkeit und Freiheit der Satire.'

NOTES TO CHAPTER 6

1 Cf Liselotte Dieckmann, *Hieroglyphics*, p 45.

2 Dieckmann, p 45.

3 Joseph Mazzeo, 'A Critique of Some Modern Theories of Metaphysical Poetry,' 93.

4 Josef Lederer, 'John Donne and the Emblematic Practice,' *RES*, 21 (1946), 183.

5 Lederer, p 186.

6 Cf pp 80–6.

7 Muriel Bradbrook, *Shakespeare and Elizabethan Poetry*, 238.

8 Cf Roy Pascal, *German Literature in the Sixteenth and Seventeenth Centuries* (London, 1968), pp 90–1.

9 Rosemary Freeman, 'George Herbert and the Emblem Books,' p 162; repeated in slightly altered wording in *English Emblem Books*, p 167.

10 Cf Dietrich Walter Jöns, 'Die emblematische Predigtweise Johann Sauberts,' in *Rezeption und Produktion zwischen 1570 und 1730, Festschrift für Günther Weydt zum 65. Geburtstag*, ed W. Rasch, et al (Bern/Munich, 1972), pp 137–58.

11 Winfried Schleiner briefly draws attention to the emblematic quality of some of the imagery of Donne's sermons. He writes: 'The practice of relating point by point the various parts of an emblematic picture to some spiritual meaning is not unlike the procedure outlined above [Donne's exegetical method]. On a purely rhetorical level, this similarity to an emblem might be claimed for the more elaborate figures of the kind examined here' (*The Imagery of John Donne's Sermons* [Providence, 1970], p 180). The similarity is more than a matter of rhetoric. One wishes that the author had investigated this aspect more fully, especially as reference is made to the work of both Ohly and Schöne. The recent book by Gale H. Carrithers, *Donne at Sermons: a Christian Existential World* (Albany, 1972), does not consider the possibly emblematic structure of Donne's sermons.

12 Cf Maria Fürstenwald, *Andreas Gryphius: Dissertationes funebres. Studien zur Didaktik der Leichabdankungen* (Bonn, 1967).

Selected Bibliography

CRITICAL STUDIES

Since I completed this study and its selected bibliography a *Supplement* to the Henkel-Schöne *Emblemata* (Stuttgart, 1976) has appeared. With its 2338 bibliographical entries, divided into five major sections and seventeen subsections, the *Supplement* is the most exhaustive bibliography on things emblematic that has been compiled to date. Unfortunately, it lacks an index of proper names, so that consulting the *Supplement* can be a time-consuming business.

Allen, Don C. 'Ben Jonson and the Hieroglyphics,' *PQ*, 18 (1939), 290–300

Alpaugh, David, J. 'Emblem and Interpretation in *The Pilgrim's Progress*,' *ELH*, 33 (1966), 299–314

Angress, Ruth *The Early German Epigram. A Study in Baroque Poetry* (Lexington, 1971)

Aptekar, Jane *Icons of Justice, Iconography and Thematic Imagery in Book v of 'The Faerie Queene'* (New York, 1969)

Ashcroft, Jeffrey 'Ad Astra Volandum. Emblems and Imagery in Grimmelshausen's "Simplicissimus",' *MLR*, 68 (1973), 844–62

Ayres, Robert '*Robinson Crusoe*: "Allusive Allegorik History",' *PMLA*, 82 (1967), 399–407

Beachcroft, T.O. 'Quarles – and the Emblem Habit,' *DubR*, 188 (1931), 80–96

Beachcroft, T.O. 'Crashaw and the Baroque Style,' *Cri*, 23 (1934), 407–25

Benjamin, Walter *Ursprung des deutschen Trauerspiels* (Berlin, 1928)

Bergeron, David *English Civic Pageantry* (London, 1971)

Berthoff, Ann Evans *The Resolved Soul. A Study of Marvell's Major Poems* (Princeton, 1970)

Bertonasco, Marc F. *Crashaw and the Baroque* (Alabama, 1971)

Biggins, Dennis ' "Exit pursued by a Beare": A Problem in *The Winter's Tale*,' SQ, 13 (1962), 3–13

Bircher, Martin 'Unergründlichkeit. Catharina Regina von Greiffenbergs Gedicht über den Tod der Barbara Susanna Eleonora von Regal,' in *Deutsche Barocklyrik. Gedichtinterpretationen von Spee bis Haller*, ed Martin Bircher und Alois Haas (Bern/Munich, 1973), pp 185–223.

Bircher, Martin, and Daly, Peter 'C.R.v. Greiffenberg and J.W.v. Stubenberg. Zur Frage der Autorschaft zweier anonymer Widmungsgedichte,' *Literaturwissenschaftliches Jahrbuch*, 7 (1966), 17–35

Black, Ingrid, and Daly, Peter *Gelegenheit und Geständnis. Unveröffentlichte Gelegenheitsgedichte als verschleierter Spiegel des Lebens und Wirkens der Catharina Regina von Greiffenberg*, Kanadische Studien zur deutschen Sprache und Literatur, 3 (Bern, 1971)

Bradbrook, Muriel *Shakespeare and Elizabethan Poetry* (London, 1951)

Braunmuller, R.A. 'The Natural Course of Light Inverted: an *Impresa* in Chapman's *Bussy D'Ambois*,' JWCI, 34 (1971), 356–60

Brown, C.C., and Ingoldsby, W.P. 'George Herbert's "Easter-Wings",' HLQ, 35 (1972), 131–42

Carrithers, Gale H. *Donne at Sermons: A Christian Existential World* (Albany, 1972)

Chew, Samuel 'Time and Fortune,' ELH, 6 (1939), 83–113

Chew, Samuel 'Richard Verstegan and the "Amorum Emblemata" of Otho van Veen,' HLQ, 8 (1945), 192–9

Chew, Samuel *The Virtues Reconciled* (Toronto, 1947)

Chew, Samuel 'Spenser's Pageant of the Seven Deadly Sins,' in *Studies in Art and Literature for Belle da Costa Greene*, ed D. Miner (Princeton, 1954), pp 37–54

Chew, Samuel *The Pilgrimage of Life* (New Haven and London, 1962)

Church, Margaret 'The First English Pattern Poems,' PMLA, 61 (1946), 636–50

Clark, Ira 'Samuel Daniel's "Complaint of Rosamond",' RQ, 23 (1970), 152–62

Clemen, Wolfgang *Die Tragödie vor Shakespeare. Ihre Entwicklung im Spiegel der dramatischen Rede* (Heidelberg, 1955)

Clements, Robert J. *Picta Poesis. Literary and Humanistic Theory in Renaissance Emblem Books* (Rome, 1960)

Coupe, William A. *The German Illustrated Broadsheet in the Seventeenth Century*, 2 vols (Baden-Baden, 1966)

Crompton, N.J.R. 'Sidney and Symbolic Heraldry,' CA, 8 (1965), 244–8

Daly, Peter M. 'Die Metaphorik in den Sonetten der Catharina Regina von Greiffenberg' (Diss. Zürich, 1964)

Daly, Peter M. 'Southwell's "Burning Babe" and the Emblematic Practice,' WasR, 3 (1968), 29–44, to be reprinted in *Emblemforschung*, ed Sibylle Penkert (Darmstadt)

Daly, Peter M. 'The Poetic Emblem,' Neoph, 54 (1970), 381–97

Daly, Peter M. 'Emblematic Poetry of Occasional Meditation,' *GLL*, 25 (1972), 126–39

Daly, Peter M. 'Trends and Problems in the Study of Emblematic Literature,' *M*, 5 (1972), 53–68

Daly, Peter M. 'Vom privaten Gelegenheitsgedicht zur öffentlichen Andachtsbetrachtung (zu C.R.v. Greiffenbergs *Trauer Liedlein*),' *Euph*, 66 (1972), 308–14

Daly, Peter M. 'Emblematische Strukturen in der Dichtung der Catharina Regina von Greiffenberg,' in *Europäische Tradition und deutscher Literaturbarock. Internationale Beiträge zum Problem von Überlieferung und Umgestaltung*, ed G. Hoffmeister (Bern, 1973), pp 182–215

Daly, Peter M. 'Goethe and the Emblematic Tradition,' *JEGP*, 74 (1975), 388–412

Daly, Peter M. *Dichtung und Emblematik bei Catharina Regina von Greiffenberg* (Bonn, 1976)

Daly, Peter M. 'A Note on Shakespeare's Sonnet 116: A Case of Emblematic Association,' *SQ*, 28 (1977), 515–16

Datta, Kitty Scoular 'New Light on Marvell's "A Dialogue between the Soul and Body",' *RQ*, 22 (1969), 242–59

Dieckmann, Liselotte *Hieroglyphics. The History of a Literary Symbol* (St Louis, 1970)

Doebler, John 'A Submerged Emblem in Sonnet 116,' *SQ*, 15 (1964), 109–10

Eichler, Else 'Christian Scrivers 'Zufällige Andachten,' ein Beitrag zur Geistes- und Formgeschichte des 17. Jhs? (Diss. Halle, 1926)

Fairchild, A.H.R. '*The Phoenix and Turtle*. A Critical and Historical Interpretation,' *ES*, 33 (1904), 337–84

Fairchild, A.H.R. 'A Note on *Macbeth*,' *PQ*, 4 (1925), 348–50

Feldges, Mathias *Grimmelshausens 'Landstörtzerin Courasche.' Eine Interpretation nach der Methode des vierfachen Schriftsinnes*, Basler Studien zur deutschen Sprache und Literatur, 38 (Bern, 1969)

Fingesten, Peter 'Symbolism and Allegory,' in S.Z. Buehne, J.L. Hodge, and L.B. Pinto, eds, *Helen Adolf Festschrift* (New York, 1968), pp 126–37

Forster, Leonard *The Icy Fire* (Cambridge, 1969)

Foss, Martin *Symbol and Metaphor in Human Experience* (Princeton, 1949)

Fowler, A.D.S. 'Emblems of Temperance in *The Faerie Queene*, Book II,' *RES*, 2 (1960), 143–9

Freeman, Rosemary 'George Herbert and the Emblem Books,' *RES*, 17 (1941), 150–65

Freeman, Rosemary *English Emblem Books* (London, 1948; repr 1967)

Fricke, Gerhard *Die Bildlichkeit in der Dichtung des A. Gryphius* (Berlin, 1933)

Fürstenwald, Maria *Andreas Gryphius: Dissertationes funebres. Studien zur Didaktik der Leichenabdankungen* (Bonn, 1967)

Gersch, Hubert 'Dreizehn Thesen zum Titelkupfer des *Simplicissimus*,' in *Internationaler Arbeitskreis für deutsche Barockliteratur* (Wolfenbüttel, 1973), pp 76–81

Gersch, Hubert *Geheimpoetik. Die 'Continuatio des abentheurlichen Simplicissimi'
interpretiert als Grimmelshausens verschlüsselter Kommentar zu seinem Roman*
(Tübingen, 1973)

Giehlow, Karl *Die Hieroglyphenkunde des Humanismus in der Allegorie der Renaissance, besonders der Ehrenpforte Kaisers Maximilian I*, Jahrbuch der Kunsthistorischen Sammlungen des allerhöchsten Kaiserhauses, 22, Heft 1, Leipzig, 1915)

Gilbert, Allan H. 'Falstaff's *Impresa*,' *N&Q*, 154 (1933), 389

Gilbert, Allan H. 'The Monarch's Crown of Thorns; (1) The Wreath of Thorns in
Paradise Regained,' *JWCI*, 3 (1939–40), 156–60

Gilbert, Allan H. 'The Embleme for December in "The Shepheardes Calender",' *MLN*,
63 (1948), 181–2

Gilbert, Allan H. *The Symbolic Persons in the Masques of Ben Jonson* (Durham, North
Carolina, 1948)

Gilman, Sander 'The Uncontrolled Stead: A Study of the Metamorphosis of a Literary
Image,' *Euph*, 66 (1972), 32–54

Goldman, Lloyd 'Samuel Daniel's *Delia* and the Emblem Tradition,' *JEGP*, 67 (1968),
49–63

Goldsworthy, William L. *Shakespeare's Heraldic Emblems: Their Origin and Meaning*
(London, 1928)

Gombrich, E.H. '"Icones Symbolicae." The Visual Image in Neoplatonic Thought,'
JWCI, 11 (1948), 163–92

Gordon, D.J. '"Veritas Filia Temporis": Hadrianus Junius and Geoffrey Whitney,'
JWCI, 3 (1940), 228–40

Gordon, D.J. 'The Imagery of Ben Jonson's *The Masque of Blacknesse* and *The Masque
of Beautie*,' *JWCI*, 6 (1943), 122–41

Gordon, D.J. '*Hymenaei*: Ben Jonson's Masque of Union,' *JWCI*, 8 (1945), 107–45

Graziani, René 'Philip II's "Impresa" and Spenser's Souldan,' *JWCI*, 27 (1964), 322–4

Green, Henry *Shakespeare and the Emblem Writers* (London, 1870)

Greene, David 'Medieval Backgrounds of the Elizabethan Emblem Books' (Diss. Berkeley, 1958)

Grimm, Reinhold 'Bild und Bildlichkeit im Barock,' *GRM*, 19 (1969), 379–412

Haberkamm, Klaus *Sensus astrologicus. Zum Verhältnis von Literatur und Astrologie
in Renaissance und Barock* (Bonn, 1972)

Habicht, Werner 'Becketts Baum und Shakespeares Wälder,' *Deutsche Shakespeare-
Gesellschaft West*, x (1970), 77–98

Hagstrum, Jean *The Sister Arts. The Tradition of Literary Pictorialism and English
Poetry from Dryden to Gray* (Chicago, 1958)

Harms, Wolfgang 'Wörter, Sachen und emblematische "res" im "Orbis sensualium
pictus" des Comenius,' in *Gedenkschrift für W. Foerste* (Cologne/Vienna, 1970), pp
531–42

Harms, Wolfgang 'Diskrepanzen zwischen Titel und Inhalt der "Explicatio oder Au-
ßlegung über die Wohrten Salomonis ..." (1663) des Chemikers Johann Rudolf
Glauber,' in *Rezeption und Produktion in Renaissance und Barock. Festschrift für G.
Weydt* (Bern/Munich, 1972), pp 155–67

Harms, Wolfgang 'Der Fragmentencharakter emblematischer Auslegungen und die
Rolle des Lesers. Gabriel Rollenhagens Epigramme,' in *Deutsche Barocklyrik.
Gedichtinterpretationen von Spee bis Haller*, ed Martin Bircher and Alois M. Haas
(Bern/Munich, 1973), pp 49–64

Harms, Wolfgang '*Mundus imago Dei est.* Zum Entstehungsprozeß zweier Emblembücher Jean Jacques Boissards,' *DVJs*, 47 (1973), 223–44

Harms, Wolfgang 'Der Eisvogel und die halkyonischen Tage. Zum Verhältnis von
naturkundlicher Beschreibung und allegorischer Naturdeutung,' in *Verbum et Signum. Festschrift für Friedrich Ohly* (Munich, 1975), I, 477–515

Harms, Wolfgang, and Freytag, Hartmut *Außerliterarische Wirkungen barocker
Emblembücher. Emblematik in Ludwigsburg, Gaarz und Pommersfelden* (Munich,
1975)

Hayes, Charles 'Symbol and Allegory: A Problem in Literary Theory,' *GR*, 44 (1969),
273–88

Heckman, John 'Emblematic Structures in *Simplicissimus Teutsch*,' *MLN*, 84 (1969),
876–90

Heckscher, William S. 'Renaissance Emblems,' *The Princeton University Library
Chronicle*, 15 (1954), 55–68

Heckscher, William S., and Wirth, Karl-August 'Emblem, Emblembuch,' in *Reallexikon zur Deutschen Kunstgeschichte* (Stuttgart, 1959), V, cols 85–228

Heilman, Robert B. *This Great Stage. Images and Structure in 'King Lear'* (Baton
Rouge, 1948)

Henkel, Arthur, and Schöne, Albrecht *Emblemata, Handbuch zur Sinnbildkunst des
XVI. und XVII. Jahrhunderts* (Stuttgart, 1967)

Hocke, Gustav René *Die Welt als Labyrinth Manier und Manie in der europäischen
Kunst*, rde, L/LI (Hamburg, 1957)

Hocke, Gustav René *Manierismus in der Literatur. Sprach-Alchemie und esoterische
Kombinationkunst*, rde, LXXXII/LXXXIII (Hamburg, 1959)

Höltgen, Karl Joseph 'Eine Emblemfolge in Donnes Holy Sonnet XIV,' *ASnS*, 200
(1963), 347–52

Höltgen, Karl Joseph 'Arbor, Scala und Fons vitae. Vorformen devotionaler Embleme
in einer mittelenglischen Handschrift,' in *Chaucer und seine Zeit*, Buchreihe der
Anglia, 14 (Tübingen, 1968)

Homann, Holger 'Emblematisches in Sebastian Brants *Narrenschiff*?' *MLN*, 81 (1966),
463–75

Homann, Holger 'Prolegomena zu einer Geschichte der Emblematik,' *CG*, 3 (1968), 244–57

Homann, Holger *Studien zur Emblematik des 16. Jahrhunderts* (Utrecht, 1971)

Hoole, W.S. 'Thomas Middleton's Use of "Imprese" in "Your Five Gallants",' *SP*, 31 (1934), 215–23

Hoyle, James 'Some Emblems in Shakespeare's *Henry IV* Plays,' *ELH*, 37 (1971), 512–27

Hunter, Paul J. *The Reluctant Pilgrim. Defoe's Emblematic Method and Quest for Form in Robinson Crusoe* (Baltimore, 1966)

Hough, G., and Fowler, A. 'Spenser and Renaissance Iconography,' a critical forum of *Essays in Criticism*, 11 (1961), 233–8

Iversen, Erik *The Myth of Egypt and its Hieroglyphs in European Tradition* (Copenhagen, 1961)

Jacobsen, Eric *Die Metamorphose der Liebe in Friedrich Spees Trutznachtigall* (Copenhagen, 1954)

Johnson, Edward D. 'Some Examples of Shakespeare's Use of the Emblem Books,' *B*, 29 (1945), 145–6; and 30 (1946), 65–8

Jöns, Dietrich *Das 'Sinnen-Bild.' Studien zur allegorischen Bildlichkeit bei Andreas Gryphius* (Stuttgart, 1966)

Jöns, Dietrich 'Emblematisches bei Grimmelshausen,' *Euph*, 62 (1968), 385–91

Jöns, Dietrich 'Die emblematische Predigweise Johann Sauberts,' in *Rezeption und Produktion zwischen 1570 und 1730. Festschrift für Günther Weydt zum 65. Geburtstag*, ed Wolfdietrich Rasch, Hans Geulen, and Klaus Haberkamm (Bern-Munich, 1972), pp 137–58

Kau, Joseph 'Daniel's *Delia* and the *Imprese* of Bishop Paolo Giovio: Some Iconographical Influences,' *JWCI*, 33 (1970), 325–8

Kayser, W. *Das sprachliche Kunstwerk*, 9th ed (Bern, 1963)

Kiel, Anna H. *Jesias Rompler von Löwenhalt. Ein Dichter des Frübarock*, Diss. Amsterdam (Utrecht, 1940)

Korn, A.L. 'Puttenham and the Oriental Pattern-Poem,' *CL*, 6 (1954), 289–303

Lausberg, Heinrich *Handbuch der literarischen Rhetorik* (Munich, 1960)

Lederer, Joseph 'John Donne and the Emblematic Practice,' *RES*, 22 (1946), 182–200

Lesky, Grete *Schloß Eggenberg. Das Programm für den Bildschmuck* (Graz/Vienna/Cologne, 1970)

Lewis, Arthur O. 'Emblem Books and English Drama: A Preliminary Survey 1581–1600' (Diss. Pennsylvania State College, 1951)

McManaway, James G. '"Occasion," *Faerie Queene*, II, IV, 4–5,' *MLN*, 49 (1934), 391–3

Martz, Louis *The Poetry of Meditation*, rev ed (New Haven, 1962)

Mayer, Gerhart 'Die Personalität des Simplicius Simplicissimus,' *ZdP*, 88 (1969), 497–521

Mazzeo, Joseph 'A Critique of Some Modern Theories of Metaphysical Poetry,' *MP*, (1952), 88–96

Mazzeo, Joseph 'Metaphysical Poetry and the Poetic of Correspondencies,' *JHI*, 14 (1953), 221–34

Mehl, Dieter *The Elizabethan Dumb Show* (London, 1965), translated from *Die Pantomime im Drama der Shakespearezeit* (Heidelberg, 1964)

Mehl, Dieter 'Emblematik im Englischen Drama der Shakespearezeit,' *A*, 87 (1969), 126–46, translated as 'Emblems in English Renaissance Drama,' *RD*, ns 2 (1969), 39–57

Mehl, Dieter 'Schaubild und Sprachfigur in Shakespeares Dramen,' *Deutsche Shakespeare-Gesellschaft West*, x (1970), 7–29

Miedema, Hessel 'The term *Emblema* in Alciati,' *JWCI*, 31 (1968), 234–50

Monroy, Ernst Friedrich von *Embleme und Emblembücher in den Niederlanden 1560–1630* (Utrecht, 1964)

Morgan, Gareth 'The Emblems of *Erotocritos*,' *TQ*, 10 (1967), 241–68

Mulhauser, Ruth 'The Poetic Function of the Emblems in the *Delie*,' *L'EC*, 5 (1965), 80–9

Nicoll, Allardyce *The Stuart Masques and the Renaissance Stage* (London, 1937)

Ohly, Friedrich 'Vom geistigen Sinn des Wortes im Mittelalter,' *ZfdAdL*, 89 (1958–9), 1–21

Oppel, Horst *Titus Andronicus. Studien zur dramengeschichtlichen Stellung von Shakespeares früher Tragödie*, Schriftenreihe der deutschen Shakespeare-Gesellschaft, N.F. 9 (Heidelberg, 1961)

Parker, Alexander A. *Literature and the Delinquent: the picaresque novel in Spain and Europe, 1599–1753* (Edinburgh, 1967)

Pascal, Roy *German Literature in the Sixteenth and Seventeenth Centuries* (London, 1968)

Penkert, Sibylle 'Zur Emblemforschung,' *GgA*, 224 (1972), 100–20

Penkert, Sibylle 'Grimmelshausen Titelkupfer-Fiktionen. Zur Rolle der Emblematik-Rezeption in der Geschichte poetischer Subjektivität,' in *Internationaler Arbeitskreis für deutsche Barockliteratur* (Wolfenbüttel, 1973), pp 52–75

Praz, Mario *Studies in Seventeenth Century Imagery*, 2nd ed (Rome, 1964)

Redgrave, G. 'Daniel and the Emblem Literature,' *TBS*, 11 (1912), 39–58

Reichenberger, Kurt 'Das Schlangensymbol als Sinnbild von Zeit und Ewigkeit. Ein Beitrag zur Emblematik in der Literatur des 16. Jahrhunderts,' *ZrP*, 81 (1964), 346–51

Rosenfeld, Helmut *Das Deutsche Bildgedicht*, Palaestra, CIC (Leipzig, 1935)

Ross, Lawrence J. 'The Meaning of Strawberries in Shakespeare,' *SR*, 7 (1961), 225–40

Rusche, H.G. 'Two Proverbial Images in Whitney's "A Choice of Emblems" and Marlowe's "The Jew of Malta",' *N&Q*, n.s. 11 (1964), 261

Savage, H.L. 'Heraldry in Shakespeare,' *SQ*, 1 (1950), 286–91

Schindler, Marvin *The Sonnets of Andreas Gryphius. Use of the Poetic Word in the Seventeenth Century* (Gainesville, 1971)

Schleiner, Winfried *The Imagery of John Donne's Sermons* (Providence, 1970)

Scholte, J.H. *Der Simplicissimus und sein Dichter* (Tübingen, 1950)

Schöne, Albrecht *Emblematik und Drama im Zeitalter des Barock*, 2nd rev ed (Munich, 1968)

Schöne, Albrecht 'Hohburgs Psalter-Embleme,' *DVJs*, 44 (1970), 655–69

Scott, W.O. 'Another "Heroical Devise" in *Pericles*,' *SQ*, 20 (1969), 91–4

Scott-Giles, C. Wilfred *Shakespeare's Heraldry* (London, 1950)

Seeberg, Erich *Zur Frage der Mystik* (Leipzig, 1927)

Sharrock, Roger 'Bunyan and the English Emblem Writers,' *RES*, 21 (1945), 105–16

Shearman, John *Mannerism* (Harmondsworth, 1967)

Steadman, John M. 'Una and the Clergy: The Ass Symbol in *The Faerie Queene*,' *JWCI*, 21 (1958), 134–7

Steadman, John M. 'Spenser's House of Care: A Reinterpretation,' *SR*, 7 (1960), 207–24

Steadman, John M. 'Areopagitica and the Hieroglyphica of Goropius Becanus,' *N&Q*, n.s. 7 (1961), 181–2

Steadman, John M. 'Spenser's "Errour" and Renaissance Allegorical Tradition,' *NM*, 62 (1961), 22–38

Steadman, John M. 'Dalila, the Ulysses Myth, and the Renaissance Allegorical Tradition,' *MLR*, 57 (1962), 560–5

Steadman, John M. 'Falstaff as Actaeon: A Dramatic Emblem,' *SQ*, 14 (1963), 230–44

Stemper, Anneliese *Die Medaillen des Herzogs Heinrich Julius von Braunschweig=Wolfenbüttel und ihre Beziehungen zu den 'Emblemata' des Joachim Camerarius*, Arbeitsbericht aus dem Städtischen Museum Braunschweig, no. 8 (Braunschweig, 1955).

Sulzer, Dieter 'Zu einer Geschichte der Emblemtheorien,' *Euph*, 64 (1970), 23–50

Summers, J.H. *George Herbert: His Religion and Art* (London, 1954)

Tuve, Rosemond *Allegorical Imagery: Some Medieval Books and Their Posterity* (Princeton, 1966)

Vodosek, Peter 'Das Emblem in der deutschen Literatur der Renaissance und des Barock,' *Jahrbuch des Wiener Goethe-Vereins*, 68 (1964), 5–40

Volkmann, Ludwig *Bilderschriften der Renaissance, Hieroglyphik und Emblematik in ihren Beziehungen und Fortwirkungen* (Leipzig, 1923)

Walker, Saxon 'Mime and Heraldry in *Henry IV, Part I,*' *E,* 11 (1956), 91–6

Wallerstein, Ruth *Richard Crashaw. A Study in Style and Poetic Development* (Madison, 1935)

Warnock, Robert G., and Folter, Roland 'The German Pattern Poem: A Study in Mannerism of the Seventeenth Century,' in *Festschrift für Detlev W. Schumann Zum 70. Geburtstag,* ed R. Schmitt (Munich, 1970), pp 40–73

Warren, Austin *Richard Crashaw. A Study in Baroque Sensibility* (Baton Rouge, 1939)

Weydt, Günther *Nachahmung und Schöpfung im Barock. Studien um Grimmelshausen* (Bern/Munich, 1968)

Wheelwright, Philip *The Burning Fountain* (Bloomington, 1954)

Wickham, Glynne *Early English Stages* (London, 1959)

Widmer, Kingsley 'The Iconography of Renunciation: The Miltonic Simile,' *ELH,* 25 (1958), 258–69

Wilkenfield, Roger B. 'Act and Emblem: the Conclusion of *Samson Agonistes,*' *ELH,* 32 (1965), 160–8

Wind, Edgar *Pagan Mysteries in the Renaissance* (Harmondsworth, 1967)

Windfuhr, Manfred *Die barocke Bildlichkeit und ihre Kritiker. Stilhaltungen in der deutschen Literatur des 17. und 18. Jahrhunderts* (Stuttgart, 1966)

Wittkower, Rudolf 'Hieroglyphics in the Early Renaissance,' in *Developments in the Early Renaissance,* ed Bernard S. Levy (Albany, 1972), pp 58–97

Yates, Frances 'The Emblematic Conceit in Giordano Bruno's *De Gli Eroici Furori* and in the Elizabethan Sonnet Sequences,' *JWCI,* 6 (1943), 101–21

Ziemendorff, I. *Die Metaphor bei den weltlichen Lyrikern des deutschen Barock* (Berlin, 1931)

SELECTION OF WORKS IN ENGLISH
ON GERMAN BAROQUE LITERATURE

Browning, Robert B. *German Baroque Poetry 1618–1723* (Pennsylvania, 1971)

De Capua, A.G. *German Baroque Poetry, Interpretative Readings* (Albany, 1972)

Gillespie, Gerald *German Baroque Poetry* (New York, 1971)

Pascal, Roy, *German Literature in the Sixteenth and Seventeenth Centuries* (London, 1968)

RECENT COMPARATIVE STUDIES OF EUROPEAN LITERATURE
OF THE SIXTEENTH AND SEVENTEENTH CENTURIES

Krailsheimer, A.J., ed *The Continental Renaissance, 1500–1600* (Harmondsworth, England, 1971)

Segel, Harold B. *The Baroque Poem* (New York, 1974), pp 3–139.

Warnke, Frank J. *Versions of Baroque*. European Literature in the Seventeenth Century (New Haven/London, 1972)

TRANSLATIONS OF EUROPEAN POETRY OF THE SIXTEENTH
AND SEVENTEENTH CENTURIES

Priest, Harold Martin *Renaissance and Baroque Lyrics* (Chicago, 1962); contains a useful bibliography of collections of translations from Italian, Spanish, and French
Schoolfield, George C. *The German Lyric of the Baroque in English Translation* (Chapel Hill, 1961)
Segel, Harold B. *The Baroque Poem* (New York, 1974), pp 147–315
Warnke, Frank, J., *European Metaphysical Poetry* (New Haven, 1961)

Index of Names

Aeschylus 107
Alan of Lille 33, 42
Alberti, Leon Battista 16, 17, 25, 26
  illustration
Alciatus, Andreas 4, 6, 8–11, 12–13
  illustration, 17, 23, 36, 37 illustration,
  40, 51, 55, 56, 58, 63, 107, 127, 137,
  139
Allen, Don C. 59
Alpaugh, David J. 174
Aneau, Barthelemy 58, 137
Aptekar, Jane 65, 109–11
Aristotle 50, 184
Arndt, Johann 119
Augustine 17, 43, 46

Bacon, Roger 61
Balde, Jacob 63
Beachcroft, T.O. 46, 83, 86, 93, 114, 120
Benjamin, Walter 134, 143, 147, 177, 178
Bergeron, David 162, 163
Berthod, François 63
Bertonasco, Marc F. 33, 63, 64, 68, 72,
  73, 93, 95–7, 100
Bèze, Théodore de 141
Biggins, Dennis 61, 62
Birken, Sigmund von 99, 132

Blake, William x, 89, 118
Blount, Thomas 23, 25
Bosch, Hieronimus 139
Bowles, William Lisle 64
Bradbrook, Margaret 145, 146, 185
Brant, Sebastian 112
Brentano, Clemens x, 89, 90
Brown, C.C. 125
Bruck, Jakob von 59, 169
Bruno, Giordano 33, 106, 107
Bunker, Cameron F. 7
Bunyan, John 60, 61, 76, 168, 172, 174
Buwinghausen, Margaretha Maria
  von 76

Callahan, Virgina Woods 11
Camerarius, Joachim 23, 25, 27, 46, 55,
  60, 76, 77, 141, 156, 161, 162
Caussin, Nicolas 59
Chapman, George 156
Chew, Samuel 114
Church, Margaret 124
Cicero 17
Clement of Alexandria 15
Clements, Robert J. x
Coleridge, Samuel Taylor x, 64
Colonna, Francesco 17, 18 illustration

Coornhert, Dirk Volckertszoon 56
Copernicus 33
Coustau, Pierre 56
Cramer, Daniel 63, 66, 72, 73, 104
Crashaw, Richard 46, 63, 64, 68, 93,
    95–7, 100, 102–4, 120
Crompton, N.J.R. 27
Curtius, Ernst Robert 124
Cysarz, Herbert 119

Daniel, Samuel 57, 58, 83, 107, 108, 166
Defoe, Daniel 168, 169, 174, 175
Dekker, Thomas 145, 166
Demetz, Peter 55
Descartes 33
Dieckmann, Liselotte 16
Diodorus 15, 17
Doebler, John 104, 105
Donne, John 65, 91, 105, 106, 188
Drayton, Michael 106
Durant, Geoffrey 65
Dürer, Albrecht 17–19

Eichendorff, Josef Freiherr von x
Eichler, Else 80
Eliot, T.S. 185
Erasmus 11, 43
Estienne, Henri, Sieur de Fossez 23, 25,
    34, 35, 43, 79, 85

Fairchild, A.H.R. 55
Ficino, Marsilio 16
Fingesten, Peter 65
Fischart, Johann 5
Fleming, Paul 187
Folter, Roland 124, 127, 132
Fowler, A.D.S. 93, 109
Franciscus, Erasmus 34
Freeman, Rosemary 5, 9, 33, 39, 52, 57,
    70, 83–5, 88–9, 103, 114, 116–18, 125,
    150, 173, 186
Freytag, Hartmut 28
Fricke, Gerhard 81, 82, 119

Galileo 33
Gersch, Hubert 184
Giehlow, Karl 5, 8, 11, 81
Gilbert, Allan H. 59, 60
Giovio, Paulo 21, 22, 39, 79, 101, 102,
    154
Glauber, Johann Rudolf 34
Gloner, Samuel 83
Goethe, Johann Wolfgang von x, 87, 118,
    178
Goldman, Lloyd 57, 58, 83, 107, 108
Gordon, D.J. 144, 145, 164, 165
Green, Henry ix, 10, 55, 57, 82, 134
Greiffenberg, Catharina Regina von 176,
    187; Sonnette, Lieder und Gedichte 68,
    69, 70, 73, 79, 86, 87, 90, 94, 96–100,
    118, 130–1 illustration, 132, 133; ms
    poems 70, 72; Tugend–Ubung 78, 79;
    Leiden und Sterben CHRISTI 97, 100–1
Grimm, Reinhold 7, 50, 52
Grimmelshausen, Hans Jakob Christoffel
    von 58, 86, 168, 169, 170, 172, 175,
    176, 179–84, 181 illustration
Gryphius, Andreas 60, 71, 81, 90, 91,
    118, 119, 135, 140, 142, 159–62, 188
Günther, Johann Christian 101

Habicht, Werner 156
Haeften, Benedikt van 66, 68, 72, 73, 105
Hagstrum, Jean 22, 114, 138, 166
Hall, Joseph 76
Hallmann, Johann Christian 60, 135,
    149, 150
Harms, Wolfgang 5, 27, 28, 32–4
Harsdörffer, Georg Philipp 22, 39, 46, 82,

84, 86, 162; *Frauenzimmer Gespräch-spiele* 28, 32, 43, 71, 75, 77, 78, 92, 98, 99, 132, 180
Haugwitz, August Adolph von 60
Heckman, John 177, 178, 179
Heckscher, William S. 5–7, 9, 27, 31–3, 38, 55
Heilman, Robert B. 142, 143
Helwig, Johann 127
Henkel, Arthur 138
Herbert, George 39, 84, 114, 125, 126 *illustration*, 176, 186
Herder, Johann Gottfried 185
Herodotus 15
Hocke, Gustav René 5, 51
Hofmannswaldau, Hoffman von 65, 120, 121, 122
Höltgen, Karl Josef 105, 106
Holtzwart, Mathias 5
Homann, Holger 112
Hoole, W.S. 56
Horace 185
Horapollo 8, 11, 14–18, 59, 79, 85
Hough, G. 83
Hoyle, James 139, 148
Hughes, Thomas 152
Hunter, Paul J. 168, 169, 174, 175

Ingoldsby, W.P. 125
Isselburg, Peter 60
Iversen, Erik 11, 14, 15, 20

Jacobsen, Eric 62, 63
Johnson, Edward D. 56
Jolles, André 54
Jones, Inigo 166
Jöns, Dietrich Walter 5–7, 9, 38, 42, 83, 127; *Das 'Sinnen-Bild.' Studien zur allegorischen Bildlichkeit bei Andreas Gryphius* 18, 21, 22, 25, 32, 33, 35, 36,

51–3, 86, 119; 'Emblematisches bei Grimmelshausen' 58, 59, 169–72
Jonson, Ben 59, 60, 144, 145, 157, 164–6

Kayser, Wolfgang 83
Keil, Anna 81, 82, 114
Kircher, Athanasius 18, 20
Klaj, Johann 124
Kornfeld, Theodor 127, 128–9 *illustration*, 132

Lausberg, Heinrich 4
Lederer, Joseph 83
Ledesma, Alonso de 75
Lohenstein, Daniel Caspar von 60, 135, 141, 147
Löwenhalt, Rompler von 81, 82, 114
Lucan 15

Magnus, Albertus 46
Maier, Michael 4
Mannich, Johann 66
Männling, Johann Christoph 127
Marino, Giambattista 103
Marlowe, Christopher 102, 153, 154
Marvell, Andrew 88, 89
Mayer, Gerhart 183
Mazzeo, Joseph 51
Mehl, Dieter 54, 134, 136, 145, 146, 148–52, 157, 159
Meisner, Daniel 6
Middleton, Thomas 56, 57
Miedema, Hessel 7
Mignault, Claude 10, 63
Milton, John 68, 108, 112
Monroy, Ernst Friedrich von 81
Montenay, Georgette de 47 *illustration*, 66, 67 *illustration*
More, Henry 40

Mourgues, Odette de 95
Mulhauser, Ruth 111, 112

Nashe, John 102
Nicoll, Allardyce 166, 167

Ohly, Friedrich 38
Opitz, Martin 55, 73, 74, 187
Oppel, Horst 137, 138, 154

Palladius 59
Pallavicino 51
Panofsky, Erwin 5, 6, 18, 64
Paradin, Claude 23, 24 illustration, 151
Parker, A.A. 172
Peacham, Henry 28, 30 illustration, 31, 32, 62, 163
Penkert, Sibylle 5, 7, 80, 176, 180, 181, 183, 184
Perrière, Guillaume de la 46, 48–9 illustration, 55
Picinelli, Filippo 59
Pirckheimer, Willibald 17, 18
Plato 15, 184
Pliny 15, 34, 85
Plotinus 15
Plutarch 15
Pongs, Hermann 80, 83
Praz, Mario ix, 4–6, 8, 9, 18, 21–3, 32, 42, 55, 75, 82, 83, 106, 150

Quarles, Francis 39, 60, 61, 84, 105, 106

Reimann, Jakob Friedrich 113
Reusner, Nicolas 23, 56, 58, 139
Ripa, Caesar 59, 60, 144, 164
Rollenhagen, Gabriel x, 25
Rosenfeld, Helmut 9, 182

Saavedra Fajardo, Diego de 60

Sambucus, Joannes 76, 137
Saubert, Johann 59
Scève, Maurice 111, 112
Scholte, Jan Hendrik 183
Schöne, Albrecht x, 5, 6, 50, 53, 58, 79, 83, 127, 134, 138, 177–9; Emblematik und Drama im Zeitalter des Barock ix, 6, 9, 14, 15, 21–3, 32–4, 36, 38–40, 42, 55, 60, 70, 74, 93, 94, 101, 102, 140–3, 147, 149, 150, 162, 163, 164
Schoonhovius, Florentius 141
Scriver, Johann 76, 80
Seeberg, Erich 80–2
Shaftesbury, Third Earl of 185
Shakespeare, William 55, 56, 61, 62, 104, 134, 136–9, 142–6, 148, 149, 154–6, 158, 159, 171
Sharrock, Roger 60, 61, 83
Shearman, John 54
Sidney, Sir Philip 102, 106, 107
Silesius, Angelus 122, 123
Southwell, Robert 99, 104
Spee von Langenfeld, Friedrich 62, 63
Spenser, Edmund 63, 93, 108–11
Stabius 18
Steadman, John M. 63, 136, 137
Stegemeier, Henri 3, 5, 8, 28
Stubenberg, Johann Wilhelm 69
Sudermann, Daniel 83
Sulzer, Dieter 5, 7, 22, 23, 25, 46, 54, 65

Taurellus, Nicolaus 25, 34, 40, 41 illustration, 76
Tesauro, Emmanuelle 50, 51
Thompson, Elbert N.S. 5
Tourneur, Cyril 153, 159
Typotius, Jakob 60, 71

Valerianus, Pierius 18, 59, 109
Vaughan, Henry 88, 89, 103, 116

Veen, Otto van x
Verstegen, Richard 114
Vodosek, Peter 83
Volkmann, Ludwig 5, 8, 11, 14, 18, 81
Vries, Anne Gerard Christian de 6

Walker, Saxon 139
Wallerstein, Ruth 83, 102–4
Warnock, Robert G. 124, 127, 132
Warren, Austin 71, 83
Webster, John 153
Weckherlin, Georg Rudolf 187
Weydt, Günther 180
Wheelwright, Philip 4
Whitney, Geoffrey 57, 58, 60, 61, 63,
    127, 137, 139, 151, 163
Wickham, Glynne 134, 145, 155, 162
Widmer, Kingsley 68, 112

Wiedemann, Conrad 124
Wilkenfield, Roger B. 108
Wimsatt, W.K. 64, 65
Wind, Edgar 43
Windfuhr, Manfred 113, 114, 118
Wirth, Karl-August 5, 6, 7, 9, 27, 31, 32,
    33, 38, 55
Wither, George x, 44–5 illustration, 60,
    61, 116–18
Wittkower, Rudolf 17, 25
Wölfflin, Heinrich 23
Wordsworth, William x, 65

Yates, Frances 106, 107

Zesen, Philipp von x, 63, 127
Ziemendorff, Ingeborg 119
Zincgref, Julius Wilhelm 32, 59, 171, 172

Index of Emblem Motifs

(including personifications, biblical and classical figures used as motifs)

Aaron 145
Actaeon 56–8, 136, 137
adder 141
Aeneas 56
Affections 164, 165
altar 125, 164
ambergris 70
anchor 17, 25, 65, 102, 115. See also
    dolphin and anchor, golden 173
Anima. See Cupid and
anvil. See hammer and
apple 58, 86, 175
Arithmetic 144
ark of the heart 73
Arrogance 135
arrow 157
ass 83, 183

ball 135
basilisk 18
bear 14, 35
bear and storm 61–2
beaver 15
bee 14, 16
bee and rose 73, 74
bees and spiders 59, 169
bellows 106

black 144, 145
black man 173
blood 43, 64, 65, 99
blue 31, 87, 144, 164
book 182, 183
branches 73, 111, 137, 138
breasts and suckling 64, 96
bridle 109, 157
Brutus 146
bull 15, 18, 59, 170

Cadmus 36
candle 106, 156
cedar 96, 97, 138, 153
chain 78, 79
chain, golden 157, 165
chicken 61, 173
circle 16, 17
coach (in shape of cross) 69
cock 18
compass 104, 105
compasses 105, 135
corn 76, 77
corpse 147
crane 15, 18
crocodile 15, 110, 111
crocodile's teeth 34

cross 66, 68, 69, 77
cross, pattern poem 77, 132
crown 18, 75, 77, 99
crucible 68, 90
crystal 79
Cupid and Anima 64
cushion 148

dagger 159
Desire 157
dew 18, 103, 123
diamond 42, 43, 142
dog 14, 18, 99, 111
dolphin 17
dolphin and anchor 25, 79
dove 77, 104
duck 182, 183

eagle 18, 21, 25, 27, 28, 39, 78, 182
eagle and mole 70, 75
earthquake 175
'Easter-Wings' 125
eel 14
egg 77
elder-tree 156
elephant 14
Envy 111, 135, 163
Eris 163
ermine 25
Eschyia 144
Europa 163
eye 16, 17. See also winged eye
eye and sceptre 14

falcon 14
falcon on the orb 18
Fame 58
feet 18
fire 58, 61, 66, 68, 99, 108, 173, 175. See
    also salamander in

fire and water 14
fish 65
flame 161
fleurs-de-lis 28
flint 114
flower 169, 170
flower bulbs 59, 172
fly 113
flying fish 154
forget-me-not flower 87
Fortuna 58, 146
Fortune 135, 163
fountain 99
frog 76
frankincense 96

garden, enclosed 65
glass 91
glass ball 135
globe 60
goat 15, 43, 182
goblet 127
gold 31, 89–91, 99, 109, 122. See also
    anchor, golden; chain, golden
goose 14, 15
grafting 27, 138
Greed 163
green 87

halcyon 144
hammer 65, 106, 161
hammer and anvil 106
hare 14, 27, 46, 139
hawk 14, 17
heart 66, 73, 103. See also name written
    in a heart; roses growing out of a heart
heart in a nest of thorns 71, 72
Hercules 11, 36, 58, 109, 111
hill 155
hippopotamus hooves 14

holm oak 59
horn 153
horse 109
horse's carcass 15
hourglass 127
Humours 164, 165
Hypocrisy 163

ibis 14
Icarus 36
incense 34, 100
iron 78, 79
ivy 39, 74

Justice 163

kingfisher 144
knife 148

lamp 59, 144, 164, 170, 171
laurel 70, 75, 95
lead 122
level 144
levelling instrument 106
lightning 175
lily 31, 72
lion 15, 18, 28, 32, 43, 84, 99, 110, 139
lodestone 78

marigold 116–18
Mars 98
mask 182
Medea 36, 50
medlar 153
mole. See eagle and
moon 139
mortar and rammer 106
mountain 175
muckrake 61, 173
Murder 146
myrrh 97

name written in a heart 62, 63
Narcissus 58
Nemesis 58
nest 144
Nile 95, 96
Noah's ark 73
nut-tree 127, 132

oak 155, 171
oak and palm 156
oil 123, 170, 171, 173
olive 73
opportunity 56
Orpheus 56
ox 14, 16
oyster 70, 123

palm 70, 73, 88, 102, 127, 140, 183. See
    also oak and
palm wine 175
papyrus bundle 15, 18
Paris 36
Passion 61
Patience 61
Peace 163
pearl 74, 123
Pegasus 56
pelican 15, 98, 152
phallus 65
phoenix 15, 21, 23, 25, 35, 69, 85, 108,
    182, 183
pilgrim 60
pitcher 76
plum tree 153
pomegranate 75, 86, 175
porcupine 99
Prometheus 58, 107, 198

rammer. See mortar and
Rape 146

Reason 144, 157, 164, 165
red 158
Revenge 146
rhinoceros 99
robin and spider 61
rock 94, 98, 99, 113
rock of virtue 70, 135
rose 27, 97, 158, 161. *See also* bee and
rose and thorn 74, 99, 171
rose en soleil 139
roses growing out of a heart 72
rudder (in shape of cross) 69

saffron 55
salamander 15, 25
salamander in fire 21
salt 86, 87
satyr 182, 184
scales 148
sceptre 70. *See also* eye and
sea 114, 115, 175
serpent 18, 46
setsquare 109
sextant 105
shield 28
ship 114, 115
ship's masts 69
Sisyphus 58
skull 65, 148, 158, 159
snake 18, 43, 135, 140, 141, 159
snake biting tail 15, 16
spark 114
spider 61, 169, 173. *See also* bees and;
    robin and
stag 21, 137, 153
stag's head 137
star 18, 105, 144, 164
steel 69, 114
sticks, bundle of 151

stone 98, 175
stone of the cross 69
stork 15, 144
storm 114, 115. *See also* bear and
suckling. *See* breasts and
sun 27, 69, 116, 119, 135, 139
sunburst 139
sun clouded 139, 140
sunflower 27, 99
sun in splendour 139
sun's rays 79, 110
swan 182, 183
sword 110, 144, 161, 164, 182
syringe 157

Tantalus 36
taper 156
tears 118
thorn 86, 97. *See also* heart in a nest of
    thorns
thorny bush 69
thunder 175
thunderbolts 110
tiger 98, 141
time 163
torch 100, 106, 156
tree 27, 59, 111, 155, 184

unicorn 84

Venus 98
vulture 14–16, 58, 107

water 61
water and wine 109
waterfall 116
wave 70, 135
wheel 65
wheelcross 65
white 144, 158, 164

wick 123
wine. *See* water and
wine press 69, 113
wing 135
winged eye 25

winter 135
woman 104
wounds 64, 97

yew 156

P9-CRY-781

LEADERSHIP AT THE CROSSROADS

LEADERSHIP AT
THE CROSSROADS

Joanne B. Ciulla, Set Editor

Volume 1

Leadership and Psychology

Edited by Crystal L. Hoyt, George R. Goethals,
and Donelson R. Forsyth

Praeger Perspectives

PRAEGER

Westport, Connecticut
London

Library of Congress Cataloging-in-Publication Data

Leadership at the crossroads.
   v. cm.
  Includes bibliographical references and index.
  Contents: v. 1. Leadership and psychology / edited by Crystal L. Hoyt,
  George R. Goethals, and Donelson R. Forsyth – v. 2. Leadership and politics / edited by
  Michael A. Genovese and Lori Cox Han – v. 3. Leadership and the humanities /
  edited by Joanne B. Ciulla.
  ISBN 978-0-275-99760-1 ((set) : alk. paper) – ISBN 978-0-275-99762-5 ((vol. 1) :
  alk. paper) – ISBN 978-0-275-99764-9 ((vol. 2) : alk. paper) – ISBN 978-0-275-99766-3
  ((vol. 3) : alk. paper)
  1. Leadership. I. Forsyth, Donelson R., 1953-
HM1261.L422 2008
303.3′4—dc22   2008018976

British Library Cataloguing in Publication Data is available.

Library of Congress Catalog Card Number: 2008018976
ISBN: Set: 978-0-275-99760-1
    Vol. 1: 978-0-275-99762-5
    Vol. 2: 978-0-275-99764-9
    Vol. 3: 978-0-275-99766-3

First published in 2008

Praeger Publishers, 88 Post Road West, Westport, CT 06881
An imprint of Greenwood Publishing Group, Inc.
www.praeger.com

Printed in the United States of America

The paper used in this book complies with the
Permanent Paper Standard issued by the National
Information Standards Organization (Z39.48–1984).

10 9 8 7 6 5 4 3 2 1

Contents

Preface   ix

Introduction: A Contemporary Social Psychology of Leadership   1
Crystal L. Hoyt, George R. Goethals, and Donelson R. Forsyth

Part I. The Personal Characteristics of Leaders   11

1. Personality and Leadership   13
Stephen J. Zaccaro, Lisa M. V. Gulick, and Vivek P. Khare

2. Social Psychology and Charismatic Leadership   30
Ronald E. Riggio and Heidi R. Riggio

3. Knocking on Heaven's Door: The Social Psychological Dynamics   45
of Charismatic Leadership
Sheldon Solomon, Florette Cohen, Jeff Greenberg, and Tom Pyszczynski

4. Social Identity Theory of Leadership   62
Michael A. Hogg

5. Emotional Intelligence and Leadership: Implications for Leader   78
Development
Paulo N. Lopes and Peter Salovey

Part II. Perceiving Leaders   99

6. Social Cognitive Perspectives on Leadership   101
   Tiane L. Lee and Susan T. Fiske

7. Seeing and Being a Leader: The Perceptual, Cognitive, and   116
   Interpersonal Roots of Conferred Influence
   Donelson R. Forsyth and Judith L. Nye

8. Presidential Greatness and its Socio-Psychological Significance: 132
   Individual or Situation? Performance or Attribution?
   Dean Keith Simonton

9. The Unbearable Lightness of Debating: Performance Ambiguity   149
   and Social Influence
   Matthew B. Kugler and George R. Goethals

10. Social Stigma and Leadership: A Long Climb Up a Slippery   165
    Ladder
    Crystal L. Hoyt and Martin M. Chemers

11. Deifying the Dead and Downtrodden: Sympathetic Figures as   181
    Inspirational Leaders
    Scott T. Allison and George R. Goethals

Part III. What Leaders Do   197

12. Persuasion and Leadership   199
    James M. Olson and Graeme A. Haynes

13. What it Takes to Succeed: An Examination of the Relationship   213
    Between Negotiators' Implicit Beliefs and Performance
    Laura J. Kray and Michael P. Haselhuhn

14. Presidential Leadership and Group Folly: Reappraising the Role   230
    of Groupthink in the Bay of Pigs Decisions
    Roderick M. Kramer

15. Self-Regulation and Leadership: Implications for Leader   250
    Performance and Leader Development
    Susan Elaine Murphy, Rebecca J. Reichard, and Stefanie K. Johnson

Part IV. Interactions between Leaders and Followers   265

16. Evolution and the Social Psychology of Leadership: 267
    The Mismatch Hypothesis
    *Mark Van Vugt, Dominic D. P. Johnson, Robert B. Kaiser,
    and Rick O'Gorman*

17. Harnessing Power to Capture Leadership   283
    Adam D. Galinsky, Jennifer Jordan, and Niro Sivanathan

Contents

vii

18. Morality as a Foundation of Leadership and a Constraint on
    Deference to Authority   300
    Linda J. Skitka, Christopher W. Bauman, and Brad L. Lytle

About the Editor and Contributors   315

Index   325

Preface

The spring of 2006 found the three of us ensconced as a cabal of social psychologists in a school dedicated to the study of leadership: the Jepson School of Leadership Studies at the University of Richmond. Crystal had joined the faculty in 2003 fresh from her graduate studies at UC Santa Barbara. Don took the Colonel Leo K. and Gaylee Thorsness Chair in Ethical Leadership in the fall of 2005 after long service at Virginia Commonwealth University. Then, in the spring of 2006, Al left Williams College to join the group as the E. Claiborne Robins Distinguished Chair. Different in backgrounds and research interests, we shared a social psychologically framed perspective on leadership.

As a trio, we constituted a sizeable coalition of like-minded leadership scholars in our new academic home. With 12 professors, we comprised a quarter of the faculty. The Jepson School of Leadership Studies is dedicated to the study of leadership, interdisciplinary education, and the liberal arts. The faculty in this intellectually vibrant school hail from a number of traditional disciplines (e.g., philosophy, political science, history, religion, English, economics), and together explore fundamental questions about who we are, how we live together, and how we influence the course of history. As new colleagues in this school of leadership studies, we knew three things for certain: First, most of what social psychologists study is related to our understanding of leadership. Second, the connections between social psychology and leadership needed to be made more apparent. Third, the three of us wanted to work collaboratively on a project to such ends. It was at this auspicious moment that our colleague, Joanne Ciulla, a philosopher at Jepson, approached us about contributing a volume on social psychology and leadership to the Praeger set *Leadership at the Crossroads.* We jumped on the opportunity.

The result is that 41 social psychologists, including ourselves, have contributed 19 chapters on the intersection of leadership and social psychology. The chapters revolve around the following four themes: the characteristics of leaders, people's perceptions of leaders, what leaders do, and the interaction between leaders and followers. Our collective goal in this volume was to communicate not only to our social psychology colleagues but also to a larger audience of social scientists, well-read laypersons, and advanced undergraduate students who are interested in leadership but who may not know very much about social psychology and how it can inform that interest. The chapters in our book integrate conceptual approaches to leadership, but they stress the importance of empirical evidence in evaluating theoretical understandings. Thus, our goal was not to offer another "airport book" (a book, often purchased when one is stuck on a layover in an airport, typically written by a former leader who draws largely on personal experience to pontificate about leadership) full of unsubstantiated claims about leadership, but rather an accessible book with claims that are backed up with empirical evidence.

The process of editing this book has been invigorating. Merely choosing the topics we should include in the book reaffirmed our belief that issues of leadership are at the heart of most research in social psychology. The process of editing this volume has also provided us opportunities both to reconnect with old friends and to make new ones. It has also given the three of us an opportunity to strengthen our own bonds—with the added benefit of instilling fear in our leadership colleagues about what happens when the "three social psychologists" meet behind closed doors.

We owe a debt of gratitude to many individuals who have helped us in this process. Joanne Ciulla's wide-ranging understanding of leadership prompted her to consider social psychology as a source of insights, and she secured the relationship with our publisher. We never would have undertaken this project without her support and her leadership. We also recognize and appreciate the leadership of the Jepson School, including former Dean Kenneth Ruscio (now president of Washington and Lee) and our new dean, Sandra Peart, who have worked to create an amazing configuration of scholars dedicated to leadership. Tammy Tripp was instrumental in the final stages of the project, patiently and cheerfully providing the editorial guidance needed to turn our rough manuscript pages into clean copy. We also thank Tom

Matthews, Robert Jepson, and the Robins family whose vision and support provided us with the means to join together to pursue our studies of leaders and leadership.

Finally, on a more personal note, we also thank our families and loved ones for tolerating our need to sneak away from time to time to work on these chapters. This project has been more fun for us than for them. We appreciate their support and understanding.

Introduction: A Contemporary Social Psychology of Leadership

CRYSTAL L. HOYT, GEORGE R. GOETHALS, AND
DONELSON R. FORSYTH

From its inception as a distinct discipline devoted to the scientific study of how people influence and are influenced by others, social psychology has explored the nature of leadership. After noting the origins of leadership research in the work of such early theorists as Le Bon, Freud, and Lewin, we discuss the four key themes addressed in this volume: (1) the characteristics of the leader; (2) people's perceptions of their leaders or their potential leaders; (3) what it is that leaders actually do; and (4) the nature of the interaction between leaders and followers.

No one discipline can claim the analysis of leadership as its sovereign dominion, but social psychology's emphasis on the scientific study of how people influence and respond to the influence of others makes it entirely appropriate that a collection of chapters written by the best minds in that field should stand beside ones examining leadership from the humanities on the one hand and political science on the other. Social psychology has much to say about leadership, hence its inclusion in the interdisciplinary Praeger set *Leadership at the Crossroads*.

How has the social psychological study of leadership evolved over the years? When psychology and social psychology emerged from philosophy as distinctive disciplines in the late nineteenth century, leadership was a central concern for many in the field of social psychology. Allport (1968, p. 1), writing in his classic historical analysis of social psychology, noted that the field's intellectual ancestors were the political philosophers who understood that "governments must conform to the nature of the men governed." Thomas Hobbes, John Locke, David Hume, Jean-Jacques Rousseau, and other social philosophers speculated about the nature of humans and their societies, but it remained for the emerging social sciences—economics, sociology, psychology, social psychology, political science, and anthropology—to seek out data to test the validity of their conjectures. For example, Le Bon in his 1895 book *Psychologie des Foules* described the way leaders can hold sway over individuals who have been transformed by their membership in a mob or crowd. Wilhelm Wundt, the recognized founder of scientific psychology, turned his attention in the early 1900s to the study of Volkerpsychologie, which included within it substantial conceptual material pertaining to leadership, particularly with regards to the subordination of the individual to the will of the leader. One of the first textbooks in social psychology, Ross's (1908) *Social Psychology,* included detailed discussions of the heroic leader and the leader with natural authority, as did Allport's classic 1924 text. Freud (1921), although known primarily for his work on personality and psychodynamics, provided a provocative theoretical perspective on leadership in his *Group Psychology and the Analysis of Ego.*

As the field matured, journals began to carry research reports with such titles as "The social psychology of leadership" (Bartlett, 1926), "Psychology, leadership, and democracy" (Tait, 1927), and "A psychological description of leadership" (Nafe, 1930), and some of the new field's most iconic studies focused on leadership. This gradual increase in research was underscored by the 1939 publication of the classic work of Lewin, Lippitt, and White, which examined the consequences of different styles of leadership on productivity and satisfaction. In light of this early work, editions of the *Handbook of Social Psychology* and the highly influential series on *Readings in Social Psychology* from the 1940s and 1950s accorded leadership a significant place in the overall concerns of the discipline.

In recent decades, leadership has been upstaged as a topic of concern among social psychologists, but this respite is now over. Social psychologists' renewed interest in leadership points to the centrality of the topic in a field dedicated to understanding processes of social influence. The essays collected here show that many of the finest scholars in social psychology are exploring leadership and its connection to such central topics as attitudes and social cognition, group dynamics and interpersonal processes, and personality and individual differences. We also include chapters that look at leadership from such relatively new perspectives as evolutionary social psychology, terror management theory, emotional intelligence, and social identity theory. In sum, we are delighted to include here contributions illuminating leadership from the most distinguished scholars doing work in the most central areas of the discipline of social psychology.

The chapters lend themselves to a variety of organizational schemes, depending on the readers' interests and orientation, but we have settled on an approach that pays homage to the earliest social psychological studies of leadership: (1) the characteristics of the leader; (2) people's perceptions of their leaders or their potential leaders; (3) what it is that leaders actually do; and (4) the nature of the interaction between leaders and followers. Most of our chapters fall clearly into one of these four categories. Those by Zaccaro, Gulick, and Khare; by Riggio and Riggio; and by Hogg, for example, discuss various leader qualities, such as charisma and prototypicality, that affect both their emergence as leaders and their success as leaders. Lee and Fiske and Forsyth and Nye deal squarely with perceptions of leaders, and concepts such as implicit theories of leadership. And so forth. On the other hand, some chapters may have required a bit of forcing to fit into one of the groupings. Kramer's chapter on "group folly," for example, touches on several themes, but pays particularly close attention to the intricacy of leader-follower interactions. Having been as sensible as we could about organizing the book, let us provide an overview of what follows.

THE PERSONAL CHARACTERISTICS OF LEADERS

Freud (1921), in his seminal analysis of leadership, said that groups crave leadership and the strong exercise of authority, and that this need carries the group "half-way to meet the leader, yet he too must fit in with it in his personal qualities." Five of our chapters consider these personal qualities. Zaccaro, Gulick, and Khare ask a very old question—is leadership determined by one's personality?—but offer a very new set of answers. Although for many years experts maintained that there is no such thing as a "born leader"—that is, that temperament and personality are unrelated to leadership—more sophisticated approaches that recognize the interaction of personality and situational factors reach a different conclusion. New research designs allow investigators to differentiate the effects of various personality factors from background causes, resulting in clearer estimates of the strength of the personality-leadership relationship.

The chapters by Riggio and Riggio and by Solomon, Cohen, Greenberg, and Pyszczynski address aspects of a leaders' charisma. The Riggios consider the characteristics of charismatic leaders but also how group dynamics and attribution processes affect perceptions of charismatic leadership. Charisma therefore has a great deal to do with personal qualities, but even more to do with perception and interaction within the group. Solomon and his colleagues use their terror management theory to explain the allure of charismatic leaders. According to terror management theory, people manage the potential terror invoked by awareness of one's mortality by reaffirming a belief in a meaningful worldview and one's place in that world. Accordingly, people follow charismatic leaders because these leaders make them feel like a valued part of something great. The authors provide empirical evidence supporting this motivational account of the appeal of charismatic leaders.

Hogg's chapter explores the identity functions of leadership, and in so doing introduces the importance of group members' prototypicality, or the extent to which, in Freud's terms, they possess "the typical qualities of the individuals concerned in a particularly clearly marked and pure form." His social identity theory-based approach maintains that as membership in a group or category becomes more important to one's sense of self, one is more influenced by group members, or leaders, who best embody the prototypical qualities of the group. Highly prototypical leaders have an effectiveness advantage over less prototypical leaders because they are well-liked, they are influential and gain compliance from followers, they earn their followers' trust, they are perceived as charismatic, and they are in a position to be both innovative and maintain their prototypicality.

Lopes and Salovey, in the final chapter dealing with personal qualities, consider the importance of a newly studied individual capacity, "emotional intelligence." Emotional intelligence consists of a number of closely related abilities, namely the abilities: (1) to perceive accurately one's own and others' emotions; (2) to understand how emotions influence cognition and behavior; (3) to use emotions to stimulate thinking; and (4) to manage our own emotions and those of others. Lopes and Salovey clarify the importance of emotional intelligence in leadership, and how developing emotional intelligence contributes to the development of effective leadership.

PERCEIVING LEADERS

As Kurt Lewin aptly noted, "social action no less than physical action is steered by perception" (Lewin, 1997, p. 51). Indeed, leadership has long been considered to principally exist in the eye, or the mind, of the beholder. Le Bon, Freud, and other early scholars in social psychology believed that people's perceptions of leaders are complicated. Most are drawn to group members who match their expectations of what a leader should be, even if that image suggests the leader may be despotic or motivated by a desire to control others. These notions have evolved into concepts of implicit leadership theories or leader schemas, which are the focus of chapters by Lee and Fiske and Forsyth and Nye. These authors help us begin to examine the perceptual and cognitive processes that help both leaders and followers interpret the nature of their joint social situation. Both chapters view people as processors of information who continually seek data about important others. This cognitive perspective assumes that people search for information that will help them understand the motives, actions, and emotions of others, and that they organize the clues they have available to them from their perceptions and their memories. Lee and Fiske provide an introduction to the importance of mental representations in the leadership process. Their general overview of social cognition focuses on three mental representations that are key in person perception: schemas, prototypes, and exemplars. They then demonstrate that, although leader perceptions vary across contexts, there are two main dimensions that underlie most leader images: competence and warmth. Forsyth and Nye extend this analysis by asking if people's cognitive expectations about leaders substantially influence the veridicality of their social inferences. They find that people's personal theories about leaders exert a strong influence in leadership situations, and that these cognitive schemas affect people's thinking about leaders across a wide variety of cultures and contexts.

Leader schemas also play an important conceptual role in Simonton's chapter on perceptions of presidential greatness. Simonton's work suggests that in rating U.S. presidents supposedly expert historians use many of the same implicit theories of leadership as laypeople, and that both groups are highly influenced by salient information, such as whether there was a scandal during a president's term. Simonton further suggests that situational rather than personal variables account for many of these ratings. For example, presidents who were assassinated tend to get favorable ratings. While this finding certainly points toward the impact of situations, there is an intriguing relationship between a personal variable, need for power, and assassination. Simonton unravels the complexities of historians' judgments in some of the familiar terms of social cognition.

Kugler and Goethals also consider what we might call political social cognition. Their research on assessments of performance in presidential and vice-presidential debates suggests that a large number of personal and situational variables combine and interact to affect viewers' perceptions. Most impressive, perhaps, is the extent to which those perceptions are influenced by the opinions of others. Their findings suggest that debates are often quite ambiguous, and different people's performance appraisals are affected in subtly different ways by what they learn from both peers and pundits.

A chapter by Hoyt and Chemers addresses the unique experiences of nondominant, or stigmatized, leaders such as women and minorities. It begins with the problem that leader schemas or prototypes are typically male and typically of a socially dominant race/ethnicity. They examine how people respond to and perceive stigmatized leaders as well as the experiences of those leaders themselves. Negative stereotypes of individuals based on skin color, gender, or other devaluing characteristics are incompatible with expectations of effective leadership and can result in negative judgments by others. Additionally, members of stigmatized groups are fully aware of these stereotyped expectations, and their awareness often influences the way they behave, both negatively and positively, and the attributions they make in leadership positions.

Even though individuals tend to more strongly endorse leaders who match their personal beliefs about what makes for good leadership, their emotions and motivations can also prompt them to throw their support behind one type of leader and not another. In their chapter, Allison and Goethals review findings that suggest followers who feel sympathy, adoration, or concern for a leader tend to support that leader. These emotional foundations of leadership endorsement extend, for example, to underdog leaders who must overcome significant obstacles on their way to office or position. Similarly, and perhaps more surprisingly, followers are also more positive toward leaders after they have died, particularly if they were martyrs for a noble cause.

WHAT LEADERS DO

Social psychologists, skeptical of the principles of leadership so frequently offered by sages and self-proclaimed experts, early on sought to distinguish between prescriptive, normative analyses of leadership and descriptive, data-based analyses of leadership. Those studies of what leaders actually do as they strive to guide, organize, and inspire others suggest that leadership is more than just the traditional duality of socioemotional work and initiating structure. The role of leader is a multifaceted one, for one must be able to persuade others, make decisions, resolve conflicts, and effectively regulate oneself.

Freud (1921) emphasized that the most influential leaders had great faith in an idea and were able to articulate it in a way that appealed primarily to people's emotions. He wrote of "the truly magical power of words" and that while those words needed to use powerful images, they did not need to appeal to rationality. He articulated one of the most powerful principles of persuasion, repetition: the leader "must repeat the same thing again and again." In accord with this emphasis on oratory, Olson and Haynes open this section with their look at leadership and persuasion. Their discussion of the attitude change literature relevant to leadership certainly points to the importance of nonrational factors in persuasion, particularly the idea that much of persuasion happens through the less deliberative "peripheral route" rather than the more thoughtful "central route." On the other hand, they argue that using strong, cogent, and clear arguments is the leader's most effective path to persuasion. They also point to the personal characteristics that make leaders maximally effective, including charisma, likability, poise, and self-assurance.

Although Freud focused on persuasion, he also understood the importance of perceptions of justice in effective leadership. For example, he discussed the idea that the leader had to foster an illusion of fairness, that is, that he loved "all the individuals in the group with an equal love" so that rivalries among followers would not disrupt the group, or induce them to challenge the leader. In effect, leaders had to be skillful negotiators. John F. Kennedy reminded us of this critical element of leadership when he asserted "let us never negotiate out of fear. But let us never fear to negotiate." Kray and Haselhuhn contribute a chapter on negotiation as a critical skill in leadership, and emphasize the cognitive underpinnings of effective negotiation. They explore the importance of negotiator beliefs in determining negotiation effectiveness. Such beliefs include conceptions of the resource pool as fixed or expandable, whether an issue is even thought to be negotiable, and people's implicit beliefs about the traits needed to be an effective negotiator. Kray and Haselhuhn discuss their research examining the importance of implicit negotiation beliefs about whether negotiators are born (fixed ability) or made (malleable ability). Their work resonates with the age-old question of whether leaders are born or made. (We think the short answer is, both.)

Social psychologists have made a number of important contributions to our understanding of group decision-making processes and the role of leaders in those processes. Notably, Irving Janis's concept of *groupthink* has made a substantial impact on the field. Kramer's chapter reconsiders the role of groupthink in President John F. Kennedy's decision making leading to the Bay of Pigs fiasco during the first three months of his administration. Recent documents suggest that groupthink was less a dynamic in the covert plan to overthrow Castro's regime in Cuba than Kennedy's own political calculations and the ability of advisers in various agencies, including the CIA and the military, to manipulate Kennedy by playing on his political concerns. Kramer's work suggests that in the aftermath Kennedy understood that his own way of thinking was ultimately responsible for the decision to proceed with the operation. Furthermore, it suggests that Kennedy's awareness that he was "the responsible officer of the government" during the operation led to him being much more thoughtful about decision making during the Cuban missile crisis a year and a half later.

The first three chapters of this section emphasize behaviors leaders engage in with others: persuasion, negotiation, and decision making. The final chapter in this section speaks to the importance of leaders' self-oriented behaviors. Effective leadership demands both the motivation and capacity for effective self-regulation. Murphy, Reichard, and Johnson focus on this often overlooked aspect of leader behavior. They begin with a consideration of how leaders' own self-perceptions affect their behavior and demonstrate the importance of using theories of the self, such as self-schema or identity theories, in understanding leader effectiveness. Their primary focus becomes the relationship of Bandura's notion of self-regulation to the domain of leadership and the significant roles of leadership self-efficacy, self-management, and self-awareness in effecting more constructive leader behavior. Finally, they examine leader self-development through the lens of self-regulation techniques.

INTERACTIONS BETWEEN LEADERS AND FOLLOWERS

Freud once more is the source of insightful ideas about the relative power of the leader to exert influence over others. In some cases, he suggested, when followers are transformed into the primal horde, leaders can indulge their own wishes and their narcissism, and treat group members quite severely. Such a leader is "free. His intellectual acts were strong and independent . . . and his will needed no reinforcement from others . . . he loved no one but himself, or other people only as they served his needs." In this final section, the authors more closely examine these interactions between leaders and followers by focusing on how evolutionary processes result in contemporary leaders who may be unfit to provide for the needs of their followers, how power can alter the dynamics between leaders and followers, and how followers' moral convictions guide their interactions with leaders.

Van Vugt, Johnson, Kaiser, and O'Gorman's chapter considers research on the evolutionary underpinnings of leadership that suggests a more complicated and balanced view of the development of relations between leaders and followers. They suggest that leadership is an evolutionarily stable adaptation that enhanced the fitness of human beings across long spans of time and a variety of situations. Actions that help others organize their communal activities and reduce conflict among members benefit the group but also increase the leader's access to resources and increase the likelihood that the leader will survive long enough to procreate. Leadership also benefits those who follow, for in scarce resource environments competition among members over resources, constant struggles for dominance, and uncoordinated defensive and domestic activities will be deadly to all. As Van Vugt and his colleagues note, however, leadership and followership processes evolved in human groups that existed in an environment of evolutionary adaptiveness (EEA) that differs in dramatic ways from the groups and communities where humans currently live. The result is that contemporary leaders sometimes fail because the psychological and interpersonal reactions of both followers and leaders are influenced by genetic tendencies that are not as behaviorally adaptive as they were in earlier evolutionary contexts: the evolutionary mismatch hypothesis of leadership.

Consistent with the focus on the failures of contemporary leaders, the chapter by Galinsky, Jordan, and Sivanathan implicitly details Freud's view of a despotic leader who fully illustrates Lord Acton's famous warning that "power tends to corrupt; absolute power corrupts absolutely." Galinsky et al. explain that since leaders tend to be more powerful than their followers, they are psychologically and behaviorally activated: more proactive, more self-promoting, and more likely to seek out rewards and exploit opportunities. Followers, in contrast, are more inhibited, for they tend to be more reactive, cautious, and vigilant. Galinsky and his colleagues identify a number of negative side effects of the acquisition of power by leaders, but they also suggest ways that power can be harnessed to energize positive forms of leadership.

In the final chapter of our volume, Skitka, Bauman, and Lytle provide a useful counterpoint in focusing on the follower's capacity to resist the demands of the powerful leader. Social psychologists have demonstrated that powerful leaders can extract obedience from their followers, to the point that they undertake actions that most would consider to be morally questionable. Skitka and her colleagues, however, note that leaders who direct their followers in ways that violate the followers' own core moral values will likely fail as a source of influence. Moral conviction, they suggest, is a more potent guide to behavior than more general attitudes and beliefs, and thereby provides followers with guides for action as well as criteria for the evaluation of a leader. Not only will they refuse to follow the direction of a leader who asks them to act in ways that are inconsistent with their convictions, but they will also come to question the legitimacy of that leader.

AN OVERVIEW

Although we can distinguish four aspects of leadership for the purposes of organizing the work of our colleagues in this volume, they are, in fact, very much interrelated, even intertwined. An understanding of the connections between these aspects is suggested by considering our chapters as a whole. The leader's personal characteristics are surely important, but what matters more is how they are perceived. There must be some correspondence between what followers or potential followers expect and desire, and what qualities leaders or potential leaders have, or are perceived to have. People have expectations not only about what leaders are like but also about what they do. They expect leaders to persuade, to push and prod, and to innovate. Furthermore, followers hold leaders responsible for success and failure, and so leaders, like President Kennedy, carefully weigh how actions are likely to affect their perceived competency and legitimacy. And then beyond mutual sets of expectations, leaders and followers actually interact. Evolutionary analyses suggest that groups have developed highly adaptive ways for coordinating leading and following, in the interests of goal accomplishment, tranquility within the group, and protection from outside threats. Despite the evident adaptive nature of leader/follower coordination, the power leaders obtain leads to several varieties of exploitation of followers. Effective resistance by followers and effective self-regulation by leaders reduce these destructive aspects of power.

In conclusion, we are extremely pleased that the chapters in this book provide insight into the interrelated processes of leadership. They represent the state of the art of the social psychology of leadership. We are grateful to our contributors and excited for our readers. We hope that the latter will develop a useful and stimulating understanding of leadership from the work of the former.

REFERENCES

Allport, F. (1924). *Social psychology*. Boston, MA: Houghton Mifflin.

Allport, G. W. (1968). The historical background of modern social psychology. In G. Lindzey & E. Aronson (Eds.), *Handbook of social psychology* (2nd ed., Vol. 1, pp. 1–80). Reading, MA: Addison-Wesley.

Bartlett, F. C. (1926). The social psychology of leadership. *Journal of the National Institute of Industrial Psychology, 3*, 188–193.

Freud, S. (1921). *Group psychology and the analysis of the ego* (J. Strachey, Trans.). London: Hogarth Press and the Institute of Psycho-analysis.

Le Bon, G. (1895). *Psychologie des Foules* [*The Crowd*]. London: Unwin.

Lewin, K. (1997). Conduct, knowledge and the acceptance of new values. In G. Lewin (Ed.), *Resolving social conflicts: Selected papers on group dynamics* (pp. 48–55). Washington, DC: American Psychological Association.

Lewin, K., Lippitt, R., & White, R. (1939). Patterns of aggressive behavior in experimentally created 'social climates.' *Journal of Social Psychology, 10*, 271–299.

Nafe, R. W. (1930). A psychological description of leadership. *Journal of Social Psychology, 1*, 248–266.

Ross, E. A. (1908). *Social psychology: an outline and source book*. New York: Macmillan.

Tait, W. D. (1927). Psychology, leadership and democracy. *The Journal of Abnormal and Social Psychology, 22*, 26–32.

PART I

THE PERSONAL CHARACTERISTICS OF LEADERS

1

Personality and Leadership

STEPHEN J. ZACCARO, LISA M. V. GULICK, AND VIVEK P. KHARE

The question of personality influences on leadership has been oft-studied but still presents a source of controversy. In this chapter, we briefly review the history of this question in social and organizational psychology. We also provide a rationale, based on variance in situation strength, for the viability of personality as a predictor of leadership. We then articulate some conceptual frames for the specification of personality attributes that predict leader role occupancy and leader role effectiveness. While the predictors of leader role occupancy will overlap somewhat with those of leader role effectiveness, we point to some important differences in the two sets of variables. We conclude this chapter by arguing that, when examining leader traits, researchers should explore multiple attributes and how these attributes interact with one another, rather than relying on traditional univariate or additive approaches.

The topic of leadership has waxed and waned in prominence over the historical breadth of social psychology. The first handbook of social psychology (Murchison, 1935) included limited references to leadership patterns in animal colonies and in nursery school children. Murphy and Murphy's (1932) chapter in that handbook was also one of the earliest sources to discuss research suggesting that leadership derived from situational dynamics in addition to, or rather instead of, stable or trait characteristics of the individual (e.g., Parten, 1933). Over the next three decades, leadership emerged as a major topic in social psychology, enough to warrant separate chapters (Gibb, 1954, 1969) in the next two handbooks (Lindzey, 1954; Lindzey & Aronson, 1969). However, the latest edition of the handbook (Gilbert, Fiske, & Lindzey,

1998) relegated leadership to small sections in two chapters (Pfeffer, 1998; Levine & Moreland, 1998).

This ebb and flow corresponded to countervailing shifts in this literature regarding the focus on personality and individual differences as prominent influences on leadership (Zaccaro, 2007). Indeed, the role of personality in leadership has remained a consistent and controversial topic in social and organizational psychology through the whole of the twentieth century and into the first decade of the present century. We revisit this question in this chapter; we first review traditional conceptions of the personality and leadership connection before offering a revitalized perspective that takes into account both the coherence of personality and the power of the situation where leadership occurs.

LEADERSHIP AND PERSONALITY: A HISTORICAL REVIEW

The earliest scientific research on leadership focused on the stable qualities that distinguished leaders from nonleaders (Terman, 1904). For some, leadership reflected an identifiable personality attribute of the individual. For example, Gibb (1947, p. 267) summarized this approach well: "Leadership has usually been thought of as a specific attribute of personality, a personality trait, that some persons possess and others do not, or at least that some achieve in high degree while others scarcely at all." For others, leadership activities were defined as being derived from stable individual qualities, mostly including personality traits, but other stable characteristics as well (e.g., intelligence, physical characteristics). Thus, an early study by Craig and Charters (1925) described the individual attributes of successful industry leaders. Bird's (1940) textbook on social psychology contained a chapter on leadership that summarized the results of "approximately twenty inquires bearing some resemblance to controlled investigations" (p. 378) into the traits that distinguish leaders from nonleaders. He reported 79 traits. However, he also reported little consistency in the literature in defining core leadership traits, citing only four general traits of leadership—"intelligence, initiative, a sense of humor, and extraversion" (p. 380).

Several reviews published in the 1940s and 1950s also summarized this literature, echoing Bird's observation of inconsistency in observed relationships between leader traits and outcomes. As a consequence, more leadership scholars began to argue for contextual approaches to leadership (Jenkins, 1947; Gibb, 1947, 1954; Stogdill, 1948; see Day and Zaccaro, 2007, for a more comprehensive review of the history of leadership traits research). These literature reviews and corresponding arguments likely instigated a changing zeitgeist in leadership theory and research away from a focus on the personality of leaders and toward the situational factors that determine leader role occupancy and leadership behavior. Day and Zaccaro (2007) argued that this change, beginning in the 1940s, possibly resulted from growing attention by social psychologists to the phenomenon of leadership. Because social psychology emphasizes social context as the sine qua non for explaining behavior, the focus in leadership research became leadership behavior and the situational influences that governed its effective enactment. For example, Day and Zaccaro noted that the classic research programs at The Ohio State University and at the University of Michigan in the 1940s and 1950s "sought to identify what leadership behaviors were likely to be most effective in different situations and in a broader sense identify the situational characteristics that demand particular patterns of leadership" (p. 390).

The situational perspective continued to dominate the study of leadership in social psychology for much of the next 20–30 years, with decreasing (or no) emphasis placed on the personality of the leader as an important driver of leadership dynamics. Fiedler's (1964, 1971) theory presented a disposition by situation model, where individuals would be effective as leaders only in situations that matched their orientation to leadership. Thus, while Fiedler still described an important role for personality in leadership, he also defined situational moderators as being critical for this relationship. Subsequent theories described leadership more purely in terms of situational parameters (e.g., Hersey & Blanchard, 1969; House, 1971; Kerr & Jermier, 1978), while others emphasized leader-follower dynamics (e.g., Graen & Cashman, 1975; Hollander, 1964; Lord, Foti, & Phillips, 1982). These latter approaches did not consider personality attributes as integral variables in the prediction of leadership.

These contributions represented the mainstream of leadership research and theory in social psychology. However, new analyses and perspectives of leadership began to rise to prominence in the 1980s that reemphasized the importance of the leader's personality in leadership. Several studies used updated measurement and statistical strategies to revise conclusions from earlier leadership research. For example, Mann (1959) reviewed research on personality and performance in small groups. While he found some consistent relationships, he noted that "in no case is the median correlation between an aspect of personality . . . and performance higher than .25, and most of the median correlations are closer to .15" (p. 266). These findings became part of the oft-cited support for the conclusion that trait approaches were not helpful in explaining leadership. However, Lord, De Vader, and Alliger (1986) used more sophisticated meta-analytical strategies to reexamine these same studies, along with those that were published since Mann's paper. They found stronger correlations between the sets of personality variables examined by Mann and several indicators of leadership. Other meta-analyses conducted since that paper yielded similar conclusions regarding personality attributes and leadership (Judge & Bono, 2000; Judge, Bono, Ilies, & Gerhardt, 2002; Keeney & Marchioro, 1998). For example, Judge, Bono, Ilies, and Gerhardt (2002) found support for a significant relationship between the five-factor model of personality and leadership (multiple correlation of .48).

Theories of inspirational leadership that began to emerge in the organizational literature offered perspectives of leadership that emphasized leader personality. For example, House (1977; also see Shamir, House, & Arthur, 1993) described how leaders use the formation and articulation of inspiring messages (e.g., vision) to motivate subordinate loyalty and commitment. Similar models were offered by Bass (1985), Conger and Kanungo (1987), and Sashkin (1988). Such charismatic influences were defined as grounded in the personality of the charismatic leader (House & Howell, 1992), specifically such attributes as socialized power needs, risk propensity, nurturing ability, and high self-esteem or confidence (Zaccaro, 2001).

More recently, leadership theorists have begun to offer theories and models that appear to place an even stronger emphasis on leader personality. For example, Avolio, Gardner, Walumbwa, Luthans, and May (2004) offered a theoretical framework of how "authentic leaders" influence follower attitudes and behaviors. Such leaders were defined as "those individuals who are deeply aware of how they think, and behave, and are perceived by others as being aware of their own and others' values/moral perspective, knowledge, and strengths, aware of the context in which they operate and who are confident, hopeful, optimistic, resilient, and high on moral character" (from Avolio, Luthans, & Walumbwa, 2004; cited in Avolio et al., pp. 802–804). This definition suggests that personal attributes of the leader play a significant role in producing perceptions of authenticity. For example, Wood (2007) argued that the character attributes of integrity and self-transcendence act as important antecedents of authentic leadership.

This summary suggests that leader personality is once again being defined as an important contribution to leadership. Reviews by Day and Zaccaro (2007), Zaccaro, Kemp, and Bader (2004), and Zaccaro (2007) describe in more detail the ebb and flow of the importance of personality and traits in leading models of leadership in different time periods. We would argue that while current perspectives of leadership no longer dismiss leader traits and personality as important influences, there is still a significant deficiency in understanding how such variables act within the context of situational parameters to affect leadership outcomes. Also, the typical approaches to studying personality and leadership still resemble the traditional univariate or additive methods applied in earlier research. For example, a number of studies cited in the meta-analysis by Judge et al. (2002) examined only a single personality attribute (such as extraversion or conscientiousness) as a predictor of leadership. Indeed, while most recent reviews of leadership acknowledge the reemergence of traits, they still tend to present such perspectives in ways fundamentally unchanged from those in the 1930s and 1940s (e.g., Den Hartog & Koopman, 2001; Levine & Moreland, 1998). For example, in their chapter in the last edition of the *Handbook of Social Psychology,* Levine and Moreland (1998, p. 443) note that "although personal characteristics can influence who becomes a leader and how the person behaves in the role, it is clear that leaders vary widely in personality and no set of critical characteristics determines leadership in all situations." This summary varies little in tone and consequence from the summary offered by Gibb in his review of leadership in the 1954 *Handbook of Social Psychology.*

In the remainder of this chapter, we will offer some basic premises about personality and leadership, including some arguments for why the *nature* of leadership supports an emphasis on leader traits. We will also summarize research linking personality (a) to leader role occupancy and (b) to leadership effectiveness. We do not wish to present our arguments or summaries in terms of the worn-out "personality versus situation" typology. We agree with Day and Zaccaro (2007) who stated, "any assertion that traits are irrelevant to leadership seems naïve at best" (p. 398). We also agree that any explanation of leadership that does not boldly include situational influences as central drivers would fail several tests of conceptual and practical validity. As Vroom and Jago (2007) argue, "viewing leadership in purely dispositional or purely situational terms is to miss a major portion of the phenomenon" (p. 23). Models of leadership need to offer more complex integrations of leader traits and situations. In this chapter we summarize research on constructions of leader personality that (a) demark most leaders from nonleaders, and (b) could fit into such integrations.

PERSONALITY AND THE NATURE OF LEADERSHIP SITUATIONS

Several personality theorists (e.g., Bem & Allen, 1974; Mischel, 1977, 2004) have argued that the strength of situational demands in a context can act to mitigate the expression of strong disposition-based behavior. The essence of leadership, particularly at executive and middle levels of organizations involves making decisions in situations that allow choices among viable alternatives. For example, individuals working at different levels of organizations experience different environmental constraints that pose unique skill requirements. Upper level leadership positions often involve a greater amount of ambiguity (Hambrick, 1989) and discretion (Jacobs & Jaques, 1990), while lower level leadership positions are often associated with more concrete instructions from supervisors and more well-defined tasks, leaving little room for deviation or choice (Jacobs & Jaques, 1987). House and Aditya

(1997) compared higher degrees of leader discretion to the weak situations outlined by Mischel (1977). Weak situations are those contexts that lack structure and concrete direction of how one is supposed to behave (Mischel, 1977). In weak situations, individual traits become more prominent and are therefore stronger determinants of behavior (Mischel, 1973). This line of thinking suggests that personal attributes will be especially important in leadership, particularly at upper levels of organizational leadership.

A leader who is operating in a strong situation may be more certain of the appropriate behaviors to demonstrate than a leader operating in a weak, or ambiguous, situation. The strength of the situation thus provides a sense of clarity that reduces discretionary choice in selected leadership behaviors. Mischel (2004) summarized his approach as reflecting "more situation-qualified characterizations of persons in contexts, making dispositions situationally hedged, and interactive with the situations in which they were expressed" (pp. 4–5). Mischel (1977) argued that in "strong" situations, contextual cues and normative expectations provide clear guidance to participants regarding appropriate behavior, and thus constrain the expression of personality. Individuals in such situations have little real choice and autonomy in what behaviors they need to display in order to remain socially effective. In "weak" situations, no such guidance or cues are available. Barrick and Mount (1993) noted that in such situations, "the person has considerable discretion in determining which behaviors, if any, to undertake" (p. 12). Behavioral expectations are at best ambiguous, providing individuals with more choice and autonomy in their choice of responses. Thus, when situations allow behavior discretion, personality and individual differences are likely to play a more prominent role in determining the content of behavior.

Several studies have provided evidence for this moderating influence in terms of work performance. For example, Barrick and Mount (1993) examined the relationships between conscientiousness and extraversion, respectively, with managerial performance under conditions of high and low autonomy. As expected, they found that when midlevel managers and first-line supervisors experienced more autonomy in their jobs, the association of each personality variable with performance was much higher than when managers indicated their jobs had low autonomy. Beaty, Cleveland, and Murphy (2001) examined associations between conscientiousness, extraversion, agreeableness, and neuroticism, respectively, and contextual performance, defined as the "behaviors associated with helping coworkers perform their assigned tasks" (p. 126). They completed a laboratory study in which they varied the strength of situational cues and a field study in which they measured the strength of normative expectations. In the laboratory study, they found that when expectations about how to behave were unclear in organizational scenarios, extraversion was more strongly related to choices to engage in helping behavior than when task performance expectations were very clear. Similar findings of stronger personality-behavior correlations in "weaker" situations were reported in the field study.

This argument suggests that when examining the effects of personality on leadership, one needs to take considerable account of the degree to which situations afford the display of leadership. Indeed, leadership substitutes theory is premised on the notion that a large number of situational variables can minimize the appropriateness or necessity of leadership behaviors (Kerr & Jermier, 1978). However, this conclusion ignores a defining feature of such behavior that we have noted—leadership as a phenomenon occurs almost exclusively in situations where individuals have choices and autonomy in their decisions and responses. That is, leadership is, by definition, the province of weak group and organizational situations.

This defining feature of leadership is not a new one. Katz and Kahn (1978) defined leadership as "the influential increment over and above mechanical compliance with the routine directives of the organization" (p. 528). In light of the aforementioned definitions of strong situations, they can be considered as containing "routine directives" and inducing "strong compliance." Thus, leadership by this definition refers to activities that reflect social influence beyond that exerted by a situational press. Indeed, most definitions of leadership define such influence in part as providing direction for collective action (Yukl, 2006). The provision of direction implies choice in determining among different action paths (or even inaction), which is most appropriate for reaching collective goals. For example, Jacobs and Jaques (1990) noted that leadership involved "an exchange of information about what ought to be done (or how it ought to be done, or some other *discretionary* issue)" (p. 282, italics added). Finally, Mumford (1986) captures this aspect of leadership when he defines it as "a form of discretionary behavior which involves some significant element of choice in whether or not and what kind of action will be taken. This constraint is based on the fact that actions which are completely specified by normative role requirements are a property of the organization rather than of the individual" (p. 513).

The idea that acts of leadership inherently involve choice and autonomy strengthens the pure case for personality influences on leadership outcomes. However, these influences, and the particular mix of personality variables specified as precursors of leadership, will likely vary depending upon the particular outcome being examined. For example, the personality attributes that predict the attainment of leader roles, or leader role occupancy, may be distinct from those that predict effectiveness in these roles. Also, single personality variables will rarely exert strong influences on leadership. Instead, personality attributes are likely to affect leadership in concert with other attributes as part of an integrated constellation. This latter perspective has been labeled the "pattern" approach to leadership and personality (Foti & Hauenstein, 2007; Smith & Foti, 1998: see also Zaccaro, 2007, and Zaccaro, Kemp, & Bader, 2004).

We examine these ideas more closely in the next sections. Specifically, we have argued that leadership situations are weak in the sense that they typically do not provide clarity in terms of expected behavior. Instead, they offer individuals choices in (a) whether or not to assume the leader role, and (b) what decisions to make in such roles. When greater ambiguity exists for the leader in making these choices (e.g., at higher levels of organizational leadership, where leaders typically face greater complexity and decision choices), personality attributes should more strongly predict leadership role occupancy and leadership effectiveness. Accordingly, in the next sections we examine how multiple personality attributes, acting jointly, influence these leadership outcomes.

PERSONALITY AND LEADER ROLE OCCUPANCY

We have noted that leadership criteria can include leader role occupancy, or the attainment of leader roles, and leadership effectiveness, or the success of the leader role occupant (Judge et al., 2002; Lord et al., 1986). Further distinctions can also be made in each of these sets of criteria. For example, most studies of leader role occupancy have used peer rankings or ratings to determine leadership attainment (i.e., leader emergence). Others have examined the successive occupancy of leader roles over a career span (i.e., leader promotion, leader selection). However, few studies have examined criteria related to an individual's motivation to obtain leadership roles (i.e., leadership seeking) (Chan & Drasgow, 2001).

Leadership role seeking derives from a set of individual attributes that reflect an individual's willingness or motivation to actively obtain the leadership role in a team or organization. The grounding of this leadership in personality attributes is supported by Schneider's Attraction-Selection-Attrition (ASA) model (Schneider, 1987; Schneider, Goldstein, & Smith, 1995). This model argues that individuals are differentially attracted to careers and organizations as a result of different mixes of personality attributes. As applied to leadership, individuals with certain personality attributes would likely be more attracted to leadership roles. A recent study by Arvey, Rotundo, Johnson, Zhang, and McGue (2006) provides some evidence for this premise. They found that significant variance in leadership role attainment was based in part on social potency, which was measured as the degree to which an individual "enjoys or would enjoy leadership roles" (Arvey et al., 2006, p. 17).

Related dispositional variables that should predict systematic variance in seeking leadership include *motivation to lead* (Chan & Drasgow, 2001), *need for power* (McClelland & Boyatzis, 1982), and *dominance* (Lord et al., 1986; Mann, 1959). Each of these personality attributes increases the likelihood that an individual will choose to pursue a leadership role if a situation provides the choice or opportunity to do so. Motivation to lead refers to a personal construct "that affects a leader's or leader-to-be's decision to assume leadership training, roles, and responsibilities, and that affect his or her intensity of effort at leading and persistence as a leader" (Chan & Drasgow, 2001, p. 482). Chan and Drasgow reported that such motivation influenced ratings of leadership potential. Need for power refers to personal motives to seek and use power and influence (cf. McClelland and Boyatzis, 1982)). Yukl (2006) noted that "someone with a high need for power enjoys influencing people and events and is more likely to seek positions of authority" (p. 193). Longitudinal studies by Howard and Bray (1988) and McClelland and Boyatzis (1982) found significant relationships between variables elated to personal need for power and managerial promotion rates. Dominance, or the stable desire to impose one's influence and will on situations, has been prominently linked to leadership emergence in a number of studies (Foti & Hauenstein, 2007; Keeney & Marchioro, 1998; Lord et al., 1986; Mann, 1959).

Note that while a number of studies support the importance of personality attributes that predict one's attraction to leadership roles, most of them use leader emergence or actual role attainment (through selection or promotion) as criteria. Few studies have examined leader role-seeking behaviors directly. This distinction is important because leader emergence rests on attributes in addition to one's motivation to seek leadership roles. Leader emergence requires some form of endorsement from potential followers—Judge et al. (2002, p. 767) note that "leader emergence refers to whether (or to what degree) an individual is viewed as a leader by others." This need for support from followers suggests that leader emergence is predicted by personal attributes that systematically impact how one is perceived by others, in addition to those influencing attraction to leader roles. Potential leaders need to understand the leadership needs of followers and be able to respond accordingly (Zaccaro, Foti, & Kenny, 1991). Accordingly, Zaccaro et al. reported significant positive associations between self-monitoring dispositions and leader rankings and ratings in small groups. Likewise, in their meta-analysis, Judge et al. reported significant correlations between leader emergence scores and such attributes as extraversion and sociability. These attributes predispose the leader to favor interactions with others and to conduct those interactions more effectively.

These studies share a common theme—the use of either a single variable or an additive approach to an examination of personality and leader role occupancy. That is, these studies have typically examined only one personality attribute, or looked at the independent contributions of several attributes. Smith and Foti (1998) argued, instead, that particular combinations or patterns of personality attributes ought to be examined for their association with leader emergence. Similarly, Zaccaro (2007) argued that researchers need to examine how multiple traits can be "combined in optimal ways to jointly influence leadership" (p. 12). Foti and Hauenstein (2007) provided evidence for this approach by showing that combining attributes such as intelligence, dominance, self-monitoring, and self-efficacy in particular ways explained significant incremental variance in leader emergence scores over simple additive contributions of these same attributes.

In sum, a number of recent studies have documented significant links between personality attributes and leader role occupancy. We have suggested that the mix of influential dispositions will vary according to the targeted leadership criteria—leadership seeking, leader emergence, or leader selection. We have also argued that specified dispositions need to be considered as part of an integrated constellation of attributes that influence each of these criteria. Earlier, we suggested that leadership as a phenomenon reflects behaviors that are inherently displayed in weak group or organizational situations. However, at this point we should offer a possible qualifier to this premise for leader emergence and leader selection. Both of these processes reflect endorsements of leader role occupancy by others. In some instances, situational demands can preclude a particular person from assuming the leadership role regardless of his or her predisposition for the role. For example, an individual may possess all of the aforementioned personality attributes that promote leadership seeking behavior, but if the position also requires particular functional knowledge that he or she does not have, or if that person cannot gain the endorsement of a powerful patron in the organization, then he or she will not gain the position.

PERSONALITY AND LEADERSHIP EFFECTIVENESS

Several studies have demonstrated significant associations between personality attributes and measures of leader effectiveness (e.g., Foti & Hauenstein, 2007; Judge et al., 2002). Zaccaro (2007) has asserted that much of the earlier work on leader traits and leadership criteria has been atheoretical with little or no explanation for *why* certain attributes should relate to particular indices of leadership effectiveness. Mumford and his colleagues (Mumford, 1986; Mumford, Zaccaro, Harding, Jacobs, & Fleishman, 2000) have provided one such conceptual rationale based on a perspective of leadership as complex social problem solving. This perspective argues that the central role of leaders is to help their constituent teams and organizations achieve collective goals (Hackman & Walton, 1986). The contexts of organizational action can present threats to goal progress or opportunities for goal advancement. Likewise, organizational environments can change significantly such that group and organizational structures and processes become misaligned with environment requirements (Katz & Kahn, 1978; Mumford, 1986). Accordingly, leaders facilitate the progress of their followers by helping them resolve threats to goal progress, take advantage of goal opportunities, and correct misalignments with operating environments.

Based on this perspective Mumford (1986; Mumford, Zaccaro, Harding, et al., 2000) argued that leadership can be defined in terms of problem solving processes that promote organizational adaptation. These processes include the definition of problem components and the generation and evaluation of potential solutions. They also include the implementation of solutions in complex social domains and monitoring the effects of such implementation.

Defining leadership in terms of such social or organizational problem solving processes provides a basis for hypothesizing the nature and direction of influences on leadership effectiveness by particular personality attributes. For example, because organizational contexts are typically complex, attributes that predispose the leader toward a willingness to tackle tough problems, persist in their resolution, and be comfortable with complexity should promote leadership processes related to problem definition and solution generation. Mumford, Zaccaro, Harding, et al. (2000) specified several such attributes, including mastery motives, dominance, openness, tolerance for ambiguity, curiosity, and an orientation toward abstract conceptualization (e.g., intuition on the Myers-Briggs scale, Gardner & Martinko, 1996). Studies that have affirmed the effects of these attributes on leader effectiveness include Gardner and Martinko (1996), Lord et al. (1986), and Judge et al. (2002).

Other personality attributes should foster solution implementation processes. Because such processes involve facilitating complex social dynamics and carefully monitoring the effects of solutions in social contexts, variables such as extraversion, sociability, and conscientiousness should be significant predictors of leader effectiveness. In support of this premise, Judge et al. (2002) reported that extraversion and conscientiousness yielded significant corrected correlations with indices of leadership effectiveness.

Note that most studies supporting the proposed effects of these personality attributes have used a univariate or additive approach. However, we have argued here (and elsewhere by the first author; Zaccaro, 2001, 2007; Zaccaro et al., 2004) that leadership researchers need to explore how personality affects leadership jointly with other cognitive, social, and motivational attributes. We noted earlier that Foti and Hauenstein (2007) reported support for this approach when using leader emergence as the criterion. They also found similar support for joint effects of individual differences on leadership effectiveness criteria. We suggest, though, that the pattern trait approach needs to be extended to consider not only the joint effects of personality and nonpersonality attributes but also the joint effects of multiple personality variables. If different personality variables are more likely to foster effectiveness of different leadership processes, then overall leader success will likely result from the combined influences of several attributes. For example, leader effectiveness is likely to be maximized when (a) leaders possess motives to lead, an orientation for abstract conceptualization, mastery motives, openness, extraversion, *and* conscientiousness; *and* (b) these leaders also possess other attributes such as cognitive ability, social capabilities, problem solving skills, and expertise (Mumford, Zaccaro, Harding, et al., 2000; Zaccaro, 2007).

Personality theorists have argued for such combinations in discussion of "types" (e.g., Magnusson, 1988). Mumford, Zaccaro, Johnson, et al. (2000) identified several types that distinguished leader rank and leadership effectiveness among army officers. Specifically, they found two types that were more likely to be evident in senior officers than among their junior counterparts—*motivated communicators* and *thoughtful innovators*. Motivated communicators were those officers who scored high on measures of extraversion, responsibility, achievement, dominance, verbal reasoning skills, and problem solving skills. Note that this type contains several of the personality attributes that we described earlier as linked to different aspects of leader problem solving effectiveness. This type contained cognitive capacity and skills as well. The second type reflected officers who scored high on introversion, preferences for abstract conceptualization, achievement, dominance, verbal reasoning and problem solving skills. Of particular note is that opposing attributes (introversion-extraversion) appear in different types. Mumford, Zaccaro, Johnson, et al. noted that each type corresponded to different aspects of the leadership role–tactical operations (motivated communicators) and operational planning (thoughtful innovators). This study demonstrated the complexity of how personality attributes can relate to leadership criteria. We urge more research on such joint and integrated effects of different personality attributes and with other nonpersonality variables.

SUMMARY

We have noted in this chapter that the premise that personality attributes are significant predictors of leadership has been substantially revived in the organizational literature. We have also argued that because leadership refers to sets of processes that occur in response to organization problems that do not have routine solutions, and that require discretion and choices by the leader (i.e., "weak" situations), personality and individual differences should have a stronger role in these processes than in other situations fully constrained by normative expectations. We would add that this does not diminish or obviate the role of situations in leadership, for situational events define the parameters of organizational problems and the constraints on their solutions. We suggest accordingly that when leadership researchers examine personality and leadership, they should focus on individual differences that allow stability in leader role occupancy but variability in enacted leadership activities (Zaccaro, 2007; Zaccaro et al., 1991).

We would also suggest leadership researchers devote attention to developing more sophisticated conceptual frames that describe how personality attributes differentially predict leader role occupancy and leader effectiveness. We have argued that different models likely apply to leader role occupancy and leader effectiveness, but current theories and models do not specify these differences in terms clear enough to develop testable propositions. We have offered some ideas here based on more complex integrations of multiple personality attributes. Because leadership activities are situationally bound, these attribute patterns need to be constructed around individual qualities that predict stability in role occupancy, but also adaptability and flexibility to situational demands (Zaccaro, 2007; Zaccaro et al., 1991). We would encourage researchers to continue along this research path and to develop leadership models that specify further integrations of personality attributes with other sets of variables such as cognitive capacities, social competencies, and expertise. We believe these prescriptions can advance our current understanding of how leaders differ from nonleaders, and how they persist in being effective across diverse situations.

REFERENCES

Arvey, R. D., Rotundo, M., Johnson, W., Zhang, Z., & McGue, M. (2006). The determinants of leadership role occupancy: Genetic and personality factors. *Leadership Quarterly, 17,* 1–20.

Avolio, B. J., Gardner, W. L., Walumbwa, F. O., Luthans, F., & May, D. R. (2004). Unlocking the mask: A look at the process by which authentic leaders impact follower attitudes and behaviors. *Leadership Quarterly, 15*(6), 801–823.

Avolio, B. J., Luthans, F., & Walumbwa, F. O. (2004). *Authentic leadership: Theory-building for veritable sustained performance.* Working paper, Gallup Leadership Institute, University of Nebraska, Lincoln.

Barrick, M. R., & Mount, M. K. (1993). Autonomy as a moderator of the relationships between the big five personality dimensions and job performance. *Journal of Applied Psychology, 78,* 111–118.

Bass, B. M. (1985).*Leadership and performance beyond expectations.* New York: Free Press.

Beaty, J. C., Jr., Cleveland, J. N., & Murphy, K. R. (2001). The relation between personality and contextual performance in "strong" versus "weak" situations. *Human Performance, 14*(2), 125–148.

Bem, D., & Allen, A. (1974). On predicting some of the people some of the time: The search for cross-situational consistencies in behavior. *Psychological Review, 81,* 506–520.

Bird, C. (1940). *Social psychology.* New York: Appleton-Century.

Chan, K., & Drasgow, F. (2001). Toward a theory of individual differences and leadership: Understanding the motivation to lead. *Journal of Applied Psychology, 86,* 481–498.

Conger, J. A., & Kanungo, R. N. (1987). Toward a behavioral theory of charismatic leadership in organizations. *Academy of Management Review, 12,* 637–647.

Craig, D. R., & Charters, W. W. (1925). *Personal leadership in industry.* New York: McGraw-Hill.

Day, D. V., & Zaccaro, S. J. (2007). Leadership: A critical historical analysis of the influence of leader trait. In L. L. Koppes (Ed.), *The history of industrial and organizational psychology: The first 100 years.* Mahwah, NJ: Erlbaum.

Den Hartog, D. N., & Koopman, P. L. (2001). Leadership in organizations. In N. Anderson, D. Oniz, & C. Viswesvaran (Eds.), *The International Handbook of Work and Organizational Psychology* (Vol. 2, pp. 166–187). London: Sage.

Fiedler, F. E. (1964). A contingency model of leadership effectiveness. *Advances in Experimental Social Psychology, 1,* 149–190.

Fiedler, F. E. (1971). Validation and extension of the contingency model of leadership effectiveness: A review of the empirical findings. *Psychological Bulletin, 76,* 128–148.

Foti, R. J., & Hauenstein, N. M. A. (2007). Pattern and variable approaches in leadership emergence and effectiveness. *Journal of Applied Psychology, 92,* 347–355.

Gardner, W. L., & Martinko, M. J. (1996). Using the Myers-Briggs Type Indicator to study managers: A literature review and research agenda. *Journal of Management, 22,* 45–83.

Gibb, C. A. (1947). The principles and traits of leadership. *Journal of Abnormal and Social Psychology, 42,* 267–284.

Gibb, C. A. (1954). Leadership. In G. Lindzey (Ed.), *Handbook of social psychology.* Cambridge, MA: Addison-Wesley.

Gibb, C. A. (1969). Leadership. In G. Lindzey and E. Aronson (Eds.), *Handbook of social psychology* (2nd ed., pp. 205-282). Reading, MA: Addison-Wesley.

Gilbert, D. T., Fiske, S. T., & Lindzey, G. (Eds.). (1998). *The handbook of social psychology* (4th ed.). Boston: McGraw-Hill.

Graen, G. B., & Cashman, J. F. (1975). A role making model in formal organizations. In J. G. Hunt & L. L. Larson (Eds.), *Leadership frontiers* (pp. 143–165). Kent, OH: Kent State University.

Hackman, J. R., & Walton, R. E. (1986). Leading groups in organizations. In P. S. Goodman & Associates (Eds.), *Designing effective work groups.* San Francisco: Jossey-Bass.

Hambrick, D. C. (1989). Guest editor's introduction: Putting top managers back in the strategy picture. *Strategic Management Journal, 10,* 5–15.

Hersey, P., & Blanchard, K. H. (1969). *Management of organizational behavior.* Englewood Cliffs, NJ: Prentice-Hall.

Hollander, E. P. (1964). *Leaders, groups, and influence*. New York: Oxford University Press.

House, R. J. (1971). A path-goal theory of leader effectiveness. *Administrative Science Quarterly, 16,* 321–338.

House, R. J. (1977). A 1976 theory of charismatic leadership. In J. G. Hunt & L. L. Larson (Eds.), *Leadership: The cutting edge* (pp. 189–207). Carbondale, IL: Southern Illinois University.

House, R. J., & Aditya, R. (1997). The social scientific study of leadership: Quo vadis? *Journal of Management, 23,* 409–474.

House, R. J., & Howell, J. M. (1992). Personality and charismatic leadership. *Leadership Quarterly, 3,* 81–108.

Howard, A., & Bray, D. W. (1988). *Managerial lives in transition: Advancing age and changing times*. New York: Guilford Press.

Jacobs, T. O., & Jaques, E. (1987). Leadership in complex systems. In J. Zeidner (Ed.), *Human productivity enhancement* (Vol. 2, pp. 7–65). New York: Praeger.

Jacobs, T. O., & Jaques, E. (1990). Military executive leadership. In K. E. Clark & M. B. Clark (Eds.), *Measures of leadership* (pp. 281–295). Greensboro, NC: Center for Creative Leadership.

Jenkins, W. O. (1947). A review of leadership studies with particular reference to military problems. *Psychological Bulletin, 44,* 54–79.

Judge, T. A., & Bono, J. E. (2000). Five-factor model of personality and transformational leadership. *Journal of Applied Psychology, 85,* 751–765.

Judge, T. A., Bono, J. E., Ilies, R., & Gerhardt, M. W. (2002). Personality and leadership: A qualitative and quantitative review. *Journal of Applied Psychology, 87,* 765–780.

Katz, D., & Kahn, R. L. (1978). *The social psychology of organizations*. New York: Wiley.

Keeney, M. J., & Marchioro, C. A. (1998). *A meta-analytic review of the traits associated with leadership emergence: An extension of Lord, De Vader, and Alliger (1986)*. Paper presented at the 13th annual meeting of the Society for Industrial and Organizational Psychology, Dallas, TX.

Kerr, S., & Jermier, J. M. (1978). Substitutes for leadership: Their meaning and measurement. *Organizational Behavior and Human Performance, 22,* 375–403.

Levine, J. M., & Moreland, R. L. (1998). Small groups. In D. T. Gilbert, S. T. Fiske, & G. Lindzey (Eds.), *The handbook of social psychology* (4th ed., pp. 415–469). Boston: McGraw-Hill.

Lindzey, G. (Ed.). (1954). *The handbook of social psychology*. Cambridge, MA: Addison-Wesley.

Lindzey, G., & Aronson, E. (Eds.). (1969). *The handbook of social psychology* (2nd ed.). Reading, MA: Addison-Wesley.

Lord, R. G., De Vader, C. L., & Alliger, G. M. (1986). A meta-analysis of the relation between personality traits and leadership perceptions: An application of validity generalization procedures. *Journal of Applied Psychology, 71,* 402–409.

Lord, R. G., Foti, R. J., & Phillips, J. S. (1982). A theory of leadership categorization. In J. G. Hunt, U. Sekaran, & C. Schriesheim (Eds.), *Leadership: Beyond establishment views* (pp. 104–121). Carbondale, IL: Southern Illinois University.

Magnusson, D. (1998). The logic and implications of a person-oriented approach. In R. B. Cairns, L. R. Bergman, & J. Kagan (Eds.), *Methods and models for studying the individual* (pp. 33–64).Thousand Oaks, CA: Sage.

Mann, R. D. (1959). A review of the relationships between personality and performance in small groups. *Psychological Bulletin, 56,* 241–270.

McClelland, D. C., & Boyatzis, R. E. (1982). Leadership motive pattern and long term success in management. *Journal of Applied Psychology, 67,* 737–743.

Mischel, W. (1973). Toward a cognitive social learning reconceptualization of personality. *Psychological Review, 80,* 252–283.

Mischel, W. (1977). The interaction of personal and situation. In D. Magnusson & N. S. Endler (Eds.), *Personality at the crossroads: Current issues in interactional psychology* (pp. 333–352). Hillsdale, NJ: Erlbaum.

Mischel, W. (2004). Toward an integrative science of the person. *Annual Review of Psychology, 55,* 1–22.

Mumford, M. D. (1986). Leadership in the organizational context: Conceptual approach and its application. *Journal of Applied Social Psychology, 16,* 212–226.

Mumford, M. D., Zaccaro, S. J., Harding, F. D., Jacobs, T. O., & Fleishman, E. A. (2000). Leadership skills for a changing world: Solving complex social problems. *Leadership Quarterly, 11,* 11–35.

Mumford, M. D., Zaccaro, S. J., Johnson, J. F., Diana, M., Gilbert, J. A., & Threlfall, K. V. (2000). Patterns of leader characteristics: Implications for performance and development. *Leadership Quarterly, 11,* 115–133.

Murchison, C. (Ed.). (1935). *Handbook of social psychology.* Worcester, MA: Clark University Press.

Murphy, L. B., & Murphy, G. (1935). The influence of social situations upon the behavior of children. In C. Murchison (Ed.), *Handbook of social psychology.* Worcester, MA: Clark University Press.

Parten, M. P. (1933). Leadership among preschool children. *Journal of Abnormal and Social Psychology, 27,* 430–442.

Pfeffer, J. (1998). Understanding organizations: Concepts and controversies. In D. T. Gilbert, S. T. Fiske, & G. Lindzey (Eds.), *The handbook of social psychology* (4th ed.; pp. 733–777). Boston, MA: McGraw-Hill.

Sashkin, M. (1988). The visionary leader. In J. A. Conger & R. N. Kanungo (Eds.), *Charismatic leadership: The elusive factor in organizational effectiveness.* San Francisco: Jossey-Bass.

Schneider, B. (1987). The people make the place. *Personnel Psychology, 40,* 437–454.

Schneider, B., Goldstein, H. W., & Smith, D. B. (1995). The ASA framework: An update. *Personnel Psychology, 48,* 747–773.

Shamir, B., House, R. J., & Arthur, M. (1993). The motivational effects of charismatic leadership: A self-concept based theory. *Organization Science, 4,* 577–594.

Smith, J. A., & Foti, R. J. (1998). A pattern approach to the study of leader emergence. *Leadership Quarterly, 9,* 147–160.

Stogdill, R. M. (1948). Personal factors associated with leadership: A survey of the literature. *Journal of Psychology, 25,* 35–71.

Terman, L. M. (1904). A preliminary study in the psychology and pedagogy of leadership. *Pedagogical Seminary, 11,* 413–451.

Vroom, V. H., & Jago, A. G. (2007). The role of situation in leadership. *American Psychologist, 62,* 17–24.

Wood, G. M. (2007). *Authentic leadership: Do we really need another leadership theory?* Unpublished doctoral dissertation, George Mason University.

Yukl, G. A. (2006). *Leadership in organizations* (6th ed.). Upper Saddle River, NJ: Pearson Prentice Hall.

Zaccaro, S. J. (2001). *The nature of executive leadership: A conceptual and empirical analysis of success.* Washington, DC: APA Books.

Zaccaro, S. J. (2007). Trait-based perspectives in leadership. *American Psychologist, 62,* 6–16.

Zaccaro, S. J., Foti, R. J., & Kenny, D. A. (1991). Self-monitoring and trait-based variance in leadership: An investigation of leader flexibility across multiple group situations. *Journal of Applied Psychology, 76,* 308–315.

Zaccaro, S. J., Kemp, C., & Bader, P. (2004). Leader traits and attributes. In J. Antonakis, A. T. Cianciolo, and R. J. Sternberg (Eds.), *The nature of leadership* (pp. 101–124). Thousand Oaks, CA: Sage.

2

Social Psychology and Charismatic Leadership

RONALD E. RIGGIO AND HEIDI R. RIGGIO

Charisma and charismatic leadership can be understood as a social psychological phenomenon. Charismatic leadership only occurs with follower identification with the social group, from which follows a tendency to attribute power and causal influence to the leader, intense liking of the leader, modeling of leader behavior, increasing commitment to group goals, and shared emotions with the leader. Leader charisma is enhanced as followers discount discrepant leader behaviors, reciprocate leader self-sacrifice, and self-fulfill leader expectations. Situational factors enhance leader charisma, including comparison with less successful leaders and situational uncertainty or threat. Individual factors also come into play because charisma can be viewed as a set of behaviors and characteristics, including sensitivity to the environmental context, sensitivity to followers' needs and concerns, ability to articulate a compelling, shared vision, unconventional behavior, personal risk taking, and skills in social and expressive communication. Viewing charisma as resulting from the interplay between individual leader characteristics and behaviors, and features of followers, situations, and interactions, may guide future research on charisma and facilitate our understanding of the powerful effects, historical ramifications, and memorable nature of charismatic leadership.

Ask any assembled group to generate a list of famous charismatic leaders and you will find remarkable agreement. In the United States, Presidents John F. Kennedy and Ronald Reagan will usually top the list, as will World War II leaders Franklin Delano Roosevelt and Winston Churchill. The names of leaders of national and international social movements—Martin Luther King Jr. and Mohandas Gandhi—will also be mentioned. These are then usually followed by local politicians and, depending upon the group, business leaders, sports leaders, religious leaders, and sometimes entertainers.[1] But then it gets troublesome. Adolf Hitler usually makes the list, followed by notorious, Svengali-like figures such as the Peoples Temple leader, Jim Jones, and religious cult leader David Koresh. If you look at the personal qualities or personalities of this diverse group, there is seemingly little in common. If you consider that the list contains individuals who are perceived to be both morally good (King, Gandhi) and bad (Hitler, Jones), it gets even more confusing. Although many hold formal leadership positions (U.S. presidents or other heads of state), others do not. This suggests that charisma is not about personality, nor is it associated with a particular role. Much of what constitutes charismatic leadership is social psychological in nature, although it is clear that these leaders possessed certain elements in common that contributed to their charisma. Yet, even these personal elements are tied to social psychological constructs.

This chapter will examine charisma and charismatic leadership. Although charismatic leadership has been studied by sociologists, psychoanalytic-oriented and personality psychologists, and management scholars, social psychologists have paid scant attention to charisma and charismatic leadership. Yet, many of the elements of charismatic leadership, and the relationship between charismatic leader and followers, are better understood through the application of social psychological theories and constructs.

Charisma is both "smoke" and substance. We maintain that charisma is partly a social construction, but that there is also some true substance—individual and social factors that contribute to a leader's charisma. We will begin by exploring how shared perceptions of a leader result in attributions that a particular leader is or is not charismatic. We will then look at how situational factors play a part in helping to create charismatic leaders. Because charismatic leadership is a relationship-based type of leadership, we will look at how the social psychology of relationships helps us understand the process of charisma. Finally, we will look at the substance—the skills and behaviors that distinguish charismatic leaders from those who do not possess charisma.

The notion of charisma has Christian religious roots, and the word itself means "a divine gift of grace." Social scientific analyses of charisma, however, began with the work of sociologist Max Weber (1947), who, in his conceptualization of "charismatic authority," suggested that during times of unrest or inertia followers latch onto an individual who has some reason to draw their collective attention. The followers then imbue this individual with extraordinary powers and qualities. The devotion of followers to charismatic leaders is very strong, but Weber puts the real source of the charismatic authority in the situation ("crisis" conditions; the leader has notable success) and in followers' shared perceptions of the leader. Weber's perspective foreshadows the more recent research on charismatic leadership by social psychologists that apply social identity theory to the study of leadership (Hogg, 2001; van Knippenberg & Hogg, 2003).

SOCIAL IDENTITY THEORY AND CHARISMATIC LEADERSHIP

According to social identity theory, group members who are highly prototypical, that is, members who embody the beliefs, values, and norms of the group, are more likely to emerge as group leaders. These emergent leaders are well liked and are attractive to group members. As a result, they can become persuasive and powerful. When a leader is seen as attractive, the potential attractiveness of the entire group increases, increasing the positive distinctiveness of the group and bolstering follower social identity (Tajfel & Turner, 1986). According to social identity theory, this perceived attractiveness can evolve into perceptions of the leaders possessing "charisma." This is particularly true in the U.S. and Western cultures that have a "romance of leadership"—making leaders into heroic figures and viewing them as the primary cause of a group or organization's success or failure (Meindl, Ehrlich, & Dukerich, 1985). The celebrity status given to U.S. companies' chief executive officers (CEOs) and their enormous salaries, often tied to the companies' performance, support the romance of leadership concept.

The strong focus on the leader common in Western cultures often leads to overattributing a group's successful (or failed) outcome to the leader and is an example of the well-known social psychological construct of the fundamental attribution error (Jones & Nisbett, 1972; Ross, 1977). The fundamental attribution error, in brief, is the tendency to make personal (or "dispositional") attributions for the causes of particular actions or outcomes, and to minimize the role that situational factors play in the outcome. Leaders, who are the focal point of attention, particularly in a society that has a romance of leadership, are more likely to be viewed as primary agents or causes of the group's success or failure. Social identity theory and the fundamental attribution error seem to clearly explain the charisma of U.S. President Ronald Reagan. Reagan was elected at a time in U.S. history when morale was low due to poor economic conditions and a decline in U.S. influence abroad. For many Americans, Reagan represented the prototype of the confident, "get-tough" individual. His unabashed patriotism made him the perfect example of the proud American. Coupled with his celebrity status as a former actor, Reagan was enormously popular and was elected over the incumbent president, Jimmy Carter. At the same time, blame for a stalled economy and the failed attempt to rescue U.S. hostages being held in Iran was attributed to Carter (who is often mentioned as a "noncharismatic" leader). Reagan, on the other hand, has been attributed by many with reviving the economy (via "Reaganomics") and causing the collapse of the Soviet Union and the tearing down of the Berlin wall—consistent with the fundamental attribution error, which downplays the situational and other factors that impacted these outcomes.

Social identity theory also suggests that the highly prototypical, charismatic leader is viewed by followers as the embodiment of the group's norms and values (Hogg, 2004; Hogg & van Knippenberg, 2003). As a result, followers develop a great deal of trust that the leader will work in the best interests of the group or organization. Yet, leaders are afforded greater latitude than regular members to violate shared group norms by using what Edwin Hollander (1958) termed "idiosyncrasy credits." It is these idiosyncrasy credits that are earned by leaders, but perhaps received in greater numbers by charismatic leaders, which allow leaders to be forgiven for violations of group norms. This is consistent with supporters' willingness to forgive certain transgressions of their leaders, such as the sexual indiscretions of Presidents Kennedy and Clinton. Reagan seemingly had built enough idiosyncrasy credits that he was nicknamed the "Teflon president" because of the public's willingness to forgive the Iran-Contra scandal and other missteps. It seems that followers are more likely to discount inconsistent behavior by charismatic leaders because it allows them to maintain their extremely positive schema of the leader, thereby maintaining positivity of the group as a whole (Lord, Ross, & Lepper, 1979).

Charismatic leaders impact followers by serving as positive role models. Leadership typically involves clear status differences between leaders and followers, so leaders are the focus of followers' attention and they are scrutinized constantly and often emulated. As noted in the social identity theory of leadership, leaders are expected to embody the norms and values of the group. To be seen as a charismatic leader, it is particularly important that the leader be visible and seen as greatly involved in the group's functioning. They become exemplars for group behavior. For example, charismatic military leader Alexander the Great typically led the offensive charges in battle. As a result, Alexander was often wounded, which not only inspired his followers to equal Alexander's boldness but also served to increase his charismatic appeal to his followers. Recent research has demonstrated that leaders who are seen as sacrificing themselves or their self-interests for the good of the group tend to be viewed as more charismatic and more trustworthy (DeCremer & van Knippenberg, 2005; Halverson, Holladay, Kazama, & Quinones, 2004). In the business world, charismatic CEOs, such as Apple's Steve

Jobs and Chrysler's Lee Iacocca, became models of self-sacrifice when they elected to take one dollar as annual salary to demonstrate their commitment to helping lead their companies out of difficult times, a practice that has been adopted by the founders of Google, Inc. (not withstanding that all of these leaders are well-compensated via stock options and other revenue streams).

Self-sacrificial behavior and demonstrating extraordinary commitment to the group and the group's mission on the part of the charismatic leader also serves a social learning, role-modeling function (Bandura, 1977). Followers model the leader's behavior, and with a strong commitment to the group's goals and purposes, they are likely to follow their leader's example of self-sacrifice. Further, when leaders themselves make sacrifices, it encourages followers to make their own sacrifices in service to the group as a method of reciprocation (viewing the leader's sacrifice as a favor that should be returned). It seems probable that self-sacrificing leaders are well aware that these behaviors may lead to increased compliance from followers (Cialdini & Trost, 1998).

In summary, as suggested by social identity theory, charismatic leadership (and leadership in general) is part social construction. Individuals who are perceived to be prototypical group members emerge as leaders, and if they seem the embodiment of all that the group or organization stands for, they are prone to be labeled as charismatic. Engaging in bold or self-sacrificial behavior enhances followers' perceptions of a leader's charisma. However, situational and individual factors also contribute to charismatic leadership, and we will discuss each of these separately.

SITUATIONAL FACTORS AND CHARISMATIC LEADERSHIP

A number of situational factors have been hypothesized to contribute to both the emergence of charismatic leaders and the perception of a leader's charisma. As mentioned, crisis situations represent opportunities for a charismatic leader to emerge as noted by Weber (1947) and others (Burns, 1978; House, 1977). Charismatic leaders of destructive cult groups, including Jim Jones and David Koresh, create beliefs about crisis situations among their followers, including beliefs about external threats of destruction to the group from purported enemies (Layton, 1998; Tabor & Gallagher, 1995). Shamir and Howell (1999) outline a number of additional situational factors. For example, charismatic leaders are more likely to occur in situations where there is a weak group or organization structure, such as in entrepreneurial organizations or groups that lack a rigid, bureaucratic-like structure. It is not surprising then that Silicon Valley has seemingly produced a number of charismatic CEOs in high-tech, start-up organizations and in an environment that thrives on constant change, new technology, and a lack of rules.

Charismatic leaders may also benefit from a contrast effect. Specifically, a charismatic individual is more likely to emerge as leader if he or she follows a particularly noncharismatic individual (Shamir & Howell, 1999). Perceptions of the charismatic leader can intensify when directly contrasted with a leader who is not charismatic. A classic example is the Nixon-Kennedy televised debates during the 1960 presidential election. Kennedy emerged from the debates with his charisma intensified, while Nixon's stilted performance led to him being labeled as noncharismatic. There is also evidence that Kennedy emerged from the debates being viewed by voters as a more "ideal President" (see Goethals, 2005)—consistent with social identity theory's emphasis on prototypicality. A similar process may have occurred in the 2004 election with presidential hopeful John Kerry being labeled as particularly noncharismatic in comparison to George W. Bush (e.g., Safire, 2004).

A leader's charisma can also change depending on situational factors. For example, Winston Churchill was viewed as more charismatic during wartime than during times of peace. Similarly, George W. Bush's popularity rose, presumably along with perceptions of his charisma, following the terrorist attacks of September 11, 2001 (Bligh, Kohles, & Meindl, 2004). And again, dangerous cult leaders have often used increasing perceptions of group crisis and threat among followers as a way to periodically increase their authority and control over followers (Layton, 1998; Lofland, 1977; Tabor & Gallagher, 1995).

A common misconception is that charisma is a phenomenon that only occurs when followers are distant from a leader. Adolf Hitler's charismatic appeal, for example, was carefully managed by keeping him physically distant from followers. Billboard photos and other propaganda materials were crafted in order to portray him as powerful and handsome. Yet, research has demonstrated that charisma can occur at all levels, including in direct one-on-one relationships. For example, House, Spangler, and Woycke (1991) showed that charismatic U.S. presidents were not only seen as charismatic by the distant public, but also by their close cabinet members and advisors.

SOCIAL RELATIONSHIP PROCESSES AND CHARISMATIC LEADERSHIP

Although all forms of leadership involve an interaction of leaders and followers, there are peculiarities to the charismatic leadership relationship that are somewhat unique. Charismatic leaders and their followers have a deeper, more emotional relationship than do other leaders and followers. Moreover, charismatic leaders have important effects on the self-concepts of followers, which then translate into increased devotion to the charismatic leader and higher levels of follower commitment and performance (Bass, 1985; Bass & Riggio, 2006). We will discuss the effects of charismatic leaders on followers in some depth.

Shamir, House, and Arthur (1993) explained key aspects of the relationship that occurs between a charismatic leader and followers. They describe people in social psychological terms, suggesting that while humans are goal-oriented and practical (seeking rewards and avoiding pain), they are also motivated to enhance their self-esteem and sense of self-efficacy over their environment. Self-concept is formed in part by membership in various social groups. The charismatic leader builds the relationship with followers by emphasizing that the follower is a member of a special social collective, particularly one that has admirable values. Mohandas Gandhi, Martin Luther King Jr., and Nelson Mandela appealed to followers as members of a social collective—a universal brotherhood—that advocated nonviolence and basic human rights. Jim Jones consistently presented a mission of revolutionary socialism (i.e., a world without racial and class discrimination) to his followers. This leads followers to feel a sense of collective identity as a member of a group with a noble cause, which enhances their self-esteem and sense of self-worth.

The charismatic leader also expresses confidence in followers and their abilities to achieve outcomes, which builds followers' self-esteem and individual and collective senses of self-efficacy (Bandura, 2000; Walumbwa, Wang, Lawler, & Shi, 2004). This then leads to greater shared commitment to the values and goals of the collective, as espoused by the charismatic leader. In communicating the collective mission, the charismatic leader suggests that there is intrinsic value in the attainment of performance-related goals. For the followers, then, accomplishing goals is not just performing duties, but is intrinsically valued as part of the larger purpose. Moreover, because the goals are a basis for the group's identity, the bond between the individual follower and the group is very strong. Individual identity becomes merged with group identity (Bass & Riggio, 2006), with followers developing self-schemas of themselves as group members (Markus, 1977), making them more likely to continue to behave consistently with group goals and commitments (Cialdini & Trost, 1998).

In addition, the charismatic leader tends to communicate positive affect toward followers. As charismatic leaders express positive regard and liking for their followers, followers increasingly like the leader; as followers liking for the leader increases, their compliance with leader directives will also increase (Cialdini & Trost, 1998). The leader's communication of positive regard and high performance expectations for followers also triggers a self-fulfilling prophecy—the well-researched process popularly termed the "Pygmalion effect" (Rosenthal, 1994; Rosenthal & Jacobson, 1968)—whereby the leader's expectations are communicated directly and subtly to followers, which in turn influences their sense of self-efficacy and subsequent performance (Eden & Sulimani, 2002; McNatt, 2000). The leader can convey positive expectations through subtle nonverbal cues of approval, or more directly by spending time encouraging and challenging followers to become more engaged and focused on the task at hand. Simply put, the leader expects that followers will perform well, and these expectations get communicated to followers through expression of positive feelings and encouragement. This causes followers to be more motivated and to believe that they can indeed perform at high levels, and performance follows. There is evidence that charismatic-transformational leaders are better able to improve follower performance via the Pygmalion effect than are noncharismatic leaders (Dvir, Eden, Avolio, & Shamir, 2002).

The relationship between charismatic leaders and followers is also quite distinct from other leader-follower bonds because of the characteristic emotional connection. Charismatic leaders are, by definition, inspirational. Much of the charismatic leader's ability to inspire has been encapsulated in the emotional contagion process (Hatfield, Cacioppo, & Rapson, 1994). Specifically, charismatic leaders are able to express emotions[2]—typically positive emotions—to followers in such a way that followers are "infected" by their leader's emotions, creating a sympathetic emotional state in the followers. This emotional contagion process has been captured in several studies (e.g., Bono & Ilies, 2006; Cherulnik, Donley, Wiewel, & Miller, 2001; Friedman & Riggio, 1981). For example, Bono and Ilies (2006) demonstrated that charismatic leaders' expression of positive emotions was correlated with ratings of the leaders' effectiveness, as well as its having a positive influence on improving the moods of followers. Friedman and Riggio (1981) found that emotional expressiveness was a necessary component for transmission of moods/emotions to occur. Specifically, only the emotionally expressive individuals in each group were able to influence the moods of the other group members.

It is likely that the contagion process goes both ways, with the charismatic leader sensing followers' emotions and their emotional reactions in order to better connect with followers, although this has not been empirically verified. A vivid example is when a charismatic leader is making an inspiring and emotional speech to a crowd of followers, with the leader attuned to the crowd's reaction and "feeding off" of their reaction to incite the crowd further. Martin Luther King Jr.'s last speech in Memphis ("I've been to the mountaintop") is a good example where he begins slowly (he was ill), but both the crowd and King himself become more and more emotional as the speech progresses.

As this suggests, an important and often overlooked aspect of charismatic leadership is the ability to empathize and "connect" with followers on a deep, emotional level. Individuals who have had face-to-face interactions with charismatic U.S. presidents commonly remark how the president made them "feel like they were the only person in the room." Dozens of individuals have commented that presidents Kennedy and Clinton were particularly adept at making this one-on-one connection (e.g., Hayden, 2002; Sorenson, 1965), as have former and surviving members of the Peoples Temple about Jim Jones (Layton, 1998). We will explore these aspects of charismatic leaders further when focusing on their behaviors and particular charismatic qualities.

CHARISMATIC LEADER BEHAVIORS AND SKILLS

What accounts for the seeming agreement of followers concerning a given leader's charisma? Not just notable success. Truman is considered a highly effective and successful president, but he is rarely mentioned as charismatic. Conversely, the charismatic John F. Kennedy was a popular president, but is not considered by historians to have had a great deal of success. This suggests that there are indeed some individual differences that are driving both shared perceptions of charisma and the unique behaviors demonstrated by charismatic leaders.

An ongoing line of research has tried to list the behaviors that distinguish charismatic leaders from other types of leaders. Many of these distinguishing characteristics have been identified in the work of Conger and Kanungo (1998), which focuses primarily on charismatic leadership in work organizations. According to Conger and Kanungo, charismatic leaders possess certain qualities and behaviors. These include: *sensitivity to the environmental context, sensitivity to followers' needs and concerns, ability to articulate a compelling, shared vision, unconventional behavior,* and *personal risk taking.*

By being sensitive to the environmental context, charismatic leaders look for opportunities to move followers and the organization forward in substantial and often dramatic ways. This can involve moving the group from a period of stagnation or noticing an opportunity for a new endeavor, a course of action, or, in business, a new product or service. In politics, President Kennedy's exhortation to "get America moving again" is a good example. This is then used as a focal point for the leader to draw followers' attention and leads to their perception of the leader's charisma (Conger & Kanungo, 1998).

In addition, charismatic leaders are sensitive to followers' needs and concerns, and these are factored into the process. Charismatic leaders directly communicate their caring and sympathy to followers, both verbally and nonverbally. These leader behaviors help build the strong, emotional bonds between charismatic leaders and followers that were discussed earlier. Research has demonstrated that charismatic/transformational leaders foster higher-quality leader-follower relations than do other types of leaders (Graen & Uhl-Bien, 1995; Howell & Hall-Merenda, 1999).

There has long been a connection between charismatic and visionary leadership, with being visionary viewed as a component of charismatic leadership. The ability of charismatic leaders to articulate a compelling vision may appeal to followers because the vision provides some sort of direction or helps to make sense out of an uncertain and often complex social environment. It is a well-known social psychological finding that under conditions of uncertainty, people look to others for cues that help define the situation and provide guidance and direction (Cialdini & Trost, 1998). Given that charismatic leaders stand out (i.e., they are easily able to attract attention due to their unconventionality and some of the expressive qualities that we will discuss later), and by virtue of their abilities to create and communicate an exciting vision, it makes sense that uncertain followers (and followers during times of uncertainty) would be persuaded by the charismatic leader's compelling vision. Further, by nature of being in a leadership position, leaders also offer authority in times of uncertainty, increasing follower compliance in these kinds of situations (Cialdini & Trost, 1998).

Finally, Conger and Kanungo (1998) note the risk-taking behavior associated with charismatic leaders. Risk taking can involve both the new, unconventional direction that the charismatic leader is advocating the group take, as well as the personal sacrifice that the leader makes to show commitment to the course of action, as noted earlier. The leader's self-sacrifice can serve as a sign to followers that the leader is committed to the group and to the vision and can invoke a sense of reciprocity in followers who become more committed to the group's direction and goals.

Other scholars have noted that charismatic leaders tend to have a "charismatic delivery style" in public speaking (Holladay & Coombs, 1993, 1994). This consists of a speaking style that is viewed as dramatic and dominant, but also friendly, attentive to the audience, and relaxed. Research has demonstrated that charismatic delivery style is related to both perceptions of the speaker's charisma and to perceptions that the individual will be an effective leader (Bligh, Kohles, & Pillai, 2005). In another study, charismatic U.S. presidents were found to use more metaphors in their speech than noncharismatic presidents, presumably in an effort to make their speeches more dramatic and clearer (Mio, Riggio, Levin, & Reese, 2005).

It is interesting to note that although it is popularly believed that charisma has something to do with an individual's personality, few scholars have explored the role of personality in charisma. Riggio (1987, 1998), however, has argued that charismatic individuals possess highly developed skills in emotional communication and exceptional verbal and social skills. Particularly important is the possession of emotional expressiveness and facility in verbal communication, consistent with the research on delivery style. However, charismatic individuals have also been found to be emotionally sensitive and to be sensitive to their social environments. This sensitivity clearly plays a part in developing the strong interpersonal relationships between charismatic leaders and followers that were discussed earlier. Finally, and particularly important for charismatic leaders, there is the ability to play important social roles, what is commonly referred to as "social competence" or "savoir-faire" (Riggio & Reichard, in press). Snyder (1987) has also noted the importance of social role-playing and leadership in his construct of self-monitoring. Leadership itself can be seen as a complex social role. Bass (2002) has argued that the personal qualities associated with charismatic leaders are likely a combination of verbal, emotional, and social intelligences—a point of view that is consistent with the notion that charismatic leaders possess well-developed emotional and social skills.

CONCLUSION

Although charismatic leadership has not received much direct attention from social psychologists, our understanding of charisma and charismatic

Social Psychological Constructs Involved in Charismatic Leadership and How Each Affects the Leadership Process

Social Psychological Construct	Process and Results
Social Identity	Followers join positive groups, enhancing feelings of positive self-esteem
Fundamental Attribution Error	Followers attribute causal influence to the leader, increasing his/her charisma
Discounting	"Idiosyncrasy credits" for the leader
Modeling	Leaders model desired behaviors, and demonstrate rewards for desired behaviors
Social Influence	Leaders become increasingly influential under uncertain or threatening conditions
Contrast Effect	Appeal of leaders is enhanced when they follow a particularly poor leader
Identity Formation	Followers become schematic for membership in the group; they behave consistently with their commitment to the group
Self-Fulfilling Prophecy	Leaders emphasize goals for followers and their abilities to attain them
Emotional Contagion	Followers take on the emotions of leaders; leaders read and emulate the emotions of followers
Compliance	Liking of the leader; reciprocation of self-sacrifice; appeal of authority in conditions of uncertainty

leadership processes can be increased through the application of social psychological theories and constructs. Leadership, and charismatic leadership in particular, is extremely complex. It occurs at multiple levels—the group, the dyad, and at the individual level. The general public has been fascinated with and mystified by charisma and charismatic leadership. Looking at charismatic leadership through the lens of social psychology allows us to see clearly that it is a product of the interplay of the social, interpersonal, cognitive, and emotional processes of human beings.

NOTES

1. Sadly, relatively few women are mentioned initially in lists of charismatic leaders, although this is likely due to relatively few women holding national and international leadership positions until recent years.

2. Negative emotions can also be part of the emotional contagion process as evidenced by Adolf Hitler's use of strong negative emotions—anger, outrage, frustration—to build follower commitment and fuel followers' hatred for scapegoated groups such as Jews, gypsies, and gays.

REFERENCES

Bandura, A. (1977). *Social learning theory.* Englewood Cliffs, NJ: Prentice-Hall.

Bandura, A. (2000). Exercise of human agency through collective efficacy. *Current Directions in Psychological Science, 9,* 75–78.

Bass, B. M. (1985). *Leadership and performance beyond expectations.* New York: Free Press.

Bass, B. M. (2002). Cognitive, social, and emotional intelligence of transformational leaders. In R. E. Riggio, S. E. Murphy, & F. J. Pirozzolo (Eds.), *Multiple intelligences and leadership* (pp. 105–118). Mahwah, NJ: Erlbaum.

Bass, B. M., & Riggio, R. E. (2006). *Transformational leadership* (2nd ed.). Mahwah, NJ: Erlbaum.

Bligh, M. C., Kohles, J. C., & Meindl, J. R. (2004). Charisma under crisis: Presidential leadership, rhetoric, and media responses before and after the September 11th terrorist attacks. *Leadership Quarterly, 15,* 211–239.

Bligh, M. C., Kohles, J. C., & Pillai, R. (2005). Crisis and charisma in the California recall election. *Leadership, 1,* 323–352.

Bono, J. E., & Ilies, R. (2006). Charisma, positive emotions and mood contagion. *Leadership Quarterly, 17,* 317–334.

Burns, J. M. (1978). *Leadership.* New York: Harper & Row.

Cherulnik, P. D., Donley, K. A., Wiewel, T. R., & Miller, S. (2001). Charisma is contagious: The effect of leaders' charisma on observers' affect. *Journal of Applied Social Psychology, 31,* 2149–2159.

Cialdini, R. B., & Trost, M. R. (1998). Social influence: Social norms, conformity, and compliance. In D. T. Gilbert, S. T. Fiske, & G. Lindzey (Eds.), *Handbook of social psychology* (4th ed., Vol. 3, pp. 151–192). New York: McGraw-Hill.

Conger, J. A., & Kanungo, R. N. (1998). *Charismatic leadership in organizations.* Thousand Oaks, CA: Sage.

De Cremer, D., & van Knippenberg, D. (2005). Cooperation as a function of leader self-sacrifice, trust, and identification. *Leadership & Organization Development Journal, 26,* 355–369.

Dvir, T., Eden, D., Avolio, B. J., & Shamir, B. (2002). Impact of transformational leadership on follower development and performance: A field experiment. *Academy of Management Journal, 45,* 735–744.

Eden, D., & Sulimani, R. (2002). Pygmalion training made effective: Greater mastery through augmentation of self-efficacy and means efficacy. In B. J. Avolio, & F. J. Yammarino (Eds.), *Transformational and charismatic leadership: The road ahead* (pp. 287–308). Oxford, UK: JAI/Elsevier.

Friedman, H. S., & Riggio, R. E. (1981). Effect of individual differences in nonverbal expressiveness on transmission of emotion. *Journal of Nonverbal Behavior, 6,* 96–104.

Goethals, G. R. (2005). Nonverbal behavior and political leadership. In R. E. Riggio & R. S. Feldman (Eds.), *Applications of nonverbal behavior* (pp. 95–115). Mahwah, NJ: Erlbaum.

Graen, G. B., & Uhl-Bien, M. (1995). Relationship based approach to leadership: Development of leader-member exchange (LMX) theory of leadership over 25 years: Applying a multi-level, multi-domain perspective. *Leadership Quarterly, 6,* 219–247.

Halverson, S. K., Holladay, C. L., Kazama, S. M., & Quinones, M. A. (2004). Sacrificial behavior in crisis situations: The competing roles of behavioral and situational factors. *Leadership Quarterly, 15,* 263–275.

Hatfield, E., Cacioppo, J. T., & Rapson, R. (1994). *Emotional contagion.* Cambridge: Cambridge University Press.

Hayden, J. (2002). *Covering Clinton: The President and the press in the 1990s.* Westport, CT: Praeger.

Hogg, M. A. (2001). A social identity theory of leadership. *Personality and Social Psychology Review, 5,* 184–200.

Hogg, M. A. (2004). Social identity theory. In G. R. Goethals, G. J. Sorenson, & J. M. Burns (Eds.), *Encyclopedia of Leadership* (Vol. 4, pp. 1457–1462). Thousand Oaks, CA: Sage Press.

Hogg, M. A., & van Knippenberg, D. (2003). A social identity model of leadership effectiveness in organizations. In R. M. Kramer & B. M. Staw (Eds.), *Research in organizational behavior: Vol. 25* (pp. 243–295). Oxford: Elsevier.

Holladay, S. J., & Coombs, W. T. (1993). Communicating visions: An exploration of the role of delivery in the creation of leader charisma. *Management Communication Quarterly, 6,* 405–427.

Holladay, S. J., & Coombs, W. T. (1994). Speaking of visions and visions being spoken: An exploration of the effects of content and delivery on perceptions of leader charisma. *Management Communication Quarterly, 8,* 165–189.

Hollander, E. P. (1958). Conformity, status, and idiosyncrasy credit. *Psychological Review, 65,* 117–127.

House, R. J. (1977). A 1976 theory of charismatic leadership. In J. G. Hunt & L. L. Larson (Eds.), *Leadership: The cutting edge* (pp. 189–207). Carbondale, IL: Southern Illinois University Press.

House, R. J., Spangler, W. D., & Woycke, J. (1991). Personality and charisma in the U.S. presidency: A psychological theory of leader effectiveness. *Administrative Science Quarterly, 36,* 364–396.

Howell, J. M., & Hall-Merenda, K. E. (1999). The ties that bind: The impact of leader-member exchange, transformational and transactional leadership, and distance on predicting follower performance. *Journal of Applied Psychology, 84,* 680–694.

Jones, E. E., & Nisbett, R. E. (1972). The actor and the observer: Divergent perceptions of the causes of the behavior. In E. E. Jones, D. E. Kanouse, H. H. Kelley, R. E. Nisbett, S. Valins, and B. Weiner (Eds.), *Attribution: Perceiving the causes of behavior* (pp. 79–94). Morristown, NJ: General Learning Press.

Layton, D. (1998). *Seductive poison: A Jonestown survivor's story of life and death in the Peoples Temple.* New York: Anchor Books.

Lofland, J. (1977). *Doomsday cult: A study of conversion, proselytization, and maintenance of faith.* New York: Halsted.

Lord, C. G., Ross, L., & Lepper, M. (1979). Biased assimilation and attitude polarization: The effects of prior theories on subsequently considered evidence. *Journal of Personality & Social Psychology, 37,* 2098–2109.

Markus, H. R. (1977). Self-schemata and processing information about the self. *Journal of Personality & Social Psychology, 35,* 63–78.

McNatt, D. B. (2000). Ancient Pygmalion joins contemporary management: A meta-analysis of the result. *Journal of Applied Psychology, 85,* 314–322.

Meindl, J. R., Ehrlich, S. B., & Dukerich, J. M. (1985). The romance of leadership. *Administrative Science Quarterly, 30,* 78-102.

Mio, J. S., Riggio, R. E., Levin, S., & Reese, R. (2005). Presidential leadership and charisma: The effects of metaphor. *Leadership Quarterly, 16,* 287–294.

Riggio, R. E. (1987). *The charisma quotient.* New York: Dodd, Mead.

Riggio, R. E. (1998). Charisma. In H. S. Friedman (Ed.), *Encyclopedia of mental health* (Vol. 1, pp. 387–396). San Diego, CA: Academic Press.

Riggio, R. E., & Reichard, R. J. (2008). The emotional and social intelligences of effective leadership: An emotional and social skill approach. *Journal of Managerial Psychology, 23*(2), 169–185.

Rosenthal, R. (1994). Interpersonal expectancy effects: A 30-year perspective. *Current Directions in Psychological Science, 3,* 176–179.

Rosenthal, R., & Jacobson, L. (1968). *Pygmalion in the classroom: Teacher expectations and pupils' intellectual development.* New York: Holt, Rinehart & Winston.

Ross, L. (1977). The intuitive psychologist and his shortcomings: Distortions in the attribution process. In L. Berkowitz (Ed.), *Advances in experimental social psychology* (Vol. 10, pp. 173–240). Orlando, FL: Academic Press.

Safire, W. (2004, July 7). The body politic will reject a 'charisma transplant.' *The New York Times.*

Shamir, B., House, R. J., & Arthur, M. B. (1993). The motivational effects of charismatic leadership: A self-concept based theory. *Organization Science, 4,* 577–594.

Shamir, B., & Howell, J. M. (1999). Organizational and contextual influences on the emergence and effectiveness of charismatic leadership. *Leadership Quarterly, 10,* 257–283.

Snyder, M. (1987). *Public appearances, private realities: The psychology of self-monitoring.* New York: W. H. Freeman.

Sorenson, T. C. (1965). *Kennedy.* New York: Harper & Row.

Tabor, J. D., & Gallagher, E. V. (1995). *Why Waco? Cults and the Battle for Religious Freedom in America.* Berkeley: University of California Press.

Tajfel, H., & Turner, J. C. (1986). The social identity theory of intergroup behavior. In S. Worchel & W. Austin (Eds.), *Psychology of intergroup relations* (pp. 7–24). Chicago: Nelson-Hall.

van Knippenberg, D., & Hogg, M. A. (2003). A social identity model of leadership effectiveness in organizations. In R. M. Kramer & B. M. Staw (Eds.), *Research in organizational behavior, Vol. 25* (pp. 243–295). Oxford: Elsevier.

Walumbwa, F. O., Wang, P., Lawler, J. J., & Shi, K. (2004). The role of collective efficacy in the relations between transformational leadership and work outcomes. *Journal of Occupational and Organizational Psychology, 77,* 515–530.

Weber, M. (1947). *The theory of social and economic organizations* (A. M. Henderson & T. Parsons, Trans.). New York: Free Press.

3

Knocking on Heaven's Door: The Social Psychological Dynamics of Charismatic Leadership

SHELDON SOLOMON, FLORETTE COHEN, JEFF GREENBERG, AND TOM PYSZCZYNSKI

Charismatic leaders have a way of appearing in times of great distress. They usually espouse a decidedly radical vision that promises to resolve the crisis . . . a charismatic leader offering a solution, however radical, is particularly welcome in difficult times . . . in the turmoil and anxiety that keep company with crisis, anyone who confidently proposes a solution is likely to be looked upon as charismatic . . . followers' response to charismatics [is] a devotion born of distress.

(Lipman-Blumen, 1996, p. 30)

In this chapter we present a social psychological account of charismatic leadership from an existential psychodynamic perspective based on terror management theory and empirical research in support of this conceptual analysis. We start with Max Weber's depiction of charismatic leadership as a fundamentally social psychological process consisting of a dynamic interpersonal relationship with a specific kind of leader serving the needs of particular followers in the context of unsettling historical moments. Specifically, a charismatic leader generally arises in times of uncertainty and distress, and proclaims supernatural powers or is imbued with them by her/his followers, who then take psychological solace basking in the reflected heroic glory of the divinely ordained leader's effort to identify and eliminate evil. And following Ernest

Becker, we argue that fear of death is a central determinant of the motivational impetus of a substantial proportion of human behavior and the psychological impetus for the allure of charismatic leadership. In accord with these claims, we describe research demonstrating that reminders of death increase Americans' support for charismatic leaders in general and for President George W. Bush and his policies in Iraq in particular. Finally, we briefly consider the implications of these ideas for democratic political institutions and future inquiry in leadership studies.

The German sociologist Max Weber initiated contemporary scientific analysis of leadership by distinguishing between authority based on tradition (e.g., kings and family patriarchs), rationality (i.e., power legally acquired through existing bureaucratic structures), and charisma. Weber (1922/1947; see also 1925/1968) characterized charisma as "a certain quality of an individual personality, by virtue of which he is set apart from ordinary men and treated as endowed with supernatural, superhuman, or at least specifically exceptional powers or qualities," and stipulated that charismatic leaders can range from saintly (e.g., Jesus, Mohandas Gandhi, Mother Teresa) to diabolical (e.g., Adolf Hitler, Charles Manson). Weber also posited that charismatic leaders often emerged in times of historical upheaval.

In this chapter we present a social psychological account of charismatic leadership from an existential psychodynamic perspective based on terror management theory (Greenberg, Pyszczynski, & Solomon, 1986; Solomon, Greenberg, & Pyszczynski, 1991).

TERROR MANAGEMENT THEORY

Terror management theory (TMT) is derived primarily from work by cultural anthropologist Ernest Becker (1962, 1971, 1973, 1975). Becker asserted that although we humans share with all other forms of life a basic biological predisposition toward continued existence in the service of survival and reproduction, we possess cognitive capabilities that enable us to engage in abstract, symbolic thought (Deacon, 1997), rendering us explicitly aware of our own existence and enabling us to ponder the past, imagine possible futures, and conceive of that which does not presently exist and then transform our imaginative conceptions into concrete reality.

These remarkable cognitive capabilities, however, also produced problematic consequences, specifically, the awareness of the following: (1) the inevitability of death; (2) the fact that death can occur at any time for unpredictable and uncontrollable reasons; and (3) that humans are, from a biological perspective, transient creatures no more durable or noteworthy than porcupines or paramecia. These disquieting revelations subjected early humans to potentially debilitating terror that would undermine effective instrumental behavior (Solomon, Greenberg, Schimel, Arndt, & Pyszczynski, 2004a).

Becker hypothesized that humans solved the problem of death through the creation and maintenance of cultural worldviews: beliefs about the nature of reality shared by individuals within a group that provide an explanation of the origin of the universe, prescriptions for obtaining a sense of personal significance (self-esteem), and assurances of invulnerability and immortality to those of value—either literally through various conceptions of afterlives common to almost all religions (Burkert, 1996), and/or symbolically by being part of something greater and longer lasting than oneself, such as children, fortunes, works of art or science, and identification with a culture that will persist after one's own demise.

In sum, the juxtaposition of an inclination toward self-preservation with the sophisticated intellectual abilities that make humans aware of death creates the potential for paralyzing terror. One of the most important functions of cultural worldviews is to manage the terror associated with this awareness of death. Effective "terror management" requires two components: (a) faith in a meaningful conception of reality; and (b) belief that one is meeting the standards of value prescribed by that worldview. Because of the protection from the potential for terror afforded by these psychological structures, people are motivated to maintain faith in their cultural worldviews and satisfy the standards of value associated with them.

Faith in cultural worldviews, and their effectiveness as buffers against anxiety, is increased when others share one's worldview and decreased when others hold worldviews different from one's own. This is one reason why people often feel uncomfortable and even hostile toward those who are different. Additionally, because no symbolic cultural construction can actually overcome the physical reality of death, residual anxiety is unconsciously projected onto other group(s) of individuals as scapegoats: designated diabolical repositories of evil, the eradication of which would make earth as it is in heaven. This leads us to respond to people with different beliefs by berating them, trying to convert them to our system of beliefs, and/or just killing them to show that "my God is stronger than your God and we'll kick your ass to prove it."

Empirical assessments of TMT. Over 300 experiments by independent researchers in at least 16 countries have produced findings in accord with hypotheses derived from TMT (for recent reviews, see Greenberg, Solomon, & Arndt, 2008; Solomon, Greenberg, & Pyszczynski, 2004b). This research has shown that: (a) increasing self-esteem reduces anxiety in response to threats (e.g., watching gory death images or anticipating electrical shocks); (b) subtle reminders of mortality lead to more positive reactions to those who support one's worldview, more negative reactions to those who threaten it, and increased striving for self-esteem; (c) threats to self-esteem or one's worldview increase the accessibility of death-related thoughts, and boosts to self-esteem or faith in one's worldview reduce the accessibility of death-related thoughts; and (d) increasing the plausibility of life after death decreases the effect of reminders of death on self-esteem striving and worldview defense. Because much of our research on the role of terror management processes in the appeal of charismatic leaders has focused largely on the *mortality salience hypothesis* [described in (b) above], we provide a more thorough review of previous research that has taken this approach.

The mortality salience hypothesis states that if cultural worldviews and the personal significance they afford serve a death-denying function, then asking someone to think about their own death (*mortality salience* [MS]) should increase the need for the protection normally provided by the cultural worldview and the self-worth derived from it, and, accordingly, evoke judgments and behaviors that uphold faith in that worldview and one's self-worth within the context of that worldview. Participants in a typical study are told that we are investigating personality traits; consequently they will complete some standard personality assessments. Embedded in these personality inventories to obscure the true purpose of the study is what is described as a new projective measure consisting of two open-ended questions to render mortality momentarily salient: "Please briefly describe the emotions that the thought of your own death arouse in you"; and "Jot down, as specifically as you can, what you think will happen to *you* as you physically die." Participants in control conditions complete parallel questions about other topics. Participants are then given an opportunity to evaluate others who either share or differ from their cultural worldviews or to assert their self-worth.

For example, Greenberg et al. (1990, Study 1) had Christian participants rate Christian and Jewish targets (who were portrayed as quite similar except for religious background) after a mortality salience or control induction. In the control condition there were no differences in participants' evaluations of the targets; however, a reminder of death in the experimental condition produced increased affection for the fellow Christian target and exaggerated hostility for the Jewish target. Greenberg et al. (1990, Study 3) then exposed American college students to essays supposedly written by an American author who either praised or condemned the American way of life, following a mortality salience or control induction. Participants rated the author of the pro-U.S. essay more favorably than the author of the anti-U.S. essay in the control condition; however, in response to MS this tendency was exaggerated in both directions; specifically, more positive and negative reactions to pro- and anti-U.S. authors, respectively.

Ochsmann and Mathy (1994) demonstrated behavioral effects of MS: German university students sat closer to a German confederate and farther away from a Turkish confederate after MS relative to a control condition in which there was no difference in physical distance as a function of the ethnicity of the confederate; McGregor et al. (1998) showed that MS produced greater physical aggression against someone who did not share one's political orientation; and Greenberg, Simon, Porteus, Pyszczynski, and Solomon (1995) demonstrated that participants were more uncomfortable sifting sand through an American flag or using a crucifix as a hammer following a MS induction.

Mortality salience effects have been obtained using a wide variety of operationalizations of MS, e.g., subliminal reminders of death (Arndt, Greenberg, Pyszczynski, & Solomon, 1997) or interviews in front of a funeral parlor (Pyszczynski et al., 1996). Additionally, studies have found MS effects to be quite different from reminders of other aversive events, such as uncertainty, failure, intense pain, social exclusion, and paralysis.

FATAL ATTRACTION: THE ALLURE OF CHARISMATIC LEADERS

Allegiance to charismatic leaders may be one particularly effective mode of terror management. In *Escape from Freedom*, Eric Fromm (1941) proposed that loyalty to charismatic leaders results from a defensive need to feel a part of a larger whole, and surrendering one's freedom to a larger-than-life leader can serve as a source of self-worth and meaning in life. Following Fromm, Becker (1971, 1973) posited that when mainstream worldviews are not serving people's need for psychological security, concerns about mortality impel people to devote their psychological resources to following charismatic leaders who bolster their self-worth by making them feel like they are valued participants in a great heroic mission, such that "[group] ... members do not feel that they are alone with their own smallness and helplessness, as they have the powers of the hero-leaders with whom they are identified" (Becker, 1973, p. 133).

To test this hypothesis, Cohen, Solomon, Maxfield, Pyszczynski, and Greenberg (2004) had participants read campaign statements purportedly written by three gubernatorial candidates after a MS or control induction. The candidates varied in leadership style, following Yukl's (1998) distinction between charismatic (visionary), task-oriented (instrumentally effective), and relationship-oriented (emphasizing the need for leaders and followers to work together and accept mutual responsibility) leadership styles. For example, the charismatic leader stated: "You are not just an ordinary citizen, you are part of a special state and a special nation ...." The task-oriented leader stated: "I can accomplish all the goals that I set out to do. I am very careful in laying out a detailed blueprint of what needs to be done so that there is no ambiguity." The relationship-oriented leader stated: "I encourage all citizens to take an active role in improving their state. I know that each individual can make a difference . . . ."

Participants then selected the candidate they would vote for. The results were striking. In the control condition, only 4 of 95 participants voted for the charismatic candidate, with the rest of the votes split evenly between the task and relationship oriented leaders. However, following MS, there was almost an 800 percent increase in votes for the charismatic leader (31); votes for the task-oriented leader were unaffected, but the relationship-oriented leader's votes significantly declined (perhaps because MS participants were disinclined to support a leader who asked them to share responsibility for the affairs of state, rather than assuring them that they are special by virtue of merely belonging to it).

These findings led us to wonder if President George W. Bush's tremendous popularity following the September 11, 2001, attacks on the Pentagon and World Trade Center was partially a consequence of the dramatic and ongoing reminder of death and vulnerability provided by that fateful event. Prior to 9/11, Bush's presidency was viewed as ineffectual and uninspired, even to many of his Republican supporters. Indeed, in a front-page story in the Sunday *New York Times* published on September 9, 2001, Berke and Sanger wrote:

> As White House officials move to refocus President Bush's energies on the precarious economy, they are working to present him as a more commanding leader in what may be the most treacherous stretch of his first year in the White House. The economic and political challenges facing Mr. Bush were underscored earlier this week when his senior adviser, Karl Rove, joined more than a dozen prominent Republicans for a private dinner and heard an unvarnished critique of Mr. Bush's style and strategy. . . . As Mr. Bush faces narrowing economic options at home and rising challenges abroad, some of his advisers said they feared he still did not project the image of a commanding leader. These advisers cite polls showing that many people still view Mr. Bush not as decisive but as tentative and perhaps overly scripted.

However, within a few weeks of declaring that the nation was at war and warning other nations to join the "crusade" to "rid the world of the evildoers" or face, in Vice President Dick Cheney's words, the "full wrath of the United States" (Purdum, 2001), President Bush's approval ratings reached historically unprecedented heights. Summarizing the aggregated findings of over 300 national surveys taken in September and October 2001, Jacobson (2003, pp. 5–6) observed:

> Americans of all political stripes rallied around the president. Bush's approval ratings shot up from the 50s to the highest levels ever recorded, topping

90 percent in some September and October polls. The largest change by far occurred among Democratic identifiers, whose ratings of Bush jumped by more than 50 percentage points, from an average of 30 percent in the period before September 11 to an average of 81 percent in the month following the attacks. Support also rose among Republicans (to 98 percent in polls taken through October) but it was already so high (89 percent) that the Republican contribution to the overall rise could be only modest.

This remarkable transformation of the President from an awkward lame duck in-the-making to a courageous, self-assured, decisive chief executive was described in the cover story in *Time Magazine* on October 22, 2001 (Carney and Dickerson)—*A Work In Progress: Bush is growing—and graying—before our eyes. An inside report on the making of a leader:*

> The President is growing before our eyes . . . . The changing President is the perfect mirror of a changing country. He's trying to become the leader that America needs right now, just as America is trying to become the nation it needs to be. Though his hair seems grayer since Sept. 11, his face a touch more careworn, Bush has told a number of friends and advisers that he has never known such clarity of purpose, such certainty that he is the right person for the moment. He is buoyed by his faith that God has chosen him to lead the country during this perilous time.

This fits nicely with Weber's account of the dynamics of charismatic leadership: Bush became a charismatic leader by declaring that God had chosen him to rid the world of evil at a historical moment, when due to the 9/11 terrorist attacks, most Americans were experiencing great psychological duress.

To determine if President Bush's popularity and support for his policies in Iraq was influenced by defensive reactions to subtle reminders of death, Landau et al. (2004; Study 1) asked participants to read the following "Opinion Survey" after a MS or aversive control induction:

> It is essential that our citizens band together and support the President of the United States in his efforts to secure our great Nation against the dangers of terrorism. Personally I endorse the actions of President Bush and the members of his administration who have taken bold action in Iraq. I appreciate our President's wisdom regarding the need to remove Saddam Hussein from power and his Homeland Security Policy is a source of great comfort to me. It annoys me when I hear other people complain that President Bush is using his war against terrorism as a cover for instituting policies that, in the long run, will be detrimental to this country. We need to stand behind our President and not be distracted by citizens who are less than patriotic. Ever since the attack on our country on September 11, 2001, Mr. Bush has been a source of strength and inspiration to us all. God bless him and God bless America.

While President Bush and his policies in Iraq were not highly regarded by participants in the control condition, there was a dramatic increase in support for the President and his Iraq policies following a MS induction.

In Study 2, participants were exposed to subliminal terrorism primes (the numbers 911 or the letters WTC) or subliminal control primes (numbers and letters of equivalent familiarity), followed by a word stem completion task to assess the accessibility of implicit death-related thoughts; e.g., C O F F _ _ and S K _ _ _ could be completed as coffin and skull rather than coffee and skill. Results indicated greater numbers of death-related words for participants in the subliminal terrorism prime conditions; for Americans then, even nonconscious intimations of the events of 9/11 aroused concerns about mortality. Accordingly, in Study 3 we asked participants to think about death (MS), the events of 9/11 (terrorism prime), or an aversive control topic (an upcoming exam) before reading the same "Opinion Survey" employed in Study 1, and found that both mortality and 9/11 salience produced substantial increases in support for President Bush and his policies in Iraq (results graphically depicted in Figure 3-1).

Then in Study 4, whereas participants rated John Kerry more favorably than George Bush in a control condition, Bush was more favorably evaluated than Kerry after a reminder of death. These findings were then replicated and extended by Cohen, Ogilvie, Solomon, Greenberg, and Pyszczynski (2005) in a sample of registered voters who intended to vote in a study conducted six weeks before the 2004 presidential election. Whereas control participants

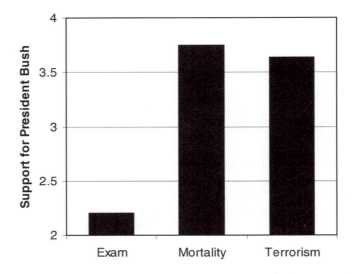

Figure 3-1 Support for President Bush as a function of priming condition

reported they would be voting for Senator Kerry by a 4:1 margin, President Bush was favored by a 2.5:1 margin after a MS induction.

From a TMT perspective, these findings reflect the psychological security afforded by Bush's self-confident public image, his message of being divinely ordained on the right side in the battle of good versus evil, his high status as President, the psychological insecurity associated with the popularized image of Kerry as an indecisive waffler, or a combination of these factors. Regardless of the specific reasons, Cohen et al. (2005) argued that the 2004 presidential election was decisively influenced by nonconscious defensive reactions to relentless reminders of death and the events of September 11, 2001, by Republican political strategists aided by the release of a video by Osama bin Laden the weekend before the election; from a purely political perspective, death has been very good to President Bush. Indeed, Senator Kerry came to the same conclusion when reflecting on the election on January 30, 2005, observing that: "the attacks of Sept. 11 were the 'central deciding thing' in his contest with President Bush and that the release of an Osama bin Laden videotape the weekend before Election Day had effectively erased any hope he had of victory" (Nagourney, 2005).

Some (e.g., Jost, 2006) have interpreted the Bush finding as indicating that MS leads people toward political conservatism. However, existing evidence does not support this conclusion. First, in all of the MS-Bush studies, a single item measure of political orientation was included after the MS manipulation and the evaluation of Bush. MS did not shift participants toward conservatism on this self-report measure in any of these studies. This suggests that the Bush effect did not reflect a general shift toward political conservatism, but rather an increased preference for either the current leader of the nation or for a more charismatic candidate. Indeed, Pyszczynski et al. (2006) found that although MS led conservative Americans to advocate more extreme military measures against potentially threatening nations, it had no such effect on moderate or liberal Americans.

To more directly determine if MS affects political orientation or the appeal of charismatic candidates, Kosloff, Greenberg, Weise, and Solomon (2008) examined the effects of MS on American liberals' and conservatives' evaluations of two gubernatorial candidates. In one condition, candidate A was a charismatic conservative and candidate B was a conflicted liberal. In the other condition, candidate A was a charismatic liberal and candidate B was a conflicted conservative. Following Cohen et al. (2004), the charismatic candidates exuded self-confidence and emphasized the specialness and greatness of the nation. The conflicted candidates expressed concerns and uncertainty about the future and guarded optimism about what s/he could accomplish. The liberal candidates emphasized protecting the environment, freedom of speech, privacy, and civil rights for all. The conservative candidates

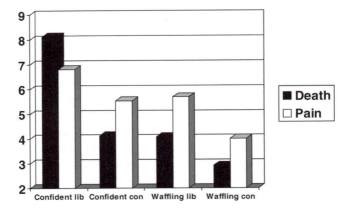

Figure 3-2 Liberal participants' evaluations of confident liberal, confident conservative, waffling liberal, and waffling conservative candidates, as a function of mortality salience

emphasized secure streets and borders, family values, religious freedom, and the right to bear arms.

The results for liberal participants, depicted in Figure 3-2, showed that MS significantly increased the appeal of the charismatic liberal and significantly reduced liking for the conflicted liberal or either conservative candidate. The data for the conservative participants, depicted in Figure 3-3, showed a parallel pattern. MS significantly increased liking for the charismatic conservative and tended to reduce liking for the conflicted conservative

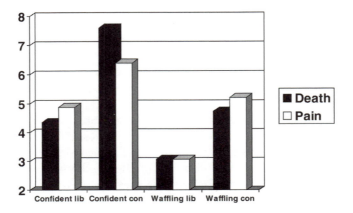

Figure 3-3 Conservative participants' evaluations of confident liberal, confident conservative, waffling liberal, and waffling conservative candidates, as a function of mortality salience

and the charismatic liberal, although the latter two simple effects were not significant.

MS therefore appears to increase the appeal of charismatic leaders who promote one's preferred political ideology. There was no hint of an MS-induced shift toward the conservative candidate. In fact, consistent with the idea that reminders of death lead to rejection of those who espouse different worldviews, MS made liberals more negative toward the conservative candidates (and tended to make conservatives a bit more negative toward liberal candidates).

TMT research thus indicates that reminders of mortality often lead to increased support for charismatic leaders and their efforts to elevate the ingroup above all others by vanquishing the evil they attribute to particular outgroups. But the picture is complicated. Sometimes these effects are moderated by political orientation (e.g., Kosloff et al., 2008; Pyszczynski et al., 2006), but sometimes they are not (e.g., Cohen et al., 2005; Landau et al., 2004). This has led us to investigate other variables that might determine which aspects of one's worldview a person gravitates toward when the need for existential protection is increased by reminders of death. Weise et al. (2008) recently integrated insights from attachment theory (Bowlby, 1969) and Lakoff's (2002) analysis of moral politics to show that both chronic and acute accessibility of attachment representations can play an important role in this process. Based on Lakoff's (2002) reasoning, we posited that a liberal worldview reflects values congruent with secure attachment, and that values of a conservative worldview reflects less secure attachment patterns. In accord with this notion, Study 1 showed that following MS, securely attached participants increased both self-reported liberalism and support for a Democratic presidential candidate, and less securely attached participants tended to increase self-reported conservatism and support for a Republican presidential candidate.

Other recent studies have shown that when the value of compassion is primed, reminders of death lead fundamentalist Americans to reduce their support for violent tactics in the war on terror and fundamentalist Iranians to less negative attitudes toward the United States in particular and the Western world in general (Rothschild, Abdollahi, & Pyszczynski, 2007). Similarly, Motyl et al. (2007) have shown that the effects of MS on implicit anti-Arab prejudice and anti-immigration attitudes can be reversed or eliminated when a sense of common humanity is activated by means of thoughts of families and childhood. These findings show that although reminders of death often push people to support charismatic leaders and their outgroup-derogating policies, this effect is not inevitable and can even be reversed when elements of one's worldview that counter such tendencies, such as secure attachment, compassionate religious values, or a sense of common humanity, are activated.

CONCLUSION

All of the great leaders have had one characteristic in common: it was the willingness to confront unequivocally the major anxiety of their people in their time. This, and not much else, is the essence of leadership.

(Galbraith, 1977, p. 330)

We concur with Max Weber's depiction of charismatic leadership as a fundamentally social psychological process involving a dynamic interpersonal relationship with a specific kind of leader serving the needs of particular followers in the context of unsettling historical moments. To Weber's cogent analysis of charismatic leadership we added Ernest Becker's insights about denial of death as the underlying motivational impetus for the allure of charismatic leaders; in other words, while Weber *describes* charismatic leadership, Becker *explains* it. And terror management theory affords the methodology to provide empirical corroboration of this explanatory account via the mortality salience paradigm. Specifically, our research demonstrated that reminders of death increase support for charismatic leaders in general and President George W. Bush and his policies in Iraq in particular. Subsequent research demonstrated that reminders of death increase devotion to charismatic leaders who share one's political orientation, and that following a mortality salience induction, securely attached individuals became more liberal and more supportive of a Democratic candidate, while less securely attached individuals became more conservative and more supportive of a Republican candidate.

As we have argued elsewhere (Solomon, Greenberg, & Pyszczynski, 2004c), these findings should be interpreted with caution. We do not mean to argue that all support for charismatic leaders in general, or President Bush and his policies in Iraq in particular, is necessarily the result of mortality salience induced defensive reactions. Many conservatives and Republicans insist that their support for President Bush is based on reasoned agreement with Bush's policies, and this may certainly be the case. However, social psychologists (not to mention Freud and anyone working in the psychoanalytic tradition) are very much aware that people are very poor accountants of their own higher order mental processes (e.g., Nisbett & Wilson, 1977). So given that people really do not and cannot know *why they do what they do when they do it,* claims to the effect that support for President Bush or any charismatic leader have a rational basis must be viewed with skepticism. And this is equally true for liberals making comparable claims about the "rational" basis of support for their leaders as well as their reflexive disdain for Bush, which may also be partially attributable to defensive reactions to mortality salience.

Also important to note is that, following Weber, our analysis of the psychological appeal of charismatic leaders makes no explicit inference about the quality of such leadership. Recall that Weber viewed charismatic leaders on a continuum from heavenly saints to satanic monsters, with benign and/or banal charismatics somewhere in between. Sometimes a fairly unambiguous determination can be made; most people, for example, view Jesus and Gandhi as timely and profoundly positively influential leaders; and Attila the Hun, Ivan the Terrible, Peter the Cruel, and Adolf Hitler as good exemplars of evil incarnate. But other leaders are more difficult to characterize and are often viewed in diametrically different ways by their supporters and their detractors. President George W. Bush is such a leader: to his staunch supporters, he is a heroic stalwart in an unwavering heroic quest to rid the world of evil; while to his detractors, Bush is more akin to an inarticulate Hitler in his demagogic ideology, totalitarian predilections, and imperialist genocidal intentions.

Obviously, both views of the president are overstated, but the general question of how to distinguish between benevolent and malevolent charismatic leadership is worthy of serious theoretical consideration and empirical research, especially in light of Galbraith's claim above that all great leaders confront the most urgent anxieties of their followers at particular historical moments. Jean Lipman-Blumen, in *The Allure of Toxic Leaders: Why We Follow Destructive Bosses and Corrupt Politicians—and How We Can Survive Them* (2005), provides a descriptive account of the behavioral and dispositional tendencies of "toxic" leaders. Behaviorally, such leaders are commonly guilty of the following: violating basic standards of human rights; consciously feeding followers illusions to augment their powers and undermine follower's capacity to act independently; appealing to basest fears of followers; muffling constructive criticism; misleading followers with deliberate falsehoods and misdiagnosis of issues and problems; engaging in unethical, illegal, and criminal acts; building totalitarian or dynastic regimes; targeting scapegoats; ignoring or promoting incompetence, cronyism, and corruption. Personally, such leaders are typically lacking in integrity (specifically, they tend to be cynical, corrupt, hypocritical, or untrustworthy), insatiably ambitious, egotistical in ways that blind him/her to his/her shortcomings, arrogantly unable to recognize mistakes, avaricious, recklessly disregarding of costs of their actions, and unable to understand the nature of relevant problems and to act efficiently and effectively in difficult situations.

Regardless of the level of President Bush's "toxicity" as a leader according to these criteria, future research should be directed to examining the effects of reminders of death on the appeal of charismatic and other types of leaders across the "saint" to "sinner" spectrum, granting that there will always be spirited disagreement about where a particular leader might fall along this continuum. Other individual difference variables in addition to attachment style that might moderate the relationship between mortality salience and the appeal of charismatic leadership should also be investigated. Cross-cultural inquiry is also surely warranted and essential.

Meanwhile, the fact that subtle brief manipulations of psychological conditions—asking people to think about their own death or the events of 9/11—produced such striking differences in political preferences for charismatic leaders in general and President Bush in particular suggests that close elections could be decided as a result of nonrational terror management concerns. This has portentous implications for democratic political institutions. We fervently hope that Americans across the political spectrum could agree that winning elections as a result of nonconscious defensive psychological processes is antithetical to the democratic ideal that voting behavior should be a consequence of rational choice based on an informed understanding of the relevant issues.

The best protection against such outcomes may be to monitor and take pains to resist any efforts by candidates to capitalize on fear-mongering. As David Myers so eloquently put it in a 2004 op-ed piece in the *Los Angeles Times:* "It is perfectly normal to fear purposeful violence from those who hate us. When terrorists strike again, we will all recoil in horror. But smart thinkers also will want to check their intuitive fears against the facts and to resist those who serve their own purposes by cultivating a culture of fear." Additionally as a culture, we should teach our children and encourage our citizens to vote with their "heads" rather than their "hearts," as we know from prior research that mortality salience effects are eliminated when people are asked to think rationally (Simon et al., 1997). And it may also be helpful to raise awareness of how concerns about death affect human behavior in general in order to inoculate individuals to minimize defensive reactions to mortality salience. Hopefully, such measures will encourage citizens to make electoral choices based on the qualifications and political positions of the candidates rather than on the urge to preserve psychological equanimity in response to intimations of mortality.

REFERENCES

Arndt, J., Greenberg, J., Pyszczynski, T., & Solomon, S. (1997). Subliminal presentation of death reminders leads to increased defense of the cultural worldview. *Psychological Science, 8,* 379–385.

Becker, E. (1962). *The birth and death of meaning.* New York: Free Press.

Becker, E. (1971). *The birth and death of meaning: An interdisciplinary perspective on the problem of man* (2nd ed.). New York: Free Press.

Becker, E. (1973). *The denial of death*. New York: Free Press.

Becker, E. (1975). *Escape from evil*. New York: Free Press.

Berke, R., & Sanger, D. (2001, September 9). Bush's aides seek to focus efforts on the economy. *The New York Times*, p. 1A.

Bowlby, J. (1969). *Attachment*, Attachment and Loss (Vol. 1). New York: Basic Books.

Burkert, W. (1996). *Creation of the sacred: Tracks of biology in early religions*. Cambridge, MA: Harvard University Press.

Carney, J., & Dickerson, J. F. (2001, October 22). A work in progress. *Time Magazine*.

Cohen, F., Ogilvie, D. M., Solomon, S., Greenberg, J., & Pyszczynski, T. (2005). American roulette: The effect of reminders of death on support for George W. Bush in the 2004 presidential election. *Analyses of Social Issues and Public Policy, 5,* 177–187.

Cohen, F., Solomon, S., Maxfield, M., Pyszczynski, T., & Greenberg, J. (2004). Fatal attraction: The effects of mortality salience on preferences for charismatic, task-focused, and relational leaders. *Psychological Science, 15,* 846–851.

Deacon, T. (1997). *The symbolic species: The co-evolution of language and the brain*. New York: Norton.

Fromm, E. (1941). *Escape from freedom*. New York: Henry Holt.

Galbraith, J. K. (1977). *The age of uncertainty*. Boston: Houghton Mifflin.

Greenberg, J., Pyszczynski, T., & Solomon, S. (1986). The causes and consequences of a need for self-esteem: A terror management theory. In R. F. Baumeister (Ed.), *Public self and private self* (pp. 189–212). New York: Springer-Verlag.

Greenberg, J., Pyszczynski, T., Solomon S., Rosenblatt, A., Veeder, M., Kirkland, S., & Lyon, D. (1990). Evidence for terror management theory II: The effects of mortality salience on reactions to those who threaten or bolster the cultural worldview. *Journal of Personality and Social Psychology, 58,* 308–318.

Greenberg, J., Simon, L., Porteus, J., Pyszczynski, T., & Solomon, S. (1995). Evidence of a terror management function of cultural icons: The effects of mortality salience on the inappropriate use of cherished cultural symbols. *Personality and Social Psychology Bulletin, 21,* 1221–1228.

Greenberg, J., Solomon, S., & Arndt, J. (2008). A basic but uniquely human motivation: Terror management. In J. Y. Shah & W. L. Gardner (Eds.), *Handbook of Motivation Science* (pp. 114–134). New York: The Guilford Press.

Jacobson, G. C. (2003). The Bush presidency and the American electorate. Paper prepared for delivery at the conference on "The George W. Bush Presidency: An Early Assessment" at the Woodrow Wilson School, Princeton University, April 25–26, 2003. Retrieved June 18, 2007, from http://www.wws.princeton.edu/bushconf/JacobsonPaper.pdf

Jost, J. T. (2006). The end of ideology. *American Psychologist, 61,* 651–670.

Kosloff, S., Greenberg, J., Weise, D., & Solomon, S. (2008). The effects of mortality salience on political preferences: The roles of charisma and political orientation. Manuscript submitted for publication, University of Arizona, Tucson, AZ.

Lakoff, G. (2002). *Moral politics: How liberals and conservatives think* (2nd ed.). Chicago: University of Chicago Press.

Landau, M. J., Solomon, S., Greenberg, J., Cohen, F., Pyszczynski, T., Arndt, J., Miller, C. H., Ogilvie, D. M., & Cook, A. (2004). Deliver us from evil: The effects of mortality salience and reminders of 9/11 on support for president George W. Bush. *Personality and Social Psychology Bulletin, 30,* 1136–1150.

Lipman-Blumen, J. (1996). *The connective edge: Leading in an interdependent world.* San Francisco: Jossey-Bass.

Lipman-Blumen, J. (2005). *The allure of toxic leaders: Why we follow destructive bosses and corrupt politicians—and how we can survive them.* New York: Oxford University Press.

McGregor, H. A., Lieberman, J. D., Greenberg, J., Solomon, S., Simon, L., Arndt, J., & Pyszczynski, T. (1998). Terror management and aggression: Evidence that mortality salience motivates aggression against worldview-threatening others. *Journal of Personality and Social Psychology, 74,* 590–605.

Motyl, M., Pyszczynski, T., Cox, C. Seidel, A., Maxfield, M., Solomon, S., & Greenberg, J. (2007). *One big family: The effects of mortality salience and a sense of common humanity on anti-Arab prejudice and attitudes toward immigration.* Manuscript submitted for publication, University of Colorado, Colorado Springs, CO.

Myers, D. (2004, March 9). Do we fear the right thing? *The Los Angeles Times.*

Nagourney, A. (2005, January 31). Kerry says Bin Laden tape gave Bush a lift. *New York Times,* p. A21.

Nisbett, R. E., & Wilson, T. D. (1977). Telling more than we can know: Verbal reports on mental processes. *Psychological Review, 84,* 231–259.

Ochsmann, R., & Mathy, M. (1994). *Depreciating of and distancing from foreigners: Effects of mortality salience.* Unpublished manuscript, Universitat Mainz, Mainz, Germany.

Purdum, T. S. (2001, September 17). After the attacks: The White House. *New York Times,* p. A2.

Pyszczynski, T., Abdollahi, A., Solomon, S., Greenberg, J., Cohen, F., & Weise, D. (2006). Mortality salience, martyrdom, and military might: The Great Satan vs. the Axis of Evil. *Personality and Social Psychology Bulletin, 32,* 525–537.

Pyszczynski, T., Wicklund, R., Floresku, S., Gauch, G., Koch, H., Solomon, S., & Greenberg, J. (1996). Whistling in the dark: Exaggerated consensus estimates in response to incidental reminders of mortality. *Psychological Science, 7,* 332–336.

Rothschild, Z., Abdollahi, A., & Pyszczynski, T. (2007). *Does peace have a prayer? Effects of mortality salience, religious fundamentalism, and compassionate values on hostility toward the outgroup in the United States and Iran.* Manuscript submitted for publication, University of Colorado at Colorado Springs.

Simon, L., Greenberg, J., Harmon-Jones, E., Solomon, S., Pyszczynski, T., Arndt, J., & Abend, T. (1997). Terror management and cognitive-experiential self-theory: Evidence that terror management occurs in the experiential system. *Journal of Personality and Social Psychology, 72,* 1132–1146.

Solomon, S., Greenberg, J., & Pyszczynski, T. (1991). A terror management theory of social behavior: The psychological functions of self-esteem and cultural worldviews. In M. Zanna (Ed.), *Advances in experimental social psychology* (Vol. 24, pp. 91–159). Orlando, FL: Academic Press.

Solomon, S., Greenberg, J., Schimel, J., Arndt, J., & Pyszczynski, T. (2004a). Human awareness of death and the evolution of culture. In M. Schaller and C. Crandal (Eds.),

The psychological foundations of culture (pp. 15–40). Mahwah, NJ: Lawrence Erlbaum Associates.

Solomon, S., Greenberg, J., & Pyszczynski, T. (2004b). The cultural animal: Twenty years of terror management theory and research. In J. Greenberg, S. Koole, & T. Pyszczynski (Eds.), *Handbook of existential experimental social psychology* (pp. 13–34). New York: The Guilford Press.

Solomon, S., Greenberg, J., & Pyszczynski, T. (2004c). Fatal Attraction: A new study suggests a relationship between fear of death and political preferences. *American Psychological Society Observer, 17,* 13–15.

Weber, M. (1947). *Max Weber: The theory of social and economic organization* (A. M. Henderson & T. Parsons, Trans.). New York: The Free Press. (Original work published 1922.)

Weber, M. (1968). The types of legitimate domination. In G. Roth & C. Wittich (Eds.), *Economy and society: An outline of interpretive sociology* (pp. 212–301). New York: Bedminster Press. (Original work published in 1925.)

Weise, D. R., Pyszczynski, T., Cox, C. R., Arndt, J., Greenberg, J., Solomon, S., & Kosloff, S. (2008). Interpersonal politics: The role of terror management and attachment processes in shaping political preferences. *Psychological Science, 19,* 448–455.

Yukl, G. (1998). *Leadership in organizations* (4th ed.). Upper Saddle River, NJ: Prentice-Hall.

4

Social Identity Theory of Leadership

MICHAEL A. HOGG

Scientific leadership research increasingly focuses on organizational and corporate leadership and the role of the chief executive officer (CEO). It pays less attention to public leadership, the role of followers, and the way that leaders forge and express people's identity. Contextualized by a recent resurgence of interest among social psychologists in leadership, this chapter describes the social identity theory of leadership—a theory that pivots on the critical importance of self-definition as a group member (social identity) in processes within and between groups. The more important a group is to one's sense of self in a particular context, the more that leadership effectiveness rests on followers' perceptions that the leader embodies the group's defining or prototypical attributes. Under these conditions prototypical leaders are consensually liked, are able to gain compliance, are the source, not the target, of influence, are trusted to be acting in the group's best interest, are attributed with charismatic characteristics, are able to be innovative, and are well positioned to manage their prototypicality and the group's identity. The chapter describes some empirical support for these ideas and closes with a focus on intergroup leadership as a particularly challenging aspect of identity-related leadership. The social identity theory of leadership is championed as contributing to a new agenda for leadership research.

Why do we follow leaders, what do they do for us, why do we seem so often to need them, and why is it that groups rarely last long or function effectively without some type of leadership structure? Leaders do many things for us—

for example, they can coordinate the actions of many to achieve a shared goal. However, it is not coordination that is key—coordination is more management than leadership. It is the shared goal aspect that goes to the heart of leadership. Leaders are able to reflect, clarify, and redefine our own goals, or set entirely new goals that we come to cherish as our own. They are able to transform individual goals into shared or collective goals that transcend individuality, and they are able to motivate us to work selflessly toward the achievement of these goals. Mohandas Gandhi's role in leading India to independence from Britain in 1947 is an excellent example. He was able to focus and unite a wide array of interests within India around the shared goal of independence, and motivate enormous numbers of people to engage in dangerous nonviolent protests against the British colonial administration and its formidable military apparatus.

Because leadership has such an influence on people's goals and behaviors, and on the structure and functioning of society, it is not only an enduring focus of self-help and "airport" books but also of scientific inquiry—for example, Goethals, Sorenson, and Burns's (2004) four-volume *Encyclopedia of Leadership* has 1,927 pages, 1.2 million words, and 373 substantive (1,000– 6,000 word) entries written by 311 scholars. One notable feature of scientific leadership research is that although leadership is a fundamentally social psychological process where an individual has disproportionate influence over a group, the overwhelming majority of leadership research is not conducted by social psychologists, but by organizational and management scientists who focus primarily on business leadership in corporate and organizational contexts (e.g., Yukl, 2006). Such a focus on leadership through the lens of organizational and management concerns necessarily and understandably prioritizes certain agendas over others—for example, there is a heavy emphasis on the behavior of CEOs and on factors such as organizational commitment and turnover.

One important aspect of leadership that this approach to and perspective on leadership underemphasizes is its identity dimension. In a great many contexts, particularly public leadership contexts (e.g., national, political, ethnic, or ideological leadership), leaders play a pivotal role in defining our identity: what kind of people we are, what attitudes we should hold, how we should behave, what customs we should adopt, how we should interact with and treat others, and so forth (cf. Gardner, 1995). Because people look to their leaders to define who they are, followers, or rank-and-file group members, play a key role in the identity dynamic of leadership—they pay close attention to and provide parameters for the identity being constructed and promulgated by the leader.

In recent years there has been a revival of interest among social psychologists in leadership (e.g., Chemers, 1997; Hogg, 2007, Hogg, in press a; Lord

& Brown, 2004; Messick & Kramer, 2005; also see Northouse, 2007), which is helping reconfigure the agenda for research. Because this resurgence has been noticeably influenced by the social identity theory of leadership (Hogg, 2001; Hogg & van Knippenberg, 2003), which is an analysis of the identity function of leadership, it has naturally focused attention on the identity dimension of leadership.

The social identity theory of leadership also attributes a significant role in effective leadership to the perceptions and behaviors of group members as followers—a focus on followers that resonates in some ways with recent literature on "followership" (e.g., Riggio, Chaleff, & Lipman-Blumen, 2008; Shamir, Pillai, Bligh, & Uhl-Bien, 2006). Another key feature of leadership that is often overlooked is that more often than not leaders need to forge a single group identity out of disparate individual identities or, more usually, disjunctive group identities that describe groups that may have a history of conflict or antipathy—much leadership can be characterized as intergroup leadership (e.g., Pittinsky, in press).

In this chapter, I briefly overview social identity theory to lay the groundwork for a full description of the social identity theory of leadership that follows. I also describe what sort of empirical support there is for the various components of the social identity theory of leadership and comment on gaps in the empirical literature. The chapter closes with summary comments, an assessment of social identity theory's contribution to our understanding of leadership, and a pointer for future research on the important question of intergroup leadership: how do leaders provide unifying leadership to diverse subgroups that often have conflicting identities and agendas, and sometimes a history of hatred and suspicion?

SOCIAL IDENTITY THEORY

Social identity theory is a social psychological theory. It specifies how cognitive, motivational, and social interactive processes interact with knowledge we have about the nature of and relations among social groups and categories in society to construct a self-concept grounded in the groups we belong to, and generate behaviors characteristically associated with people in groups. Originally developed in the early 1970s, social identity theory is now one of social psychology's most significant theories of group processes, intergroup relations, and collective self (Tajfel & Turner, 1979; Turner, Hogg, Oakes, Reicher, & Wetherell, 1987; for contemporary overview see Hogg, 2006). One of its key insights, which distinguishes it from other social psychological accounts of group processes and intergroup relations, is its emphasis on the role of social identity.

Social identity refers to a representation and evaluation of oneself in terms of shared attributes that define the group one belongs to, one's ingroup. For example, one's social identity as a member of the Democratic Party in the United States might include some combination of value placed on universal health care, support for immediate action to prevent climate change, support for women's reproductive rights, and adherence to a more general ideology of social justice. These attributes would to a lesser or greater extent be valued and shared with other Democrats and distinguish one from Republicans. For treatments of social identity theory in the context of organizational science see Ashforth and Mael (1989) and Hogg and Terry (2000), and in the context of sociological social psychology see Hogg, Terry, and White (1995).

In order to deal with the incredible diversity of humanity, the mind represents the social world in terms of categories of people (e.g., Italians, men, Hindus, attorneys). The technical social identity term for these representations is *prototype*—a prototype is a loose or "fuzzy" set of attributes (e.g., attitudes, behaviors, dress, customs) that we believe go together to characterize a group and distinguish it from relevant other groups. Typically, people in one group agree on their prototype of their own group (ingroup) and of relevant other groups (outgroups). They also exaggerate differences between their own group and relevant outgroups and exaggerate how similar members of a specific outgroup are to one another.

In situations where, for example, we are involved in a group activity or intergroup encounter, we meet a stranger who we know little about, we feel proud of our own group, or we despise a particular outgroup, group memberships are psychologically *salient,* and we use people's category membership to configure our perceptions, program our behavior, anticipate their behavior, and structure our interaction. Under these circumstances we relatively automatically categorize people as group members and assign them the attributes of our prototype of their group—we stereotype them and treat them as embodiments of their group rather than as unique individuals (a process that social identity theorists call *depersonalization*). For example, on the basis of accent we might categorize someone as Italian and immediately assume and expect them to conform to our stereotype of Italians—that they, like all Italians, are emotionally expressive, use hand gestures, dress with style, and are passionate about soccer.

A fundamental tenet of social identity theory is that the process of depersonalization can apply to oneself—we contextually categorize ourselves in precisely the same way as we categorize others, and thus we assign to ourselves the prototypical attributes of our own group. The consequence of this is clear; self-categorization transforms our perceptions, beliefs, attitudes, feelings, and behaviors to conform to the prescriptions of the prototype we have of our group.

Because prototypes define groups, in group contexts people thirst for prototype-relevant information. Because the ingroup prototype defines and evaluates one's own group, and thus via self-categorization one's own self and identity, people are particularly vigilant for information about the ingroup prototype. There are many sources of this information, among which the most immediate and reliable is the behavior of fellow ingroup members who one has already learned are highly prototypical of the group. People rely heavily on the behavior of such people to learn what to think, how to behave, and how to view themselves as group members. To foreshadow the argument below, in many group contexts the group leader is viewed by his or her followers to be just such a highly prototypical member.

Social identity theory helps us understand a wide range of group and intergroup phenomena, including prejudice, discrimination, intergroup conflict, stereotyping, conformity, group cohesion, group decision making, and normative deviance; for recent empirical reviews see Abrams, Hogg, Hinkle and Otten (2005), Hogg and Abrams (2007), and Hogg, Abrams, Otten, and Hinkle (2004).

SOCIAL IDENTITY THEORY OF LEADERSHIP

Social identity theory has direct implications for the psychology of leadership, which have recently been formalized as the social identity theory of leadership (Hogg, 2001; Hogg & van Knippenberg, 2003; also see van Knippenberg & Hogg, 2003). The key idea is that as group membership becomes increasingly salient and important to members of the group and as members identify more strongly with the group, effective leadership rests increasingly on the leader being considered by followers to possess prototypical properties of the group. In this analysis, group members as followers play a significant role in configuring the characteristics of the group's leadership or even creating the leadership itself—members are more likely to follow leaders whom they consider most able to construct a group identity that is acceptable to them (Hogg, 2008).

As people identify more strongly with a group, they pay more attention to the group prototype and to what and who is more prototypical (research shows that under these circumstances members have good knowledge about the relative prototypicality of group members—e.g., Haslam, Oakes, McGarty, Turner, & Onorato, 1995). As explained above, this is because the prototype defines the group's membership attributes and thus members' own self-concept and identity. In these contexts where group membership is psychologically salient, being perceived to be a highly prototypical leader makes one more influential. There are a number of basic social identity and social psychological reasons for this.

Appearance of Influence

First, depersonalization means that people conform to the group prototype—there is good evidence that self-categorization produces conformity, because members of a group typically share the same ingroup prototype and each member assigns this same prototype to oneself via self-categorization (e.g., Abrams, Wetherell, Cochrane, Hogg, & Turner, 1990). Thus, members appear to be influenced by the prototype and, therefore, by those members who are actually more group prototypical. Prototypical members are perceived to have disproportionate influence over the rest of the members of the group. Prototypical leaders appear to be more effective sources of influence.

Prototype-Based Popularity

Second, prototypical group members are liked, as group members, more than less prototypical members, and, because there is usually significant agreement on the prototype, the group as a whole likes prototypical members—they are consensually popular in group terms. Research shows that identification and group salience produce relatively consensual liking for more prototypical group members over less prototypical members (e.g., Hogg, 1993). Such popularity facilitates influence—research shows we are significantly more likely to comply with requests from people we like (Berscheid & Reis, 1998). Thus, prototypical leaders are popular in the eyes of their followers and are readily able to gain compliance with their ideas—they can exercise effective leadership. Furthermore, this popularity instantiates an evaluative status difference between the consensually popular leader and his or her followers. Where there is a leadership clique rather than a solo leader, as is often the case, this status differential may become a genuine intergroup status differential within the group, in which case the seeds of destructive leader-follower conflict may be sown.

Legitimacy, Trust, and Innovation

Third, prototypical members find the group more central and important to self-definition, and, therefore, identify more strongly with it. They have a greater investment in the group and, thus, are more likely to behave in group-serving ways. They embody group norms more precisely, and they are more likely to favor the ingroup over outgroups, to treat ingroup members fairly, and to act in ways that promote the ingroup. Research confirms that enhanced identification is associated with greater conformity to norms and stronger ingroup favoritism (e.g., see Hogg & Abrams, 2007) and with fairer treatment of fellow ingroup members and more pronounced promotion of the group's goals and welfare (e.g., see Tyler, 1997). These behaviors confirm members' prototypicality and membership credentials, and encourage other members of the group to trust them to be acting in the best interest of the group even when it may not appear that they are—they are furnished with legitimacy (Tyler, 1997; Tyler & Lind, 1992; see Platow, Reid, & Andrew, 1998; Platow & van Knippenberg, 2001). Thus, followers invest their trust in prototypical leaders, which paradoxically allows such leaders to diverge from group norms and be less conformist and more innovative and transformational than non- or less prototypical leaders (cf. Hollander, 1958). Innovation and transformation are, of course, key components of effective leadership (e.g., Avolio & Yammarino, 2003).

Social Construction of Charisma

Finally, because the prototype is so central to group life, information related to the prototype subjectively stands out against the background of other information in the group. Prototypical leaders are probably the most direct source of prototype information, and so prototypical leaders are figural against the background of the group. Members pay close attention to their leaders and, as in other areas of social perception and inference, attribute their behavior to invariant underlying personality attributes or "essences" (e.g., Gilbert & Malone, 1995; Haslam, Rothschild, & Ernst, 1998). In the context of leadership this causes followers to construct a charismatic leadership personality for their leader—after all, the general class of behaviors that is being attributed to personality include being the source of influence, being able to gain compliance from others, being popular, having higher status, being innovative, and being trusted.

In this way charisma, which plays an important role in transformational leadership (e.g., Avolio & Yammarino, 2003), is constructed by group processes (see Haslam & Platow, 2001) rather than being a static personality attribute that is brought by individuals to the group. The perception of charisma further facilitates effective and innovative leadership on the part of a prototypical leader. For example, a new departmental chair promoted from the ranks might initially seem just like the rest of us, but if members identified strongly with the department and he happened to be highly prototypical then we might gradually attribute his influence over us to his charismatic personality rather than his prototypicality.

Leaders as Entrepreneurs of Identity

These social identity leadership processes extend considerable power to leaders to maintain their leadership position. Because they are trusted, given latitude to be innovative, and invested with status and charisma, prototypical leaders are very effective prototype managers, or entrepreneurs of identity (Reicher & Hopkins, 2003). They can define what the group stands for and what the social identity of its members is, by consolidating an existing prototype, modifying it, or dramatically reconstructing it. One of the key attributes of effective leadership is precisely this visionary and transformational activity in which leaders are able to change what the group sees itself as being. For example, during the 1980s the British Prime Minister, Margaret Thatcher, constructed a new more imperially assertive and proud British identity around an iconic image of herself as Boadecia—a first century British Queen who led a British uprising against the occupying forces of the Roman Empire.

There are many strategies that prototypical leaders can employ to manage their prototypicality and shape their group's identity. There is evidence that they can talk up their own prototypicality and/or talk down aspects of their own behavior that are nonprototypical; identify deviants or marginal members to highlight their own prototypicality or to construct a particular prototype for the group that enhances their own prototypicality; secure their own leadership position by vilifying contenders for leadership and casting the latter as nonprototypical; and identify as relevant comparison outgroups, those outgroups that are most favorable to their own prototypicality (e.g., Reicher & Hopkins, 1996, 2003).

Leaders can also engage in a discourse that raises or lowers salience. If you are highly prototypical, then raising salience and strengthening members' identification with the group will provide you with the leadership benefits of high prototypicality; if you are not very prototypical, then lowering salience and weakening members identification will protect you from the leadership pitfalls of not being very prototypical. Generally, leaders who feel they are not, or are no longer, prototypical strategically engage in a range of group-oriented behaviors to strengthen their membership credentials (e.g., Platow & van Knippenberg, 2001).

In concluding this description of the social identity theory of leadership, there is one important caveat to bear in mind. Social identity leadership processes only, or more strongly, occur in groups that members identify more strongly with. As the group's salience or members' strength of identification with the group weakens, social identity leadership processes also weaken. Leadership becomes less strongly based on how prototypical the leader is of the group, and more strongly based on other factors, such as how charismatic they are, and how well they match people's general or more specific schemas of the properties a leader should possess to fulfill a particular group function.

EMPIRICAL EVIDENCE

Overall, the social identity theory of leadership, although a relative new-comer to the leadership scene, has already attracted solid empirical support from laboratory experiments and more naturalistic studies and surveys. I have mentioned some of this support above; for detailed summaries of empirical work, see Ellemers, de Gilder, & Haslam, 2004; Hogg, 2001; Hogg & van Knippenberg, 2003; van Knippenberg & Hogg, 2003; van Knippenberg, van Knippenberg, De Cremer, & Hogg, 2004.

Perhaps the most critical body of evidence comes from studies showing that, as people identify more strongly with their group, prototypical members are more likely to be (effective) leaders and more prototypical leaders are more effective than less prototypical leaders. For example, Hains, Hogg, and Duck (1997) conducted a laboratory experiment in which participants (N = 184) who anticipated joining a small group for a discussion were given some controlled information about the group. To manipulate strength of iden-tification, the psychological salience of the group was varied—information referred to groups or to loose aggregates of individuals, to the existence of commonalities or differences among people in the group, and to participants in group terms or individual terms. Participants were also told that one of them had been randomly selected as leader and were given information ostensibly about that person—the person's attributes were a close match to the group's attributes (high prototypicality leader) or a poor match (low pro-totypicality leader). Before joining the group they rated the leaders on 10 gen-eral leadership effectiveness items (α = .88). Hains and colleagues found, as predicted, that under high salience the prototypical leader was significantly more strongly endorsed than the less prototypical leader (see Figure 4-1).

Fielding and Hogg (1997) replicated this finding in a naturalistic measurement-based field study of "outward bound" groups, and Hogg, Fielding, Johnson, Masser, Russell, and Svensson (2006) found the same thing in a laboratory study with gender groups in which salience was manipulated in a similar way to Hains et al. (1997) and the leader's group prototypicality was operationalized as the extent to which the participant's (N = 257) gender stereotypical assumptions about the leader matched the group's agentic (male stereotypic) or communal (female stereotypic) norm. Under high salience the prototypical leader was significantly more strongly endorsed (16-item leadership effectiveness scale, α = .92), than the less prototypical leader (see Figure 4-2).

In a similar vein to these studies, studies by Duck and Fielding (1999, 2003) and Van Vugt and De Cremer (1999) have found that as identification strengthens ingroup leaders (more ingroup prototypical) are endorsed more strongly than outgroup leaders (less ingroup prototypical). Other studies

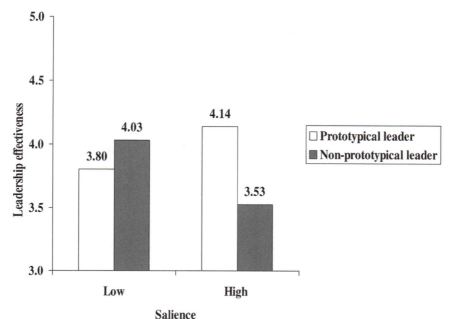

Figure 4-1 Leadership effectiveness as a function of group salience and group prototypicality of the leader (Hains, Hogg, & Duck, 1997)

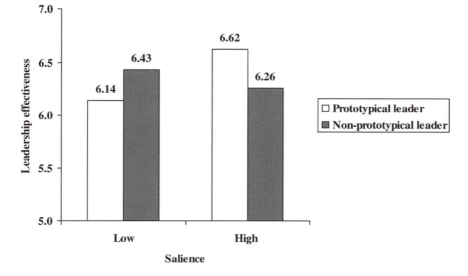

Figure 4-2 Leadership effectiveness as a function of group salience and group prototypicality of the leader (Hogg, Fielding, Johnson, Masser, Russell, & Svensson, 2006)

have shown that as identification increases leaders are more strongly endorsed if they favor their ingroup over outgroups (Platow, Hoar, Reid, Harley, & Morrison, 1997), express strong commitment to the group (De Cremer & Van Vugt (2002), and treat group members as a group rather than individualizing them as separate from the group (Hogg, Martin, Epitropaki, Mankad, Svensson, & Weeden, 2005). In support of the role of trust in social identity related leadership, Platow and van Knippenberg (2001) report a study showing that as people identify more with their group they are more likely to provide unqualified endorsement of their leader to the extent that the leader is highly prototypical of the group.

CONCLUDING COMMENTS AND FUTURE DIRECTIONS

Scientific leadership research has increasingly tended to focus on organizational and corporate contexts and the role of the CEO. Other contexts of leadership, such as public leadership, and other aspects of leadership, such as the role of followers and the identity dimension of leadership, have a lower profile in the leadership literature and are less well explored. However, in recent years there has been a resurgence of interest among social psychologists in leadership; a resurgence built partly on what we now know about social cognition (how people mentally process, represent, and use information about other people), but also very significantly on the social identity analysis of group processes and intergroup relations.

In this chapter I argue that identity management is a key function of leadership—people derive a sense of who they are from the groups they belong to, and they overwhelmingly look to their leaders to define their group's attributes (its attitudes, values, and customs) and thus their identity in society. National leadership campaigns are a good example of this process—there is a dynamic in which the electorate seeks an image of what the nation stands for, what its true identity is, and presidential and prime ministerial contenders vie to provide this identity and to show how they best embody its attributes.

Drawing on social identity theory, which focuses on the generative role of group belongingness and social identity in group behaviors, I described the social identity theory of leadership. The most fundamental premise of the social identity theory of leadership is that when a group is psychologically important to your sense of self you pay close attention to and are influenced by those people who you consider to best embody the group's prototype. Thus, prototypical members are more influential than nonprototypical members (they are effectively leaders) and prototypical leaders are more influential than nonprototypical leaders.

In newly formed salient groups or groups that have a leadership vacuum, members probably evaluate leadership somewhat exclusively against their perception of the prototype. However, in groups with established or incumbent leaders a variety of social identity related processes provide leaders with the ability to take the lead in defining the prototype themselves and, thus, their own prototypicality. I described how prototypicality can be associated with consensual positive regard, status, and the process of compliance; unqualified trust and the potential to be innovative; the construction of a charismatic personality; and the power to use a variety of strategies to protect and promote prototypicality and function as an entrepreneur of identity. Evidence in support of the social identity theory of leadership was briefly touched on to show that there is already relatively good support for the main features of the theory.

To conclude, let me discuss one area where more research is needed. From a social identity point of view one challenge faced by leaders is that to be effective they need to be considered prototypical, and yet in many leadership situations they need to appeal to diverse groups that in many cases simply do not get on and have very different views of the superordinate category prototype. More often than not the great challenge of leadership is being an effective *intergroup* leader—being able to provide effective leadership across multiple groups (Hogg, in press b). The challenge here is in making multiple groups consider themselves a single group or to have a single identity, but at the same time not to feel that their existing identities have been devalued or erased. For example, the current (2008) presidential race in the United States is to some extent an exercise in persuading polarized political groups to have a shared prototype of being American—a prototype that one candidate can claim to represent better than other candidates (Hohman, Hogg, & Bligh, in press). In Iraq the issue is more dramatic: how can a single leader appear prototypical to warring factions hell-bent on each other's annihilation?

The question here is part of the wider issue of building social harmony and common identities from conflict. Social psychologists invest a great deal of research effort on the questions of reducing conflict and building harmony —for example, they study the dynamics of schisms (e.g., Sani & Reicher, 1998), organizational mergers and acquisitions (e.g., Terry, Carey, & Callan, 2001), cultural pluralism (e.g., Moghaddam, 2008; Verkuyten, 2006), and the construction of common ingroup identities (e.g., Hewstone, 1996). However, the key role of leaders and leadership is rarely mentioned—one exception is in the study of social dilemmas where identity-based leadership has been studied as an effective solution to some dilemmas (e.g., De Cremer & Van Vugt, 2002). The role of leaders in building common identities that bridge deep cultural divides remains to be fully explored and is, of course, a critical issue for society.

In this chapter I hope that I have not only shown how the social identity theory of leadership contributes to our understanding of leadership, but also how it helps reconfigure the agenda for leadership research, allowing us to ask different questions and focus on different aspects and contexts of leadership—specifically the identity function of leadership.

REFERENCES

Abrams, D., Hogg, M. A., Hinkle, S., & Otten, S. (2005). The social identity perspective on small groups. In M. S. Poole & A. B. Hollingshead (Eds.), *Theories of small groups: Interdisciplinary perspectives* (pp. 99–137). Thousand Oaks, CA: Sage.

Abrams, D., Wetherell, M. S., Cochrane, S., Hogg, M. A., & Turner, J. C. (1990). Knowing what to think by knowing who you are: Self-categorization and the nature of norm formation, conformity, and group polarization. *British Journal of Social Psychology, 29,* 97–119.

Ashforth, B. E., & Mael, F. A. (1989). Social identity theory and the organization. *Academy of Management Review, 14,* 20–39.

Avolio, B. J., & Yammarino, F. J. (Eds.). (2003). *Transformational and charismatic leadership: The road ahead.* New York: Elsevier.

Berscheid, E., & Reis, H. T. (1998). Attraction and close relationships. In D. T. Gilbert, S. T. Fiske, & G. Lindzey (Eds.), *The handbook of social psychology* (4th ed., Vol. 2, pp. 193–281). New York: McGraw-Hill.

Chemers, M. M. (1997). *An integrative theory of leadership.* Mahwah, NJ: Erlbaum.

De Cremer, D., & Van Vugt, M. (2002). Intergroup and intragroup aspects of leadership in social dilemmas: A relational model of cooperation. *Journal of Experimental Social Psychology, 38,* 126–136.

Duck, J. M., & Fielding, K. S. (1999). Leaders and sub-groups: One of us or one of them? *Group Processes and Intergroup Relations, 2,* 203–230.

Duck, J. M., & Fielding, K. S. (2003). Leaders and their treatment of subgroups: Implications for evaluations of the leader and the superordinate group. *European Journal of Social Psychology, 33,* 387–401.

Ellemers, N., de Gilder, D., & Haslam, S. A. (2004). Motivating individuals and groups at work: A social identity perspective on leadership and group performance. *Academy of Management Review, 29,* 459–478.

Fielding, K. S., & Hogg, M. A. (1997). Social identity, self-categorization, and leadership: A field study of small interactive groups. *Group Dynamics: Theory, Research, and Practice, 1,* 39–51.

Gardner, H. (1995). *Leading minds: An anatomy of leadership.* New York: Basic Books.

Gilbert, D. T., & Malone, P. S. (1995). The correspondence bias. *Psychological Bulletin, 117,* 21–38.

Goethals, G. R., Sorenson, G. J., & Burns, J. M. (Eds.). (2004). *Encyclopedia of leadership.* Thousand Oaks, CA: Sage.

Hains, S. C., Hogg, M. A., & Duck, J. M. (1997). Self-categorization and leadership: Effects of group prototypicality and leader stereotypicality. *Personality and Social Psychology Bulletin, 23,* 1087–1100.

Haslam, N., Rothschild, L., & Ernst, D. (1998). Essentialist beliefs about social categories. *British Journal of Social Psychology, 39,* 113–127.

Haslam, S. A., Oakes, P. J., McGarty, C., Turner, J. C., & Onorato, S. (1995). Contextual changes in the prototypicality of extreme and moderate outgroup members. *European Journal of Social Psychology, 25,* 509–530.

Haslam, S. A., & Platow, M. J. (2001). Your wish is our command: The role of shared social identity in translating a leader's vision into followers' action. In M. A. Hogg & D. J. Terry (Eds.), *Social identity processes in organizational contexts* (pp. 213–228). Philadelphia, PA: Psychology Press.

Hewstone, M. (1996). Contact and categorization: Social-psychological interventions to change intergroup relations. In C. N. Macrae, C. Stangor, & M. Hewstone (Eds.), *Stereotypes and stereotyping* (pp. 323–368). New York: Guilford.

Hogg, M. A. (1993). Group cohesiveness: A critical review and some new directions. *European Review of Social Psychology, 4,* 85–111.

Hogg, M. A. (2001). A social identity theory of leadership. *Personality and Social Psychology Review, 5,* 184–200.

Hogg, M. A. (2006). Social identity theory. In P. J. Burke (Ed.), *Contemporary social psychological theories* (pp. 111–136). Palo Alto, CA: Stanford University Press.

Hogg, M. A. (2007). Social psychology of leadership. In A. W. Kruglanski & E. T. Higgins (Eds.), *Social psychology: Handbook of basic principles* (2nd ed., pp. 716–733). New York: Guilford.

Hogg, M. A. (2008). Social identity processes and the empowerment of followers. In R. E. Riggio, I. Chaleff, & J. Lipman-Blumen (Eds.), *The art of followership: How great followers create great leaders and organizations* (pp. 267–276). San Francisco: Jossey-Bass.

Hogg, M. A. (in press a). Influence and leadership. In S. T. Fiske, D. T. Gilbert, & G. Lindzey (Eds.), *The handbook of social psychology* (5th ed.). New York: Wiley.

Hogg, M. A. (in press b). Leading across diverse and conflicting social identities. In T. Pittinsky (Ed.), *Crossing the divide: Intergroup leadership in a world of difference.* Cambridge, MA: Harvard Business School Publishing.

Hogg, M. A., & Abrams, D. (2007). Intergroup behavior and social identity. In M. A. Hogg & J. Cooper (Eds.), *The Sage handbook of social psychology: Concise student edition* (pp. 335–360). London: Sage.

Hogg, M. A., Abrams, D., Otten, S., & Hinkle, S. (2004). The social identity perspective: Intergroup relations, self-conception, and small groups. *Small Group Research, 35,* 246–276.

Hogg, M. A., Fielding, K. S., Johnson, D., Masser, B., Russell, E., & Svensson, A. (2006). Demographic category membership and leadership in small groups: A social identity analysis. *The Leadership Quarterly, 17,* 335–350.

Hogg, M. A., Martin, R., Epitropaki, O., Mankad, A., Svensson, A., & Weeden, K. (2005). Effective leadership in salient groups: Revisiting leader-member exchange theory from the perspective of the social identity theory of leadership. *Personality and Social Psychology Bulletin, 31,* 991–1004.

Hogg, M. A., & Terry, D. J. (2000). Social identity and self-categorization processes in organizational contexts. *Academy of Management Review, 25,* 121–140.

Hogg, M. A., Terry, D. J., & White, K. M. (1995). A tale of two theories: A critical comparison of identity theory with social identity theory. *Social Psychology Quarterly, 58,* 255–269.

Hogg, M. A., & van Knippenberg, D. (2003). Social identity and leadership processes in groups. In M. P. Zanna (Ed.), *Advances in experimental social psychology* (Vol. 35, pp. 1–52). San Diego, CA: Academic Press.

Hohman, Z. P., Hogg, M. A., & Bligh, M. (in press). Identity and intergroup leadership: Asymmetrical political and national identification in response to uncertainty. *Self and Identity.*

Hollander, E. P. (1958). Conformity, status, and idiosyncracy credit. *Psychological Review, 65,* 117–127.

Lord, R. G., & Brown, D. J. (2004). *Leadership processes and follower identity.* Mahwah, NJ: Erlbaum.

Messick, D. M., & Kramer, R. M. (Eds.). (2005). *The psychology of leadership: New perspectives and research.* Mahwah, NJ: Erlbaum.

Moghaddam, F. M. (2008). *Multiculturalism and intergroup relations.* Washington, DC: American Psychological Association.

Northouse, P. G. (2007). *Leadership: Theory and practice* (4th ed.). Thousand Oaks, CA: Sage.

Pittinsky, T. (Ed.). (in press). *Crossing the divide: Intergroup leadership in a world of difference.* Cambridge, MA: Harvard Business School Publishing.

Platow, M. J., Hoar, S., Reid, S. A., Harley, K., & Morrison, D. (1997). Endorsement of distributively fair and unfair leaders in interpersonal and intergroup situations. *European Journal of Social Psychology, 27,* 465–494.

Platow, M. J., Reid, S. A., & Andrew, S. (1998). Leadership endorsement: The role of distributive and procedural behavior in interpersonal and intergroup contexts. *Group Processes and Intergroup Relations, 1,* 35–47.

Platow, M. J., & van Knippenberg, D. (2001). A social identity analysis of leadership endorsement: The effects of leader ingroup prototypicality and distributive intergroup fairness. *Personality and Social Psychology Bulletin, 27,* 1508–1519.

Reicher, S. D., & Hopkins, N. (1996). Self-category constructions in political rhetoric: An analysis of Thatcher's and Kinnock's speeches concerning the British miners' strike (1984–5). *European Journal of Social Psychology, 26,* 353–371.

Reicher, S. D., & Hopkins, N. (2003). On the science of the art of leadership. In D. van Knippenberg & M. A. Hogg (Eds.), *Leadership and power: Identity processes in groups and organizations* (pp. 197–209). London: Sage.

Riggio, R., Chaleff, I., & Lipman-Blumen, J. (Eds.). (2008). *The art of followership: How great followers create great leaders and organizations.* San Francisco: Jossey-Bass.

Sani, F., & Reicher, S. D. (1998). When consensus fails: An analysis of the schism within the Italian Communist Party (1991). *European Journal of Social Psychology, 28,* 623–645.

Shamir, B., Pillai, R., Bligh, M. C., & Uhl-Bien, M. (Eds.). (2006). *Follower-centered perspectives on leadership: A tribute to the memory of James R. Meindl.* Greenwich, CT: Information Age Publishing.

Tajfel, H., & Turner, J. C. (1979). An integrative theory of intergroup conflict. In W. G. Austin & S. Worchel (Eds.), *The social psychology of intergroup relations* (pp. 33–47). Monterey, CA: Brooks/Cole.

Terry, D. J., Carey, C. J., & Callan, V. J. (2001). Employee adjustment to an organizational merger: An intergroup perspective. *Personality and Social Psychology Bulletin, 27,* 267–280.

Turner, J. C., Hogg, M. A., Oakes, P. J., Reicher, S. D., & Wetherell, M. S. (1987). *Rediscovering the social group: A self-categorization theory.* Oxford, UK: Blackwell.

Tyler, T. R. (1997). The psychology of legitimacy: A relational perspective on voluntary deference to authorities. *Personality and Social Psychology Review, 1,* 323–345.

Tyler, T. R., & Lind, E. A. (1992). A relational model of authority in groups. In M. P. Zanna (Ed.), *Advances in experimental social psychology* (Vol. 25, pp. 115–191). New York: Academic Press.

van Knippenberg, D., & Hogg, M. A. (2003). A social identity model of leadership in organizations. In R. M. Kramer & B. M. Staw (Eds.), *Research in organizational behavior* (Vol. 25, pp. 243–295). Greenwich, CT: JAI Press.

van Knippenberg, D., van Knippenberg, B., De Cremer, D., & Hogg, M. A. (2004). Leadership, self, and identity: A review and research agenda. *The Leadership Quarterly, 15,* 825–856.

Van Vugt, M., & De Cremer, D. (1999). Leadership in social dilemmas: The effects of group identification on collective actions to provide public goods. *Journal of Personality and Social Psychology, 76,* 587–599.

Verkuyten, M. (2006). Multiculturalism and social psychology. *European Review of Social Psychology, 17,* 148–184.

Yukl, G. (2006). *Leadership in organizations* (6th ed.). Upper Saddle River, NJ: Prentice-Hall.

5

Emotional Intelligence and Leadership: Implications for Leader Development

PAULO N. LOPES AND PETER SALOVEY

We view emotional intelligence as a set of abilities that encompass perceiving, expressing, understanding, using, and managing emotions. Leaders' ability to influence others depends on their capacity to generate enthusiasm for a collective mission and establish sound communication with followers, among other factors. Because emotions are linked to motivation, influence the way people think, and facilitate communication, leaders need to attend to and manage their own and others' emotions. We review some of the ample research evidence highlighting the role of emotions in decision making, communication, and interpersonal relationships. Perhaps because it is difficult to measure emotional intelligence as a set of emotional information processing skills, there are not yet clear research findings linking ability measures of emotional intelligence to leadership effectiveness. Nonetheless, evidence suggests that it is possible to develop emotional skills, and we discuss how emotional skills training can be used to enhance leadership development.

Interest in emotional intelligence has continued to grow in business, education, and other circles. Salovey and Mayer first proposed a theory of emotional intelligence in 1990. They argued that the capacity to perceive, understand, use, and manage emotions can be viewed as an interrelated set of abilities that help people to attain adaptive goals in life and, generally, are distinct from IQ. Their theory was inspired by an expanding body of research on emotion, indicating that emotions serve adaptive functions, that IQ does not tap all the skills that contribute to intelligent behavior and adaptation in life, and that there are meaningful individual differences in the way that people deal with emotions and process emotional information (Salovey & Mayer, 1990).

Popularized in a 1995 bestselling book by Goleman, this idea seemed intuitively appealing to many readers because it resonated with their life experiences. It reinforced the notion that it is emotions that make people tick, that IQ is only part of the story of why some people are more successful than others, and that emotional and interpersonal competencies have been neglected in school and other settings. In casual conversation, the topic often generates compelling stories of individuals who excelled in school but whose career progress was undermined by difficulties with self-regulation and social relationships.

Why should leaders care about emotions? Because emotions influence the way people think and behave, and influencing behavior is what leadership is all about. Several authors have proposed that emotions and emotional intelligence play a central role in the leadership process (e.g., George, 2000; Kets de Vries, 2001). Yet, the implications for assessment and training are less obvious.

Popular interest in emotional intelligence has outpaced sound research in this area, although recent years have seen the publication of scientific articles supporting the validity and utility of the concept. One can now find different perspectives on emotional intelligence and the best way to measure it (Mayer, Salovey, & Caruso, 2000), so the term "emotional intelligence" is used to designate many different things. In this chapter, we help readers to make sense of theory and research in this area, and explore implications for assessment and training. Is there strong evidence (yet) that emotional intelligence contributes to leader effectiveness? Not really—perhaps because emotional intelligence is difficult to measure. Nevertheless, can emotional abilities contribute to leader effectiveness, and should these abilities be addressed in leader development programs? Yes—and we will discuss how.

Our analysis is largely based on an ability model of emotional intelligence (Mayer & Salovey, 1997; Salovey & Grewal, 2005) because abilities can be viewed as a form of developing expertise (Sternberg, 1999), and therefore this model offers a useful theoretical framework for leader development. We focus on leadership in organizational settings because the topic of emotional intelligence has aroused widespread interest in the business world, although most of the ideas discussed in this chapter could be applied to other realms of leadership as well. We emphasize implications for leader development to help managers interested in their professional development and faculty involved in executive education to make sense of the research on emotional intelligence. As a starting point, we synthesize a large body of research linking emotional processes to motivation, interpersonal interaction, cognition, and decision making. Afterward, we outline different models of emotional intelligence and ways to measure it. Then we map the links between the ability model and leadership theory. Finally, we discuss implications for leader development, the main focus of this chapter.

WHY SHOULD LEADERS ATTEND TO EMOTIONS?

Emotions and feelings[1] can signal important information about the environment (Lazarus, 1991; Schwarz, 1990), telling us whether it is safe or unsafe to explore, for example. They can elicit approach or avoidance tendencies, and activate goals and goal-driven behavior (Frijda, 1988). People usually seek to repeat experiences that made them feel good in the past and tend to stay away from activities, individuals, and places that have made them anxious or upset in the past. Emotions can boost physiological arousal to alert the brain and energize the body for emergency responses (Sapolsky, 2000), or dampen arousal to conserve resources. Thus, emotions are intimately linked to motivational states (Frijda, 1988) and one of leaders' functions is to motivate others.

Emotions also help people to communicate and interact with others (Keltner & Haidt, 1999). A look of fear or a smirk of contempt on someone's face can be telling because emotional expressions convey information about a person's thoughts and intentions (Ekman, 2003). Therefore, the ability to decode nonverbal cues of emotion can help people to understand and influence others (Elfenbein, Marsh, & Ambady, 2002). The capacity to express emotions can also facilitate communication (Snodgrass, Hecht, & Ploutz-Snyder, 1998) and induce liking (e.g., Friedman, Riggio, & Casella, 1988) or trust.

Emotions also are contagious (Hatfield, Cacioppo, & Rapson, 1994). A leader's enthusiasm can spread to the rest of the team because people tend to catch others' emotions through nonconscious mimicry and other forms of entrainment. This contributes to empathy and rapport, and may facilitate identification with a leader or induce a similar mind-set in a group. Thus, emotions help to coordinate social encounters and group behavior. Moreover, emotions can strengthen or disrupt social bonds. People are usually drawn to individuals who exude good spirits and tend to avoid those who are persistently negative or down (Argyle & Lu, 1990; Furr & Funder, 1998). The bonds established through rewarding experiences and positive emotions can help a team to overcome rough times and friction later. By signaling like and dislike, emotions can also facilitate identification with a group and demarcate an outgroup (Devos, Silver, Mackie, & Smith, 2002).

Furthermore, emotions direct attention and influence the way people think. For example, negative emotions can interrupt an ongoing train of thought to make an individual attend to more pressing concerns (Simon, 1967). They can focus attention on the problem at hand and induce people to scrutinize relevant information carefully and systematically (Schwarz, 1990, 2002). In contrast, positive emotions can broaden the focus of attention and facilitate free association, divergent thinking, and creative problem solving (Fredrickson, 1998; Isen, Daubman, & Nowicki, 1987). Thus, leaders can instill positive spirits in a group to enhance creativity in a brainstorming session, or instill fear to focus people on a problem and generate a sense of urgency about change (Huy, 1999).

Emotions can also facilitate problem solving by activating memories and knowledge of situations that were associated with similar emotional experiences in the past (Bower, 1981; Singer & Salovey, 1988). Emotions also facilitate learning from experience by focusing people's attention on and making them think about negative events (Baumeister, Vohs, DeWall, & Zhang, 2007). Furthermore, emotions influence decision making by signaling preferences and attitudes that may have been neglected in conscious analysis or by influencing the way that we think about past, present, and future events (Loewenstein & Lerner, 2003). Leaders' understanding and awareness of the influence of emotion on their thinking can give them a heightened capacity to manage themselves and others.

EMOTIONAL INTELLIGENCE THEORY AND RESEARCH

Salovey and Mayer (1990; Mayer & Salovey, 1997) proposed a definition of emotional intelligence focused on emotional information processing. Their model encompassed the ability to perceive emotions in self and others; to understand how emotions blend, unfold, and influence cognition and behavior; to use emotions to facilitate thinking; and to manage emotions in self and others. These abilities are thought to be interrelated because they all rely on emotional information processing and one ability can support another. For example, recognizing inner cues of emotional arousal (e.g., heart beating faster, sweating, loud voice) and understanding how anger can lead to rash decisions can inform and facilitate emotion regulation.

Mayer and Salovey (1997) sought to distinguish emotional intelligence from other constructs such as personality (Mayer et al., 2000). They also argued that emotional intelligence should be assessed by asking people to solve problems involving emotional information, rather than asking people whether they consider themselves emotionally intelligent. Self-judgments tend to be biased because people like to think well of themselves (Codol, 1975; Greenwald, 1980; Taylor, 1986). The majority of respondents consider themselves above average on a wide range of positive traits and abilities, including emotional intelligence (Brackett, Rivers, Shiffman, Lerner, & Salovey, 2006). Moreover, people may lack information to evaluate their emotional abilities accurately because they seldom receive clear or reliable feedback in this domain. As an alternative to questionnaires, respondents can be asked to decode facial expressions of emotion, identify how emotions are likely to evolve in a particular scenario, or rate the effectiveness of different responses to an emotionally challenging situation, for example. The Mayer-Salovey-Caruso Emotional Intelligence Test (MSCEIT; Mayer, Salovey, & Caruso, 2002) uses this approach to assess the four dimensions of the ability model.

Research using ability measures (mostly the MSCEIT) has yielded some evidence that emotional abilities are interrelated, distinct from personality and IQ, and associated with important outcomes—even after controlling statistically for the effect of potential confounds. A confirmatory factor analysis of MSCEIT scores found support for four distinct emotional abilities underlying a higher-order factor of emotional intelligence (Mayer, Salovey, Caruso, & Sitarenios, 2003). Several studies indicate that MSCEIT scores are associated with the quality of social relationships and interpersonal interaction, as rated by multiple informants—even after controlling for demographic factors, personality traits, and indicators of IQ (e.g., Brackett et al., 2006; Lopes, Brackett, Nezlek, Schütz, Sellin, & Salovey, 2004; Lopes, Salovey, Côté, & Beers, 2005). This evidence seems to be most consistent for the emotion regulation branch.

There is also evidence that some emotional abilities are associated with positive workplace and negotiation outcomes (for a review, see Mayer, Roberts, & Barsade, 2008). For example, a meta-analysis aggregating numerous studies suggested that emotion perception accuracy was associated with modestly higher indicators of workplace effectiveness in professions as diverse as physicians, human service workers, schoolteachers and principals, and business managers (Elfenbein, Foo, White, Tan, & Aik, 2007). In a study of 175 university employees, MSCEIT emotional intelligence scores were associated with supervisor ratings of job performance after controlling for cognitive ability, personality traits, and other confounds (Côté & Miners, 2006). In a study of 44 analysts and clerical employees of a health insurance company, MSCEIT scores were associated with higher company rank, merit increases, and peer and/or supervisor ratings of interpersonal facilitation and stress tolerance (Lopes, Grewal, Kadis, Gall, & Salovey, 2006). Further research is needed to link emotional abilities and objective indicators of work performance.

Broader views of emotional intelligence. Other authors have proposed far broader views of emotional intelligence, encompassing emotional and social skills, personality traits, and motivational and other characteristics (e.g.,

Bar-On, 2000; Goleman, 1995, 1998; Petrides & Furnham, 2003). These conceptions may be appealing precisely because they are more encompassing. Broad measures based on these conceptions can be useful for 360-degree assessments if organizations wish to assess a wide array of adaptive characteristics and competencies with a single questionnaire. These broad conceptions also avoid the difficulty of carving boundaries between partially overlapping constructs, such as emotional and social skills.

Nonetheless, there are drawbacks to this approach. For research purposes, the benefit of integrating a wide range of traits and competencies into one theoretical framework, rather than studying them separately, is generally unclear. If we lump many desirable traits and competencies into one score, we might end up with a rough indicator of perceived global adjustment (or core self-evaluation; Bono & Judge, 2003), but we do not know exactly what it measures. Research linking these overall scores to workplace outcomes is often not really informative. It is no wonder that a measure of global adjustment is associated with positive outcomes. To date, few studies examining the predictive validity of these broad measures have controlled simultaneously for the most relevant confounds, including IQ, personality, motivation, and self-enhancement. Furthermore, several measures based on broad models of emotional intelligence share substantial overlap with the Big Five personality traits (e.g., Brackett & Mayer, 2003), which also tap into emotional reactivity and self-regulation (Larsen, 2000).

For the purpose of assessment and leader development, it is far more useful to consider an individual's detailed profile of strengths and weaknesses than to aggregate this information into a single score for emotional intelligence. It is also useful to distinguish broad personality traits that tend to be difficult to change from skills that may be more amenable to training. For assessment purposes, the usefulness of questionnaire measures is limited by the fact that self-reports are biased by self-enhancement and faking, and informant ratings are prone to halo effects (people who like and admire their leaders tend to rate the leaders highly on most dimensions). In both the cognitive and emotional realms, ability tests and self-report measures correlate only weakly and thus seem to measure different things (Brackett et al., 2006; Mabe & West, 1982). For all these reasons, we focus on the ability model of emotional intelligence in this chapter and in our empirical work.

Limitations and implications of the ability model. Research focused on abilities and skills can potentially contribute to an in-depth understanding of the processes and strategies underlying emotionally intelligent behavior, and thereby help to design better leader development programs. For assessment, scores on ability measures that ask respondents to solve problems are less likely to be distorted by self-enhancement and deliberate faking than scores on self-report measures that tap into perceived self-efficacy (Brackett et al.,

2006). Yet, it is also important to consider the limitations of the ability model of emotional intelligence and the research that supports it, namely because it may help readers to devise effective training programs and use balanced assessment strategies.

In its original formulation, this model provided an integrative theoretical framework that mapped emotional abilities and made few detailed predictions. One of the advantages of this model is that it is narrowly focused on emotional abilities. As a conceptual map, however, one of its limitations is that it does not clearly chart the boundaries and overlap between emotional abilities, on the one hand, and social abilities or personality, on the other. In practice, it may be difficult to disentangle emotional abilities from personality traits that are strongly influenced by innate emotional dispositions, such as emotional stability. For example, the capacity for effective emotion regulation reflects the combined effects of innate temperamental dispositions (the foundation of personality) and emotion regulation skills acquired over the life span. The implication for assessment is that using tests of emotional abilities in combination with personality measures and 360-degree feedback may yield a better picture of an individual's emotional functioning than relying on a single assessment strategy. The implication for training is that developing emotion regulation skills may entail overcoming deeply engraved habits and dispositions, and therefore require opportunities for repeated practice and feedback as well as booster sessions.

It is difficult to disentangle emotional and social skills because emotions serve social and communicative functions and social interaction involves emotional communication. Managing emotions in interpersonal situations involves both emotion-focused and problem-focused strategies, tapping into emotional and social skills. For example, one way to regulate one's emotions is to cognitively reappraise the situation. In managing emotionally challenging interpersonal situations, effective reappraisal may draw on perspective-taking, social, communication, and negotiation skills (to elicit the other person's views and see the problem from his or her perspective, for example). Thus, it is difficult to demarcate the realm of emotional abilities clearly and disentangle it from the realms of personality and social skills. This means that, for training purposes, it may be useful to integrate emotional and interpersonal skills training, and help participants to understand that personality is also malleable to some extent (Heatherton & Weinberger, 1994).

Much of the evidence in support of the ability model (examining emotional intelligence as an integrated set of abilities) has relied on a single measure, the MSCEIT. The theory of emotional intelligence proposes that emotional abilities are interrelated and represent a distinct form of intelligence (Mayer, Salovey, Caruso, & Sitarenios, 2001). Yet, some of the evidence in support of this claim is limited because correlations among the four abilities could be inflated by common method bias associated with the use of a single measure and a particular type of scoring, for example. Measures of nonverbal decoding skills tapping into different channels of nonverbal communication (e.g., facial expression of emotion versus body language or multiple channels) correlate weakly, suggesting that they do not represent a cohesive domain of ability (see Hall & Bernieri, 2001).

Accordingly, assessing emotion decoding skills rigorously may require a more extensive battery of tests than time usually allows. For leader development programs, it may be useful to adapt existing measures of nonverbal decoding skills and use them as dynamic tests, combining assessment and training, and providing participants immediate feedback (e.g., right or wrong) after each item. Because time constraints preclude training all the skills underlying emotional intelligence through explicit classroom instruction, it is especially important to help participants to learn from experience. This could be achieved by incorporating principles of action science and reflective practice (e.g., Argyris, Putnam, & Smith, 1990; Schön, 1987) as well as individualized coaching in leader development programs.

It is also important to keep in mind that existing tests of emotional intelligence do not assess all the skills that underlie emotionally intelligent behavior. For example, with regard to emotion regulation, a test such as the MSCEIT measures knowledge of effective strategies for handling emotionally challenging situations more than the capacity to implement these strategies effectively in real life. Thus, scores on existing tests should be interpreted with great caution because they might not provide a full or balanced picture of a person's emotional competencies. Further validation and perhaps test development are needed before these measures can be used reliably for selection purposes. A balanced assessment strategy should rely on multiple measures, including multirater feedback, personality questionnaires, and observations, for example. Observing how individuals manage emotionally challenging group work can be useful for both assessment and training purposes because it brings to the surface issues that can then be discussed in the classroom.

EMOTIONAL ABILITIES AND LEADERSHIP

Theories of transformational leadership and leader-member exchange, which are associated with leadership effectiveness (see meta-analyses by Gerstner & Day, 1997; Judge & Piccolo, 2004; Lowe, Galen Kroeck, & Sivasubramaniam, 1996), suggest important links between emotional abilities and leadership. We review these theoretical links briefly before considering the research evidence.

The full range leadership model (Bass & Avolio, 1994) maps leadership styles from laissez-faire management to transactional and transformational leadership, ranked from least to most effective. Laissez-faire management amounts to an absence of leadership. Transactional leadership involves influencing others by rewarding desired behavior and the fulfillment of contractual obligations, planning for the attainment of organizational goals, and intervening when things go wrong. Transformational leadership involves motivating and inspiring members to go beyond contractual obligations, deliver exceptional performance, and attain their full potential. Insofar as transactional leaders rely on the capacity to dispense rewards associated with a formal position of power and a rigid command-and-control structure, they may not be concerned about developing emotional abilities. Nonetheless, the effective use of emotional rewards involving encouragement, praise, and support for employees' feelings of self-worth may draw on emotional abilities and dispositions to some extent.

Transformational leadership includes the dimensions of idealized influence (charisma), inspirational motivation, intellectual stimulation, and individualized consideration (Bass, 1985; Bass & Avolio, 1994). Whereas intellectual stimulation may rely to a large extent on cold cognition, the other dimensions of transformational leadership are likely to involve an emotional substrate related to emotional communication and identification (e.g., empathy), and the orchestration of emotions (including the arousal of positive attitudes and positive emotions toward a collective mission or goal). The dimension of individualized consideration, in particular, highlights the importance of understanding members' needs, hopes, and fears, in order to coach them effectively and help them develop.

Conger and Kanungo's (1998) work on charismatic leadership, which is closely linked to transformational leadership (Rowold & Heinitz, 2007), outlines three stages of the leadership process. First, leaders need to assess the environment and evaluate followers' needs. Second, they must generate a strategic vision and communicate it in a way that inspires others. Third, they must act as role models by defying conventional wisdom, taking risks, revealing integrity, and devoting full effort to the attainment of a collective mission. It can be argued that emotional abilities facilitate these three tasks and contribute to most of the capacities outlined in accounts of transformational and transactional leadership. In particular, emotional abilities can help leaders to understand others' motivations and concerns, enabling effective analysis, decision making, communication, and influence.

From the perspective of the leader-member exchange theory (Graen & Uhl-Bien, 1995), a leader's influence is enhanced by developing a high quality working relationship or true partnership with followers, involving mutual trust, open communication, and coaching. By stressing the quality of the relationship between leader and follower, leader-member exchange theory suggests that emotional abilities facilitate leadership insofar as they contribute to positive interpersonal interactions. As discussed above, there is empirical evidence from several studies linking emotional abilities (in particular emotion regulation ability) and the quality of interpersonal interaction.

The emotional intelligence framework fits well into the skills approach to the study of leadership. Early writings on leadership skills emphasized the distinction between technical, conceptual, and people skills (see Katz, 1955), just as early research on leadership styles focused on task-oriented versus relationship-oriented behavior. Viewing leadership as an interpersonal phenomenon suggests that effective leadership depends upon the leader's ability to solve the complex social problems that arise in organizations, and this entails creative problem solving, social judgment, and knowledge (Mumford, Zaccaro, Harding, Jacobs, & Fleishman, 2000). Once again, emotional abilities should contribute to social judgment skills.

Also relevant to our discussion is the basic principle of the situational approach to leadership: to be effective, leaders must adapt their style and behavior to the demands of different situations. This idea is in line with one of the basic principles of social psychology, that people's behavior and responses to any event are influenced by the social situation to a greater extent than is usually recognized (Ross & Nisbett, 1991). The importance of individualized consideration and sensitivity to members' needs highlighted in accounts of transformational and charismatic leadership, and leader-member exchange theory, suggests that leaders must interact differently with each follower in order to build effective working relationships. This requires flexibility, adaptability, and attunement to people and to the situation (Hooijberg, Hunt, & Dodge, 1997). The ability to process emotional information is likely to contribute to this interpersonal attunement and flexibility.

Several authors have discussed theoretical links between emotional intelligence and leadership in greater depth than we can do here. For example, George (2000) argued that moods and emotions play a central role in the leadership process. She further proposed that emotional intelligence contributes to effective leadership in several ways, including the development of collective goals and a meaningful identity for an organization, communication and persuasion, the enhancement of enthusiasm, confidence, optimism, cooperation, and trust, sound decision making, and the implementation of organizational change. Huy (1999) argued that building motivation for organizational change requires balancing negative and positive emotions skillfully because it is often necessary to induce a sense of urgency and focus people on a better future so as to energize people rather than paralyze them with fear.

Research. Theoretically, then, there are strong reasons to expect emotional abilities to contribute to leadership effectiveness. At present, however, the empirical evidence for this link is still limited. Few studies have been published in peer-reviewed journals showing significant associations between ability measures of emotional intelligence and indicators of leadership effectiveness, controlling for possible confounds. Moreover, we do not know of any rigorous studies examining the causal effect of emotional intelligence training on leadership effectiveness, although studies of this kind may be in the works.

A few studies provide suggestive and preliminary evidence for the link between emotional abilities and leadership but should be viewed with caution until the findings are replicated and extended. For example, in a study of 145 managers of a biotechnology/agricultural company, managers' ability to recognize facial expressions of emotion in photographs was associated with subordinate ratings of transformational leadership (Rubin, Munz, & Bommer, 2005). Two studies indicated that total emotional intelligence scores on the MSCEIT were associated with leader emergence in undergraduate work groups—controlling for gender, personality, and IQ (Côté, Lopes, Salovey, & Miners, 2008; still under review at the time of writing). In a study of 41 executives from a large Australian public service organization, emotional intelligence scores on the MSCEIT were associated with positive multi-rater feedback on some dimensions (e.g., "cultivates productive working relationships," but not with supervisor ratings of goal achievement; Rosete & Ciarrochi, 2005).

There is evidence linking self-report measures of emotional intelligence and leadership. This research is often less informative than we would wish for the reasons discussed above (e.g., self-enhancement bias, confounds with personality and motivation, halo effects, and conceptual overlap between predictor and outcomes). Nonetheless, some studies using questionnaire measures have yielded interesting findings. For example, a study conducted in four countries indicated that subordinates' ratings of their managers' empathy were associated with different subordinates' ratings of the same managers' leadership effectiveness (Rahim & Psenicka, 2005). Some qualitative studies have also generated provocative findings. For example, a case study tracked 104 middle managers in an information technology service company that was adapting to global competition after deregulation. The analysis highlighted the importance of managers' attending to employees' emotions and personally committing to change projects in order to balance continuity and change, and keep employees motivated (Huy, 2002).

Despite these suggestive findings, rigorous evidence linking scores on ability measures of emotional intelligence and leader effectiveness is still scarce in peer-reviewed journals.[2] Based on a review of meta-analyses, an American

Psychological Association task force concluded that researchers studying complex human behavior should be satisfied with small effects (e.g., accounting for 1 percent to 4 percent of the variance in outcome measures; Meyer et al., 2001). However, most studies rely on samples that are too small to detect weak effects.

There are several reasons why emotional abilities might be only weakly related to leadership effectiveness (see also Antonakis, 2003). Many factors beyond a leader's control influence his or her effectiveness as a leader. The list of skills that contribute to effective leadership is very large, and it is possible to be an effective leader by capitalizing on different skills. Leaders can also recruit people with complementary skills and develop emotional capabilities at the group or organizational levels to compensate for their own personal deficits (Druskat & Wolff, 2003; Huy, 1999). The interpretation of research findings is further complicated by the fact that individuals may develop emotional skills to compensate for traits that might hinder their emergence as leaders (for example, developing interpersonal sensitivity to compensate for social anxiety or low social dominance). Moreover, emotional abilities are difficult to measure and existing ability measures only capture some of the skills that contribute to emotionally intelligent behavior. For all these reasons, we should expect statistical associations between any one ability and leadership effectiveness to be weak, and future research should use larger samples to detect such weak effects. Weak effects should not be neglected when the outcomes are important, as is the case of leadership. A small change in some leaders' behavior could make a difference to millions of people.

SUMMARY AND IMPLICATIONS FOR LEADER DEVELOPMENT

It is difficult to study broad and complex phenomena such as leadership and emotional intelligence through the traditional scientific paradigm of isolating different aspects of the problem and examining these with high precision and reliability. Therefore leader development programs cannot rely exclusively on available research findings. Although there is little direct evidence that emotional abilities contribute to leader effectiveness, there is abundant evidence that effective problem solving, decision making, interpersonal interaction, and communication draw on emotional processes involving the perception, understanding, use, and regulation of emotion. Therefore, it makes sense to integrate emotional skills training in leader development programs.

People will not make a real effort to learn unless they are convinced that learning is possible. Is there evidence that emotional skills can be trained? Ekman's Facial Action Coding System or Micro Expression Training Tool has been used to train people to recognize basic, universal facial expressions and more complex blends of emotion (Ekman, 2003). Decoding nonverbal communication in ongoing social interaction entails not only knowing how to interpret the cues but also attending to these cues. The type of training that Ekman proposes may also help to develop a habit of attending to others' emotions. The ability to understand emotions relies largely on knowledge (about emotional dynamics and display rules, for example). This knowledge can be acquired through explicit instruction or through discussions of emotionally loaded personal experiences, for example (see Caruso & Salovey, 2004, for other training ideas).

There is some evidence that programs of social and emotional learning for school children and adolescents can have beneficial effects (e.g., Greenberg, Kusché, Cook, & Quamma, 1995; Hawkins, Catalano, Kosterman, Abbott, & Hill, 1999; Weissberg & Greenberg, 1998). Adults often seek psychotherapy because of difficulties with emotion regulation, and outcome studies indicate that several forms of psychotherapy and emotion regulation training can be effective (Bergin & Garfield, 1994; Deffenbacher, Oetting, Huff, & Thwaites, 1995; Seligman, 1995). Although emotion-based personality traits are fairly stable over time, there is more room for change in adulthood than people commonly recognize (see Heatherton & Weinberger, 1994). The fact that people usually do not change much does not mean that one cannot change if there is a good enough reason to change. There is evidence from meta-analyses aggregating a large number of studies that training can be effective in several realms related to emotional abilities, including stress inoculation training, sensitivity and self-awareness training, management education, and cross-cultural training (Burke & Day, 1986; Deshpande & Viswesvaran, 1992; Faith, Wong, & Carpenter, 1995; Niemiec, Sikorski, Clark, & Walberg, 1992; Saunders, Driskell, Johnston, & Salas, 1996). A few field experiments also suggest that people can be trained to act as transformational leaders with a positive impact on followers (e.g., Barling, Weber, & Kelloway, 1996; Dvir, Eden, Avolio, & Shamir, 2002). In sum, there is evidence from several lines of research that emotional skills and skills related to emotional intelligence can be learned.

Nevertheless, it is important to recognize the challenges of helping people to develop emotional abilities and to consider the implications for training. The challenges are especially noteworthy with regard to emotion regulation. Characteristics such as the propensity to experience positive and negative emotions seem to be driven in large part by one's genetic endowment and are fairly stable over time (Watson, 2000). Some emotional reactions have been deeply engraved through traumatic or quasi-traumatic experiences or countless reenactments, to the point that they have become automatic and habitual, and are therefore difficult to change. Individual differences in the

tendency to attend to one's own and others' feelings, which may be associated with nonconscious defense mechanisms or emotion regulation strategies
(Singer & Sincoff, 1990; Vaillant, 1977), can preclude the full use of emotional
information. In adulthood, people seldom receive clear feedback about their
emotional behavior, and thus often lack the awareness and motivation
required to develop skills in this realm. All this suggests that it is difficult to
bring about change through short training programs and that overselling
the benefits of emotional skills training can backfire. Providing individualized coaching, incorporating repeated opportunities for practice within
formal training sessions, or spacing out sessions over time to allow participants to practice new strategies between sessions, can facilitate change. Considering that it may be difficult to develop some emotional skills and that
leaders can capitalize on their strengths to compensate for some deficits,
leader development programs should avoid overly preoccupying participants with correcting mild deficits in emotional skills.

The existing research base does not tell us how emotional skills should be
integrated into leader development programs. It is possible to devise specific
activities and exercises to train the skills mapped by the ability model of emotional intelligence (see Caruso & Salovey, 2004; Lopes, Côté, & Salovey, 2005).
The emotional intelligence framework may also be useful for leader development programs that emphasize self-awareness and self-regulation as the
foundations for self-development (e.g., Avolio, 2004). For example, developing the ability to recognize one's own and others' emotions can enhance
self-awareness. Developing the ability to manage emotions can facilitate
other forms of self-regulation and give people the strength and resilience to
take on new challenges and experiment with different behaviors, which are
crucial steps for leader development.

Many executives are action-oriented and have little patience for theory or
training that they do not perceive to be of real practical benefit. Because people seldom receive feedback about their emotional skills, and are usually not
aware of their strengths and weaknesses in this realm, intensive feedback
from 360-degree assessments and observations of group work can be used
to develop self-awareness and generate buy-in for emotional skills training.
Interest and motivation can also be enhanced by letting participants opt into
a workshop on emotional intelligence after receiving 360-degree feedback,
and by tailoring content and methods to address participants' concerns.

People often find it difficult to recognize or talk about how they are
processing emotional cues or managing emotions. Using challenging group
work or other experiential learning exercises to stir up emotions in the classroom can help to surface relevant issues and make ideas easier to grasp. Considering the links between emotion, cognition, and social interaction, it is
possible to discuss emotions while addressing a range of topics relevant to

leader development (such as organizational change, communication, negotiation, or teamwork), instead of offering workshops devoted exclusively to emotion and emotional intelligence. However, instructors need expertise on emotion and practice dealing with emotions in the classroom.

It is probably impossible to train all of the skills that contribute to emotionally intelligent behavior through explicit classroom instruction within a reasonable time frame. Thus, helping participants to learn from experience is likely to maximize the benefits of training and ensure lasting impact. For this purpose, leader development programs should prepare participants to attend to others' emotional reactions, try different strategies, seek formal and informal feedback often, and reflect on their experiences and the impact of their own behavior. Leader development can be viewed as a form of personal development that requires the ability and willingness to learn from experience (Van Velsor & McCauley, 2004), and the basic principles of action science can enhance this capacity (Argyris et al., 1990; Schön, 1987).

Developing emotional abilities can enrich one's professional and personal life, and contribute to one's continuing personal development. Even if the effects are small, the cumulative benefits could be huge over the life span. When people consider whether changing a counterproductive pattern of behavior is worth the effort, they should keep in mind that this initial effort could benefit them for the rest of their lives. Yet, when people receive multi-rater feedback for the first time, highlighting deficits that they were not aware of, they often feel threatened or pressured to change against their will. That is particularly likely if the deficits relate to emotional characteristics that they perceive to be part of their personality or sense of self. Several authors have argued that people should strive to build on their strengths rather than correct mild deficits, because the latter strategy can take a lot of effort and yield only modest improvement (e.g., Zenger & Folkman, 2002). Although this idea makes sense, it might also lead people to underestimate their tremendous capacity for learning and growth. Leader development programs should help participants to view learning and change as part of an ongoing process of self-motivated personal development. In this context, the idea of emotional intelligence offers an appealing and useful framework to get people to think about using and managing emotions and emotional information more intelligently in their personal and professional lives.

NOTES

The authors thank Jochen Menges and Nicholas Emler for their comments on an earlier version of this manuscript.

1. In the psychological literature, "emotion" refers to a rather short-lived and intense organized response integrating physiological, behavioral, and cognitive

dimensions, which is triggered by an event perceived to influence one's well-being and is accompanied by a conscious feeling. "Affect" is a broader term that encompasses emotions, more subtle feelings, and more diffuse and long-lasting moods that are not associated with a specific event. For the sake of simplicity and to avoid jargon, in this chapter we use the term "emotion" to designate affect.

2. This is a concern, especially considering how much interest this topic has generated. It is possible that a number of studies have not been published because the results did not conform to expectations and nonsignificant findings are difficult to publish in peer-reviewed journals. For this chapter we were unable to review unpublished research, but future literature reviews should consider it.

REFERENCES

Antonakis, J. (2003). Why "emotional intelligence" does not predict leadership effectiveness: A comment on Prati, Douglas, Ferris, Ammeter, and Buckley (2003). *The International Journal of Organizational Analysis, 11,* 355–361.

Argyle, M., & Lu, L. (1990). Happiness and social skills. *Personality and Individual Differences, 11,* 1255–1261.

Argyris, C., Putnam, R., & Smith, D. M. (1990). *Action science: Concepts, methods, and skills for research and intervention.* San Francisco: Jossey-Bass.

Avolio, B. J. (2004). Examining the full range model of leadership: Looking back to transform forward. In D. V. Day, S. J. Zacarro, & S. M. Halpin (Eds.), *Leader development for transforming organizations: Growing leaders for tomorrow* (pp. 71–98). Mahwah, NJ: Erlbaum.

Barling, J., Weber, T., & Kelloway, E. K. (1996). Effects of transformational leadership training on attitudinal and financial outcomes: A field experiment. *Journal of Applied Psychology, 81,* 827–832.

Bar-On, R. (2000). Emotional and social intelligence: Insights from the Emotional Quotient Inventory. In R. Bar-On & J. D. A. Parker (Eds.), *The handbook of emotional intelligence* (pp. 363–388). San Francisco: Jossey-Bass.

Bass, B. M. (1985). *Leadership and performance beyond expectations.* New York: Free Press.

Bass, B. M., & Avolio, B. J. (1994). *Improving organizational effectiveness through transformational leadership.* Thousand Oaks, CA: Sage.

Baumeister, R. F., Vohs, K. D., DeWall, C. N., & Zhang, L. (2007). How emotion shapes behavior: Feedback, anticipation, and reflection, rather than direct causation. *Personality and Social Psychology Review, 11*(2), 167–203.

Bergin, A. E., & Garfield, S. L. (1994). *Handbook of psychotherapy and behavior change* (4th ed.). New York: Wiley.

Bono, J. E., & Judge, T. A. (2003). Core self-evaluations: A review of the trait and its role in job satisfaction and job performance. *European Journal of Personality, 17,* S5–S18.

Bower, G. H. (1981). Mood and memory. *American Psychologist, 36,* 129–148.

Brackett, M. A., & Mayer, J. D. (2003). Convergent, discriminant, and incremental validity of competing measures of emotional intelligence. *Personality and Social Psychology Bulletin, 29,* 1147–1158.

Brackett, M. A., Rivers, S. E., Shiffman, S., Lerner, N., & Salovey, P. (2006). Relating emotional abilities to social functioning: A comparison of self-report and performance measures of emotional intelligence. *Journal of Personality and Social Psychology, 91,* 780–795.

Burke, M. J., & Day, R. R. (1986). A cumulative study of the effectiveness of managerial training. *Journal of Applied Psychology, 71,* 232–245.

Caruso, D. R., & Salovey, P. (2004). *The emotionally intelligent manager.* San Francisco: Jossey-Bass.

Codol, J. P. (1975). On the so-called superior conformity of the self behavior: Twenty experimental investigations. *European Journal of Social Psychology, 5,* 457–501.

Conger, J. A., & Kanungo, R. N. (1998). *Charismatic leadership in organizations.* Thousand Oaks, CA: Sage.

Côté, S., Lopes, P. N., Salovey, P., & Miners, C. T. H. (2008). *Emotional intelligence and leadership emergence.* Manuscript submitted for publication.

Côté, S., & Miners, C. T. H. (2006). Emotional intelligence, cognitive intelligence, and job performance. *Administrative Science Quarterly, 51,* 1–28.

Deffenbacher, J. L., Oetting, E. R., Huff, M. E., & Thwaites, G. A. (1995). Fifteen-month follow-up of social skills and cognitive-relaxation approaches to general anger reduction. *Journal of Counseling Psychology, 42,* 400–405.

Deshpande, S. P., & Viswesvaran, C. (1992). Is cross-cultural training of expatriate managers effective: A meta analysis. *International Journal of Intercultural Relations, 16,* 295–310.

Devos, T., Silver, L. A., Mackie, D. M., & Smith, E. R. (2002). Experiencing intergroup emotions. In D. M. Mackie & E. R. Smith (Eds.), *From prejudice to intergroup emotions* (pp. 111–134). New York: Psychology Press.

Druskat, V. U., & Wolff, S. B. (2003). Group emotional intelligence and its influence on group effectiveness. In C. Cherniss & D. Goleman (Eds.), *The emotionally intelligent workplace: How to select for, measure, and improve emotional intelligence in individuals, groups, and organizations* (pp. 132–155). San Francisco: Jossey-Bass.

Dvir, T., Eden, D., Avolio, B. J., & Shamir, B. (2002). Impact of transformational leadership on follower development and performance: A field experiment. *Academy of Management Journal, 45,* 735–744.

Ekman, P. (2003). *Emotions revealed: Recognizing faces and feelings to improve communication and emotional life.* New York: Times Books.

Elfenbein, H. A., Foo, M. D., White, J. B., Tan, H. H, & Aik, V. C. (2007). Reading your counterpart: The benefit of emotion recognition ability for effectiveness in negotiation. *Journal of Nonverbal Behavior, 31.*

Elfenbein, H. A., Marsh, A. A., & Ambady, N. (2002). Emotional intelligence and the recognition of emotion from facial expressions. In L. Feldman Barrett & P. Salovey (Eds.), *The wisdom in feeling: Psychological processes in emotional intelligence* (pp. 37–59). New York: Guilford Press.

Faith, M. S., Wong, F. Y., & Carpenter, K. M. (1995). Group sensitivity training: Update, meta-analysis, and recommendations. *Journal of Counseling Psychology, 42,* 390–399.

Fredrickson, B. L. (1998). What good are positive emotions? *Review of General Psychology, 3,* 300–319.

Friedman, H. S., Riggio, R. E., & Casella, D. F. (1988). Nonverbal skill, personal charisma, and initial attraction. *Personality and Social Psychology Bulletin, 14,* 203–211.

Frijda, N. H. (1988). The laws of emotion. *American Psychologist, 43,* 349–358.

Furr, R. M., & Funder, D. C. (1998). A multimodal analysis of personal negativity. *Journal of Personality and Social Psychology, 74,* 1580–1591.

George, J. M. (2000). Emotions and leadership: The role of emotional intelligence. *Human Relations, 53,* 1027–1055.

Gerstner, C. R., & Day, D. V. (1997). Meta-analytic review of Leader-Member Exchange Theory: Correlates and construct issues. *Journal of Applied Psychology, 82,* 827–844.

Goleman, D. (1995). *Emotional intelligence.* New York: Bantam.

Goleman, D. (1998). *Working with emotional intelligence.* New York: Bantam.

Graen, G. B., & Uhl-Bien, M. (1995). Relationship-based approach to leadership: Development of Leader-Member Exchange (LMX) theory of leadership over 25 years: Applying a multi-level multi-domain perspective. *Leadership Quarterly, 6,* 219–247.

Greenberg, M. T., Kusché, C. A., Cook, E. T., & Quamma, J. P. (1995). Promoting emotional competence in school-aged children: The effects of the PATHS curriculum. *Development and Psychopathology, 7,* 117–136.

Greenwald, A. G. (1980). The totalitarian ego: Fabrication and revision of personal history. *American Psychologist, 35,* 603–618.

Hall, J. A., & Bernieri, F. J. (2001). *Interpersonal sensitivity: Theory and measurement.* Mahwah, NJ: Erlbaum.

Hatfield, E., Cacioppo, J. T., & Rapson, R. L. (1994). *Emotional contagion.* New York: Cambridge University Press.

Hawkins, J. D., Catalano, R. F., Kosterman, R., Abbott, R., & Hill, K. G. (1999). Preventing adolescent health-risk behaviors by strengthening protection during childhood. *Archives of Pediatric & Adolescent Medicine, 153,* 226–334.

Heatherton, T. F., & Weinberger, J. L. (Eds.). (1994). *Can personality change?* Washington, DC: American Psychological Association.

Hooijberg, R., Hunt, J. G., & Dodge, G. E. (1997). Leadership complexity and development of the Leaderplex Model. *Journal of Management, 23,* 375–408.

Huy, Q. N. (1999). Emotional capability, emotional intelligence, and radical change. *Academy of Management Review, 24,* 325–345.

Huy, Q. N. (2002). Emotional balancing of organizational continuity and radical change: The contribution of middle managers. *Administrative Science Quarterly, 47,* 31–69.

Isen, A. M., Daubman, K. A., & Nowicki, G. P. (1987). Positive affect facilitates creative problem solving. *Journal of Personality and Social Psychology, 52,* 1122–1131.

Judge, T. A., & Piccolo, R. F. (2004). Transformational and transactional leadership: A meta-analytic test of their relative validity. *Journal of Applied Psychology, 89,* 755–768.

Katz, R. L. (1955). Skills of an effective administrator. *Harvard Business Review, 33,* 33–42.

Keltner, D., & Haidt, J. (1999). Social functions of emotions at four levels of analysis. *Cognition and Emotion, 13*, 505–521.

Kets de Vries, M. F. R. (2001). *The leadership mystique: A user's manual for the human enterprise.* London: Financial Times Prentice Hall.

Larsen, R. J. (2000). Toward a science of mood regulation. *Psychological Inquiry, 11*, 129–141.

Lazarus, R. (1991). *Emotion and adaptation.* New York: Oxford.

Loewenstein, G., & Lerner, J. S. (2003). The role of affect in decision making. In R. J. Davidson, K. R. Scherer, & H. H. Goldsmith (Eds.), *Handbook of affective sciences* (pp. 619–642). New York: Oxford University Press.

Lopes, P. N., Brackett, M. A., Nezlek, J. B., Schütz, A., Sellin, I., & Salovey, P. (2004). Emotional intelligence and social interaction. *Personality and Social Psychology Bulletin, 30*, 1018–1034.

Lopes, P. N., Côté, S., & Salovey, P. (2005). An ability model of emotional intelligence: Implications for assessment and training. In V. U. Druskat, F. Sala, & G. Mount (Eds.), *Linking emotional intelligence and performance at work: Current research evidence with individuals and groups* (pp. 53–80). Mahwah, NJ: Lawrence Erlbaum Associates.

Lopes, P. N., Grewal, D., Kadis, J., Gall, M., & Salovey, P. (2006). Evidence that emotional intelligence is related to job performance and affect and attitudes at work. *Psicothema, 18*, 132–138.

Lopes, P. N., Salovey, P., Côté, S., & Beers, M. (2005). Emotion regulation ability and the quality of social interaction. *Emotion, 5*, 113–118.

Lowe, K. B., Galen Kroeck, K., & Sivasubramaniam, N. (1996). Effectiveness correlates of transformational and transactional leadership: A meta-analytic review of the MLQ literature. *Leadership Quarterly, 7*, 385–425.

Mabe, P. A., & West, S. G. (1982). Validity of self-evaluation of ability: A review and meta-analysis. *Journal of Applied Psychology, 67*, 280–296.

Mayer, J. D., Roberts, R. D. & Barsade, S. G. (2008). Emerging research in emotional intelligence. *Annual Review of Psychology, 59*, 507–536.

Mayer, J. D., & Salovey, P. (1997). What is emotional intelligence? In P. Salovey & D. Sluyter (Eds.), *Emotional development and emotional intelligence: Implications for educators* (pp. 3–31). New York: Basic Books.

Mayer, J. D., Salovey, P., & Caruso, D. (2000). Models of emotional intelligence. In R. J. Sternberg (Ed.), *Handbook of intelligence* (pp. 396–420). New York: Cambridge.

Mayer, J. D., Salovey, P., & Caruso, D. (2002). *Mayer-Salovey-Caruso Emotional Intelligence Test (MSCEIT): User's Manual.* Toronto: Multi-Health Systems.

Mayer, J. D., Salovey, P., Caruso, D. R., & Sitarenios, G. (2001). Emotional intelligence as a standard intelligence. *Emotion, 1*, 232–242.

Mayer, J. D., Salovey, P., Caruso, D. R., & Sitarenios, G. (2003). Measuring emotional intelligence with the MSCEIT V2.0. *Emotion, 3*, 97–105.

Meyer, G. J., Finn, S. E., Eyde, L. D., Kay, G. G., Moreland, L. K., & Dies, R. R. (2001). Psychological testing and psychological assessment: A review of evidence and issues. *American Psychologist, 56*, 128–165.

Mumford, M. D., Zaccaro, S. J., Harding, F. D., Jacobs, T. O., & Fleishman, E. A. (2000). Leadership skills for a changing world: Solving complex social problems. *Leadership Quarterly, 11*, 11–35.

Niemiec, R. P., Sikorski, M. F., Clark, G., & Walberg, H. J. (1992). Effects of management education: A quantitative synthesis. *Evaluation and Program Planning, 15*, 297–302.

Petrides, K. V., & Furnham, A. (2003). Trait emotional intelligence: Behavioural validation in two studies of emotion recognition and reactivity to mood induction. *European Journal of Personality, 17*, 39–57.

Rahim, M. A., & Psenicka, C. (2005). Relationship between emotional intelligence and effectiveness of leader role: A dyadic study in four countries. *The International Journal of Organizational Analysis, 13*, 327–342.

Rosete, D., & Ciarrochi, J. (2005). Emotional intelligence and its relationship to workplace performance outcomes of leadership effectiveness. *Leadership and Organization Development Journal, 26*, 388–399.

Ross, L., & Nisbett, R. E. (1991). *The person and the situation: Perspectives of social psychology.* New York: McGraw-Hill.

Rowold, J., & Heinitz, K. (2007). Transformational and charismatic leadership: Assessing the convergent, divergent and criterion validity of the MLQ and the CKS. *The Leadership Quarterly, 18*, 121–133.

Rubin, R. S., Munz, D. C., & Bommer, W. H. (2005). Leading from within: The effects of emotion recognition and personality on transformational leadership behavior. *Academy of Management Journal, 48*, 845–858.

Salovey, P., & Grewal, D. (2005). The science of emotional intelligence. *Current Directions in Psychological Science, 14*, 281–285.

Salovey, P., & Mayer, J. D. (1990). Emotional intelligence. *Imagination, Cognition, and Personality, 9*, 185–211.

Sapolsky, R. M. (2000). *Why zebras don't get ulcers: An updated guide to stress, stress-related diseases, and coping.* New York: W. H. Freeman.

Saunders, T., Driskell, J. E., Johnston, J. H., & Salas, E. (1996). The effect of stress inoculation training on anxiety and performance. *Journal of Occupational Health Psychology, 1*, 170–186.

Schön, D. A. (1987). *Educating the reflective practitioner: Toward a new design for teaching and learning in the professions.* San Francisco: Jossey-Bass.

Schwarz, N. (1990). Feelings as information: Information and motivational functions of affective states. In E. T. Higgins & R. M. Sorrentino (Eds.), *Handbook of motivation and cognition: Vol. 2. Foundations of social behavior* (pp. 527–561). New York: Guilford Press.

Schwarz, N. (2002). Cognitive tuning. In L. Feldman Barrett & P. Salovey (Eds.), *The wisdom in feeling: Psychological processes in emotional intelligence* (pp. 144–166). New York: Guilford Press.

Seligman, M. E. P. (1995). The effectiveness of psychotherapy: The *Consumer Reports* study. *American Psychologist, 50*, 965–974.

Simon, H. A. (1967). Motivational and emotional controls of cognition. *Psychological Review, 74*, 29–39.

Singer, J. A., & Salovey, P. (1988). Mood and memory: Evaluating the Network Theory of Affect. *Clinical Psychology Review, 8*, 211–251.

Singer, J. L., & Sincoff, J. L. (1990). Summary chapter: Beyond repression and the defenses. In J. L. Singer (Ed.), *Repression and dissociation*. Chicago: University of Chicago Press.

Snodgrass, S. E., Hecht, M. A., & Ploutz-Snyder, R. (1998). Interpersonal sensitivity: Expressivity or perceptivity? *Journal of Personality and Social Psychology, 74*, 238–249.

Sternberg, R. J. (1999). Intelligence as developing expertise. *Contemporary Educational Psychology, 24*, 359–375.

Taylor, S. E. (1986). *Positive illusions: Creative self-deception and the healthy mind.* New York: Basic Books.

Vaillant, G. E. (1977). *Adaptation to life.* Boston: Little, Brown.

Van Velsor, E., & McCauley, C. D. (2004). Introduction: Our view of leadership development. In C. D. McCauley & E. Van Velsor (Eds.), *The Center for Creative Leadership handbook of leadership development* (2nd ed., pp. 1–22). San Francisco, CA: Jossey-Bass.

Watson, D. (2000). *Mood and temperament.* New York: Guilford Press.

Weissberg, R. P., & Greenberg, M. T. (1998). School and community competence-enhancement and prevention programs. In W. Damen (Series Ed.) & I. E. Sigel & K. A. Renninger (Vol. Eds.), *Handbook of child psychology: Vol. 4. Child psychology in practice* (5th ed., pp. 877–954). New York: John Wiley & Sons.

Zenger, J., & Folkman, J. (2002). *The extraordinary leader: Turning good managers into great leaders.* New York: McGraw-Hill.

PART II

PERCEIVING LEADERS

6

Social Cognitive Perspectives on Leadership

TIANE L. LEE AND SUSAN T. FISKE

Leadership perception comprises various forms of mental representation, or the structure of how people remember and think of their leaders. These representations include schemas, prototypes, and exemplars. A schema is a general representation that specifies necessary and sufficient attributes for who qualifies as a leader. Another summary representation, a prototype, is constructed from leader-typical traits abstracted from previously encountered leaders. Unlike a schema, a prototype provides a comparison standard by which perceivers judge the degree of typicality of each encountered leader. Exemplars, on the other hand, are a set of concrete examples in the perceiver's memory. Across these structures, leader images contain similar content: warmth and competence are two core dimensions with which perceivers are concerned. Leadership perception is context sensitive—culture and gender are main moderators—but a social cognitive approach makes sense of and organizes what at first glance are idiosyncratic leader images. Traits expected of leaders can be organized into a dimensional framework of warmth and competence. Contingency research also highlights their central role: leaders who demonstrate competence and trustworthiness gain "idiosyncrasy credits," and a leader's primary concern, either task accomplishment (competence) or interpersonal relations (warmth), interacts with degree of control to determine effective performance.

People expect certain things of their leaders. When their leaders deliver on those expectations—or do not—those follower beliefs have consequences.

Presidents get reelected or not; CEOs rise and fall; juries reach verdicts or hang; teams win or lose. Social cognitive perspectives focus on beliefs, especially followers' beliefs, but also on societal and cultural beliefs, about who leaders are and who they should be.

Social cognitive approaches rely on concepts of mental representation. The first section reviews three major psychological frameworks that explain how people categorize and remember others: schemas, prototypes, and exemplars. Each of these representations contains the images people have of what a leader is like. We explain the theoretical structure of leader images within each viewpoint, but we also describe the general *content* of leader images, which these perspectives all share—it turns out that two dimensions underlie the characteristics that leaders are expected to exemplify. Finally, we provide an overview of two types of leadership research, trait studies and contingency research, showing that leader images contain these two core dimensions. Social cognitive principles reconcile and organize various research findings on leader images.

MENTAL REPRESENTATIONS

Leader images are a type of mental representation or knowledge structure, which is information encoded and constructed by individuals, later accessed and used in various ways—including to evaluate or interpret the target stimulus (Smith, 1998). Schemas are one type of mental representation. They are cognitive structures—organized prior knowledge—representing abstract understanding of a complex concept or type of stimulus (Fiske & Taylor, 2008). The schema concept is derived from Gestalt psychology (Koffka, 1935), which recognizes perception as holistic and treats concepts as coherent wholes (rather than the sum of their parts). Likewise, the information represented in schemas includes general knowledge, extracted from one's own previous experiences or from societal beliefs, and organized into an integrated whole.

As such, schemas are lay theories, or individuals' understanding about how their world works, that help people simplify their environment (Markus & Zajonc, 1985). Schemas allow people to fill in missing details and remember highlights. They facilitate top-down cognitive processes, a way to understand and experience complex stimuli through relying on more general knowledge. Schemas both facilitate the perception of expectancy-consistent information and make people attend to schema-inconsistent information, in an effort to understand and explain it. For example, people expect presidents to be dignified, so it is easy for them to encode a president acting formal at a diplomatic dinner, whereas a president who appears in a clown suit requires explanation. People may recall exceptions like this, but when they have to guess or estimate under uncertainty, they tend to fall back on their schematic expectations. People tend to interpret ambiguous information as fitting their schematic expectations, thereby maintaining their schemas. For example, the president who cracks a joke at a state dinner is putting people at ease, not forfeiting his or her dignity.

Leader schemas are a type of role schema; examples of other role schemas are the group helper and the group watchdog. A leader schema specifies leaders' expected traits, attributes, and appropriate behaviors. People apply schemas to instances that they have classified as category members. That is, people must first recognize an individual as a leader before applying a leader schema to that person. (The categorization is based on prototypes or exemplars, described below.) Thus, if a perceiver considers a leader to be someone who initiates meetings and makes decisions, then he or she will classify a person exhibiting those behaviors as a leader. The perceiver then may have other knowledge in his or her leader schema (e.g., leaders like to be respected), which they also apply to help them understand the person. A schema is a unitized representation, in that the represented information is activated as all or nothing. So if a perceiver has a leader schema that depicts a leader as someone who likes to be respected and who is a top-notch multitasker, both of these expectations are applied to individuals the perceiver classifies as a leader.

Schemas share many properties with prototypes, which are another form of person representation. Prototypes are similar to schemas in that they contain expectations (traits and attributes) about a concept (leader). However, unlike schemas, which specify necessary and sufficient attributes for what constitutes a category member, prototypes do not have such hard set guidelines for categories. Rather, perceivers interpret targets by the extent to which they are typical or atypical category members. For example, a person who (1) initiates meetings and (2) makes decisions may be a more typical leader than one who (3) is a top-notch multitasker. These three characteristics range in the degree to which they are typical of leader qualities.

Similar to a schema, a prototype contains features abstracted from societal beliefs, or from previous encounters with category members. So a person's prototypical leader is constructed from encounters with different types of leaders: politicians, business owners, community activists. The result is a prototypical leader with traits abstracted from across those various leaders (e.g., charismatic, in the public eye). Although a prototype is generally understood to be the most representative member (Cantor & Mischel, 1979), a prototype can also be an extreme ideal category member (Fiske & Taylor, 1991). As a result, leader prototypes may represent more typical examples (e.g., chief executive officer [CEO] of a company), or they may resemble more extreme examples (e.g., president of a country).

Because prototypical features are abstracted from category members and then compiled into a prototype, two characteristics are noteworthy. First, perceivers do not need to have encountered a prototypical category member in order to construct a prototype (Posner & Keele, 1968). In fact, no actual category member may be a perfect prototype; instead, each instance contains some typical features that contribute to the construction of the prototypical category member. Second, a prototype may include features that are not diagnostic of category membership. For example, it is not necessary that leaders be male, and being male is not sufficient to be a leader. Yet for some perceivers the prototypical leader may embody the image of a man. In addition, some prototypical features may not exist at all in some category members. For example, being Protestant may be prototypical of American presidents, but not all presidents have been Protestant. This is a major difference between prototypes and schemas: prototypes are average or idealized instances with all attributes filled in, including category-irrelevant features (e.g., male, Protestant), whereas schemas contain only the focal, category-relevant features. Consequently, prototypes may refer to more detailed (yet, less organized and fuzzier) images while schemas are internally coherent.

Still another social cognitive view depicts person representation as a set of exemplars. Recall that schemas and prototypes are generalized representations; while they are constructed from specific instances, they do not represent specific instances. Exemplars are the specific instances and are, therefore, context sensitive. The exemplar view holds that people judge each target based on its similarity to specific, previously encountered examples.

Rather than summary representations such as a generalized image (schemas), or averaged or idealized prototypes, exemplars emphasize the role of concrete examples and specific previous experiences of the perceiver. This idea is best represented by norm theory (Kahneman & Miller, 1986), in which each new instance or experience activates the most relevant and similar exemplars to that experience, and against which perceivers judge the new instance. The degree of similarity to the activated exemplars reflects how normal or unusual the new instance is.

The exemplar view highlights aspects of social cognitive evidence that neither the schema nor the prototype view emphasizes. First, it supports the observation that people refer to specific examples (rather than the category itself) to make judgments about another category member. For example, a person curious to know whether Bill Clinton was the youngest American president would have to recall at least one of two specific presidents (Theodore Roosevelt and John F. Kennedy) to realize that he was not. To be sure, the prototype view acknowledges that people remember specific instances but does not give specific instances much more consideration, whereas the exemplar view gives them a central role in person perception because it holds that new instances are compared against these remembered instances.

In addition, the exemplar view accounts for people's knowledge of within-category variation because they are aware of specific instances. People know that most American presidents were elected into office but that only a handful became president by default: Andrew Johnson after Abraham Lincoln's assassination and Lyndon B. Johnson after John F. Kennedy's, etc. Again, the prototype view acknowledges that people know of variability when it comes to presidents but posits that people gloss over this variability to form a prototype of the presidency as an elected office. People's understanding of within-category variability allows them to appreciate the correlation between certain features in a category. For example, they are aware that presidents who were not popularly elected into office tended to have been vice presidents.

For our purposes, leader images, whether they come from prototypes and schemas, or constitute a set of exemplars, will appear together for the remainder of the chapter; their dissimilarities matter less than what they have in common. These mental representations demonstrate the perceiver as an active observer, who makes sense of, constructs impressions of, and evaluates leaders. People use prototypes or exemplars as comparison standards against which new instances are contrasted and possibly classified as category members, activating schematic representations of that category. Subsequently, they rely on the activated schema to make inferences about the stimulus: filling in missing details with schema-consistent information; interpreting ambiguous information as schema-consistent; and directing attention to schema-inconsistent information, in order to dedicate special processing, for example. These attentional, interpretational, and retrieval processes usually take place without conscious effort by the perceiver. In person perception, people employ some combination of these representations (Smith & Medin, 1981), and leader perception is one example.

Applied to leadership, implicit leader theories draw on these stored concepts. People hold *implicit leadership theories* (ILTs; Calder, 1977; Kenney, Schwartz-Kenney, & Blascovich, 1996; Offermann, Kennedy, & Wirtz, 1994; Phillips & Lord, 1981), which specify the characteristics and behaviors that leaders should exhibit. Leadership categorization theory (Lord, Foti, & Phillips, 1982; Lord, Foti, & de Vader, 1984) examines recognition-based leadership perceptual processes in which ILTs are used to categorize targets as leaders. When a perceiver encounters an individual in a leadership position or a target individual who displays schema-consistent or prototypical qualities of a leader, these leader images are activated and affect the perceiver's further expectations of the target as well as the subjective experience of the interaction (Foti & Lord, 1987; Kenney et al., 1996; Rush & Russell, 1988). Thus, leaders are recognized based on how well they fit into perceivers' expectations of a leader. Once perceivers recognize a leader's prototypical traits and categorize the target as a leader, categorization affects attention, encoding, and retrieval of schema-consistent information such that it biases subsequent behavioral expectations and responsibility attributions, even if they are inaccurate (Foti & Lord, 1987; Lord et al., 1984).

Another commonality among these representations is their two-dimensional content, not always self-evident but extractable. We apply social cognitive findings on person perception to leader images in prototypical trait studies and contingency studies, both of which reveal two underlying dimensions. We now turn to the content of these leader representations.

CORE DIMENSIONS IN PERSON PERCEPTION

If people have prior knowledge—and therefore expectations—about leaders, what exactly are their expectations? To answer this question, we look at person perception more generally, as we did with leader images. In the latter half of the twentieth century, across a wide variety of different social science disciplines and research groups, a similar pair of dimensions recurred: one revolving around the theme of competence (e.g., ability, intelligence) and another revolving around warmth (e.g., trustworthiness, sociability).

In early person perception research, warm-cold emerged as a primary dimension (Asch, 1946), and contrasted with competence-related adjectives (Hamilton & Fallot, 1974); multidimensional scaling of trait descriptions replicated these dimensions (Rosenberg, Nelson, & Vivekananthan, 1968).

Group research discovered the same two dimensions—labeled task and social—in describing small group interactions, although they added a third, non-trait-based dimension: sheer amount of interpersonal interaction (Bales, 1970). Likewise, personality psychology discovered two modes of being in the world, agency and communion (Bakan, 1956), which soon appeared in gender research as masculine and feminine, respectively (Carlson, 1971; Spence, Helmreich, & Holahan, 1979). Subsequent work built on Bakan's research to identify comparable dimensions of self-profitability (e.g., confident, ambitious) and other-profitability (e.g., tolerant, trustworthy) (Peeters, 1983), which appear in both interpersonal perception (Vonk, 1999; Wojciszke, 1997) and intergroup perception (Phalet & Poppe, 1997).

These two dimensions again appear prominently in the Stereotype Content Model (SCM; Fiske, Cuddy, Glick & Xu, 2002; Fiske, Cuddy, & Glick, 2007). In the SCM, social perception immediately answers two key questions. The first reveals concern about the target's warmth: Are the other's intentions good or bad toward me (and my group)? The second question reveals another primary concern about the target's competence: Is the person able or unable to enact these intentions? The answers to these questions result in four general images of the target: warm and competent; warm and incompetent; not trustworthy and competent; neither trustworthy nor competent.

The model further posits that the target's status strongly predicts competence assessments; a similar element appears in leader images (see below). And, perceived cooperation predicts warmth assessments; leaders who cooperate and do not exploit their subordinates are also seen as warm. In a series of experiments, manipulating interpersonal status and cooperation within a team led, respectively, to perceived competence and warmth (Russell & Fiske, in press).

Useful in various instances of intergroup perception (Clausell & Fiske, 2005; Cuddy, Norton, & Fiske, 2005; Eckes, 2002; Lee & Fiske, 2006), the SCM also applies to leader images, which (1) reveal these two recurring dimensions, and (2) involve factors (cooperation, power, status) that also closely relate to attributions of warmth and competence. We suggest that the SCM provides one way to organize the various findings from leadership research into a manageable framework. Many of these findings fit into a two-dimensional structure, one dimension akin to warmth, and one akin to competence.

CONTROVERSY: NO UNIVERSAL LEADER IMAGE IN THE FACE OF CONTEXT SENSITIVITY?

Researchers have noted many mixed and unclear results in leadership research, rendering it difficult to find consensus in leader images (Chemers, 2000). In addition, it remains unclear how perceivers account for the range of contextual factors when they think about leadership, which suggests that no prototypical leader image exists (Lord, Brown, Harvey, & Hall, 2001). One theory argues that the individual perceived to be most prototypical of a particular group, as opposed to one who resembles a generic prototypical leader image, is attributed, ascribed, or conferred leadership (see social identity theory of leadership; Hogg, 2001). The implication is that leader images are group-specific and that single-prototype-based leadership research may leave some gaps. Further, other studies suggest people's prototypes differ based on, and as a result of, their specific experiences with leaders (Nye & Simonetta, 1996).

That people's own experiences provide the meaning of leadership and expectations about leaders implies that, indeed, there is no consensus of a prototypical leader. This is not surprising given the context-sensitive nature of leadership. Certainly, some factors moderate leader images, of which culture and gender are two of the most common and influential (Chemers, 2000). For the purpose of understanding the underlying patterns in leader image content despite these moderators, we briefly explore the impact of culture and gender.

Cross-national studies show that leader prototypic traits vary systematically at societal, organizational, and task levels (Bayazit, 2004). While particular prototypical traits may be unique, one can extract a general pattern of warmth-related and competence-related dimensions. For example, a traditional Latin American leader prototype is a leader who is autocratic, directive, relationship-oriented, assertive, and aggressive; seldom delegates work or uses teams; prefers formal top-down communication; and avoids conflict (Romero, 2004). We emphasize two general themes across these traits: showing relationship concerns and avoiding conflict compose an interpersonally oriented dimension, and being autocratic, directive, and assertive compose a task-oriented dimension, similar to competence.

Gender also moderates leader images. Lay theories of leadership and stereotypes about leaders include characteristics and behaviors that resemble stereotypically masculine traits (Miner, 1993; Powell, 1988). Descriptive (what men are like) and prescriptive (what men should be like) stereotypes of men depict them as assertive, confident, aggressive, agentic, and possessing self-direction (e.g., Williams & Best, 1990). Overall, men are, and should be, competent, as are leaders, revealing a perceived fit between stereotypical male attributes and expected leadership qualities (Heilman, 2001).

In addition, two major differences expected of men and women leaders align with gender stereotypes (for a review, see Eagly & Johnson, 1990). First, people expect men to be task-oriented (or higher on the Initiating Structure; see below) and women to be relationship-oriented (or higher on the Consideration Structure; see below). Second, they expect men to lead autocratically, and women, democratically. But contrary to perceivers' expectations for male versus female leaders, there is no gender difference in task versus relationship orientations in organizational studies, although there is a gender difference in survey and laboratory studies—women are more relationally oriented and democratic in their approach to leadership.

The findings are again mixed, depending on the type of setting. But one way to interpret these findings is to see the pattern (warmth and competence) in how images interact with context. The two dimensions persist across the different studies. The net effect is that the gender of the leader creates unique contingencies in the perception of the leader, along warmth and competence dimensions. In gender stereotypes, the counterpart to the stereotypic competent male is a stereotypically warm female: descriptive and prescriptive stereotypes of women reveal that people expect *and* prefer women to be nice, kind, sensitive, and nurturing, among other things (e.g., Heilman, 2001; Prentice & Carranza, 2002). Again, we see warmth and competence. For the remainder of the chapter, we focus on these two dimensions across various examples of two types of leadership research: trait studies and contingency research.

LEADER IMAGES IN TRAIT STUDIES PARALLEL PERSON PERCEPTION'S PRIMARY DIMENSIONS

Studies of actual leaders produce a competence theme and a warmth theme. Early studies of emergent leadership show that people with different personalities take on one of two leadership roles: task leader and socioemotional leader (Bales, 1958), fitting the competence-warmth dimensions of social cognition research. In a study on one specific political figure, Polish respondents ascribed various personality traits to their current president (Wojciszke & Klusek, 1996). These ratings produced three factors: competence, morality, and likability. A competence factor consisted of traits such as ingenious and clever. One can see that the other two factors, morality and likability, estimate a warm person. Traits that made up the morality factor were fair, honest, sincere, righteous, and unselfish. Traits that made up the likable factor were good-looking and pleasant. There were also overlaps between these two factors: modest and likable were related to both.

For ideal leader traits, Americans also hold a prototypic image (competent and trustworthy) of a president (Kinder, Peters, Abelson, & Fiske, 1980). In this study, people chose the six most important attributes for an ideal president from a list of 32 traits (16 good, 16 bad) and 32 behaviors (16 good, 16 bad). Selected items referred to success and competence-related traits (e.g., smart, *not* unstable) and behaviors (e.g., provide strong leadership; *not* get into unnecessary wars), and political trustworthiness, exemplified through traits (e.g., warm, *not* power-hungry) and behaviors (e.g., communicate openly with the people, *not* use office for personal gain).

In work teams, organizational researchers identify *Initiating Structure* and *Consideration* as the two predominant dimensions in describing leader behavior (Fleishman, 1953; Halpin & Winer, 1957). These two dimensions interact with work outcomes: a leader's provision of task-related guidance and socioemotional support impact subordinate motivation and performance (see path-goal theory of leader effectiveness; House, 1971). (For more contingency theories, see next section.)

If we examine these two dimensions, we see that they approximate competence and warmth dimensions. Initiation is equivalent to the competence dimension in person perception. It refers to a leader who uses standard operating procedures, criticizes poor work, and emphasizes high levels of performance. These behaviors are related to leaders' focus on building a structure for task accomplishment, being directive, and assigning tasks (specifying procedures to be followed, clarifying expectations of subordinates, and scheduling work to be done). This dimension includes planning, organizing, directing, and controlling. Consideration fits the warmth dimension. It entails leaders showing concern for feelings of subordinates, making sure that minority viewpoints are considered in decision making, and attempting to reduce conflict in the work environment. These behaviors relate to a concern with positive group morale and follower satisfaction: being supportive and helpful, and generally creating an environment of warmth by doing such things as being friendly and approachable, looking out for the personal welfare of the group, and doing little things for subordinates.

To be sure, some theories of leader images analyze more than these two primary dimensions. A literature review of early studies on leadership traits found that leadership was associated with six general factors: capacity, achievement, responsibility, participation, status, and situation (Stogdill, 1948). Three of the factors—capacity, achievement, and responsibility—may relate to competence traits. Capacity refers to traits such as intelligence, alertness, and originality; achievement refers to a leader's scholarship and knowledge; responsibility includes demonstration of dependability, initiative, and persistence. Thus, these three factors consist of characteristics that researchers have found to constitute competence. Status also typically relates to competence. Other characteristics could compose warmth. Participation refers to sociability, cooperation, and adaptability, while situation refers to a leader's interaction with followers' skills, needs, and interests.

In a more recent study, six factors represented leader prototypic traits. Again, some relate most to competence. Intelligence (e.g., intelligent, clever), dedication (e.g., dedicated, disciplined), and strength (e.g., strong, forceful) are prototypic, whereas tyranny (e.g., domineering, power-hungry) and masculinity (e.g., male, masculine) were deemed unprototypical. Other factors relate to warmth such as sensitivity (e.g., sympathetic, sensitive), attractiveness (e.g., attractive, classy), and charisma (e.g., charismatic, inspiring; Offermann et al., 1994).

Thus, one could summarize leader prototype traits as following the same dimensions as the vast majority of person perception and group perception research.

SITUATION-CONTINGENT (OR PROCESS-ORIENTED) LEADERSHIP RESEARCH CORROBORATES SOCIAL COGNITION RESEARCH FINDINGS

Leadership operates in the context of situational parameters such as specific groups, genders, and cultures. But the contingency models that follow show that the two core social cognition dimensions are important, in concordance with the leader image studies above. These two dimensions are the ones that interact with follower or situational characteristics.

One contingency theory looks at how these dimensions contribute to leadership legitimacy in the eyes of followers. The "idiosyncrasy credit" model of innovative leadership (Hollander, 1958) argues that competence and trustworthiness (through demonstrating loyalty to group values) help an individual gain status in his or her group. A social exchange concept, the theory points to the key role of these two dimensions in helping the leader earn "idiosyncrasy credits," which can then be accumulated and exchanged for innovative actions down the road. An individual who demonstrates competence and trustworthiness early on reaps the rewards of receiving legitimacy as the leader.

Still another contingency theory emphasizes the role of task-related competence and warmth. According to the Contingency Model of Leadership Effectiveness, the interaction between the leader's primary concern (task accomplishments or interpersonal relations) and the degree of leader situational control determines effective performance. Effective performance results from task-motivated leaders in situations with either very low or very high control, or from relationship-oriented leaders in situations with moderate control (Fiedler, 1993). The leader's task and interpersonal motivations are measured through the Least Preferred Co-worker Scale (LPC), which assesses the leader's view of his or her least favorite co-worker ("the one person with whom you have had the most difficulty in getting the job done") on 18 bipolar scales of personality traits (e.g., friendly–unfriendly) (Fiedler, 1964). People with low LPC scores are task-motivated; they show concern for getting the job done. They tell people what to do, are punitive, and are not too concerned about others' feelings. These leaders emphasize effective and competent task performance. People with high LPC scores, on the other hand, tend to be considerate, provide rewards, are nondirective, and invite subordinate participation. These leaders show greater concern with interpersonal relationships.

CONCLUSION

People's leader images are both generic—what they expect of leaders in general—and contingent—what they expect of particular leaders in particular settings as a result of culture, gender, and social group, among other contextual variables. Leadership, from a social cognition perspective, entails the interplay among a variety of expectations, but some core principles apply, such as the recurring dimensions of competence and warmth expectations. Although the leader image literature may appear incoherent and limit the idea of universal leader images, we stress two points: that prototypes and exemplars are context sensitive, and that two main dimensions appear in most of these representations.

REFERENCES

Asch, S. E. (1946). Forming impressions of personality. *Journal of Abnormal and Social Psychology, 41,* 1230–1240.

Bakan, D. (1956). *The duality of human existence: An essay on psychology and religion.* Oxford, England: Rand McNally.

Bales, R. F. (1958). Task roles and social roles in problem solving groups. In E. F. Maccoby, T. M. Newcomb, and E. L. Hartley (Eds.), *Readings in Social Psychology* (3rd ed., pp. 437–447). New York: Holt, Rinehart & Winston.

Bales, R. F. (1970). *Personality and interpersonal behavior.* New York: Holt, Rinehart & Winston.

Bayazit, M. (2004). Conditioning the eye of the beholder: Are leader prototypes context-sensitive? *Dissertation Abstracts International: Section B: The Sciences and Engineering, 64*(9-B), 4660.

Calder, B. J. (1977). An attribution theory of leadership. In B. M. Staw & G. R. Salancik (Eds.), *New directions in organizational behavior.* Chicago, IL: St. Clair Press.

Cantor, N., & Mischel, W. (1979). Prototypes in person perception. In L. Berkowitz (Ed.), *Advances in experimental psychology* (pp. 3–52). New York: Academic Press.

Carlson, R. (1971). Sex differences in ego functioning: Exploratory studies of agency and communion. *Journal of Consulting and Clinical Psychology, 37,* 267–277.

Chemers, M. M. (2000). Leadership research and theory: A functional integration. *Group Dynamics: Theory, Research, and Practice, 4,* 27–43.

Clausell, E., & Fiske, S. T. (2005). When do subgroup parts add up to the stereotypic whole? Mixed stereotype content for gay male subgroups explains overall ratings. *Social Cognition, 23,* 161–181.

Cuddy, A. J. C., Norton, M., & Fiske, S. T. (2005). This old stereotype: The pervasiveness and persistence of the elderly stereotype. *Journal of Social Issues, 61,* 267–285.

Eagly, A. H., & Johnson, B. T. (1990). Gender and leadership style: A meta-analysis. *Psychological Bulletin, 108,* 233–256.

Eckes, T. (2002). Paternalistic and envious gender stereotypes: Testing predictions from the stereotype content model. *Sex Roles, 47,* 99–114.

Fiedler, F. E. (1964). A contingency model of leadership effectiveness. In L. Berkowitz (Ed.), *Advances in experimental social psychology* (Vol. 1, pp. 149–190). New York: Academic Press.

Fiedler, F. E. (1993). The leadership situation and the black box in contingency theories. In M. M. Chemers & R. Ayman (Eds.), *Leadership theory and research: Perspectives and directions* (pp. 1–28). San Diego: Academic Press.

Fiske, S. T., Cuddy, A. J. C., & Glick, P. (2007). Universal dimensions of social perception: Warmth and competence. *Trends in Cognitive Science, 11,* 77–83.

Fiske, S. T., Cuddy, A. J. C., Glick, P., & Xu, J. (2002). A model of (often mixed) stereotype content: Competence and warmth respectively follow from perceived status and competition. *Journal of Personality and Social Psychology, 82,* 878–902.

Fiske, S. T., & Taylor, S. E. (1991). *Social cognition* (2nd ed.). New York: McGraw-Hill.

Fiske, S. T., & Taylor, S. E. (2008). *Social cognition: From brains to culture.* New York: McGraw-Hill.

Fleishman, E. A. (1953). The description of supervisory behavior. *Journal of Applied Psychology, 37,* 1–6.

Foti, R. J., & Lord, R. G. (1987). Prototypes and scripts: The effects of alternative methods of processing information on rating accuracy. *Organizational Behavior and Human Decision Processes, 39,* 318–340.

Halpin, A. W., & Winer, B. J. (1957). A factorial study of the leader behavior descriptions. In R. M. Stogdill & A. E. Coons (Eds.), *Leader behavior: Its description and measurement.* Columbus: Ohio State University Bureau of Business Research.

Hamilton, D. L., & Fallot, R. D. (1974). Information salience as a weighting factor in impression formation. *Journal of Personality and Social Psychology, 30,* 444–448.

Heilman, M. E. (2001). Description and prescription: How gender stereotypes prevent women's ascent up the organizational ladder. *Journal of Social Issues, 57,* 657–674.

Hogg, M. A. (2001). A social identity theory of leadership. *Personality and Social Psychology Review, 5,* 184–200.

Hollander, E. P. (1958). Conformity, status, and idiosyncrasy credit. *Psychological Review, 65,* 117–127.

House, R. J. (1971). A path-goal theory of leader effectiveness. *Administrative Science Quarterly, 16,* 321–338.

Kahneman, D., & Miller, D. T. (1986). Norm theory: Comparing reality to its alternatives. *Psychological Review, 93,* 136–153.

Kenney, R. A., Schwartz-Kenney, B. M., & Blascovich, J. (1996). Implicit Leadership Theories: Defining leaders described as worthy of influence. *Personality and Social Psychology Bulletin, 22,* 1128–1143.

Kinder, D. R., Peters, M. D., Abelson, R. P., & Fiske, S. T. (1980). Presidential prototypes. *Political Behavior, 2,* 315–336.

Koffka, K. (1935). *Principles of Gestalt psychology.* New York: Harcourt, Brace, & World.

Lee, T. L., & Fiske, S. T. (2006). Not an outgroup, but not yet an ingroup: Immigrants in the stereotype content model. *International Journal of Intercultural Relations, 30,* 751–768.

Lord, R. G., Brown, D. J., Harvey, J. L., & Hall, R. J. (2001). Contextual constraints on prototype generation and their multilevel consequences for leadership perceptions. *Leadership Quarterly, 12,* 311–338.

Lord, R. G., Foti, R. J., & de Vader, C. L. (1984). A test of Leadership Categorization Theory: Internal structure, information processing, and leadership perceptions. *Organizational Behavior and Human Performance, 34,* 343–378.

Lord, R. G., Foti, R. J., & Phillips, J. S. (1982). A theory of leadership categorization. In J. G. Hunt, U. Sekaran, & C. Schriesheim (Eds.), *Leadership: Beyond establishment views.* Carbondale, IL: Southern Illinois University Press.

Markus, H. R., & Zajonc, R. B. (1985). The cognitive perspective in social psychology. In G. Lindzey & E. Aronson (Eds.), *Handbook of social psychology* (3rd ed., Vol. 1, pp. 137–230). New York: Random House.

Miner, J. B. (1993). *Role motivation theories*. New York: Routledge.

Nye, J. L., & Simonetta, L. G. (1996). Followers' perceptions of group leaders: The impact of recognition-based and inference-based processes. In J. L. Nye & A. M. Brower (Eds.), *What's social about social cognition? Research on socially shared cognition in small groups* (pp. 124–153). Thousand Oaks, CA: Sage Publications.

Offermann, L. R., Kennedy, J. K., & Wirtz, P. W. (1994). Implicit leadership theories: Content, structure, and generalizability. *Leadership Quarterly, 5,* 43–58.

Peeters, G. (1983). Relational and informational patterns in social cognition. In W. Doise and S. Moscovici (Eds.), *Current issues in European Social Psychology* (pp. 201–237). Cambridge, England: Cambridge University Press; and Paris: Maison des Sciences de l'Homme.

Phalet, K., & Poppe, E. (1997). Competence and morality dimensions of national and ethnic stereotypes: A study in six eastern-European countries. *European Journal of Social Psychology, 27,* 703–723.

Phillips, J. S., & Lord, R. G. (1981). Causal attributions and perceptions of leadership. *Organizational Behavior and Human Performance, 28,* 143–163.

Posner, M. I., & Keele, S. W. (1968). On the genesis of abstract ideas. *Journal of Experimental Psychology, 77,* 353–363.

Powell, G. N. (1988). *Women & men in management*. Newbury Park, CA: Sage.

Prentice, D. A., & Carranza, E. (2002). What women and men should be, shouldn't be, are allowed to be, and don't have to be: The contents of prescriptive gender stereotypes. *Psychology of Women Quarterly, 26,* 269–281.

Romero, R. J. (2004). Latin American leadership: El Patron & El Lider Moderno. *Cross-Cultural Management, 11,* 25–37.

Rosenberg, S., Nelson, C., & Vivekananthan, P. S. (1968). A multidimensional approach to the structure of personality impressions. *Journal of Personality and Social Psychology, 9,* 283–294.

Rush, M. C., & Russell, J. E. A. (1988). Leader prototypes and prototype-contingent consensus in leader behavior descriptions. *Journal of Experimental Social Psychology, 24,* 88–104.

Russell, A. M., & Fiske, S. T. (in press). It's all relative: Competition and status drive interpersonal perception. *European Journal of Social Psychology.*

Smith, E. E., & Medin, D. L. (1981). *Categories and concepts*. Cambridge, MA: Harvard University Press.

Smith, E. R. (1998). Mental representation and memory. In D. T. Gilbert, S. T. Fiske, & G. Lindzey (Eds.), *Handbook of social psychology* (4th ed., Vol. 1, pp. 391–445). New York: McGraw-Hill.

Spence, J. T., Helmreich, R. L., & Holahan, C. K. (1979). Negative and positive components of psychological masculinity and femininity and their relationships to self-reports of neurotic and acting out behaviors. *Journal of Personality and Social Psychology, 37,* 1673–1682.

Stogdill, R. M. (1948). Personal factors associated with leadership: A survey of the literature. *Journal of Psychology, 25,* 35–71.

Vonk, R. (1999). Effects of self-profitability and other-profitability on evaluative judgments of behaviours. *European Journal of Social Psychology, 29,* 833–842.

Williams, J. E., & Best, D. L. (1990). *Measuring sex stereotypes: A multination study.* Newbury Park, CA: Sage.

Wojciszke, B. (1997). Parallels between competence- versus morality-related traits and individualistic versus collectivistic values. *European Journal of Social Psychology, 27,* 245–256.

Wojciszke, B., & Klusek, B. (1996). Moral and competence-related traits in political perceptions. *Polish Psychological Bulletin, 27,* 319–325.

7

Seeing and Being a Leader: The Perceptual, Cognitive, and Interpersonal Roots of Conferred Influence

DONELSON R. FORSYTH AND JUDITH L. NYE

Are leaders intelligent or unintelligent, outgoing or introverted, understanding or insensitive, cooperative or inflexible, strict or undisciplined? Group members answer these questions by drawing on their beliefs about leaders. These implicit leadership theories, or ILTs, are intuitive assumptions about the naturally occurring relationships among various traits, behaviors, and characteristics associated with leadership, and evidence suggests that they often influence who emerges as a leader and how that leader is perceived and evaluated. Each person's ILT, depending on past experiences and cultural background, may include some idiosyncratic elements, but most people expect leaders to be dynamic, conscientious people with superior intellectual, social, and motivational skills. ILTs generally help followers process information efficiently, but ILTs can distort perceptions and interfere with identification of the best leader for a given situation. Biases against leaders who are women, for example, may be rooted in followers' implicit assumptions about men, women, and leadership. Because leaders' endorsement by followers depends on how followers perceive them, skilled leaders tailor their self-presentations to match their followers' ILT-based expectations.

In 1968 Henry Kissinger did not think that Richard M. Nixon, the newly elected U.S. president, could ever succeed as a world leader. Kissinger was confident that he knew what it took to be a good leader, and those preconceptions did not mesh with what he knew about Nixon's intellect, skill, and personality (Kissinger, 1979). But when they met in a private conference, Nixon disconfirmed Kissinger's long-held expectations. They discussed trade relations, nuclear weapons, and the war in Vietnam, and by the end of the conference, Kissinger changed the way he thought of Nixon: "I was struck by his perceptiveness and knowledge so at variance with my previous image of him" (1979, p. 12). Later Kissinger would agree to join his staff when Nixon asked him.

This historic encounter highlights the cognitive side of leadership. Leadership is a profoundly interpersonal process whereby cooperating individuals influence and motivate others to promote the attainment of group and individual goals, but perceptual and cognitive processes sustain these social outcomes. A cognitive approach to leadership recognizes that people are active processors of information about the social situations they face. When people meet for the first time, they quickly appraise each others' potential as leaders, and within the first few minutes those with more potential are permitted to exert more influence over the group than others. When viewers watch politicians engage in debate before elections, they intuitively appraise each candidate's strengths and weaknesses. In corporate settings employees take note of their bosses' words and deeds, and over time come to a relatively stable conclusion about their strengths and weaknesses. Few of us ever have the chance to meet a president-elect, but all of us actively seek, process, and store information about the leaders who surround us.

What mental processes lie at the core of people's perceptions of leaders? We explore this question here, with a particular focus on the cognitive mechanisms that perceivers rely on as they formulate their impressions of each leader and potential leader they encounter. As sages have long realized and researchers have recently confirmed empirically, people do not passively absorb information from each new situation they face. They are, instead, mentally prepared for the task of social perception, with each new experience observed and interpreted within a context provided by preexisting expectations, goals, plans, preconceptions, attitudes, beliefs, and so on. Kissinger, for example, gathered information about the president-elect during their conversation, but his previous experiences with leaders had written deeply on his mind's model of leaders and leadership. Here we briefly review the way that intuitive mental models about leaders and leadership work to shape both the way people perceive those who influence them and the way leaders present themselves to those they lead (see, too, Schyns & Meindl, 2005).

SEEING LEADERS: IMPLICIT LEADERSHIP THEORIES (ILTs)

Most people think that they will know a leader when they see one, because they intuitively assume that leaders possess certain qualities. Are leaders intelligent or unintelligent? Outgoing or introverted? Task-oriented or indecisive? Cooperative or Machiavellian? Strong or weak? People readily answer these questions by drawing on their *implicit leadership theories* (ILTs), which are their tacit beliefs about the traits, qualities, and characteristics leaders possess. These beliefs are described as *implicit* because these intuitive assumptions are usually unrecognized rather than stated explicitly. These beliefs are called *theories* because, like theories developed by experts and scientists, these cognitive frameworks include law-like generalities about leadership and more specific hypotheses about the types of qualities that characterize most leaders.

What qualities, skills, and characteristics are part of people's ILTs? When Eden and Leviatan (1975) first examined this question by asking people to describe a leader they had never met, they discovered that people's ratings converged on certain common qualities pertaining to structuring the work to be done (e.g., maintains high standards, offers to solve problems) and consideration for the relations with and between members (e.g., is friendly and easy to approach, encourages teamwork). Lord and his colleagues, across a series of studies, consistently found that people's ratings in a variety of settings coalesce around these same themes of initiating structure for the task and concern for relations (e.g., Rush, Thomas, & Lord, 1977). In our own research (Nye & Forsyth, 1991) we, too, have found that people associate leadership with instrumentality (analytical, task-oriented, problem-solving) and social sensitivity (egalitarian, positive, extroverted).

ILTs also include more specific, trait-level qualities, such as integrity and competence (Chemers, 1997), decisiveness (Hogan & Kaiser, 2005), and willingness to shape group goals and norms (Den Hartog, House, Hanges, Ruiz-Quintanilla, & Dorfman, 1999). Lord, Foti, and De Vader (1984), in their analysis of people's perceptions of leaders in various domains (e.g., military, political, educational, media, minority), identified ten key qualities: dedicated, goal-oriented, informed, charismatic, decisive, responsible, intelligent, determined, organized, and verbally skilled. Offermann, Kennedy, and Wirtz's (1994) research on this issue revealed sensitivity, dedication, tyranny, charisma, attractiveness, masculinity, intelligence, and strength as important qualities in ILTs. Epitropaki and Martin (2004) refined the list of Offerman et al. (1994) through confirmatory factor analysis and structural equations modeling. They identified four key leadership qualities—sensitivity, intelligence, dedication, and dynamism—that were relatively consistent across time and contexts, as well as some qualities that are associated with poor, ineffective leadership (tyrannical and masculine).

The culture where one lives also influences the kinds of qualities that become embedded in one's ILT, but despite these culture-centered nuances there is a striking degree of agreement across people world-wide. Researchers in the Global Leadership and Organizational Behavior Effectiveness (GLOBE) Program, for example, asked 15,022 managers in 62 different countries around the world to describe desirable and undesirable characteristics in a leader (House & Javidan, 2004). They then identified those qualities that nearly all of the individuals agreed were critical by calculating indexes of agreement for each country: visionary (acts with foresight, plans ahead), inspirational (dynamic, positive, encouraging, confidence builder, motivational), integruous (trustworthy, just, honest), team-focused (informed, communicative, coordinator, team builder), diplomatic (win-win problem solver, effective bargainer), administratively competent, decisive, and performance-oriented.

The GLOBE researchers also identified some qualities that were specific to a particular country or region. For example, whereas most people surveyed expected effective leaders to be charismatic (visionary/inspirational) and team-focused, in some cultures these qualities were stressed more than in others, and these variations reflected broader cultural differences in emphasis on power relations, tolerance of uncertainty, and masculinity (e.g., Hofstede, 1980). Highly collectivistic societies, for example, favored charismatic leaders more so than more individualistic ones. Cultures that displayed higher levels of gender egalitarianism and lower levels of uncertainty avoidance stressed participative, team-focused leadership. Those individuals who lived in cultures marked by hierarchical power structures and greater levels of elitism were more tolerant of self-centered leaders who were status conscious and formalistic. The GLOBE researchers also discovered that certain specific traits were highly valued in some cultures but dismissed as harmful to leadership in others. Risk taking, for example, was considered a quality that enhanced leadership effectiveness in some countries, but in others this quality was viewed as a quality that would disqualify a person from a leadership role. Other culturally contingent ILT traits included ambitious, cunning, elitist, intuitive, micromanaging, procedural, ruling, self-effacing, subdued, and willful (Dorfman, Hanges, & Brodbeck, 2004).

ILTs are also sensitive to the specifics of a given situation. Lord et al. (1984) point out that some leadership traits, such as persistence, likability, and charisma, are considered to be essential qualities only in particular contexts, such as politics, business, or sports. Moreover, people's ILTs appear to augment and discount specific qualities to take into account the kinds of qualities a leader will need to deal with a particular leadership setting. When people are asked to describe the qualities a person needed to be successful as a CEO of a large company and those that are needed for skillful management or supervision of a department, their ILTs shift accordingly to take into account these variations in situational demand (Den Hartog & Koopman, 2005). Similarly, different qualities are expected in a newly appointed group leader in comparison to one who has occupied this role for some time (Kenney, Schwartz-Kenney, & Blascovich, 1996).

Finally, evidence suggests that individual differences also play a role in leadership perceptions. Men's and women's ILTs differ to some degree, in that sensitivity is less central and power more central in men's ILTs (Epitropaki & Martin, 2004). Children are more likely to emphasize task-related competences as key determinants of leadership, more so than concern for people (Ayman-Nolley & Ayman, 2005). Individuals who are leaders themselves stress dynamism (dynamic, strong, energetic) in their ILTs more than those who are not leaders of a group or organization (Epitropaki & Martin, 2004). Moreover, our ILTs change over time, as we have more contact with leaders (Lord & Maher, 1991).

These studies suggest that ILTs, like any cognitive process occurring in a complex social situation, are highly sensitive to interpersonal context and the dynamic interplay between participants. However, even though ILTs often shift to fit a particular setting, in most settings members expect that their leaders will have certain qualities that set them apart from others. In general, they expect that leaders will be dynamic people who are conscientious about pursuing group goals by drawing on an ample supply of intellect, enthusiasm, interpersonal skill, and integrity.

ILTs AND LEADERSHIP APPRAISALS

People would have considerable difficulty navigating a range of social settings if they did not have an accurate conception of the qualities to consider when identifying a leader. Without ILTs, followers would be unable to identify whose influence they should accept or situations where *they* should step forward into a leadership role. Asch (1946, p. 258), a pioneer in the field of person perception, explained:

> We look at a person and immediately a certain impression of his character forms itself in us. A glance, a few spoken words are sufficient to tell us a story about a highly complex matter. We know that such impressions form with remarkable rapidity and great ease. Subsequent observations may enrich or upset our first view, but we can no more prevent its rapid growth than we can avoid perceiving a given visual object or hearing a melody.

Thus, ILTs are extensions of often-practiced habits of perception that we use, on a daily basis, to make sense of our social world.

In his information processing theory of leadership perceptions, Lord suggests that ILTs provide followers with a psychological standard or *prototype* they can use to distinguish between effective and ineffective leaders and leaders and followers (Lord, 2005; Lord & Maher, 1991). If, for example, a follower's ILT maintains that a prototypical leader should be bold, energetic, and daring, then she will likely rate an enthusiastic leader more positively than a low-key consensus builder. In contrast, if the follower believes that a leader should be considerate and reflective, then he will respond more positively to one who shows concern for others and deliberates extensively before making a decision. As the *prototype-matching hypothesis* suggests, followers evaluate their leaders and potential leaders by noting the actions and characteristics of the individuals in their group, comparing their findings to their implicit leadership theories, and then favoring those individuals who most closely match their intuitive conception of an ideal or prototypical leader (Lord & Maher, 1991).

Researchers have found support for the prototype-matching hypothesis in a number of studies using various methods. Lord et al. (1984), for example, asked people to evaluate one of three hypothetical leaders. One, the prototypical leader, displayed qualities that were congruent with most people's ILTs: he set goals, provided directive information, talked with subordinates a great deal, and identified problems that needed a solution. The second leader displayed qualities that were inconsistent with most ILTs; he admitted mistakes, paid little attention to details, was critical without reason, and withheld rewards. A third leader displayed positive qualities that were neither consistent nor inconsistent with most ILTs. This leader sought out information, clarified his attitudes, and prevented conflicts. As the prototype-matching hypothesis predicts, the prototypical leader was judged to be more effective than the atypical leader, with match to ITL explaining the majority of the variance in leadership evaluations.

We (Nye & Forsyth, 1991) extended these findings by asking followers to judge the leadership effectiveness and collegiality of an administrator with leadership responsibilities during a simulated performance appraisal review. Recognizing that different individuals' ILTs may vary in their inclusion of one trait or another, we first measured followers' beliefs about leaders using a series of adjectives drawn from Bales' Systematic Multiple Level Observation of Groups inventory, or SYMLOG (Bales, Cohen, & Williamson, 1979). Followers used the adjectives from SYMLOG to describe their own personal view of an ideal business or small organization leader, and we determined their relative emphasis on dominance (active, assertive, talkative), social sensitivity (egalitarian, positive, extroverted), and instrumental control (analytical, task-oriented, problem-solving). The followers were then given the annual review materials for a leader who was described, by his or her own supervisor, as hardworking, competent, and creative. For some followers these materials suggested that the leader was strong on initiating structure, but for others the review stressed the leader's interpersonal, socioemotional skills.

The prototype-matching hypothesis was supported, particularly for the socioemotional component of followers' ILTs. As shown in Figure 7-1, an outgoing, socioemotional leader was viewed more positively by followers whose ILTs emphasized the importance of people skills, but less positively by those whose intuitive theories did not stress this aspect of leadership. The prototype-matching hypothesis was also supported for the remaining two dimensions—dominance and instrumental control—but only for men in the study. Men who believed that an ideal leader should be dominant and high in instrumental control rated the task-oriented leader more positively than the socioemotional leader. Some of the women, in contrast, rated a leader who disconfirmed their ILTs more positively than those who confirmed their ILTs. Specifically, women who did not emphasize dominance or instrumental control rated the task-oriented leader more positively than a socioemotional one. Because the discrepancy occurred on the two masculine-oriented power dimensions (dominance and instrumental control) and not the interpersonal dimension of friendliness, women may have been reluctant to use their ILTs in these domains as guides for evaluating a relatively successful leader.

Although speculative, this explanation is consistent with other research that suggests that information about a leader's successfulness plays a key role in shaping leadership perceptions. When leaders have been successful in the past, perceivers expect them to always be successful leaders (Nye, 2005).

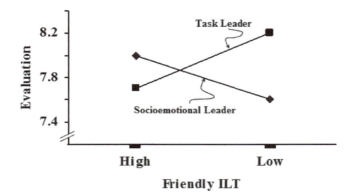

Figure 7-1 Mean effectiveness ratings of socioemotional and task leaders by followers who endorsed either high or low friendliness prototypes

Essentially, performance information is a key perceptual cue that allows perceivers to take an important leap of faith and infer that certain leaders are good. This inference is not surprising, in that we naturally assume that a leader's primary responsibility is to meet group goals. This inferential process is often called the performance cue effect, and it is well documented in leadership research (Lord & Maher, 1991). For example, leaders of successful groups were rated as more effective and collegial than were leaders of unsuccessful groups (Nye & Simonetta, 1996, Study 1), and leaders were judged as being more responsible for group outcomes when the outcomes were positive (Nye, 2002).

ILTs, ACCURACY, AND BIAS

A cognitive approach to leadership assumes that followers are information processors who rationally gather information about leaders by using their existing implicit beliefs about leadership as a helpful guide. Yet, research and everyday experience reveal that people's choices of leaders, and their perceptions of those leaders' effectiveness, often defy logic. Unfortunately, when individuals first meet as a group and must select one individual to act as their leader, they tend to select the talkative one—even if what he or she says is not particularly clever (Mullen, Salas, & Driskell, 1989). When followers judge leaders who are women, they tend to rate them as less effective compared to men who perform the identical types of behaviors (Eagly & Karau, 2002). When voters must select a leader, they sometimes fall prey to the "Warren Harding Effect"—thinking that a handsome candidate has great leadership potential, even when he is thoroughly incompetent (Gladwell, 2005).

Thus, although implicit leadership theories can be quite helpful, allowing followers to sift through and organize a welter of information about current or future leaders, they provide this service at a cost. They can bias followers' perceptions so that they become overly sensitive to information that confirms their initial expectations and ignore information that conflicts with their initial beliefs about leaders. Kissinger, for example, knew that Nixon was a leader, so his ILT about world leaders was primed and ready to be used as a structure for incoming information. Because Kissinger's ILT included patriotism, he was ready to recognize Nixon's strong national pride because it was consistent with his expectations. Conversely, he may have forgotten characteristics that are inconsistent with his ILT; since he did not expect a famous leader to be timid or friendly, he may have forgotten that Nixon displayed these qualities. Kissinger's ILT may have even distorted his memory; as he wrote his memoirs he may have clearly remembered (confabulated) traits, characteristics, and actions that he never even observed (being tough, obsessive).

Research provides ample evidence of the biasing effects of ILTs on perceptions of leadership. Foti and Lord (1987), for example, arranged for raters to watch a videotape of a group interaction before asking them to identify behaviors that the leader had or had not performed. As would be expected, when the leader acted in ways that matched raters' ILTs (prototypical behaviors were present or antiprototypical behaviors were absent), their accuracy and confidence levels were relatively high. However, when leader behavior violated raters' ILTs (prototypical behaviors were absent or antiprototypical behaviors were present), accuracy suffered. Raters recalled more prototypical behaviors than actually occurred, and did not recall antiprototypical behaviors that occurred. Interestingly, rater confidence was not always a reliable indicator of accuracy, which suggests that biased perceptions may be exacerbated by inflated confidence in them.

The biasing influence of ILTs on followers' perceptions and evaluations of leaders may explain continuing sex differences in leadership. Even though studies of men and women in positions of leadership reveal no convincing evidence of male superiority (Chemers, 1997; Eagly, 2007), evaluative and perceptual biases among group members persist. Both men and women, when surveyed, express a preference for male bosses. When men and women join in so-called leaderless groups, the leader who gradually emerges over time is more often than not a man. When subordinates describe their leaders, they rate leaders who are women as less dominant and less effective than male leaders. Perhaps consequently, women receive lower evaluations and fewer promotions than men even when their performance and behaviors are identical. Eagly's social-role theory suggests that people's leadership prototypes are more congruent with their assumptions about the roles men traditionally occupy (Eagly & Karau, 2002). Because women have traditionally been excluded from leadership positions, group members may be more familiar with men in positions of leadership. In consequence, group members may question the leadership ability of women because they view women "as lacking the stereotypical directive and assertive qualities of good leaders—that is, as not being tough enough or not taking charge" (Eagly, 2007, p. 4).

Do group members' ILTs, coupled with their stereotypes about men and women, contribute to their bias against female leaders? We (Forsyth, Heiney, & Wright, 1997) examined this possibility by exposing individuals with differing views about women's roles to a woman who used either a relationship-oriented leadership style or a task-oriented leadership style. The female leader worked with two men and two women on a series of group and individual tasks in a laboratory setting. The leader, who was selected from among the group members on the basis of her scores on a leadership test, was in actuality a confederate of the experimenter. In some groups she enacted a task-oriented leadership style, but in others she focused on the socioemotional side of leadership. Each group included two individuals who were conservative in their attitudes toward the role of women in contemporary society and two more liberal-minded individuals.

As the prototype-matching hypothesis would suggest, individuals who possessed more traditional stereotypes about women judged their leader more harshly than individuals whose attitudes were less stereotyped. Conservative participants liked their leaders less than the more liberal group members, and they felt she would be harder to work with. Conservative participants were also more negative than the liberal participants when the leader enacted a relationship-oriented style. They felt such leaders were friendlier, but they nonetheless gave higher effectiveness ratings to the task-oriented leader. Moreover, men exhibited somewhat more prejudice toward the leader.

ILTs AND BEING A LEADER

Savvy leaders, recognizing the importance of being seen as having the qualities that qualify them to be leaders, carefully manage the impressions they create in others' eyes. They do not simply let their followers draw their own conclusions about their strengths and weaknesses. Instead, they usually regulate their outward actions in order to project a particular image. As Calder (1977, p. 202) wrote, "to teach leadership is to sensitize people to the perceptions of others."

The inconsistency between ILTs and people's stereotypes about men and women, however, suggests that women are caught in a self-presentational bind when they take on the leadership role. For men the leader image–maintenance process is a relatively straightforward one; the skills and qualities that make up most people's ILTs are consistent with their stereotypes about men. Women, in contrast, must choose between enacting behaviors that are consistent with their followers' ILT or their stereotypes about women.

We (Forsyth, Schlenker, Leary, & McCown, 1985) investigated this interpersonal dilemma in a study of ad hoc groups working on a series of problem-solving tasks. The members of these groups first completed a face-valid leadership inventory and learned that they had been selected to be the group's leader on the basis of their responses to the inventory. We told some leaders that their scores indicated they were task-oriented leaders who would be instrumental in helping the group reach its goals. We told others that they were relationship-oriented leaders who were skilled in helping group members work well together. We told still others that they had both of these skill sets. (When subsequently asked if they considered themselves to be task or relational, the leaders' responses indicated that they accepted the feedback as valid.)

After receiving the feedback about their leadership skills but before actually getting down to work, the leaders were told that to simulate groups that had been working together for a longer period of time they would be given the chance to exchange personal information about themselves with the other members. The exchange of information would be highly structured, however, with leaders using a series of adjectives to describe themselves to their followers. The adjective list paralleled those used to measure ILTs in other research, and included such qualities as powerful, influential, dominant, skilled (dynamism), self-disclosing, open, moving toward others (social sensitivity), and fair, truthful, responsible, and pleasant (social responsibility).

How did these leaders' present themselves to their followers? Unexpectedly, they did not emphasize the strengths that the leadership inventory told them they possessed. Instead, their claims conformed to traditional expectations based on sex roles rather than leadership roles. The men described themselves as task-oriented, even when they were told that they were socially sensitive and responsible. The women, in contrast, described themselves as socially sensitive and responsible, but not as task-oriented (even when they knew that they were, in fact, highly competent task leaders). Moreover, those leaders who were told that they were task-oriented were more confident when evaluating their chances of success as a leader. Those who believed that they were relationship-oriented leaders doubted their ability to lead their groups.

These findings suggest that ILTs and stereotypes about men and women can, in some cases, act as interpersonal self-fulfilling prophecies that guide the self-descriptions and overt self-presentational claims leaders make to their followers. Men, even when they believe they are socially skilled, may nonetheless describe themselves in ways that match the demands of the masculine sex role. Women, in contrast, may discount their task-oriented abilities in their self-presentations by displaying qualities that are more consistent with the feminine sex role. These self-presentations, paired with the prototype-matching process described earlier, result in men being favored as leaders rather than women.

ILTs AND THE EYE OF THE FOLLOWER

The strong impact of ILTs on followers' perceptions raises an intriguing question: Which came first: leaders' traits and actions or followers' beliefs about leaders' traits and actions? For many years researchers who wanted to know how leaders actually behaved did not ask the leaders to describe their own actions; they assumed that the leaders' reports would be too biased and possibly self-aggrandizing. Instead, they turned to those they thought would be a more objective source of information: followers. In the Ohio State University Leadership Studies, for example, investigators asked members of various groups to indicate how many of these behaviors their leaders displayed. They then narrowed down the original nine types of behaviors to two essential components: consideration and initiating structure (Halpin & Winer, 1952). Other researchers using similar procedures confirmed Ohio State's basic findings, all the while assuming that followers' reports of what their leaders do were excellent proxies for what their leaders actually did. To know what a leader did on a daily basis, one needed only to ask subordinates to describe their leaders' actions, and then tally the results.

Studies of ILTs, however, suggest that leadership may be in the eye of the beholder—the follower—rather than in the actions of the leader. That is, when researchers ask subordinates to describe their leaders, these ratings may reflect the subordinates' implicit leadership theories more than their leaders' actions. Why do individuals, even when judging leaders in remarkably different contexts that should demand widely divergent types of skills, abilities, and actions from leaders, nonetheless tend to report that their leaders are task-focused and relationship-oriented? This is because followers' implicit leadership theories include these two components (Eden & Leviatan, 1975; Schyns & Meindl, 2005). Thus, consistent with the distinction between task and relationship that is revealed in past research, leadership may rest more in group members' minds than in leaders' actual behaviors. Some researchers go so far as to define leadership as a perceptual process rather than a behavioral one; as a social construction, existing solely in the minds of the social thinker. Lord and Maher (1991, p. 11) write: "we define leadership as the process of being perceived by others as a leader."

Do people sometimes see leadership when none actually exists and overlook leadership when they do not expect it? Leadership is, undeniably, partly a perceptual process. People believe in leaders and in leadership, sometimes expressing more faith in the unique qualities of leaders than is warranted by reality. Consider the notion of the charismatic leader. For leaders to be considered charismatic, they must be so recognized by their followers as leaders with unique, almost miraculous, qualities. Charisma, as a concept, originally described a special power given by God to certain individuals. These individuals were capable of performing extraordinary, miraculous feats, and they were regarded as God's representatives on earth (Weber, 1946). Weber argued that charismatic leaders do not have unique, wondrous powers, but they succeed because their followers think they have unique, wondrous powers.

Similarly, Meindl's research on the "romance of leadership" suggests that people believe so strongly in the concept of leadership that they virtually ignore the influence of other potential factors and focus on leaders as causal agents. This romantic view of leadership ignores both the limited influence wielded by most leaders and the many other factors that influence a group and its dynamics (Meindl, 1995; Meindl, Ehrlich, & Dukerich, 1985). In her research, Emrich (1999) found that this faith in leaders applies to potential leaders as well as incumbents. Particularly when they were members of turbulent groups, people saw leadership potential where none existed. They exaggerated the potential of possible leaders, misremembered crucial details, recalled their future leader having performed any number of leader-consistent behaviors, and forgot any past behaviors that conflicted with their image of the person as a suitable leader. Thus, trying situations can conspire with ILTs to create leaders both interpersonally and psychologically.

SEEING LEADERSHIP AND BEING A LEADER

In the years since Eden and Leviatan (1975) coined the term "implicit leadership theory" (apparently by accident; Eden & Leviatan, 2005), the preponderance of evidence suggests that *ILTs matter*. Researchers have known for years that leadership cannot be understood by examining only the qualities and actions of the leader, for followers have a significant say in the leadership process, and their allegiance to their leader can make or break a group. Although few would accept the claim that leadership exists solely as a perception, most researchers would acknowledge the critical role that followers' perceptions play in the leadership process. If individuals' ILTs favor individuals who are dynamic, socially sensitive, dedicated, or just highly vocal, then people with these qualities will rise to positions of authority in the group—even when these qualities are not relevant to group needs. People will find that they are led by people they deserve, or, at least, by people they expect.

If ILTs were like actual scientific theories, individuals would discard them when they failed to explain who is and who is not an effective leader. But because they are implicit, ILTs are rarely subjected to scrutiny or revised. At the same time, social thinkers are capable of breaking out of the cognitive miser mode when properly motivated, opening up their implicit theories to revision and engaging in more complex and thorough patterns of thinking. This view explains why Henry Kissinger was able to revise his assessment of Richard Nixon and accept the president's offer to join his administration. If he had been blinded by his ILT, he would have never been able to see that some of Nixon's most nonleaderlike qualities were his great strengths. Kissinger's cognitive transformation provides a standard for followers to emulate. Although they may find that they are drawn to leaders who match their ILTs, they should be aware that their beliefs about their leaders may be based on outmoded ways of thinking about the leadership process, and be willing to give leaders who do not fit their traditional conception of a leader an opportunity to take on the role.

REFERENCES

Asch, S. (1946). Forming impressions of personality. *Journal of Abnormal and Social Psychology, 41,* 258–290.

Ayman-Nolley, S., & Ayman, R. (2005). Children's implicit theories of leadership. In B. Schyns & J. R. Meindl (Eds.), *Implicit leadership theories: Essays and explorations* (pp. 227–274). Greenwich, CT: Information Age Publishing.

Bales, R. F., Cohen, S. F., & Williamson, S. A. (1979). *SYMLOG: A system for the multiple level observation of groups.* New York: The Free Press.

Calder, B. J. (1977). An attribution theory of leadership. In B. M. Staw & G. R. Salancik (Eds.), *New directions in organizational behavior* (pp. 179–204). Chicago: St. Clair Press.

Chemers, M. M. (1997). *An integrative theory of leadership.* Mahwah, NJ: Erlbaum.

Den Hartog, D. N., House, R. J., Hanges, P. J., Ruiz-Quintanilla, S. A., & Dorfman, P. W. (1999). Culture specific and cross-culturally generalizable implicit leadership theories: Are the attributes of charismatic/transformational leadership universally endorsed? *Leadership Quarterly, 10,* 219–258.

Den Hartog, D. N., & Koopman, P. L. (2005). Implicit theories of leadership at different hierarchical levels. In B. Schyns & J. Meindl (Eds.), *Implicit leadership theories: Essays and explorations* (pp. 135–158). Greenwich, CT: Information Age Publishing.

Dorfman, P. W., Hanges, P. J., & Brodbeck, F. C. (2004). Leadership and cultural variation. In R. J. House, P. J. Hanges, M. Javidan, P. W. Dorfman, & V. Gupta (Eds.), *Culture, leadership, and organizations: The GLOBE study of 62 societies* (pp. 669–719). Thousand Oaks, CA: Sage Publications.

Eagly, A. H. (2007). Female leadership advantage and disadvantage: Resolving the contradictions. *Psychology of Women Quarterly, 31,* 1–12.

Eagly, A. H., & Karau, S. J. (2002). Role congruity theory of prejudice toward female leaders. *Psychological Review, 109,* 573–598.

Eden, D., & Leviatan, U. (1975). Implicit leadership theory as a determinant of the factor structure underlying supervisory behavior scales. *Journal of Applied Psychology, 60,* 736–741.

Eden, D., & Leviatan, U. (2005). From implicit personality theory to implicit leadership theory: A side-trip on the way to implicit organization theory. In B. Schyns & J. R. Meindl (Eds.), *Implicit leadership theories: Essays and explorations* (pp. 3–14). Greenwich, CT: Information Age Publishing.

Emrich, C. G. (1999). Context effects in leadership perception. *Personality and Social Psychology Bulletin, 25,* 991–1006.

Epitropaki, O., & Martin, R. (2004). Implicit leadership theories in applied settings: Factor structure, generalizability, and stability over time. *Journal of Applied Psychology, 89,* 293–310.

Forsyth, D. R., Heiney, M. M., & Wright, S. S. (1997). Biases in appraisals of women leaders. *Group Dynamics: Theory, Research, and Practice, 1,* 98–103.

Forsyth, D. R., Schlenker, B. R., Leary, M. R., & McCown, N. E. (1985). Self-presentational determinants of sex differences in leadership behavior. *Small Group Behavior, 16,* 197–210.

Foti, R. J., & Lord, R. G. (1987). Prototypes and scripts: The effects of alternative methods of processing information on rating accuracy. *Organizational Behavior and Human Decision Processes, 39,* 318–340.

Gladwell, M. (2005). *Blink: The power of thinking without thinking.* New York: Little, Brown and Co.

Halpin, A. W., & Winer, B. J. (1952). The leadership behavior of the airplane commander. Columbus, OH: Ohio State University Research Foundation.

Hofstede, G. (1980). *Culture's consequences: International differences in work-related values.* Newbury Park, CA: Sage.

Hogan, R., & Kaiser, R. B. (2005). What we know about leadership. *Review of General Psychology, 9,* 169–180.

House, R. J., & Javidan, M. (2004). Overview of GLOBE. In R. J. House, P. J. Hanges, M. Javidan, P. W. Dorfman, & V. Gupta (Eds.), *Culture, leadership, and organizations: The GLOBE study of 62 societies* (pp. 9–28). Thousand Oaks, CA: Sage Publications.

Kenney, R. A., Schwartz-Kenney, B. M., & Blascovich, J. (1996). Implicit leadership theories: Defining leaders described as worthy of influence. *Personality and Social Psychology Bulletin, 22,* 1128–1143.

Kissinger, H. (1979). *The White House years.* New York: Little Brown.

Lord, R. G. (2005). Preface: Implicit leadership theory. In B. Schyns & J. R. Meindl (Eds.), *Implicit leadership theories: Essays and explorations* (pp. ix–xiv). Greenwich, CT: Information Age Publishing.

Lord, R. G., Foti, R. J., & De Vader, C. L. (1984). A test of leadership categorization theory: Internal structure, information processing, and leadership perceptions. *Organizational Behavior and Human Performance, 34,* 343–378.

Lord, R. G., & Maher, K. J. (1991). *Leadership and information processing: Linking perceptions and performance.* Boston, MA: Unwin Hyman, Inc.

Meindl, J. R. (1995). The romance of leadership as a follower-centric theory: A social constructionist approach. *Leadership Quarterly, 6,* 329–341.

Meindl, J. R., Ehrlich, S. B., & Dukerich, J. M. (1985). The romance of leadership. *Administrative Science Quarterly, 30,* 78–102.

Mullen, B., Salas, E., & Driskell, J. E. (1989). Salience, motivation, and artifact as contributions to the relation between participation rate and leadership. *Journal of Experimental Social Psychology, 25,* 545–559.

Nye, J. L. (2002). The eye of the follower: Information processing effects on attributions regarding leaders of small groups. *Small Group Research, 33,* 337–360.

Nye, J. L. (2005). Implicit theories and leaderships in the thick of it: The effects of prototype matching, group setbacks, and group outcomes. In B. Schyns & J. R. Meindl (Eds.), *Implicit leadership theories: Essays and explorations* (pp. 39–61). Greenwich, CT: Information Age Publishing.

Nye, J. L., & Forsyth, D. R. (1991). The effects of prototype-based biases on leadership appraisals: A test of leadership categorization theory. *Small Group Research, 22,* 360–379.

Nye, J. L., & Simonetta, L. G. (1996). Followers' perceptions of group leaders: The impact of recognition-based and inference-based processes. In J. L. Nye & A. M. Brower (Eds.), *What's social about social cognition? Research on socially shared cognition in small groups* (pp. 124–153). Thousand Oaks, CA: Sage Publications.

Offerman, L. R., Kennedy, J. K., Jr., & Wirtz, P. W. (1994). Implicit leadership theories: Content, structure, and generalizability. *Leadership Quarterly, 5,* 43–58.

Rush, M. C., Thomas, J. C., & Lord, R. G. (1977). Implicit leadership theory: A potential threat to the internal validity of leader behavior questionnaires. *Organizational Behavior & Human Performance, 20,* 93–110.

Schyns, B., & Meindl, J. R. (Eds.). (2005). *Implicit leadership theories: Essays and explorations.* Greenwich, CT: Information Age Publishing.

Weber, M. (1946). The sociology of charismatic authority. In H. H. Gert & C. W. Mills (Trans. & Eds.), *From Max Weber: Essay in sociology* (pp. 245–252). New York: Oxford University Press. (Originally published in 1921.)

8

Presidential Greatness and Its Socio-Psychological Significance: Individual or Situation? Performance or Attribution?

DEAN KEITH SIMONTON

The chapter reviews the empirical research on the leadership exhibited by presidents of the United States. This research attempted to identify the predictors of presidential performance as gauged by "greatness" ratings. Obtained from surveys of experts, these ratings represent a strong, stable, and valid consensus on the global performance of these chief executives. A series of studies spanning a 30-year period eventually generated a six-variable prediction equation that explains between 77 and 83 percent of the variance in presidential greatness for all presidents from Washington to Clinton. The six predictors are as follows: (a) the number of years the president served; (b) the number of years he served as wartime commander in chief; (c) whether or not the administration experienced a major scandal; (d) whether or not the incumbent was the victim of a successful assassination; (e) whether the president was a war hero; and (f) the president's assessment on a measure of intellectual brilliance. The chapter then treats some methodological issues before turning to a theoretical interpretation of the empirical findings. Any theoretical explanation has to address two distinct questions: First, to what extent does each predictor variable represent an individual or situational factor?

Second, to what degree do presidential greatness ratings reflect objective leader performance rather than subjective attributions of leadership?

Leadership adopts many forms. At one extreme, we might speak of "little-l" leadership. This kind is what appears in everyday decision-making groups, such as a meeting of the local Parent Teacher Association. At the other extreme, we can talk of "Big-L" leadership. Leaders in this category exert the kind of leadership that "makes history." Their successes (and failures) leave a permanent mark on the course of human events. Such leaders eventually become the subject of biographies, histories, and scholarly evaluations. Big-L leadership can include generals who win major battles, entrepreneurs who found new industries, religious figures who establish new faiths, and political leaders who serve as the heads of state of powerful nations. In the last category we can include dictators of totalitarian states, prime ministers of parliamentary systems, and presidents occupying the executive branch of a tripartite government that also includes legislative and judicial branches. Perhaps the most conspicuous example of the latter is the chief executive who serves as president of the United States. As the most influential leader of one of the world's most prominent nations, U.S. presidents provide an ideal research site for investigating big-L leadership. It is for this reason that I have devoted over a quarter century to studying those select leaders who have managed to serve in this high office.

These studies were devoted to addressing two major theoretical issues— issues that apply to both little-l and Big-L leadership. The first question concerned the relative importance of individual and situational variables. To what extent is leadership a matter of being the "right person" versus being at the "right place and the right time"? To what degree do they actively shape events rather than being passively shaped by those events? The second question concerns the relative influence of objective performance and subjective attribution. Is leadership largely rooted in the actual leadership behavior of the leader? Or is it mostly situated in the "eyes of the beholders"—in the followers who are engaged in making attributions that may or may not closely correspond with objective acts of leadership?

In this chapter I wish to report the progress that has been made in addressing these two issues with respect to the chief executives of the United States of America. I begin by discussing the main criterion by which presidential leadership is assessed. I then turn to a treatment of the main predictors of this specific criterion. After a brief methodological discussion, I close by examining what these predictors imply with respect to the individual-situational and performance-attribution questions.

PRESIDENTIAL GREATNESS

The leadership of U.S. presidents can be judged by numerous standards (Bailey, 1966; Simonton, 1987b). Most concern the highly specialized duties laid out in the nation's Constitution. How well does the president carry out his responsibility as commander in chief? How well does he execute the laws of the land? How good are the president's appointments to high offices, such as ambassadors, cabinet officials, and federal judgeships? Each of these criteria can then be given an appropriate operational definition. For instance, presidents might be judged according to the manner in which they used their veto power to shape legislation passed by Congress (Simonton, 1987a). How many bills did they veto and how many of these vetoed bills were overturned by a two-thirds majority in both houses? The major problem with using these specialized measures of presidential leadership is that they do not strongly correlate with each other (Simonton, 1987b, 1993). One of the reasons why they do not highly correlate is that each specific measure may not apply to all presidents. For example, a president cannot demonstrate leadership as commander in chief unless the nation is at war.

These problems have led many researchers to focus on a more global criterion of leadership, namely, *presidential greatness* (e.g., Deluga, 1997, 1998; McCann, 1990; Nice, 1984). This assessment represents an overall judgment of the chief executive's performance, an assessment that presumably integrates all relevant criteria into a single score. In fact, the chief executives have been subjected to this very kind of systematic evaluation for well over 60 years. For example, experts in the American presidency will often offer their personal judgments of the relative standing of various occupants of that office. Thus, Rossiter (1956) rated the presidents from Washington to Eisenhower, deleting only three presidents who had extremely short terms in office (William Harrison, Zachary Taylor, and James Garfield). He identified eight presidents as "great" (e.g., George Washington, Abraham Lincoln, and Franklin Roosevelt) and five presidents as "failures" (e.g., Warren Harding, Ulysses S. Grant, and James Buchanan). A little later Sokolsky (1964) extended the ratings to John F. Kennedy (deleting W. Harrison and Garfield but not Taylor), and placed Washington, Franklin Roosevelt, and Lincoln at the top, Grant and Harding at the bottom. Only a couple of years later Bailey (1966) offered his own assessments in his book specifically titled *Presidential Greatness*. Washington was deemed the greatest, Andrew Johnson the worst. Naturally, it is easy to raise the objection that these judgments represent only a single person's opinion. How can we be assured that the assessments do not reflect personal or political biases?

This subjectivity problem can be circumvented by surveying multiple experts rather than relying on the views of any single expert. Given enough survey respondents, the bias of any one expert will be counterbalanced by the contrary biases of other experts. The first researcher to adopt this superior method was Schlesinger (1948), who had 55 historians rate all presidents up to Franklin Roosevelt, with the exception of W. Harrison and Garfield. Lincoln came in first and Harding last. Later Schlesinger (1962) repeated the process, this time using 75 experts and extending the presidents to Eisenhower. Again, Lincoln came out on the top, Harding at the bottom. Since Schlesinger's pioneering surveys, the presidential greatness ratings have expanded by having even more experts evaluate ever more chief executives. For example, Murray and Blessing (1983) had 846 diverse experts rate all presidents from Washington to Nixon (again with the exclusion of W. Harrison and Garfield) and obtained greatness ratings along an interval scale (see also Murray & Blessing, 1988). As in Schlesinger's polls, Lincoln rated the highest, Harding the lowest.

Indeed, despite some disagreements here and there, the entire set of greatness ratings exhibit a remarkable degree of consensus (Simonton, 1986b, 1987b, 2006). This consensus was first demonstrated by Kynerd (1971) using the evaluations published by Schlesinger (1948, 1962), Rossiter (1956), Sokolsky (1964), and Bailey (1966), where necessary translating qualitative judgments into ordinal scales. The correlations among the five ratings ranged from .734 to .963. Moreover, if Bailey's assessments are omitted, then the correlations range from .894 to .963, an even better degree of agreement. The deletion of Bailey's ratings can be justified on the grounds that his judgments were published as an explicit criticism of the earlier ratings, and thus may have a contrarian bias. Later assessments also correlate with these earlier ratings. For example, the Ridings and McIver (1997) survey of 719 experts produced ratings that correlate .94 with Schlesinger (1948), .92 with Schlesinger (1962), .80 with Rossiter (1956), .78 with Bailey (1966), and .96 with Murray and Blessing (1983; Simonton, 2001). In addition, confirmatory factor analysis demonstrates that alternative greatness measures can be explained using a single latent variable with high factor loadings (Simonton, 1991a).

Some research has also given some insight into the components of these global assessments. For instance, Maranell (1970) had 571 historians rate the presidents on seven dimensions: general prestige, administration accomplishments, strength of action, presidential activeness, idealism versus practicality, flexibility, and respondents' information. The first four items correlate between .89 and .98, and thus can be said to define a greatness factor, a conclusion reinforced by a factor analysis of the same ratings (Wendt & Light, 1976; see also Simonton, 1981). Moreover, this greatness factor correlates .94 with Schlesinger (1948), .93 with Schlesinger (1962), .88 with Rossiter (1956), .94 with Sokolsky (1964), and .72 with Bailey (1966; Simonton, 1981). Hence, presidential greatness appears to involve some combination of general prestige, administration accomplishments, strength of action, and presidential activeness.

GREATNESS PREDICTORS

Given this strong consensus on the relative leadership merits of the U.S. presidents, what variables account for the variation? Why are some presidents great and others failures? To what extent are any predictor variables individual or situational in nature? Wendt and Light (1976) were the first investigators to attempt to answer this question. Using the greatness factor derived from the Maranell (1970) survey results, they found that these scores correlated positively with wars declared or sanctioned by Congress ($r = .57$), the number of unilateral military interventions ($r = .48$), the number of assassination attempts ($r = .59$), and a number of other predictors. Nonetheless, this investigation suffered from two major limitations: (a) it only looked at recent presidents who were elected to office ($n = 15$), and (b) it did not conduct a multiple regression analysis but rather merely calculated zero-order correlations. Yet this investigation inspired a series of studies devoted to teasing out the predictors using a larger sample of presidents and implementing more sophisticated analytical strategies. These studies fall into three consecutive decades: the 1980s, the 1990s, and the 2000s. These decades are set apart not just by the publication dates of the investigations but also by the greatness measures used and the presidents included (e.g., more recent chief executives).

The 1980s

The first attempt to advance beyond the Wendt and Light (1976) inquiry was conducted by Simonton (1981). As in their study, greatness was assessed using the general factor derived from the Maranell (1970) survey of 571 historians. A huge database was then compiled regarding a large number of potential predictors. These concerned variables regarding each president's term in office (e.g., manner of entering and leaving the presidency and all relevant events between) as well as potential biographical predictors (viz. both preelection and postadministration variables). The systematic search began by looking at the ordinary correlation coefficients. After identifying the variables that had significant correlations, these were then entered into a multiple regression analysis. The latter allows the estimation of any given variable's effect on the criterion after controlling for all other variables. If a variable had no predictive value after making this statistical adjustment, it was deleted as a possible predictor.

The upshot of the foregoing selection procedure was a five-variable equation that accounted for 75 percent of the variance in presidential greatness. The predictors were as follows (β representing the standardized partial regression coefficients or "betas," which are similar to correlations except with adjustments for the other variables also in the equation): the number of years the president served in office ($\beta = .24$), the number of years that he served as wartime commander in chief ($\beta = .36$), the occurrence of a major administration scandal ($\beta = -.20$), the occurrence of unsuccessful assassination attempts ($\beta = .30$), and the number of books that the president had published prior to entering office ($\beta = .28$). Additional analyses showed that the resulting equation was transhistorically invariant. In other words, the impact of the five predictors was not moderated by the date in which they assumed office.

Although this 1981 study could be said to have made some progress, it still left much to be desired. Most conspicuously, the dependent variable was defined for only 33 presidents. Just a couple of years later it had become apparent that this sample size could be increased by about 10 percent. To be specific, Murray and Blessing (1983) had published their survey results that allowed the sample size to be increased to 36 presidents—all the presidents to Nixon with the commonplace exception of W. Harrison and Garfield. This investigation also included the results of two other recent surveys covering the same presidents: One was a survey of 41 experts conducted by Porter in 1981 and the other a survey of 49 experts published by the *Chicago Tribune* in 1982. As a consequence, it was possible to determine whether any prediction equation would replicate across three alternative presidential leadership evaluations.

These three surveys provided the impetus for Simonton's (1986b) follow-up inquiry. The investigation began by using factor analysis to show that all evaluations of presidential leadership from Schlesinger (1948) to Murray and Blessing (1983) yielded a single greatness factor. The next step was to define and measure over 300 potential predictors. Besides the variables examined in earlier investigations, numerous new predictors were defined on the basis of subsequent inquiries into other forms of political leadership, such as that displayed by absolute monarchs (Simonton, 1983, 1984). Because the number of variables was so large, a systematic set of stringent criteria was imposed on the search for predictors. Most critical was the imposition that any prediction equation had to replicate across all three survey results. The outcome was another five-variable equation, but one that did not completely overlap with the 1981 results. Replicating the previous findings were the three predictors of years in office (βs = .37 to .41), war years (βs = .37 to .45), and scandals (βs = −.48 to −.48). However, two new variables emerged as predictors. First, successful assassination replaced unsuccessful attempts as a predictor (βs = .25 to .32), a change that reflects the addition of Gerald Ford to the sample (the target of two unsuccessful assassination attempts). Second, prior status as a war hero—as in the cases of Washington, Andrew Jackson, Grant, and Dwight Eisenhower—entered the equation (βs = .31 to .32). The new five-variable equation explained 77–78 percent of the variance in the three greatness criteria. And, again, the predictors were transhistorically invariant.

The foregoing study can be considered an improvement insofar as it used the same number of predictors to explain more variance in the greatness ratings of more presidents. But it still suffered from one major liability: It incorporated hardly any variables that directly assessed the personality traits of the 36 chief executives. This deficiency is especially critical if we want a fair gauge of the relative contribution of individual and situational factors to presidential leadership. Accordingly, a second investigation introduced new methods for at-a-distance personality assessment (Simonton, 1986c). Specifically, a team of independent raters applied the 300-descriptor Adjective Check List (Gough & Heilbrun, 1965) to personality profiles abstracted from biographical sources. These profiles had all identifying material removed and were placed in random order. The raters were provided reliable scores on 110 adjectives. A factor analysis of these scores yielded 14 orthogonal dimensions. Using the Murray and Blessing (1983) survey evaluations, the study then determined whether any of these factors enhanced the prediction of presidential greatness. The outcome was a six-variable prediction equation (Simonton, 1986c). Besides the five predictors of years in office (β = .36), war years (β = .35), scandal (β = −.40), assassination (β = .20), and war hero (β = .33), a new one was added, namely, Intellectual Brilliance (β = .26). The variable was defined by such descriptors as intelligent, inventive, insightful, curious, interests wide, artistic, sophisticated, and complicated. The magnitude of the effect for this variable was almost the same as that for the pre-presidential book publication record in the 1981 study, suggesting that the latter variable was serving as a proxy for Intellectual Brilliance. In any case, with this addition, 82 percent of the variance could be explained, a decided improvement. The new equation was also transhistorically invariant. Just as importantly, Intellectual Brilliance was the only one of the 14 personality factors that correlated with all assessments of presidential greatness published over a 35-year period.

For the remaining years of the 1980s several attempts were made to augment or modify this six-variable equation. For example, Simonton (1987b, 1988) himself tested the possible impact of other individual and situational variables, but found that the same six predictors emerged unscathed. Likewise, Kenney and Rice (1988) and Holmes and Elder (1989) attempted to identify additional predictors, but these could not account for any more variance than already explained by the six-variable equation (Simonton, 1991b). The equation emerging from the Simonton (1986c) investigation appeared very robust.

The 1990s

In this decade there was something of a lull in research regarding the predictors of presidential greatness. To be sure, several investigators proposed new variables or new equations as alternatives to the six-variable model (e.g., Deluga, 1997, 1998; McCann, 1990, 1992; Spangler & House, 1991). Yet for reasons that will be discussed later, none of these rival predictors provided an improvement over the earlier equation (see, e.g., Simonton, 1992). The only original contribution that Simonton himself made to the literature related to this subject was an investigation into the differential greatness of the presidential First Ladies (Simonton, 1996). It was shown that her greatness rating was a function of her personal and political assets and her president's performance rating. A by-product of this inquiry was yet another replication of the same six-variable equation using a new criterion of presidential performance. Specifically, greatness was a function of years in office ($\beta = .35$), war years ($\beta = .38$), scandals ($\beta = -.53$), assassination ($\beta = .21$), war hero ($\beta = .34$), and Intellectual Brilliance ($\beta = .16$). Fully 83 percent of the criterion variance could be so explained, and the effects were again invariant across historical time.

One of the reasons why research stagnated a bit during this period is that new presidential greatness ratings are hard to come by. Comprehensive surveys are expensive to execute and thus cannot be justified unless more former presidents are added to the list. Normally, such additions only take place every four or eight years. But finally, in 1997, Ridings and McIver published their greatness assessments based on the survey of 719 experts. Unlike previous investigations, these ratings pertained to all presidents from Washington through William Clinton, including the often omitted William Harrison and Garfield. This meant that for the first time the model could be tested on a sample 10 percent larger than that available for the investigations of the mid-1980s.

The 2000s

Very early in this decade Simonton (2001) used the Ridings and McIver (1997) survey to test whether the six-variable equation would replicate on a more extensive sample. The outcome was confirmatory. About 77 percent of the variance in presidential greatness could be attributed to the same six predictors, namely years in office ($\beta = .53$), war years ($\beta = .30$), scandal ($\beta = -.38$), assassination (β = .21), war hero (β = .22), and Intellectual Brilliance (β = .21). Furthermore, Simonton was able to take advantage of the fact that Ridings and McIver had the presidents rated on more specialized performance criteria, namely, assessed leadership, accomplishment, political skill, appointments, and character and integrity. Because these five criteria correlate highly with each other and with the overall assessment, they can be viewed as the components of presidential greatness. Accordingly, it was possible to determine which of the six predictors were most strongly associated with which criteria. To illustrate, war hero status was most predictive of assessed leadership, the number of years as wartime commander in chief was most predictive of accomplishment, and the occurrence of administration scandals was most predictive of character and integrity (in a negative direction). By comparison, the number of years the president served in the White House was more evenly predictive of all five criteria.

The preceding investigation had two limitations. First, because Clinton was still in office at the time Ridings and McIver (1997) carried out their survey, his rating was deleted from the analysis. This deletion was especially justified given that the Monica Lewinsky scandal broke the year after the survey results were published. Second, Intellectual Brilliance scores were not available for the presidents who served after Ronald Reagan (Simonton, 1986c). Both of these deficiencies were remedied in another investigation published the following year (Simonton, 2002). In the former case, the inquiry took advantage of a recent survey conducted after Clinton left office (C-Span Survey of Presidential Leadership, 2000). In the latter case, the investigation built upon a study by Rubenzer, Faschingbauer, and Ones (2000) that asked experts to rate U.S. presidents on the Big Five Personality Factors. Among these factors is Openness to Experience, which correlates .71 with the Intellectual Brilliance measure. Therefore, scores on Openness were used to reconstruct the missing values on the Intellectual Brilliance measure (via regression methods). It was thus possible to test the full six-variable equation on all 41 presidents between Washington and Clinton, inclusively. All six predictors replicated, again accounting for 77 percent of the variance. In particular, greatness was a function of years in office (β = .55), war years (β = .24), scandal (β = −.36), assassination (β = .24), war hero (β = .18), and Intellectual Brilliance (β = .29).

In 2006 Simonton confirmed this last replication with a new set of Intellectual Brilliance estimates that were extended all the way to George W. Bush (using the Openness to Experience scores reported in Rubenzer & Faschingbauer, 2004). The standardized regression coefficients (βs) were virtually identical and the same amount of variance explained (viz. 77 percent).

So far it seems that Simonton is the only one replicating Simonton's six-variable equation, but that is not the case. Cohen (2003) applied the same model to two separate greatness assessments, one based on a 2000 CNN poll of 58 experts and the other on a poll of 1145 CNN viewers. The six-variable equation replicated across both assessments, with very similar regression weights across both. Hence, the six-predictor model has survived an empirical test by an independent investigator. And both Cohen (2003) and Simonton (2002) have shown that it applies to all presidents from Washington through Clinton.

METHODOLOGICAL ISSUES

Before I can return to the two theoretical issues posed at the beginning of this chapter, I first must address two methodological issues. The failure to do so would otherwise cast doubt on any theoretical interpretation.

The first question concerns the exact degree to which we can say that the various investigations published between 1986 and 2006 can be considered genuine replications. In the first place, the amount of variance explained appears to have declined from 82 percent to 77 percent. In addition, the standardized partial regression coefficients for some of the predictors have tended to either enlarge or shrink across the 20-year period. Thus, years in office and assassination have tended to increase in effect while war years and war hero have tended to decrease in effect. It would seem that these trends would contradict the earlier assertion that the effects of the six variables are transhistorically invariant. Yet this conclusion would be invalid. There are two complicating factors. First, some of the variables have undergone a decline in variance since the earlier investigations. For instance, no president has been a former war hero since Eisenhower, a fact that may partly explain why the impact of this variable has declined from above .30 to below .20. Second, the later studies not only add more recent presidents but also use more recent survey respondents to judge greatness. It is conceivable that experts have modified slightly the weights they assign the six predictors. For example, the experiences associated with the Vietnam War might have undermined somewhat the importance of war years and even war hero as greatness predictors. Even so, such shifts in weights could still apply to all presidents from Washington through Clinton, and thereby remain invariant across historical time.

The second methodological question involves the causal status of rival predictors. As noted earlier, many investigators have identified correlates of presidential greatness that did not end up in the final equation. How can this be? There are two causal models that can explicate this outcome: spuriousness and mediation.

According to the spuriousness explanation, a variable might correlate with presidential greatness because both that variable and greatness are caused by another variable, a variable that is already a predictor in the equation. For example, a number of investigators have suggested that presidential greatness correlates with leader charisma (e.g., Emrich, Brower, Feldman, & Garland, 2001; Simonton, 1988). Although the zero-order correlations are positive, charisma does not enter the equation with the six predictors (Simonton, 1988). It turns out that charisma is strongly correlated with Intellectual Brilliance. In fact, the correlation between greatness and charisma reduces to nonsignificance after partialling out the variance they both share with Intellectual Brilliance.

According to the mediation account, a variable might not enter the multiple regression equation because its impact is mediated by one or more variables that did enter the equation. In other words, the variable's effect is indirect rather than direct. For instance, Winter (2003) has indicated that presidential greatness is positively associated by power motivation (as assessed by content analysis of inaugural addresses). But the power motive is also correlated with a president entering the United States in a war and becoming a target of assassination attempts (Winter, 2003). Because war years and assassination are already in the equation, the consequence of this motive variable can only function through these direct effects.

THEORETICAL INTERPRETATION

I now wish to discuss a substantive account of the six-predictor model. That is, I want to interpret these consistent findings in terms of the two issues mentioned at the beginning, namely, individual versus situational factors and performance versus attribution.

Individual Versus Situational Factors

What do the six predictors imply about the relative contribution of personal and social variables to presidential greatness? To address this question, let us look at each predictor separately:

1. *Years in office*—At first glance, the length of a president's tenure in the White House might be said to reflect his personal qualities as a political leader. After all, the single most important predictor of years in office is the number of times the president has been elected to that office (Simonton, 1986b). Yet this inference becomes more problematic on further examination. For instance, most of the predictors of a president's reelection are situational rather than individual in nature. A case in point is the fate of the so-called "accidental president," that is, chief executives who enter the presidency through the death or resignation of their predecessor. Even though vice presidents do not

differ from presidents on any relevant criterion of leadership, those vice presidents who enter the Oval Office through vice-presidential success are less likely to be nominated to serve a full term (Simonton, 1985). In the main, a detailed analysis of the factors underlying years in office suggests that this variable may be far more situational than individual in nature (Simonton, 1987b).

2. *War years*—This predictor is also somewhat ambivalent. As noted earlier, presidents who score high in power motivation are more likely to enter the nation into war (Winter, 2003). Yet it is also the case that much of this variable is governed by situational determinants. Although most presidents prefer to fight short (and victorious) wars, all too often they are obliged to fight long wars. Certainly this was the case in the U.S. Civil War as well as the Vietnam War, both of which dragged on far longer than anticipated. So it is difficult to determine how much of this predictor can be considered individual rather than situational in nature.

3. *Scandals*—Unlike the previous two, this predictor appears to be more obviously individual in nature. As pointed out earlier, scandals are associated with low scores on character and integrity (Simonton, 2001), and scandals are also associated with high scores on need for affiliation (Winter, 2003). Presidents with strong moral principles who appoint experts rather than friends to high office are less likely to experience a major administration scandal. Nevertheless, it should also be acknowledged that some portion of this variable may be situational. At least, we will never know how many presidents had scandalous activities going on in the White House but were fortunate enough never to be detected.

4. *Assassination*—Because assassination attempts are positively associated with the president's power motivation (Winter, 2003), it would appear that this predictor would count as an individual factor. Nonetheless, it should also be clear that this variable must have a prominent situational component. After all, if it were entirely individual in nature—powerful presidents attracting their potential killers—we would expect assassination *attempts* to be the primary predictor of presidential greatness, and that is not the case. Because only a single inch or just one second may separate a successful from an unsuccessful assassination attempt, a huge part of this predictor must contain pure luck.

5. *War hero*—This predictor is perhaps the most peculiar. On the one hand, we would usually expect war heroes to display personal characteristics that set them apart from everyone else (e.g., courage). On the other hand, it is not always clear that national war heroes have such traits. Thus, while there can be no doubt that generals like Washington and Jackson displayed tremendous individual courage, it is not so clear that Eisenhower did so. The latter's military leadership was predicated more on the organizational skills required to launch a large-scale attack on the beaches of Normandy. Furthermore, it is not obvious that the qualities underlying military leadership are identical to those behind political leadership.

6. *Intellectual Brilliance*—Of all the six predictors, this seems to be the most pa-
    tently individual in status. In support of this categorization I need only men-
    tion that intelligence is the one individual-difference variable that has been
    most consistently shown to correlate with leadership in a wide range of situa-
    tions (Simonton, 1995). Moreover, the correlation between this variable and
    presidential greatness is about the same magnitude as seen in most empirical
    research. The only counterargument would be that Intellectual Brilliance is
    assessed after the fact, and so the assessment could be influenced by greatness
    judgments that are themselves influenced by situational factors.

In light of the above discussion, it is difficult to make any precise statement
of the relative contribution of individual and situational factors. The best
guess, in my present opinion, is that being at the right place at the right time
has some priority over being the right person. The degree of that differential
is much less easily specified.

Objective Performance Versus Subjective Attribution

The variables making up the six-predictor equation are odd in at least three
ways. First, the list excludes many objective performance criteria that would
be expected to form part of any overall assessment (Bailey, 1966; Simonton,
1987a). For instance, what about the number of administration-sponsored
bills signed into law? What about the number of successful treaties negotiated? Second, the list includes some variables that do not appear on anyone's
inventory of relevant criteria. For example, no one has claimed that assassinated presidents are superior to those having luckier fates. Nor has anyone
argued that former war heroes make better chief executives than those lacking that distinction. Furthermore, there is not a shred of evidence that either
assassination or war hero status is associated with any more pertinent leader
behavior. Third and last, even when it can be argued that a specific variable
has some indirect relevance, it seems peculiar that a more directly relevant
variable did not enter the prediction equation. One might argue that the number of years in office serves as a proxy for other more germane criteria, such as
reelection, which serves as a direct measure of how well the president performed in his first term. Yet when both years in office and reelection are put
into the equation together, only the former variable comes out as a significant
predictor. Hence, reelection cannot be a direct effect.

Although the six variables seem odd from the standpoint of assessing
objective performance, they do not seem so strange if we were to look at them
from the perspective of subjective attributions. Most represent the kinds of
facts that are most likely to be available in even the shortest biographical
entry. The reader will soon discover how long the president served, whether

he served as a wartime commander in chief, whether any scandals had broken out in his administration, and whether or not he was assassinated. Even the president's Intellectual Brilliance can be inferred from any signs of precocious behavior, his educational history—including attendance at prestigious colleges and the receipt of academic honors—and such adulthood behaviors as writing books, the variable that emerged as a predictor in the original 1981 equation (Simonton, 1981). Furthermore, if these are the kinds of information that are most likely to be read, they may also constitute the facts that are most likely to be recalled when asked to pass judgments on the leaders who have occupied the White House. They are both highly salient and highly available. As a consequence, the six-variable equation might be better explicated in terms of an attributional model.

That possibility was examined in an experimental simulation of the predictive model (Simonton, 1986a). The simulation began by specifying a hypothetical process by which salient information activates three separate components of a leadership schema—namely, strength, activity, and goodness—that are presumed to mediate the relation between the salient facts and the summary attribution of leadership. The strength, activity, and goodness components were hypothesized on the basis of specialized research on the prototype of presidential leadership (Kinder, Peters, Abelson, & Fiske, 1980) as well as on more general inquiries into the principal dimensions underlying meaning (Osgood, Suci, & Tannenbaum, 1957).

College participants were then given the task of evaluating leaders based on descriptive vignettes that contained each leader's standing on the six predictors. The leader described by each vignette was anonymous, and in one experimental condition the judges were not even told that the descriptions applied to U.S. presidents. Strikingly, on the basis of this minimal information the assessors were able to reproduce the greatness ratings actually received by the presidents corresponding to the vignettes. Indeed, the students, though blind to the identity of those they were evaluating, produced scores that correlated .84 with the Murray and Blessing (1983) survey results. More concretely, the greatness ratings of blind raters correlated almost as highly with the historians' ratings as the historians' ratings correlate with each other.

Furthermore, the weights assigned the six descriptors paralleled those assigned by the presidential experts. The only exception was a tendency for the student raters to bestow somewhat less weight to years as a wartime commander in chief. In addition, when the raters were given information that the experts do not use in their judgments, the agreement with the greatness ratings actual declined—further evidence that these data are not relevant to global presidential performance evaluations. Finally, the investigation showed that the impact of the six items of salient information was largely mediated by the three semantic assessments of strength, activity, and goodness. For instance, wartime leaders and former war heroes are judged as stronger, whereas leaders with major scandals are judged as less good. The impact of the six predictors on the overall performance rating became negligible once the effects of the strength, activity, and goodness assessments were taken into account.

All in all, the above investigation provides an empirical argument for the conclusion that expert ratings of the U.S. presidents tell us more about how leaders are perceived than how they actually perform. Presidential greatness may represent more a subjective attribution than an objective performance. Joining this inference with that drawn in the preceding section, we might also conjecture that situational factors dominate over individual factors in the activation of this leadership schema. Presidents are viewed as great largely because they happen to be at the right place and at the right time.

REFERENCES

Bailey, T. A. (1966). *Presidential greatness*. New York: Appleton-Century.

C-Span Survey of Presidential Leadership. (2000). Retrieved November 17, 2000, from www.americanpresidents.org/survey/historians/overall.asp.

Cohen, J. E. (2003). The polls: Presidential greatness as seen in the mass public: An extension and application of the Simonton model. *Presidential Studies Quarterly, 33*, 913–924.

Deluga, R. J. (1997). Relationship among American presidential charismatic leadership, narcissism, and related performance. *Leadership Quarterly, 8*, 51–65.

Deluga, R. J. (1998). American presidential proactivity, charismatic leadership, and rated performance. *Leadership Quarterly, 9*, 265–291.

Emrich, C. G., Brower, H. H., Feldman, J. M., & Garland, H. (2001). Images in words: Presidential rhetoric, charisma, and greatness. *Administrative Science Quarterly, 46*, 527–557.

Gough, H. G., & Heilbrun, A. B., Jr. (1965). *The Adjective Check List manual*. Palo Alto, CA: Consulting Psychologists Press.

Holmes, J. E., & Elder, R. E. (1989). Our best and worst presidents: Some possible reasons for perceived performance. *Presidential Studies Quarterly, 19*, 529–557.

Kenney, P. J., & Rice, T. W. (1988). The contextual determinants of presidential greatness. *Presidential Studies Quarterly, 18*, 161–169.

Kinder, D. R., Peters, M. D., Abelson, R. R., & Fiske, S. T. (1980). Presidential prototypes. *Political Behavior, 2*, 315–338.

Kynerd, T. (1971). An analysis of presidential greatness and "President rating." *Southern Quarterly, 9*, 309–329.

Maranell, G. M. (1970). The evaluation of presidents: An extension of the Schlesinger polls. *Journal of American History, 57*, 104–113.

McCann, S. J. H. (1990). Threat, power, and presidential greatness: Harding to Johnson. *Psychological Reports, 66*, 129–130.

McCann, S. J. H. (1992). Alternative formulas to predict the greatness of U.S. presidents: Personological, situational, and zeitgeist factors. *Journal of Personality and Social Psychology, 62,* 469–479.

Murray, R. K., & Blessing, T. H. (1983). The presidential performance study: A progress report. *Journal of American History, 70,* 535–555.

Murray, R. K., & Blessing, T. H. (1988). *Greatness in the White House: Rating the presidents, Washington through Carter.* University Park, PA: Pennsylvania State University Press.

Nice, D. C. (1984). The influence of war and party system aging on the ranking of presidents. *Western Political Quarterly, 37,* 443–455.

Osgood, C. E., Suci, G., & Tannenbaum, P. (1957). *The measurement of meaning.* Urbana, IL: University of Illinois Press.

Ridings, W. J., Jr., & McIver, S. B. (1997). *Rating the presidents: A ranking of U.S. leaders, from the great and honorable to the dishonest and incompetent.* Secaucus, NJ: Citadel Press.

Rossiter, C. L. (1956). *The American presidency.* New York: Harcourt Brace.

Rubenzer, S. J., & Faschingbauer, T. R. (2004). *Personality, character, & leadership in the White House: Psychologists assess the presidents.* Washington, DC: Brassey's.

Rubenzer, S. J., Faschingbauer, T. R., & Ones, D. S. (2000). Assessing the U.S. presidents using the revised NEO Personality Inventory. *Assessment, 7,* 403–420.

Schlesinger, A. M. (1948, November 1). Historians rate the U.S. presidents. *Life,* pp. 65–66, 68, 73–74.

Schlesinger, A. M. (1962, July 29). Our presidents: A rating by 75 historians. *New York Times Magazine,* pp. 12–13, 40–41, 43.

Simonton, D. K. (1981). Presidential greatness and performance: Can we predict leadership in the White House? *Journal of Personality, 49,* 306–323.

Simonton, D. K. (1983). Intergenerational transfer of individual differences in hereditary monarchs: Genes, role-modeling, cohort, or sociocultural effects? *Journal of Personality and Social Psychology, 44,* 354–364.

Simonton, D. K. (1984). Leaders as eponyms: Individual and situational determinants of monarchal eminence. *Journal of Personality, 52,* 1–21.

Simonton, D. K. (1985). The vice-presidential succession effect: Individual or situational basis? *Political Behavior, 7,* 79–99.

Simonton, D. K. (1986a). Dispositional attributions of (presidential) leadership: An experimental simulation of historiometric results. *Journal of Experimental Social Psychology, 22,* 389–418.

Simonton, D. K. (1986b). Presidential greatness: The historical consensus and its psychological significance. *Political Psychology, 7,* 259–283.

Simonton, D. K. (1986c). Presidential personality: Biographical use of the Gough Adjective Check List. *Journal of Personality and Social Psychology, 51,* 149–160.

Simonton, D. K. (1987a). Presidential inflexibility and veto behavior: Two individual-situational interactions. *Journal of Personality, 55,* 1–18.

Simonton, D. K. (1987b). *Why presidents succeed: A political psychology of leadership.* New Haven, CT: Yale University Press.

Simonton, D. K. (1988). Presidential style: Personality, biography, and performance. *Journal of Personality and Social Psychology, 55,* 928–936.

Simonton, D. K. (1991a). Latent-variable models of posthumous reputation: A quest for Galton's G. *Journal of Personality and Social Psychology, 60,* 607–619.

Simonton, D. K. (1991b). Predicting presidential greatness: An alternative to the Kenney and Rice Contextual Index. *Presidential Studies Quarterly, 21,* 301–305.

Simonton, D. K. (1992). Presidential greatness and personality: A response to McCann (1992). *Journal of Personality and Social Psychology, 63,* 676–679.

Simonton, D. K. (1993). Putting the best leaders in the White House: Personality, policy, and performance. *Political Psychology, 14,* 537–548.

Simonton, D. K. (1995). Personality and intellectual predictors of leadership. In D. H. Saklofske & M. Zeidner (Eds.), *International handbook of personality and intelligence* (pp. 739–757). New York: Plenum.

Simonton, D. K. (1996). Presidents' wives and First Ladies: On achieving eminence within a traditional gender role. *Sex Roles, 35,* 309–336.

Simonton, D. K. (2001). Predicting presidential greatness: Equation replication on recent survey results. *Journal of Social Psychology, 141,* 293–307.

Simonton, D. K. (2002). Intelligence and presidential greatness: Equation replication using updated IQ estimates. *Advances in Psychology Research, 13,* 143–153.

Simonton, D. K. (2006). Presidential IQ, Openness, Intellectual Brilliance, and leadership: Estimates and correlations for 42 US chief executives. *Political Psychology, 27,* 511–639.

Sokolsky, E. (1964). *Our seven greatest presidents.* New York: Exposition Press.

Spangler, W. D., & House, R. J. (1991). Presidential effectiveness and the leadership motive profile. *Journal of Personality and Social Psychology, 60,* 439–455.

Wendt, H. W., & Light, P. C. (1976). Measuring "greatness" in American presidents: Model case for international research on political leadership? *European Journal of Social Psychology, 6,* 105–109.

Winter, D. G. (2003). Measuring the motives of political actors at a distance. In J. M. Post (Ed.), *The psychological assessment of political leaders: With profiles of Saddam Hussein and Bill Clinton* (pp. 153–177). Ann Arbor, MI: University of Michigan Press.

9

The Unbearable Lightness of Debating: Performance Ambiguity and Social Influence

MATTHEW B. KUGLER AND GEORGE R. GOETHALS

This chapter considers three sets of studies on how social influence affects perceptions of candidates' performances in presidential debates. The first set shows that perceptions are influenced markedly by the reactions of peers watching the debate at the same time or by televised audiences shown on broadcast debates. The second set shows that expectations created by news accounts prior to debates also have significant impact and that different kinds of news accounts affect different viewers in distinct ways. Individuals with a high need for cognition respond well to more complicated messages that advance some reason as to why an apparently negative candidate characteristic may actually work in his or her favor. Those individuals do not respond well to simple assertions that a particular candidate will perform well. On the other hand, individuals with a low need for cognition show the opposite pattern. They respond to the simple but not the more complex messages. The third set of studies considers postdebate spin as well as predebate predictions. Although campaigns often use the strategy of lowering expectations before a debate by arguing that their candidate is disadvantaged and will not perform well, and then after the debate declare a surprising victory, our research suggests that this strategy is unlikely to work. It appears too manipulative. Generally, when campaigns set expectations low, viewers perceive their candidate's performance as weak.

In the spring of 2007, Joseph Biden scored points on newscasts with a one-word answer to a debate question. The long-serving senator from Delaware was debating his rivals for the 2008 Democratic presidential nomination. Questions had been raised about his seemingly uncontrolled verbosity. Biden was asked whether he could assure worried voters that he had sufficient self-discipline to be president. He simply said: "Yes." His answer—just one word—provided an impressive example of restraint. For the broadcast media, it was an effective, though minimal, sound bite. There have been many other brief exchanges that have had similar impact: Lloyd Bentsen telling Dan Quayle, "You're no Jack Kennedy," or Ronald Reagan saying that he would "not exploit, for political purposes, my opponent's youth and inexperience." These exchanges addressed issues of great concern in a discrete and direct manner, and so have passed into debate lore.

We think moments such as these are memorable and influential for two reasons. First, debates have become ever more important in our political process; as voters, we would very much like to know how to assess them. This is made difficult by the second reason. For the most part, the candidates' relative performances are unclear. Crystallizing moments such as those above are rare. The typical lack of clarity means that while debates are important, they are also ambiguous. Research in social psychology going back to Allport and Postman's (1947) studies of rumors has shown that the importance/ambiguity combination creates an extremely ripe occasion for social influence (see Baron, Vandello, & Brunsman, 1996, for a more recent study). Allport and Postman argue that in those situations people seek guidance in creating a simple summary of the facts. Consistent with this research, we would predict that people will be easily influenced by other people's evaluations (media reports, campaign spin, water cooler gossip) of debate performances. This chapter reports several studies addressing that hypothesis.

The importance of debates. Presidential debates are seen by increasingly large numbers of people, with an estimated 62.5 million viewers seeing the first debate of 2004 (Commission on Presidential Debates, 2008). Though debates are often derided as being uninformative, the evidence shows that voters learn at least a little from them—especially about candidates with whom they are not very familiar (Holbrook, 1999). There is also a strong correlation between a person's view of who won a debate and his/her choice on Election Day (Sears & Chaffee, 1979; Schrott, 1990). Coupled with a large viewership, these findings suggest that debates have the potential to swing close elections.

Debate evaluations. But debate evaluations are far from objective. Many variables come into play. Research on the Kennedy-Nixon debates in 1960 suggests that "the medium is the message" and that Kennedy benefited greatly from the way he appeared on television, relative to Richard Nixon (Kraus,

1962). That is, it is widely believed that John F. Kennedy benefited most among voters who watched the debates on television rather than those who listened on the radio. For example, after the first debate, undecided television viewers were more likely to perceive Kennedy rather than Nixon as similar to the "ideal leader" (Tannenbaum, Greenberg, & Silverman, 1962).

Another factor is prior political leanings and attitudes toward the candidates (Sears & Chaffee, 1979; Sigelman & Sigelman, 1984). In a representative study Fazio and Williams (1986) found high correlations between predebate candidate favorability ratings and postdebate ratings of candidate performance in the 1984 election cycle. In fact, the general conclusion of the political science literature is that perceptions of all political actions are strongly influenced by one's initial leanings (e.g., Kinder, 1998; Bartels, 2002). So while there is a strong relationship between your perception of who won the debate and who you will eventually vote for, you are generally inclined to believe your favored side won.

Media reports are also important. For example, Ranney (1983) and Steeper (1978) documented the effect of news stories on perceptions of President Gerald Ford's Eastern Europe gaffe in the 1976 debates. Ford had said that Eastern Europe was not under the domination of the Soviet Union. While this remark did not hurt Ford immediately after the debate, news coverage convinced people that he had made a serious mistake and he was subsequently perceived to have lost. Media coverage similarly changed an Al Gore debate victory over George W. Bush into a defeat during the 2000 election (Jamieson & Waldman, 2002).

Other research on media commentary continues to underline its importance. Such commentary lessened Bill Clinton's perceived margin of victory (McKinnon, Tedesco, & Kaid, 1993) in the 1992 debates. Similar research on the 1996 debates between Clinton and Republican challenger Bob Dole showed that network commentary raised viewers' assessments of both candidates (McKinnon & Tedesco, 1999). In general, debate research suggests that contextual features—such as media commentary and whether people watch the debates on television or listen to them on the radio—make a substantial difference (Kaid & Bystrom, 1999; Lemert, Elliot, Bernstein, Rosenberg, & Nestvold, 1991; Schroeder, 2000). These findings are consistent with the notion that debate perceptions are inherently somewhat fragile. It does not take much to shift people's opinions.

In the aftermath of the election of 1960, Sidney Kraus argued that the debates mattered whether people watched them or not (1962). A narrative was constructed about Kennedy's cool confidence and command in the first debate, and that story weighed heavily in a close election. What happened in the debate mattered, but the way the public and the media digested and constructed the debate performances was crucial—more crucial, in fact, than whether a person had actually seen the debate. In light of the subsequent research discussed above, Kraus's comment seems prescient.

Our research explores multiple facets of how people's perceptions of debates are affected by what they learn about others' views. It shows that people can be highly influenced by information that they receive about others' assessments before, during, and after the debate itself. Its focus is on the influence of both other debate viewers and media commentators. In addition, it considers the possible influence of debate moderators and questioners. Our first set of studies considers one of the simplest forms of influence, that in which other people's opinions are made known without any rationale or argument. In these studies, those opinions are revealed during the debates themselves. We find that they produce a great deal of influence, influence that is best characterized as conformity (e.g., McGuire, 1968). Our second set of studies considers how different individuals are affected by media-created expectations. It tests the hypothesis that different kinds of people react differently to messages of varying complexity. Our final set of studies considers how people might be affected by two kinds of "spin"—predebate prediction about relative performance and postdebate assessment of that performance.

SIMPLE CONFORMITY AND DEBATE PERCEPTIONS

Televised debates give audiences an hour or more to assess presidential candidates both by sound and sight as they are confronted with challenging questions. It could be argued that this should give viewers ample opportunity to form strong and coherent impressions about both the show and the actors. Further, it could be argued that—so extensive is the evidence presented in a televised debate—any attempts to influence the opinions of viewers during or after a debate would be overwhelmed by the sheer magnitude of audiovisual data presented. In fact, given null results in the following experiments, that is precisely what psychologists would have argued. What the following experiments suggested, however, is that debates are highly ambiguous. For both specific events within debates (Experiments 1+2) and global evaluations of debates (Experiments 3+4), our viewers looked to the reactions of both their peers and distant debate audiences when making their assessments.

Sound Bites: No One Could Forget When. . .

As noted above, there are moments in presidential and vice-presidential debates that have passed into debate lore as unforgettable. Even many current high school and college students know something of the Kennedy-Nixon debates, and textbooks on political science, American government, and political communication mention supposedly decisive moments in debates to illustrate one concept or another. From our perspective, the question of decisive moments is an interesting one. If there are exchanges in debates that are of such clarity in and of themselves, then it is hard to argue that the ambiguity of debates is high.

Yet, a moment may not need to be inherently special to enter into debate lore as pivotal. It could be that instead of *being* critical some moments are *made* critical. Perhaps audience reaction or postdebate interpretation is necessary to turn a one-liner from mundane to pivotal. To examine the degree to which pivotal sound bites stand on their own, two studies were run on Williams College undergraduates using the second presidential debate of 1984 (Fein, Goethals, & Kugler, 2007).

Let us recall briefly the election of 1984. The Republican candidate was President Ronald Reagan and the Democratic candidate was Walter Mondale, a former vice president and senator. Throughout the campaign, Reagan enjoyed a substantial lead (and ultimately won by an impressive margin). There was, however, one dark period for the Reagan campaign. In the first debate, Reagan had an unexpectedly poor showing, appearing confused. Combined with his age, this confusion sparked some second thoughts in the electorate and Mondale's numbers began to climb. In the second debate, exactly two weeks later, Henry Trewhitt, a correspondent for *The Baltimore Sun,* asked Reagan directly about his age.

Mr. Trewhitt: Mr. President, I want to raise an issue that I think has been lurking out there for two or three weeks, and cast it specifically in national security terms. You already are the oldest president in history, and some of your staff say you were tired after your most recent encounter with Mr. Mondale. I recall, yet that President Kennedy had to go for days on end with very little sleep during the Cuban missile crisis. Is there any doubt in your mind that you would be able to function in such circumstances?[1]

This question cut straight to the heart of the resurgent concerns about Reagan's age. Reagan's answer was telling:

Reagan: Not at all, Mr. Trewhitt, and I want you to know that also I will not make age an issue of this campaign. I am not going to exploit for political purposes my opponent's youth and inexperience.

The audience erupted in laughter. Mondale, recognizing the mood, joined in. Trewhitt said, "Mr. President, I'd like to head for the fence and try to catch that one before it goes over, but I'll go on to another question."

In many ways, this is the prototypical critical moment. Reagan's response was widely reported and the slight slump disappeared from tracking polls. It appeared that his words were universally received as clever and on topic. Our studies, however, showed that the story was slightly more complicated.

These experiments each had three conditions: an unedited version containing the key sound bite and the audience reaction to it, an edited version in which the sound bite was included but audience and commentator reaction was excluded, and a second edited version lacking the sound bite altogether. If the one-liner stood on its own and participants did not require "help" from the audience to recognize its importance, then it should not make any difference if the audience reaction and Trewhitt's "home run" comment are deleted. If, on the other hand, audience and commentator reaction were necessary to persuade viewers that the sound bite was important, then taking them out should have the same effect as taking out both the sound bite and the audience and commentator reactions.

The participants in our experiment judged Reagan the winner of the debate in the control condition (with the unedited sound bite). However, they did not believe Reagan performed better than Mondale when the sound bite was included but the audience applause and moderator reaction were excluded. There was a dramatic drop in Reagan's performance ratings when his comments were not stamped with the audience's approval. This would seem to indicate that the sound bite did not stand well on its own. When the sound bite was not included at all, Mondale was again seen as doing better in the debate—unsurprising since Reagan's best lines had been omitted.

Interestingly, only 15 percent of participants in the condition where the reaction had been deleted listed the sound bites as among the highlights of the debate, as opposed to 78 percent of participants in the control condition that included audience applause. In this case, the supposed defining moments had little impact if they were not endorsed by others. In the same way, television sitcoms depend on canned laughter. The jokes themselves do not have the same impact if they are presented without other viewers' reactions.

From these studies, we learned something very important about how one-liners are perceived. Specifically, we saw that it was not so much the exchange itself but rather how it was perceived by the audience that most influenced how viewers saw it. But many debates do not have such decisive moments. How susceptible to influence are viewers when the debate content is less dramatic and more even?

We conducted two studies investigating that question. One was a simple lab study. Participants came into the lab in small groups to watch a short segment of the same 1984 Reagan-Mondale debate. They were given wireless handheld dials with digital displays of the type commonly used in marketing and persuasion studies. Mirroring a procedure used by CNN in their live coverage of the 1992 debates, participants were told that they should use the dials to track their reactions during the course of the debates (turning them one direction in favor of the Republican candidate and the other direction in favor of the Democratic candidate) and that a graph showing the average of their group members' reactions would be superimposed over the debate video itself. This way they would have constant feedback letting them know how well each candidate was doing at various points in the debate.

For our study, we ignored the group's actual responses and manipulated the feedback displayed. The "audience" feedback always began at the neutral midpoint and during the course of the segment reached a value that was solidly in either Reagan or Mondale territory. This false feedback had a huge effect on audience perceptions. Participants who saw their "peer's reactions" favor Reagan rated his performance (on 100 point scales) as being 20 points above Mondale's. Participants who thought that their peers favored Mondale said that he outperformed Reagan by 20 points.

Both this study and the sound bite studies can be criticized for being artificial. But our final study, run during the 1992 campaign, had groups of participants watch a presidential debate live in the presence of a few confederates who had been told to cheer subtly for either Bush or Clinton, and jeer the other very quietly but audibly. Participants in the "pro-Bush" room rated Bush's performance far better (and Clinton's far worse) than did participants in the "pro-Clinton" room. On a 100 point scale, Clinton's performance was rated as 51 points higher than Bush's in the "pro-Clinton" group but only 6 points higher in the "pro-Bush" group. None of the participants said that they were influenced by other people's reactions, and most reported that they barely noticed the reactions of the confederates. Interestingly, the confederates themselves were affected by their own behavior. They were more pro-Clinton in the "pro-Clinton" group than in the "pro-Bush" group. This study, using a simple, natural manipulation in the midst of an active campaign cycle shows how powerfully debate perceptions can be shaped by social influence.

Conclusions

These four studies show that debate perceptions are highly malleable, which suggests in turn that they are very ambiguous. Even when they seem quite clear, they are subject to considerable social influence. Perceptions of even a rather stark and memorable physical reality are shaped by social reality. Specifically, moments in debate history that are later called decisive can be easily cast into oblivion by removing the reactions of the audience. Showing people the reactions of their peers during the course of debates (a feat that is now trivial technologically) *creates* a consensus position. And exposing debate watchers to a biased crowd will dramatically shift their perceptions. In these findings, we have substantial support for the ambiguity of debates based on the extent to which even modest social influence changes debate perceptions.

TRAIT-FOCUSED SPIN

The next pair of studies (Kugler & Goethals, in press) addresses two new elements in debate perceptions. The first is inspired by Laswell's (1948) classic formulation that the study of persuasion concerns "who says what to whom and with what effect." So we can begin to think about how different audiences are affected by different messages under different conditions. Second, we want to examine a hard case for social influence in debates: candidates who had obviously negative traits.

One individual difference measure from the persuasion literature can be seen as being particularly important in addressing the first question: Need for Cognition (NFC). NFC measures how much a person is intrinsically driven to think, separating "chronic cognizers" from "cognitive misers" (Cacioppo, Petty, & Kao, 1984). It figures prominently in several models of persuasion, including the Elaboration Likelihood Model (Cacioppo, Petty, Kao, & Rodriguez, 1986). We proposed that people who are high in NFC, those who are highly motivated to think carefully, would prove resistant to the effects of simple persuasion attempts that ignored candidates' negative qualities. These people would be willing and presumably able to counter-argue against a glib pronouncement favoring one candidate over another, a pronouncement that did not provide any backup. On the other hand, their low NFC counterparts would show the usual cooperative effects in response to simple messages. This finding would be consistent with effects found regarding NFC in priming studies (Petty, 2001).

We are also concerned here with how spinners might devise convincing messages when the candidates they support have obvious negative attributes. Examples include John F. Kennedy's inexperience, Bob Dole's aggressiveness, and George W. Bush's vagueness. In each of these cases, a simple positive spin might be suspect. These candidates had real problems and all of the cheering crowds in the world could only do so much to counter them. And those people a candidate would most need to impress—news reporters, pundits, potential funders—would certainly be paying close attention, emulating the harder to persuade high NFC audiences.

For these sophisticated and involved viewers, we proposed a new approach to pre-debate spin. These individuals might be more influenced by more complex framings that cast specific potentially negative qualities in a favorable light. Such trait-focused spin (TFS) essentially attempts to spin straw into gold. A real-world example of this type of spin can be seen in the work of Jamieson and Waldman (2002) on media framing in the 2000 presidential campaign. They discuss how the media created a narrative that provided an interpretive frame for George W. Bush's performance in the 2000 debates. The issue was Bush's vagueness about specific policies. This attribute could be seen as a sign of intellectual shallowness, but it could also be portrayed as part of a particular management style. In the summer before the debates, the Bush campaign promoted their candidate as the MBA president, concerned with the big picture and not trivial details. This created a positive frame. When the press later saw Bush's performance in the debates, his vagueness cued memories of his business school background as opposed to doubts about his intelligence.

Chronic cognizers might enjoy the complexity of the counterintuitive interpretations. The elaborate nature of the persuasive message sidesteps their defenses. After trait-focused spin they can say, "Yes, I think he did well, not surprising given his top-down management style." Yet this very advantage could have the reverse effect on cognitive misers. They could easily become lost in the complexity of the message.

We tested these hypotheses in two studies. In the control conditions, participants were given a simple introductory article about the debate they were about to view. In the positive spin conditions, they were given the same article, but with a section inserted saying that the target candidate was favored over his opponent. No real reason was offered for this assertion. There were also trait-focused spin conditions in which a potentially negative trait was described, and then integrated into a positive prediction. In the first case (Dole vs. Mondale, 1976) the trait was Bob Dole's aggressiveness, and in the second case (Bush vs. Dukakis, 1988) the trait was Michael Dukakis's cold, intellectual detachment.

In the first study, then, the goal was to influence perceptions of Senator Bob Dole in his 1976 vice-presidential debate against Senator Walter Mondale. As indicated above, Dole was seen as being very aggressive. Historically, his aggressiveness was very poorly received and, after the election, even he acknowledged that he had gone too far. His performance was such that viewers at the time understood exactly what Mondale was talking about when he referred to Dole's reputation as a "hatchet man." Participants were brought into the lab for a study on perceptions of presidential debates. They were told which debate they would be watching and were given a news article with one of the following headlines: "TV Producer Says Clash May be 'Liveliest of All'" (control); "Senate Watcher: Dole to 'Overwhelm' Mondale" (simple positive spin); and "Senate Watcher: 'Aggressive' Dole to 'Overwhelm' Mondale" (trait description as part of positive message, TFS). The simple positive spin article simply reported that Dole was favored. The trait-focused spin article said that Dole would effectively use his quick wit and sharp invective to overwhelm Mondale. After participants finished watching the selected segment of the debate, in this case the closing third, they were given a questionnaire asking various questions about the debate.

We predicted that high need for cognition participants would not be influenced by the simple positive spin article, but that they would be moved by the trait-focused spin article. In contrast, we expected that low need for cognition participants would be moved by the simple positive spin article, but might find the trait-focused spin article too involved, and might not be influenced by it. All participants (100 percent) in the control condition said that Mondale won the debate. In contrast, those who had been told that Dole would perform well, or that he would do well because he was aggressive, were generally more favorable toward Dole than were control participants. However, there was an interesting difference based on the participants' need for cognition. High NFC participants found simple positive spin unpersuasive. Again, none of them thought Dole won. But as predicted, they were positively influenced by the trait-based spin. In that instance, 50 percent thought Dole won. Low NFC participants were more or less equally persuaded by both types of spin. In the simple positive spin condition, 50 percent said Dole won. In the trait-based spin condition, 43 percent said Dole won. Thus the more complex message was slightly—although not significantly—less effective for the low NFC participants.

Study 2 employed largely the same design and procedure. Its main goal was to replicate the results of Study 1, especially the difference based on NFC status, in the context of a different debate and a different trait. The performance selected for this study was that of Governor Michael Dukakis in the second presidential debate of 1988. While the 1988 election was largely unexceptional—if not quite as one-sided as 1984—there were a few memorable exchanges in the second debate. These resulted from a framing that the Republicans had been constructing for some time. In the first debate, when Dukakis seemed to laugh derisively at Bush's momentary confusion, Bush said, "Wouldn't it be nice to be the iceman and never make a mistake." This iceman framing can be seen as having prompted the first question in the second debate, the well-known "Kitty question." Governor Dukakis was asked, "If Kitty Dukakis were raped and murdered, would you favor an irrevocable death penalty for the killer?" A difficult question in the best of times, but made worse by Dukakis's cold and analytic answer. Even he later admitted that he had flubbed the response. A later question, like one given to Reagan in 1984, asked him to reflect upon his performance in the previous debate. It alluded to a belief that Dukakis had "won the first debate on intellect, and yet [he] lost it on heart."

Both of these exchanges are reflective of a general problem created by the "iceman" framing. Dukakis had a very analytic style that played poorly with the electorate. Thus in our articles for this study, the overarching trait into which we attempted to assimilate Dukakis's analytical detachment was "intelligent." A generally positive word that undeniably applies to Dukakis, "intelligent" can also carry with it the air of detachment, intellectualism, and lack of warmth. This captures both the positive and negative aspects of his performance in the debate and throughout the campaign.

Once again articles were drafted for the three categories used in Experiment 1. The results were slightly different in this study. Compared to the control condition, the simple spin condition produced only modest influence for both high and low need for cognition participants. Twenty-five percent of the high NFC participants thought that Dukakis won in the control condition, and 38 percent of them thought he won in the simple spin condition, an increase of 13 percent. The low NFC participants showed a nearly identical increase of 12 percent from 11 percent in the control condition to 23 percent in the simple spin condition. Neither of these represented a statistically significant improvement. However, the trait-focused spin condition was highly effective for the high NFC participants. Fifty-seven percent of them thought that Dukakis won. However, none (zero percent) of the low NFC participants in the trait-focused spin condition thought Dukakis won. The trait-focused spin article talked about both the upsides (he will not get lost in the passions of the moment) and downsides (he is aloof) of Dukakis's intelligence. This message was persuasive to the high NFC participants who can look at issues from both sides. For low NFC participants, all that seemed to matter was that Dukakis was aloof, i.e., cold.

Conclusions

Presidential candidates have strengths that can be highlighted, but also weaknesses that cannot be hidden. Results from the two studies reported here suggest clear strategies for working with these weaknesses. Both experiments showed that participants who are high in NFC are willing to be persuaded to incorporate specific potentially negative character traits into positive general frames. But what of those debate watchers who are not intensely motivated to think carefully about politics? The results of the 2000 election, where George W. Bush's inarticulacy was early and often framed in terms of his "big picture" approach, suggest that with enough repetition, the electorate as a whole can be brought around to embrace a particular framing. Thus, while trait-focused spin did not work for low NFC participants in our second study, it might be more effective in real campaigns. Also, there is a considerable literature on public opinion, some of which focuses on models of elite-driven attitude assessments (e.g., Kinder, 1998). In these models, involved citizens spread their carefully formed opinions to their less dedicated peers, a kind of water cooler postdebate spin. This downstream spin may be the key for those who are less engaged. The next section investigates a related form of social influence in assessments of presidential debate performance.

INTERACTIONS OF PREDEBATE AND POSTDEBATE SPIN

While our studies of trait-focused spin (TFS) employed positive appraisals of the competing candidates, such favorable predebate evaluations are probably less common than more modest candidate descriptions from campaign sources who try to set low expectations. For example, prior to the 1992 vice-presidential debate between Dan Quayle and Al Gore (and, memorably, Admiral James Stockdale, running mate of Ross Perot), Republican sources tried to lower expectations for Quayle. They claimed that Al Gore had been educated at elite schools (he was a Harvard graduate) and had lifetime advantages that made it difficult for Quayle to compete on a fair or equal basis. Why is the expectations game played this way?

There are probably two related reasons. First, when a poor performance really is expected, the campaign may try to lower its impact by creating a frame in which it can charitably be understood. In 1992, Republican campaign managers were well aware of Quayle's disappointing vice-presidential debate performance during the 1988 campaign, in which Democrat Lloyd Bentsen leveled Quayle with the well-remembered put-down, "Senator, you're no Jack Kennedy." Something had to be done. Setting low expectations might help. Low expectation frames can often be understood as a form of negative trait-focused spin. The frame says, our candidate will likely perform poorly, but here is why it should not be taken too seriously. Second, a negative performance expectation creates a low bar over which a candidate may leap, even with a mediocre performance. The hope is that the performance will be enough better than predicted to create a contrast effect (Schwartz & Bless, 1992). That is, the performance may look even better than it was if it is compared to and contrasted with a low expectation.

Creating low performance expectations for debates quite probably extends from the utility of creating low expectations for primary results. Over the years, the expectations game has been played most vigorously in the New Hampshire primary. In 1968, Eugene McCarthy was perceived as the effective "winner" of that primary even though incumbent president Lyndon Johnson got more votes, all write-ins. Though Johnson was not even on the ballot, and he got more votes, he was deemed the loser. McCarthy exceeded expectations. In 1972, George McGovern lost the New Hampshire primary to Edmund Muskie, but did better than expected, and celebrated the result. In 1992, Bill Clinton did better than expected, following the Gennifer Flowers and draft-dodging controversies, and declared himself "The Comeback Kid" even though he lost to Paul Tsongas.

However, an important difference between primaries and debates would seem to render playing the low expectations game perilous in the debate context. In primaries, there is a clear outcome, measured precisely in terms of the percentage of votes going to each candidate. In debates, as we have argued, the outcome is quite ambiguous. When an outcome is ambiguous, it is generally assimilated to, rather than contrasted with, any expectation that has been created (Schwartz & Bless, 1992). That is, if potential voters are led to expect a candidate to debate poorly, they may be very likely to perceive the candidate's performance just that way. A study by Norton and Goethals (2004) explored precisely this possibility.

Undergraduate research participants watched about half of a 1996 Massachusetts senatorial debate between the incumbent senator, John Kerry, and the incumbent governor, William Weld. Pretests showed that Kerry was clearly perceived as the winner of this portion of the debate. In the study itself, participants watched the same debate segments, with some additions. During the introductions, a supposed TV station political commentator, Jack Harper, reported either "low pitch" (negative) or "high pitch" (positive) dubbed-in messages regarding Kerry's performance. Furthermore, these messages were based on information either from "members of the media" or Kerry aides. In the low pitch version, it was stated that Kerry had been ill and unable to prepare, and was the clear underdog. In the high pitch version, the message stated that Kerry was well-rested and "raring to go," and that he was the clear favorite. The results of the study were quite clear. Kerry's margin of victory was less when participants heard a low pitch for him. Setting expectations low effectively turned Kerry from a winner into a loser.

While creating low expectations prior to an ambiguous performance can lower perceptions of the performance, campaign aides generally do not rest simply on the impact of low initial expectations. Positive postdebate spin is often combined with lowering expectations before the debate to create an opportunity for campaign "spinners" or "framers" to say, in effect, we were very pleasantly surprised at how well our candidate performed. How well does this work?

Not very. A follow-up study addressed this question. The low-pitch, high-spin combination, where campaigns set a low bar, with a negative expectation, and then declare a surprising victory, does not work very well. Observers watched the same video of the Kerry-Weld debate discussed above. This time, not only were predebate pitches included, but also postdebate spin was added. At the end of the actual debate there were a few seconds of televised applause with no comment from the actual broadcasters. In this interval Jack Harper's (the alleged commentator's) postdebate assessment was dubbed in. He reported that either "members of the press" or "the Kerry people" thought that Kerry had won the debate. These reports followed earlier predebate pitches, from either the press or the Kerry campaign, that were either positive or negative. When the positive postdebate spin for Kerry followed the earlier positive pitch, Harper reported that "as expected he outperformed Governor Weld and gained a clear victory." When the spin followed an earlier negative pitch, Harper reported "he performed better than expected and gained a clear victory."

The result produced by the various combinations of predebate pitches and postdebate spins was quite clear. Kerry's margin of victory grew following the positive postdebate spin, except in one instance. When the postdebate spin was attributed to Kerry aides, following a low pitch by these same aides, Kerry gained nothing. Viewers seemed to think that Kerry's aides lacked credibility and were obviously trying to manipulate the audience. Some data on viewer ratings of the overall quality of the network coverage also suggest their skepticism in this condition. First, coverage ratings were higher when Harper reported the views of the press rather than those of campaign aides. Viewers trust the media more than campaign spinners. Furthermore, the quality of coverage was rated particularly poorly when Harper reported the campaign aides' low-pitch/high-spin combination. They did not believe these attempts at influence, and they preferred that Harper not report them.

In line with this skepticism about campaign spinners, it is interesting that following the 2004 presidential debates between John Kerry and President George Bush, ABC News refused to interview aides from either campaign. They relied instead on their own commentators and instant viewer poll results. Of course, this does not take social influence out of the equation. The findings from all of our experiments suggest that the perceptions of media commentators and the perceptions of other viewers, as conveyed in polls, will have a great impact on those who are tuning in to postdebate coverage. It is not clear whether the media commentators reflect the viewer poll results or vice versa. Either way, the combination is likely to have a powerful influence on those watching the televised coverage.

CONCLUSION

Taken together, our results from three sets of studies show that people's perceptions of debate performances are highly susceptible to social influence. They suggest that debates are inherently ambiguous and that people are open to guidance even when interpreting supposedly crystal clear debate moments. In 2007 Joe Biden had the good sense to respond to the question about his verbosity with brevity, creating a perfect media sound bite. His response actually said very little about his capacity for restraint, just as Reagan's famous age comment was not necessarily indicative of his mental acuity and Lloyd Bentsen's "you're no Jack Kennedy" put-down of Dan Quayle explained nothing about the latter's leadership ability. Yet all of these moments are excellent examples of how the media shapes public perceptions of our quadrennial presidential debates. This shaping is not necessarily—or even likely—for the good, but understanding its form and the magnitude of its impact is essential, especially if we wish to make debates into something more than an exchange of sound bites.

A recent column in *The New York Times* ridiculed coverage of a 2008 Republican primary debate, lamenting the emphasis on how candidates "came across" at the expense of analyzing the veracity of what the candidates actually said (Krugman, 2007). The single most important lesson from our research is that how a candidate comes across is as much a function of what is said *about* them as what *they* themselves say. If media coverage of debates focuses on the trivial, then so will public evaluations. This is to no one's benefit.

NOTES

1. Transcript courtesy of the Commission on Presidential Debates. http:// www.debates.org/pages/trans84c.html

REFERENCES

Allport, G. W., & Postman, L. (1947). *The psychology of rumor.* New York: Henry Holt & Co.

Baron, R. S., Vandello, J. A., & Brunsman, B. (1996). The forgotten variable in conformity research: Impact of task importance on social influence. *Journal of Personality & Social Psychology, 71,* 915–927.

Bartels, L. M. (2002). Beyond the running tally: Partisan bias in political perceptions. *Political Behavior, 23,* 117–150.

Cacioppo, J. T., Petty, R. E., & Kao, C. (1984). The efficient assessment of need for cognition. *Journal of Personality Assessment, 48,* 306–307.

Cacioppo, J. T., Petty, R. E., Kao, C., & Rodriguez, R. (1986). Central and peripheral routes to persuasion: An individual difference perspective. *Journal of Personality and Social Psychology, 51,* 1032–1043.

Commission on Presidential Debates. (2008). 2004 Debates. Webpage. Retrieved February 10, 2008, from http://www.debates.org/pages/his_2004.html

Fazio, R. H., & Williams, C. J. (1986). Attitude accessibility as a moderator of the attitude-perception and attitude-behavior relations: An investigation of the 1984 presidential election. *Journal of Personality and Social Psychology, 51*(3), 505–514.

Fein, S., Goethals, G. R., & Kugler, M. B. (2007). Social influence on political judgments: The case of presidential debates. *Political Psychology, 28*(2), 165–192.

Holbrook, T. M. (1999). Political learning from presidential debates. *Political Behavior, 21*(1), 67–89.

Jamieson, K. H., & Waldman, P. (2002). *The press effect: Politicians, journalists, and the stories that shape the political world.* Cambridge: Oxford University Press.

Kaid, L. L., & Bystrom, D. G. (1999). *The electronic election: Perspectives on the 1996 campaign communication.* Mahwah, NJ: Erlbaum.

Kinder, D. R. (1998). Opinion and action in the realm of politics. In D. Gilbert, S. Fiske, & G. Lindzey (Eds.), *The handbook of social psychology* (pp. 778–867). New York: McGraw-Hill.

Kraus, S. (1962). *The great debates: Background, perspectives, effects.* Bloomington: Indiana University Press.

Krugman, P. (2007, June 8). Lies, sighs and politics. *The New York Times*, p. A29.

Kugler, M. B., & Goethals, G. R. (in press). "Trait-focused spin in presidential debates: Surviving the kisses of death." *Basic and Applied Social Psychology.*

Laswell, H. (1948). *The structure and function of communication and society: The communication of ideas.* New York: Institute for Religious and Social Studies.

Lemert, J. B., Elliot, W. R., Bernstein, J. M., Rosenberg, W. L., & Nestvold, K. J. (1991). News verdicts, the debates, and presidential campaigns. New York: Praeger.

McGuire, W. J. (1968). The nature of attitudes and attitude change. In G. Lindzey & E. Aronson (Eds.), *Handbook of social psychology* (2nd ed., Vol. 3, pp. 136–314). Reading, MA: Addison-Wesley.

McKinnon, L. M., & Tedesco, J. C. (1999). The influence of medium and media commentary on presidential debate effects. In L. L. Kaid, & D. G. Bystrom (Eds.), *The electronic election: Perspectives on the 1996 campaign communication* (pp. 191–206). Mahwah, NJ: Erlbaum.

McKinnon, L. M., Tedesco, J. C., & Kaid, L. L. (1993). The third 1992 presidential debate: Channel and commentary effects. *Augmentation and advocacy, 30,* 106–118.

Norton, M., & Goethals, G. R. (2004). Spin (and pitch) doctors: Campaign strategies in televised political debates. *Political Behavior, 26*(3), 227–244.

Petty, R. E. (2001). Subtle influences on judgment and behavior: Who is most susceptible? In J. Forgas and K. Williams (Eds.), *Social influence: Direct and indirect processes* (pp. 129–146). New York: Psychology Press.

Ranney, A. (1983). *Channels of power.* New York: Basic Books.

Schroeder, A. (2000). *Presidential debates: Forty years of high-risk TV.* New York: Columbia University Press.

Schrott, P. R. (1990). Electoral consequences of "winning" televised campaign debates. *Public Opinion Quarterly, 54*(4), 567–585.

Schwartz, N., & Bless, H. (1992). Constructing reality and its alternatives: An inclusion/exclusion model of assimilation and contrast effects in social judgment. In L. Martin & A. Tesser (Eds.), *Construction of social judgments* (pp. 217–245). Hillsdale, NJ: Erlbaum.

Sears, D. O., & Chaffee, S. H. (1979). Uses and effects of the 1976 debates: An overview of the empirical studies. In S. Kraus (Ed.), *The great debates: Carter versus Ford, 1976.* Bloomington: Indiana University Press.

Sigelman, L., & Sigelman, C. K. (1984). Judgments of the Carter-Reagan debate: The eyes of the beholders. *Public Opinion Quarterly, 48*(3), 624–628.

Steeper, F. T. (1978). Public response to Gerald Ford's statements on Eastern Europe in the second debate. In G. F. Bishop, R. G. Meadow, & M. Jackson-Beeck (Eds.), *The presidential debates: Media, electoral, and policy perspectives* (pp. 81–101). New York: Praeger.

Tannenbaum, P. H., Greenberg, B. S., & Silverman, F. R. (1962). Candidate images. In S. Kraus (Ed.), *The great debates.* Bloomington: Indiana University Press.

10

Social Stigma and Leadership: A Long Climb Up a Slippery Ladder

CRYSTAL L. HOYT AND MARTIN M. CHEMERS

I am really thrilled to be running at a time in our history when, on a stage, you can see an African American man, a Hispanic man, and a woman.

—Hillary Clinton

In this chapter we explore the difficulties women and minorities face in the leadership domain simply because they belong to social groups that are subordinated in our society. The stereotypes, prejudice, and discrimination faced by these nondominant, "stigmatized" individuals contribute to their underrepresentation in top leadership roles. In this chapter, we address stigma and leadership from the following two perspectives: (1) perceptions of and responses to stigmatized leaders by others, and (2) experiences of stigmatized leaders. Regardless of whether they are endorsed or not, the culturally dominant stereotypes surrounding stigmatized groups are pervasive and impact both dominant and subordinated members of society. Judgments of others based on skin color, gender, or other salient stigmatizing characteristics disadvantage individuals in the leadership domain. In addition, members of stigmatized social groups are keenly aware of the stereotypes surrounding their social group and are aware that others may treat them according to those beliefs. The incompatibility of negative stereotypes with expectations for effective leadership places challenges on stigmatized individuals at the outset. A greater understanding of social stigma and leadership will help us close the leadership gap; if leadership is in as short supply as many fear, utilizing all of our potential resources is required.

Senator Hillary Clinton's quote, referring to fellow 2008 presidential hopefuls Barack Obama and Bill Richardson, is quite telling of the lack of diversity in U.S. political and economic leadership. The prevalence of white males in top leadership positions (far beyond their percentage of the population as a whole) extends well beyond presidential candidates, to many other influence-wielding bodies such as Congress, boards of directors, and the C-suite (CEOs, COOs, CFOs, . . .). In this chapter we explore the difficulties that women and minorities face in the leadership domain because of their membership in subordinated social groups.

THE GLASS CEILING TURNED LABYRINTH

The well-known term "glass ceiling," originally coined to refer to the invisible barrier preventing women from ascending the corporate leadership ladder, now refers to barriers preventing people who are not members of society's dominant groups from reaching elite leadership positions. Eagly and Carli (2007) find the metaphor of a glass ceiling troublesome in that it implies that it is an absolute, impassable barrier, that everyone has equal access to lower level positions, and that there is one large obstacle rather than a number of challenges along the way. Instead, they proffer the image of the leadership labyrinth conveying the image of a journey.

Although women and minorities are successfully finding their way through the labyrinth in record numbers, they remain underrepresented, particularly in the upper echelons of American business and politics. For example, only 23.4 percent of the chief executive officers (CEOs) in American organizations are women, and African Americans and Latinos represent a mere 3.1 percent and 4.6 percent of all CEOs, respectively (U.S. Bureau of Labor Statistics, 2006). At Fortune 500 companies, these statistics are even bleaker. Women represent less than 3 percent of CEOs, they hold only 14.7 percent of Fortune 500 board seats, and women of color hold merely 3.4 percent of board seats (Catalyst, 2006; CNNMoney, 2007). Less than 2 percent of the F500 CEOs are African American, and African Americans hold only 8.3 percent of Fortune 500 board seats (Executive Leadership Council, 2004; Fortune Press Center, 2006). These numbers are even more dismal for Latino leaders who occupy a mere 3.1 percent of F500 board seats (Latinas occupy 0.8 percent) and only 1 percent of CEO positions (Hispanic Association on Corporate Responsibility, 2007).

On the political front the numbers are not much better. Women currently hold only 87 of the 535 seats in the U.S. Congress (16.3 percent; 16 percent in

employed (Ridgeway, 2001). In terms of gender, these status judgments create implicit performance expectations that can have a substantial impact on mixed-sex group interactions such that women's input is given less attention and evaluated more poorly than men's. It is sometimes the case that any positive input of women, particularly in masculine tasks, is attributed more to luck than to her ability, making women less willing than men to speak up and contribute to tasks. All of these factors result in less influence and lower likelihood of leadership emergence for women than men.

Not all people respond to women in leadership positions in the same manner. A recent 2006 Gallup poll asking Americans about their gender preferences in bosses revealed that 37 percent of those polled preferred a male boss, 18 percent prefer a female boss, and 43 percent do not have a preference. One factor that determines how people respond to women in leadership positions is their expectations about the roles of men and women in society. For example, compared to more liberal individuals, people with conservative views of gender roles like female leaders less, think they would be more difficult colleagues, and rate them more negatively when they lead in a relationship-oriented style (Forsyth, Heiney, & Wright, 1997). Similarly, follower attitudes have been shown to be important in the evaluation and performance of first year female cadets at West Point (Rice, Bender, & Vitters, 1980). Female leaders' group performance and follower satisfaction were the same as that of male leaders when followers held progressive attitudes about women in leadership positions, but female leaders performed more poorly than male leaders and had less satisfied followers when those followers held the more traditional attitudes, hostile to women in leadership positions.

Discrimination against women in leadership positions often comes in subtle forms. In one study, Supino and Goethals (2007) presented people with a vignette of either a male or a female candidate for U.S. Secretary of Defense during either a peace context or a terror context. Although the male participants found the male and female candidates equally competent across conditions, they were less likely to vote for the female candidate. In other words, male participants showed a subtle form of discrimination against the female candidate in that their willingness to vote for her was not on par with their perceptions of competency as it was for the male candidate. Further analyses revealed that the male participants rated the female candidate as less intelligent across contexts, and they rated her as less able to cope with stress and more passive than the male candidate in the terror context. Gender discrimination in the leadership domain is indeed still prevalent, yet its contemporary form is more subtle and pernicious.

In addition to evaluating women more negatively and being less likely to select them for leadership positions, successful women leaders engender hostility in terms of not being liked and being personally derogated, which ultimately has implications for career outcomes such as evaluations and reward allocations (Heilman, Wallen, Fuchs, & Tamkins, 2004). These penalties women incur for success at male tasks result from the perceived violation of the female gender role. Thus, women leaders are in a double bind: they need to show agency to be perceived as an effective leader but not too much agency or they will be disliked; they also need to show communion to be liked but not too much or they will be seen as an ineffective leader. This hostility that women encounter for violating the prescription of femininity was clearly illustrated in the 1989 Supreme Court case *Price Waterhouse v. Ann Hopkins*. Hopkins was told by Price Waterhouse that she was too "macho" and that she should be more feminine. They went as far as to advise her to go to charm school, wear jewelry and makeup, and be less aggressive. Hopkins was told that she would not make partner because she was too masculine, and in the end, the court ruled that Price Waterhouse was discriminating based on gender stereotypes.

Stigma and Attributions

Another way stigma impacts perceptions of leaders is through the attributions people make for others' behaviors. People have an intrinsic need to explain behavior and, when searching for these explanations, stereotypes can significantly bias attributions. For example, a large review of the attributional research demonstrates that people attribute success at masculine tasks to skill when rating men, but attribute women's success to luck (Swim & Sanna, 1996). These biased attributions extend to ethnic/racial minorities as well. For example, researchers have shown that people are more likely to attribute a successful banking career to ability and less likely to attribute it to effort and luck when the banker is a White man compared to a White woman or a Black woman or man (Yarkin, Town, & Wallston, 1982). These attributions play an important role in people's evaluations of leaders. For example, when followers make external attributions, such as luck, for poor leader performance or internal attributions, such as ability, for good performance, they evaluate the leader better than when the opposite attributions are made.

Attributions also play an important role when leaders are viewed as being the beneficiary of preferential treatment, a perception that often surrounds affirmative action. Justice Clarence Thomas's appointment on the Supreme Court has been viewed by many to be a result of preferential treatment rather than based solely on merit. Regarding Thomas, Democratic Senator Joseph Biden remarked, "Had Thomas been white, he never would have been nominated. The only reason he is on the court is because he is black." Justice Thomas, however, has repeatedly denied that he has been the beneficiary of preferential treatment. This fervent denial is understandable considering how attributions of preferential treatment impact stigmatized leaders. When individuals selected for leadership roles are thought to have been given preferential treatment, or what some call "reverse discrimination," their abilities and deservingness of the leadership role may be discounted in the attribution process (Crosby, Iyer, Clayton, & Downing, 2003). When leaders are perceived to have been selected for the leadership role preferentially, they are rated lower in leadership characteristics and effectiveness and are more likely to be recommended to be replaced (DeMatteo, Dobbins, Myers, & Facteau, 1996). However, these negative effects can be compensated for when followers are given positive feedback about leader performance. Considerable research indicates that when considerations of merit are indicated along with social group membership, reactions are much more positive.

EXPERIENCES OF STIGMATIZED LEADERS

I could not at any age be content to take my place by the fireside and simply look on.

—Eleanor Roosevelt

Regardless of whether they are endorsed or not, the culturally dominant stereotypes surrounding stigmatized groups are pervasive and impact both dominant and subordinated members of society. Members of stigmatized social groups are keenly aware of the stereotypes surrounding their social group and are aware that others may treat them according to those beliefs. Secretary of State Condoleezza Rice grew up in Birmingham, Alabama, during racial segregation and was fully aware of racial hostility. Rice's success as a leader depended in part on her responses to the deeply ingrained racism in her childhood, and she credits her parents for her determination to succeed: "My parents had me absolutely convinced that, well, you may not be able to have a hamburger at Woolworth's, but you can be President of the United States."

Stereotype Threat

Stigmatized leaders may perform less well when they think they are being evaluated through the lens of negative stereotypes. Stereotype-based expectations of inferiority can place a large psychological burden on leaders. "Stereotype threat" is the name given to the apprehension individuals experience when they are at risk of confirming a negative social stereotype (Steele & Aronson, 1995). Examining the role of stereotype threat within the domain of leadership, Davies, Spencer, and Steele (2005) exposed undergraduate women to either gender stereotypic commercials (e.g., a female college

student dreaming of becoming the homecoming queen) or neutral commercials (e.g., a cell phone commercial). They found that those women who were
exposed to gender stereotypic commercials had lower leadership aspirations
for an upcoming task. Correspondingly, other researchers found similar stereotype threat effects such that women performed less well than men on a
masculine sex role-typed managerial task (Bergeron, Block, & Echtenkamp,
2006) and on a negotiation task when the stereotype was *implicitly* activated
(Kray, Thompson, & Galinsky, 2001).

We have further investigated the psychological burden that the gender
leader stereotype places on women in the leadership role. In one study,
undergraduate participants were exposed to magazine advertisements portraying women in either gender stereotypic (e.g., taking care of families,
shopping) or counterstereotypic (e.g., being an entrepreneur, making millions
of dollars) roles (Hoyt & Simon, 2008). Subsequently, in an ostensibly second
study, participants were "randomly assigned" to the leadership role of a
three-person group task wherein the leader's charge was to lead a discussion
and reach consensus with two female followers on a controversial topic at the
university (the followers were confederates of the experimenter trained to
provide standardized feedback in all conditions). The results demonstrated
the negative impact of the gender-stereotypic advertisements. The women
in the stereotypic advertisement condition reported that they performed
worse on the leadership task and they reported lower levels of self-esteem
and well-being than those in the counterstereotypic condition.

Using a different method to activate the gender leader stereotype and a different task, we demonstrated similar effects of stereotype activation on
women in the leadership role in another experiment (Simon & Hoyt, 2007).
In this study female participants completed a modified version of the Remote
Associates Test. Although this test was originally developed as a test of creativity, participants were told that the task was a reliable measure of
decision-making abilities in leadership situations. The gender leader stereotype was activated for half of the participants by telling them that the task
had shown robust gender differences, and the stereotype was nullified for
the other half by telling them that the task had shown no gender differences.
Participants in the stereotype activation condition took longer to complete the
task, reported lower levels of perceived performance, identified less with
leadership, and reported lower levels of self-esteem and higher disappoint-
ment scores compared to those in the nullified condition.

Stereotype Reactance

Despite the well-documented stereotype threat effects, stereotypes do not
always result in deleterious responses from the negatively stereotyped

individual. For example, while Davies et al. (2005) found that exposure to stereotypic commercials undermines women's leadership aspirations, presenting the task as identity safe, that is, telling participants that there are no gender differences in the leadership task, eliminates this vulnerability. Additionally, Bergeron and colleagues (2006) found that women do not underperform men on the managerial task when it is feminine sex role-typed.

Furthermore, some leaders from nondominant social groups actually react to negative stereotypes and discrimination with constructive responses. Oprah Winfrey embodies this beneficial "I'll show you" response: "I was raised to believe that excellence is the best deterrent to racism or sexism. And that's how I operate my life." When individuals are confronted with a negative stereotype and they engage in counterstereotypical behavior, they are engaging in what has been termed "stereotype reactance." For example, women have demonstrated reactance by outperforming men at the bargaining table when they were *explicitly* presented with the gender and negotiation stereotype (Kray et al., 2001).

Not all stigmatized individuals will respond to negative stereotypes in the same manner. In a series of studies, we examined the role of leadership self-efficacy, or confidence one has in her/his leadership abilities, in women's responses to the leader-gender stereotype (Hoyt & Blascovich, 2007; Hoyt, 2005). In two experimental studies, we selected women with high or low leadership self-efficacy to serve as leaders of an ostensible three-person group undertaking an employee hiring decision task. Half of the leaders were primed with the gender leader stereotype by perusing a folder containing media images of male leaders, and they were given information on the gender gap in top leadership roles. The results showed that, unlike low efficacy leaders, high efficacy leaders exhibited positive, "I'll show you!" responses and reported higher levels of perceived performance, identification with leadership, and well-being as well as performing better.

Stigmatized Leaders' Attributions

Another approach to understanding the impact of stigma on low status group members is to examine the attributions they make. The belief that one is the beneficiary of preferential selection can have harmful effects. Shelby Steele, a vocal opponent of affirmative action, argues that being the recipient of preferential treatment can be harmful to the well-being of African Americans:

> Even when the black sees no implication of inferiority in racial preferences, he knows that whites do, so that—consciously or unconsciously—the result is virtually the same. The effect of preferential treatment—the lowering of normal standards to increase black representation—puts blacks at war with an

expanded realm of debilitating doubt, so that the doubt itself becomes an unrecognized preoccupation that undermines their ability to perform, especially in
integrated situations.

These potentially damaging effects of preferential selection have been
shown to generalize beyond race and extend into the realm of leadership.
For example, when women believe they are preferentially selected to leadership roles, they undermine their advancement by being less likely to choose
demanding work assignments and they are more likely to undervalue their
work-related abilities and task orientation (Heilman, Rivero, & Brett, 1991).
These negative effects, however, were not found when the preferential selection was accompanied with positive assessment of their work-related abilities. Examining the role of affirmative action on leadership selection, Major,
Feinstein, and Crocker (1994) found that women selected for a leader role
based on sex only were more likely to devalue the importance of being a
leader compared to those selected on merit. However, the negative impact
of preferential treatment is attenuated when consideration of merit is
included with the group-based membership—a procedure that mimics
affirmative action procedures in the real world (Crosby et al., 2003).

When faced with negative feedback, stigmatized leaders may wonder
whether the feedback is truly in response to their ability or due in part to
the prejudicial attitudes of the person giving it. This uncertainty is termed
"attributional ambiguity"; these nondominant leaders are uncertain of the
motives underlying other's reactions to them, and the attributions they make
can have important implications for their psychological well-being. Crocker
and Major (1989) hypothesized that attributing negative feedback to prejudice can be self-protective by buffering stigmatized individuals from negative
self-evaluation. Although making these attributions may be self-protective
when confronting negative feedback, these same attributions can undermine
leaders' ability to take credit for positive feedback from followers.

To take a close look at these predictions, we experimentally examined the
attributions and subsequent well-being of Latino leaders (Hoyt, Aguilar, Kaiser, Blascovich, & Lee, 2007). These two studies were conducted using immer-
sive virtual environment technology that allows for computer-generated
visual input. Participants donned headsets that immersed them in a virtual
conference room ostensibly with two other participants who were actually
physically located in other locations in the laboratory. The individuals who
were playing the leadership role were made aware whether their "virtual
identity" was as a White person or a Latino. In the first study, participants
(whether portrayed as Latino or White) were given negative performance
feedback during a leadership role. The participants who were represented as
Latino attributed the negative feedback more to discrimination and reported
greater well-being than nonstigmatized participants. In other words, blaming

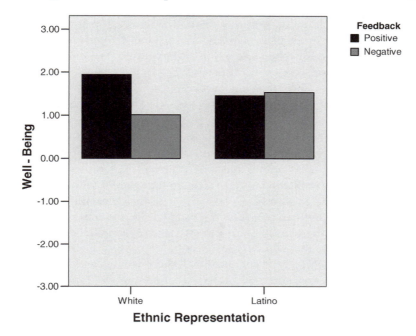

**Figure 10-1 The effects of positive and negative performance feedback
and stigma (ethnic representation) on well-being**

poor performance on discrimination protected the self-esteem of the participants in the face of negative feedback.

The second experiment was restricted to only Latino participants who were
given either negative or positive feedback. Latinos with their stigma revealed
(portrayed as Latino in the virtual conference room) again showed the self-
protective effects after receiving negative leadership feedback. However, in
addition, Latinos with a revealed stigma also discounted positive feedback
and reported lower well-being (see Figure 10-1). These findings show that
members of socially devalued groups are acutely aware that others might be
responding on the basis of group membership. Attributing feedback to one's
group membership can buffer leaders against negative feedback but can
undermine their ability to take credit for positive feedback.

CONCLUSION

Effective leadership involves (a) establishing one's credibility and influence, (b) building a relationship that, through coaching and support, enables
followers to contribute to group goals, and (c) fully utilizing all of the

resources available to the group by matching leadership strategies to the environment appropriately and creating a strong belief among team members of the collective competency and value of the group (Chemers, 1997). Each one of these elements presents obstacles, barriers, and hurdles for aspiring leaders who are members of stigmatized groups.

The incompatibility of negative stereotypes with expectations for effective leadership places challenges on stigmatized individuals at the outset. It may take longer or even be impossible for nontraditional leaders to convince others that they are right for the role and worthy of leadership status and influence. The basis for enabling and empowering followers to contribute to group goals requires that the leader is able to understand followers' capabilities and needs and to supply support and guidance. The ability to achieve these functions heavily depends on building strong authentic relationships. Animosities, negative expectations, and resistance from followers and superiors make garnering that ability very difficult.

However, the picture is not completely bleak for women and minority leaders. Affirmative action programs, especially those that are careful to remind both leaders and followers of competency as the basis for appointment, will put more currently stigmatized individuals into leadership roles. The findings are clear that as followers have a chance to evaluate their leaders on the basis of work-relevant performance, judgments based on irrelevant social categories become less prevalent (Lord & Maher, 1991). Additionally, the mere presence of more women and minorities in top leadership positions will begin to break down the negative stereotypes against these leaders. If leadership is in as short supply as many fear, utilizing all of our potential resources is required.

REFERENCES

Berger, J., Rosenholtz, S. J., & Zelditch, M. (1980). Status organizing processes. *Annual Review of Sociology, 6,* 479–508.

Bergeron, D. M., Block, C. J., & Echtenkamp, A. (2006). Disabling the able: Stereotype threat and women's work performance. *Human Performance, 19,* 133–158.

Catalyst. (2006). 2005 *Catalyst census of women board directors of the Fortune 500.* New York: Catalyst.

Chemers, M. M. (1997). *An integrative theory of leadership.* Mahwah, NJ: Erlbaum.

CNNMoney. (2007). *Women CEOs for Fortune 500 companies.* Retrieved July 9, 2007, from http://money.cnn.com/magazines/fortune/fortune500/2007/womenceos/

Crocker, J., & Major, B. (1989). Social stigma and self-esteem: The self-protective properties of stigma. *Psychological Review, 96,* 608–630.

Crosby, F., Iyer, A., Clayton, S., & Downing, R. (2003). Affirmative action: Psychological data and the policy debates. *American Psychologist, 58,* 93–115.

Davies, P. G., Spencer, S. J., & Steele, C. M. (2005). Clearing the air: Identity safety moderates the effects of stereotype threat on women's leadership aspirations. *Journal of Personality and Social Psychology, 88,* 276–287.

Deaux, K. (1984). From individual differences to social categories: Analysis of a decade's research on gender. *American Psychologist, 39,* 105–116.

DeMatteo, J. S., Dobbins, G. H., Myers, S. D. & Facteau, C. L. (1996). Evaluation of leadership in preferential and merit-based leader selection situations. *Leadership Quarterly, 7*(1), 41–62.

Eagly, A. H., & Carli, L. L. (2007, September). Women and the labyrinth of leadership. *Harvard Business Review,* 62–71.

Eagly, A. H., & Karau, S. (2002). Role congruity theory of prejudice toward female leaders. *Psychological Review, 109,* 573–598.

Executive Leadership Council. (2004). Institute for leadership development and research: 2004 Census of African American on boards of directors of Fortune 500 companies. Retrieved July 9, 2007, from http://www.elcinfo.com/ExecSummary.pdf

Forsyth, D. R., Heiney, M. M., & Wright, S. S. (1997). Biases in appraisals of women leaders. *Group Dynamics, 1,* 98–103.

Fortune Press Center. (2006). *Key Fortune 500 findings and stats.* Retrieved July 9, 2007, from http://www.timeinc.net/fortune/information/presscenter/fortune/press_releases/20060403_fortune500.html

Goffman, E. (1963). *Stigma.* Englewood Cliffs, NJ: Prentice-Hall.

Heilman, M. E., Block, C. J., Martell, R. F., & Simon, M. C. (1988). Has anything changed? Current characterizations of men, women, and managers. *Journal of Applied Psychology, 74,* 935–942.

Heilman, M. E., Rivero, J. C., & Brett, J. F. (1991). Skirting the competence issue: Effects of sex-based preferential selection on task choices of women and men. *Journal of Applied Psychology, 76,* 99–105.

Heilman, M. E., Wallen, A. S., Fuchs, D., & Tamkins, M. M. (2004). Penalties for success: Reactions to women who succeed at male gender-typed tasks. *Journal of Applied Psychology, 89,* 416–427.

Hispanic Association on Corporate Responsibility. (2007). *2007 Corporate governance study.* Retrieved July 9, 2007, from http://www.hacr.org/research/pageID.87/default.asp

Hogg, M. A. (2001). A social identity theory of leadership. *Personality and Social Psychology Review, 5,* 184–200.

Hogg, M. A., Fielding, K. S., Johnson, D., Masser, B., Russell, E., & Svensson, A. (2006). Demographic category membership and leadership in small groups: A social identity analysis. *The Leadership Quarterly, 17,* 335–350.

Hoyt, C. L. (2005). The role of leadership efficacy and stereotype activation in women's identification with leadership. *Journal of Leadership and Organizational Studies, 11*(4), 2–14.

Hoyt, C., Aguilar, L., Kaiser, C., Blascovich, J., & Lee, K. (2007). The self-protective and undermining effects of attributional ambiguity. *Journal of Experimental Social Psychology, 43,* 884–893.

Hoyt, C., & Blascovich, J. (2007). Leadership efficacy and women leaders' responses to stereotype activation. *Group Processes and Intergroup Relations, 10,* 595–616.

Hoyt, C., & Simon, S. (2008). The dark side of exposure to role models: Will female leaders guide you to the top or just let you down? Manuscript in preparation.

Kenney, R. A., Schwartz-Kenney, B. M., & Blascovich, J. (1996). Implicit leadership theories: Defining leaders described as worthy of influence. *Personality and Social Psychology Bulletin, 22,* 1128–1143.

Kray, L. J., Thompson, L., & Galinsky, A. (2001). Battle of the sexes: Gender stereotype confirmation and reactance in negotiations. *Journal of Personality & Social Psychology, 80,* 942–958.

Leary, M. R. (1995). *Impression management and interpersonal behavior.* Dubuque, IA: Brown & Benchmark.

Lord, R. G., & Maher K. J. (1991). *Leadership and information processing: Linking perceptions and performance.* Boston, MA: Unwin Hyman.

Major, B., Feinstein, J., & Crocker, J. (1994). The attributional ambiguity of affirmative action. *Basic and Applied Social Psychology, 15,* 113–141.

Major, B., & O'Brien, L. (2005). The social psychology of stigma. In S. T. Fiske (Ed.), *Annual Review of Psychology* (Vol. 56, pp. 393–421). Chippewa Falls, WI: Annual Reviews.

Rice, R. W., Bender, L. R., & Vitters, A. G. (1980). Leader sex, follower attitudes toward women, and leadership effectiveness: A laboratory experiment. *Organizational Behavior and Human Performance, 25,* 46–78.

Ridgeway, C. L. (2001). Gender, status, and leadership. *Journal of Social Issues, 57,* 637–655.

Schein, V. E. (1973). The relationship between sex role stereotypes and requisite management characteristics. *Journal of Applied Psychology, 57,* 95–100.

Simon, S., & Hoyt, C. (2007). *Women's responses to gender-leader stereotype activation.* Unpublished manuscript.

Steele, C. M., & Aronson, J. (1995). Stereotype threat and the intellectual test performance of African Americans. *Journal of Personality and Social Psychology, 69,* 797–811.

Supino, A., & Goethals, G. (2007). *The war on inequality: Subtleties in the perceptions of women leaders.* Unpublished manuscript.

Swim, J. K., & Sanna, L. J. (1996). He's skilled, she's lucky: A meta-analysis of observer's attributions for women's and men's successes and failures. *Personality and Social Psychology Bulletin, 22,* 507–519.

U.S. Bureau of Labor Statistics. (2006). *Current population survey, annual averages–household data.* (Table 11: Employed persons by detailed occupation, sex, race, and Hispanic or Latino ethnicity.) Retrieved July 6, 2007, from ftp://ftp.bls.gov/pub/special.requests/lf/aat11.txt

Yarkin, K., Town, J., & Wallston, B. (1982). Blacks anti women must try harder: Stimulus persons' race and sex attributions of causality. *Personality and Social Psychology Bulletin, 8,* 21–24.

11

Deifying the Dead and Downtrodden: Sympathetic Figures as Inspirational Leaders

SCOTT T. ALLISON AND GEORGE R. GOETHALS

There is nothing sweeter than to be sympathized with.

—George Santayana

In my country, we go to prison first and then become President.

—Nelson Mandela

This chapter proposes that leaders often derive their most inspirational qualities from events or actions that transpire before and after, rather than during, their tenure as leaders. These events or actions engender sympathy, emotional support, and adoration for the leader. We identify three types of individuals whose effectiveness as leaders stem from actions that elicit sympathetic responses from others: underdog leaders who attract sympathy from their ability to overcome significant obstacles before they assume their leadership; deceased leaders who attract sympathy and whose deaths elicit reverence and inspiration long after they are gone; and martyrs who make the ultimate sacrifice for noble causes and whose appeal is derived from combined elements of both underdog and deceased leaders. We propose that the self-sacrifice of all three types of leaders cements these leaders' positive legacy, and that these leaders' values both reflect and become a central part of their community's social identity.

A vast body of leadership research has focused on inspirational leaders and the actions they take, during their tenure as leaders, to motivate and arouse passion among their followers (see Avolio & Yammarino, 2002, for a review). These leaders have been characterized as charismatic (Shamir, 1991), transformational (Burns, 1978), or inspirational (Yukl, 2006), and they connect emotionally with their followers by engaging behaviors such as articulating a clear and appealing vision (Raelin, 1989); persuading followers to fulfill that vision (House & Shamir, 1993); using strong and expressive forms of communication (Nadler, 1988); acting confidently and optimistically (Mumford & Strange, 2002); expressing confidence in followers (Eden, 1990); using symbolic, dramatic actions to emphasize key values (Yukl, 2006); leading by example (House & Howell, 1992); and empowering people to achieve the vision (Riggio & Conger, 2005).

Whereas these inspiring actions occur during one's term as leader, we argue in this chapter that a leader's most transforming actions often occur *before* and *after,* rather than during, his or her tenure as leader. To be effective sources of inspiration, these actions must be emotionally powerful to followers, engendering sympathy, respect, and veneration for the leader. A prominent example is the leadership of Nelson Mandela, who endured 27 years of imprisonment before assuming the presidency of South Africa. While imprisoned, he and other inmates performed hard labor in a lime quarry. Prison conditions were harsh; prisoners were segregated by race, with black prisoners receiving the least rations. Political prisoners such as Mandela were kept separate from ordinary criminals and received fewer privileges. Mandela has described how, as a D-group prisoner (the lowest classification) he was allowed one visitor and one letter every six months. Mandela's ability to prevail after such long-term suffering made him an inspirational hero. His remarkable triumph over adversity, occurring before his presidency, propelled him to international fame and adoration.

Whereas Mandela's inspirational qualities derived from events that transpired before his formal leadership, other leaders inspire others based on occurrences after their tenure as leaders. Consider the intriguing case of Missouri governor Melvin Carnahan, who was elected to the U.S. Senate on November 7, 2000. Ordinarily, there is nothing noteworthy about voters electing an individual to office, except in this instance the individual had perished in a plane crash three weeks prior to the election. Even more extraordinary was the fact that Carnahan was trailing his opponent by several percentage points in opinion polls just prior to the plane crash. Polls clearly showed that his popularity soared as a result of his death. How could Carnahan have achieved a level of support in death that he could not achieve in life?

We argue that Mandela and Carnahan inspired their followers largely because their experiences engendered sympathetic responses. According to

Eisenberg (2004), sympathy is "an affective response that consists of feeling sorrow or concern for the distress or needy other" (p. 678). Typically, the target of the sympathetic response has experienced a significant setback or suffered a calamitous outcome. Sympathy often derives from empathy, a related affective response that Eisenberg defines as "the comprehension of another's emotional state" that leads the perceiver to feel emotions that are "identical or very similar to what the other person is feeling or would be expected to feel" (p. 678). Batson and his colleagues have found that people display preferential treatment toward those with whom they sympathize. Specifically, sympathizers value the welfare of the persons in need (Batson, Turk, Shaw, & Klein, 1995) and allocate resources preferentially to targets of sympathy, even if these allocations violate principles of justice (Batson, Klein, Highberger, & Shaw, 1995).

From these considerations, it appears that targets of sympathetic responses are often the beneficiary of prosocial actions. When a person suffers, observers vicariously feel some of that suffering and may come to care deeply about the ultimate fate of the affected individual. But if the person faces a challenging situation over which observers have no control, they may be relegated to noting how the challenged person responds to the setback. For those challenged individuals who triumph over their setbacks, our sympathy and prosocial wishes for them can evolve into respect, admiration, and even adoration. If the setback is death itself, our sympathy can evolve into reverence and idealization. In short, negative outcomes experienced before or after one's tenure as leader can engender strong sympathetic responses and have a transforming, inspiring effect on followers.

In this chapter, we identify three types of individuals whose effectiveness as leaders derive from actions that elicit sympathetic responses from others. The first is an *underdog leader,* of which Mandela is a classic example. People sympathize with underdogs and admire those underdogs who defy expectations by overcoming significant obstacles. The second type of leader who attracts sympathy is a *deceased leader.* As in the case of Mel Carnahan, death invokes sorrowful responses and elevates the status of the deceased. The third type of leader who elicits sympathy is a *martyr,* who makes the ultimate sacrifice for a noble cause and whose appeal is derived from combined elements of both underdog and deceased leaders. We describe each of these three leader types in some detail below.

UNDERDOGS AS INSPIRATIONAL LEADERS

Success is to be measured not so much by the position that one has reached in life as by the obstacles which he has overcome.

—Booker T. Washington

Although most social psychological theory and research has focused on the human tendency to associate with winners and successful others (e.g., Cialdini et al., 1976), our recent research findings point to the opposite tendency, namely, the appeal of the underdog (Kim et al., in press; see also Vandello, Goldschmied, & Richards, 2007). Stories about underdogs seem to touch something deep in the human psyche (Spencer, 1873). People, animals, and even inanimate objects that face difficult challenges, against a strong opponent or a demanding situation, inspire our support. The publishers of the children's classic *The Little Engine That Could* (Piper, 1930) suggest that the phrase "I think I can" is as central to our collective culture as "I have a dream" and "One small step for man."

What are underdogs, and why might people sympathize with them? We define underdogs as social entities whose struggles engender sympathy with others (Kim et al., in press). The notion of struggle is central to the definition of an underdog; the struggle can be against either a difficult situation or a formidable opponent, which we define as the top dog. Across many cultures underdog stories abound. Many cultural narratives relate stories of people facing difficult challenges, such as King Sisyphus condemned in Hades to roll a stone toward the top of a hill for eternity. Similarly, "The American Dream" and the Horatio Alger stories of "rags to riches," embodied by individuals such as Andrew Carnegie, captivate our dreams to overcome the imposed limitations of underdog status (Scharnhorst, 1980). Cultural icons featured in films such as *Rocky, The Karate Kid, Erin Brockovich, Seabiscuit,* and *Million Dollar Baby* provide sympathetic and inspiring portrayals of successful underdogs. We believe that such narratives reflect an archetype of struggle, derived from the Jungian hero archetype (Jung, 1964), and that these archetypical narratives elicit sympathy and support. These heroic accomplishments of underdogs inspire us and may underscore our hope that the world can be a fair place in which all individuals have the potential to succeed.

Are underdog leaders more inspirational than top dog leaders? To answer this question, Allison and Heilborn (2007, Study 1) gave participants descriptions of business and political leaders and experimentally manipulated the biographical backgrounds of the leaders, with half the participants learning that the leaders endured an impoverished upbringing (underdog condition) and the other half learning that the leaders enjoyed an affluent upbringing (top dog condition). Although participants did not differ in their ratings of the basic competence of underdog and top dog leaders, they did differ significantly on measures of sympathy and inspiration. Specifically, participants reported that they sympathized more with underdog leaders than with top dog leaders, and that they liked and respected underdog leaders more than top dog leaders. In addition, participants were significantly more inspired by the underdog leaders, more motivated to work for underdog leaders, more inspired by the underdog leader's vision, and more convinced that the underdog leaders would achieve long-term success.

Allison and Heilborn (2007, Study 2) also asked a different group of 50 participants to generate lists of real-world underdog and top dog leaders. The five underdog leaders most frequently mentioned were Muhammad Ali (listed 27 times), Steve Jobs (24), Martin Luther King Jr. (23), Nelson Mandela (21), and Oprah Winfrey (17). The five top dog leaders most frequently mentioned were Bill Gates (28), George Steinbrenner (20), Donald Trump (20), George W. Bush (19), and Michael Bloomberg (12). These ten individuals were then rated by other participants on dimensions of sympathy, liking, respect, competence, and inspiration. The results showed that, compared to the group of top dog leaders, the group of underdog leaders were significantly more sympathized with, liked, respected, and inspiring.

Do all underdogs—leaders as well as nonleaders—inspire us? We have conducted several studies showing that people are significantly more likely to root for and sympathize with many types of underdog entities (e.g., teams, artists, and businesses) than they are to root for and sympathize with top dog entities (Kim et al., in press, Study 1). Most importantly, we found that people's sympathy for the underdog was the psychological mechanism responsible for this underdog effect (Study 3). It is noteworthy that increased sympathy and emotional support for the underdog does not translate into increased perceived competence for the underdog. We found that although people were more likely to root for an underdog artist than for a top dog artist in an upcoming competition, they judged the top dog artist's painting to be superior in quality to that of the underdog (Kim et al., Study 2). Importantly, we have found in a follow-up study that this negative view of the quality of underdogs' work may be limited to pre-outcome measures of quality. When people are asked to judge the quality of underdog and top dog work *after* the successful outcome of a competition, we discovered that people judge underdogs' work as superior to that of top dogs. These findings suggest that underdogs attract our sympathy but must prove themselves worthy of our admiration by triumphing over their obstacles.

One of our most revealing studies underscored the psychologically powerful effect of underdogs on human judgments (Kim et al., in press, Study 3). Employing a methodology reminiscent of that used by Heider and Simmel (1944), the study involved showing participants clips of animated shapes that appeared to chase or bump other shapes. Heider and Simmel's participants inferred causality from the movement of these shapes and also assigned dispositional attributes to the shapes as a result of their behavior toward each other. The beauty of Heider and Simmel's work is that it illustrated just how pervasive and natural the attribution process is, emerging in judgments of simple lifeless objects. We presented their participants with moving shapes

Figure 11-1 A geometric shape appearing to struggle to attain a goal

to determine whether people naturally bestow underdog status and under-dog qualities upon shapes that move more slowly than others. The study included four conditions: (1) a single nonstruggling geometric shape (see Figure 11-1); (2) a single struggling geometric shape; (3) a struggling geometric shape together with a benign nonstruggling shape; and (4) a struggling geometric shape together with a "malicious" nonstruggling shape that appeared to intentionally block the struggling shape (see Figure 11-2).

The results of this study showed that people showed more emotional support for a single struggling shape than for a single nonstruggling shape. This finding suggests that an entity's struggle, by itself, is enough to engender support, even when the entity is by itself. Kim et al. also found that the social context heightened participants' emotional support for the struggling entity, such that participants were especially likely to root for a struggling entity when paired with a nonstruggling one. Finally, the strongest underdog effect emerged when participants viewed a struggling shape whose progress toward achieving its apparent goal was overtly thwarted by a nonstruggling shape (Figure 11-2). Even more importantly, for the purposes of this chapter, Kim et al. found that participants were more likely to sympathize with the single struggling shape than with the single nonstruggling shape. Moreover,

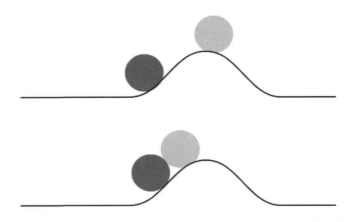

Figure 11-2 A struggling geometric shape's goal appearing to be thwarted by a nonstruggling shape

participants showed the greatest degree of sympathy for the struggling shape paired with the malicious circle that impeded the struggling shape's progress.

In summary, the results of several studies suggest that underdogs are viewed as highly respected and inspirational leaders. They derive their appeal from their ability to overcome difficult situations that attract our sympathy. Underdogs who prevail over their circumstances and later become leaders have earned our respect and support, and they are judged to be inspiring leaders.

THE DEAD AS INSPIRATIONAL LEADERS

Death openeth the gate to good fame.

—Francis Bacon

In June 2004, the death of former U.S. President Ronald Reagan triggered an outpouring of praise and admiration from former political allies and adversaries alike (Von Drehle, 2004). These tributes and adulations caught many anti-Reagan liberals by surprise (Troy, 2005). One study of media coverage of Reagan found that it was significantly more positive after his death than during his tenure as president (Lichter, 2004). The media were rarely kind to Reagan and his policies during his presidency, and yet the very same media posthumously showered him and his legacy with many accolades. In fact, a 2007 Gallup poll ranked him as second best all-time U.S. president, trailing only Abraham Lincoln (Polling Report, 2008). How has Reagan attracted more widespread respect in death than he was able to attract in life?

In several studies, we have found that people form more favorable impressions of dead leaders than of equivalent living leaders (Allison, Eylon, Beggan, & Bachelder, in press; Allison & Eylon, 2005; Eylon & Allison, 2005). This finding, moreover, emerges in evaluations of fictitious leaders as well as real-world leaders, and it emerges in judgments of competent as well as incompetent leaders. The results of these studies also show that positive judgments of the dead are significantly correlated with judgments of sympathy. Interestingly, the only condition we have been able to identify under which the death positivity bias does not appear is in evaluations of immoral leaders, who are judged *less* favorably after death than in life. We have proposed that the death of immoral individuals engenders far less sympathy than the death of moral individuals, thus leading to posthumous judgments that are less favorable for the immoral dead (Allison et al., in press).

We have called people's tendency to inflate their evaluations of the dead *the death positivity bias* (Allison et al., in press). The death positivity bias nicely explains why Reagan's posthumous media coverage was so positive, and why Carnahan was able to come from behind posthumously to defeat his opponent in Missouri's 2000 U.S. Senate election. Reagan's and Carnahan's deaths elicited sympathy and activated the norm of speaking only "well" of the dead. We have found that this norm may explain why press coverage of dead celebrity leaders, such as Princess Diana, John F. Kennedy Jr., and Tupac Shakur, is significantly more positive after death than before death (Allison et al., in press, Study 3). We speculate that the death of young leaders is especially likely to heighten death positivity biases. Moreover, death not only inflates our evaluations, it also makes them impervious to change, a phenomenon we call the *frozen in time effect* (Eylon & Allison, 2005).

Philosophers have long been keenly aware of this norm prescribing reverence for deceased individuals. For example, the great playwright Sophocles warned his audiences "not to insult the dead." Athenian statesman and legislator Solon echoed this sentiment when he implored citizens to "speak no ill of the dead." The eminent Greek historian Thucydides went beyond this simple admonition by observing that "all men are wont to praise him who is no more." In more modern times, American poet John Whittier noted that "death softens all resentments, and the consciousness of a common inheritance of frailty and weakness modifies the severity of judgment."

Our analysis of death positivity phenomena is consistent with the theoretical mechanisms implicated in terror management theory (Arndt, Greenberg, Schimel, Pyszczynski, & Solomon, 2002; Solomon, Cohen, Greenberg, & Pyszczynski, Chapter 3 of this volume). Terror management theory proposes that when people think about death, they experience terror and thus engage in worldview-validating behaviors aimed at reducing the terror. As Greenberg, Solomon, & Pyszczynski (1997) note, "Cultural worldviews ameliorate anxiety by imbuing the universe with order and meaning, by providing standards of value that are derived from that meaningful conception of reality, *and by promising protection and death transcendence* to those who meet those standards of value" (italics added, p. 65). In short, a person's cultural worldview allows behaviors deemed valuable to take on higher order meaning, providing the person with a means for achieving symbolic immortality (Arndt et al., 2002).

This tendency to support one's cultural worldview when thinking of death leads to a more favorable evaluation of those who uphold the values and norms of the worldview, and harsher judgments of those who violate the worldview (Rosenblatt, Greenberg, Solomon, Pyszczynski, & Lyon, 1989). Although terror management researchers have not yet investigated positivity biases in evaluations of dead targets, it seems reasonable that if a deceased target were a meaningful contributor to society—and hence affirmed the perceiver's worldview—then the perceiver may be motivated to form heightened posthumous appraisals of the deceased target. Following the tenets of TMT, when perceivers honor the dead, particularly dead leaders whose actions in life affirmed and validated the perceiver's cultural worldview, these enhanced evaluations may mitigate perceivers' own terror of death that arises from the sheer exposure to the thought of death. Honoring dead leaders who upheld the perceiver's worldview allows the perceiver to evoke the sense of security provided by adhering to the cherished principles of the cultural worldview. It may also serve to reduce peoples' fear of their own mortality by assuring them that they will be well regarded after their death.

Effective leaders have long been known to shape the values and emotions of those who follow (Dasborough, 2006), and the death positivity bias may represent one source of emotional connection between leaders and followers. To the extent that leaders embody the values of their groups or organizations, their deaths may inspire followers to create permanent positive remembrances of their leaders. These remembrances can take the form of statues, shrines, buildings, city and road names, epic stories, and visages on currency and stamps. Actions taken to honor dead leaders are consistent with the tenets of terror management theory and its emphasis on the impact of mortality salience in validating one's cultural worldview (Arndt et al., 2002). A great leader affirms the values of the group (Hogg, Chapter 4 in this volume), and when the leader passes away, followers may be motivated to ensure that these affirmations endure by elevating the status of the leader beyond that which existed when he or she was alive (Allison & Eylon, 2005).

MARTYRS AS INSPIRATIONAL LEADERS

The tyrant dies and his rule is over; the martyr dies and his rule begins.

—Soren Kierkegaard

Surprisingly, very little research has been conducted on the psychologically rich concept of martyrdom. We define martyrs as people who sacrifice their lives in support of a principle or cause. Droge and Tabor (1992) have outlined three defining characteristics of a martyr's death. First, the death usually occurs as a sign of persecution and is seen by similarly persecuted others as noble and heroic. Second, martyrs die with the notion that others will benefit as a result of their suffering. Third, martyrs make their sacrifice with the expectation of an eternal vindication, which is often their prime motivation.

Martyrdom has its roots in ancient Greek and Roman cultural values. Socrates, called the "saint and martyr of philosophy" by Gottlieb (2000), willingly accepted his death sentence and took his own life to uphold his belief system. The suicide of Socrates "has stood for 2400 years as a symbol of dying for one's principles" (DeSpelder & Strickland, 1996, p. 455). Greeks and Romans valued the idea of meeting death with both courage and acceptance. Romans revered both the bloody deaths in the gladiator arenas as well as intellectual suicides in the tradition of Socrates. The Roman belief system contained the idea that life "was a treasure that gained value or power only when expended" and that martyrdom "transformed weakness into power" (Cormack, 2001, p. 26).

In modern times, martyrdom is probably most often considered in the context of religious extremism, but this religious context also has ancient origins. Two thousand years ago, Christianity was metamorphosed from a peripheral offshoot of Judaism to a beleaguered underdog religious sect. Early Christians were put to death in great numbers for preaching their illegal faith to their fellow Roman citizens. This era of persecution spurred the growth of Christianity, as each publicly executed martyr attracted a new cult of converts. For early Christians, the suffering and death of Jesus held a "fatal attraction" (Kastenbaum, 2004, p. 62) and was a strong advertisement for a threatened faith. Paralleling the choice of martyrs, Jesus willingly chose his suffering and death, according to the Gospel of John (10:18): "No one takes my life, but I lay it down of my own accord." The redemptive value of suffering became part of the "Christian heroic ideal" (Cormack, 2001, p. 43). Martyrs did not just expect to be resurrected in the next life, but also for their memories to be resurrected for all of time. The unshakable determination of these early Christian martyrs shamed the Roman Empire's tactics of brutality, garnered sympathy for the Christian cause, and fueled the growth of Christianity.

Virtually all religions feature at least some history of martyrdom or suggestion of martyrdom in their belief systems. In Scripture there are numerous accounts of Jewish martyrs resisting the Hellenizing of their Seleucid overlords, being executed for such crimes as observing the Sabbath, circumcising their children, or refusing to eat pork or meat sacrificed to idols. In Hinduism, the term *sati* refers to a woman's act of immolating herself on the funeral pyre of her husband, as remaining alive after one's husband's death carries with it the feared social sanction of being "an alluring or lustful widow who might tarnish the family reputation" (Cormack, 2001, p. 120). Satis are venerated as martyrs for being those who "embody and affirm the truth" (Cormack, 2001, p. 119). The Islamic conceptualization of martyrdom delineates specific rewards for those who would die for their God; the Qur'an specifies that the Muslim martyr, or *shahid,* is spared the pain of death and receives immediate entry into paradise. Islam accepts a much broader view of what constitutes a martyr, including anyone who succumbs in territorial conflicts between Muslims and non-Muslims. There is widespread disagreement in the Muslim community about whether suicide bombers should be considered martyrs (Cormack, 2001).

Martyrs who die for their causes would appear to derive much of the sympathy and support they attract through mechanisms associated with the death positivity bias (Allison et al., in press). Moreover, from our review of the history of martyrdom, it appears that most martyrs embrace underdog causes. Indeed, a "top dog martyr" would seem to be an oxymoron, inasmuch as the desperation of dying for one's cause suggests a minority or underdog position under great siege. Thus martyrs may be especially powerful in attracting sympathy because they derive it from mechanisms implicated in people's responses to the sacrifice and suffering of underdogs and of the dead.

Witnessing others make extreme sacrifices appears to be psychologically powerful. A prominent example can be found in our evaluations of those who died in the terrorist attacks of September 11, 2001. Hundreds of firefighters, emergency rescue workers, and law enforcement personnel sacrificed their lives to save others from the World Trade Center. Although roughly 3,000 people perished in this tragedy, a disproportionate amount of media attention, and national mourning, focused on the loss of these emergency personnel. Their morally courageous and heroic actions at the time of their deaths sealed our impressions of them forever. Clearly, living emergency rescue workers have our great admiration, but our greatest veneration is reserved for individuals whose deaths occur in the performance of their moral, altruistic services.

We investigated martyrdom in the laboratory by asking participants to evaluate an individual who died while engaged in a fierce political fight against poverty. Half the participants learned that this individual was a financially disadvantaged person (underdog condition), whereas the other half learned that this individual was a financially advantaged person (top dog condition). Moreover, half these two groups of participants learned that this person took his own life for the cause he championed (suicide condition), whereas the other half learned that this person was killed by opponents of his cause (nonsuicide condition). The results revealed that the martyr who attracted the highest degree of sympathy and support was the underdog martyr whose death was caused by the opponents to his cause. Martyrs who took their own lives—whether underdog or top dog in status—were viewed the least sympathetically and received the weakest emotional support. The top dog martyr who died at the hands of his opponent was the recipient of a moderate amount of sympathy and support. As in our studies of the underdog - (e.g., Kim et al., in press), we found that sympathy judgments mediated the effects of underdog status on support judgments.

These findings suggest that martyrs can inspire others, but they also underscore an important boundary to the effect, namely, that (at least among our American participants) committing suicide to advance a cause is viewed as unacceptable regardless of underdog or top dog status. The most powerful martyrs are those whose deaths occur at the hands of their opponents, and these deaths are viewed especially sympathetically when the martyrs are underdogs. As noted above, this finding may be culture specific. For example, Palestinian suicide bombers have been treated like celebrities, their legacies cemented by community-wide celebrations, and their personal items coveted as objects of worship-like devotion (Israeli, 2003).

In summary, martyrdom has a long and storied history in human tales of sacrifice, heroism, and religious persecution. Martyrs inspire others, and their self-sacrificing actions often promote their causes so effectively that their beliefs can become a central part of their community's social identity. The death of a martyr can attract sympathy and support for the martyr's cause, but death by suicide is far less likely to tug on the heartstrings of western observers than death caused by opponents of the cause.

SUMMARY AND CONCLUDING COMMENTS

Next to love, sympathy is the divinest passion of the human heart.
—Edmund Burke

Leaders of all three types described in this chapter—underdogs, the dead, and martyrs—share in common the experience of great sacrifice and suffering. Underdogs face daunting challenges and must sacrifice their time, energy, and strength to overcome those challenges. Leaders who perish make the ultimate sacrifice, as do martyrs. We propose that the self-sacrificing actions of all three types of leaders cement these leaders' positive legacies to such a degree that their values become imbedded into their community's social identities. Borrowing a phrase from Aronson and Mills's (1959) classic study of cognitive dissonance, suffering does indeed lead to liking.

Our three types of leaders embody some of western society's most cherished values. Successful underdogs are a living testament to the puritan work ethic, and dead leaders and martyrs nourish our images of fallen heroes who sacrifice themselves for the greater good. Effective leadership and moral conduct are inextricably linked (Burns, 1978), and our analysis would seem to have several implications for promoting better and more responsible leadership. First, the death positivity bias would underscore the importance of leaders proactively engaging in activities aimed at validating the moral values of the group or organization. A leader's moral conduct may be a more central determinant of perceived leadership effectiveness than other, more traditional, criteria for evaluating leadership (Allison & Eylon, 2005). A second implication of the death positivity bias is that enhanced posthumous evaluations of a leader may influence employee attitudes and behavior in the workplace long after the leader has passed away. Leadership has long been known to shape the values and performance of those who follow (Gardner, 1995), and moral leadership posthumously inspires followers. A third implication of the death positivity bias is that it suggests strategies for leaders to craft constructive posthumous legacies for themselves and for their organizations (Allison, Eylon, & Markus, 2004). Although firms and individuals work hard at building reputations, it is clear that the focus needs to be on long-term meaningful issues (e.g., morality) that will eventually elicit respect and sympathy from followers.

We would like to end this chapter on a cautionary note. Although the resounding message from the research reported here points to the propensity of sympathetic figures to attract emotional support and adulation, there is the possibility that these responses to sympathetic leaders have a fragile quality. As we have noted, Kim et al. (in press) did find that people show strong emotional support for underdogs, but Kim et al.'s Study 4 demonstrated that under certain conditions people's emotional support did not translate into *behavioral* support. Specifically, when the outcome of a competition had important consequences for perceivers, the top dog received significantly more tangible, monetary support than did the underdog. Only when the outcome had no effect on perceivers did perceivers' emotional connection to the underdog translate into increased behavioral assistance to the underdog. Leaders should take note that suffering may lead to liking, but it does not always lead to unconditional following.

REFERENCES

Allison, S. T., & Eylon, D. (2005). The demise of leadership: Death positivity biases in posthumous impressions of leaders. In D. Messick & R. Kramer (Eds.), *The psychology of leadership: Some new approaches* (pp. 295–317). New York: Erlbaum.

Allison, S. T., Eylon, D., Beggan, J. K., & Bachelder, J. (in press). The demise of leadership: Positivity and negativity in evaluations of dead leaders. *The Leadership Quarterly.*

Allison, S. T., Eylon, D., & Markus, M. (2004). Leadership legacy. In J. M. Burns, G. R. Goethals, & G. Sorenson (Eds.), *The encyclopedia of leadership* (pp. 894–898). New York: Berkshire Publishing.

Allison, S. T., & Heilborn, J. (2007). *The smaller they come, the better they lead: Underdogs as inspirational leaders.* Unpublished manuscript, University of Richmond.

Arndt, J., Greenberg, J., Schimel, J., Pyszczynski, T., & Solomon, S. (2002). To belong or not to belong, that is the question: Terror management and identification with gender and ethnicity. *Journal of Personality and Social Psychology, 83,* 26–43.

Aronson, E., & Mills, J. (1959). The effect of severity of initiation on liking for a group. *Journal of Abnormal and Social Psychology, 59,* 177–181.

Avolio, B. J., & Yammarino, F. J. (2002). *Transformational and charismatic leadership: The road ahead.* Oxford, UK: Elsevier Science.

Batson, C. D., Klein, T. R., Highberger, L., & Shaw, L. (1995). Immorality from empathy-induced altruism: When compassion and justice conflict. *Journal of Personality and Social Psychology, 68,* 1042–1054.

Batson, C. D., Turk, C. L., Shaw, L., & Klein, T. R. (1995). Information function of empathic emotion: Learning that we value the other's welfare. *Journal of Personality and Social Psychology, 68,* 300–313.

Burns, J. M. (1978). *Leadership.* New York: Harper & Row.

Cialdini, R. B., Borden, R. J., Thorne, R. J., Walker, M. R., Freeman, S., & Sloan, L. R. (1976). Basking in reflected glory: Three football field studies. *Journal of personality and social psychology, 34,* 366–375.

Cormack, M. (2001). *Sacrificing the self: Perspectives on martyrdom and religion.* Oxford: University Press.

Dasborough, M. T. (2006). Cognitive asymmetry in employee emotional reactions to leadership behaviors. *The Leadership Quarterly, 17,* 163–178.

DeSpelder, L. A., & Strickland, A. L. (1996). *The last dance: Encountering death and dying.* California: Mayfield Publishing.

Droge, A., & Tabor, J. (1992). *A noble death.* San Francisco: Harper Publishing.

Eden, D. (1990). *Pygmalion in management: Productivity as a self-fulfilling prophecy.* Lexington, MA: Lexington Books.

Eisenberg, N. (2004). Empathy and sympathy. In M. Lewis & J. M. Haviland-Jones (Eds.), *Handbook of emotions* (pp. 677–691). New York: The Guilford Press.

Eylon, D., & Allison, S. T. (2005). The frozen in time effect in evaluations of the dead. *Personality and Social Psychology Bulletin, 31,* 1708–1717.

Gardner, H. (1995). *Leading minds: An anatomy of leadership.* New York: Basic.

Gottlieb, A. (2000). *The dream of reason.* New York: W. W. Norton.

Greenberg, J., Solomon, S., & Pyszczynski, T. (1997). Terror management theory of self-esteem and cultural worldviews: Empirical assessments and conceptual refinements. In M. Zanna (Ed.), *Advances in Experimental Social Psychology* (Vol. 29, pp. 61–139). San Diego: Academic Press.

Heider, F., & Simmel, M. (1944). An experimental study of apparent behavior. *American Journal of Psychology, 57,* 243–259.

House, R. J., & Howell, J. M. (1992). Personality and charismatic leadership. *Leadership Quarterly, 3,* 81–108.

House, R. J., & Shamir, B. (1993). Toward the integration of charismatic, visionary, and transformational leadership theories. In M. M. Chemers & R. Ryman (Eds.), *Leadership theory and research: Perspectives and directions* (pp. 81–107). San Diego: Academic Press.

Israeli, R. (2003). *Islamikaze: Manifestations of Islamic martyrology.* London: Frank Cass.

Jung, C. G. (1964). *Man and his symbols.* New York: Doubleday.

Kastenbaum, R. (2004). *On our way: The final passage through life and death.* Berkeley: University of California Press.

Kim, J., Allison, S. T., Eylon, D., Goethals, G., Markus, M., McGuire, H., & Hindle, S. (in press). Rooting for (and then abandoning) the underdog. *Journal of Applied Social Psychology.*

Lichter, S. R. (2004). *Press praised Reagan only after death.* Retrieved July 15, 2007, from the Center for Media and Public Affairs Web site, http://www.cmpa.com/pressReleases/StudyFindsPressPraise ReaganOnlyAfterDeath.htm

Mumford, M. D., & Strange, J. M. (2002). Vision and mental models: The case of charismatic and ideological leadership. In B. Avolio & F. Yammarino (Eds.), *Transformational and charismatic leadership: The road ahead* (pp. 109–142). Oxford, UK: Elsevier Science.

Nadler, D. A. (1988). Organizational frame bending: Types of change in the complex organization. In R. Kilmann & T. Covin (Eds.), *Corporate transformation: Revitalizing organizations for a competitive world* (pp. 66–83). San Francisco: Jossey-Bass.

Piper, W. (1930). *The little engine that could.* New York: Platt & Munk.

Polling Report. (2008). *Presidents and history.* Retrieved January 8, 2008, from the Polling Report Web site, http://www.pollingreport.com/wh-hstry.htm

Raelin, J. A. (1989). An anatomy of autonomy: Managing professionals. *Academy of Management Executive, 3,* 216–228.

Riggio, R. E., & Conger, J. A. (2005). Getting it right. The practice of leadership. In J. Conger & R. Riggio (Eds.), *The practice of leadership: Developing the next generation of leaders* (pp. 331–344). San Francisco: Jossey-Bass.

Rosenblatt, A., Greenberg, J., Solomon, S., Pyszczynski, T., & Lyon, D. (1989). Evidence for terror management theory I: The effects of mortality salience on reactions to those who violate or uphold cultural values. *Journal of Personality and Social Psychology, 57,* 681–690.

Scharnhorst, G. (1980). *Horatio Alger, Jr.* Boston: Twayne Publishers.

Shamir, B. (1991). The charismatic relationship: Alternative explanations and predictions. *Leadership Quarterly, 2,* 81–104.

Spencer, H. (1873). *The principles of psychology* (Vol. 2). New York: Appleton.

Troy, G. (2005). *Legacy of Ronald Reagan* (#62462). Retrieved July 15, 2007, from the History News Network Web site, http://hnn.us/readcomment.php?id=62462#62462

Vandello, J. A., Goldschmied, N. P., & Richards, D. A. R. (2007). The appeal of the underdog. *Personality and Social Psychology Bulletin, 33,* 1603–1616.

Von Drehle, D. (2004, June 5). Ronald Reagan dies. *Washington Post.* Retrieved July 15, 2007, from http://www.washingtonpost.com/wp-dyn/articles/A18566-2004Jun5.html

Yukl, G. (2006). *Leadership in organizations.* Upper Saddle River, NJ: Prentice-Hall.

PART III

WHAT LEADERS DO

12

Persuasion and Leadership

JAMES M. OLSON AND GRAEME A. HAYNES

In this chapter, we discuss the implications of social psychological research on persuasion for leaders. For example, how can leaders maximize their influence in a group? How can they successfully convince people to follow recommended courses of action? We address these questions by analyzing the effectiveness of former Vice President Al Gore in the film *An Inconvenient Truth*. What characteristics of the film and of Gore account for the persuasiveness of his message? We show that research findings on persuasion illuminate some of the mechanisms through which *An Inconvenient Truth* changes viewers' beliefs and attitudes. We begin our analysis by differentiating between two types of persuasion, one based on strong arguments and one based on cues that imply the position is correct. We then discuss some of the source characteristics that influence the persuasive impact of a communication, including the source's credibility and presentational style, as well as some of the message characteristics that influence persuasive impact, including the explicit drawing of conclusions and the elicitation of a state known as "protection motivation." In the final section of the chapter, we offer some concrete suggestions for leaders who want to persuade and influence group members.

In the documentary film *An Inconvenient Truth* (Bender, Burns, David, Skoll, & Guggenheim, 2006), former U.S. Vice President Al Gore presents evidence to support the claims that global warming is a serious threat to humanity and that such warming is caused in large part by human activities. The film has been enormously successful (it grossed about $50 million at the box office) and very influential, persuading many viewers to learn more about the issue and even to change their behavior to reduce greenhouse gas emissions. Not surprisingly, the film has been more favorably received by Democrats than Republicans in the United States; for example, a survey in December 2006 showed that 82 percent of Democrats supported legislation that would set limits for greenhouse gas emissions, whereas 61 percent of Republicans supported such legislation. There has also been some controversy about Gore's arguments and data (e.g., the critical documentary *The Great Global Warming Swindle*, Durkin, 2007), but no one can dispute the impact of the film. Indeed, in October 2007, Gore was awarded the Nobel Peace Prize for his role in bringing the issue of global warming into the international spotlight.

Our goal in this chapter is to discuss the implications of social psychological research on persuasion for leaders. For example, how can leaders maximize their influence in a group? How can they successfully convince people to follow recommended courses of action? We will address these questions by analyzing the effectiveness of *An Inconvenient Truth*. What characteristics of the film and of Gore account for the persuasiveness of the message? (Gore's effectiveness is particularly interesting given his prior reputation as a wooden speaker.) We will argue that research findings on persuasion illuminate some of the mechanisms through which *An Inconvenient Truth* changes viewers' beliefs and attitudes.

We will begin by defining some of the key concepts that we will discuss. Social psychologists define *attitudes* as individuals' evaluations (good-bad judgments) of a target (Zanna & Rempel, 1988). For example, an individual's attitude toward global warming is the judgment that global warming is bad or good (and the extremity of that evaluative judgment). Social psychologists define *beliefs* as individuals' cognitive links between an attribute and a target (Fishbein & Ajzen, 1975). That is, beliefs represent the characteristics or features that an individual associates with a target. For example, an individual's beliefs about global warming are the associations that come to mind when he or she thinks about global warming, such as hotter temperatures, rising sea levels, more frequent hurricanes, air pollution, and so on. Attitudes and beliefs are related constructs; indeed, attitudes are often based on beliefs (e.g., an unfavorable evaluation of global warming based on such perceived negative consequences as rising sea levels and air pollution). In the remainder of this chapter, we use the term *persuasion* to refer to changes in either attitudes or beliefs in response to a message. We do not differentiate between changing attitudes and changing beliefs because the distinction does not matter to most people attempting influence (e.g., leaders), so long as the message is accepted and the recommendations are embraced. Moreover, techniques that facilitate a change in attitudes also facilitate a change in beliefs.

We will begin our analysis by differentiating between two types of persuasion. We will then discuss some of the features of messages and sources that

influence the persuasive impact of a communication. In both sections, we will apply the theoretical concepts to *An Inconvenient Truth,* treating Al Gore as a model for leaders whose goal is to persuade. We close the chapter with a more general summary of the implications of these findings for leaders.

TWO TYPES OF PERSUASION

When laypersons think about *persuasion,* they normally imagine changes in attitudes or beliefs that result from a convincing message. That is, most people think of persuasion as involving a written or oral communication that contains strong arguments, which then elicit favorable thoughts and agreement based on rational analysis. Although such persuasion is common, social psychologists have also identified a second type of persuasion that is not as rational or argument-based. Specifically, people sometimes adopt an attitude or accept the recommendations of a message simply because there are cues or features that imply the position is correct. This type of influence occurs when we read a newspaper article in which a new car model is favorably evaluated by an auto expert. We do not question the evaluation or scrutinize the evidence offered in the article (unless, perhaps, we happen to be looking for a car). The expert is a person who knows about cars, and that is that. This is also the type of influence that can be exerted by someone we admire or like. For example, when a popular singer endorses a product, fans may purchase the product simply because they identify with the singer.

These two "types" of persuasion—one based on strong arguments and one based on cues that imply the position is correct—have been integrated by Petty and Cacioppo (1986) in the *elaboration likelihood model* (see also Chaiken's 1980 *systematic-heuristic model*). The elaboration likelihood model is probably the most influential theory of persuasion today. It has been tested in many studies and applied to many persuasion domains (for a review, see Petty & Wegener, 1998).

The elaboration likelihood model distinguishes between two "routes" to persuasion. The *central route* refers to persuasion that is based on information and strong arguments. The *peripheral route* refers to persuasion that is based on simple cues and assumptions (e.g., the car reviewer is an expert). Persuasion that occurs via the central route is effortful because the person must pay attention to the message and think carefully about the arguments. Therefore, to conserve psychological resources, the central route is useful primarily when the issue is important or personally relevant to the individual. The peripheral route involves less effort, so people are likely to use it when the issue is not as important. When attitude change results from central processing, it is more likely to be long-lasting and to affect behavior than when attitude change results from peripheral processing.

Petty and Cacioppo hypothesized that the rational, argument-based type of attitude change (central route) will occur only when an individual is *both* (1) motivated to engage in the necessary thinking *and* (2) capable of understanding the arguments. For example, the issue must be at least somewhat important to the individual (to motivate him or her to exert the effort to think carefully), and the arguments must be simple enough and presented clearly enough that the individual is able to understand them. If either requirement is missing, then the peripheral route is the only avenue by which persuasion can occur.

Numerous researchers have documented both central route persuasion and peripheral route persuasion in the same study. Typically, these researchers have shown that the strength of the arguments in a message is very influential when recipients are motivated to listen and the arguments are clear, but if recipients are not interested in the topic or cannot understand the arguments, then persuasion occurs only when there is a cue implying that the message is valid, such as a highly credible source.

For example, Hafer, Reynolds, and Obertynski (1996) conducted a study in St. Catharines, Ontario, Canada, that presented participants with a persuasive message on *plea bargaining* (which occurs when an accused person pleads guilty in return for a reduced charge). At the time the study was conducted, a well-publicized case of plea bargaining had recently occurred in St. Catharines, involving an individual who was implicated in the murder of two teenage girls but received a relatively short sentence in return for testifying against another defendant. This deal was widely criticized for being too lenient. Thus, the issue of plea bargaining was salient to participants, and their preexisting attitudes were probably unfavorable.

Participants listened to a taped message that presented either five strong or five weak arguments in favor of plea bargaining. Within each message, all of the arguments were either stated clearly (e.g., "There is often an overly long time period before a case comes to trial. Plea bargaining can help to cut down on this waiting period") or in complex and hard-to-understand language (e.g., "Plea bargaining can facilitate the avoidance of trial delays of unacceptable magnitude"). Finally, the source of the message was either an expert judge who was a graduate of Harvard Law School (high credibility) or a second-year law student (low credibility).

The researchers predicted that all participants would be highly motivated to process the message (due to the salience of the issue), but that those who read a complex message would have trouble understanding it. (Consistent with this reasoning, a memory test taken at the end of the study showed that participants who read a hard-to-understand message recalled less information than participants who read a clear message.) How were these messages expected to affect attitudes toward plea bargaining? When the message was clear and comprehensible, strong arguments were expected to persuade more effectively than weak arguments, and source credibility was not expected to make much difference. But when the message was difficult to understand, strong versus weak arguments were not expected to matter, whereas participants would be persuaded more by the high credibility source than by the low credibility source. Results on the attitude measure supported these predictions. Thus, persuasion occurred via the central route when the arguments were clear but via the peripheral route when they were not.

How does the distinction between central and peripheral routes to persuasion apply to *An Inconvenient Truth*? Most people who see the film are probably highly motivated by the issue of global warming because they or their children, or both, are likely to be personally affected. Thus, most viewers engage the central route while watching the film. Gore presents many arguments, often accompanied by graphs and dramatic photos. These arguments are generally comprehensible and compelling, especially because most viewers lack specific knowledge to counterargue Gore's claims. Therefore, the film is very effective in producing persuasion via the central route.

But *An Inconvenient Truth* is skillful because it also includes many cues that imply the validity of the conclusions, which facilitate persuasion via the peripheral route. Perhaps the most important cue for peripheral persuasion is source credibility (see Eagly, Wood, & Chaiken, 1978). Credibility consists of two principal components: expertise (e.g., knowledge, experience) and trustworthiness (e.g., honesty, no ulterior motives). Al Gore is a former vice president who is clearly intelligent and articulate. His self-deprecating humor early in the film increases his perceived trustworthiness. Most of the scientists cited in the film are authoritative and associated with prestigious universities. All of these cues of source credibility induce viewers to accept the conclusions as valid. Also, the movie is long and includes numerous statistics; people sometimes infer that a message is valid simply because it is long, based on the reasoning that at least some of the arguments must be valid (see Petty & Cacioppo, 1984).

Thus, Gore covers all the bases in *An Inconvenient Truth*. He presents strong, compelling arguments on an issue that is highly motivating for most viewers, and his status and intelligence serve as cues implying validity for those viewers who are either not motivated or unable to understand the persuasive information. The significant impact of the film may be attributable to its effective intermixing of these substantive and stylistic factors.

SOURCE CHARACTERISTICS THAT INCREASE PERSUASIVENESS

Some people are more persuasive than others. Having strong, compelling arguments for one's position is paramount, of course, but what additional, noncontent characteristics of the source of a message are associated with greater persuasiveness? In this section, we will summarize some of the social psychological research that has investigated source variables (for reviews, see Johnson, Maio, & Smith-McLallen, 2005; Perloff, 2003; Petty & Wegener, 1998) and consider their applicability to Gore's role as leader and advocate in *An Inconvenient Truth*.

We mentioned credibility in the previous section as one important source variable. Other source characteristics that have been studied include likability, attractiveness, similarity (to the recipients of the message), and power. Not surprisingly, likable, attractive, similar, and powerful sources are generally more influential than dislikable, unattractive, dissimilar, and weak sources—especially in the context of persuasion via the peripheral route, such as when the issue is not important to the recipient of the message (see Petty & Wegener, 1998). Although these factors all facilitate persuasion, they probably do so by different psychological mechanisms. For example, Kelman (1958) distinguished between *internalization, identification,* and *compliance.* Internalization represents true, enduring persuasion, wherein the recipients conclude that the message content is valid. Source credibility often facilitates internalization. Identification occurs when the recipients accept the message's recommendations because they admire or want to establish a relationship with the source. The acceptance is genuine, but it does not necessarily reflect belief in the veridicality of the arguments. Likable, attractive, and similar sources may often facilitate identification. Finally, compliance occurs when the recipient endorses the message publicly but not privately. Powerful sources may often produce compliance.

How do these source characteristics apply to *An Inconvenient Truth?* Al Gore is an ideal presenter of the film's content. We have already noted that his intelligence, articulateness, and status give him credibility. His humor and likability heighten his attractiveness. His casual, friendly style and frequent references to family engender feelings of similarity in viewers. Finally, his position as a famous politician increases viewers' admiration and gives him additional credibility as a powerful, influential person. Gore's success at eliciting simultaneous perceptions of authority, honesty, and likability serves as a model for leaders aiming to influence their followers.

There is one final source characteristic we want to discuss, which relates to presentational style. Charismatic, persuasive individuals often have distinct speech styles, which make them appear more self-confident and well-informed than other communicators. What features of their speeches create these impressions? Perhaps the most important feature of speech is the extent to which it is "powerless" or "powerful" (Erickson, Lind, Johnson, & O'Barr, 1978; Hosman, 1989). *Powerless speech* contains sounds, words, or phrases that communicate uncertainty, lack of knowledge, or low status. For example, statements such as "I haven't thought about this a lot, but. . ." and "You probably know more about this than I do, but. . ." (often called *disclaimers*) suggest that the speaker's comments are preliminary and may not be valid. Similarly, phrases such as "I guess" and "maybe" (often called *hedges*) indicate a lack of confidence and imply that the speaker is uncertain about the accuracy of his or her comments. Also, *speech hesitations* such as "uh" and "well" indicate nervousness and perhaps even attempted deception. Finally, *polite forms* such as "Please consider. . ." and "Thank you for your attention. . ." imply low status, as well as possible uncertainty. In contrast to powerless speech, *powerful speech* does not include these features and gives the impression of credibility, expertise, self-confidence, honesty, and high status.

Many studies have tested the impact of powerless versus powerful speech. For example, Erickson et al. (1978) investigated the impact of powerless versus powerful speech in a simulated courtroom setting. Participants were given some background information about a civil damages trial and then either read a written transcript or listened to an audiotape of the testimony of a witness. The content of the witness's testimony was taken from a real trial. The witness supported the person who was suing the defendant for damages, so if the witness was credible and influential, then participants should have awarded larger damages to the plaintiff. The witness adopted either a powerless or powerful style of speech. For example, in response to the question "Approximately how long did you stay there before the ambulance arrived?" the witness who used powerless speech said: "Oh, it seems like it was about, uh, twenty minutes. Just long enough to help my friend Mrs. Davis, you know, get straightened out." The witness who used powerful speech responded to the same question by saying: "Twenty minutes. Long enough to help get Mrs. Davis straightened out." In response to another question, the witness using powerless speech said, "Yes, I guess I do," whereas the powerful speech witness simply said, "Yes."

After reading the background information and then reading or listening to testimony, participants rated the credibility of the witness and estimated the amount of damages, if any, that should be awarded to the plaintiff. Analyses of these measures showed that the powerless/powerful speech manipulation had a significant impact. Participants rated the witness who used powerful (versus powerless) speech as more credible, and participants awarded larger values to the plaintiff when the witness used powerful (versus powerless) speech.

In *An Inconvenient Truth,* Gore consistently employs a powerful speech style. He avoids hedges and hesitations, and speaks clearly and confidently without disclaimers. Of course, a recorded speech allows editing and consequent elimination of verbal miscues. Nonetheless, Gore's presentational style is excellent.

MESSAGE CHARACTERISTICS THAT INCREASE PERSUASIVENESS

Some messages are more persuasive than others. Once again, the inclusion of strong arguments to support one's points constitutes the foremost quality of influential messages, but social psychologists have also identified other features of effective messages (for reviews, see Johnson et al., 2005; Perloff, 2003; Petty & Wegener, 1998). In this section, we will review some of this work and consider the implications for Gore and *An Inconvenient Truth*.

One factor relates to whether messages should include an explicit statement of conclusions. Researchers have compared messages in which conclusions are explicitly stated versus messages in which conclusions are not stated (with the hope that recipients will draw the conclusions themselves, which might increase the impact of the conclusions). For example, a speaker who presents information on crime rates and wants the audience to conclude that more police should be hired can either state the recommendation explicitly or hope that the audience will make this inference on their own. O'Keefe (1997) identified past studies on this issue and conducted a "meta-analysis" of the findings—a technique that combines the results of many studies and tests whether the overall pattern is significant. O'Keefe's meta-analysis showed that explicit conclusions are generally more persuasive than unstated or implicit conclusions. Presumably, explicit conclusions leave no doubt about the implications of the speaker's arguments, whereas at least some recipients are unlikely to draw those conclusions on their own.

A second factor involves the one-sided versus two-sided nature of the message. Given that there are almost always two sides to important issues, should a speaker who is arguing for one side acknowledge both sides in the message, or should he or she mention only the preferred side? Further, if the speaker mentions both sides, should the other side be explicitly refuted or simply stated? For example, a speaker who argues in favor of reducing tuition at a college can choose to present a one-sided message, mention that some people support higher tuition but say little else, or state that some people support higher tuition but then refute the arguments for that side. In a meta-analysis of the literature, Allen (1991) concluded that two-sided messages that refute the other side are most effective; interestingly, two-sided messages that simply state the other side without any refutation are actually less persuasive than one-sided messages. Presumably, a two-sided message that refutes the other side shows both that the speaker is well-informed about the issue (e.g., knows there are two sides) and that the arguments for the opposing side are weak. Two-sided messages may also be effective because they show that the speaker is honest and is not trying to hide the opposing side.

A third factor relates to the use of metaphors in a message. Metaphors are comparisons or connections drawn between two objects, implying that the objects are conceptually similar. For example, referring to a person as "a snake in the grass" implies that he or she may be sneaky, dangerous, and ready to strike unexpectedly. Researchers have tested whether the use of metaphors influences the effectiveness of messages. On the one hand, metaphors are colorful, might increase attention, and can clarify or organize the main points in the message. On the other hand, metaphors can be subtle and potentially confusing. Sopory and Dillard (2002) conducted a meta-analysis of research on metaphors, which revealed that metaphors generally increase the effectiveness of persuasive messages. Metaphors are usually vivid and interesting (e.g., "he has the heart of a lion"), thus increasing attention while also helping the recipient to organize and understand the arguments in a message.

The final factor we want to discuss in this section concerns the use of threat or fear in a message to motivate attitude and behavior change. Social psychologists have long been interested in the effectiveness of threatening messages, but early research on fear appeals yielded inconsistent results (see McGuire, 1969). Fortunately, order was imposed on the literature by Rogers (1983) in his *protection motivation theory.* Rogers hypothesized that in order for a threatening message to be effective, it must create four beliefs or perceptions in the recipient: (1) the problem is *severe,* (2) the recipient is *susceptible* to the problem, (3) the recommended actions will be *effective* in avoiding the problem, and (4) the recipient is *personally capable* of performing the recommended actions. If these four beliefs are created, then the individual will feel motivated to protect himself or herself.

Many researchers have tested protection motivation theory by manipulating some of the critical beliefs and then measuring participants' attitudes toward the recommended actions and/or their intentions to perform the actions. These studies have generally supported the model. For example, Das, de Wit, and Stroebe (2003) manipulated the first two perceptions listed above: severity and susceptibility. Participants read an article about the health implications of stress. In the low severity condition, the article stated that stress can cause a variety of relatively mild consequences, such as fevers and cold hands. In the high severity condition, the article stated that stress can cause a variety of serious consequences, such as heart disease and ulcers. Next, participants were told that a new scale had recently been developed to measure people's susceptibility to developing stress-related health problems in the future. Participants then completed this alleged stress susceptibility scale, after which they were told that their future risk of developing stress-related illnesses was either low (low susceptibility condition) or quite high (high susceptibility condition).

All participants then read a fictitious letter that had allegedly been submitted to an American health journal, which described stress management training as an effective way to reduce the risk of stress-related illnesses. Finally, participants rated their attitude toward stress management training (e.g., the extent to which they thought stress management training was useful, important, and positive) and were asked whether they would like to receive more information about stress management training (yes or no).

Results showed that participants' attitudes were least favorable toward stress management training when both severity and susceptibility were low. That is, when participants learned that stress has only mild consequences and they were not personally susceptible, they did not rate stress management training as highly useful or important. In contrast, when either severity or susceptibility was high (the other three conditions), participants' attitudes toward stress management training were more favorable. The results on participants' requests for more information on stress management training showed the same pattern. In the "low severity/low susceptibility" condition, only 25 percent of the participants requested additional information, whereas the other three conditions yielded an average of 60 percent who requested additional information.

We have identified four characteristics of effective messages: they state conclusions explicitly; they mention both sides of the issue but refute the nonpreferred side; they use metaphors; and they generate four beliefs to arouse protection motivation. Does Al Gore employ these techniques in *An Inconvenient Truth?* The short answer is yes. The longer answer follows.

First, Gore is explicit about the consequences of global warming and the actions that must be taken to combat the problem. He presents graphs and photos to underscore the urgency of corrective actions. In short, he leaves very little to the imagination of the audience. Second, Gore both mentions and refutes the other side of the issue. Regarding the claim that scientists are divided on the issue, Gore counters with evidence suggesting that there is near unanimity in the scientific community. Regarding the argument that combating global warming will damage the economy, Gore states that new technologies will soften the economic consequences. Third, Gore uses numerous metaphors in his presentation. For example, he calls the Arctic region "a canary in a coal mine" to imply that current changes in the Arctic are early signs of danger and must be taken seriously. He also tells the story of his father's difficult decision to stop growing tobacco after his sister Nancy died of lung cancer. It is understood that this decision serves as a metaphor for the current choices facing the world with regard to global warming.

Finally, Gore's message on global warming effectively targets the beliefs identified as crucial by protection motivation theory. His graphs, photographs, and commentary support each of the four perceptions: if unchecked, global warming will have devastating consequences (it is a serious problem); global warming is happening now (the world is susceptible); there are things we can do to significantly reduce and even halt global warming (the recommendations will be effective at solving the problem); and small, individual actions to reduce greenhouse gas emissions will ultimately make the difference (individuals can perform the recommended actions). Together, these perceptions arouse protection motivation: viewers often leave the theatre shaken by the realization of the severity of the global warming problem but also energized to reduce their own CO_2 emissions.

PERSUASION AND LEADERSHIP

We have reviewed diverse social psychological research on persuasion and used these findings to explain Gore's effectiveness in the documentary *An Inconvenient Truth*. Gore uses persuasion techniques skillfully to maximize the impact of the film's message. In this final section of the chapter, we will briefly consider the implications of the reviewed research for other leaders who want to persuade and influence group members.

First, we should note that leaders vary a great deal in their oratorical skills, charisma, and self-confidence. They also vary in the nature of their leadership role. Some have considerable power over group members, whereas others are weak; some are popular with their subordinates, whereas others are disliked; and some are experienced in the role, whereas others are new. These differences affect leaders' abilities to employ specific persuasion techniques, so the following comments are meant as general guides to be adapted for particular leaders and groups.

The first point is that strong arguments are the best, most surefire way to persuade. When clear, cogent reasoning supports a leader's recommendations, persuasive success is likely. This point is particularly true when recipients of the message are motivated and able to process information carefully, such as when the issue is personally relevant (which probably encompasses most instances of leaders influencing group members). Recommending that leaders have strong arguments to support their conclusions may not be particularly helpful, however, because all of us strive to be convincing when possible, and sometimes strong arguments are simply lacking. Nevertheless, leaders may underestimate the importance of presenting strong arguments, assuming instead (sometimes wrongly) that group members will accept their conclusions at face value and implement their decisions with alacrity.

A second point is that leaders can exploit cues that lend credibility to the message, such as their own leadership expertise and authority. When group members are not processing the message carefully (due to low motivation or low ability), credibility cues can induce acceptance of the recommendations via the peripheral route. It may also be possible to emphasize features of the message (rather than the leader) that give it additional weight, such as its long developmental history or the fact that input was received from various experts.

Leaders are also more likely to have persuasive success if they are liked and perceived as similar. Although these qualities cannot be achieved by all leaders, they can be cultivated over time. Of course, likability and similarity can have benefits beyond increasing the leader's persuasive impact, such as improving group morale and cohesiveness.

Charismatic speakers often speak clearly and confidently, communicating their ideas with poise and self-assurance. One key aspect of such communication is powerful rather than powerless speech. In general, leaders should strive to avoid disclaimers, hedges, and hesitations in their written and oral presentations. They should speak clearly and succinctly, without apologies or other polite forms of speech. Powerful speech not only increases persuasiveness, but also enhances perceived competence and attractiveness (e.g., Holtgraves & Lasky, 1999), which are themselves desirable traits for leaders to possess (or to be seen as possessing).

Leaders can build certain features into messages to enhance persuasion. For example, explicit conclusions should typically be drawn for the audience. Two-sided messages including a refutation of the nonpreferred side should be employed when possible. And metaphors can be used occasionally, so long as they are clear in meaning and implication.

Finally, when the domain of influence involves self-protective actions (e.g., health behaviors, job security), leaders should aim to create the beliefs identified as critical by protection motivation theory. Recipients must perceive that the problem is serious, that they, the group, or both are susceptible, that recommended actions will effectively deal with the problem, and that they are personally capable of performing the recommended actions. Leaders can use these four perceptions as a framework for creating persuasive messages.

Research on attitudes and persuasion has been abundant in social psychology. There is now a growing literature that can be accessed for practical advice on both being persuasive and resisting persuasion. By definition, leaders must influence other people (lead them). Therefore, leaders can benefit from the knowledge that social psychologists have gathered on effective persuasion techniques. Al Gore's success in *An Inconvenient Truth* provides a real-life demonstration that these techniques work.

REFERENCES

Allen, M. (1991). Meta-analysis comparing the persuasiveness of one-sided and two-sided messages. *Western Journal of Speech Communication, 55,* 390–404.

Bender, L. (Producer), Burns, S. (Producer), David, L. (Producer), Skoll, J. (Producer), & Guggenheim, D. (Producer/Director). (2006). *An inconvenient truth* [Motion picture]. United States: Lawrence Bender Productions.

Chaiken, S. (1980). Heuristic versus systematic processing and the use of source versus message cues in persuasion. *Journal of Personality and Social Psychology, 39,* 752–766.

Das, E. H. H. J., de Wit, J. B. F., & Stroebe, W. (2003). Fear appeals motivate acceptance of action recommendations: Evidence for a positive bias in the processing of persuasive messages. *Personality and Social Psychology Bulletin, 29,* 650–664.

Durkin, M. (Director). (2007, March 8). *The great global warming swindle* [Television broadcast]. United Kingdom: Independent Broadcasting Authority.

Eagly, A. H., Wood, W., & Chaiken, S. (1978). Causal inferences about communicators and their effect on opinion change. *Journal of Personality and Social Psychology, 36,* 424–435.

Erickson, B., Lind, E. A., Johnson, B. C., & O'Barr, W. M. (1978). Speech style and impression formation in a court setting: The effects of "powerful" and "powerless" speech. *Journal of Experimental Social Psychology, 14,* 266–279.

Fishbein, M., & Ajzen, I. (1975). *Belief, attitude, intention, and behavior: An introduction to theory and research.* Reading, MA: Addison-Wesley.

Hafer, C. L., Reynolds, K. L., & Obertynski, M. A. (1996). Message comprehensibility and persuasion: Effects of complex language in counterattitudinal appeals to laypeople. *Social Cognition, 14,* 317–337.

Holtgraves, T., & Lasky, B. (1999). Linguistic power and persuasion. *Journal of Language and Social Psychology, 18,* 196–205.

Hosman, L. A. (1989). The evaluative consequences of hedges, hesitations, and intensifiers: Powerful and powerless speech styles. *Human Communication Research, 15,* 383–406.

Johnson, B. T., Maio, G. R., & Smith-McLallen, A. (2005). Communication and attitude change: Causes, processes, and effects. In D. Albarracín, B. T. Johnson, & M. P. Zanna (Eds.), *The handbook of attitudes* (pp. 617–669). Mahwah, NJ: Erlbaum.

Kelman, H. C. (1958). Compliance, identification, and internalization: Three processes of attitude change. *Journal of Conflict Resolution, 2,* 51–60.

McGuire, W. J. (1969). The nature of attitudes and attitude change. In G. Lindzey & E. Aronson (Eds.), *Handbook of social psychology* (2nd ed., Vol. 3, pp. 136–314). Reading, MA: Addison-Wesley.

O'Keefe, D. J. (1997). Standpoint explicitness and persuasive effect: A meta-analytic review of the effects of varying conclusion articulation in persuasive messages. *Argumentation and Advocacy, 34,* 1–12.

Perloff, R. M. (2003). *The dynamics of persuasion: Communication and attitudes in the 21st Century* (2nd ed.). Mahwah, NJ: Erlbaum.

Petty, R. E., & Cacioppo, J. T. (1984). The effects of involvement on responses to argument quantity and quality: Central and peripheral routes to persuasion. *Journal of Personality and Social Psychology, 46,* 69–81.

Petty, R. E., & Cacioppo, J. T. (1986). The elaboration likelihood model of persuasion. In L. Berkowitz (Ed.), *Advances in experimental social psychology* (Vol. 19, pp. 123–205). New York: Academic Press.

Petty, R. E., & Wegener, D. T. (1998). Attitude change: Multiple roles for persuasion variables. In D. T. Gilbert, S. T. Fiske, & G. Lindzey (Eds.), *The handbook of social psychology* (4th ed., Vol. 1, pp. 323–390). New York: McGraw-Hill.

Rogers, R. W. (1983). Cognitive and physiological processes in fear appeals and attitude change: A revised theory of protection motivation. In J. T. Cacioppo & R. E. Petty (Eds.), *Social psychophysiology: A sourcebook* (pp. 153–176). New York: Guilford.

Sopory, P., & Dillard, J. P. (2002). Figurative language and persuasion. In J. P. Dillard & M. Pfau (Eds.), *The persuasion handbook: Developments in theory and practice* (pp. 407–426). Thousand Oaks, CA: Sage.

Zanna, M. P., & Rempel, J. K. (1988). Attitudes: A new look at an old concept. In D. Bar-Tal & A. W. Kruglanski (Eds.), *The social psychology of knowledge* (pp. 315–334). Cambridge, UK: Cambridge University Press.

13

What It Takes to Succeed: An Examination of the Relationship Between Negotiators' Implicit Beliefs and Performance

LAURA J. KRAY AND MICHAEL P. HASELHUHN

The ability to successfully negotiate with others is a key skill for leaders in today's rapidly changing organizational, political, and social environ- ments. Decades of research have demonstrated that the beliefs negotiators bring to the bargaining table have strong effects on how value is created and claimed. In this chapter, we begin by reviewing previous research linking cognition and negotiation, exploring how negotiators' beliefs regarding themselves, their counterparts, and the negotiation situation affect conflict resolution. Building on this previous work, we introduce recent research that explores how negotiators' implicit beliefs regarding the malleability or fixedness of negotiation ability affect multiple aspects of the negotiation process. We present research demonstrating that nego- tiators who believe that negotiation ability can be developed have a clear and consistent advantage over negotiators who believe that negotiation ability is a fixed trait, as gauged by value creation, value claiming, and negotiation course mastery. We conclude with an eye toward future research, arguing that leaders' implicit beliefs in other domains (e.g., emotion, personality, morality) may have important implications for how leaders negotiate and interact with others.

One of the most important attributes of a successful leader is the ability to negotiate effectively. We make this bold assertion fully recognizing the complex analytic and strategic decisions that characterize a leader's job because, in order to sell ideas, secure resources, and implement strategy, leaders must work interdependently with others. This observation is especially true in today's business environment where the rapid pace of change is unprecedented. The complexity and pace of leaders' decision making has been exacerbated by constantly changing technology, increased job mobility, greater access to information, and more diversity in the workplace (Thompson, 2005). Whenever individuals require the buy-in and assistance of others, the ability to negotiate effectively increases the chances of success. This assertion holds true both within and between organizations and regardless of the power relations between parties.

Given the importance of negotiation as a core leadership competency, it is worthwhile to consider what the negotiation process involves. In its simplest form, negotiations enable two or more parties to divide up a fixed pie of resources in such a way that both parties have exceeded their next-best alternative. If a house seller has an existing offer for $250,000 and only aspires to maximize the sale price, then her decision of whether to accept a competing offer entails assessing whether it exceeds this dollar value. More complex yet equally common negotiations might involve multiple issues and multiple parties with differing priorities, expectations about the future, and attitudes about risk and time. For example, a more typical negotiation over property includes issues such as the closing date, inspection terms, and type of financing. Whereas the seller may prioritize the closing date, the buyer may care more about the inspection terms, thus creating an opportunity to expand the pie by granting each negotiator her most preferred concession. Across myriad configurations of issues and parties, the negotiation process enables interdependent parties with likely conflicting desires to reach agreement over the division of scarce resources.

Achieving success in negotiations requires diverse leadership skills. Negotiations are challenging because they involve a fundamental tension between claiming and creating value (Lax & Sebenius, 1986). Whereas claiming value involves maximizing one's share of a pool of resources, creating value involves expanding the pie through creative problem solving. Value that is created must be claimed, meaning that negotiators must learn to balance both competitive and cooperative motives. Yet the behaviors associated with claiming value are often in opposition to the behaviors associated with creating value. For example, claiming value often involves inflating demands with an assertive opening offer that anchors the negotiation (Galinsky & Mussweiler, 2001), whereas creating value involves openly sharing information to facilitate logrolling (Thompson, 1991) or identifying interests underlying stated positions (Fisher, Ury, & Patton, 1991). By striking a delicate balance between these two approaches, negotiators succeed at securing resources and expanding the pie.

With this brief introduction to negotiation as a backdrop, the focus of the current chapter is the relationship between negotiators' beliefs and their performance. We recognize that the past 20 years of research on negotiation has been largely cognitive in orientation (cf. Bazerman & Carroll, 1987). Much attention has been paid to negotiators' beliefs about the zone of possible agreements and characteristics of the parties involved. We briefly review several key findings related to negotiator beliefs and the impact that they have on performance as a way of laying a foundation for current research that expands the scope of theorizing about negotiator cognitions. Specifically, we describe recent research identifying implicit negotiation beliefs, which concern individuals' assumptions about whether negotiating ability is a skill that can be developed as opposed to being a fixed trait, as powerful predictors of how well negotiators perform, both in terms of claiming and creating value and in learning negotiation theory. We then lay out a research agenda for further exploration of the role of negotiators' implicit beliefs in a wide range of negotiation processes and outcomes.

NEGOTIATOR BELIEFS: A REVIEW OF THE RESEARCH

Researchers have long appreciated the importance of negotiators' beliefs in determining how resources are divided and whether they are expanded in such a way that negotiators avoid leaving money on the table. Negotiators' beliefs can either provide them with the confidence and efficacy they need to persevere or undermine their ability to succeed. Just as self-fulfilling prophecies can produce outcomes consistent with expectations (Rosenthal & Jacobson, 1968), negotiators' cognitions do more than just describe reality; they shape it. Although a comprehensive review of the literature on cognition in negotiations is beyond the scope of this chapter, we consider three classes of negotiator beliefs that support the thesis that beliefs matter. Rather than focusing on the beliefs that negotiators may have about specific issues that are on the table in a particular negotiation, we restrict our discussion to beliefs that define situations and what it calls for to succeed, as a way of laying a foundation for current research on implicit beliefs in negotiations.

Fixed pie belief. One of the earliest findings in the cognitive revolution was the observation that negotiators often assume that the pool of resources to be divided is fixed. The fixed-pie bias is characterized by a belief that the interests of negotiators are opposed, and therefore, that resources are zero-sum (Bazerman & Neale, 1983; Pinkley, Griffith, & Northcraft, 1995; Thompson & Hastie, 1990). If negotiators assume that a negotiation is fixed-sum in nature (even though this may not be the case), they tend to align their behaviors entirely with the goal of claiming value and often leave money on the table. However, it may be the case that the parties' priorities differ across issues, and that there are opportunities for trade-offs. A lose-lose outcome (Thompson & Hrebec, 1996) is often the result of a fixed-pie perception because negotiators fail to explore opportunities to satisfy each party's interests. Rather than expending the effort and working to build on differences, negotiators prematurely settle for suboptimal outcomes. Implicit in the notion of a fixed-pie bias is the recognition that negotiators' beliefs about the issues on the table affect how well they perform.

Negotiability beliefs. Negotiators' beliefs about whether a situation or issue is potentially negotiable have powerful effects on whether effort is expended to improve offers initially put on the table. Instead of accepting the first offer presented to them, people who believe that an issue is negotiable are more likely to engage in a process characterized by reciprocal concessions. Researchers examining these types of beliefs have focused most of their attention on exposing a perceptual asymmetry between women and men (Babcock, Gelfand, Small, & Stayn, 2006). In general, much variability exists among individuals in the recognition of the potential to negotiate, which contributes to a gender gap in negotiation performance whereby men tend to reap more favorable outcomes than women (Kray & Thompson, 2005). In much of the experimental research done on negotiation, role-playing simulations make it obvious to participants that they are in a negotiation situation. In contrast, the real world is colored by the ambiguity of whether a situation has the potential to be a negotiation. For example, students enrolled in negotiations courses often fret over how they can know which aspects of a job offer are negotiable. Some employers make standard offers to all entry-level candidates, and other employers personalize their offers. Implicit in the belief that a situation is negotiable is the assumption that efforts to improve outcomes will be worthwhile.

Effective negotiator beliefs. A third example of the importance of beliefs in determining how well negotiators perform has to do with the traits they associate with effective negotiators. When a negotiation is thought to be diagnostic of inherent abilities, negotiators' naïve theories about what it takes to succeed at the bargaining table are activated. Kray, Thompson, and Galinsky (2001) determined that many of the traits associated with effective negotiators are consistent with gender stereotypes. For example, students in a negotiations class in an MBA program ascribed stereotypically masculine traits, such as assertiveness, rationality, and a lack of emotionality, to effective negotiators. When a negotiation is thought to be diagnostic of core abilities, these stereotypes are automatically activated, and negotiators implicitly question whether they possess the attributes required for success. When negotiators question their own ability to succeed, it affects their confidence, the assertiveness of their opening offers, and ultimately how well they perform. This research suggests that negotiators' beliefs about what it takes to succeed, and whether they possess those traits, dictate how well they do when the stakes are highest.

Implicit Negotiation Beliefs

The research previously discussed suggests that beliefs about the fixedness of the pie, offers, and traits associated with effective negotiators have robust effects on how negotiators perform. Each of the aforementioned findings regarding negotiator cognition supports the view that beliefs about the rigidity of the negotiation situation and what it takes to succeed undermine effective performance. Negotiators who believe that the pie can be expanded, that anything is negotiable, and that a wide range of traits and styles contribute to success are indeed more successful at the bargaining table. Next we expand on these observations by exploring negotiators' beliefs about the ability of individuals to improve as negotiators. We review research examining general theories about human personality and aptitude and then explore the implications of implicit theories about negotiation.

In a highly influential approach to examining self-theories, Carol Dweck and her colleagues (Dweck, 1996; Dweck & Leggett, 1988) proposed that implicit beliefs are rarely articulated thoughts regarding the malleability of personality and intelligence that nonetheless have powerful effects on motivation, affect, and behavior. According to Dweck, implicit beliefs fall along a continuum, with entity and incremental beliefs representing the endpoints. Entity theorists are individuals who endorse the belief that an attribute, such as personality or intelligence, is a fixed entity that is difficult—if not impossible—to change. In contrast, incremental theorists believe that personal attributes are malleable to such a degree that anyone can change even their most basic characteristics through hard work and persistence. Whereas the entity theorist endorses a "nature" viewpoint, the incremental theorist favors a "nurture" viewpoint. Although some evidence suggests that individuals hold "implicit person beliefs" that generalize across contexts (e.g., Chiu, Hong, & Dweck, 1997; Heslin, VandeWalle, & Latham, 2006), individuals are clearly capable of modifying their viewpoint depending on the domain under consideration. For example, an individual may believe that intelligence is a fixed trait, but that people can demonstrate different sides of their personality depending on the situation. Likewise, an individual may be an incremental theorist with regard to intelligence but an entity theorist with regard to athletic ability. Implicit beliefs regarding personality, morality, intelligence, and emotion have been identified (e.g., Chiu, Dweck, Tong, & Fu, 1997; Hong, Chiu, Dweck, & Sacks, 1997; Tamir, John, Srivastava, & Gross, 2007).

Applying the lens of self-theories to negotiations, our research has examined implicit negotiation beliefs and their influence on negotiation processes and outcomes (Kray & Haselhuhn, 2007). Implicit negotiation beliefs refer to the belief that an individual's ability to negotiate is fixed (i.e., the idea of the "born negotiator") versus the belief that anyone can become a good negotiator through training and hard work. We expected implicit negotiation beliefs to affect negotiation performance in two ways. First, we expected that implicit negotiation beliefs would affect the types of goals negotiators adopted at the bargaining table. Drawing on previous research on more general forms of implicit beliefs (e.g., Dweck & Leggett, 1988), we expected that because incremental theorists believe that people can grow and gain negotiation ability, they would approach negotiations with *mastery goals,* or the desire to learn new things and improve. In contrast, because entity theorists believe that negotiation ability is relatively fixed, we anticipated that they would approach negotiations with *performance goals,* or the desire to demonstrate how well they can negotiate.

Second, we expected implicit negotiation beliefs to determine the amount of effort negotiators dedicated to the conflict resolution process. Effort affects how long negotiators hold out for a concession, how many offers are put on the table, and how persistent negotiators are in reaching agreement versus declaring an impasse. In general, effort has a negative connotation for entity theorists because it can be interpreted as a sign that one has little intrinsic ability. Incremental theorists, on the other hand, place a high value on effort. They believe that learning and growing are effortful processes that require dedication and commitment, and, indeed, more value is placed on the process of achievement than on the ultimate achievement itself (Hong, Chiu, Dweck, Lin, & Wan, 1999). Based on the links between implicit beliefs and effort, we predicted that incremental theorists would exert greater effort in negotiations. Because effort and perseverance have been linked to negotiation success (Bazerman, Magliozzi, & Neale, 1985; Huber & Neale, 1986), we expected incremental theorists to outperform their entity counterparts.

To test our hypotheses regarding the relationship between implicit negotiation beliefs and goals, we designed a three-pronged approach. First, we sought to establish a causal relationship between implicit negotiation beliefs and performance by manipulating beliefs. An additional benefit of this experimental approach is that it allowed us to examine mediating processes that link implicit beliefs to performance. Second, because we believe implicit negotiation beliefs operate within the real world in a fairly stable manner, we examined the impact of dispositional implicit beliefs on performance in a nonexperimental setting. Third, because we expected incremental theorists to be more learning-oriented than entity theorists, we sought to determine what effect implicit negotiation beliefs have on actual learning in a classroom setting. In combination, this multipronged approach contributes to a robust understanding of the role of implicit negotiation beliefs at the bargaining table.

In our experimental research, we presented novice negotiators with an essay designed to manipulate their endorsement of an entity versus incremental viewpoint and then examined their goals and performance in negotiations. Specifically, participants read an essay designed to spur either incremental or entity beliefs. The essays were titled "Negotiation Ability Is Changeable and Can Be Developed" and "Negotiation Ability, Like Plaster, Is Pretty Stable over Time." Each essay included reports from fictitious studies supporting the main thesis of the article. In our first study, after reading one of the essays, participants were given an opportunity to select a negotiation task that they expected to perform. One task was labeled a "learning negotiation task" and was described as an opportunity to learn new concepts and practice their skills, although it would also expose them to the risk of failure. The second task was labeled a "performance negotiation task" and was described as an opportunity for them to demonstrate their ability as a negotiator, although it would also limit their ability to learn anything new. Consistent with our theorizing, implicit negotiation beliefs predicted which task negotiators selected: incremental theorists were significantly more likely to prefer a negotiation task that would offer them an opportunity to learn and grow as a negotiator, even if it meant they might not succeed initially. In a follow-up study, we had participants actually complete a distributive negotiation task after being exposed to our essay manipulation. We predicted that the incremental theorists' greater willingness to expend effort to overcome obstacles would lead them to outperform their entity theorist counterparts. Consistent with this hypothesis, we found that negotiators who read a fictitious article asserting the fixedness of negotiation ability claimed less of the negotiation pie than did negotiators who read an article describing negotiation ability as malleable.

We also examined the relationship between implicit negotiation beliefs and both value claiming and value creating in a classroom setting. We measured implicit negotiation beliefs on the first day of a negotiation class and then examined their correlation with negotiation performance throughout the course. Entirely consistent with our experimental findings, we observed that individuals who naturally endorsed an incremental viewpoint claimed more of the bargaining pie than their entity counterparts. To explore value creating, negotiators engaged in a simulation characterized by a negative bargaining zone, which exists when a seller's minimum requirement is greater than the buyer's maximum willingness to pay. Specifically, the seller in this negotiation required a minimum of $580,000 for a gas station, but the buyer was only authorized to pay up to $500,000. Although a negotiation with a negative bargaining zone typically ends in impasse, in our simulation negotiators could overcome their initial impasse if they discussed the interests underlying their stated positions and introduced additional terms into the agreement that satisfied these interests. In this simulation, part of the rationale for the seller's asking price was that he would be taking a trip around the world and wanted to have money in the bank for when he returned and needed to find employment. Because the buyer wanted to purchase a significant number of stations that had to be managed and the seller had established a good reputation as a station owner, negotiators could expand the pie by having the buyer offer a job to the seller upon returning from his travels. By discussing the rationale underlying their offers, negotiators had more information from which they could construct a viable agreement. Notably, success on this task required negotiators to persevere beyond initial stalemates and to expend effort to craft a workable deal. Consistent with our expectations, incremental theorists were more successful at this task than entity theorists. Specifically, we found that the more dyads collectively endorsed an incremental viewpoint, the more likely the negotiators were to avoid impasses and instead create an agreement that expanded the pie.

We also showed that implicit negotiation beliefs affect more than negotiation performance; they also affect a person's ability to learn about negotiation theory and to analyze negotiation situations. By correlating implicit negotiation beliefs measured on the first day of a semester-long course with final course grades determined 15 weeks later, we found that the implicit negotiation beliefs of students at the beginning of a semester predicted their learning. In particular, the more adamantly students believed that negotiating ability is a skill that can be developed, the more successfully they learned course concepts and the better they performed in school.

To understand why implicit negotiation beliefs have the power that they do, we examined the contribution of negotiators' beliefs about their own ability. We reasoned that entity theorists are most vulnerable to underperforming relative to their incremental counterparts when they doubt their own ability to succeed. As our finding regarding negotiation achievement goals suggests, entity theorists are relatively unwilling to put themselves in a situation where they run the risk of failure. Rather than persevering to overcome an obstacle that could potentially lead to failure, we expected entity theorists to give up when they encountered challenges to their success. To test this hypothesis, we measured negotiators' confidence in their ability to succeed before they engaged in a distributive negotiation. We found an interaction between perceived ability and implicit negotiation beliefs; entity theorists performed well only when they perceived themselves to be strong negotiators, while incremental theorists performed at a relatively high level regardless of their perceived ability. As shown in Figure 13-1, entity theorists performed on par

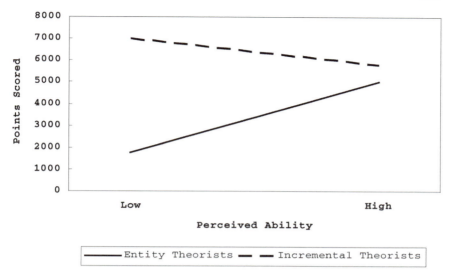

Figure 13-1 Relationship between implicit beliefs, perceived ability, and performance

with incremental theorists when they were confident in their ability. The pernicious effect of entity beliefs was most pronounced when they doubted their abilities.

Overall, these studies strongly support the idea that implicit negotiation beliefs affect how successfully people negotiate. The belief that negotiation ability can be changed promotes effort and perseverance in all facets of the negotiation process. Value claiming, value creating, and the learning of negotiation concepts are facilitated by the belief that negotiating ability is a skill that can be developed. Next we broaden the scope of investigation of implicit beliefs beyond the negotiation domain to better understand their impact across a variety of leadership settings and to identify directions for future research.

A Wide-Lens Examination of Implicit Beliefs

In this section, we consider several areas of research that speak to the vast impact of implicit beliefs, specifically on negotiations and more generally on leadership behavior.

Conflict Handling Styles

In addition to the effects of implicit beliefs on transactional negotiations, beliefs also affect how individuals approach conflict resolution in interpersonal relationships (Kammrath & Dweck, 2006). In this context, implicit beliefs refer not to negotiation ability in particular, but rather to beliefs regarding whether people can change their basic attributes. In the broader conflict resolution domain, incremental theorists tend to respond to conflict by openly discussing potentially contentious issues and trying to constructively address the situation, whereas entity theorists are less likely to approach conflict in such a straightforward manner. In Kammrath and Dweck's investigation of real-world conflicts, this divergence in how entity versus incremental theorists approach conflict was strongest when the issues were most important—precisely when constructive problem solving may be most desirable. They theorized that these responses are a direct result of beliefs regarding the efficacy of the effortful conflict resolution process. Incremental theorists, who believe that a counterpart in a conflict can change the traits or behaviors at the source of the conflict, are willing to exert effort in important situations because they believe the effort may pay off. Entity theorists, on the other hand, see attempts at change as a wasted effort as well as futile.

Implicit Emotion Beliefs

Researchers have recently identified individual differences in beliefs regarding the malleability of emotion. In this context, incremental theorists believe that the emotions one feels can be controlled, while entity theorists believe that emotions cannot be changed (Tamir et al., 2007). Emotions are critical for understanding negotiation behavior (Barry, Fulmer, & Goates, 2006; Barry, Fulmer, & Van Kleef, 2004). The ability to control anger or frustration at a counterpart's moves is crucial for effectively separating the person from the problem, a key part of the problem-solving negotiation style prescribed by practitioners and scholars alike (Fisher et al., 1991). Because the belief that emotions can be changed is so closely tied to the belief that one can personally control his or her emotions (Tamir et al., 2007), incremental theories of emotion can lead to greater confidence and self-efficacy at the bargaining table.

Implicit Morality Beliefs

Implicit beliefs regarding morality may be an important factor in negotiations as well. In this context, entity theorists believe that a person's moral character is fixed and that morality and honesty are ingrained aspects of an individual's personality, whereas incremental theorists believe that moral character is something that can change (Chiu, Hong, & Dweck, 1997). Because entity theorists believe that moral character is a fixed attribute, they place great weight on single instances of moral or immoral behavior. In contrast, incremental theorists focus their attention on the contextual factors that may lead a person to act morally or immorally in a given situation. In light of the growing importance that researchers and practitioners place on the ethics of negotiation (Shell, 2006), these beliefs are of particular interest. While incremental theorists may view a negotiator's past ethical transgressions as one-off occurrences, entity theorists will likely interpret a previous instance of unethical behavior as a strong predictor that the negotiator will not hesitate to act unethically in any future interaction, regardless of the context. Likewise, if incremental theorists have a more contextualized view of morality, they may be more likely to engage in ethically questionable behavior without considering the reputational consequences of even one transgression. In support of this view, a recent study examined the use of deception in a negotiation simulation designed to pose an ethical dilemma. In this study, more than 40 percent of negotiators who held incremental beliefs regarding morality reported misrepresenting material information. In contrast, less than 15 percent of negotiators who held entity beliefs regarding morality reported engaging in similar deception (Haselhuhn, Schweitzer, & Kray, 2007). These initial findings suggest that implicit morality beliefs have strong implications for how ethically people behave, how reputations form, what negotiators expect of others, and negotiators' willingness to forgive past transgressions in dispute situations.

Implicit Subordinate Beliefs

Moving beyond the specific context of negotiations, implicit beliefs impact interactions between superiors and subordinates in organizational contexts (VandeWalle, 1997; Heslin, Latham, & VandeWalle, 2005; Heslin et al., 2006). VandeWalle found that a person's implicit beliefs extend to perceptions of others. For example, managers with incremental theories believe that their subordinates can change and grow, while entity theorists place greater weight on initial impressions. As a result, incremental theorists are more likely to coach their subordinates and teach them important skills that are mutually beneficial. Rather than entering into contentious discussions regarding suboptimal performance, incremental managers are willing to work with their subordinates to improve the situation to a greater degree than entity managers (Heslin et al., 2006). As part of this feedback and coaching process, incremental theorists are more sensitive to changes in performance, both positive and negative, of their subordinates. Entity theorists base their evaluations of subordinates primarily on initial performance outcomes. When it is assumed that people are unable to drastically change their ability, these initial impressions are thought to generalize to future behaviors as well. Incrementalists, on the other hand, believe that subordinates can change, and therefore place greater weight on more recent performance (Heslin et al., 2005). These findings suggest that the entity viewpoint prevents people from updating their beliefs about others and may result in less accurate evaluations of others over time.

Implicit Leadership Beliefs

We have recently begun examining beliefs regarding the malleability of leadership by adapting our scale measuring implicit negotiation beliefs specifically to the leadership domain (Kray & Haselhuhn, 2008). In our first investigation of how these beliefs may impact leadership behavior, we focused on one critical skill for effective leadership: the ability to process information in an unbiased fashion and avoid the tendency to attend to and give great weight to information consistent with a preexisting hypothesis. Previous research has determined that the confirmation bias is a robust affliction resulting from motivated information processing (Schulz-Hardt, Frey, Luthgens, & Moscovici, 2000). After measuring the implicit beliefs of MBA students enrolled in an introductory organizational behavior course, we correlated their beliefs with their decision-making process in a simulation designed to gauge the tendency to engage in biased information processing. Based on the space shuttle Challenger disaster in which decision makers failed to appreciate information that suggested conditions were not favorable for a safe launch, the Carter Racing simulation challenges participants to question the decision to "launch" by considering information that could potentially disconfirm this dominant hypothesis. Since making strategic decisions is a central job of leaders, we expected that implicit leadership beliefs would impact how participants approached the task. Our analyses suggest that incremental theorists were significantly more likely than entity theorists to process information in a balanced manner. As a result, incremental theorists were significantly less likely to make a decision consistent with the ill-fated Challenger launch. These findings clearly suggest that implicit beliefs affect the manner in which information is processed.

A Research Agenda

Given the importance of implicit negotiation beliefs on negotiation and leadership performance, we encourage future research that broadens the breadth and depth of our understanding of their impact. Although the possible avenues for future research are vast, we restrict our discussion to three possible paths. Specifically, we consider the impact of implicit beliefs on assessments of negotiating parties, negotiator preferences, and willingness to negotiate.

Negotiator Assessments

Reputations matter in negotiations (Tinsley, O'Connor, & Sullivan, 2002). Knowing what to expect from one's negotiating partner helps to determine what information to reveal and when to do so. If negotiators expect their partners to be weak because they have not been effective in the past, they may be overconfident in their ability to prevail without sufficient consideration of alternatives or preparation. We expect that negotiators who hold entity beliefs will believe that past negotiation outcomes are stronger predictors of future success or failure compared to incremental theorists. If, however, the contexts of two negotiations are different enough that these assumptions prove faulty, then entity theorists may be more likely to fall victim to the fundamental attribution error (Ross, 1977). A negotiator who has performed poorly in the past may improve in future negotiations, or may try new things at the bargaining table that could lead to different results. Similarly, a negotiator who has performed well in the past could improve or regress if they try new tactics or strategies. These differences in how past performance is evaluated may lead to differences in negotiation preparation.

Negotiator Risk Attitudes

Implicit beliefs may impact negotiators' attitudes toward risk at the bargaining table. Virtually all methods of creating value in negotiations require that negotiators accept some degree of risk. Specifically, negotiators assume *strategic risk* when they reveal information about their preferences that their counterpart could exploit (Roth, 1977). For example, a car buyer who reveals her preference for a red vehicle may pay more if a car dealer claims that he cannot keep red cars in stock. Negotiators assume *contractual risk* when they structure a deal on the basis of their uncertain forecasts of the future (Bottom, 1998). For example, a buyer's willingness to pay for a vehicle may be based on her estimates of the car's resale value in 5 years. Because this value will not be known until the future unfolds, the buyer may overpay if her estimates are overly optimistic. Kray, Paddock, and Galinsky (2007) determined that past performance influences how negotiators respond to these two types of risk. Negotiators who have experienced a history of failures are more drawn to contractual risk, and its delay of outcomes, than to strategic risk. This effect may be moderated by negotiators' implicit beliefs. Because entity theorists endorse a fixed belief about abilities, we expect that past performance will have a larger influence on current risk attitudes of entity theorists than on incremental theorists. Future research that explores how implicit beliefs shape attitudes about various types of risk in negotiations would be worthwhile.

Along similar lines, many negotiations involve trade-offs between short-term and long-term performance concerns. Negotiators may have to relinquish some of what they want in a negotiation in favor of developing a long-term relationship with a negotiation counterpart that will bring returns over an extended period. Entity theorists, who are more focused on demonstrating their ability, may be concerned about short-term outcomes since any loss with no guarantee of a future gain is threatening to one's self-esteem. Incremental theorists, on the other hand, approach situations with the goal of learning and gaining competence over time, which suggests that they may be more focused on long-term relationships than entity theorists. Examining how implicit beliefs affect the trade-offs negotiators make over time is also a promising direction for future research.

Willingness to Negotiate

A third direction for future research involves how implicit beliefs affect the willingness of individuals to solve problems through negotiations. For example, consumers looking to purchase a new car often have the choice between making their purchase at a regular dealership or purchasing the same car at a "no negotiation" dealership. The option that does not involve negotiation appears to be quite successful. Indeed, when General Motors introduced the Saturn brand, a large facet of the marketing campaign focused on the fact that customers would pay the price on the tag, no haggling required (or allowed). Assuming that dealerships like this are not benevolently putting their lowest price on the tag, shoppers are essentially paying the dealership a premium to avoid negotiation (Purohit & Sondak, 1999). We hypothesize that entity theorists will have a greater preference for the dealership that does not allow negotiation relative to incremental theorists for at least two reasons. First, incrementalists will likely see more value in the negotiation process itself because it provides an opportunity to learn and improve for future negotiations. Entity theorists, on the other hand, will likely see the time and effort spent negotiating as an additional cost to buying the car because they perceive little value from the negotiation process. Second, in contrast to incrementalists' views of the negotiation as a learning experience, entity theorists view the negotiation as an opportunity to demonstrate their negotiation prowess (or avoid showing the lack thereof). This view suggests that highly confident entity theorists will be more likely to purchase a car from a regular dealership (since they aim to demonstrate their high level of ability), while entity theorists with lower self-evaluations will be more likely to choose the option that does not require negotiation. Incrementalists' choices, conversely, should be unrelated to perceived ability.

CONCLUSION

We began this chapter by highlighting the intimate relationship between leadership effectiveness and negotiating ability. With this appreciation of the art and science of negotiation front and center, we then explored one of the most important contributors to negotiation success: the set of beliefs that negotiators bring with them to the bargaining table. First, we acknowledged the deep cognitive roots of early negotiation research with its emphasis on assessing negotiators' beliefs about the fixedness of offers, pies, and contributors to success. Second, we attempted to motivate the next generation of negotiator cognition research by introducing implicit negotiator beliefs as a powerful determinant of negotiation performance. Finally, we laid out an agenda for expanding the scope of investigations regarding implicit beliefs at the bargaining table. In so doing, we call attention to the fact that what it takes to succeed is a belief that success is within reach through hard work and perseverance.

REFERENCES

Babcock, L., Gelfand, M. J., Small, D., & Stayn, H. (2006). Gender differences in the propensity to negotiate. In D. D. Cremer, M. Zeelenberg, & J. K. Murnighan (Eds.), *Social psychology and economics* (pp. 239–259). Mahwah, NJ: Erlbaum.

Barry, B., Fulmer, I. S., & Goates, N. (2006). Bargaining with feeling: Emotionality in and around negotiation. In L. Thompson (Ed.), *Negotiation theory and research* (pp. 99–127). New York: Psychology Press.

Barry, B., Fulmer, I. S., & Van Kleef, G. (2004). I laughed, I cried, I settled: The role of emotion in negotiation. In M. J. Gelfand and J. M. Brett (Eds.), *The handbook of negotiation and culture* (pp. 71–94). Stanford, CA: Stanford University Press.

Bazerman, M. H., & Carroll, J. S. (1987). Negotiator cognition. In L. L. Cummings & B. M. Staw (Eds.), *Research in organizational behavior* (Vol. 9, pp. 247–288). Greenwich, CT: JAI.

Bazerman, M. H., Magliozzi, T., & Neale, M. A. (1985). Integrative bargaining in a competitive market. *Organizational Behavior and Human Decision Processes, 35*, 294–313.

Bazerman, M. H., & Neale, M. A. (1983). Heuristics in negotiation: Limitations to effective dispute resolution. In M. H. Bazerman & R. J. Lewicki (Eds.), *Negotiating in organizations* (pp. 342–365). Beverly Hills, CA: Sage.

Bottom, W. P. (1998). Negotiator risk: Sources of uncertainty and the impact of reference points on negotiated agreements. *Organizational Behavior and Human Decision Processes, 76*, 89–112.

Chiu, C., Dweck, C. S., Tong, J. Y., & Fu, J. H. (1997). Implicit theories and conceptions of morality. *Journal of Personality and Social Psychology, 73*, 923–940.

Chiu, C., Hong, Y., & Dweck, C. S. (1997). Lay dispositionism and implicit theories of personality. *Journal of Personality and Social Psychology, 73*, 19–30.

Dweck, C. S. (1996). Implicit theories as organizers of goals and behavior. In P. M. Gollwitzer & J. A. Bargh (Eds.), *The psychology of action: Linking cognition and motivation to behavior* (pp. 69–90). New York: The Guilford Press.

Dweck, C. S., & Leggett, E. L. (1988). A social-cognitive approach to motivation and personality. *Psychological Review, 95*, 256–273.

Fisher, R., Ury, W., & Patton, B. (1991). *Getting to yes: Negotiating agreement without giving in.* New York: Penguin Books.

Galinsky, A. D., & Mussweiler, T. (2001). First offers as anchors: The role of perspective-taking and negotiator focus. *Journal of Personality and Social Psychology, 81*, 657–669.

Haselhuhn, M. P., Schweitzer, M. E., & Kray, L. J. (2007). *Exploring the moral chameleon: Implicit negotiation beliefs and perceptions of ethics at the bargaining table.* Unpublished manuscript, University of Pennsylvania.

Heslin, P. A., Latham, G. P., & VandeWalle, D. (2005). The effect of implicit person theory on performance appraisals. *Journal of Applied Psychology, 90*, 842–856.

Heslin, P. A., VandeWalle, D., & Latham, G. P. (2006). Keen to help? Managers' implicit person theories and their subsequent employee coaching. *Personnel Psychology, 59*, 871–902.

Hong, Y., Chiu, C., Dweck, C. S., Lin, D. M.-S., & Wan, W. (1999). Implicit theories, attributions, and coping: A meaning system approach. *Journal of Personality and Social Psychology, 77*, 588–599.

Hong, Y., Chiu, C., Dweck, C. S., & Sacks, R. (1997). Implicit theories and evaluative processes in person cognition. *Journal of Personality and Social Psychology, 33*, 296–323.

Huber, V., & Neale, M. (1986). Effects of cognitive heuristics and goals on negotiator performance and subsequent goal setting. *Organizational Behavior and Human Decision Processes, 38*, 342–365.

Kammrath, L. K., & Dweck, C. S. (2006). Voicing conflict: Preferred conflict strategies among incremental and entity theorists. *Personality and Social Psychology Bulletin, 32*, 1497–1508.

Kray, L. J., & Haselhuhn, M.P. (2007). Implicit negotiation beliefs and performance: Longitudinal and experimental evidence. *Journal of Personality and Social Psychology, 93*, 49–64.

Kray, L. J., & Haselhuhn, M. P. (2008). *Born leader or lifelong learner? An examination of implicit leadership beliefs.* Unpublished manuscript, University of California, Berkeley.

Kray, L. J., Paddock, L., & Galinsky, A. D. (2007). The effect of past performance on expected control and risk attitudes in integrative negotiations. Unpublished manuscript, University of California, Berkeley.

Kray, L. J., & Thompson, L. (2005). Gender stereotypes and negotiation performance: An examination of theory and research. *Research in Organizational Behavior, 26*, 103–182.

Kray, L., Thompson, L., & Galinsky, A. (2001). Battle of the sexes: Gender stereotype confirmation and reactance in negotiations. *Journal of Personality and Social Psychology, 80*, 942–958.

Lax, D., & Sebenius, J. (1986). *The manager as negotiator: Bargaining for cooperation and competitive gain.* New York: Free Press.

Pinkley, R. L., Griffith, T. L., & Northcraft, G. B. (1995). "Fixed pie" a la mode: Information availability, information processing, and the negotiation of suboptimal agreements. *Organizational Behavior and Human Decision Processes, 62*, 101–112.

Purohit, D., & Sondak, H. (1999). Fear and loathing at the car dealership: The perceived fairness of pricing policies. Unpublished manuscript, Duke University.

Rosenthal, R., & Jacobson, L. (1968). *Pygmalion in the classroom: Teacher expectation and pupils' intellectual development.* New York: Rinehart and Winston.

Ross, L. (1977). The intuitive psychologist and his shortcomings. In L. Berkowitz (Ed.), *Advances in experimental social psychology* (Vol. 10, pp. 173–220). New York: Academic.

Roth, A. E. (1977). Bargaining utility, the utility of playing a game, and models of coalition formation. *Journal of Mathematical Psychology, 16*, 153–160.

Schulz-Hardt, S., Frey, D., Luthgens, C., & Moscovici, S. (2000). Biased information search in group decision making. *Journal of Personality and Social Psychology, 78*, 655–669.

Shell, G. R. (2006). *Bargaining for advantage.* New York: Penguin Books.

Tamir, M., John, O. P., Srivastava, S., & Gross, J. J. (2007). Implicit theories of emotion: Affective and social outcomes across a major life transition. *Journal of Personality and Social Psychology, 92*, 731–744.

Thompson, L. (1991). Information exchange in negotiation. *Journal of Experimental Social Psychology, 27*, 161–179.

Thompson, L. (2005). *The mind and heart of the negotiator* (3rd ed.). Upper Saddle River, NJ: Pearson Prentice Hall.

Thompson, L., & Hastie, R. (1990). Social perception in negotiation. *Organizational Behavior and Human Decision Processes, 47*, 98–123.

Thompson, L., & Hrebec, D. (1996). Lose-lose agreements in interdependent decision making. *Psychological Bulletin, 120*, 396–409.

Tinsley, C. H., O'Connor, K. M., & Sullivan, B. A. (2002). Tough guys finish last: The perils of a distributive reputation. *Organizational Behavior and Human Decision Processes, 88*, 621–642.

VandeWalle, D. M. (1997). Development and validation of a work domain goal orientation instrument. *Educational and Psychological Measurement, 57*, 995–1015.

14

Presidential Leadership and Group Folly: Reappraising the Role of Groupthink in the Bay of Pigs Decisions

RODERICK M. KRAMER

"What do you think about this damned invasion?"
"I think about it as little as possible."

—President Kennedy's response to Arthur Schlesinger Jr.'s query on March 28, 1960, prior to the Bay of Pigs invasion (Schlesinger, 2007, p. 108)

Social scientists have afforded considerable attention to identifying the antecedents or determinants of effective presidential decision making. Recognizing that nearly all consequential presidential decisions are made within the context of group deliberations, they have focused particular attention on understanding how presidential advisors influence decision making. Within this literature, Janis's groupthink hypothesis remains by far the most cited and influential framework. Janis regarded the Bay of Pigs decision as one example of a perfect decision fiasco and one that could be attributed to the effects of dysfunctional group dynamics. This chapter reexamines the adequacy of Janis's groupthink explanation in light of recently declassified evidence. I conclude the preponderance of the evidence does not favor groupthink as a necessary or sufficient explanation for the Bay of Pigs decisions.

In a reflective moment during his presidency, President John F. Kennedy observed, "The essence of ultimate decision remains impenetrable to the observer—often, indeed, to the decider himself.... There will always be the dark and tangled stretches in the decision-making process—mysterious even to those who may be most intimately involved" (quoted in Allison & Zelikow, 1999, p. i). Kennedy's observation notwithstanding, social scientists have afforded considerable attention to the antecedents or determinants of presidential decision making (e.g., Burns, 2006; Burke & Greenstein, 1989). Recognizing that nearly all important and consequential presidential decisions are made within the context of group deliberations, political scientists and presidential historians have been particularly interested in understanding how presidential advisors influence presidential decision making.

Although the lion's share of research in this important area has been done by political scientists (Cronin & Greenberg, 1969; George, 1980), social psychologists have made a number of important contributions as well (e.g., Raven, 1974). Among these social psychological contributions, Janis's (1972, 1983) groupthink hypothesis remains by far the most cited and influential framework. Indeed, more than four decades after its conception, the groupthink hypothesis remains an enduring fixture in the social psychological literature on decision-making fiascoes involving presidential decisions, including those made by Presidents Kennedy, Richard Nixon, Lyndon Johnson, Jimmy Carter, Ronald Reagan, and George W. Bush (Hart, 1990).

In many respects, the resilience of the groupthink hypothesis is not altogether surprising. Among its alluring features is that it appears to offer a set of *prima facie* plausible assumptions regarding the dynamics of dysfunctional decision making. Additionally, it identifies a set of compelling symptoms for diagnosing the sources of defective deliberation. Moreover, it offers a series of concrete and useful prescriptions for avoiding them. Perhaps most impressively, support for the theory is buttressed by a set of dramatic and compelling case studies. Janis's original case studies include some of the most formative events in American history—the tragic escalation of the Vietnam War, the ill-fated Bay of Pigs operation, and the nefarious Watergate cover-up. The conjunction of defining events in history with a seemingly parsimonious and robust theory to explain them has proven a powerful lure to both theorists and practitioners alike.

In each of these cases, unfortunately, the evidence available to Janis for constructing his inductive analysis was fragmentary and incomplete. Additionally, in some instances, we now know relevant data were suppressed and/or sanitized by various governmental agencies. Janis himself recognized the constraining limitations of the evidence available to him. Consequently, he urged future scholars to reappraise the groupthink hypothesis as new, relevant evidence emerged. It is in this spirit that the present analysis proceeds.

There are several reasons why revisiting the original case studies might prove fruitful today. First, Janis's qualitative studies constituted the core empirical foundation for his conjectures about groupthink. However incomplete the evidence might have been, Janis believed his case studies offered compelling evidence for the validity of the groupthink hypothesis. His arguments and assembly of the evidence were so persuasive that groupthink remains among the most influential explanations for these fiascoes even today. Indeed, so successful and compelling has the groupthink account been that it continues to exert explanatory sway over conventional wisdom regarding the origins and dynamics of a variety of contemporary presidential fiascoes (e.g., Hart, 1990; Moorehead, 1991; Neck, 1992).

Reexamining the original case studies seems particularly appropriate at this time for two other reasons. First, the scholarly literature on group and organizational decision making has made impressive theoretical strides in the decades since Janis originally articulated the groupthink hypothesis (see, e.g., Hackman, 2003; March, 1995; Tetlock, 1991, 1995; Turner, Pratkanis, Probasco, & Leve, 1992; Turner, Pratkanis, & Struckman, 2007; Whyte, 1989). Thus, scholars today have a much richer set of theoretical perspectives from which to survey the hypothesis and the evidence for it. Second, and of particular relevance to the present study, with the passage of time a considerable amount of fresh archival material bearing on these fiascoes has become available to scholars. With respect to the Bay of Pigs decisions made by President Kennedy and his advisors, for example, this material includes a treasure trove of recently declassified records, such as presidential logs, memos, and transcripts of crucial meetings (Kornbluh, 1998; Reeves, 1993). Further, comprehensive oral histories are also now available for the Kennedy presidency (e.g., Strober & Strober, 1993). Additionally, there are new reassessments by historians and political scientists, as well as detailed memoirs from principal participants in the Kennedy years that were not available when Janis conceived the groupthink hypothesis (Burns, 2006; Fursenko & Naftali, 1997; Kornbluh, 1998; Naftali, 2001).

For all of these reasons, the time seems ripe to revisit the Bay of Pigs decision-making process and, in particular, the adequacy of the groupthink hypothesis to explain it.[1] How well has Janis's construal of the Bay of Pigs decision-making process weathered nearly four decades of theoretical advances and emerging empirical evidence? This is the central question I engage in this chapter.

ADVICE, DISSENT, AND DECISION IN THE BAY OF PIGS CASE: REASSESSING THE JANIS BRIEF

Janis regarded the decision by President Kennedy and his advisors to approve the CIA's plan to land a contingent of Cuban exiles on the shores of Cuba in 1961 as the prototypic example of groupthink. As he later recounted, many of his initial intuitions regarding groupthink were inspired by this case. Moreover, he felt the Bay of Pigs case most explicitly represented all of the relevant features of the hypothesis. In his eyes, therefore, the Bay of Pigs constituted a "perfect failure" in decision making—and an equally perfect example of groupthink in action.

Janis's arguments regarding groupthink were woven around a series of critical questions that should be used, he proposed, as guidelines for deciding whether groupthink was present in any presidential decision. First, it was important to examine *who* made the policy decision. Did the evidence show, for example, that the critical decisions were made primarily by a president acting alone, or did it indicate instead that an advisory group participated to a significant extent? Second, it was important to determine whether this group constituted a tightly knit, cohesive group. Third, were the antecedent conditions and symptoms of groupthink discernible in the group's deliberations? Fourth, were the decisions avoidable errors? In other words, was there sufficient countervailing evidence available to the group members to indicate that their decisions entailed unacceptable risks, or were in other ways seriously flawed? If not, Janis noted reasonably, any critique reduces to mere hindsight bias and would not constitute a true instance of groupthink.

With these evaluative criteria in mind, it is useful to explicate some of the major points in Janis's analysis and argument. First, Janis's characterization of the decision-making process leading up to the Bay of Pigs attached considerable importance to a specific series of meetings involving President Kennedy and some of his advisors during which the Bay of Pigs was discussed. Janis implied that the planning for the invasion occurred *primarily* within the context of these deliberations and that they could be characterized, in turn, as discussions by a small, cohesive, and relatively isolated group that consisted, moreover, of a fixed cast of advisors.

In recent years, the release of new and detailed records have provided scholars with much more information regarding the actual scale, scope, duration, and content of the planning sessions leading up to the Bay of Pigs. These records also reveal the magnitude of Kennedy's efforts to decide what to do about the Cuban operation *outside* the context of these meetings (see, e.g., Higgins, 1987; Neustadt & May, 1986; Reeves, 1993; Strober & Strober, 1993). Viewed in aggregate, these new sources provide a detailed—and in some instances almost hour-by-hour—chronicle of the decision-making process, including not only with whom Kennedy discussed the Bay of Pigs, but how often and for how long, as well as the specific content of some of those discussions.

This recently available material suggests—to an extent much less apparent in the fragmentary data then available to Janis—that President Kennedy did not rely exclusively, or even predominantly, on a small, fixed, tightly knit group of advisors in making his ultimate decisions regarding the Bay of Pigs operation. Instead, he employed a broad and complex—even if also somewhat idiosyncratic and unsystematic—advisory process. This new evidence, in fact, shows that Kennedy prudently sought advice from a wide corridor of diverse opinions. These included soliciting the views of President Dwight Eisenhower, the views of a number of prominent journalists and magazine editors he respected, various senators, and even close friends and colleagues (see, e.g., Dallek, 2003; George, 1980; Reeves, 1993).

To be sure, Kennedy remained secretive regarding the extent of his advisory process. He had a tendency, as presidential scholar Reeves (1993) noted, to compartmentalize his associations and discussions, probably to retain control over his decision-making process. Kennedy was also prudently cautious when it came to revealing his own thinking about the operation when soliciting others' views, most likely in order to keep his options open until the very end. As a result, individuals around Kennedy often underestimated the extent to which he sought the advice of others beside themselves. At the same time, they also overestimated the extent to which his opinion mirrored their own views (Reeves, 1993).

The new evidence also suggests that the comparatively few group planning sessions devoted specifically to the Bay of Pigs might better be characterized as a "series of *ad hoc* meetings" involving a "small but shifting set of advisers" (Neustadt & May, 1986, p. 142). Thus, they were hardly the sort of sustained deliberations involving a single, tightly knit and isolated group, as Janis argued (Kornbluh, 1998).

Janis also faulted Kennedy and his advisors for not attending more diligently to the details of the CIA plan and uncovering its prospective flaws. However, with the release of classified documents over the past four decades, scholars are now in a much better position to appreciate that the planning for this operation occurred during a period of what Reeves (1993) has aptly characterized as "an astonishing density of [simultaneous or co-occurring] events" (pp. 74–75). Specifically, at the very same time that he was dealing with planning the Bay of Pigs operation, Kennedy was also confronting a growing crisis in Southeast Asia, an extremely risky and uncomfortably fluid situation in Berlin, and a rapidly emerging "race for space" in which the United States seemed stuck in the starting blocks (Reeves, 1993, p. 85). Thus, the planning sessions for the Bay of Pigs occurred within the context of a series of other critical events that claimed the attention of Kennedy and his advisors.

As a consequence of this astonishingly packed agenda, Kennedy's advisors had to make difficult—but necessary—discriminations as to how best to allocate their limited and strained attentional resources. There was, as a result, somewhat of a tendency to delegate and defer to other experts when necessary. Even Secretary of Defense Robert McNamara, an individual legendary for his hands-on, detailed-oriented, attentive approach to decision making, has recently confessed, "I had entered the Pentagon with a limited grasp of military affairs and even less grasp of covert operations. This lack of understanding, coupled with my preoccupation with other matters and my deference to the CIA on what I considered an agency operation, led me to accept the [Bay of Pigs] plan uncritically" (p. 26). In fairness to himself, McNamara said he felt that Cuba was not his turf, nor was it his role to attend to the operational details of the Bay of Pigs planning, especially given the operational control of the CIA and the military experts advising it. Moreover, he felt his job was to attend to the more urgent and critical tasks President Kennedy had already assigned to him (including, among other things, reassessing U.S. nuclear deterrent capabilities and revamping its strategic policy regarding their use).

Janis's critique of the overall quality of the decision-making process, moreover, was predicated on his assumption that available evidence was sufficient to indicate serious problems with the proposed CIA operation. Thus, in his view, the decision to proceed with it reflected an avoidable decision error of the sort that defined groupthink. Janis used Kennedy's spontaneous exclamation (made to speechwriter Ted Sorensen as they strolled around the White House grounds after the failure), "How could I have been so stupid to let this thing go forward?" to suggest that this was Kennedy's own *post hoc* assessment. When Kennedy's complete statement is examined, however, it is clear he was referring specifically to his stupidity over trusting the recommendations of his military and CIA experts on the feasibility of the operation and its odds for success. As Neustadt and May (1986) noted more broadly, Kennedy was "scarcely stupid to think Castro a problem. *Most Americans thought so too, not least Eisenhower and Nixon*" (p. 270, emphases added). Newly available evidence suggests, in fact, that President Eisenhower had warned Kennedy in the strongest of terms at one of their early secret briefings (classified at the time of Janis's analysis) that it was Kennedy's "responsibility to do whatever was necessary to overthrow Castro because the United States could not let the present government go on there" (Higgins, 1987, p. 76). The former President communicated a sense of urgency for action to Kennedy, cautioning him against weakening commitment to the contest in Cuba. "Should we support guerrilla operations in Cuba?" Kennedy asked

Eisenhower. "To the utmost," Eisenhower replied (Reeves, 1993, p. 32). Eisenhower further warned Kennedy to "avoid any reorganization until he could become acquainted with the problems" (p. 32).

As Neustadt and May (1986) further noted, Kennedy was hardly stupid for trying to "hold firm against the overt use of American Force [during the invasion itself]. Law and morality were buttressed by military considerations" (p. 270). Thus, they concluded, "so the stupidity for which [Kennedy] blamed himself comes down to a small handful of judgments and presumptions on a handful of particulars" (p. 270).

Based upon all of the evidence available to him, Janis also assumed that the CIA had been at most simply a bit naive and overly optimistic in its assessments of the prospects for success of the planned Cuban operation. The recently declassified records and materials indicate, however, that Kennedy and his advisors were actively and intentionally misled about the operation by Richard Bissell, the primary proponent and operational officer in charge of the action, and other advisory elements with the CIA. There is strong evidence, for example, that Bissell, acting largely on his own initiative, transformed the operation from an initially small-scale covert infiltration into a substantial invasion (Neustadt & May, 1986). Moreover, the CIA was determined to proceed with its aggressive agenda of covert operations in Cuba and perfectly willing, if necessary, to provide bogus or inflated accounts of anti-Castro activities, civilian unrest, and lack of support for Castro to the President and his advisors in order to secure their commitment (Neustadt & May, 1986). Thus, the CIA representatives said nothing when President Kennedy expressed reservations about the original parameters for the operation and failed to act in good faith in complying with Kennedy's directives (Reeves, 1993, p. 263). Instead, as Reeves (1993) has nicely put it, the CIA started "making it up as they went along." In fact, Bissell and the CIA were quite adept at "reading" Kennedy's concerns and responding in the most persuasive way to assuage them. For example, as soon as Kennedy revealed a proclivity toward viewing acceptance or rejection of the original plan in terms of its political ramifications (e.g., risks to his image as president), the CIA and Bissell were quick to reframe the options available to him in similar terms. Detecting, for example, that the new President was sensitive to possible domestic political repercussions of the venture's failure, CIA Director Allen Dulles skillfully positioned the trade-offs associated with going forward versus calling off the operation in precisely such terms: "There would be a political price, as well as a military one," he shrewdly reminded the President, "for calling off the invasion" (Reeves, 1993, p. 71).

Moreover, and relatedly, Dulles knew how to prick Kennedy's anxieties about being compared to Eisenhower as the nation's commander in chief and coming up short in that comparison. When discussing the plan's prospects for success, for example, Dulles told Kennedy, "Mr. President, I know you're doubtful about this . . . but I stood at this very desk and said to President Eisenhower about a similar operation in Guatemala, 'I believe it will work.' And I say to you now, Mr. President, that the prospects for this plan are even better" (p. 73). Bissell and the CIA were also convinced that, because Kennedy was so concerned about appearing weak against communism and indecisive as a military leader, he would commit to the much larger operation they had in mind once it was too late to call it off. In other words, "when push came to shove," Kennedy would do whatever necessary to save face and avoid a military defeat (Reeves, 1993, p. 72).

Janis also made much of Kennedy's tendency to ignore expert advice that questioned the wisdom of the operation. According to Janis, this critical advice should have factored more heavily into Kennedy's deliberation process. In Janis's eyes, it also constituted further evidence that the Bay of Pigs was an avoidable decision error. Janis affords particular attention, in this regard, to the fact that Kennedy gave little weight to Chester Bowles's reservations regarding the logistics of the operation—concerns that in retrospect turned out to be quite prescient. However, recent documents indicate that President Kennedy had little confidence in Bowles's judgment or his strategic acumen with respect to such matters. Bowles had acquired a general reputation within the Kennedy administration and the State Department for gloomy, fatalistic analyses. "Chet was just telling me there are four revolutions [going on around the world] that we need to worry about," Kennedy once humorously quipped after one encounter with Bowles (Reeves, 1993, p. 53). Moreover, as revealed in recently released oral history of this period, Bowles had also acquired a reputation for making arguments that were perceived as containing serious strategic flaws (R. F. Kennedy, 1988). As a consequence, Bowles had "slipped in the President's esteem" (Higgins, 1987, p. 107). Indeed, he had become the sort of risk-averse, gloomy analyst who had simply cried wolf too many times. It is hardly surprising, therefore, that Kennedy chose to discount Bowles's advice in this particular instance. And, significantly, Kennedy was not alone in doing so. Dean Rusk and others also chose to give little credence to Bowles's forebodings about the Bay of Pigs.

In contrast, Kennedy and those around him had a great deal of confidence in Richard Bissell's operational abilities and his strategic acumen regarding covert operations. By all accounts, Bissell was a brilliant and compelling speaker. He displayed a deft grasp of strategic issues and a confident command of operational details. Whenever doubts were expressed about the wisdom or feasibility of some aspect of the Bay of Pigs operation or the logic of its assumptions, Bissell was able to provide convincing and reassuring answers. His answers, moreover, seemed amply supported by the CIA's seemingly objective and independent assessments (which we now know were intentionally disinformative; the CIA was determined to secure presidential commitment in the belief that once his feet were in the water, Kennedy would never pull them out).

Even the military advisors in the room—whom Kennedy scrutinized for reactions of reservation or doubt—revealed little ambivalence or concern regarding the operation as it was articulated by Bissell. Of them, Kennedy later commented, and with some justifiable bitterness, "Those sons-of-bitches with all the fruit salad just sat there nodding, saying it would work" (Reeves, 1993, p. 103).

This last point merits emphasis because Janis concluded that the deferential treatment accorded Bissell reflected a "taboo against antagonizing new members of the group" (Janis, 1972, p. 31). However, Kennedy accepted Bissell's judgment not because there was some sort of irrational or inflated trust of the members of his inner circle. Rather, and more simply, Kennedy felt Bissell made the keenest and most compelling arguments regarding going forward rather than backing away from the proposed CIA operation. Along with Eisenhower's strong urgings and support of the operation, Bissell's leadership and assessment of his prospects were viewed as significant endorsements by the new President.

In trying to further assess why President Kennedy proceeded with what seemed such an obviously flawed plan, Janis also afforded considerable attention to the role that overconfidence and unrealistic optimism played in the deliberation process. There was, as Janis aptly noted, some evidence of buoyant optimism in the early months of the Kennedy administration. However, much of the evidence Janis cites refers to a *general* mood in the White House about what might be accomplished in the four years that lay ahead. Significantly, the new evidence indicates that this uncritical or unrealistic optimism did *not* extend to Kennedy's deliberations about the Bay of Pigs operation. Presidential insider and historian Arthur Schlesinger was particularly adamant about this distinction. In support of this point, the new evidence indicates that President Kennedy expressed significant reservations about the plan from the outset. As soon as the operation had been presented to him, he immediately appreciated the serious political risks it posed and discerned the need to "turn down the noise" level on it (Reeves, 1993, p. 70). By "noise level" Kennedy meant the magnitude of the proposed invasion and the fact that it would occur during the day. He thus countered Bissell's ambitious proposed operation with a "scaled down" plan that included "no invasion, *just infiltration*" (p. 82, emphases added). He called for a change to a remote landing, and informed the CIA to make it a "quieter" landing, preferably even conducting the operation at night. He determined from the outset that there should be no U.S. military intervention. Additionally, he insisted on having a call-off option up until the last minute if he was not satisfied with the confluence of emerging factors. The CIA disapproved of these changes, but remained silent.

Kennedy's ongoing ruminations regarding the operation were not unrealistically optimistic nor was his acceptance of the parameters of the plan uncritical. Instead, he was, if anything, clearly dysphoric about the "hot potato" that Eisenhower had passed to him. Thus, when confronted with the question, "What do you think of this damned invasion idea?" he replied, "I think about it as little as possible" (Reeves, 1993, p. 76). Even up to the last minute, Kennedy expressed skepticism regarding important features of the plan (White, 1999). However, he also felt it was impossible to avoid proceeding with some version of the operation if he was to avert a potentially catastrophic political loss. Moreover, given the tightly compressed "window of opportunity" outlined by the CIA and Bissell, Kennedy felt there was little time for more leisurely reflection or equivocation. Higgins (1987) succinctly characterized his mood in the following terms, "Although profoundly doubtful about his first major presidential decision, two hours after Bissell's official deadline for the final Go–No Go deadline, Kennedy, with a heavy heart, released the invading fleet approaching the Bay of Pigs" (p. 131).

Janis suggests that Kennedy and his advisors suffered from unrealistic optimism and displayed symptoms of an "illusion of invulnerability" when deciding ultimately to proceed with the operation. However, new evidence indicates that Kennedy's evaluation of the prospects for success of this operation was influenced not only by the deliberately misleading CIA intelligence assessments but also by the fact that the plan had been developed under the leadership of President Eisenhower. Dwight Eisenhower was, after all, the primary architect and organizational genius behind the largest, most complex, and most successful military invasion in U.S. history—the invasion of Europe that led to Hitler's defeat. On first hearing the operational details of the proposed Cuban operation, Kennedy commented, somewhat sardonically, "Just like D-day." It was almost inconceivable to Kennedy that a plan developed under Eisenhower's watchful eye—and that Eisenhower now seemed to endorse unconditionally during their two top secret briefings together—could be so inherently flawed.

Kennedy's assessment of the prospects for success of the scaled down infiltration that he envisioned and authorized reflected, moreover, a reasonable reading of the history of U.S. covert operations up until that point. It is noteworthy to remember that this was a history that Janis and the American public had no inkling of at the time the groupthink hypothesis was conceived. With respect to the military risks of failure, for example, there had been, up until this point, a series of historical top secret but successful covert operations of exactly this sort (see Reeves, 1993). The idea of the Cuban operation was therefore simply to duplicate the role the CIA had played in other successful covert overthrows (p. 70). CIA Director Dulles reassured the president that the Cuban operation was even more likely to succeed than these past operations.

Second, with respect to the political risks associated with the invasion, U.S. presidents up until this time had been extraordinarily successful, especially given the number of risky covert operations around the world, at maintaining "plausible denial." The pre-Watergate press was far more trusting of U.S. institutions and less aggressive at investigating presidential indiscretions.

Viewed in aggregate, this new evidence suggests more clearly why President Kennedy felt *ex ante* that he had little reason to reflect upon the possibility of a *catastrophic* failure—either militarily or politically—of the sort that unfolded.

New evidence reinforces the view that President Kennedy's assessment of the merits of the CIA plan was dominated by political considerations. Kennedy was keenly cognizant, for instance, of the political implications of the operation's success. He was especially appreciative of the political repercussions associated with its failure. As Reeves (1993) concluded in a recent assessment of all of the available evidence, Kennedy was "concerned about the politics of the invasion—he wanted the least possible political risks—even though that meant military risks would be greatest" (p. 134). In Kennedy's eyes, the decision he faced was whether to continue with an ongoing covert operation that already enjoyed considerable institutional momentum—and that had been developed under Eisenhower's leadership—or "turn it off," thereby risking enormous scorn and imperiling an already fragile reputation.

Kennedy's tendency to construe this decision primarily in political terms, it is essential to note, was entirely consonant with all of the political instincts and judgments that had propelled him—against great odds—into the White House in the first place. Throughout his political career, Kennedy—despite his campaign rhetoric to the contrary—was a reluctant and circumspect cold warrior. He believed in cautious appraisal and conservative action. When it came to controversial or costly political issues, he avoided action whenever possible, or, if need be, selected the most moderate course available. Kennedy believed, as Schlesinger (1965) once noted [and aptly quoting one of Kennedy's own conclusions from *Profiles in Courage*], that those who go down to defeat in vain defense of a principle "will not be on hand to fight for that or any other principle in the future" (p. 110).

Throughout his campaign, Kennedy had self-consciously projected an identity as a cold warrior. He had also decried repeatedly the complacent and indecisive leadership of President Eisenhower and Vice President Nixon whom, he asserted, had allowed a communist regime to fester unchallenged only 90 miles from American soil. In his inaugural address, moreover,

Kennedy noted that he "welcomed" and "would not shrink" from his responsibility in dealing with the communist menace, a point he reiterated during press conferences and in other speeches.

Kennedy was also fully aware of the fact that he was under scrutiny. Both the American public and the international community were still forming impressions of this young and inexperienced leader. Thus, although "Ike's approval was not necessary," Kennedy felt, "his disapproval would be devastating" (Reeves, 1993, p. 33). Kennedy knew that his international adversaries, as well as his domestic rivals, would use evidence of weakness or indecisiveness to potentially devastating effect. Thus, from Kennedy's perspective, undoing the decision was much worse than letting it go forward in its scaled down form.[2]

In many ways, Kennedy's advisors tended to evaluate both the Cuban operation, as well as the options *they* confronted, in similar terms. Janis identified a number of important aspects of the psychological "climate" within the advisory group meetings, which, he argued, contributed directly to its defective deliberations. He suggested, for example, that Kennedy's advisors often suppressed personal doubts *because* of group pressures and group dynamics. In particular, he argued that group members were motivated to protect a valued but fragile *esprit de corp*.

There is no doubt that some members of Kennedy's group entertained reservations about the wisdom of going forward with the CIA operation. Nor is there any doubt that they sometimes elected not to fully express those concerns in the planning sessions. However, recent evidence suggests that political considerations, more than group dynamics *per se*, shaped the reticence of Kennedy's advisors to reveal their thoughts. For example, McGeorge Bundy's acquiescence to Kennedy's decision did not reflect a suppression of personal doubt that was predicated on a lack of willingness to disrupt the group's cohesiveness or *esprit de corps*, as Janis suggested. Rather, it was based on his perception that the "noise level" (i.e., scale and scope) of the covert operation had been reduced sufficiently to overcome his skepticism (Neustadt & May, 1986). Bundy, like Kennedy, was attuned primarily to the political risks public exposure of the covert operation posed. When reassured those risks were reasonably "contained," he opted for going forward. Moreover, in a later and more general discussion of his philosophy about serving a president as an advisor, Bundy noted, regarding the suppression of doubt or "self-censorship," that he felt his role was that of a

> staff officer who knows the big decision is made and is working to help in its execution. Obviously I have had my own views on what ought to be done and how, but since on balance I am in favor of trying harder, not heading for the exit, I am ready to help the president do it his way. He's the boss. (p. 123)

Other accounts emphasize strenuously that Bundy was always ready to express and defend his doubts when he felt doing so was essential (Valenti, 1975).

Similarly, although Secretary of State Dean Rusk indicated significant reservations about the operation after the fact, his decision not to voice them vociferously at the time did not reflect group dynamics so much as a carefully considered political calculus. As Frankel (1994) noted, Dean Rusk had developed a "formula" for political resilience in the competitive Washington bureaucracy, and that formula "was to endure and survive, to keep playing a mediocre hand rather than risk all for a better one, and to stand around for greater achievement another day." From the vantage point of a purely political calculus, it should be emphasized, this formula served Rusk remarkably well: he enjoyed the reins of power as secretary of state longer than anyone ever had before him.

Even advisor and historian Arthur Schlesinger noted that, although he felt badly *ex post* about having remained silent during the planning meetings, "my feelings of guilt were tempered by the knowledge that a course of objection would have accomplished little save to gain me a name as a nuisance" (Schlesinger, 1965, p. 144).

Thus, participants' self-censorship and suppression of personal doubts reflected a political motive more than a group-centered motive. When in doubt, each member of Kennedy's inner circle decided to conserve political capital and not draw attention to himself, especially for a cause that was not really his turf. Each reasoned, why weaken political credibility on later, more personally relevant issues? As Thomson (1968) astutely observed about the utility of such a calculus in the White House (or other competitive political settings), "The inclination to remain silent or to acquiesce . . . to live to fight another day, to give on this issue so that you can be 'effective' on later issues—is overwhelming" in such situations (p. 49).

In some respects, the very public exit of Chester Bowles—the most vocal public critic of the invasion plan—was ample validation for this point of view. Bowles was the one official ceremoniously "hung out to dry" by Kennedy when the house cleaning came. From the perspective of the pragmatic politician, a highly visible "profile in courage" (expressing one's doubts and going against the grain) may be highly desirable from the standpoint of high quality decision making, but it may be fatal to one's long-term political effectiveness and even survival.

Having covered a fair bit of ground in reviewing Janis's original arguments and the new evidence available to scholars that is pertinent to evaluating them, it may be useful here to attempt briefly to pull the strands of argument and evidence more tightly together. First, there is no doubt, as Janis aptly observed, that group deliberations played an important role in Kennedy's decision making. However, it is also clear that Kennedy reached far and wide beyond any one seemingly isolated and insulated inner circle for advice. Instead, he drew on diverse networks and contacts that he had carefully cultivated during his rise to political power and that had served him well in the past.

Second, it is clear that Kennedy trusted his advisors and relied on their assessments (although to varying degrees). Thus, his final decisions were influenced by the advice he received from them, as Janis argued. However, it is also clear that he deeply trusted his own political instincts and judgments, especially when it came to protecting his political power as president and his image in history. As Reedy (1970) concluded in a thoughtful assessment of presidential decision making, "The fact is that a president makes his decisions as he wishes to make them, under conditions he himself has established, and at times of his determination" (p. 31). Kennedy made his own decisions—and his decision to proceed with the Bay of Pigs was a considered, individual decision by a tough-minded political pragmatist who wished to avoid political loss.

Although Kennedy made his own decisions after what he might have regarded as prudent and reasoned reflection, this is not to claim that his decision-making process was necessarily always systematic or coherent. As presidential scholar and Kennedy observer Burns (2006) aptly noted:

> Crisis followed crisis [in the Kennedy administration] . . . The main fault lay in Kennedy's fluid, informal management style, which placed enormous burdens of coordination and follow-through on the president . . . He insisted that everything be brought to him. He was governing alone and he was overwhelmed by it. There was little chance for reflection, planning, or anticipation. (p. 50)

Thus, although it is true that Kennedy sometimes repudiated what from the outside might seem like expert advice (e.g., the advice of Chester Bowles), these tendencies did not reflect the operation of groupthink-like factors such as an illusion of vulnerability and unrealistic optimism. Rather, they reflected the same sort of cautious, risk-averse political appraisal of options available to him that had helped Kennedy reach the presidency in the first place. Thus, Kennedy did not "avoid" or "minimize" painful trade-offs, as Janis suggested, so much as opt for the less politically risky alternative. If anything, in fact, Kennedy ruminated intensely about his decisions. Relatedly, there seems pervasive evidence of an asymmetry in the salience of political gains and losses driving his judgment and choice. Specifically, in each case, the prospect of political losses often seemed to loom much larger than the prospect of potential gains from a given course of action. In some instances, this led decision makers to favor the status quo (e.g., Kennedy's decision to continue with rather than "turn off" the Cuban operation). Thus, when in doubt,

Kennedy almost always opted for the course of action that averted or mini-
mized, to the greatest degree possible, the prospect of political losses. To a
sometimes surprising extent, Kennedy tended to engage in "worse case"
thinking about the political risks and losses associated with certain decisions
like the Bay of Pigs. Kennedy might more aptly be considered a cautious warrior rather than a cold warrior.

Along related lines, much of the new evidence points, rather consistently,
to the conclusion that many of the individual members in Kennedy's advisory group also operated out of a similar, pragmatic, political calculus—a
calculus honed by years of experience in the political trenches. Thus, behaviors such as suppression of doubt and self-censorship reflected political considerations as much as they did concerns about disrupting the cohesiveness
or *esprit de corps* of the groups they were in. Although interesting, this pattern
is hardly surprising: Kennedy had been careful to select those individuals
who had the pragmatic intellect and tough-minded optimism and confidence
he felt they needed to be effective.

In sum, the present chapter argues that Janis's original analysis of the Bay
of Pigs decisions tends to overstate the causal importance of small group
dynamics, while underestimating the significance that *political* psychological
factors played in the unfolding of these fiascoes.[3] In asserting that the groupthink hypothesis fails to provide either a parsimonious or powerful theoretical account of this fiasco, I do not intend to cast aspersions on Janis's
observational skills. As Janis himself repeatedly noted throughout both editions of the groupthink work, the available historical records on the Bay of
Pigs were frustratingly fragmentary and equivocal regarding many key
points. As a consequence, he was required on many points to make inferential
leaps of faith in building his brief for the groupthink hypothesis. And it
should be remembered that it was Janis himself who encouraged future
scholars to revisit the Bay of Pigs decision-making process as more evidence
about it became available.

CONCLUSION

If repudiating the groupthink hypothesis, we are left in this chapter with
the nagging question, what, if anything, does the study of such fiascoes tell
us? As Whyte (1989) succinctly put the matter, "The critical question from
an analytic point of view [becomes] whether or not any pattern can be recognized from decisions of this sort, or are these simply difficult decisions that
unfortunately went awry" (p. 40). To put this question in perspective, it is
useful to remember that Janis characterized the Bay of Pigs invasion as "one
of the worst fiascoes ever perpetrated by a responsible government" (p. 14).
Scholars today continue to agree the decisions leading up to the invasion

were deeply flawed. However, when viewed in aggregate, the new evidence suggests that the Bay of Pigs fiasco was, at best, an *imperfect* failure of choice among imperfect alternatives. Most importantly, it emerges as a far from perfect example of groupthink. It is perhaps better characterized, as a failure of judgment and decision that flowed from political rather than group folly. When viewed from that perspective, the contributions of the present research can be framed in terms of both the theoretical and practical implications of these findings. I begin with the theoretical.

Broadly construed, the results of the present research provide additional support for a number of influential theoretical perspectives that have been brought to bear on risky decision making in organizations. At the time Janis conceived the groupthink hypothesis, it should be recalled, theory and research on organizational decision making were dominated largely by subjective utility theory. According to this perspective, organizational decision makers are motivated to maximize their prospective gains through their actions. More recent work on organizational decision making, however, has offered an alternative view of the political decision-making calculus, and one in which loss avoidance figures prominently in judgment and choice (e.g., Farnham, 1994; Kramer, 1989; Kramer, Meyerson, & Davis, 1990). Other studies (e.g., Stein & Pauly, 1993; Whyte, 1989) have buttressed the argument that decision makers are often motivated to minimize economic, social, and political losses in their actions. Particularly compelling work was done by Whyte (1989) with his thoughtful group polarization perspective. Whyte argued, consistent with prospect theory, "for each of the fiascoes discussed by Janis, the frame adopted by decision makers led them to perceive their decision as between a certain [i.e., sure] loss and potentially greater [but uncertain] losses" (p. 48). Much of the new evidence presented in this chapter supports Whyte's argument.

Such considerations engage, more generally, recent conceptions of rationality in organizational decision making. As Tetlock (1991) and March (1995) have noted, decisions in group and organizational settings are complex *social* events. As such, logics of appropriateness and concerns about accountability often influence decision makers' concerns about what it means for a decision to be "good." Decisions that seem poorly conceived when viewed through one theoretical lens may glisten when viewed from another. As Tetlock (1991) has crisply put it, "Response tendencies that look like judgmental flaws from one metaphorical perspective frequently look quite prudent from another" (p. 454). In other words, a decision that looks thoroughly irrational when viewed from the perspective of an "intuitive economist" might look quite reasonable when viewed from the perspective of the "intuitive politician." Thus, how attractive or unattractive a decision appears may vary with the analytic framing or conceptual categorization used by a decision maker when evaluating it. Along these lines, the analysis advanced in this chapter also resonates with recent perspectives on intelligent or adaptive decision making, in particular the work by Sternberg and his associates on the role practical intelligence plays in real-world problem solving (Sternberg, 1985; Sternberg, Wagner, Williams, and Hovarth, 1995; Wagner & Sternberg, 1986). Sternberg (1985) argues that intelligent behavior in real-world settings is often "directed toward purposive adaptation to . . . real-world environments relevant to one's life" (p. 45). In developing this idea, Sternberg et al. (1995) draw an important distinction between formal, academic knowledge and tacit knowledge. As defined by them, tacit knowledge is "action-oriented knowledge . . . that allows individuals to achieve goals they personally value. The acquisition and use of such knowledge appears to be uniquely important to competent performance in real-world endeavors" (p. 916). President Kennedy was, at heart, a pragmatic intellect in exactly this vein. His political intelligence was shaped by years of a cautious climb through a series of risky encounters and highly competitive political contests. Along the way, he derived significant tacit knowledge that helped him navigate through and around the political crises he confronted. Almost everyone who knew Kennedy and worked with him was struck by the cautious approach he took to political risks: When in doubt, he tended to take the less risky road (see, e.g. Dallek, 2003; Reeves, 1993). In contrast with previous work on practical intelligence, which has largely extolled the virtues of practical intelligence; the present research suggests some ways in which such hard-won and often adaptive forms of tacit knowledge, acquired on the road to power, may impede sensemaking and effective action once power is achieved.

Turning to the matter of practical implications, one might ask, "Does it really matter all that much which model or metaphor we use when viewing decision-making fiascoes of this sort?" To the extent such models and metaphors serve as templates that guide real-world policy makers as they wrestle with difficult and complex sensemaking predicaments of the sort Janis studied, the answer is yes. Janis himself remained optimistic about the utility of groupthink as a remedy for reducing avoidable decision error in organizations. His framework could, he suggested, provide a "new perspective for preventing Watergate-like fiascoes in government, private industry, and public welfare organizations" (1983, p. 204). But if, in fact, the theory is wrong, it may quite obviously lead policy makers to focus on irrelevant factors and even stimulate wrongheaded interventions or solutions. In this sense, when the status of a conceptual model is elevated to metaphor, it can obscure important relationships and hinder understanding as much as illuminate it. Along these lines, Hart (1990) lamented the tendency to use the concept of groupthink, "loosely and indiscriminately as a symbolically powerful pejorative label . . . a kind of analytical garbage can for commentators and analysts in need of a powerful metaphor" when trying to explain ill-fated institutional or organizational actions (p. ix).

Even to this day, groupthink remains among the most influential metaphors for understanding major policy fiascoes. As Tetlock (1995) aptly noted, "Janis' case studies represent the most sustained effort to apply work on group dynamics to elite political settings" (p. 46). The evidence assembled here suggests there is value in revisiting such theories and the qualitative evidence in their favor, lest we (paraphrasing George Eliot) get our thoughts hopelessly "entangled in metaphors," and "act fatally on the strength of them" (quoted in Hardin, 1980, p. 261).

NOTES

The initial development of these ideas was stimulated by a series of animated discussions with the late Irving Janis, while he and I were members of a small research group that met at the Center for Advanced Studies in the Behavioral Sciences (see Kahn & Zald, 1990, for the final report of our efforts). I owe a special thanks to Irv for his encouragement and enthusiasm in pursuing these ideas. I also owe a special debt to Robert McNamara, Carl Kaysen, Alain Entoven, the late Jack Valenti, the late McGeorge Bundy, the late John Gardner, and the late Richard Neustadt for their generosity and willingness to discuss their recollections of the Kennedy and Johnson Vietnam decisions with me. I appreciate the support of the John F. Kennedy School of Government and in particular its Center for Public Leadership, while I was researching this paper during visits in 2001 and 2006. Finally, the librarians at the John F. Kennedy Presidential Library were extremely helpful in locating pertinent documents for this research.

1. A preliminary analysis of the Bay of Pigs decision-making process was reported earlier in Kramer (1998). However, the completeness and validity of that analysis was limited by the unavailability of several key reports, including the critical CIA study and an independent study commissioned by the Attorney General Robert F. Kennedy (the so-called Taylor Study). Those documents have now been declassified and their major findings incorporated into this chapter.

2. Such political calculations undoubtedly influenced Kennedy's assessment of the so-called "disposal problem" (i.e., what to do with the fully trained guerrillas if they were not used). Janis viewed Kennedy's assessment of this issue as a major example of defective appraisal. The disposal problem, however, had a number of significant political ramifications in Kennedy's calculus. Once it became public knowledge that the young president had failed to carry through on an invasion plan designed by the master of invasion plans—four star General Eisenhower—he appeared weak and inexperienced, just as Nixon had repeatedly asserted during the presidential campaign.

3. In fairness to him, Janis (1983) was very mindful of the role that political factors played in the Bay of Pigs (see, e.g., his discussion of the four-factor model, pp. 30–32). However, from the standpoint of the newly available evidence, the political factors he considered were too narrow and afforded too little weight.

REFERENCES

Allison, G., & Zelikow, P. (1999). *Essence of decision* (2nd ed.). New York: Addison-Wesley.

Burke, J. P., & Greenstein, F. I. (1989). *How presidents test reality: Decisions on Vietnam, 1954 and 1965*. New York: Russell Sage Foundation.

Burns, J. M. (2006). *Running alone: Presidential leadership from JFK to Bush II (Why it has failed and how we can fix it)*. New York: Basic Books.

Cronin, T. E., & Greenberg, S. D. (1969). *The presidential advisory system*. New York: Harper & Row.

Dallek, R. (2003). *An unfinished life: John F. Kennedy, 1917–1963*. New York: Little, Brown.

Farnham, B. (1994). *Avoiding losses/take risks: Prospect theory and international conflict*. Ann Arbor, MI: University of Michigan Press.

Frankel, M. (1994, December 22). "Dean Rusk, Secretary of State, is dead at 85." Obituary, *New York Times*, pp. A1 and A16.

Fursenko, A., & Naftali, T. (1997). *One hell of a gamble: The secret history of the Cuban Missile Crisis, Khrushchev, Castro, and Kennedy, 1958–1964*. New York: Norton.

George, A. (1980). *Presidential decision-making in foreign policy: The effective use of information and advice*. Boulder, CO: Westview.

Hackman, R. (2003). *Leading teams*. Boston, MA: Harvard Business School Press.

Hardin, G. (1980). The tragedy of the commons. *Science, 43*, 257–264.

Hart, P. 't (1990). *Groupthink in government: A study of small groups and policy failure*. Baltimore, MD: Johns Hopkins University Press.

Higgins, T. (1987). *The perfect failure: Kennedy, Eisenhower, and the CIA at the Bay of Pigs*. New York: Norton.

Janis, I. L. (1972). *Victims of groupthink*. Boston: Houghton Mifflin.

Janis, I. L. (1983). *Groupthink: Psychological studies of policy decisions and fiascoes* (2nd ed.). Boston: Houghton Mifflin.

Kahn, R. L., & Zald, M. (1990). *Organizations and nation-states*. San Francisco: Jossey-Bass.

Kennedy, R. F. (1988). *In his own words: The unpublished recollections of the Kennedy years*. New York: Bantam Press.

Kornbluh, P. (1998). *Bay of Pigs declassified: The secret CIA report on the invasion of Cuba*. New York: The New Press.

Kramer, R. M. (1989). Windows of vulnerability or cognitive illusions? Cognitive processes and the nuclear arms race. *Journal of Experimental Social Psychology, 25*, 79–100.

Kramer, R. M., Meyerson, D., & Davis, G. (1990). How much is enough? Psychological components of "guns versus butter" decisions in a security dilemma. *Journal of Personality and Social Psychology, 58*, 984–993.

March, J. G. (1995). *A primer on decision making*. New York: Free Press.

Moorehead, G. (1991). Group decision fiascoes continue: Space shuttle Challenger and a revised groupthink framework. *Human Relations, 44*, 539–550.

Naftali, T. (2001). *The presidential recordings of JFK*. New York: Norton.

Neck, C. P. (1992). Jury deliberations in the trial of *U.S. v. John DeLorean:* A case analysis of groupthink avoidance and an enhanced framework. *Human Relations, 45,* 1077–1091.

Neustadt, R. E., & May, E. R. (1986). *Thinking in time: The uses of history for decision makers.* New York: Free Press.

Raven, B. H. (1974). The Nixon group. *Journal of Social Issues, 30,* 297–320.

Reedy, G. E. (1970). *The twilight of the presidency: An examination of power and isolation in the White House.* New York: World.

Reeves, R. (1993). *President Kennedy: Profile of power.* New York: Simon & Schuster.

Schlesinger, A. M., Jr. (1965). *A thousand days.* New York: Fawcett.

Schlesinger, A. M., Jr. (2007). *Journals: 1952–2000.* New York: Penguin.

Stein, J. G., & Pauly, L. W. (1993). *Choosing to cooperate: How states avoid loss.* Baltimore, MD: Johns Hopkins University Press.

Sternberg, R. J. (1985). *Beyond IQ: A triarchic theory intelligence.* New York: Cambridge University Press.

Sternberg, R. J., Wagner, R. K., Williams, W. M., & Horvath, J. A. (1995). Testing common sense. *American Psychologist, 50,* 912–927.

Strober, G. S., & Strober, D. H. (1993). *Let us begin anew: An oral history of the Kennedy administration.* New York: Harper.

Tetlock, P. E. (1991). An alternative metaphor in the study of judgment and choice: People as politicians. *Theory and Psychology, 1,* 451–475.

Tetlock, P. E. (1995). Social psychology and world politics. In D. Gilbert, S. Fiske, & G. Lindzey (Eds.), *Handbook of social psychology* (4th ed., Vol. 2, pp. 868–912). New York: McGraw-Hill.

Thomson, J. C. (1968, April). How could Vietnam happen? An autopsy. *Atlantic Monthly, 221,* 47–53.

Turner, M. E., Pratkanis, A. R., Probasco, P., & Leve, C. (1992). Threat, cohesion, and group effectiveness: Testing a social identity maintenance perspective on groupthink. *Journal of Personality and Social Psychology, 63,* 781–796.

Turner, M. E., Pratkanis, A. R., & Struckman, C. K. (2007). Groupthink as social identity maintenance. In A. R. Pratkanis (Ed.), *The science of social influence* (pp. 223–246). New York: Psychology Press.

Valenti, J. (1975). *A very human president.* New York: Norton.

Wagner, R. K., & Sternberg, R. J. (1986). Tacit knowledge and intelligence in the everyday world. In R. J. Sternberg & R. K. Wagner (Eds.), *Practical intelligence: Nature and origins of competence in the everyday world.* New York: Cambridge University Press.

White, M. J. (1999). *The Kennedys and Cuba: The declassified documentary history.* New York: Ivan Dee.

Whyte, G. (1989). Groupthink reconsidered. *Academy of Management Review, 14,* 40–56.

15

Self–Regulation and Leadership: Implications for Leader Performance and Leader Development

SUSAN ELAINE MURPHY, REBECCA J. REICHARD, AND
STEFANIE K. JOHNSON

Leader behavior is a social influence process and, as such, requires an understanding of social factors that affect perceptions. Social cognitive theory has been used in the past to describe followers' perceptions of leader behavior, effectiveness, and prototypicality. However, much less research has examined how social cognitive views of leader self-perception impact leader behavior. This chapter explores the continued and potential contribution of theories of self-regulation for leadership performance and development. Social psychological principles explaining both the structure and function of the self have vast implications for leadership; therefore, we overview theorizing incorporating ideas of the self, including leader self-schema and identity, as well as components of self-regulation such as self-efficacy and self-awareness within current theories of leadership.

Goal-driven, self-motivated, accomplishment-oriented, self-disciplined are common words used to describe successful individuals, and especially individuals who rise to positions of organizational and political leadership. Underlying these concepts is the belief that the key to success lies in one's own hands. Although popular writing underscoring preferred leadership skills and abilities identifies both the self-regulation of goal-directed behaviors and emotions as important components of success, little research has investigated the role of self-regulation in leadership theory (Boyatzis, Goleman, & McKee, 2002). Self-determination and self-management are major topics explained by a social psychological self-regulative view of motivation and have important implications for the study of leadership. This chapter examines specific components of self-regulation that play a role in effective leadership, including leadership self-efficacy, leader self-schema, and the role of self-awareness. We discuss the effects of these constructs on both leader performance and leader development within a model of self-regulation of leadership.

Social cognitive theory focuses on how people perceive both others and themselves in social situations (Fiske & Taylor, 1991). Given that leadership is a social activity that includes both leaders and followers, perceptual processes are important. In leadership and management, social cognitive theory has been used to understand followers' perceptions of leader behavior, including the affective and cognitive processing strategies used in the social perception of leaders (Lord & Emrich, 2001). Specifically, leaders whose behavior and attitudes match leadership prototypes are perceived more positively than leaders whose behavior and attitudes do not (Lord & Maher, 1993). Hogg's (2001) recent work on the Social Identity Theory of Leadership (SITL) supports the idea that the group is more likely to perceive a prototypic leader as an effective leader, and finds that group members will endorse leaders who behave in a prototypical manner (see also Hogg, Chapter 4 in this volume). A recent study has used SITL to investigate a specific leadership theory, that of charismatic leadership, showing that one becomes a charismatic leader when the group agrees that he or she, in fact, looks like a charismatic leader (Platow, D. van Knippenberg, Haslam, B. van Knippenberg, & Spears, 2006).

Somewhat neglected in this social cognitive "revolution" of leadership research has been the role of social cognitive factors from the leader's perspective. In other words, what effects do leaders' perceptions of their own behavior have in leadership situations? How do social cognitive factors affect how leaders think about themselves and how they engage in behaviors to enact the leadership role? Two broad areas of study with respect to the self provide some answers to these questions and have important implications for leader behavior (Fiske & Taylor, 1991). The first refers to the structure of the self and includes a person's personality attributes, social roles, past experiences, and future goals. Cantor and Kihlstrom (1987) argue that the mental representation of the self consists of a hierarchy of context-specific self-concepts with each representing one's beliefs about oneself in a different set of situations. This specific structure of the self is often called a person's self-schema or the "cognitive-affective structure that represents a person's experience in a given domain" (Fiske & Taylor, 1991, p. 182). Knowledge about the self can develop through socialization, reflected appraisals through others' views of us, explicit feedback from others, and from a process of social comparison (Taylor, Peplau, & Sears, 2006).

The second broad area of study in relation to the self is how the self enacts behavior, revises behavior, and alters the environment through self-regulation (Markus & Wurf, 1987). Self-regulation recognizes that individuals have self-control over their actions by setting internal standards and also by evaluating the discrepancy between the standard and personal performance (Carver & Scheier, 1998). Individuals control their actions through goal setting, cognitive strategies of planning or rehearsing, and monitoring goal attainment. In the next section we overview the effects of the structure of the self on leadership performance.

STRUCTURE OF THE SELF: DEVELOPING PERCEPTIONS OF SELF-SCHEMA AND LEADER IDENTITY

A small number of leadership researchers have utilized theories of the self for understanding leader behavior, although little empirical work has been done in this area. An early theoretical contribution came from Gardner and Avolio's (1998) dramaturgical view of charismatic leadership in which they outlined the role of the self system (specifically, leader identity, or self-schema for leadership) for a leader's ability to manage followers' impressions and to demonstrate particular leader behaviors. In addition to a thorough review of the self literature as applied to leadership, Gardner and Avolio suggested ideas for future research. For example, they propose that leaders' perceptions of situations and audiences are directly affected by their leader identity. That is, those who strongly identify themselves as leaders would readily pick out followers in a group or others who need their leadership guidance.

Another important contribution in this area came from a review of cognitive psychology's contribution to leadership research by Lord and Emrich (2001) who proposed that these same structures of leader identity were important, but went further to suggest that how one thinks about himself or herself as leader, or metacognitive processes, affect changes in leader behavior. As an example of these metacognitive processes, Wofford, Joplin, and Comforth (1996) showed that a leader's script for leadership changed depending upon situational demands. Furthermore, leaders who regularly interact with group members must behave in connection with some predetermined self script or schema that is part of their working self-concept (Wofford & Goodwin, 1994). A study by Wofford, Goodwin, and Whittington (1998), in fact, showed that a leader's behavior is dictated by leader self-schema; specifically, leaders with a transformational leader self-schema were seen as more transformational by their subordinates than those whose leadership schema did not match the features of transformational leadership. Murphy and Ensher (in press) found some support for this idea in a qualitative investigation that showed specific types of leadership schema as articulated in leader interviews were important for charismatic leader behavior.

Recent theorizing on the self has also been incorporated into models of authentic leadership (Chan, Hannah, & Gardner, 2005; Gardner, Avolio, Luthans, May, & Walumbwa, 2005). According to authentic leadership theory as developed by Luthans and Avolio (2003), authentic leaders display transparency, openness, and trust, provide guidance toward worthy objectives, and take an active role in follower development. In fact, to be an effective leader, authentic leadership researchers argue that one must be genuine with respect to his or her identity through self-awareness and self-acceptance. Therefore, within authentic leadership theories issues of the self become very important for effective leadership.

In understanding the application of leader self-schema or identity to our understanding of leadership effectiveness, researchers must also consider the complex nature of these constructs. Leader schemata or leader identity are most likely multifaceted, exist at multiple levels, and change over time as leaders engage in leadership developmental experiences that build leadership skills as well as the ability to view the complexity of leadership challenges. Building on work by Brewer and Gardner (1996), Lord and Brown (2004) identified three levels within leader identity that are important to leader behavior. These are individual level, relational identity, and collective leader identities. To some extent these are also considered developmental levels as Lord and Hall (2005) assert that the individual level, where one is emphasizing "their uniqueness and differentiation of the self from others," is usually held by novice leaders. As one becomes more comfortable in the relationship, leader identity is expected to take on a more relational emphasis that is manifested in specific roles or relationships, where, as Lord and Hall put it, "the leader include[s] others in the definition of one's own self-identity." Finally, as leaders develop and become responsible for larger groups or causes, a collective identity will develop, as well as the qualities that are prototypical of these collectives. In other words, collective identity is characterized by a leader who adopts and manifests the agreed upon behaviors of the group.

The ideas surrounding self-construal, especially independent versus interdependent self, may also affect leader identity and behavior (D. van Knippenberg, B. van Knippenberg, De Cramer, & Hogg, 2004). For example, it may be that leaders with extreme independent self-construals will find it difficult to connect with followers along either relational or collective identities because of their overwhelming motivation to see followers and leaders as being independent (Sedikides & Brewer, 2001). It may be that in addition to a changing schema surrounding how a leader might behave in general, there may also be a deeper schemata surrounding how relationships work that is important to leadership effectiveness. Leaders who think of themselves as more intertwined with the fate of their group members (interdependent self-construal) may be more effective at leading teams.

FUNCTION OF THE SELF: SELF-REGULATION AND LEADER PERFORMANCE

In his social cognitive theory, Albert Bandura (1997) portrayed a triadic model of reciprocal causation by stating that (1) the person, (2) the environment, and (3) past behavior have reciprocal impacts on one another. Self-regulation is one of the five human capabilities outlined in social cognitive theory (symbolizing, forethought, observational, self-regulatory, and self-reflective) that affect individuals' behavior by enabling them "to exercise some control over their thoughts, feelings, motivation, and actions" (Bandura, 1991, p. 249). According to Bandura, the process of self-regulation begins with the level of self-awareness in which individuals observe their thoughts and behaviors (Bandura, 1986). Next, they make judgments of their capabilities within a domain—or estimates of self-efficacy. Self-efficacy is defined by Bandura (1986) as "judgments of capabilities to organize and execute courses of action required to attain designated types of performances" (p. 391; Bandura, 1991). High self-efficacy has been shown to lead to increased performance in a wide range of situations (Bandura, 1997). Differences in levels of self-efficacy also explain individual reactions to discrepancies between personal standards and attainments. For those individuals low in self-efficacy, failure to attain a personal standard is discouraging, whereas for those individuals high in self-efficacy, it is motivating (Bandura & Cervone, 1983; Stajkovic & Luthans, 1998). Finally, they engage in the thoughts, affect, motivation, and action.

Murphy (2002) introduced a model of self-regulation for leaders based on ideas of the self, especially focused on the role that leadership self-efficacy would play in leader performance when leaders were faced with situational challenges that produced stress. The model, adapted from Markus, Cross, and Wurf (1990) begins with the structure of the self with respect to the domain of leadership. The structure requires that a leader holds a prototype of the role of leaders in general and second, must hold a self-schema with respect to his or her own required behavior in that role. Those who either choose or find themselves in a leadership role must understand role requirements and make an assessment of their current complement of skills to fulfill that role. With respect to the leadership domain, the leader must make self-efficacy assessments of his or her capabilities to fulfill the leadership role under various conditions or situations (Murphy, 1992). Leadership self-efficacy has been shown to be related to leader effectiveness and group effectiveness. For example, Murphy and Ensher (1999) found that female supervisors with higher self-efficacy were rated as more effective than those with low self-efficacy, whereas self-efficacy made no difference for male supervisors. Hoyt, Murphy, Halverson, and Watson (2003) showed that leadership self-efficacy increased collective self-efficacy of followers. Therefore, not only did self-efficacy work to increase the leader's effectiveness, it in turn increased the self-efficacy of followers. In these studies, leadership self-efficacy was centered around the task of small group leadership. Paglis and Green (2002) found that leadership self-efficacy, specific to leading change, predicted leader effectiveness. Recently, Foti and Hauenstein (2007) found that even general self-efficacy was predictive of leader emergence and ratings of leader effectiveness.

In addition to the key role of self-efficacy in understanding leadership effectiveness, another important component is found in the work on self-management. Techniques including self goal-setting, rehearsal, self-observation, and self-reward and self-punishment have been shown to be effective ways to change workplace behavior (Manz, 1986). For example, self-management strategies have been shown to reduce absenteeism (Frayne & Latham, 1987; Latham & Frayne, 1989); increase sales performance (Frayne & Geringer, 2000); and improve newcomers' organization socialization (Saks & Ashforth, 1996). As the leader moves to organize behavior and plan actions, issues of self-management become even more important. Self-management has been show to be an effective tool for understanding leadership effectiveness (Manz & Sims, 1989), improving joint venture general manager performance (Frayne & Geringer, 1994) and enhancing team effectiveness (Cohen, Chang & Ledford, 1997; Uhl-Bien & Graen, 1998). Given the consistent effects of self-management techniques for employees in general, the application to leadership provides an important addition to current theorizing.

THE SELF AND MOTIVATION TO DEVELOP LEADERSHIP

While the concepts of self and self-regulation are important for leadership performance, they each also have implications for leadership development. Because the responsibility of leadership development has largely shifted from the organization to the individual, leader self-development is becoming a key strategy for leader development (Reichard & Murphy, 2008). Based on social cognitive theory, Reichard (2006) defined leader self-development as any self-initiated and/or self-structured developmental activity of a leader focused on expanding his or her leadership. Leader self-development covers a broad range of behaviors and thoughts and can be differentiated from other types of leader development. Specifically, as contrasted to formal training, leader self-development offers a continuous, flexible strategy to develop leaders in today's complex organizational environment. Given the high levels of self-initiation and self-control needed to engage in leader self-development, self-regulation plays a central role in this process as well.

An important precursor to engaging in leader self-development behaviors is the level of motivation to develop possessed by the individual. Maurer and Lippstreu (2005) asserted that participation in leader development activities, such as leadership training, is predicted by one's motivation to develop leadership, which is different from motivation to lead. These authors stated that motivation to develop leadership capability is defined as "the desire to develop or improve leadership skills and attributes through effort" (Maurer, Weiss, & Barbeite, 2003). Motivation is needed to drive a leader to improve. A leader with high motivation to develop expends large amounts of energy on development and persists in the face of failure. As a key predictor of the success of leader self-development, the intensity and direction of a leader's motivation to develop may be the result of two interrelated yet distinct self-processes: self-discrepancy and leader identity.

First, motivation to develop can be described in terms of self-discrepancy theory (Higgins, 1987). According to self-discrepancy theory, there are three domains of the self: actual, hoped for, and feared. While the actual self refers to one's representation of the attributes believed to be actually possessed, the hoped-for possible self is one's representation of the attributes one would ideally like to possess and the feared possible self represents what the leader wishes to avoid becoming (Markus & Nurius, 1986a). These latter two possible selves allow leaders to be "active producers" of their own development by trying out different "provisional selves" (Markus & Nurius, 1986b; Ibarra, 1999). By contrasting the hoped for or feared leader self to the actual leader self, salience is placed on the discrepancy resulting in motivation for improvement (Cross & Markus, 1991). Therefore, the salience of the discrepancy between actual and possible leader selves may be one explanation for the intensity of one's motivation to develop leadership.

Specifically, the actual-to-possible self-discrepancy may impact a leader's motivation to develop through the desire to reduce tension caused by the discrepancy. When the gap between one's actual leadership ability and one's possible leadership ability becomes salient, tension results. Related to cognitive dissonance theory, the size of the discrepancy impacts the amount of tension felt (Festinger & Carlsmith, 1959). The tension provides a basis for energy, direction, and persistence—that is, motivation to develop (Ryan & Deci, 2000). Therefore, tension created from the increased salience of the actual-to-possible self-discrepancy will motivate the leader to develop in order to reduce the tension or uneasiness. It is in this way that enhanced self-awareness serves as a tool for evaluation of current leadership skills and abilities and a springboard for development (Hall, 2004).

Second, the intensity and direction of motivation to develop leadership may be a result of the strength of one's leader identity. As Lord and Hall note:

> Identity is a central focus because it (a) provides an important structure around which relevant knowledge can be organized; (b) is a source of motivational and directional forces that determine the extent to which the leader voluntarily puts himself or herself in developmental situations; and (c) may provide access to personal material (i.e., stories, core values, etc.) that can be used to understand and motivate subordinates. (p. 592)

Reichard found that leader identity strength, defined as the number of leader behaviors that the leader endorsed as characteristic of him or her self, was positively and significantly correlated with motivation to develop leadership (Reichard, 2006). Those who see leadership as central to their identity were better versed in the various behaviors involved in leadership than individuals who thought only a handful of behaviors were descriptive of their leadership. Therefore, as an alternative to focusing on a self-discrepancy as a key motivational factor behind self-development, future researchers may want to focus on building individuals' positive identity as a leader, which includes a range of behaviors both positive and negative. Building a strong leader identity may include such things as opportunities to experience more and difficult leadership challenges, enhancement of leader self-efficacy through success, verbal persuasion, and observation of similar role models, and an increase in knowledge about various leadership styles.

Although an individual identifies as a leader, the likelihood that he or she actually engages in leader self-development may be dependent on efficacy beliefs, both in terms of developmental efficacy and means efficacy. While one's belief in his/her ability to develop leadership skills is an internal efficacy belief (Maurer, Weiss, & Barbeite, 2003), means efficacy, an external efficacy belief, refers to one's belief in the tools available to perform a task (Eden & Granat-Flomin, 2000). The level of developmental efficacy may be influenced by one's beliefs regarding the stability of leadership ability. High developmental efficacy requires that the individual holds the assumption that leaders are made rather than born, also referred to as an incremental theory of ability. Developmental efficacy may also increase through successful attempts at development or observation of such in similar others. Similarly required for effective leader self-development, individuals with high means efficacy are confident that the tools and resources to which they have access will work effectively in improving their leadership. In fact, Reichard demonstrated that means efficacy was a significant moderator of the relationship between the quality of leader self-developmental goals and intentions to self-develop (Reichard, 2006). Taken together, important "self" variables for leader development, especially self-development, include leader identity, self-discrepancy, motivation to develop leadership, and both developmental and means efficacy.

SELF-AWARENESS IN LEADERSHIP PERFORMANCE AND DEVELOPMENT

A final important aspect in issues of self and self-regulation as applied to leadership is self-awareness. Within leadership and managerial performance and development, many employees receive formalized feedback from multiple sources. How they use this feedback, however, varies. Some may disregard it, while others use the information to further develop their skills. According to Gardner et al. (2005) feedback makes one aware of both one's strengths and weaknesses, along the many facets of leader identity, which could include one's unique values, identity, emotions, goals, knowledge, talents, and/or capabilities.

Wicklund's (1975) theory of self-awareness suggests that self-aware persons attend more to others' perceptions of them and, therefore, can utilize this information to appropriately change their behavior. More recently, self-awareness has been conceptualized as the similarity or difference between the way one sees oneself and the way he or she is seen by others (Atwater, Roush, & Fischthal, 1995; Atwater & Yammarino, 1992). The information used to assess self-awareness often stems from the 360-degree evaluation process, in which leaders rate themselves on a variety of dimensions and receive ratings from peers, subordinates, and supervisors. Estimates suggest that 12–29 percent of organizations use 360-degree feedback based on the assumption that providing leaders with feedback on how others view them will facilitate the improvement of their performance (Church, 2000).

The research on self-awareness has offered insights into the relationship between self-awareness and other individual differences, leadership performance, and the use of feedback. In terms of self-awareness and individual differences, more self-aware individuals also tend to be higher in intelligence, achievement status, and internal locus of control (Mabe & West, 1982). Researchers Atwater and Yammarino (1992) also suggest that self-ratings provide some insight into raters' traits or dispositions, such as self-esteem or self-consciousness. However, self-ratings are not generally seen as accurate predictors of performance and often suffer from a leniency bias (Harris & Schaubroeck, 1988; Hough, Keyes, & Dunnette, 1983; Podsakoff & Organ, 1986). But, when coupled with information from others' ratings, they can provide information about the raters and their leadership performance.

Self-aware individuals also report greater levels of trust than others, while individuals who underestimate their abilities tend to elicit lower levels of trust (Sosik, 2001). Further, self-aware leaders (those whose self-ratings are in agreement with others) tend to receive higher leadership ratings than others, followed by underraters (those who rate themselves lower than others rate them) and overraters (those who rate themselves higher than others rate them) who receive the lowest ratings (Atwater, Roush, & Fischthal, 1995; Atwater & Yammarino, 1992). Sosik also found that self-aware individuals display greater levels of charismatic leadership that relate positively to ratings of managerial performance by superiors (Sosik, 2001). In addition, Ostroff, Atwater, and Feinberg (2004) found that self-aware individuals earned more money than less self-aware individuals.

In terms of using feedback, Atwater and Yammarino (1992) suggest that self-aware individuals are better able to incorporate others' assessments into their self-perception and, therefore, are better able to adjust their behavior and improve their shortcomings. Conversely, overraters and underraters may avoid seeking feedback and, therefore, are less able to make self-improvements. Further, overraters' confidence causes them to ignore feedback from others and makes them unlikely to set self-improvement goals (Fedor, Rensvold, & Adams, 1992). In one study, Johnson and Ferstl (1999) examined the effects of receiving subordinate feedback on managers' self-assessment and performance over a year-long period. They found that overraters decreased their self-ratings after receiving 360-degree feedback, whereas their subordinates' ratings increased. Underraters tended to have higher self-ratings but lower subordinate ratings after receiving feedback. Finally, self-aware individuals decreased their self-ratings over time, although their subordinate ratings increased.

Self-awareness, then, is another important concept surrounding the self with social cognition that has implications for both leadership behavior and leadership development. Because, as we noted earlier, leaders and managers receive feedback on their leadership behavior, how they choose to use that information in behavior change or as an impetus for development is important. Coupled with a leader's level of self-efficacy, and perhaps strength of leadership identity, feedback and increasing self-awareness become important tools for improving behavior.

IMPLICATIONS FOR RESEARCH IN SOCIAL PSYCHOLOGY AND LEADERSHIP

In this chapter we sought to explore the importance of self-regulation for leadership performance and leadership development. We overviewed ideas of the self including leader identity and self-schema, which are important components of leadership, but have been somewhat overlooked in many theories of leadership. We also briefly overviewed ideas of self-regulation including the role of leadership self-efficacy and self-regulation techniques for increasing leadership performance and provided specific examples of these concepts as applied to leader self-development.

This chapter, however, has merely scratched the surface of the possible contribution of social psychology with respect to social cognitive theories of leadership from the leader's perspective. We are encouraged that researchers are beginning to incorporate these ideas into their leadership research, but there is still more that could be done. As we noted earlier in the chapter, Gardner and Avolio presented a comprehensive list of research studies that would explore many of the ideas they proposed in their dramaturgical model of charismatic leader behavior. Their research suggestions are not limited to charismatic leadership theory, but also have implications for further research in transformational leadership theory as well as other popular theories such as leader member exchange. For example, it is easy to imagine the difficulty in developing high quality leader member exchanges characterized by fairness, similarity in values, or employee development when the leader has no leader self-schema around those concepts but instead considers leadership as a tool exclusively for personal gain. The contribution of the self especially in understanding leadership behavior underscores the importance of appropriately matching leader self-schema and the leadership culture required within an organization.

Within this chapter we did not, however, address issues of self-presentation or impression management, but we recognize the large role they play in all social interactions, and possibly to an even larger extent in leadership situations. A final area for continued research is on the development of leadership identity and schema. Understanding initial leadership identity development and how identity progresses from an individual, relational, and collective level has implications for improving leadership effectiveness and leadership development.

There are a few existing roadblocks to full utilization of social psychology in current leadership theorizing. First, it remains difficult to generalize the results of the type of laboratory research that needs to be done to "real" organizational leaders. However, continued programs of research such as that done by Wofford and colleagues that move from laboratory to field studies will make worthwhile contributions. Second, vast research literatures in leadership may be unintentionally ignored by social psychologists when conducting leadership research, and similarly, leadership researchers fail to consider applicable social psychological research. Researchers are making inroads in addressing this problem, and this volume represents an important step. And finally, theoretical offerings as applied to particular leadership theories sometimes fail to integrate understanding of self-concepts and self-regulation because the ideas were introduced within a particular leadership theory and it is not always clear how the concepts might apply to other theories. One exception to this trend comes from Lord and his colleagues, who provide theoretical explanations within cognitive and social cognitive theory that transcends specific leadership theories. Comprehensive modeling of leadership self-regulation across leadership theories could make an invaluable contribution to the field.

REFERENCES

Atwater, L. E., Roush, P., & Fischthal, A. (1995). The influence of upward feedback on self and follower ratings of leadership. *Personnel Psychology, 48*, 35–59.

Atwater, L. E., & Yammarino, F. J. (1992). Does self-other agreement on leadership perceptions moderate the validity of leadership and performance predictions? *Personnel Psychology, 45*, 141–164.

Bandura, A. (1986). *Social foundations of thought and action.* Englewood Cliffs, NJ: Prentice-Hall.

Bandura, A. (1991). Social cognitive theory of self-regulation. *Organizational Behavior and Human Decision Processes, 50*, 248–287.

Bandura, A. (1997). *Self-efficacy: The exercise of control.* New York: W. H. Freeman.

Bandura, A., & Cervone, D. (1983). Self-evaluative and self-efficacy mechanisms governing the motivational effects of goal systems. *Journal of Personality and Social Psychology, 45*(5), 1017–1028.

Boyatzis, R., Goleman, D., & McKee, A. (2002). *Primal leadership: Realizing the power of emotional intelligence.* Boston, MA: Harvard Business School Publishing.

Brewer, M. B., & Gardner, W. (1996). Who is this "we"? Levels of collective identity and self representation. *Journal of Personality and Social Psychology, 71*, 83–93.

Cantor, N., & Kihlstrom, J. F. (1987). *Personality and social intelligence.* Englewood Cliffs, NJ: Prentice-Hall.

Carver, C. S., & Scheier, M. F. (1998). *On the self-regulation of behavior.* Cambridge: Cambridge University Press.

Chan, A., Hannah, S. T., & Gardner, W. L. (2005). Veritable authentic leadership: Emergence, functioning, and impacts. In W. L. Gardner, B. J. Avolio, & F. Walumbwa (Eds.), *Authentic leadership practice: Origins, effects, and development. Monographs in leadership and management* (Vol. 3, pp. 3–31). New York: Elsevier Ltd.

Church, A. H. (2000). Do higher performing managers actually receive better ratings? A validation of multirater assessment methodology. *Consulting Psychology Journal: Practice and Research, 52*, 99–116. Mercer's fax facts survey results: Multisource assessment. (Available from William M. Mercer, Inc., 1166 Avenue of the Americas, New York, NY 10036.)

Cohen, S. G., Chang, L., & Ledford, G. E. (1997). A hierarchical construct of self-management leadership and its relationship to quality of work life and perceived work group effectiveness. *Personnel Psychology, 50*, 275–309.

Cross, S., & Markus, H. (1991). Possible selves across the lifespan. *Human Development, 34*(4), 230–255.

Eden, D., & Granat-Flomin, R. (2000). Augmenting means efficacy to improve service performance among computer users: A field experiment in the public sector. Presented at SIOP, New Orleans.

Fedor, D., Rensvold, R., & Adams, S. (1992). An investigation of factors expected to affect feedback seeking: A longitudinal field study. *Personnel Psychology, 45,* 779–805.

Festinger, L., & Carlsmith, J. M. (1959). Cognitive consequences of forced compliance. *Journal of Abnormal Psychology, 58,* 203–210.

Fiske, S. T., & Taylor, S. E. (1991). *Social cognition.* New York: McGraw-Hill.

Foti, R. J., & Hauenstein, N. M. A. (2007). Pattern and variable approaches in leadership emergence and effectiveness. *Journal of Applied Psychology, 92,* 347–355.

Frayne, C. A., & Geringer, J. M. (1994). A social cognitive approach to examining joint venture general manager performance. *Group & Organization Management, 19*(2), 240–262.

Frayne, C. A., & Geringer, J. M. (2000). Self-management training for improving job performance: A field experiment involving salespeople. *Journal of Applied Psychology, 85*(3), 361–372.

Frayne, C. A., & Latham, G. (1987). Application of social learning theory to employee self-management of attendance. *Journal of Applied Psychology, 72,* 387–392.

Gardner, W., & Avolio, B. J. (1998). The charismatic relationship: A dramaturgical perspective. *Academy of Management Review, 23,* 32–58.

Gardner, W., Avolio, B. J., Luthans, F., May, D., & Walumbwa, F. (2005). Can you see the real me? A self-based model of authentic leadership development. *Leadership Quarterly, 16,* 343–372.

Hall, D. T. (2004). Self-awareness, identity, and leader development. In D. V. Day, S. J. Zaccaro, & S. M. Halpin (Eds.), *Leadership development for transforming organizations: Grow leaders for tomorrow* (pp. 71–98). Mahwah, NJ: Erlbaum.

Harris, M., & Schaubroeck, J. (1988). A meta-analysis of super-supervisor, self-peer, and peer-supervisor ratings. *Personnel Psychology, 41,* 43–62.

Higgins, E. T. (1987). Self-discrepancy: A theory relating self and affect. *Psychological Review, 94*(3), 319–340.

Hogg, M. A. (2001). A social identity theory of leadership. *Personality and Social Psychology Review, 5,* 184–200.

Hough, L., Keyes, M., & Dunnette, M. (1983). An evaluation of three "alternative" selection procedures. *Personnel Psychology, 36,* 261–275.

Hoyt, C. L., Murphy, S. E., Halverson, S. K., & Watson, C. B. (2003). Group leadership: Efficacy and effectiveness. *Group Dynamics, Theory, Research, and Practice, 7,* 259–274.

Ibarra, H. (1999). Provisional selves: Experimenting with image and identity in professional adaptation. *Administrative Science Quarterly, 44*(4), 764–791.

Johnson, J. W., & Ferstl, K. L. (1999). The effects of interrater and self-other agreement on performance following upward feedback. *Personnel Psychology, 52,* 272–303.

Latham, G. P., & Frayne, C. A. (1989). Self-management training for increasing job attendance: A follow-up and replication. *Journal of Applied Psychology, 74,* 411–416.

Lord, R. G., & Brown, D. J. (2004). *Leadership processes and follower self-identity.* Mahwah, NJ: Lawrence Erlbaum.

Lord, R. G., & Emrich, C. G. (2001). Thinking outside the box by looking inside the box: extending the cognitive revolution in leadership research. *Leadership Quarterly, 11* (4), 551–579.

Lord, R. G., & Hall, R. J. (2005). Identity, deep structure and the development of leadership skill. *Leadership Quarterly, 16,* 591–615.

Lord, R. G., & Maher, K. J. (1993). *Leadership and information processing: Linking perceptions and performance.* New York: Routledge.

Luthans, F., & Avolio, B. J. (2003). Authentic leadership: A positive developmental approach. In K. S. Cameron, J. E. Dutton, & R. E. Quinn (Eds.), *Positive organizational scholarship* (pp. 241–261). San Francisco: Barrett-Koehler.

Mabe, P., & West, S. (1982). Validity of self-evaluation of ability: A review and meta-analysis. *Journal of Applied Psychology, 67,* 280–286.

Manz, C. C. (1986). Self-leadership: Toward an expanded theory of self-influence processes in organizations. *Academy of Management Review, 11*(3), 585–600.

Manz, C. C., & Sims, H. P., Jr. (1989). *SuperLeadership: Leading others to lead themselves.* New York: Prentice-Hall.

Markus, H., Cross, S., & Wurf, E. (1990). The role of the self-system in competence. In R. J. Sternberg & J. Kolligian Jr. (Eds.), *Competence considered* (pp. 205–225). New Haven, CT: Yale University Press.

Markus, H., & Nurius, P. (1986a). Possible selves. *American Psychologist, 41*(9), 954–969.

Markus, H., & Nurius, P. (1986b). Possible selves. *American Psychologist, 41*(9), 955.

Markus, H., & Wurf, E. (1987). The dynamic self-concept: A social psychological perspective. *American Review of Psychology, 38,* 299–337.

Maurer, T. J., & Lippstreu, M. (2005, August). *Differentiating motivation to lead from motivation to develop leadership capability: Relevance of 'born vs. made' beliefs.* Paper presented at the meeting of the Academy of Management, Honolulu, HI.

Maurer, T. J., Weiss, E. M., & Barbeite, F. G. (2003). A model of involvement in work-related learning and development activity: The effects of individual, situational, motivational, and age variables. *Journal of Applied Psychology, 88*(4), 707–724.

Murphy, S. E. (1992). *The contribution of leadership experience and self-efficacy to group performance under evaluation apprehension.* Unpublished doctoral dissertation, University of Washington, Seattle.

Murphy, S. E. (2002). Leader self-regulation: The role of self-efficacy and multiple intelligences. In R. E. Riggio, S. E. Murphy, & F. J. Pirozzolo (Eds.), *Multiple intelligences and leadership* (pp. 163–186). Mahwah, NJ: Erlbaum.

Murphy, S. E., & Ensher, E. A. (1999). The effects of leader and subordinate characteristics in the development of leader-member exchange quality. *Journal of Applied Social Psychology, 29*(7), 1371–1394.

Murphy, S. E., & Ensher, E. A. (2008). A qualitative analysis of charismatic leadership in creative teams: The case of television directors. *Leadership Quarterly, 19*(3), 336–352.

Ostroff, C., Atwater, L. E., Feinberg, B. J. (2004). Understanding self-other agreement: A look at rater and rate characteristics, context, and outcomes. *Personnel Psychology, 57,* 333–375.

Paglis, L. L, & Green, S. G. (2002). Leadership self-efficacy and managers' motivation for leading change. *Journal of Organizational Behavior, 23,* 215–235.

Platow, M. J., van Knippenberg, D., Haslam, S. A., van Knippenberg, B., & Spears, R. (2006). A special gift we bestow on you for being representative of us: Considering leader charisma from a self-categorization perspective. *British Journal of Social Psychology, 45*(2), 303–320.

Podsakoff, P., & Organ, D. (1986). Self-reports in organizational research: Problems & prospects. *Journal of Management, 12,* 531–544.

Reichard, R. J. (2006). *Leader self-development intervention study: The impact of self-discrepancy and feedback.* Unpublished doctoral dissertation: University of Nebraska.

Reichard, R. J., & Murphy, S. E. (2008). *Leader self-development as organization strategy.* Manuscript submitted for publication.

Ryan, R. M., & Deci, E. L. (2000). Self-determination theory and the facilitation of intrinsic motivation, social development, and well-being. *American Psychologist, 55,* 68–78.

Saks, A. M., & Ashforth, B. E. (1996). Proactive socialization and behavioral self-management. *Journal of Vocational Behavior, 48,* 301–323.

Sedikides, C., & Brewer, M. B. (2001). *Individual self, relational self, collective self.* Philadelphia, PA: Psychology Press.

Sosik, J. J. (2001). Self-other agreement on charismatic leadership: Relationships with work attitudes and managerial performance. *Group & Organization Management, 26,* 484–511.

Stajkovic, A. D., & Luthans, F. (1998). Self-efficacy and work-related performance: A meta-analysis. *Psychological Bulletin, 124,* 240–261.

Taylor, S. E., Peplau, L. A., & Sears, D. O. (2006). *Social psychology* (12th ed.). Upper Saddle River, NJ: Prentice-Hall.

Uhl-Bien, M., & Graen, G. B. (1998). Individual self-management: Analysis of professionals' self managing activities in functional and cross-functional work teams. *Academy of Management Journal, 41*(3), 340–350.

van Knippenberg, D., van Knippenberg, B., De Cramer, D., & Hogg, M. (2004). Leader, self, and identity: A review and research agenda. *Leadership Quarterly, 15,* 825–856.

Wicklund, R. (1975). Objective self-awareness. In L. Berkowitz (Ed.), *Advances in experimental social psychology* (Vol. 8, pp. 233–275). New York: Academic Press.

Wofford, J. C., & Goodwin, V. L. (1994). A cognitive interpretation of transactional and transformational leadership theories. *Leadership Quarterly, 5,* 161–186.

Wofford, J. C., Goodwin, V. L., & Whittington, J. L. (1998). A field study of a cognitive approach to understanding transformational and transactional leadership. *Leadership Quarterly, 9,* 55–84.

Wofford, J. C., Joplin, J. R. W., & Comforth, B. (1996). Use of simultaneous verbal protocols in analysis of group leaders' cognitions. *Psychological Reports, 79,* 847–858.

PART IV

INTERACTIONS BETWEEN LEADERS AND FOLLOWERS

16

Evolution and the Social Psychology of Leadership: The Mismatch Hypothesis

MARK VAN VUGT, DOMINIC D. P. JOHNSON, ROBERT B. KAISER, AND RICK O'GORMAN

An evolutionary perspective on leadership assumes that leadership consists of a constellation of adaptations for solving different coordination problems in human ancestral environments, most notably pertaining to group movement, social cohesion, and intergroup relations. Our evolved leadership psychology influences the way we think about and respond to modern leadership, which creates the potential for a mismatch between leadership requirements in modern versus ancestral environments. This chapter provides some evidence for this mismatch hypothesis and notes some implications for leadership theory and practice.

When Tony Blair stepped down as prime minister of Britain in 2007 after a decade in office, most British voters were glad to see him go. Despite his numerous contributions to reforms of the health care system, education, civil law, and government, he will be remembered mostly for his decision to send British troops into Iraq. Matters of life and death ultimately determine the historical judgment of leadership. In times of crises we turn to leaders to give us comfort, hope, and a sense of direction—and if they fail, they must go.

Leadership failure is common in modern society. Scholars estimate a 60 to 75 percent failure rate in business and political leadership with sometimes dire consequences for the welfare of followers (Hogan, Curphy, & Hogan, 1994). Why does modern leadership fail so often and sometimes so spectacularly? There are many possible answers but we focus on one here. Perhaps the failure of modern leadership is a consequence of it sometimes being at odds with aspects of our evolved leadership psychology (Van Vugt, Hogan, & Kaiser, in press).

It is argued that we have a "natural way" of thinking about and responding to leadership that has been shaped by several millions of years of human evolution. But because modern human environments are so dramatically and suddenly different from ancestral environments in which leadership and followership evolved, this creates the potential for a mismatch. As a result, the way leaders and followers interact in modern societies might not always produce adaptive outcomes. This mismatch hypothesis can explain many counterintuitive findings in leadership research with various implications for leadership theory and practice.

EVOLUTIONARY SOCIAL PSYCHOLOGY

Evolutionary social psychology has its roots in social psychology, evolutionary psychology, and evolutionary biology (Schaller, Simpson, & Kenrick, 2006). Evolutionary social psychology (ESP) is based on the Darwinian assumption that human psychology is the product of evolution through natural selection in the same way that natural selection has shaped human physiology. Because the environment in which humans evolved was primarily social—humans are first and foremost a group-living species (Dunbar, 2004)—ESP proposes that the human mind is essentially social, comprising many functional psychological adaptations specifically designed to solve particular adaptive problems of ancestral group life. Examples of such adaptations include parental care, language, social cooperation, and social intelligence (Buss, 2005; Van Vugt & Schaller, in press). Individuals possessing these traits would have been better equipped to extract valuable resources from group life needed for their survival and reproduction. This then enabled these traits to spread through the population and reach fixation. Here we entertain the possibility that leadership and followership have evolved as adaptive solutions to a range of group problems.

EVOLUTIONARY ORIGINS OF LEADERSHIP

The human species is estimated be 2 to 2.5 million years old. For most of this period, humans probably lived in small kin-based bands in savannah-type environments (Dunbar, 2004; Johnson & Earle, 2000). These family-level groups were connected to others, forming clans and tribes that came together at seasonal gatherings to exchange mates, goods, and information (Richerson & Boyd, 2006). For ancestral humans, group life was the best survival strategy in a hostile environment in which predation by animals as well as aggression by other human groups was high and resources scarce (Alexander, 1987; Foley, 1997).

Collective action in the form of hunting, sharing food, and defending the group may have provided a buffer against these threats and created a niche for leadership to organize group activities (Van Vugt, 2006). For instance, in planning a group hunt people must decide who will join the hunting party, where they will go, when they go, and when they return. Such decisions create coordination problems that can be better solved if an individual initiates and coordinates the group's decision-making process. In recent papers (Van Vugt, 2006; Van Vugt, Hogan, & Kaiser, in press) we have identified three ancestral coordination problems for which leadership would have been critical—group movement (e.g., hunting), group cohesion (e.g., promoting cooperation, managing conflict), and intergroup politics (e.g., warfare, peacemaking).

There is some suggestion that leadership predates humans. The phylogenetic evidence suggests that preadaptions for leadership and followership— such as the waggle dance in honey bees and flying formations in migrating bird species (Van Vugt, 2006)—are found in quite primitive social species. These examples suggest that species lacking complex cognitive capacities can display followership using a decision rule as simple as "follow the one who moves first."

Leadership is also observed in our closest genetic relative, the chimpanzee, with whom we shared a common ancestor approximately 5–7 million years ago. Chimpanzees live in fission-fusion societies of about 30–50 individuals in a large territory. They frequently form coalitions with each other for activities such as hunting and foraging, internal politics, and protecting territory boundaries. Leadership is prominently displayed in these situations by usually the most dominant troop member, the alpha male (Boehm, 1999; De Waal, 1996).

Environment of Evolutionary Adaptedness

The social complexity of leadership most likely increased with the arrival of early humans some 2 million years ago. This period marks the beginning of the Pleistocene period, which ended as recently as 13,000 years ago with the agricultural revolution. This period is sometimes referred to as the environment of evolutionary adaptedness or EEA for humans (Foley, 1997; Van Vugt, Hogan, & Kaiser, in press).[1] Modern hunter-gatherer societies such as the !Kung San of the Kalahari desert, the Shoshone of the American Great Basin, the Yanomamö of the Amazon river basin, the Inuit of the Arctic coasts, and the Aborigines in Northern Australia may provide the best model we have for human social organization in this stage (Boehm, 1999; Chagnon, 1997; Johnson & Earle, 2000).

Extrapolating from this evidence, conditions in the EEA were largely egalitarian and there was no formal leadership structure. There were so-called "Big Men," often the best hunters or warriors in the band, who could exercise disproportionate influence on group decision making within and sometimes even outside their domain of expertise, but their power was severely curtailed (Diamond, 1997; Johnson & Earle, 2000). Attempts by Big Men to dominate group discussion—dominance is a legacy of our primate past—were met with fierce resistance from the rest of the group. Anthropologists talk about a reversal of the dominance hierarchy to indicate that, unlike in nonhuman primates, subdominants can band together and limit a leader's power through various strategies—so-called "leveling mechanisms" (Boehm, 1999; Bowles, 2006). For instance, to keep overbearing leaders in place, they use instruments such as gossip, ridicule, criticism, ostracism, and the threat of punishment and sometimes even assassination (Boehm, 1999). Across evolutionary time these leveling mechanisms may have paved the way for a more democratic, participatory group decision-making process in which dominance hierarchies were replaced by a more consensual leader-follower decision structure (Van Vugt, Hogan, & Kaiser, in press).

THE MISMATCH HYPOTHESIS

We believe that the EEA reflects our natural way of thinking about and responding to leadership and that there are substantial implications for modern leadership theory and practice. If humans are mostly adapted to Pleistocene environments, this means that some aspects of our evolved leadership and followership psychology may not be very well adjusted to modern environments. Remember that human psychological mechanisms evolved because they produced reproductive and survival benefits in ancestral environments. Because genetic evolution tends to be a slow cumulative process, such mechanisms might not produce adaptive behaviors in modern environments, particularly if these environments differ in important ways. This logic applies particularly to human activities because our social and physical environments have changed dramatically in the past 13,000 years or so since the agricultural revolution (Diamond, 1997).

The discrepancy between modern and ancestral environments potentially creates a *mismatch* between aspects of our evolved psychology and the challenges of modern society. This may have substantial implications for a range of social traits such as leadership. Mismatch theory is an evolutionarily informed concept. It applies to all organisms possessing traits (including behavioral, cognitive, and biological) that have been passed down through generations favored by natural selection because of their adaptive advantages in a given environment. Yet the evolutionary environment may be quite unlike the current environment. Therefore, traits that were adaptive in ancestral times are often no longer adaptive in the new environment. As Pinker writes, "our ordeals come from a mismatch between the sources of our passions in evolutionary history and the goals we set for ourselves today" (2002, p. 219).

We illustrate this mismatch hypothesis with two examples from human psychology that can be interpreted as supportive evidence. One classic example is the fear of snakes and spiders, which were common threats for humans in ancestral environments. But in modern societies like the United States they kill less than 20 individuals per year, most of whom are owners of dangerous snakes and spiders. In contrast, car accidents kill about 40,000 to 50,000 people a year (National Highway Traffic Safety Administration, 2005). Yet decades of research has shown that fear of snakes and spiders is more readily learned than fear of more lethal, recent dangers such as cars, guns, or electrical appliances (Ohman & Mineka, 2001).

Another example of a potential mismatch is our trust in strangers (Burnham & Johnson, 2005; Hagen & Hammerstein, 2006). Lab research shows that people readily cooperate with anonymous strangers in one-shot prisoner dilemma games (De Cremer & Van Vugt, 2002). This defies fundamental assumptions of economic and evolutionary theory—people are expected to maximize their personal payoffs in anonymous exchanges because their altruism could be exploited. However, single encounters with strangers were presumably very rare for ancestral humans. They probably mostly interacted with family members and therefore did not evolve the cognitive machinery to deal with novel situations like interacting with strangers. Our research shows that people are more likely to trust strangers if they look familiar—for instance, if they share the same facial features, speak the same language, or wear the same clothes (Park, Schaller, & Van Vugt, in press). Thus behaviors that were adaptive in ancestral environments—sharing resources with people who looked and behaved like you—may have potentially maladaptive consequences in present society.

CONTEMPORARY EVIDENCE FOR ANCESTRAL LEADERSHIP PSYCHOLOGY

Our leadership psychology evolved over several million years during which time people lived in small, kin-based egalitarian bands where leadership was informal, consensual, and situational. Since the agricultural period there has been a steady increase in the size and complexity of societies. Simple band structures have been replaced by complex social structures of chiefdoms, states, nations, and empires in which thousands or even millions of people must live and work peacefully together. Such problems, brand new on an evolutionary time scale, create new leadership challenges to which our evolved leadership psychology may not be well adjusted (Van Vugt, Hogan, & Kaiser, in press).

Next we review evidence for the influence of our ancestral past in the way we evaluate and respond to modern leadership challenges. To the extent that these challenges are novel in an evolutionary sense, there exists the potential of a mismatch with negative implications for leadership practice and group welfare.

Prototypical Band Leadership

Since humans evolved in small scale societies without any formal leadership structure and almost equal power relations between (adult male) group members, it should in theory be reflected in the way modern humans evaluate leadership. In particular, there should be universal agreement on what followers regard as positive leadership qualities. These qualities should then closely match the prototype of band leadership. The GLOBE (Global Leadership and Organizational Behavior Effectiveness) research project data are useful to test this hypothesis (http://www.thunderbird.edu/wwwfiles/ms/globe/). In a study of leadership in 61 cultures GLOBE researchers found that leaders, across many cultures, were described in certain terms, many of which were positive. Examples of terms people used are integrity—good leaders can be trusted; fairness—good leaders are just and equitable; diplomatic—good leaders handle conflict well; decisiveness—good leaders make sound and timely decisions; intelligence and competence—good leaders contribute to the group's performance; and, finally, vision—good leaders can describe a desirable future (Den Hartog, House, Hanges, Ruiz-Quintanilla, & Dorfman, 1999; see also Epitropaki & Martin, 2004; Hogan & Kaiser, 2005; Lord & Maher, 1993). These leader prototypes closely match the perception of respected Big Men in traditional band societies (Boehm, 1999; Johnson & Earle, 2000; Sahlins, 1963).

Dominance Is the Antithesis of Leadership

An important aspect of band leadership is that, except in special circumstances, one band member cannot tell others to do something they do not want to do. Members of hunter-gatherer societies are fiercely autonomous. It is not uncommon for them to ignore or disobey a person who assumes too much power and authority. Anthropologists report that the rank and file sometimes simply ignore chiefs who issue commands as opposed to making suggestions (Freeman, 1970). If a chief becomes too bossy, group members sometimes literally "vote with their feet" and leave the overbearing individual behind (Moore, 1972).

Echoing our ancestral past there should be a general aversion against bossy, self-centered leaders in modern environments. Again, the GLOBE project data are useful here. Tyranny, dominance, and selfishness are universally regarded as negative leader attributes (Den Hartog et al., 1999; Epitropaki & Martin, 2004; Hogan & Kaiser, 2005). But why do such leaders emerge in modern organizations? One explanation derived from the mismatch hypothesis is that, unlike in traditional Big Men societies, in modern organizations leaders often do not emerge from the bottom up but are imposed on a group by people higher up the hierarchy. Top-down selection may produce leaders who have other types of qualities and, therefore, we sometimes find examples of leaders and managers who are the antithesis of good leadership (Hogan & Kaiser, 2005). Indeed, hiring decisions for executive leaders are more likely to be successful if subordinates of the position are given an active role in the hiring process (Sessa, Kaiser, Taylor, & Campbell, 1998). Herein lies an important lesson for leadership practice.

Leadership Is Prestige-Based

In hunter-gatherer societies, the person who gets to lead is determined by his ability to help the group move toward specific goals. For instance, the best hunter exercises more influence on hunting decisions and the best warrior exercises more influence on warfare decisions. Positions of power and influence are often attained through leading by example, putting the concept of leadership firmly within the domain of prestige (Henrich & Gil-White, 2001). This prestige theory suggests that leaders are innovators who allow other individuals—followers—to learn from them and, in return, they earn prestige, which is paid out in greater reproductive opportunities.

The prestige dimension of leadership is echoed in modern life with effects that are sometimes beneficial, sometimes detrimental. In the world of business, politics, and warfare, individuals who have shown great expertise within that domain are more likely to be endorsed as leaders. Low task ability often automatically disqualifies people from certain leadership positions (Palmer, 1962). In modern complex environments the emphasis on task skills may backfire, however, because leadership roles are arguably more varied and complex, involving such diverse activities as coaching, communicating, motivating, problem solving, planning, making decisions, acting as a figurehead, and so forth. Thus, there is the potential for a mismatch when an individual has gained status by demonstrating skill in one domain but upon promotion to a leadership position must be skilled in a number of other, possibly unrelated, domains (cf. Berger's expectation-states theory, 1977).

Good examples of prestige-based leadership can be found in sports and politics. In team sports like football (soccer) the best players earn a lot of prestige, giving them an edge in the competition for management jobs when they retire from active play. However, there is little or no evidence to suggest that good players actually make good managers. Quite the contrary, in fact. Some of the best managers in English football—Sir Alex Ferguson at Manchester United, Arsene Wenger at Arsenal, Sven-Goran Eriksson at Manchester City —were mediocre players themselves and began their management careers at an early age. Similarly, in ancestral warfare good warriors often made good commanders by leading from the front in battles and raids. Today, however, good soldiers often falter once elevated to the entangling webs of Washington politics (Wrangham, 1999).

Leadership in Intergroup Relations

In traditional societies an important function of leadership is to manage relationships with neighboring groups. Forming alliances with other bands and clans is essential for exchanging resources and defending territories against mutual enemies. Raiding and warfare were indeed common threats in ancestral environments, leading to the extinction of many bands and societies (Keeley, 1996; Van Vugt, De Cremer, & Janssen, 2007). In traditional societies that frequently experience intergroup conflict (e.g., Yanomamö in the Amazon Basin) there is evidence of a more authoritarian leadership structure with Big Men roles often being occupied by fierce warriors (Chagnon, 1997). Intergroup conflict requires a highly coordinated group. Some degree of coercion might be necessary to maintain group unity, which paves the way for a more aggressive leader (Van Vugt, 2007).

The tribal function of ancestral leadership still plays a role in modern society with sometimes devastating consequences because the scale of warfare has grown dramatically. There is good evidence for changing leadership perceptions during intergroup conflict (Hogg, 2001). During intergroup threats groups prefer ingroup over outgroup leaders—even when it is clear to all that the latter are more competent (De Cremer & Van Vugt, 2002). Leaders have been known to strengthen their power base by starting a conflict with another group (Rabbie & Bekkers, 1978). Intergroup threats increase the support for prototypical leaders who share the norms and values of the ingroup (Hogg, 2001). And when reminded of their mortality, people are more likely to endorse a charismatic leader (Cohen, Solomon, Maxfield, Pyszcynski, & Greenberg, 2004). In analyzing the U.S. presidential elections McCann (1992) discovered that at times of crises voters were more supportive of a hawkish president. Finally, the well-known rally phenomenon describes how a leader's approval rating can spike dramatically when a nation is under attack, as with Franklin D. Roosevelt after Pearl Harbor and George W. Bush after 9/11 (Johnson & Tierney, 2006).

Although it could have been adaptive in small scale ancestral societies to endorse a more aggressive leader during times of war, this may not be the case anymore because the costs of modern warfare are so much greater—even for the winning side. Hawkish leaders can increase the probability of war without increasing the probability of reaping any benefits (Johnson, 2004). Also, remember that ancestral leadership was essentially situational, and once the threat had gone, a person lost his influence. However, in modern environments leadership positions are often formalized, and once the threat is gone, societies may be stuck with these leaders for a long time. Many figures from Stalin to Musharraf in Pakistan offer examples of military leaders who refused to shed their power once they attained it.

Separating the Person from the Role of Leader

Another example of a potential mismatch is that modern humans may have difficulties separating the role of the leader from the person occupying the role. Extrapolating from the hunter-gatherer evidence, there were no formally recognized leadership roles in ancestral times, and there was little distinction between private and public life. In fact, a person's personality and his personal norms, values, and ambitions were critical in determining whether he should get the chance to lead the group because this was the only information available. In modern society we may be consciously aware that, for instance, middle-level managers have only limited influence because they are simply following the orders of senior management. Because our psychological machinery is not very well adapted to these complex multilayered group hierarchies, we nevertheless tend to make trait inferences whenever we see leaders or managers act in certain ways. This distortion is akin to the fundamental attribution error (Tetlock, 1985), which might be another product of our ancestral past in which group environments were arguably less complex. Clearly such attribution errors can undermine group objectives when leaders are held responsible for successes or failures that were beyond their control (cf. Hackman & Wageman, 2007).

Odd Correlates of Leadership

The mismatch hypothesis might also explain why leadership correlates consistently with seemingly irrelevant factors such as age, height, weight, and health. Traditional leadership theories have some difficulty explaining these correlations and tend to see them as spurious (Bass, 1990). An evolutionary perspective might provide answers. In ancestral environments making a bad leader choice was potentially so costly that any significant beneficial personal trait would be taken into consideration in following a particular individual. The possession of some piece of specialized knowledge would have been extremely useful, like knowing about a long-forgotten water hole in case of a drought (Boehm, 1999). This knowledge was more likely to be held by older, more experienced individuals, so age was associated with prestige and leadership.[2] In modern society, the relation between age and leadership is still observed in professions that require a considerable amount of specialized knowledge such as science, technology, and arts (Bass, 1990). For leadership activities requiring physical strength and stamina, like a group hunt or warfare, our ancestors would presumably pay attention to indices of physical fitness, and someone's height, weight, energy, and health might have been important markers.

However, this might cause a potential mismatch in modern leadership environments. Although the physical aspects of modern-day leadership may seem relatively less important to the task at hand, it still matters a great deal in terms of the *perception* of leadership. For instance, men who are more physically fit and taller have an edge in leadership elections although there is little evidence that these traits are beneficial for the kind of jobs they are supposed to do (Ilies, Gerhardt, & Le, 2004; Judge & Cable, 2004). The health status of leadership candidates also plays an important role in their election— for example, for presidential elections in the United States—and that is perhaps why negative health information is very likely to be suppressed (cf. Simonton, 1994).

Gender and Leadership

Our ancestral leadership psychology might also explain why male leadership is still the norm in modern societies, essentially for two reasons. In hunter-gatherer societies, leadership often included a physical component, for example, leading group hunts, organizing raids, and breaking up group fights. In light of the obvious physical differences between men and women, the chances for men to emerge as leaders in these situations would have been considerably higher. In addition, the different reproductive interests of men and women would favor male leadership emergence. In ancestral environments men's social status was probably a good predictor of their reproductive success. Evidence from band societies, like the Yanomamö, indicates a link between male social status and number of wives and offspring (Chagnon, 1997). One way to enhance social status is to earn prestige in a valued domain, for example, through taking on a leadership role.

The evolved differences in status sensitivity between men and women might contribute to an even greater male bias in leadership emergence in modern environments. In modern societies the payoffs for leaders are often so much higher than for followers that men will go to extreme lengths to attain such positions (e.g., in modern American corporations, average salaries for CEOs are almost 200 times the average pay for workers).

It remains to be seen how adaptive this male leadership bias is in the modern world since interpersonal skills and network building are emphasized as primary leadership functions (Eagly & Carli, 2003). There is some evidence that females have better empathy and communication skills (Van Vugt, 2006) and are more likely to adopt a democratic leadership style (Eagly & Johnson, 1990). However, the male leadership bias may be difficult to overcome if one assumes that it is part of an evolved leadership psychology. Research indicates that when women and men work together on group tasks men are quicker to assume leadership roles—even if the women are better qualified for the job (Mezulis, Abramson, Hyde, & Hankin, 2004). Regardless of talent, men are also more likely to assume leadership roles when being observed by women, perhaps because women prefer status in potential mates (Campbell, Simpson, Stewart, & Manning, 2002). Finally, women are sometimes penalized for excelling at stereotypically masculine tasks, and leadership might be an example of a masculine task (Eagly & Karau, 2002; Heilmann, 2001).

Importance of Charisma

A final example of a potential mismatch is the role of charisma in modern leadership. Research on traditional societies suggests that Big Men are often extremely charismatic (Johnson & Earle, 2000; Nicholson, 2005). Being intimate, inspiring, persuasive, and visionary would have been important attributes of aspiring leaders in small face-to-face groups. In large modern organizations it is extremely hard to achieve the same levels of intimacy between leaders and followers. Yet even in large bureaucratic organizations we still demand from our leaders that they adopt a personalized style of leadership (Burns, 1978; Bass, 1985). The media obviously plays a large role in reducing the distance between leaders and followers in modern society. This, however, creates opportunities for charismatic leaders to exploit followers' susceptibility to their influence to sometimes devastating effects (e.g., Adolf Hitler).

CONCLUSION

Our main argument is that modern leadership is influenced by key aspects of our evolved leadership psychology, which has been shaped by millions of years of human evolution. Because society today is much larger and socially more complex, there is the potential for a mismatch between our innate leadership psychology that was shaped in small scale societies and modern leadership requirements. However much we may employ our intellect, our cognition remains constrained by ancestral adaptations for conducting, perceiving, and responding to leadership and followership. We reviewed several lines of leadership research that offer support for the ancestral leadership hypothesis.

A broader aim of this chapter is to start a constructive dialogue between social psychologists and other behavioral scientists studying leadership who have hardly influenced each other. Evolutionists theorize about the origins of leadership based on the principle of natural selection but have not collected much data to support their claims. In contrast, social psychology has gathered a wealth of reliable empirical nuggets about leadership, but this has not produced many overarching conceptual frameworks that can make sense of the richness of data (Van Vugt, 2006). In our view, evolutionary theory provides an excellent integrative framework that can explain the diversity of empirical findings and generate many novel testable hypotheses about leadership. Any proximate psychological theory of leadership must ultimately turn to evolutionary theory to explain its own assumptions (e.g., why people have selfish or tribal motives, or where leader prototypes come from).

A more specific contribution of our work is to show that our evolved leadership psychology is still influencing modern leadership today. We have identified several areas where there is some evidence for a *mismatch* between ancestral and modern leadership requirements such as in the influence of charisma and the relation between leadership emergence with age, height, and gender. We are not in support of the idea that leadership and followership adaptations are somehow set in stone. Evolution has afforded humans a great deal of flexibility to adapt successfully to novel environments—such as through culture, social learning, and general intelligence—and this is why humans can function in environments that seem so radically different from our Pleistocene past. This should be reflected in the diversity of leadership and followership styles that emerge in response to local environmental and cultural factors (Van Vugt, Hogan, & Kaiser, in press).

More research on the evolution of leadership is obviously needed. It would be interesting to see, for example, if leadership systematically varies with the ancestral group problems that we have identified (e.g., group movements, group cohesion, and intergroup relations). We suspect that leadership and followership should emerge more quickly in these evolutionarily relevant situations. Also, we believe that perceptions of leadership will vary with the nature of these threats. For instance, a preliminary experimental study by one of us revealed that the presence of an intergroup conflict automatically activates a male leadership prototype but that an *intragroup* conflict activates a female leadership prototype (Van Vugt & Spisak, in press).

From an applied perspective we believe that organizations will fare better if they take into account our evolved leadership psychology and find ways to work either *with* or *around* its limitations. For instance, the knowledge that men are more likely to compete for leadership positions when the status benefits are high suggests that a reduction in the rewards might encourage more women to assume leadership roles. Finally, some modern organizations, such as GoreTex, Virgin Group, and ABB, are already discovering the utility of an evolutionary approach by mimicking aspects of traditional band leadership. They delegate substantial responsibility to managers far down the chain of command so that the actual unit size that is being managed does not exceed about 150 people—precisely the size of a typical hunter-gatherer band.

NOTES

1. The term *environment of evolutionary adaptedness* refers to the environment to which a particular evolved mechanism is adapted. Evolutionary psychology proposes that the majority of human psychological mechanisms are adapted to reproductive problems frequently encountered in Pleistocene environments in which humans spent 95 percent of their history. These problems include those of mating, parenting, social coordination, and cooperation.

2. Group movement in nomadic species like baboons and elephants is indeed often decided by the older troop members.

REFERENCES

Alexander, R. D. (1987). *The biology of moral systems.* Aldine, NY: Hawthorne.

Bass, B. M. (1985). *Leadership and performance beyond expectations.* New York: Free Press.

Bass, B. M. (1990). *Bass and Stogdill's handbook of leadership: Theory, research, and managerial applications* (3rd ed.). New York: Free Press.

Berger, J. (1977). *Status characteristics and social interaction: An expectation-states approach.* New York: Elsevier.

Boehm, C. (1999). *Hierarchy in the forest.* London: Harvard University Press.

Bowles, S. (2006). Group competition, reproductive leveling, and the evolution of human altruism. *Science, 314,* 1569–1572.

Burnham, T. C., & Johnson, D. D. P. (2005). The biological and evolutionary logic of cooperation. *Analyse & Kritik, 27,* 113–135.

Burns, J. M. (1978). *Leadership.* New York: Harper & Row.

Buss, D. M. (2005). *Handbook of evolutionary psychology.* Hoboken, NJ: Wiley.

Campbell, L., Simpson, J., Stewart, M., & Manning, J. (2002). The formation of status hierarchies in leaderless groups. *Human Nature, 13,* 345–362.

Chagnon, N. A. (1997). *Yanomamö*. London: Wadsworth.

Cohen, F., Solomon, S., Maxfield, M., Pyszcynski, T., & Greenberg, J. (2004). Fatal attraction: The effects of mortality salience on evaluations of charismatic, task-oriented, and relationship-oriented leaders. *Psychological Science, 15*, 846–851.

De Cremer, D., & Van Vugt, M. (2002). Intra- and intergroup dynamics of leadership in social dilemmas: A relational model of cooperation. *Journal of Experimental Social Psychology, 38*, 126–136.

De Waal, F. B. M. (1996). *Good natured: The origins of right and wrong in humans and other animals*. Cambridge, UK: Cambridge University Press.

Den Hartog, D. N., House, R. J., Hanges, P. J., Ruiz-Quintanilla, S. A., & Dorfman, P. W. (1999). Culture-specific and cross-culturally generalizable implicit leadership theories: A longitudinal investigation. *Leadership Quarterly, 10*, 219–256.

Diamond, J. (1997). *Guns, germs and steel*. London: Vintage.

Dunbar, R. I. M. (2004). *Grooming, gossip, and the evolution of language*. London: Faber & Faber.

Eagly, A. H., & Carli, L. L. (2003). The female leadership advantage: An evaluation of the evidence. *Leadership Quarterly, 14*, 807–834.

Eagly, A. H., & Johnson, B. T. (1990). Gender and leadership style: A meta-analysis. *Psychological Bulletin, 108*, 233–256.

Eagly, A. H., & Karau, S. J. (2002). Role congruity theory of prejudice toward female leaders. *Psychological Review, 109*, 573–598.

Epitropaki, O., & Martin, R. (2004). Implicit leadership theories in applied settings: Factor structure, generalizability and stability over time. *Journal of Applied Psychology, 89*, 293–310.

Foley, R. A. (1997). The adaptive legacy of human evolution: A search for the environment of evolutionary adaptedness. *Evolutionary Anthropology, 4*, 194–203.

Freeman, D. (1970). *Report on the Iban. LSE mongraphs on social anthropology No. 41.* New York: Humanities Press.

Hackman, J. R., & Wageman, R. (2007). Asking the right questions about leadership. *American Psychologist, 62*, 43–47.

Hagen, E., & Hammerstein, P. (2006). Game theory and human evolution: A critique of some recent interpretations of experimental games. *Theoretical Population Biology, 69*, 339–348.

Heilman, M. E. (2001). Description and prescription: How gender stereotypes prevent women's ascent up the organizational ladder. *Journal of Social Issues, 57*, 657–674.

Henrich, J., & Gil-White, F. (2001). The evolution of prestige: Freely conferred deference as a mechanism for enhancing the benefits of cultural transmission. *Evolution and Human Behavior, 22*, 165–196.

Hogan, R., Curphy, G. J., & Hogan J. (1994). What we know about leadership. *American Psychologist, 49*, 493–504.

Hogan, R., & Kaiser, R. (2005). What we know about leadership. *Review of General Psychology, 9*, 169–180.

Hogg, M. A. (2001). A social identity theory of leadership. *Personality and Social Psychology Review, 5*, 184–200.

Ilies, R., Gerhardt, M., & Le, H. (2004). Individual differences in leadership emergence: Integrating meta-analytic findings and behavioral genetics estimates. *International Journal of Selection and Assessment, 12,* 207–219.

Johnson, A. W., & Earle, T. (2000). *The evolution of human societies.* Stanford, CA: Stanford University Press.

Johnson, D. D. P. (2004). *Overconfidence and war: The havoc glory of positive illusions.* Cambridge, M.A., Harvard University Press.

Johnson, D. D. P., & Tierney, D. R. (2006). Failing to win: Perceptions of victory and defeat in international politics. Cambridge, MA: Harvard University Press.

Judge, T. A., & Cable, D. M. (2004). The effect of physical height on workplace success and income: Preliminary test of a theoretical model. *Journal of Applied Psychology, 89,* 428–441.

Keeley, L. H. (1996). *Warfare before civilization: The myth of the peaceful savage.* Oxford University Press: Oxford.

Lord, R. G., & Maher, K. J. (1993). *Leadership and information processing: Linking perceptions and performance.* Boston: Unwin Hyman.

McCann, S. J. H. (1992). Alternative formulas to predict the greatness of U. S. presidents: Personologial, situational, and zeitgeist factors. *Journal of Personality and Social Psychology, 62,* 469–479.

Mezulis, A. H., Abramson, L. Y., Hyde, J. S., & Hankin, B. L. (2004). Is there a universal positivity bias in attributions? A meta-analytic review of individual, developmental, and cultural differences in the self-serving attributional bias. *Psychological Bulletin, 130*(5), 711–747.

Moore, S. F. (1972). Legal liability and evolutionary interpretation: Some aspects of strict liability, self-help, and collective responsibility. In M. Gluckman (Ed.), *The allocation of responsibility* (pp. 51–107). Manchester, UK: Manchester University Press.

National Highway Traffic Safety Administration (NHTSA). (2006, August 23). *U.S. highway death toll rises in 2005.* Retrieved January 30, 2008, from http://www.martinfrost.ws/htmlfiles/sept2006/usroad_deaths.html.

Nicholson, N. (2005). Meeting the Maasai: Messages for management. *Journal of Management Inquiry, 14,* 255–267.

Ohman, A., & Mineka, S. (2001). Fear, phobias, and preparedness: Towards an evolved module of fear and fear learning. *Psychological Review, 108,* 483–522.

Palmer, G. J. (1962). Task ability and effective leadership. *Psychological Reports, 10,* 863–866.

Park, J., Schaller, M., & Van Vugt, M. (in press). A heuristic kinship model. *Review of General Psychology.*

Pinker, S. (2002). *The blank slate.* London: Penguin Classics.

Rabbie, J. M., & Bekkers, F. (1978). Threatened leadership induces intergroup competition. *European Journal of Social Psychology, 8,* 9–20.

Richerson, P. J., & Boyd, R. (2006). *Not by genes alone: How culture transformed human evolution.* Chicago: Chicago University Press.

Sahlins, M. (1963). Poor man, rich man, big man, chief: Political types in Melanesia and Polynesia. *Comparative studies in Society and History, 5,* 285–303.

Schaller, M., Simpson, J., & Kenrick, D (2006). *Evolution and social psychology.* London: Psychology Press.

Sessa, V. I., Kaiser, R. B., Taylor, J. K., & Campbell, R. J. (1998). *Executive selection.* Greensboro, NC: Center for Creative Leadership.

Simonton, D. K. (1994). *Who makes history and why?* New York: Guilford Press.

Tetlock, P. E. (1985). Accountability: A social check on the fundamental attribution error. *Social Psychology Quarterly, 48,* 227–236.

Van Vugt, M. (2006). Evolutionary origins of leadership and followership. *Personality and Social Psychology Review, 10,* 354–371.

Van Vugt, M., De Cremer, D., & Janssen, D. (2007). Gender differences in cooperation and competition: The male warrior hypothesis. *Psychological Science, 18,* 19–23.

Van Vugt, M., Hogan, R., & Kaiser, R. (2008). Leadership, followership, and evolution: Some lessons from the past. *American Psychologist, 63,* 182–196.

Van Vugt, M., & Schaller, M. (2008). Evolutionary perspectives on group dynamics: An introduction. *Group Dynamics, 12,* 1–6.

Van Vugt, M., & Spisak, B. (in press). Sex biases in leadership emergence in within and between group conflicts. *Psychological Science.*

Wrangham, R. (1999). Is military incompetence adaptive? *Evolution and Human Behaviour 20,* 3–17.

17

Harnessing Power to Capture Leadership

ADAM D. GALINSKY, JENNIFER JORDAN, AND
NIRO SIVANATHAN

Napoleon once said, when asked to explain the lack of great statesmen in the world, that "to get power you need to display absolute pettiness; to exercise power you need to show true greatness." Such pettiness and such greatness are rarely found in one person.

—From *The Contender* motion picture (Lurie, 2001)

This chapter examines the relationship between the related yet distinct constructs of power and leadership. Although power (asymmetric control over valued resources) is often a foundation of leadership (influencing and motivating a group of individuals toward achieving a common goal), we consider power to be neither a necessary nor a sufficient condition for the emergence of leadership. We distinguish power from leadership along a number of dimensions and highlight that the relationship between power and leadership lies in power's psychological effects. A number of the psychological properties of power—action, optimism, abstract thinking—can be seen as part and parcel of effective leadership. Other psychological consequences of power—diminished perspective-taking, risk-taking, overconfidence, and the tendency to objectify others by perceiving them through a lens of self-interest—are often associated with malfeasance and are the antithesis of leadership. Our model of power and leadership contends that an effective leader is one who is able to harness the positive psychological effects of power while mitigating the negative ones. Thus, the best leaders are action-oriented, optimistic

perspective takers who see the big picture. We discuss how the springboard of power combined with perspective taking can be a particularly
constructive force that allows for the emergence of effective leadership.

The world has long been populated by powerful people striving to satisfy
their personal predilections, but *leaders* are an altogether rarer species.
Despite their intimate relationship, power and leadership are not synonymous: the mere possession of power does not qualify one as a leader and
one can lead others without possessing power. The aim of this chapter is
threefold. First, we define and distinguish between the constructs of power
and leadership. We then summarize research documenting the psychological
effects, both positive and negative, of power on cognition and behavior.
Finally, we develop a model proposing that effective leadership requires harnessing the positive psychological consequences of power while mitigating
its insidious and destructive psychological effects.

DISTINGUISHING POWER FROM LEADERSHIP

Leadership is a subject that has long captured the interest of researchers
and practitioners. In conducting a search of the psychological literature, we
found that more than 16,000 articles have been published on the topic of leadership since 1990. Although this sustained interest has led to a plethora of
research, agreement on how to define and operationalize leadership remains
elusive. This problem was best captured by Stogdill (1974) who commented
that "there are almost as many definitions of leadership as there are persons
who have attempted to define the concept" (p. 259).

Despite the lack of consensus on how to define leadership, we define it as
influencing, motivating, and enabling a group of individuals to contribute
to the success of a common goal or shared purpose (House et al., 1999; see
also Hemphill & Coons, 1957; Rauch & Behling, 1984). According to our definition, leadership is a social phenomenon—one that requires the presence
of others; a leader must have members to influence, motivate, and mobilize.

Many definitions of power involve control over resources, and we define
power as the control over important or valued resources—our own and
others' (Keltner, Gruenfeld, & Anderson, 2003; Lammers & Galinsky, in press;
Thibaut & Kelley, 1959). From this perspective, dependence is the inverse of
power; the powerless are dependent on the powerful to achieve their desired
outcomes. For example, subordinates must obtain approval from their bosses
to embark on new initiatives and children must obtain permission from
parents before they can partake in desired activities. In contrast, those who
possess power depend less on the resources of others and are therefore more
easily able to satisfy their own needs and desires. From this control over valued resources, power affords the capacity to influence others despite

resistance (French & Raven, 1959; Weber, 1947) and, it could also be said, that power provides the capacity to be uninfluenced by others (Galinsky, Magee, Gruenfeld, Whitson, & Liljenquist, in press). Without power—when one's outcomes are determined by others—one is constrained. But with power, one is relatively free of such constraint. The asymmetric interdependence of power makes it an inherently social phenomenon.

Power and leadership share two common threads. First, both constructs involve influence. A leader is, by definition, someone who influences others; influence also often emerges from control over valued resources. Second, both constructs involve a focus on goals. A leader motivates a group of individuals toward a shared objective, and numerous research findings demonstrate that power increases a focus on goals and facilitates goal-directed behavior (Galinsky, Gruenfeld, & Magee, 2003; Guinote, 2007a; Smith, Jostmann, Galinsky, & van Dijk, 2008).

But power and leadership are *not* synonymous, and they diverge on a number of important dimensions. First, power's influence is derived from the ability to provide or withhold resources or administer punishments (Keltner et al., 2003). In contrast, the influence of leadership emerges not from the lure of incentives but by inspiring through rhetoric and being the exemplar of desired behavior (Avolio & Bass, 1988). Likewise, although the concept of a powerless leader may seem anomalous, one can motivate others toward a shared goal in the absence of control over resources or the ability to administer rewards or punishments. For example, Nelson Mandela galvanized his fellow citizens to take up the fight against South African apartheid despite a 27-year imprisonment, and Rosa Parks inspired a nationwide fight for civil rights despite having neither tangible rewards to dispense nor the threat of punishments to wield.

Second, power and leadership often differ on the ultimate purpose or goal of wielding one's influence. Power's influence is often directed toward satisfying personal desires (Keltner et al., 2003; Kipnis, 1976). In contrast, leaders exert influence to help the group reach a shared goal. Thus, power is often egocentric, exercised in the service of the self, whereas leadership is directed toward elevating the common good for all its members. As a result, a power holder will often examine subordinates' assets and skills through a lens of self-interest—to discern how those strengths might be harnessed to serve his or her personal objectives. For example, a powerful male looking for female companionship may choose to have attractive female subordinates work on a task with him even if their talents are not well suited for the specific task. In contrast, a leader will seek to capitalize on subordinates' assets and skills to meet a shared objective and not for the purpose of satisfying personal desires. Within the corporate setting, such shared goals can include launching a new product or entering a new market, and within the political realm, these goals can include altering oppressive practices or producing a comprehensive immigration or health-care policy.

Third, partially as a result of these disparate goals (personal versus collective), subordinates are subjected to markedly different experiences as the targets of influence by leaders and the powerful. Since power involves rewards and punishments as vehicles of influence, members are likely to view their own behavior as externally demanded and therefore the product of extrinsic motivation. As a consequence, once the powerful's punishments or rewards are no longer present, the ability to influence will diminish and the previous displays of motivation will evaporate. In contrast, a leader moves members toward a goal through intrinsic motivation, transforming individuals through choice and commitment.

Fourth, leadership connotes status and respect, whereas such privileges do not necessarily accompany the possession of power. By virtue of a leader's ability to harness members' intrinsic motivation to reach a shared goal, a leader earns deference and esteem. The use of power, in contrast, does not guarantee positive impressions from subordinates or observers.

These distinctions between power and leadership, based in findings from empirical research, are consistent with seminal theories on what attributes define a leader. For example, Burns (1978) distinguishes between leaders and what he refers to as "power wielders." In contrast to those who "mobilize . . . resources so as to arouse, engage, and satisfy the motives of followers" (p. 18), mere power wielders prioritize their own motives, regardless of whether those motives are shared by the individuals they seek to influence. Similarly, Bass and Avolio (1994) define transformational leaders as those who consider followers' needs before their own, motivate rather than coerce, and arouse interest in a shared goal.

In this section, we distinguished power from leadership on a number of dimensions, from types of goals (personal versus collective) to the type of motivation they inspire (extrinsic versus intrinsic). In the next section, we explore how power transforms individuals' psychological processes and alters their psychological landscape. We contend that power relates to leadership through its ability to alter an individual's cognition and behavior. Whether power leads to the emergence of leadership depends on whether the positive psychological effects of power engulf the more deleterious effects.

THE PSYCHOLOGICAL CONSTRUCT OF POWER

Power has often been considered a foundational force that governs social relationships. Because power is so critical, it not only regulates social interactions but it also alters individual psychological states. Kipnis (1976) was one of the first empirical social psychologists to argue that possessing power has metamorphic consequences, and a review of the power literature by Keltner and colleagues (2003) provided ample evidence to support the idea that individuals are transformed by the experience of power. Indeed, a number of researchers have argued that because of its transformative properties, power and its effects come to reside psychologically within individuals (e.g., Bargh, Raymond, Pryor, & Strack, 1995; Chen, Lee-Chai, & Bargh, 2001; Galinsky et al., 2003; Magee, Galinsky, & Gruenfeld, 2007). An important implication of this conceptualization of power is that its effects can persist beyond the context where power was initially experienced (Anderson & Galinsky, 2006; Chen et al., 2001; Galinsky et al., 2003; Gruenfeld, Inesi, Magee, & Galinsky, 2008; Guinote, 2007a; Smith & Trope, 2006). As a result, being given control over resources (Anderson & Berdahl, 2002; Galinsky et al., 2003) or even being asked to recall a time when one had power over others (Anderson & Galinksy, 2006; Galinsky et al., 2003, in press) are all sufficient to trigger power's psychological and behavioral effects.

Our model of power is influenced by the power-approach theory (Keltner et al., 2003), which has inspired a deluge of research on how power transforms and directs individuals' psychological states. According to this theory (Keltner et al., 2003), possessing power affects the relative activation of two complementary neurobiological forces—the behavioral approach and inhibition systems—that combine to drive behavior and cognition. Power triggers behavioral approach, which is posited to regulate behavior associated with rewards. In contrast, powerlessness activates the behavioral inhibition system, which has been equated to an alarm system that triggers avoidance and response inhibition. As a result of the relative activation of these two systems, power has a number of predictable effects on cognition and behavior.

In understanding how power relates to leadership, we argue that the foundation of this relationship lies in power's psychological effects. Our model asserts that how individuals conceive or construct their ability to control important outcomes has meaningful implications for their ability to effectively lead others. What matters most are the psychological effects of power, which often constitute the proximate and driving force on the behavior of potential leaders.

A number of these psychological effects of power can be seen as part and parcel of effective leadership. Other psychological manifestations of power are associated with malfeasance and are the antithesis of leadership. Thus, we contend that an effective leader is one who is able to harness the positive effects of power while mitigating the negative effects. In the next two sections, we highlight how power alters the psychological state of individuals, beginning with the positive effects and concluding with the negative effects.

THE POSITIVE PSYCHOLOGICAL EFFECTS OF POWER

Power Increases Action

One of the most robust effects of possessing and experiencing power is that it directly translates into action. For example, Galinsky et al. (2003) found that participants who had high power in an organizational task (i.e., were managers) were more likely to "hit" in a simulated game of blackjack (an example of an action orientation) than were participants who had low power (i.e., were subordinates). The powerful are more likely to decide to negotiate an offer than to simply accept an initial proposal and are also more inclined to make the first offer in a negotiation compared to those without power (Magee et al., 2007). Both of these strategies have been repeatedly shown to garner significant financial gains to the individual (Galinsky & Mussweiler, 2001; Small, Gelfand, Babcock, & Gettman, 2007). Finally, the powerful are more likely to help in emergencies; whereas others sit back, trapped by diffusion of responsibility (thinking others will help so they do not have to) or by looking to the nonresponding pack to guide their own behavior (thinking since others are not helping, they should not either), the powerful spring into action and help those in distress (Whitson, Galinsky, Magee, Gruenfeld, & Liljenquist, 2008).

Power Makes People Optimistic

Power increases a general sense of optimism, with the powerful feeling more hopeful about their own future (e.g., getting a good job or avoiding gum disease) (Anderson & Galinsky, 2006). Power-induced optimism even extends to outcomes outside an individual's own life: power increases attention toward positive aspects of the environment and decreases attention to negative aspects of the environment. As a result, the powerful view the world as a less dangerous and threatening place. The powerful see mostly opportunity dancing in front of them, whereas the powerless are more likely to see potential hazards lurking about.

Power Increases Abstract Thinking

Power leads to a focus on the global rather than the local features of stimuli (Guinote, 2007b) and results in information being processed at higher levels of abstraction (Smith & Trope, 2006). As a result, the powerful compared to the powerless focus less on the details and more on the "big picture." They are better able to perceive patterns and to capture the gist of information (Smith & Trope, 2006). They are also more likely to focus on and attend to task-relevant information (Overbeck & Park, 2001). All of these psychological effects of power allow the powerful to see, create, and articulate a broad vision of the world—one that could potentially inspire others. By seeing the forest, the powerful are not constrained by the gnarled branches of the trees.

Power Increases Goal-Directed Behavior

Power channels thought and behavior toward accomplishing one's goals in a wide variety of situations (Bargh et al., 1995; Chen et al., 2001; Galinsky et al., 2003). Compared to those who are powerless, individuals who experience power are more likely to engage in behaviors that are consistent with currently held goals, and as a result, their observable behavior is more closely aligned with their internal states. For example, Galinsky et al. (2003) induced discomfort in participants by having a fan blow directly onto them. The experimenters constructed the situation so that the purpose of the fan was unclear to participants, thereby creating uncertainty about whether it was permissible to take action against the fan by moving it or turning it off. In their study, the powerful were more likely to remove that stimulus and satisfy their goal of reducing physical discomfort.

One consequence of this increased goal direction is that the powerful, compared to the powerless, often do not show decrements in executive functioning, which reflect attentional control mechanisms that coordinate various cognitive subprocesses (Miyake, Friedman, Emerson, Witzki, & Howerter, 2000). Proper executive functioning requires effective goal focus and impairments result from difficulty in actively maintaining a goal (Duncan, Emslie, Williams, Johnson, & Freer, 1996). As a result, lacking power produces goal neglect, which impairs executive functioning (Smith et al., 2008).

THE PERNICIOUS PSYCHOLOGICAL EFFECTS OF POWER

Based on the above effects of power, an image emerges of the powerful as focused, optimistic individuals with broad visions geared toward action. Power, however, does not always lead to beneficial outcomes (e.g., Burns, 1978). In a social context, power can also lead to dangerous and destructive behaviors. In this section we explore the less desirable consequences of power.

The Powerful Ignore Other's Perspectives and Emotions

The powerful appear to be particularly poor perspective takers. Indeed, power appears to reduce social attentiveness, placing a blind spot on considering the unique vantage points of others. Galinsky, Magee, Inesi, and Gruenfeld (2006) found that high-power participants were less likely to spontaneously adopt another's visual perspective, less likely to take into account that another person lacks their privileged knowledge, and less accurate in judging others' facial expressions of emotion. For example, Galinsky et al. asked participants to draw the letter "E" on their foreheads with a marker. Those who had been made to feel powerless were more likely to draw the "E" so that it was legible to someone facing them. Those made to feel powerful, however, drew the letter so that it looked correct from their internal perspective but was backwards from the point of view of someone facing them. Possessing power seems to almost instantly impair the ability to see things from other people's points of view. Similarly, the powerful have difficulty recognizing and adjusting for the fact that others do not share this privileged perspective. For example, the same semantic content (e.g., "nice suit!") can be received as a compliment or a thinly veiled insult, depending on knowledge of the speaker's tastes and previous interactions. Galinsky et al. presented participants with a message that on its face seemed sincere ("About the restaurant, it was marvelous, just marvelous"), but privileged background knowledge about the speaker's intentions suggested a sarcastic interpretation. They found that the powerful inaccurately predicted that others would see the world as they saw it (i.e., that the message was sarcastic) even though these others lacked access to the private knowledge held by the powerful participants.

High-power negotiators are also less accurate in perceiving (Galinsky et al., 2006) and less influenced by the emotions of others (Van Kleef, De Dreu, Pietroni, & Manstead, 2006). For example, Van Kleef et al., found that low-power negotiators conceded more to an angry opponent than to a happy one. In contrast, high-power negotiators were often uninfluenced by the type of emotion displayed by their opponents.

The Powerful Objectify Others

Power increases objectification, or the tendency to view others as a tool for one's own purpose (Gruenfeld et al., 2008). In essence, power heightens the tendency to conceive of individuals in one's social environment as possessing an instrumental and utilitarian purpose. As a result, the powerful approach and attend to useful others who will help them complete their goals (Gruenfeld et al., 2008). For example, Gruenfeld et al. assigned male participants to either a manager or subordinate and then primed half of these individuals with words related to sex (e.g., *stiff, wet, bed, skin, sweat*). They found that the managers (the high-power participants) wanted to work with an attractive female but only after being exposed to words related to sex.

This tendency toward instrumental attention was captured in a series of studies by Overbeck and Park (2006). They found that when the powerful were assigned goals related to making their workplace comfortable, they took greater effort to learn about their subordinates and remembered more distinct information about them. But when they were assigned goals related to making their workplace particularly efficient, they recalled less correct information about their subordinates and were less able to distinguish their unique characteristics. All in all, power is associated with instrumental attention driven by one's most salient, currently held goal.

This relationship between power and instrumental attention is not always undesirable. It can be dysfunctional for social relationships but functional for reaching many organizational goals. Within the corporation, as is true in nonhuman hierarchies, superiors are expected to use subordinates to complete important tasks and this power-induced tendency toward instrumental attention can improve efficiency. For example, Gruenfeld et al. (2008) found that when choosing among job candidates, high-power participants were more likely to select the candidate who best matched the position qualifications and requirements compared to those primed with low power. Similarly, instrumental attention can lead to efficient division of labor and the optimization of individual talents, and ultimately result in the maximization of wealth. By optimizing talents, the powerful can allow for and produce feelings of self-growth among subordinates. Of course, instrumental attention and behavior become less appropriate when a superior delegates professional tasks to someone who is not a direct report or delegates personal chores to or pursues his own personal desires with a professional subordinate (Bargh et al., 1995). Seeing others through the lens of self-interest can lead those others to feel alienated. Indeed, research on sexual objectification illustrates a variety of negative psychological effects for women when they are sexually objectified by men (Frederickson & Roberts, 1997; Frederickson, Roberts, Noll, Quinn, & Twenge, 1998).

The Powerful Are Overconfident

The powerful are also vulnerable to being overconfident in their judgments and decisions (Sivanathan & Galinsky, 2007). Overconfidence refers to an individual's tendency to overestimate his or her abilities or the accuracy of his or her thoughts and decisions. Sivanathan and Galinsky found converging evidence that power affected the three common strands of overconfidence—the tendency to overstate one's skills relative to the average (better than average effect, Alicke, Kotz, Breitenbecher, Yurak, & Vredenburg, 1995); the belief that chance events are subject to personal control (illusion of control, Langer, 1975); and the tendency to be overconfident in the precision of one's answers (miscalibration, Lichtenstein, Fischhoff, & Phillips, 1982). These empirical results support pejorative comments about numerous powerful CEOs and politicians making decisions fueled by hubris and a boundless sense of overconfidence.

The Powerful Are Risk Takers

Possessing power not only makes one optimistic and overconfident but it also increases people's proclivity for risk (Anderson & Galinsky, 2006). When people experience power, they attend more to information related to rewards and as a result, when presented with a risky course of action, the powerful are likely to direct their sights on the potential payoffs. At the same time, the powerful, with a subdued behavioral inhibition system, are less likely to focus on the potential threats or downsides of a risky choice. Thus, the dual focus on rewards and a lack of attention to potential dangers encourages the powerful to engage in risky choices. Across a set of five studies using myriad contexts, Anderson & Galinsky (2006) demonstrated a clear link between power and risk, such that the powerful were more likely to show greater risk preferences, make riskier gambles and choices, find risky sexual activity more attractive, and resort to risky tactics in negotiations.

One of the important implications of these findings lies in the taken-for-granted assumption that powerful individuals like CEOs engage in question-able behaviors, from unethical personal dealings or questionable corporate mergers and acquisitions, because of power's corrupting influence. Instead, as Anderson & Galinsky (2006) note, it may be an optimistic take on risk, rather than any inherent depravity, that leads power holders to engage in seemingly questionable acts.

The observed link between power, optimism, and risk taking has implications for how power, once attained, is maintained or lost. Positive illusions can lead people to achieve unlikely accomplishments by embarking on low-probability journeys and persisting when others would quit (Taylor & Brown, 1988). Such unbridled confidence can lead the powerful to make the seemingly impossible possible and, in the process, achieve leadership. The relationship between power, overconfidence, and risk taking, however, could also contribute directly to losses in power. For example, financial investments driven by overconfidence could lead to large losses, with overconfidence being one way that power often "leads to its own demise" (Winter & Stewart, 1983).

Selecting the Right Leader: Power Increases the Correspondence between Traits and Behavior

Power increases the correspondence between traits and behavior (Bargh et al., 1995; Chen et al., 2001) by reducing the strength of the situation that usually exerts pressure on and constrains the behavior of individuals (Galinsky et al., in press). Because power reduces the constraining influence of the situation on thought and expression, the personalities of high-power individuals are better predictors of their expressions and behavior than are the personalities of low-power individuals. For instance, the personalities of high-status members of a group predict the expression of both positive and negative emotions, but no such correspondence occurs for low-status members (Anderson, John, Keltner, & Kring, 2001).

This research suggests that power does not make the person but reveals the person. For example, Chen et al. (2001) found that the possession of power led those with a communal orientation to demonstrate greater generosity, but drove those with an exchange orientation to engage in more self-serving behaviors. This difference, however, was not found when individuals lacked power. Similarly, for men with a tendency to sexually harass or aggress, the psychological sense of power automatically leads to the activation of concepts associated with sex and to the perception of their female work partners in sexual terms (Bargh et al., 1995).

With power, the aggressive will become more fierce, the generous more magnanimous, and the flirtatious even more amorous. Because power leads to behavior that is consistent with existing dispositions and idiosyncratic tendencies, people should know the predispositions of those they would endow with power in hopes that they will emerge as leaders.

MODERATING THE EFFECTS OF POWER: LEGITIMACY AND CULTURE

Although our preceding analysis of the psychological effects of power suggests that power is a unitary construct with invariant effects, we posit that how power is conceptualized by the powerful and by the powerless will lead to differential downstream effects on behavior and cognition. Specifically, two variables have emerged as important moderators of the effects of power: legitimacy and culture. These moderating effects emerge from both the meaning attributed to the power relationship and the way power is acquired and exercised.

Legitimacy

The view of power as either a constructive or a destructive force often depends on whether power differences are considered to be inherently legitimate or illegitimate. Legitimate power is acquired through consensually agreed upon means and is exercised within certain established parameters. Lammers, Galinsky, Gordijn, and Otten (2008) conducted a series of studies demonstrating that the legitimacy of power determines how the powerful and the powerless think, feel, and behave. Across their studies, legitimate power consistently led to more action and risk taking than legitimate power-lessness. But when power was conceived or expressed under the shadow of illegitimacy, the powerful no longer were more likely than the powerless to embrace risk and action. For example, in one study, power was manipulated by assigning participants to either a manager or a subordinate role, and legiti-macy was manipulated either by basing these assignments on merit (the per-son assigned to the role of manager had scored well on a leadership questionnaire) or by explicitly violating merit (the person assigned to the role of manager had scored poorly on a leadership questionnaire but the experi-menter wanted that person's gender in the role of manager). After being assigned to their roles but before engaging in the managerial task, partici-pants were presented with a scenario in which they could pick a certain or risky option. Legitimate power led participants to choose a risky plan more often than legitimate powerlessness, which replicated the results of Anderson and Galinsky (2006), but this difference disappeared under illegitimacy. Importantly, the effect of legitimacy had equal and opposite effects on approach, risk, and cooperation for the powerful and for the powerless. This relationship between legitimacy and power may be one explanation for why individuals who rise to power through spurious (e.g., President Pervez Musharraf of Pakistan) or corrupt (e.g., President Robert Mugabe of Zim-babwe) pathways face resistance rather than acceptance from their subjects.

Culture

In every culture, power is an important determinant of thought and behav-ior; however, cultures vary in their conceptualizations of power (Zhong, Magee, Maddux, & Galinsky, 2006). As a result, the associations between power and attention to rewards and assertive action are culturally circum-scribed—dependent on how cultures define the "self." In some cultures, such as those found in the West, the self is defined though independent self-construals and people think of themselves as autonomous individuals defined by unique personal traits. In contrast, members of cultures in which individuals have interdependent self-construals, such as countries in East Asia, are more likely to think of themselves as embedded in social relation-ships and define themselves in terms of their group memberships and rela-tionships with others. Zhong et al. found that the basic associations with power differed by cultural background. Westerners who were subliminally primed with the word "power" (versus the word "paper") responded more quickly to reward-related words but more slowly to responsibility-related words, whereas East Asians showed the exact opposite strength of association with power: greater accessibility of responsibility-related words and weaker accessibility to reward-related words. In another study, power led to decreased cooperation for Westerners but increased cooperation for East Asians.

HARNESSING POWER TO BECOME AN EFFECTIVE LEADER

Power activates a number of positive psychological processes: it increases action and agency, optimism, and confidence. Because leaders inspire through rhetoric and action, these consequences of power may help motivate individuals toward a common goal. Indeed, visions are most effective at capturing attention and motivating behavior when they are optimistic, forecasting a better world (Bass, 1985, 1990; Berson, Shamir, Avolio, & Popper, 2001). In addition, their action orientation may inspire others to act alike, using the leader's behavior as a guide to direct their own behavior. However, unbridled overconfidence and the attractiveness of potentially costly risks must also be tempered for power to be converted into leadership. Similarly, diminished perspective taking and the myopic vision and task focus of power that propel individuals to psychologically objectify others and dismiss the non-task-related aspects of their humanity must also be reigned in, without negatively impacting a focus on the vision for the group.

We believe that a key to more effective leadership is to make perspective taking part and parcel of legitimate power. We offer the metaphor of driving a car to understand how power can be transformed into effective leadership. The agency of power is akin to pressing the gas pedal. Without acceleration, one is left standing still, unable to move forward. But one also needs a steering wheel, and the acumen for using it, to avoid crashing into obstacles along the way. Perspective taking without agency is ineffective and agency without perspective taking is dangerous and irresponsible. Effective leaders require acceleration and prudent steering—power coupled with perspective taking. We believe that the springboard of power combined with perspective taking is a particularly constructive force. The best leaders are action-oriented, optimistic, perspective takers.

One way to turn power into leadership is to make the powerful accountable because accountability increases perspective taking (Tetlock, Skitka, & Boettger, 1989). Thus, American presidents who preside over a divided government (and thus have reduced power) might be psychologically predisposed to consider alternative viewpoints more readily than those who preside over unified governments. For example, President George W. Bush clearly showed greater capacity and readiness to integrate a wider spectrum of views after the Democrats took control of Congress in 2006. Because the

American government's powers are separated into different branches, the President is dependent on and accountable to Congress and the Judiciary, and vice versa; as a result, each branch of government has incentives to consider the perspectives of the other branches. In fact, the beauty of the American constitutional system of divided government and separated powers may be that it often creates powerful perspective takers, turning presidents from potential demagogues into potential leaders.

In contrast, power that lacks accountability can lead to dangerous and foolish acts. The recent debacle involving American-hired private security contractors in Iraq illustrates this lethal combination. Unlike the U.S. military, the behavior of private security contractors has been accountable to neither the United States nor the Iraqi government and populous. This lack of accountability coupled with extreme power may have been the catalyst for the contractors' unprovoked killing of unarmed Iraqi civilians.

Some evidence to support the interaction between power and accountability in producing leadership comes from a study by Winter and Barenbaum (1985). They found that those with a high need for power—characterized by a desire to have influence and to maintain prestige—generally engaged in self-serving and self-satisfying profligate behaviors, including gambling and sexual promiscuity. However, a high need for power was transformed into responsible and socially supportive actions when those individuals faced life events—becoming a parent or having younger siblings—that increased their sense of responsibility. A high need for power combined with feelings of responsibility led individuals both to reign in their selfish desires and to display community-minded behaviors such as volunteering.

Leadership may be prevented from emerging not only when the powerful are unaccountable but also when power is achieved precipitously, without proper incubation. In the famous Stanford Prison study, for instance, volunteers who were suddenly thrust into the role of all-powerful prison guards abused their position to such an extent that the experimenters were forced to prematurely end the study (Haney, Banks, & Zimbardo, 1973). Similarly, Sivanathan, Pillutla, and Murnighan (2008) found that individuals overreacted to sudden increases in power, exercising their newly obtained control against the weak. Given that contemporary organizational life often involves dramatic increases in power, future research should examine the effect of a sudden vertical advancement in the organizational hierarchy. To become a true leader, promoted individuals will need to harness the positive elements afforded by power, while mitigating the insidious negative effects. By understanding how to bring together the acceleration of the gas pedal (i.e., the agency of power) with the guidance of the steering wheel (i.e., perspective-taking), hopefully we can understand why some individuals abuse and squander their power, whereas others harness their power in leading others toward a new horizon and a promising tomorrow.

REFERENCES

Alicke, M. D., Klotz, M. L., Breitenbecher, D.L., Yurak., T. J., & Vredenburg, D. S. (1995). Personal contact, individuation, and the better-than-average effect. *Journal of Personality and Social Psychology, 68,* 804–825.

Anderson, C., & Berdahl, J. L. (2002). The experience of power: Examining the effects of power on approach and inhibition tendencies. *Journal of Personality and Social Psychology, 83,* 1362–1377.

Anderson, C., & Galinsky, A. D. (2006). Power, optimism, and risk-taking. *European Journal of Social Psychology, 36,* 511–536.

Anderson, C., John, O. P., Keltner, D., & Kring, A. (2001). Who attains social status? Effects of personality and physical attractiveness in social groups. *Journal of Personality and Social Psychology, 81,* 116–132.

Avolio, B. J., & Bass, B. M. (1988). Transformational leadership, charisma, and beyond. In J. H. Hunt, B. R. Baliga, H. P. Dachler, & C. A. Schriesheim (Eds.), *Emerging leadership vistas* (pp. 29–49). Lexington, MA: Lexington Books.

Bargh, J. A., Raymond, P., Pryor, J. B., & Strack, F. (1995). Attractiveness of the underling: An automatic power-sex association and its consequences for sexual harassment and aggression. *Journal of Personality and Social Psychology, 68,* 768–781.

Bass, B. M. (1985). *Leadership and performance beyond expectation.* New York: Free Press.

Bass, B. M. (1990). From transactional to transformational leadership: Learning to share the vision. *Organizational Dynamics* (Winter), 19–31.

Bass, B. M., & Avolio, B. J. (1994). Introduction. In B. M. Bass & B. J. Avolio (Eds.), *Improving organizational effectiveness through transformational leadership* (pp. 1–9). Thousand Oaks, CA: Sage.

Berson, Y., Shamir, B., Avolio, B. J., & Popper, M. (2001). The relationship between vision strength, leadership style, and context. *Leadership Quarterly, 12,* 53–73.

Burns, J. M. (1978). *Leadership.* New York: Harper & Row.

Chen, S., Lee-Chai, A. Y., & Bargh, J. A. (2001). Relationship orientation as moderator of the effects of social power. *Journal of Personality and Social Psychology, 80,* 183–187.

Duncan, J., Emslie, H., Williams, P., Johnson, R., & Freer, C. (1996). Intelligence and the frontal lobe: The organization of goal-directed behavior. *Cognitive Psychology, 30,* 257–303.

Frederickson, B. L., & Roberts, T.-A. (1997). Objectification theory. *Psychology of Women Quarterly, 21,* 173–206.

Frederickson, B. L., Roberts, T.-A., Noll, S. M., Quinn, D. M., & Twenge, J. M. (1998). That swimsuit becomes you: Sex differences in self-objectification, restrained eating, and math. *Journal of Personality and Social Psychology, 75,* 269–284.

French, J. R. P., Jr., & Raven, B. H. (1959). The bases of social power. In D. Cartwright (Ed.), *Studies in social power* (pp. 118–149). Ann Arbor, MI: Institute of Social Research.

Galinsky, A. D., Gruenfeld, D. H., & Magee, J. C. (2003). From power to action. *Journal of Personality and Social Psychology, 85,* 453–466.

Galinsky, A. D., Magee, J. C., Gruenfeld, D. H., Whitson, J., & Liljenquist, K. A. (in press). Social power reduces the strength of the situation: Implications for creativity, conformity, and dissonance. *Journal of Personality and Social Psychology.*

Galinsky, A. D., Magee, J. C., Inesi, M. E., & Gruenfeld, D. H. (2006). Power and perspectives not taken. *Psychological Science, 17,* 1068–1074.

Galinsky, A. D., & Mussweiler, T. (2001). First offers as anchors: The role of perspective-taking and negotiator focus. *Journal of Personality and Social Psychology, 81,* 657–669.

Gruenfeld, D. H., Inesi, M. E., Magee, J. C., & Galinsky, A. D. (2008). Power and the objectification of social targets. *Journal of Personality and Social Psychology, 95,* 111–127.

Guinote, A. (2007a). Power and goal pursuit. *Personality and Social Psychology Bulletin, 33,* 1076–1087.

Guinote, A. (2007b). Power affects basic cognition: Increased attentional inhibition and flexibility. *Journal of Experimental Social Psychology, 43,* 685–697.

Haney, C., Banks, C., & Zimbardo, P. (1973). Interpersonal dynamics in a simulated prison. *International Journal of Criminology and Penology, 1,* 69–97.

Hemphill, J. K., & Coons, A. E. (1957). Development of the leader behavior description questionnaire. In R. M. Stogdill & A. E. Coons (Eds.), *Leader behavior: Its description and measurement* (pp. 6–38). Columbus, OH: Bureau of Business Research.

House, R. J., Hanges, P., Ruiz-Quintanilla, S. A., Dorfman, P. W., Javidan, M., Dickson, M., et al. (1999). Cultural influences on leadership and organizations: Project GLOBE. In W. F. Mobley, M. J. Gessner, & V. Arnold (Eds.), *Advances in global leadership* (Vol. 1, pp. 171–233). Stamford, CT: JAI.

Keltner, D., Gruenfeld, D. H., & Anderson, C. (2003). Power, approach, and inhibition. *Psychological Review, 110,* 265–284.

Kipnis, D. (1976). *The powerholders.* Chicago: University of Chicago Press.

Lammers, J. & Galinsky, A. D. (in press). How the conceptualization and nature of interdependency moderate the effects of power. In D. Tjosvold & B. van Knippenberg (Eds.), *Power and interdependence in organizations.* Cambridge, UK: Cambridge University Press.

Lammers, J., Galinsky, A. D., Gordijn, E. H., & Otten, S. (2008). Illegitimacy moderates the effect of power on approach. *Psychological Science, 19,* 558–564.

Langer, E. (1975). The illusion of control. *Journal of Personality and Social Psychology, 32,* 311–328.

Lichtenstein, S., Fischhoff, B., & Phillips, L. (1982) Calibration of probabilities: The state of the art to 1980. In D. Kahneman, P. Slovic, & A. Tversky (Eds.), *Judgement under Uncertainty: Heuristics and Biases.* Cambridge: Cambridge University Press.

Lurie, R. (Director). (2001). *The Contender* [Film]. Dreamworks Pictures.

Magee, J. C., Galinsky, A. D., & Gruenfeld, D. H. (2007). Power, propensity to negotiate, and moving first in competitive interactions. *Personality and Social Psychology Bulletin, 33,* 200–212.

Miyake, A., Friedman, N. P., Emerson, M. J., Witzki, A. H., & Howerter, A. (2000). The unity and diversity of executive functions and their contributions to complex "frontal lobe" tasks: A latent variable analysis. *Cognitive Psychology, 41,* 49–100.

Overbeck, J. R., & Park, B. (2001). When power does not corrupt: Superior individuation processes among powerful perceivers. *Journal of Personality and Social Psychology, 81*, 549–565.

Overbeck, J. R., & Park, B. (2006). Powerful perceivers, powerless objects: Flexibility of powerholders' social attention. *Journal of Personality and Social Psychology, 99*, 227–243.

Rauch, C. F., & Behling, O. (1984). Functionalism: Basis for an alternate approach to the study of leadership. In H. Hunt (Ed.), *Leaders and managers: International perspectives on managerial behavior and leadership* (pp. 45–62). New York: Pergamon Press.

Sivanathan, N., & Galinsky, A. D. (2007). Power and overconfidence. Unpublished manuscript.

Sivanathan, N., Pillutla, M. M., & Murnighan, J. K. (2008). Power gained, power lost. *Organizational Behavior and Human Decision Processes, 105*, 135–146.

Small, D. A., Gelfand, M., Babcock, L., & Gettman, H. (2007). Who goes to the bargaining table? The influence of gender and framing on the initiation of negotiation. *Journal of Personality and Social Psychology, 93*, 600–613.

Smith, P. K., Jostmann, N. B., Galinsky A. D., & van Dijk, W. W. (2008). Lacking power impairs executive functions. *Psychological Science, 19*, 469–475.

Smith, P. K., & Trope, Y. (2006). You focus on the forest when you're in charge of the trees: Power priming and abstract information processing. *Journal of Personality and Social Psychology, 90*, 578–596.

Stogdill, R. M. (1974). *Handbook of leadership*. New York: Free Press.

Taylor, S., & Brown, J. (1988). Illusion and well-being: A social psychological perspective on mental health. *Psychological Bulletin, 103*, 193–210.

Tetlock, P. E., Skitka, L., & Boettger, R. (1989). Social and cognitive strategies for coping with accountability: Conformity, complexity, and bolstering. *Journal of Personality and Social Psychology, 57*, 632–640.

Thibaut, J. W., & Kelley, H. (1959). *The social psychology of groups*. New York: John Wiley.

Van Kleef, G. A., De Dreu, C. K. W., Pietroni, D., & Manstead, A. S. R. (2006). Power and emotion in negotiation: Power moderates the interpersonal effects of anger and happiness on concession making. *European Journal of Social Psychology, 36*, 557–581.

Weber, M. (1947). *The theory of social and economic organization* (A. M. Henderson & T. Parsons, Trans.). New York: Oxford University Press.

Whitson, J., Galinsky, A. D., Magee, J. C., Gruenfeld, D. H., & Liljenquist, K. A. (2008). *Power and overcoming obstacles: Implications for obedience and bystander intervention.* Manuscript submitted for publication.

Winter, D. G., & Barenbaum, N. B. (1985). Personality and the power motive in women and men. *Journal of Personality, 53*, 335–355.

Winter, D. G., & Stewart, A. J. (1983). The power motive. In H. London & J. E. Exner (Eds.), *Dimensions of personality* (pp. 391–447). New York: Wiley.

Zhong, C., Magee, J. C., Maddux, W. W., & Galinsky, A. D. (2006). Power, culture, and action: Considerations in the expression and enactment of power in East Asian and Western societies. In E. A. Mannix, M. A. Neale, & Y. Chen (Eds.), *Research on Managing in Teams and Groups: 9* (pp. 53–73). Greenwich, CT: JAI Press.

18

Morality as a Foundation of Leadership and a Constraint on Deference to Authority

LINDA J. SKITKA, CHRISTOPHER W. BAUMAN, AND BRAD L. LYTLE

Stanley Milgram's classic experiments led to the widely accepted conclusion that the perceived duty and obligation to obey legitimate authorities overwhelms people's personal moral standards. We argue that this conclusion may be premature; it is impossible to know whether people are willing to compromise their moral convictions to comply with authorities' dictates unless researchers measure or manipulate the extent that people perceive a given situation to have moral relevance. Moreover, recent research supports two basic hypotheses derived from an integrative theory of moral conviction: (a) people are more likely to reject rules, commands, and decisions when they are incompatible with personal moral convictions rather than their nonmoral preferences (the authority independence hypothesis), and (b) moral decision-making contexts serve as crucial tests of the true legitimacy of authorities and authority systems (the litmus test hypothesis). Taken together, this research suggests that authorities' ability to lead rather than simply coerce compliance is tied closely to subordinates' perceptions of whether authorities share their moral vision.

Milgram's (1965, 1974) experiments often are cited as examples of the potential destructive power of obedience to authority (e.g., Kelman & Hamilton, 1989). In Milgram's studies, an authority figure commanded participants to inflict painful shocks on another person. More often than not, participants complied with the authority's commands and gave what they believed to be increasingly powerful shocks, even when the presumed victim protested that the shocks were not just uncomfortable, but were aggravating a preexisting heart problem. Milgram (1974) interpreted the results of these studies in the following way:

> Ordinary people, simply doing their jobs, and without any particular hostility on their part, can become agents in a terrible destructive process. Moreover, even when the destructive effects of their work become patently clear, and they are asked to carry out actions incompatible with fundamental standards of morality, relatively few people have the resources needed to resist authority. (p. 6)

One commonly expounded implication of Milgram's studies is that people are easily exploited puppets in the hands of authorities. People feel compelled to obey authorities, and this compulsion can trump even their normal sense of conscience or morality.

What does it mean to call something "moral" or "immoral," and how do people distinguish moral from nonmoral judgments and beliefs? People who read about the Milgram (1965, 1974) studies, for example, may interpret participants' obedience in the experiments as being "immoral" because it violated the commonly accepted rule to "do no harm." An open question, however, is whether Milgram's participants perceived the choice between defying and complying with the experimenter's requests to have moral implications (Doris, 1998). After all, the experimenter—a scientist—had informed them that although the shocks were painful, they did not cause harm. Therefore, it is unknown whether the pressure to obey the authority caused participants to transgress their moral standards because Milgram did not explicitly test whether the participants perceived the situation as a choice between upholding versus violating a personal moral value. Moreover, this interpretive ambiguity is common in the empirical literature because researchers often assert that a given behavior was or was not moral based on philosophical or theoretical grounds, but they typically do not provide any evidence that people themselves saw the situation, issue, or behavior in moral terms (e.g., Hartshorne & May, 1929; Turillo, Folger, Lavelle, Umphress, & Gee, 2002).

We believe that perceptions of morality and immorality exist as subjective judgments in the minds of perceivers, and that different people will not always see the same situations as relevant to their personal sense of morality. Moreover, whether people have a moral stake in a given situation is not something that can always (or even often) be accurately identified by third party judges without inquiry into the target's perceptions or state of mind. Therefore, to study morality, one needs to assess whether perceivers see a given situation, dilemma, or issue in moral terms. Moreover, to know whether people feel stronger needs to obey authorities than to live up to their personal moral standards, one first has to know whether people feel their personal moral standards are at stake in that given situation.

The goal of this chapter is to review research that has tested the ability of authorities and institutions to compel people to obey and to accept actions, decisions, or rules that are at odds with their personal moral standards. Before turning to a review of this research, we first discuss an integrated theory of moral conviction that explains how moral convictions differ from other kinds of attitudes or preferences, and we present specific propositions associated with the idea that there are moral limits on people's deference to authority.

AN INTEGRATED THEORY OF MORAL CONVICTION

To begin to scientifically address the psychological function and form of morality and moral convictions, we take an empirical approach to studying whether and how moral thoughts, feelings, and behavior differ from otherwise equivalent but nonmoral actions and reactions. Our theory of moral conviction begins with one key and important assumption, that is, that people can accurately report on the degree to which a given feeling or belief reflects a moral conviction (Skitka, Bauman, & Sargis, 2005). Working from this basic assumption, the task of morality research is to explore the antecedents and consequences of people's self-reported degree of moral conviction.

Our integrated theory of moral conviction (ITMC) posits a number of ways that attitudes held with strong moral conviction likely differ from equally strong but nonmoral attitudes. Our theory is an "integrated theory" because the basic framework is a synthesis of various other theories from the fields of philosophy, moral development, cultural anthropology, and psychology. One central proposition of our theory is that people tend to believe that their personal moral standards ought to apply to everyone. If one has a strong moral conviction that female circumcision is wrong, for instance, one is likely to believe that the practice is wrong not only in one's culture of origin, but in other cultures as well (e.g., Dudones, 2007; Turiel, 1983). Therefore, people should be more intolerant of diversity of opinion about attitude objects they associate with strong rather than weak moral conviction. Consistent with this idea, people prefer not to associate with morally dissimilar others, and this preference holds regardless of whether the potential relationship with the other person is intimate (e.g., marry into the family) or distant (e.g., store owner). People even sit farther away from an attitudinally dissimilar other when the dissimilarity is related to a moral as compared to a nonmoral attitude (Skitka et al., 2005).

Another distinguishing feature of people's self-identified moral convictions is that people treat their moral beliefs as if they were readily observable, objective properties of situations. For example, if you ask third-party observers why Milgram's participants should not have obeyed the experimenter, they might respond by saying something like, "Because it's wrong!" The "fact" that it is wrong is as psychologically self-evident to perceivers as $2 + 2 = 4$. Moreover, the perceived objectivity people associate with their personal moral convictions motivates them to defend their moral beliefs and feel justified for doing so, even though recognitions of fact typically do not include a motivational component (a Humean paradox; Mackie, 1977; Smith, 1994). In short, the ITMC predicts and our research finds that strong moral convictions are more motivating and are more predictive of behavior than equally strong but nonmorally convicted attitudes[1] (Skitka & Bauman, 2008; Skitka et al., 2005).

In summary, unlike attitudes rooted in social norms or personal preferences people perceive their personal moral convictions to be self-evident and motivating. As a result, people are likely to believe that others should be easily persuaded to share their moral point of view if only they were exposed to and fully appreciated the "facts" of the matter. Moreover, attitudes high in moral conviction are more likely to be motivating and lead to attitude-behavior correspondence than attitudes low in moral conviction (see Skitka & Bauman, 2008).

The ITMC also predicts that attitudes held with strong moral conviction are likely to differ from nonmoral attitudes in the magnitude if not also the type of emotion that people experience in conjunction with them. Although considerable debate exists regarding whether emotion is a cause or an epiphenomenon of moral judgment, there is overwhelming agreement that moral issues are emotionally charged. Of course, nonmoral issues can elicit a wide range of emotions, but moral issues appear to always be accompanied by intense affect. In particular, judgments of immorality are associated with strong feelings of anger, contempt, and especially disgust (Haidt, 2003a). On the other side of the same coin, positive emotions such as "elevation" and "awe," are feelings associated with particularly moral actions that may be unique to the moral domain (Haidt, 2003b). Taken together, it is clear that moral affect is a potent experience that differs from feelings associated with nonmoral beliefs and events, and affect aroused in conjunction with moral convictions can have a powerful influence on people's subsequent thoughts, feelings, and behavior (e.g., Mullen & Skitka, 2006a).

Especially important to the goals of the current paper, another distinction between moral and equally strong but nonmoral attitudes is that moral convictions are thought to be authority independent (e.g., Nucci, 2001; Nucci & Turiel, 1978). People sometimes behave in ways that might be judged by others as "moral" because they respect and adhere to the rules in a given context. However, obeying the rules may be simply behaving according to normative pressure and not because of any real personal moral commitment to those rules. For example, someone might feel that it is wrong for a 20-year-old to consume alcohol. This person's feeling about this issue would be authority dependent if it were based on a desire to adhere to the rules and legal norms of what constitutes underage drinking, or by a desire to avoid authority sanction for breaking these rules. If the rules changed, so too would this person's view about the behavior at hand. Therefore, this person's position is authority dependent. Someone whose view about this behavior was based on a sense of personal morality, however, would still think the behavior was wrong even if the rules were changed (e.g., if the legal drinking age changed to 18). In summary, attitudes rooted in moral conviction theoretically are more authority independent than otherwise strong, but nonmoral, attitudes.

THE AUTHORITY INDEPENDENCE AND LITMUS TEST HYPOTHESES

The ITMC leads to at least two novel predictions in the context of people's relationships and interactions with leaders, authorities, and institutional controls: the *authority independence* and the *litmus test* hypotheses. The authority independence hypothesis predicts that people will be more likely to reject and protest decisions made by legitimate authorities if the decisions are at odds with perceivers' core moral convictions than their equally strong but nonmoral preferences. The authority independence hypothesis is consistent with considerable anecdotal evidence in the context of moralized politics. For example, abortion remains a hotly contested issue that is hardly "settled" in the minds of those who oppose it, even though the imprimatur of the state (in the form of its highest legitimate authority) should have firmly settled the question with the 1974 Supreme Court decision in *Roe v. Wade*. Another example is the public's reaction to the verdict of the 1992 trial of the White Los Angeles police officers who beat and arrested Rodney King, a Black motorist. An onlooker captured the beating on videotape from his apartment window and released it to the press. Because of the videotape, most Americans believed that the officers were guilty of using excessive force against King (Cannon, 1999). When the police officers were acquitted of charges, riots broke out in Los Angeles that left 54 people dead, 2,000 injured, and more than 800 buildings burned (Cannon, 1999), all despite President George H. W. Bush's public announcement that, "The jury system has worked. What's needed now is calm respect for the law" (Mydans, 1992). In summary, authority wielded by the court system and even the President appeared unable to contend with people's moral outrage about the verdict.[2]

The litmus test hypothesis predicts that people use leader, authority, and institutional decisions relevant to personal moral convictions to check or verify authorities' legitimacy. People recognize that legitimate authority systems facilitate social cooperation and coordination. Therefore, people are generally willing to sacrifice a certain amount of immediate self-interest and risk exploitation to work within these systems because doing so serves their long-term self-interest (Thibaut & Walker, 1975). Due process and other procedures for handling conflict provide a way to make decisions in the absence of perfect information. When one *knows* with certainty, however, what the correct answer is to a given decision, this knowledge provides an opportunity to check how well the system works. Failure to arrive at a correct decision leads to a loss of faith in the system. The litmus test hypothesis therefore proposes that when people have strong moral convictions about the rightness or wrongness of a given decision, the legitimacy of any authority system that decides otherwise becomes suspect.

The Rodney King incident also provides anecdotal support for the litmus test hypothesis. Specifically, in addition to leading to charges against the specific police officers involved in the incident, public outrage about it prompted an independent investigation of the Los Angeles Police Department. The independent commission yielded a scathing report on the failures of the system and its leader, police commissioner Daryl Gates. Gates was ultimately forced to resign his post because of the incident (Cannon, 1999).

RESEARCH SUPPORT FOR THE AUTHORITY INDEPENDENCE AND LITMUS TEST HYPOTHESES

In addition to anecdotal support for the authority and litmus test hypotheses, a number of studies have recently found empirical support for these predictions. For example, one study examined people's reactions to the Elián González case as it unfolded over time (Skitka & Mullen, 2002). Five-year-old Elián became the center of a widely publicized custody battle after he was rescued off the Florida coastline in November 1999. Elián's mother and 10 others died when their small boat sank as they tried to travel from Cuba to the United States. Although Elián's Cuban father petitioned the United States to return Elián to his custody, Elián was put in the temporary care of Miami relatives, who filed a petition to grant him political asylum in the United States. After months of court decisions, appeals, and fruitless negotiations, federal agents took Elián by force from his Miami relatives' home. Elián finally returned to Cuba with his father in June 2000. The Elián case aroused incredible public interest and passions on both sides of the issue. Some felt that Elián should stay in the United States to grow up in freedom, whereas others felt strongly that he should be returned to his father, and therefore to Cuba.

Skitka and Mullen (2002) collected data from a nationally representative sample in the United States to assess public reactions as the case unfolded over time. Judgments were collected several weeks before the federal raid, immediately after the raid, and several weeks later when Elián ultimately was returned to Cuba. Perceptions that the justice department and other legal authorities were fair and legitimate prior to the raid did not soften the blow of people's anger if they perceived the outcome went the "wrong" way; moreover, perceptions that authorities were behaving unfairly did not undermine people's relief and acceptance if they perceived the outcome of the case went the "right" way. Analysis of open-ended comments indicated that 83 percent of people with strong moral convictions about the outcome of the case made at least one critical comment about the U.S. government, compared with only 12 percent of those without strong moral convictions. The return-Elián-to-Cuba group with strong moral convictions tended to lambast authorities for taking too long to act, whereas the stay-in-the-U.S. group with strong moral convictions criticized either specific authorities (e.g., the INS or U.S. Attorney General Janet Reno) or the decision to use force to remove Elián from his relatives' home.

In summary, the results of the Elián study supported the authority independence and litmus test hypotheses. People's reactions to the case—both their decision acceptance and postdecision levels of trust and faith in the system—were shaped primarily by their moral convictions about the "correct" decision in the case and not by pre-raid perceptions of the fairness or legitimacy of the authorities and authority systems involved. Moreover, strong moral convictions about the outcome led people to be quite critical of authorities, rather than to blindly accept or reject authorities' decision in this case.

Other evidence that supports the authority independence and litmus test hypotheses comes from another field experiment that explored people's reactions to the U.S. Supreme Court before and after it made a ruling on a case that effectively would decide whether individual states can legalize physician-assisted suicide (PAS; *Gonzales v. the State of Oregon*). Skitka (2006) assessed perceptions of the Supreme Court before and after it ruled in the case, in addition to collecting predecision measures of moral conviction about PAS, participants' religiosity, and a host of other variables. Analyses investigated two levels of reaction to the Supreme Court's decision in the case: People's reactions to the specific decision (decision fairness and acceptance) as well as their pre- and postdecision perceptions of the Court's legitimacy (assessed with three measures: trust, procedural fairness, and a direct measure of legitimacy).

Results of the PAS study supported the authority independence and litmus test hypotheses. Predecision levels of moral conviction about PAS uniquely predicted people's perceptions of decision fairness and acceptance. People whose support for PAS was held with strong moral conviction thought the decision in the case was fair, and they were quite prepared to accept it as the final word on the issue, whereas those whose opposition to PAS was held with strong moral conviction thought the decision was unfair, and they were unwilling to accept the Court's decision on the issue. Moreover, results failed to support the notion that obedience to authority would dominate people's judgment. Predecision levels of legitimacy of the Court were unrelated to perceived fairness and decision acceptance of the Court's ruling. All results for moral conviction emerged even when controlling for variables such as individual differences in participants' degree of religiosity.

Perhaps even more interesting than people's reactions to the decision itself was the impact the decision had on people's perceptions of the Supreme Court. As predicted by the litmus test hypothesis, predecision strength of moral conviction predicted people's postdecision perceptions of the Court's legitimacy. People who morally supported PAS thought that the Supreme Court was more legitimate, whereas those who morally opposed PAS thought that the Supreme Court was less legitimate after its ruling in the PAS case. Moreover, these results were unique effects of moral conviction that remained robust even when controlling for a number of alternative explanatory variables, such as strength and direction of political orientation and religiosity. In summary, when the Supreme Court ruling was at odds with people's moral convictions, they rejected the decision and perceived the Court to be less legitimate, trustworthy, and fair.

In an experimental test of the authority independence hypothesis, Bauman and Skitka (2007) assessed student participants' reactions to a decision rendered by university authorities on whether to use student fees to fund abortions at a student health clinic. Results indicated that participants who morally disagreed with the decision were prepared to petition, protest, withhold tuition and fees, and "make trouble" for the university administration, irrespective of whether they perceived the authorities as legitimate or illegitimate. Conversely, participants were fully prepared to accept a decision made by fundamentally illegitimate authorities and processes when the decision was consistent with their moral convictions.

Other studies provide further support for the litmus test hypothesis. When people were exposed to unjust laws or legal decisions, they were more likely to report intentions to flout other unrelated laws in the future (Nadler, 2005). Mullen and Nadler (2008) further tested the flouting hypothesis in an experiment that involved exposing people to legal decisions that supported, opposed, or were unrelated to participants' personal moral convictions.

Following exposure to the legal decision, participants received a pen and a questionnaire, and were asked to return both at the end of the experimental session. Consistent with the prediction that moral transgressions erode perceptions of authorities, theft of the pens was highest when the legal decision opposed rather than supported or was unrelated to participants' moral convictions.

In summary, a host of evidence indicates that people reject authorities' decisions when they are at odds with their personal moral convictions. Moreover, people use authorities' decisions in morally relevant situations as legitimacy litmus tests: When authorities make decisions, rules, or policies that are consistent with perceivers' moral convictions, perceivers accept the decision and see it as evidence of legitimacy, but when decisions, rules, or policies are inconsistent with perceivers' moral convictions, perceivers reject the decision and see it as evidence that authorities are illegitimate. Importantly, the delegitimizing effects of violating people's moral convictions generalizes: People do not just reject the decision itself, they clearly reject the authority or system that made it, and they are even less likely to comply with other unrelated laws, rules, or standards of behavior as well (Mullen & Nadler, 2008; Nadler, 2005).

MORALITY AND LEADERSHIP

Research in support of the authority independence and litmus test hypotheses complements and extends current perspectives on leader effectiveness. The litmus test hypothesis overlaps at least partially with theories that assert that leaders can induce compliance with their requests by linking tasks and values in the minds of followers. For example, transformational leaders access stakeholders' underlying ideals and engage the deeper concerns of the people around them. They move beyond instrumentalism (i.e., brokering exchanges between stakeholders) and attempt to provide a vision that aligns activities with a higher sense of purpose (e.g., Bass, 1985; Burns, 1978). Somewhat similarly, charismatic leaders successfully link tasks and values in the minds of followers and promote identification with the leader or the group (e.g., Conger, 1999; Shamir, House, & Arthur, 1993). Research from both perspectives has demonstrated that leaders who tap into followers' values increase motivation, performance, commitment, satisfaction, trust, and group promoting actions (e.g., Bass, 1985; Lowe, Kroeck, & Sivasubramaniam, 1996; Rowold & Heinitz, 2007). In sum, dominant approaches to leadership are consistent with the prosocial implications of the litmus test hypothesis, and reveal the benefits of value congruence between leaders and followers. The ability to establish a link between values and behavior is so important that some have identified it as a characteristic that differentiates leaders from authorities and allows leaders to elicit more from their followers than what they could demand based on their power alone (Fairholm, 1998; Heifetz, 1994).

Much more is known about the benefits of value-congruent leadership than about the potential liabilities of value-incongruent leadership (Conger, 1999). Although some researchers consider the deleterious effect caused by leader inauthenticity or disingenuousness (Bass & Steidlmeier, 1999; Cha & Edmondson, 2006; Price, 2003), the ITMC emphasizes that that value incongruence may go beyond limiting leader effectiveness to also affect more extreme reactions, such as outright rebellion or exiting the group (Bauman & Skitka, 2007). In addition, although theories of leadership mention the importance of values, they do not make distinctions as a function of value content (e.g., Bass, 1985; Burns, 1978; Conger, 1999; Shamir et al., 1993). Differences in the extent that leaders and followers value material gain, power, or status may have very different consequences than differences between leaders' and followers' conceptions of moral right and wrong (Skitka et al., 2005). Moreover, values are abstractions, whereas moral convictions represent concrete attitude positions or stands (Skitka et al., 2005). Two people may share a commitment to the sanctity of life, but may not share positions on physician-assisted suicide, capital punishment, or abortion. In short, value congruence between leaders and followers does not ensure moral congruence with respect to specific decisions, policies, or outcomes.

In summary, the ITMC approach complements and extends current conceptions of leadership. Moreover, the ITMC approach suggests that future research on value-driven leadership may benefit by (a) taking value content into account and exploring whether there are important differences between perceivers' and followers' congruence or incongruence of moral as compared to nonmoral values, and (b) exploring whether value congruence and incongruence as a construct might be more profitably examined at less abstract levels of analysis.

IMPLICATIONS

The goal of this chapter was to revisit the notion that the duty or obligation to obey authority can easily overwhelm people's personal moral standards or beliefs. Although Milgram's (1965, 1974) experiments were powerful demonstrations of the tendency to obey legitimate authorities, they were less persuasive demonstrations of the power of authorities to overwhelm people's personal sense of morality because morality was not directly measured or manipulated. Our review indicates that individual conceptions of morality do appear to work as safeguards against destructive obedience, at least in some situations. Specifically, when authorities or authority systems make rules or decisions that are inconsistent with people's core moral beliefs, people both rejected the decision and used this information to revise their appraisal of the authority or system's legitimacy. Even when we experimentally manipulated a situation so that there were virtually no grounds to question authorities' legitimacy predecision, people nonetheless were enraged when authorities made a decision at odds with their moral beliefs. Moreover, they were willing to take a stand against and even leave the group because of it (Bauman & Skitka, 2007). In sum, these results suggest that there may be moral limits on the power of destructive obedience.

When personal moral standards are at stake, individuals are less likely to fall prey to pressures to blindly accept authority dictates. Therefore, it is very important to know whether people perceive a given situation in moral terms. Not everyone, for example, has a moral investment in whether abortion is or is not legal. Some people might support legalized abortion simply because they prefer to have a backstop birth control method, and not because they have any particular moral agenda. Others may oppose abortion for normative or conventional reasons, for example, because it violates the dictates of their religion. If the church reversed its position on the issue, then these people likely would have no problem supporting legalized abortion instead of opposing it. In short, our approach suggests that it is important to determine whether people have a moral investment in a given situation rather than make assumptions, even in situations like abortion that are normatively understood to be moral.

Of course, there are a number of important differences between our approach and Milgram's (1965, 1974). The physical presence of authorities in Milgram's studies may have reinforced the perceived obligation to obey or reduced the extent that people perceived themselves to be responsible for their actions, each of which could have increased levels of obedience and compliance (cf. Bandura, 1999). Although there is still room for additional research to test the generalizability of our findings to situations that more closely parallel Milgram's, our results suggest that enhancing legitimacy by attending only to structural and interactional aspects of decision processes misses an important element in how people judge the legitimacy of these systems and decide whether to cooperate versus openly rebel. Leaders and authorities should be mindful about the content of their decisions, not just the procedures they use to make them. People are not so blinded by duty and obligations to obey that they do not evaluate whether the substance of decisions and laws meets the standards of personal moral litmus tests, and they will use these tests to decide whether authority systems are legitimate.

Some of our current work has begun to test hypotheses about some of the underlying processes that give rise to the "moral mandate effects" we have identified in our tests of the authority independence and litmus test hypotheses. Specifically, Mullen and Skitka (2006a) explored whether due process considerations were less important to people when they had a moral stake in decision outcomes and tested the role of three processes that may have contributed to the effect. One process they investigated was whether people with moral convictions about outcomes were motivated to justify their preferred outcome, and therefore actively distorted the way they processed available information about procedures or authorities in an effort to support their preferred conclusions. A second process they examined was whether people with moral convictions about outcomes identified or disidentified with people who shared or did not share their moral convictions, which in turn led to distributive biases that affected their perceptions of how these people deserved to be treated. A third process Mullen and Skitka evaluated was whether moral conviction about outcomes led to so much anger when authorities "got it wrong" that it subsequently biased their judgments of other aspects of the decision, such as whether authorities acted in procedurally fair ways. Results of two studies supported the notion that affect aroused by whether authorities got it "right" or "wrong" played a pivotal role in shaping people's perceptions when people had a moral stake in decision outcomes. When authorities "got it wrong," resultant anger explained not only the extent that people rejected the nonpreferred outcome, but also rejection of the procedures and the authorities that yielded them (Mullen & Skitka, 2006a; see also Bauman & Skitka, 2007; Skitka, 2006).

Other research suggests that people may become more cognitively rigid when thinking about their moral convictions than when they are thinking about other topics or issues (Lytle & Skitka, 2007), suggesting that cognitive processes may also play a role in the effects reviewed here. Although much more research is necessary to fully understand the cognitive and motivational underpinnings of moral mandate effects, these results suggest that emotion and context-specific levels of cognitive rigidity are psychological processes that underlie these results.

In closing, we should point out that it is possible to put different value spins on the conclusion that personal morality influences people's willingness to follow authority dictates. For example, rules and authorities help coordinate behavior and create social order by regulating the distribution of both the benefits and burdens of social cooperation (e.g., French & Raven, 1959; Heifetz, 1994). To be effective, however, authorities and their rules need to influence the behavior of their constituent members; followers must accept and comply with rules and dictates for authorities to have any impact on the coordination problems that are inherent in social and organizational life. Systems in which people feel free to personally decide which rules to follow and which to ignore are less likely to reap the rewards of social coordination and cooperation and may be vulnerable to chaos if not anarchy. Therefore, one spin one could place on our results is that personal moral standards pose a threat to cooperative social systems, order, and basic social cohesion.

A more positive spin on our results is that personal moral standards create a social form of checks and balances against potential exploitation on the part of malevolent authorities. People and institutions could create the artful appearance of legitimate and fair procedures without attending to the truth value, justice, or morality of what they produce and the consequences of those products for people's everyday lives. Personal moral standards may therefore act as a canary in the mine of everyday life—an early warning system that protects people from potential exploitation and protects authority systems from forgetting that authority is always at the mercy of the consent of the governed.

NOTES

Preparation of this chapter was facilitated by grant support from the National Science Foundation to the first author (NSF-0518084, NSF-0530380). Thanks to William McCready for comments on a previous draft of this manuscript and to Nick Aramovich, Edward Sargis, and the other members of the political and moral psychology lab group at the University of Illinois at Chicago for discussions about these and related ideas. Correspondence about this article should be directed to Linda J. Skitka, University of Illinois at Chicago, Department of Psychology, m/c 285, 1007 W. Harrison Street, Chicago, IL 60607-7137, lskitka@uic.edu.

1. Attitudes are surprisingly weak predictors of behavior (see Wicker, 1969, for a review).

2. Interestingly, a content analysis of editorials and letters to the editor of several national newspapers three months before and after the verdicts were announced revealed virtually no mentions of concerns about trial procedures (e.g., the change of venue to Simi Valley, or the racial composition of the jury) until *after* the verdict was announced (Mullen & Skitka, 2006b).

REFERENCES

Bandura, A. (1999). Moral disengagement in the perpetration of inhumanities. *Personality and Social Psychology Review, 3,* 193–209.

Bass, B. M. (1985). *Leadership and performance beyond expectations.* New York: Free Press.

Bass, B., & Steidlmeier, P. (1999). Ethics, character, and authentic transformational leadership behavior. *The Leadership Quarterly, 10,* 181–217.

Bauman, C. W., & Skitka, L. J. (2007). *Fair but wrong: Procedural and moral influences on group rejection and perceived fairness.* Manuscript under review.

Burns, J. M. (1978). *Leadership.* New York: Harper & Row.

Cannon, L. (1999). *Official negligence: How Rodney King and the riots changed Los Angeles and the LAPD.* Boulder, CO: Westview Press.

Cha, S. E., & Edmondson, A. C. (2006). When values backfire: Leadership, attribution, and disenchantment in a values-driven organization. *Leadership Quarterly, 17,* 57–78.

Conger, J. A. (1999). Charismatic and transformation leadership in organizations: An insider's perspective on these developing streams of research. *Leadership Quarterly, 10,* 145–179.

Doris, J. M. (1998). Persons, situation, and virtue ethics. *Nous, 32,* 504–530.

Dudones, J. (2007). The unkindest cut. *Ms. Magazine.* Retrieved June 25, 2007, from http://www.msmagazine.com/winter2007/theunkindestcut.asp

Fairholm, G. W. (1998). *Perspectives on leadership: From the science of management to its spiritual heart.* Westport, CT: Quorum Books.

French, J. R. P., Jr., & Raven, B. (1959). The bases of social power. In D. Cartwright (Ed.), *Studies in social power* (pp. 150–167). Ann Arbor: University of Michigan Press.

Haidt, J. (2003a). The moral emotions. In R. J. Davidson, K. R. Scherer, & H. H. Goldsmith (Eds.), *Handbook of affective sciences* (pp. 852–870). New York: Oxford University Press.

Haidt, J. (2003b). Elevation and the positive psychology of morality. In C. L. M. Keyes & J. Haidt (Eds.), *Flourishing: Positive psychology and the life well-lived* (pp. 275–289). Washington, DC: American Psychological Association.

Hartshorne, H., & May, M. A. (1929). *Studies in the nature of character, Volume 2: Studies in service and self-control.* New York: Macmillan.

Heifetz, R. A. (1994). *Leadership without easy answers.* Cambridge, MA: Harvard University Press.

Kelman, H. C., & Hamilton, V. L. (1989). *Crimes of obedience.* New Haven, CT: Yale University Press.

Lowe, K. B., Kroeck, K. G., & Sivasubramaniam, N. (1996). Effectiveness of correlates of transformational and transactional leadership: A meta-analytic review of the MLQ literature. *The Leadership Quarterly, 7,* 385–425.

Lytle, B., & Skitka, L. J. (2007). *Understanding the psychology of moral conviction: A test of the universalism and consequentialism hypotheses.* Paper presented at the annual meeting of the Society for Personality and Social Psychology, Memphis, TN.

Mackie, J. L. (1977). *Ethics: Inventing right and wrong.* New York: Penguin.

Milgram, S. (1965). Some conditions of obedience and disobedience to authority. *Human Relations, 18,* 57–76.

Milgram, S. (1974). *Obedience to authority: An experimental view.* New York: Harper & Row.

Mullen, E., & Nadler, J. (2008). Moral spillovers: The effect of moral mandate violations on deviant behavior. *Journal of Experimental Social Psychology,* doi:10.1016/j.jesp. 2008.04.001.

Mullen, E., & Skitka, L. J. (2006a). Exploring the psychological underpinnings of the moral mandate effect: Motivated reasoning, identification, or affect? *Journal of Personality and Social Psychology, 90,* 629–643.

Mullen, E., & Skitka, L. J. (2006b). When outcomes prompt criticism of procedures: An archival analysis of the Rodney King case. *Analyses of Social Issues and Public Policy, 6,* 1–14.

Mydans, S. (April 30, 1992). The police verdict: Los Angeles policemen acquitted in taped beating. *The New York Times.*

Nadler, J. (2005). Flouting the law. *Texas Law Review, 83,* 1440–1441.

Nucci, L. (2001). *Education in the moral domain.* Cambridge: Cambridge University Press.

Nucci, L. P., & Turiel, E. (1978). Social interactions and the development of social concepts in pre-school children. *Child Development, 49,* 400–407.

Price, T. L. (2003). The ethics of transformational leadership. *The Leadership Quarterly, 14,* 67–81.

Rowold, J., & Heinitz, K. (2007). Transformational and charismatic leadership: Assessing the convergent, divergent and criterion validity of the MLQ and the CKS. *The Leadership Quarterly, 18,* 121–133.

Shamir, B., House, R. J., & Arthur, M. B. (1993). The motivational effects of charismatic leadership: A self-concept based theory. *Organization Science, 4,* 577–594.

Skitka, L. J. (2006). *Legislating morality: How deep is the U.S. Supreme Court's reservoir of good will?* Paper presented at the meeting of the International Society for Justice Research, Berlin, Germany.

Skitka, L. J., & Bauman, C. W. (2008). Moral conviction and political engagement. *Political Psychology, 29,* 29–54.

Skitka, L. J., Bauman, C. W., & Sargis, E. G. (2005). Moral conviction: Another contributor to attitude strength or something more? *Journal of Personality and Social Psychology, 88,* 895–917.

Skitka, L. J. & Mullen, E. (2002). Understanding judgments of fairness in a real-world political context: A test of the value protection model of justice reasoning. *Personality and Social Psychology Bulletin, 28,* 1419–1429.

Smith, M. (1994). *The moral problem.* Oxford, UK: Blackwell.

Thibaut, J., & Walker, L. (1975). *Procedural justice: A psychological analysis.* Mahway, NJ: Erlbaum.

Turiel, E. (1983). *The development of social knowledge: Morality and convention.* Cambridge: Cambridge University Press.

Turillo, C. J., Folger, R., Lavelle, J. J., Umphress, E. E., & Gee, J. O. (2002). Is virtue its own reward? Self-sacrificial decisions for the sake of fairness. *Organizational Behavior and Human Decision Processes, 89,* 839–865.

Wicker, A. W. (1969). Attitudes versus actions: The relationship of verbal and overt behavioral responses to attitude objects. *Journal of Social Issues, 25,* 41–78.

About the Editors and Contributors

THE EDITORS

Donelson R. Forsyth holds the Colonel Leo K. and Gaylee Thorsness Chair in Ethical Leadership in the Jepson School of Leadership Studies at the University of Richmond. His research focuses on leadership, group processes, the social psychology of morality, environmentalism, and social cognition. He was the founding editor of the journal *Group Dynamics: Theory, Research, and Practice*. He is the recipient of the Virginia Council of Higher Education's Outstanding Faculty Award.

George R. (Al) Goethals holds the E. Claiborne Robins Distinguished Professorship in Leadership Studies at the University of Richmond. Previously at Williams College, he served as chair of the Department of Psychology, founding chair of the Program in Leadership Studies, and Provost. With Georgia Sorenson and James MacGregor Burns, he edited the *Encyclopedia of Leadership* (2004) and, with Sorenson, *The Quest for a General Theory of Leadership* (2006). Goethal's recent scholarship explores rooting for the underdog, image making in presidential debates, and the presidency of Ulysses S. Grant.

Crystal L. Hoyt is an assistant professor at the Jepson School of Leadership Studies at the University of Richmond. She completed her doctorate in social psychology at the University of California at Santa Barbara. Her research interests include examining the effects of stereotypes and discrimination on women and minority leaders. Her research has appeared in journals including *Psychological Inquiry, Group Dynamics, Small Group Research, Journal of Experimental Social Psychology,* and *Group Processes and Intergroup Relations.*

THE CONTRIBUTORS

Scott T. Allison is the MacEldin Trawick Professor of Psychology at the University of Richmond. He received his Ph.D. in social psychology at the University of California, Santa Barbara, in 1987. Dr. Allison has published over 60 articles and chapters on topics relating to group dynamics, social cognition, and individual and collective decision making. He has served on the editorial boards of the *Journal of Personality and Social Psychology, Personality and Social Psychology Bulletin,* and *Group Dynamics: Theory, Research, and Practice.* He is the recipient of the University of Richmond's Distinguished Educator Award and the Virginia Council of Higher Education's Outstanding Faculty Award.

Christopher W. Bauman received his Ph.D. in social psychology in 2006 from the University of Illinois at Chicago, and he spent two years as a postdoctoral fellow at the Dispute Resolution Research Center at the Kellogg School of Management at Northwestern University. He is currently an assistant professor in the Department of Management and Organization at the Michael G. Foster School of Business at the University of Washington. His research interests include moral conviction, justice, power, leadership, and negotiations.

Martin M. Chemers is Professor of Psychology at the University of California, Santa Cruz. Dr. Chemers came to UC Santa Cruz in 1995 to accept an appointment as the Dean of Social Sciences and Professor of Psychology. At UC Santa Cruz, he also served as Interim Executive Vice-Chancellor and Provost (December 2003–April 2004) and as Acting Chancellor (April 2004–February 2005). Prior to his tenure at UC Santa Cruz, he was the Henry R. Kravis Professor of Leadership and Organizational Psychology and Director of the Kravis Leadership Institute at Claremont McKenna College. Since receiving his Ph.D. in social psychology from the University of Illinois in 1968, he has been an active researcher and has published widely on leadership, culture, and organizational diversity.

Florette Cohen completed her doctoral studies at Rutgers University in 2008. She is now assistant professor in the Department of Psychology, Sociology, and Anthropology at The College of Staten Island of The City University of New York. She investigates how reminders of mortality influence a wide range of attitudes and behaviors, and is also interested in the psychological underpinnings of prejudice, particularly subtle forms of anti-Semitism.

Susan T. Fiske is Eugene Higgins Professor of Psychology, Princeton University (Ph.D., Harvard University; honorary doctorate, Université Catholique de Louvain-la-Neuve, Belgium). She investigates emotional prejudices at cultural, interpersonal, and neural levels. Her expert testimony was cited by the U.S. Supreme Court in a 1989 decision on gender bias. In 1998, she testified before President Bill Clinton's Race Initiative Advisory Board, and in 2001–2003, she co-authored the National Academy of Science's *Methods for Measuring Discrimination*. She edits the *Annual Review of Psychology* (with Daniel Schacter and Robert Sternberg) and the *Handbook of Social Psychology* (with Daniel Gilbert and Gardner Lindzey). She wrote *Social Beings: A Core Motives Approach to Social Psychology* (2004) and *Social Cognition* (1984, 1991, 2008, with Shelley Taylor). She won the American Psychological Association's Early Career Award for Distinguished Contributions to Psychology in the Public Interest, the Society for the Psychological Study of Social Issues' Allport Intergroup Relations Award for ambivalent sexism theory (with Peter Glick), and Harvard's Graduate Centennial Medal. She was elected President of the American Psychological Society and Fellow of the American Academy of Arts and Sciences.

Adam D. Galinsky is the Morris and Alice Kaplan Professor of Ethics and Decision in Management at the Kellogg School of Management at Northwestern University. His research focuses on power and status, negotiation and auction behavior, multicultural experience and creativity, intergroup relations, and counterfactual thinking.

Jeff Greenberg is currently Professor of Psychology and Director of the Social Psychology Program at the University of Arizona. He received his Ph.D. in psychology from the University of Kansas in 1982. His primary focus is on how basic psychological motives influence mental processes, social behavior, political preferences, and psychological health. Dr. Greenberg has over 200 publications, including four academic books. He is co-creator of the biased hypothesis testing model of human inference, the self-regulatory perseveration theory of depression, and terror management theory. He is also co-developer of a recent subdiscipline within psychology, Experimental Existential Psychology.

Lisa M. V. Gulick is completing her doctoral studies in the industrial/organizational psychology program at George Mason University. She currently works as a Consortium Research Fellow at the U.S. Army Research Institute and teaches in the George Mason School of Management. Her primary research interests include topics related to leadership, teams, diversity, and culture.

Michael P. Haselhuhn received his doctorate from the University of California, Berkeley, and is currently a postdoctoral fellow at The Wharton School at the University of Pennsylvania. Haselhuhn's research focuses on the motivational and emotional facets of human interaction, particularly as they relate to bargaining and negotiation. His work has been published in such outlets as *Cognitive Brain Research* and *Journal of Personality and Social Psychology*.

Graeme A. Haynes obtained his Ph.D. in social psychology at the University of Western Ontario in 2008. He is currently a postdoctoral fellow at Cornell University in Ithaca, New York. Graeme's primary research interests are in the areas of attitudes, judgment and decision making, justice, and social cognition. He is a member of the American Psychological Association and the Society for Personality and Social Psychology.

Michael A. Hogg is Professor of Social Psychology at Claremont Graduate University in Los Angeles, and an honorary professor of psychology at the University of Kent, United Kingdom, and the University of Queensland, Australia. He is a fellow of the Society for Personality and Social Psychology, the Society for the Psychological Study of Social Issues, and the Academy of the Social Sciences in Australia. He is the editor of *Group Processes and Intergroup Relations*, an associate editor of the *Journal of Experimental Social Psychology*, and senior consulting editor for the *Sage Social Psychology Program*. Hogg's research focuses on group processes, intergroup relations, and the self-concept and is closely associated with social identity theory. He has published 250 books, chapters, and articles on these topics. His most recent leadership book, with Daan van Knippenberg, is *Leadership and Power: Identity Processes in Groups and Organizations* (2003).

Dominic D. P. Johnson is a lecturer in international relations at the University of Edinburgh, United Kingdom. He has a D.Phil. in biology from Oxford University, and a Ph.D. in political science from Geneva University. Drawing on both disciplines, his research centers on the role of evolutionary psychology on decision making, cooperation, and conflict behavior. He has two books with Harvard University Press: *Overconfidence and War: The Havoc and Glory of Positive Illusions* (2004) and, with D. Tierney, *Failing to Win: Perceptions of Victory and Defeat in International Politics* (2006).

Stefanie K. Johnson completed her Ph.D. at Rice University in 2004 and is currently an assistant professor of Industrial/Organizational Psychology at Colorado State University in Fort Collins. Her research interests include leadership, teams, gender, and emotions at work, as well as the intersection between these domains.

Jennifer Jordan is a research fellow for the Ford Center for Global Citizenship at Northwestern's Kellogg School of Management. She previously served as the Allwin Initiative for Corporate Citizenship Postdoctoral Fellow at Dartmouth College's Tuck School. Her research interests include moral leadership, awareness, and decision making within business, as well as power and executive behavior. She co-edited (with R. J. Sternberg) *A Handbook of Wisdom: Psychological Perspectives* (Cambridge University Press, 2005). Her other writings have appeared in journals such as *Personality and Social Psychology Bulletin* and *Journal of Genetic Psychology*. Jordan is the 2005 recipient of the Academy of Management Social Issues Division Best Dissertation Award.

Robert B. Kaiser is a partner with Kaplan DeVries Inc. and was previously at the Center for Creative Leadership. He has over 90 publications and presentations on leadership. His work with Bob Kaplan on leadership versatility won runner-up for article of the year in *MIT Sloan Management Review* in 2004; they also received a U.S. patent for their innovative approach to assessing leadership. Rob also has a leadership consulting practice, specializing in developing high potentials for the executive suite. He also provides unique research-based services, which includes developing custom leadership models and assessment tools for organizations like Motorola, Unilever, and ConAgra Foods.

Vivek P. Khare is completing his doctoral studies in the industrial/organizational program at George Mason University. He teaches courses pertaining to leadership and management in both the Psychology Department and the School of Management, and his research interests include leadership and group behavior, decision making, situational influences on behavior, and self-development.

Roderick M. Kramer is the William R. Kimball Professor of Organizational Behavior at the Stanford Business School. Kramer received a Ph.D. in social psychology from the University of California Los Angeles in 1985. Kramer is the author or co-author of more than 100 scholarly articles and essays. His work has appeared in leading academic journals, such as *Journal of Personality and Social Psychology, Administrative Science Quarterly*, and the *Academy of Management Journal*, and has published in popular journals, such as the *Harvard Business Review*. He is the author or co-author of numerous books, including *Negotiation in Social Contexts, The Psychology of the Social Self, Trust in Organizations: Frontiers of Theory and Research, Power and Influence in Organizations, Psychology of Leadership, Trust and Distrust Within Organizations*, and *Trust and Distrust: Progress and Promise in Theory and Research*.

Laura J. Kray is the Harold Furst Associate Professor of Management Philosophy and Values at the Walter Haas School of Business at University of California, Berkeley. She received her Ph.D. in psychology from the University of Washington and applies this lens to her research on negotiations, gender stereotypes, counterfactual thinking, and organizational justice. She has published over 25 articles in peer-reviewed journals, and her work has been funded multiple times by the National Science Foundation and received "Best Paper" awards from the *Academy of Management* and the *International Association of Conflict Management*. She is currently on the editorial board of the *Journal of Personality and Social Psychology* and *Organizational Behavior and Human Decision Processes*.

Matthew B. Kugler is a graduate student in psychology at Princeton University. His research interests include presidential debates, the psychology of law and public policy, and political attitudes. He is currently investigating punitiveness in the United States and Europe, strict liability standards in civil cases, and the effects of mortality salience on legal decision making.

Tiane L. Lee is a Ph.D. candidate in the Department of Psychology at Princeton University (M.A. and B.A., Stanford University). A transplant of Myanmar and California, she is fascinated by diversity and intergroup dynamics, reflected in her research interests. She studies stereotypes of immigrants and minority groups; cultural understandings of friendship experiences; and the relation between close relationship preferences and ambivalent gender ideologies. She is a recipient of the Society for Personality and Social Psychology Diversity Fund Award. She was elected as a Graduate Fellow of the American Academy of Political and Social Science.

Paulo N. Lopes holds a B.A. in Economics and a Ph.D. in Psychology from Yale University and is a former Fulbright fellow. As Senior Lecturer in Psychology at the University of Surrey, he teaches social psychology with a focus on emotion and interpersonal interaction. As Visiting Assistant Professor at the Catholic University of Portugal, he teaches both MBA and executive education courses and workshops on emotional intelligence and managing people. Lopes has also taught at INSEAD, in France, as Adjunct Professor of Organizational Behavior. His research focuses on the development of interpersonal and emotional competencies in adulthood, and he has published more than 15 journal articles and book chapters on these topics. Before starting his academic career, he worked for 13 years in business and journalism, and co-directed an award-winning documentary film.

Brad L. Lytle is a graduate student at the University of Illinois at Chicago. His research interests include understanding the psychological antecedents and consequences of moral conviction, and procedural, distributive, and retributive justice.

Susan Elaine Murphy is Associate Professor of Psychology and Associate Director of Kravis Leadership Institute at Claremont McKenna College. Her research interests include self-mechanisms for leadership including self-efficacy, self-management, and stereotype threat, as well as follower perceptions. She is currently editing a book from the 2007 Kravis de Roulet conference on *The Early Seeds of Leadership: Developing the Next Generation of Leaders*. Her most recent book, *Power Mentoring: How Successful Mentors and Protégés Get the Most Out of Their Relationships* (with Dr. Ellen Ensher), was published by Jossey-Bass.

Judith L. Nye is Associate Professor of Psychology and Associate Vice President for the First-Year Experience at Monmouth University, New Jersey. Her specialization is in experimental social psychology with primary interests in social cognition and group processes. Her current research focuses on leadership as viewed through the eyes of the follower, college transitions, and how students make sense of their world.

Rick O'Gorman is a lecturer in psychology at Sheffield Hallam University, United Kingdom. His research topics include leadership, cooperation, prosociality, morality, and evolutionary models of altruism. He has published in both social and evolutionary journals including *Personality and Social Psychology Bulletin, Evolution and Human Behavior,* and *Human Nature,* as well as providing commentary to the BBC. He has served as a reviewer for a variety of journals (*British Journal of Social Psychology, Group Dynamics, Human Nature,* and *Adaptive Behavior*) and for the National Science Foundation.

James M. Olson obtained his Ph.D. at the University of Waterloo and has been a faculty member at the University of Western Ontario in London, Canada, since 1978. Jim served as Chair of the Psychology Department from 1998 to 2003. Jim has conducted research on many topics, including attitudes, justice, social cognition, and humor. He has published more than 100 articles and chapters and has edited 10 books. He is a co-organizer of the Ontario Symposium on Personality and Social Psychology, a well-known series of conferences on various topics in personality and social psychology. Jim has served as an associate editor of three scientific journals, including the *Journal of Personality and Social Psychology* (Attitudes and Social Cognition Section) from 1995 to 1998. He is a fellow of the Canadian Psychological Association, the American Psychological Association, the Association for Psychological Science, and the Society for Personality and Social Psychology.

Tom Pyszczynski received his Ph.D. in social psychology from the University of Kansas in 1980 and is currently Professor of Psychology at the University of Colorado at Colorado Springs and Director of Research for the University's Trauma, Health, and Hazard Center. He, along with Sheldon Solomon and Jeff Greenberg, has been involved in the development and testing of Terror Management Theory, which explores the role played by the fear of death in cultural beliefs and values, self-esteem, and diverse forms of human behavior. His work is currently especially focused on applying the theory to the issues of terrorism, political extremism, and rigidity in thinking. He is co-author of *The Handbook of Experimental Existential Psychology, In the Wake of 9/11: The Psychology of Terror,* and *Hanging on and Letting Go: Understanding the Onset, Progression, and Remission of Depression,* along with numerous articles in professional journals.

Rebecca J. Reichard is Assistant Professor in the School of Leadership Studies at Kansas State University. She earned her doctorate in business from the Gallup Leadership Institute at the University of Nebraska–Lincoln. She also completed a fellowship with the U.S. Army Research Institute's Leader Development Research Unit in Fort Leavenworth, Kansas, and served as postdoctoral research fellow of leadership and organizational psychology at the Kravis Leadership Institute at Claremont McKenna College. Rebecca's research emphasizes aspects of the self as related to leader development. Specifically, her dissertation examined the impact of self-discrepancy and feedback on leader self-development in the U.S. military.

Heidi R. Riggio is Assistant Professor of Psychology at California State University, Los Angeles. She earned her Bachelor and Master of Arts in Psychology at California State University, Fullerton, and her Ph.D. in Social Psychology at Claremont Graduate University. She also received a two-year postdoctoral fellowship from the Berger Institute for Work, Family, and Children at Claremont McKenna College (with Dr. Diane Halpern). Her research interests include attitudes in personal relationships, family relationships in young adulthood (including adult sibling relationships), social identity and persuasion, features of the family of origin (including maternal employment and parental divorce) and outcomes in young adulthood, and critical thinking. She has also published teaching materials focusing on critical thinking and industrial/organizational psychology.

Ronald E. Riggio is the Henry R. Kravis Professor of Leadership and Organizational Psychology and Director of the Kravis Leadership Institute at Claremont McKenna College. He received his BS in psychology from Santa Clara University and MA and Ph.D. in social/personality psychology from the University of California, Riverside. Professor Riggio is the author of over 100 books, book chapters, and research articles in the areas of leadership, assessment centers, organizational psychology, and social psychology. His research work has included published studies on the role of social skills and emotions in leadership potential and leadership success, the use of assessment center methodology for student outcome assessment, empathy, social intelligence, and charisma. His most recent books are *The Practice of Leadership* (Jossey-Bass, 2007), *Applications of Nonverbal Behavior* (co-edited with Robert S. Feldman; Erlbaum, 2005), and *Transformational Leadership (2nd ed.),* coauthored with Bernard M. Bass (Erlbaum, 2006).

Peter Salovey completed his undergraduate work in psychology and sociology at Stanford University and his doctorate in psychology at Yale University, where he was appointed to the faculty in 1986. He is now Dean of Yale College and the Chris Argyris Professor of Psychology. Salovey has authored or edited 13 books translated into seven different languages and published about 300 journal articles and essays, focused primarily on human emotion and health behavior. With John D. Mayer, he developed the framework called "Emotional Intelligence," the theory that just as people have a range of intellectual abilities, they also have a range of measurable emotional skills that profoundly affect their thinking and action. Salovey and his collaborators have developed ability tests of emotional intelligence now in use around the world. In his research on health behavior, Salovey investigates the effectiveness of health promotion messages in persuading people to change risky behaviors relevant to cancer and HIV/AIDS.

Dean Keith Simonton is Distinguished Professor of Psychology at the University of California at Davis. After earning a BA in psychology from Occidental College, he obtained a Ph.D. in social psychology from Harvard University. His research concentrates on various aspects of genius, creativity, and leadership—the leadership studies focusing on the performance of U.S. presidents. He has authored over 340 publications, including nine books. He has been honored with the William James Book Award, the George A. Miller Outstanding Article Award, the Rudolf Arnheim Award for Outstanding Contributions to Psychology and the Arts, the Theoretical Innovation Prize in Personality and Social Psychology, the Sir Francis Galton Award for Outstanding Contributions to the Study of Creativity, the President's Award from the National Association for Gifted Children, the Award for Excellence in Research from the Mensa Education and Research Foundation, and the Robert S. Daniel Award for Four Year College/University Teaching.

Niro Sivanathan is a Ph.D. candidate in the Kellogg School of Management at Northwestern University. His research focuses broadly on the impact of psychological and economic incentives on judgments and behavior, with interests in trust development, dynamics of power, reputation mechanisms, and methods to de-bias decisions. His current work examines scurrilous competitive behaviors that arise from promotion tournaments. His research has appeared or is set to appear in *Organizational Behavior and Human Decision Processes* and the *Journal of Applied Psychology*.

Linda J. Skitka received her Ph.D. in 1989 from the University of California at Berkeley. She is presently a full professor of psychology at the University of Illinois at Chicago, and her research interests include political psychology, procedural and distributive justice, and the study of moral conviction. She is currently the president of the International Society for Justice Research, and serves on numerous editorial boards, including the *Journal of Personality and*

Social Psychology, Journal of Experimental Social Psychology, Personality and Social Psychology Bulletin, and *Basic and Applied Social Psychology.*

Sheldon Solomon is Professor of Psychology and Ross Professor of Interdisciplinary Studies at Skidmore College. He received his Ph.D. in psychology from the University of Kansas in 1980. As an experimental social psychologist, his interests include the nature of self, consciousness, and social behavior. His work with Jeff Greenberg and Tom Pyszczynski exploring the effects of the uniquely human awareness of death on individual and social behavior has been supported by the National Science Foundation and Ernest Becker Foundation and was recently featured in the award-winning documentary film *Flight from Death: The Quest for Immortality;* he is co-author of *In the Wake of 9/11: The Psychology of Terror* (2003, American Psychological Association Books) and co-founder of *The World Leaders Project.*

Mark Van Vugt is Professor of Social Psychology at the University of Kent, United Kingdom. He studies leadership from an evolutionary perspective. He is the chief editor of the book *Cooperation in Society: Promoting the Welfare of Communities, States, and Organisations* with M. Snyder, T. Tyler, and A. Biel (Routledge, 2000), and co-author of the student textbook *Applying Social Psychology: From Problems to Solutions* (Sage Publishers, 2008). His work on leadership has appeared in major journals in psychology (including the *American Psychologist* and *Journal of Personality and Social Psychology*) and in the media, and it has received funding from the Economic and Social Research Council, the Leverhulme Trust, and the British Academy. He sits on the editorial boards of various journals in social psychology and is chair of the Evolution and Social Sciences group at the University of Kent.

Stephen J. Zaccaro is a professor of psychology at George Mason University. He has published widely in the areas of leadership, leader development, and team dynamics. He also serves on the editorial board of *Leadership Quarterly.* He has written a book titled, *The Nature of Executive Leadership: A Conceptual and Empirical Analysis of Success* (2001) and has co-edited three other books, *Occupational Stress and Organizational Effectiveness* (1987), *The Nature of Organizational Leadership: Understanding the Performance Imperatives Confronting Today's Leaders* (2001), and *Leader Development for Transforming Organizations* (2004). He has also consulted with the Army and various other organizations on issues related to both leadership development and team dynamics.

Index

ABB, 279
Abdollahi, A., 55
Abilities. *See* Competence
Ability model, 79–80
Aborigines, 269–70
Abortion, 304, 307, 310
Absolute monarchs, 137
Abstract conceptualization, 23, 288–89
Accountability, 295–96. *See also*
    Evaluation of leaders; Self-
    regulation
Acton, Lord, 9
Adaptation. *See* Evolutionary social
    psychology
Aditya, R., 17–18
Adjective Check List, 138
Adolescents, 90
Affect, defined, 93 n.1
Affirmative actions, 175–76, 178
African Americans, 166, 175–76. *See also*
    Minorities
Afterlife, 47

Age and leadership, 275–76
Agreeableness, 18–19
Alcohol, 304
Alexander the Great, 33
Alger, Horatio, 184
Ali, Muhammad, 185
Allen, M., 206
Alliger, G.M., 15
Allison, S. T., 184–85
Allport, G. W., 1–2, 150
The Allure of Toxic Leaders
    (Lipman-Blumen), 57
Alsop, Marin, 170
American Psychological Association,
    88–89
Ancestral environments. *See*
    Hunter-gatherer societies
Anderson, C., 292, 294
Animals, 269, 279 n.2
Ann Hopkins, Price Waterhouse v., 172
Anxiety. *See* Terror management theory
    (TMT)

Appearances (of influence), 67, 275–76.
      See also Perceiving leaders
Appearances (physical), 123, 204, 210
Apple Inc., 33–34
Appraisals. See Evaluation of leaders
Aronson, E., 2, 13, 192
Arthur, M. B., 36
Articulation skills. See Speaking and
      communications skills
Arvey, R. D., 20
ASA (Attraction-Selection-Attrition)
      model, 20
Asch, S., 120
Assassinations, 5, 105, 132, 136–41, 142–
      45, 188, 270. See also Martyrs;
      Sympathetic figures as inspirational
      leaders
Assessments. See Evaluation of leaders
Assumptions. See Implicit leadership
      theories (ILTS)
Attachment theory, 55
Attila the Hun, 57
Attitudes, 200, 312 n.1. See also
      Morality/moral convictions
Attraction-Selection-Attrition (ASA)
      model, 20
Attractiveness of leaders, 123, 204, 210
Attributional ambiguity, 176–77
Attribution errors, 32, 275
Atwater, L. E., 258, 259
Authentic leaders, 16, 253
Authority independence hypotheses,
      303–8. See also Obedience to authority
Automobile accidents, 271
Autonomy, 18–20
Avolio, B. J., 16, 252, 253, 259, 286

Baboons, 279 n.2
Bacon, Francis, 187
Bailey, T. A., 134, 135
Bakan, D., 106
Bales, R. F., 121–22
Bandura, A., 8, 254
Barenbaum, N. B., 296
Barrick, M. R., 18

Bass, B. M., 16, 40, 286
Batson, C. D., 183
Bauman, C. W., 307
Bay of Pigs invasion, 7, 230–47; CIA's
      assessments and advice, 236–40;
      concern for Kennedy's reputation,
      243; as imperfect example of
      groupthink, 245; Kennedy as a cold
      warrior, 240–41, 244, 246; Kennedy as
      pragmatic intellect, 246; Kennedy on
      failure of invasion, 235–36; Kennedy
      on presidential decision-making pro-
      cess, 231; Kennedy's advisors, 233–
      34; participants' self-censorship, 241–
      42; as "perfect failure" in decision
      making, 233; planning of the inva-
      sion, 233–34; political risks and con-
      siderations, 236–37, 239, 240–42, 243–
      44; reassessing the Janis brief, 233–44;
      simultaneous or co-occurring events,
      234–35; skepticism expressed by
      Kennedy, 236–37, 238–40; theoretical
      and practical implications of research
      on, 244–47. See also Groupthink
Beaty, J. C., Jr., 18–19
Becker, Ernest, 46–47, 49, 56
Bees, 269
Behaviors: attitudes as predictors of,
      312 n.1; increased by power, 287–88,
      292–93; moral convictions as
      predictors of, 303. See also Implicit
      leadership theories (ILTS)
Beliefs: in cultural worldviews, 47–48;
      defined, 200; as focus of social
      cognitive perspectives, 102; implicit
      morality beliefs, 222–23; moral
      convictions reflected by, 302; of
      negotiators, 215, 217–27; responses to
      people with different beliefs, 47–48.
      See also Morality/moral convictions;
      Religion
Bentsen, Lloyd, 150, 160, 162
Bergeron, D. M., 175
Berke, R., 50
Bias: in assessing presidential greatness,

134–35; implicit leadership theories (ILTS), 123–25; in self-judgments, 81–83, 88, 91, 127, 258, 259

Biden, Joseph, 150, 162, 172

Big-L leadership, 133

Big Men in traditional band societies, 270, 272, 273, 274, 277. *See also* Hunter-gatherer societies

Bin Laden, Osama, 53

Bird, C., 13

Birds, 269

Bissell, Richard, 236, 237–39

Blacks, 166, 175–76. *See also* Minorities

Blair, Tony, 267

Blessing, T. H., 135, 137, 138, 145

Blink (Gladwell), 167–68

Bloomberg, Michael, 185

Boadecia, 69

Bonaparte, Napoleon, 283

Bono, J. E., 16

Born leaders (fixed abilities), 3, 7, 218, 257

Bowles, Chester, 237, 242, 243

Boyatzi, R. E., 21

Bray, D. W., 21

Brewer, M. B., 253

Brown, D. J., 253

Buchanan, James, 134

Bundy, McGeorge, 241–42

Burke, Edmund, 192

Burns, J. M., 63, 243, 286

Bush, George H. W., 155, 157, 304

Bush, George W.: as charismatic leader, 46, 50–53, 55, 275; divided government presided over, 295–96; Kerry compared to, 35, 52–53; MS studies, 50–53, 55, 56–57; presidential debates, 151, 156–59, 162; support as result of Americans' fear of death, 46, 50–53, 55, 275; as top dog leader, 185; as wartime leader, 35

Cacioppo, J. T., 201–2

Calder, B. J., 125

Cantor, N., 251

Car accidents, 271

Carli, L. L., 166

Carnahan, Melvin, 182, 183, 187–88

Carter, Jimmy, 33

Carter Racing simulation, 224

Caruso, D. R. *See* Mayer-Salovey-Caruso Emotional Intelligence Test (MSCEIT)

Castro, Fidel. *See* Cuba

Celebrity status of leaders, 32

CEOs (chief executive officers), 32, 35, 166

Challenger disaster, 224

Challenges, overcoming. *See* Sympathetic figures as inspirational leaders

Chan, K., 21

Charisma and charismatic leadership, 30–41; allure of, 49–56; attractiveness of leaders and, 32; attributes associated with, 16; behaviors and skills, 38–40; Christian roots of, 31; compared to predecessors, 35; as component of transformational leadership, 86; constructed by group processes, 68; crisis conditions and, 34–35, 274–75; of cult leaders, 31, 34, 35; diabolical examples of, 31, 36, 57; effects on self-concepts of followers, 35–36; history of analysis of, 31; importance in hunter-gatherer societies, 277; intelligence correlating to, 142; leader effectiveness and, 7; leader identity and, 252; litmus test hypothesis and, 308; overview of, 3–4, 31; as positive role models, 33–34; presidential greatness ratings corresponding with, 142; relationships and, 35–38; risk-taking behavior by, 39; "romance of leadership," 127–28; sacrifices by leaders, 39; saintly examples of, 31, 46, 57; saint or sinner spectrum of, 57–58; of self-aware leaders, 259; social psychological dynamics of, 32–34, 40t, 45–58, 68,

251; speaking skills of, 39–40, 204–5, 210; terror management theory (TMT), 3–4, 46–58, 188–89; as viewed by inner circles, 35; visionary leaders as, 39; Weber's definition, 31–32, 34, 45, 46, 51, 56, 57, 127; women rarely at top of lists of, 41 n.1. *See also* Implicit leadership theories (ILTs); Personal characteristics of leaders; Transformational leaders

Charters, W. W., 13

Chen, S., 293

Cheney, Dick, 50

Chief executive officers (CEOs), 32, 35, 166. *See also* Upper level leadership (executive)

Children, 90, 120

Chimpanzees, 269

Choice, 18–20

Christianity, 190. *See also* Religion

Chrysler LLC, 34

Churchill, Winston, 31, 35

Cleveland, J. N., 18–19

Clinton, Bill: age at presidency, 104; emotional connection with followers, 38; greatness rating, 140; New Hampshire primary, 160; presidential debates, 151, 155; sexual indiscretions of, 33, 140, 160

Clinton, Hillary, 165, 166, 170

CNN poll, 141

Cognitive dissonance theory, 192, 256

Cognitive perspectives of leaders, 5, 116, 123. *See also* Implicit leadership theories (ILTs)

Cognitive underpinnings of moral mandate effects, 311

Cohen, F., 49–50, 52–53

Cohen, J. E., 140–41

Collective self, 64, 253

Comforth, B., 252

Communications skills. *See* Speaking and communications skills

Competence, 5, 106–11, 210. *See also* Intelligence

Competition, 8

Compliance, 204. *See also* Obedience to authority

Conducting orchestras, 170

Conflict resolution, 221–22, 274. *See also* Negotiators/negotiations; Problem solving

Conger, J. A., 16, 38, 39, 86

Congress, 166

Conscientiousness, 18–19, 23

Consideration dimensions, 109–10

Constituents. *See* Followers

The Contender (film), 283

Contextual performance, 18–19. *See also* Situational moderators

Contingency Model of Leadership Effectiveness, 111

Controversies, 5, 9, 143. *See also* Morality/moral convictions

Coordination, 63

Corruption from power, 9. *See also* Scandals

Craig, D. R., 13

Credibility, 202, 203, 209

Crisis conditions, 32, 34–35, 45, 46, 271, 275. *See also* Problem solving; Situational moderators; Terror management theory (TMT)

Crocker, J., 176

Cross, S., 254

C-Span Survey of Presidential Leadership, 140

Cuba: Cuban missile crisis, 7, 153; González, Elián, 305–6. *See also* Bay of Pigs invasion

Cult leaders, 31, 34, 35

Cultural worldviews, 47–49, 56, 108, 119, 188–89, 288, 294–95. *See also* Mortality salience (MS)

Curiosity, 23

Darwin, Charles, 268

Das, E. H. H. J., 207–8

Davies, P. G., 173–74, 175

Day, D. V., 14, 17

Death, 46, 271, 275. *See also* Crisis conditions; Deceased leaders; Terror management theory (TMT)

Debates. *See* Presidents, debates

Deceased leaders: assassinations, 5, 6, 105, 132, 136–41, 142–45, 188, 270; death positivity bias, 187–88, 189, 191, 192–93; deification of, 182, 183–89; frozen in time effect, 188; martyrs, 189–92; permanent positive remembrances of their leaders, 189, 192; posthumous legacies, crafting before death, 193; terror management theory (TMT) and, 188–89. *See also* Sympathetic figures as inspirational leaders

Decision making: authority independence and litmus test hypotheses, 303–8; influenced by emotions, 81; by overconfident leaders, 291–92; as social events, 245–46; unbiased, 224. *See also* Bay of Pigs invasion; Negotiators/negotiations; Problem solving

De Cremer, D., 70–72

Deference to authority. *See* Obedience to authority

Depersonalization, 65. *See also* Prototypes

Despotic leaders, 8, 9

De Vader, C. L., 15, 118

De Wit, J. B. F., 207–8

Diana, Princess, 188

Dillard, J. P., 207

Disclaimers, 205, 210

Discrimination. *See* Stigmatized leaders

Dole, Bob, 151, 156, 157–58

Dominance, 21, 22, 23, 272–73. *See also* Power and leadership

Drasgow, F., 21

Droge, A., 189

Duck, J. M., 70–72

Due process, 311

Dukakis, Michael, 157, 158–59

Dulles, Allen, 236–37, 240

Duty. *See* Obedience to authority

Dweck, Carol, 217, 222

Eagly, A. H., 124, 166

Eden, D., 118, 128

EEA (environment of evolutionary adaptedness), 8–9, 269–70

Effectiveness of leaders, 20–24, 308–12. *See also* Evaluation of leaders

EI. *See* Emotional intelligence

Eisenberg, N., 183

Eisenhower, Dwight: on Cuba, 234, 235–36, 238, 239, 240, 241; Kennedy's criticism of, 240; as war hero, 138, 143

Ekman, P., 89–90

Elaboration Likelihood Model, 156, 201

Elder, R. E., 138–39

Elections. *See* Presidents (U.S.)

Elephants, 279 n.2

Emotional intelligence (EI), 78–93; ability model, 79–80; bias in self-judgments, 81–82, 83, 88, 91; broader views of, 82–83; described, 4, 78; difficulty in separating from social skills, 84; emotions as contagious, 80; full range leadership model, 86; implications for leader development, 89–92; influence of emotions on the way people think, 81; IQ vs., 78–79; Laissez-faire management, 86; leader-member exchange theory, 86–87; Mayer-Salovey-Caruso Emotional Intelligence Test (MSCEIT), 82, 84–85, 88; motivational states related to, 80; nonverbal communication, 80; problem solving facilitated by, 81; situational approach to leadership, 87; skills approach, 87; theory and research, 78–79, 81–90; 360-degree assessments, 83, 91, 258, 259; as a trained skill, 90–92; transformational leadership and, 86. *See also* Emotions

Emotions: defined, 92–93 n.1; emotional communications, 39–40;

endorsements of underdogs, 6; of followers shaped by effective leaders, 37–38, 189, 192–93; implicit emotion beliefs, 222; leaders inspired by emotions of followers, 37–38; moral convictions associated with, 303; negative emotions used to build follower commitment, 41 n.2. *See also* Emotional intelligence (EI)

Empathy, 183, 277. *See also* Emotions; Sympathetic figures as inspirational leaders

Emrich, C. G., 128, 252

Encyclopedia of Leadership (Goethals et al.), 63

Endorsement from followers, 21

Ensher, E. A., 253, 255

Entity theorists, 217–27

Entrepreneurial organizations, 34–35

Environmental context, sensitivity to, 38

Environment of evolutionary adaptiveness (EEA), 8–9, 269–70

Epitropaki, O., 72, 118–19

Erickson, B., 205

Escape from Freedom (Fromm), 49

ESP (evolutionary social psychology), 268. *See also* Evolutionary social psychology

Ethics. *See* Morality/moral convictions

Ethnicity. *See* Cultural worldviews; Minorities

Evaluation of leaders: feedback from multiple sources, 258–59; implicit leadership theories (ILTS), 120–23; prestige-based leadership, 273–74; self-judgments, 81–83, 88, 91, 127, 258, 259; self-monitoring disposi-tions, 21, 22; 360-degree assessments, 83, 91, 258, 259; of women, 123, 124–26, 170–72. *See also* Accountability; Self-awareness

Evolutionary social psychology, 267–79; contemporary evidence for ancestral leadership psychology, 271–77; described, 268; early human species,

268–70; mismatch hypothesis, 268, 270–71, 273–74, 275; origins of leadership, 268–70; overview of, 8–9, 267–68

Executives. *See* Chief executive officers (CEOs); Upper level leadership

Exemplars, 101, 104–5

Extraversion, 18–19, 21, 23

Facial expressions, 89–90. *See also* Nonverbal communication

Failure of leaders, 8–9, 267–68. *See also* Scandals

Fairness, 7

Faith, 47. *See also* Beliefs; Religion

Faschingbauer, T. R., 140

Fazio, R. H., 151

Fear, 46, 271. *See also* Terror management theory (TMT)

Feedback. *See* Evaluation of leaders

Feelings. *See* Emotions

Feinstein, J., 176

Female leaders. *See* Women

Ferstl, K. L., 259

Fiedler, F. E., 15

Fielding, K. S., 70–72

First Ladies, 139

Fiske, S. T., 13–14

Five-factor model of personality and leadership, 16

Fixed abilities of leaders. *See* Born leaders

Fixed pie belief, 215–16, 217

Fleishman, E. A., 22–23

Flores, Hector M., 167

Followers: authority independence and litmus test hypotheses, 304–8; destructive power of obedience to authority, 300–302, 309–10; dominance as the antithesis of leadership, 272–73; as focus of social identity theory, 64; implicit leadership beliefs, 224; implicit subordinate beliefs, 223–24; leveling mechanisms of, 270; Milgram's

experiments, 300–301, 303, 309–10;
prototypical band leadership, 272. *See
also* Evolutionary social psychology
Ford, Gerald, 138, 151
Forsyth, D. R., 118, 121–22, 125–26
Fortune 500 companies, 166. *See also*
Chief executive officers (CEOs)
Foti, R. J., 21, 22, 23–24, 118, 124, 255
Frankel, M., 242
Freud, Sigmund: on despotic leaders, 8,
9; *Group Psychology and the Analysis of
Ego*, 2; on leaders' articulation skills,
6; on perceptions of justice in
effective leadership, 7; on personal
qualities of leaders, 3; on
self-assessments, 56; social identity
theory-based approach, 4
Friedman, H. S., 37
Fromm, Eric, 49
Frozen in time effect, 188
Full range leadership model, 86
Fundamental attribution error, 32, 275

Galbraith, J. K., 56, 57
Galinsky, A.: on negotiators, 216–17,
225; on power and leadership, 288,
289, 290, 291–92, 293–94
Gallup polls, 169, 171
Gambling, 296
Gandhi, Mohandas, 31, 36, 46, 57, 63
Gardner, W. L., 16, 23, 252, 253, 258, 259
Gates, Bill, 185
Gates, Daryl, 305
Gender: ancestral leadership
psychology, 276–77; competition for
status benefits, 279; Gallup polls on,
169, 171; ILT influenced by, 120, 122,
124–26; leader images moderated by,
108; negotiation skills by, 216–17;
perceptions and responses to
stigmatized leaders, 169–72. *See also*
Men; Stigmatized leaders; Women
General Motors, 226
Genetic evolution. *See* Environment of
evolutionary adaptiveness (EEA)

George, J. M., 87
Gerhardt, M. W., 16
Gestalt psychology, 102
Gibb, C. A., 14, 17
Gilbert, D. T., 13–14
Gladwell, Malcolm, 167–68
"Glass ceiling," 166. *See also* Stigmatized
leaders
Global warming, 199–200, 203, 204–5,
208–9, 210
GLOBE (Global Leadership and
Organizational Behavior Effective-
ness) research project, 119, 272, 273
Goals, 63, 218, 289. *See also*
Self-regulation
Goethals, G. R., 63, 161, 171
Goffman, E., 167
Goleman, D., 79
Gonzales v. the State of Oregon, 306–7
González, Elián, 305–6
Goodwin, V. L., 252–53
Google, Inc., 34
Gordijn, E. H., 293–94
Gore, Al: debates, 151, 160; on global
warming, 199–200, 203, 204–5, 208–9,
210
GoreTex, 279
Grant, Ulysses S., 134, 138
Greek culture, 188, 189
Green, S. G., 255
Greenberg, J., 48, 49–50, 52–53, 188
Group behavior: of animals, 269, 279
n.2; changing leadership during
intergroup conflict, 274; ingroups,
65–66; intergroup conflict, 274, 279;
as leveling mechanism, 270;
motivation of followers, 36–37;
outgroups, 65–66; perceived success
of leaders connected to group outcomes, 123; Pygmalion effect, 36–37;
within social identity theory, 64. *See
also* Evolutionary social psychology;
Bay of Pigs invasion
Group Psychology and the Analysis of Ego
(Freud), 2

Groupthink. *See* Bay of Pigs invasion
Gruenfeld, D. H., 290, 291
Gubernatorial candidates MS study,
    53–56

Hafer, C. L., 202–3
Hains, S. C., 70, 71f
Hall, R. J., 253, 257
Halo effects, 83, 88. *See also* Bias
Halverson, S. K., 255
Handbook of Social Psychology (Levine
    and Moreland), 17
Handbook of Social Psychology (Lindzey
    and Aronson), 2
Harding, F. D., 22–23, 135
Harding, Warren, 123, 134
Harley, K., 72
Hart, P. 't, 246–47
Hauenstein, N. M. A., 22, 23–24, 255
Health status of leaders, 275–76
Hedges (in speech), 205, 210
Heider, F., 185–86
Heilborn, J., 184–85
Heilman, M. E., 170
Heroic glory, 32, 45–46. *See also* Crisis
    conditions; Wartime leaders
Hierarchical organizations, 291
Higgins, T., 239
Hinduism, 190
Hiring decisions. *See* Selection of
    leaders
Hispanics, 166, 176–77. *See also*
    Minorities
Hitler, Adolf, 31, 35, 41 n.2, 46, 57, 277
Hoar, S., 72
Hogg, M. A., 70, 72, 169, 251
Hollander, Edwin, 33
Holmes, J. E., 138–39
Honey bees, 269
Hopkins, Ann, 172
House, R. J., 16, 17–18, 35, 36
House of Representatives, 166
Howard, A., 21
Howell, R. J., 34
Hoyt, C. L., 255

Hunter-gatherer societies: Big Men, 270,
    272, 273, 274, 277; gender and lead-
    ership, 276–77; importance of cha-
    risma, 277; leadership within
    intergroup relations, 274–75; modern
    companies following model of, 279;
    odd correlates of leadership, 275–76;
    prestige-based leadership, 273–74;
    separating the person from the role of
    leader, 275. *See also* Evolutionary
    social psychology
Huy, Q. N., 87

Iacocca, Lee, 34
Idealized influence. *See* Charisma and
    charismatic leadership
Identification and persuasion, 204
Idiosyncrasy credit model, 33, 111
Ilies, R., 16
ILTs. *See* Implicit leadership theories
Immoral behaviors. *See* Morality/moral
    convictions; Scandals
Implicit leadership theories (ILTs), 116–
    29; accuracy and bias, 123–26; being a
    leader and, 125–26; and the eye of the
    follower, 126–28; gender influenced,
    120, 122; leadership appraisals, 120–
    23; overview of, 105–6, 116–20;
    prototype-matching hypothesis, 121–
    22, 124–25; qualities associated with,
    118–19; revision of assessments,
    128–29
Implicit negotiation beliefs, 215, 217–27;
    conflict handing styles, 221–22;
    described, 217–18; implicit emotion
    beliefs, 222; implicit morality beliefs,
    222–23; implicit subordinate beliefs,
    223–24
Imprisonment, 181, 182
An Inconvenient Truth, 199–200, 203, 204–
    5, 208–9, 210
Incremental theorists, 217–27, 257
Independent self-construals, 253–54
Individual level within leader identity,
    253

Ineffective leadership, 119

Inesi, M. E., 290

Influence. *See* Motivators/motivation; Power and leadership

Ingroups, 65–66

Initiating structure dimensions, 109–10

Innovation, 24, 67–68, 111, 273

Inspiration. *See* Motivators/motivation; Sympathetic figures as inspirational leaders

Instrumental attention, 290–91

Instrumentalism, 308

Integrated theory of moral conviction (ITMC), 302–3

Integrity, 16

Intelligence, 22, 78–79, 142, 144. *See also* Competence; Emotional intelligence (EI); Presidents (U.S.), predictors of "greatness" ratings

Interdependent self-construals, 253–54

Intergroup conflict, 274, 279

Internalization, 204

Intragroup conflict, 279

Inuit, 269–70

IQ, 78–79. *See also* Intelligence

Iraq, 73, 296. *See also* Wartime leaders

Islam, 190

ITMC (integrated theory of moral conviction), 302–3

Ivan the Terrible, 57

Jackson, Andrew, 138, 143

Jacobs, T. O., 19, 22–23

Jacobson, G. C., 50–51

Jago, A. G., 17

Jamieson, K. H., 156–57

Janis, I. L., 230, 231–47. *See also* Bay of Pigs invasion

Jaques, E., 19

Jesus Christ, 46, 57, 190

Jobs, Steve, 33–34, 185

Johnson, Andrew, 105, 134

Johnson, D., 70, 71f

Johnson, J. W., 259

Johnson, Lyndon B., 105, 160

Johnson, S. J., 24

Johnson, W., 20

Jones, Jim, 31, 34, 36, 38

Joplin, J. R. W., 252

Journalists. *See* Media

Judaism, 190

Judge, T. A., 16, 21, 23

Judgments. *See* Decision making; Evaluation of leaders

Jungian hero archetype, 184

Justice, 7

Kahn, R. L., 19

Kammrath, L. K., 222

Kanungo, R. N., 16, 38, 39, 86

Katz, D., 19

Kelman, H. C., 204

Keltner, D., 287

Kennedy, J. K., Jr., 118

Kennedy, John F.: age at presidency, 104; assassination, 105, 188; as charismatic leader, 30, 38; as a cold warrior, 240–41, 244, 246; Cuban missile crisis, 7, 153; emotional connection with followers, 38; management style, 243–44; on negotiations, 7; Nixon compared to, 35, 150–52; perceived competency and legitimacy of, 9; as pragmatic intellect, 246; presidential greatness assessment, 134; sexual indiscretions of, 33; trait-focused spin, 156. *See also* Bay of Pigs invasion

Kenney, P. J., 138

Kenny, D. A., 21

Kerry, John, 35, 52–53, 161–62

Kierkegaard, Soren, 189

Kihlstrom, J. F., 251

Kim, J., 186, 193

King, Martin Luther, Jr., 31, 36, 168, 185

King, Rodney, 304–5

Kipnis, D., 286–87

Kissinger, Henry, 116–18, 123–24, 128

Knowledge structure, 102. *See also* Social cognitive perspectives

Koresh, David, 31, 34
Kosloff, S., 53
Kraus, Sidney, 151–52
Kray, L. J., 216–17, 225
!Kung San, 269–70
Kynerd, T., 135

Laissez-faire management, 86
Lakoff, G., 55
Lammers, J., 293–94
Landau, M. J., 51
Laswell, H., 156
Latinos, 166, 176–77. See also Minorities
Leadership: definitions of, 284, 285;
    leader-member exchange theory, 86–
    87; leader role occupancy, 19, 20–22;
    leadership categorization theory, 105;
    leadership role seeking, 20–21; lead-
    ership substitutes theory, 19; man-
    agement vs., 63; selection of, 123, 273
    (see also Presidents (U.S.), elections);
    skills approach, 87
Leary, M. R., 125–26
Least Preferred Co-worker Scale (LPC),
    111
Le Bon, G., 2, 4
Legacies, 193. See also Deceased leaders
Legitimacy of leaders, 9, 67–68, 293–94
Leveling mechanisms, 270
Leviatan, U., 118, 128
Levine, J. M., 17
Light, P. C., 136
Likability, 2, 7, 204, 210
Lincoln, Abraham, 105, 134, 135, 187
Lindzey, G., 2, 13–14
Lipman-Blumen, J., 45, 57
Lippitt, R., 2
Lippstreu, M., 256
Litmus test hypothesis, 304–8
The Little Engine That Could, 184
Little-l leadership, 133
Living History (Clinton), 170
Lord, R. G.: on implicit leadership
    theories (ILTS), 118, 119, 121, 124; on
    leader effectiveness, 23; leadership

definition, 127, 169; on leadership
    identity development, 253, 257; on
    metacognitive processes, 15, 252, 261
Los Angeles, 167, 304–5
Los Angeles Times, 58
Lower level leadership, 17–18, 24
LPC (Least Preferred Co-worker Scale),
    111
Luthans, F., 16, 253

Magee, J. C., 290
Maher, K. J., 127, 169
Major, B., 176
Malleable abilities of leaders, 7. See also
    Born leaders (fixed abilities)
Management vs. leadership, 63
Managerial performance, 18–19
Mandela, Nelson, 36, 181, 182, 183, 185,
    285
Mankad, A., 72
Mann, R. D., 15
Manson, Charles, 46
Maranell, G. M., 135, 136
March, J. G., 245
Markus, H., 254
Martin, R., 72, 118–19
Martinko, M. J., 23
Martyrs, 189–92. See also Deceased
    leaders; Sacrifices by leaders
Masser, B., 70, 71f
Mastery goals, 23–24, 218
Mathy, M., 49
Maurer, T. J., 256
Maxfield, M., 49–50
May, D. R., 16
May, E. R., 235, 236
Mayer, J. D., 78–79, 81–82. See also
    Mayer-Salovey-Caruso Emotional
    Intelligence Test (MSCEIT)
Mayer-Salovey-Caruso Emotional Intel-
    ligence Test (MSCEIT), 82, 84–85, 88
McCann, S. J. H., 274–75
McCarthy, Eugene, 160
McClelland, D. C., 21
McCown, N. E., 125–26

McGovern, George, 160
McGregor, H. A., 49
McGue, M., 20
McIver, S. B., 135, 139–40
McNamara, Robert, 235
Media: coverage of dead celebrity
   leaders, 187–88; distance between
   leaders and followers reduced by,
   277; presidential debate coverage,
   150–52, 156–57, 162, 163;
   pre-Watergate, 240
Meindl, J. R., 127–28
Men: competition for status benefits,
   279; expectations as leaders, 108; ILTs
   of, 120, 122, 124–26; leader
   image-maintenance by, 125; as lead-
   ers of hunter-gatherer societies, 276–
   77; male leadership prototype activated by intergroup conflict, 279;
   negotiation skills of, 216–17;
   self-efficacy ratings, 255. See also
   Gender
Mental representations. See Perceiving
   leaders
Meta-analysis, defined, 206
Metaphors, 207, 208, 210, 246–47
Micro Expression Training Tool, 89–90
Milgram, Stanley, 300–301, 303, 309–10
Military intervention, 136. See also
   Wartime leaders
Mills, J., 192
Minorities: affirmative actions, 175–76,
   178; bias attributions vs., 172–73; as
   chief executive officers (CEOs), 166;
   as nondominant leaders, 5–6;
   stereotypes used in judging the
   degree of prototypicality, 169. See also
   Stigmatized leaders
Mischel, W., 18
Mismatch hypothesis, 268, 270–71, 273–
   74, 275
Monarchs, 137
Mondale, Walter, 153–55, 157–58
Morality/moral convictions, 300–312;
   authority independence and litmus

test hypotheses, 303–8; behavior of
   constituent members influenced by,
   311–12; behaviors of leaders
   predicted by, 303; cognitive and
   motivational underpinnings of moral
   mandate effects, 311; definitions of,
   301, 309; diversity in, 302; emotions
   associated with, 303; implicit
   morality beliefs, 222–23; integrated
   theory of moral conviction (ITMC),
   302–3; leadership effectiveness and,
   308–12; Milgram's experiments, 300–
   301, 303, 309–10; moral stake of
   followers in decision outcomes, 311;
   as motivation, 303; overview of, 9;
   perceived objectivity of, 303;
   risk-taking behavior by powerful
   leaders, 292. See also Beliefs; Values
Moreland, R. L., 17
Morrison, D., 72
Mortality. See Death
Mortality salience (MS), 47–58; Bush
   studies, 50–53, 55, 56–57; effects on
   implicit anti-Arab prejudice and
   anti-immigration attitudes, 55–56;
   elections guided by, 58; liberals' vs.
   conservatives' evaluation of gubernatorial candidates, 53–56
Motivators/motivation: as component
   of transformational leadership, 86;
   Emotional intelligence (EI) related to,
   80; martyrs as, 191–92; moral
   convictions related to, 303, 311;
   motivated communicators, defined,
   24; to obtain leadership roles, 20–22;
   Pygmalion effect, 36–37; related
   dispositional variables, 21;
   self-development behaviors and,
   256–57. See also Persuasion; Power
   and leadership
Motyl, M., 55–56
Mount, M. K., 18
MSCEIT (Mayer-Salovey-Caruso Emotional Intelligence Test), 82, 83–85, 88
Mugabe, Robert, 294

Mullen, E., 306, 307–8, 311
Multiple personality attributes, 19–24
Mumford, M. D., 19, 22–23, 24
Murnighan, J. K., 296
Murphy, K. R., 18–19
Murphy, S. E., 253, 254, 255
Murphy, L. B., and Murphy, G., 13
Murray, R. K., 135, 137, 138, 145
Musharraf, Pervez, 275, 294
Muskie, Edmund, 160
Myers, David, 58

Nadler, J., 307–8
Napoleon, 283
Narcissism, 8–9
Need for Cognition (NFC), 156, 158–59
Negative leader attributes, 273
Negative stereotypes. *See* Stigmatized
    leaders
Negotiators/negotiations, 213–27;
    effective negotiator beliefs, 216–17;
    fixed pie belief, 215–16, 217; implicit
    negotiation beliefs, 215, 217–27;
    importance of reputations, 225;
    Kennedy on, 7; negotiability beliefs,
    216; overview of, 7; perceptions of
    high-power negotiators, 290; process
    described, 214–15; risk-taking behav-
    ior by powerful leaders, 225–26, 292;
    trade-off negotiators, 226; willing-
    ness to negotiate, 226–27. *See also*
    Conflict resolution
Neuroticism, 18–19
Neustadt, R. E., 235, 236
New Hampshire primary, 160
The New York Times, 50, 162
NFC (Need for Cognition), 156, 158–59
9/11 Terror attacks, 35, 50, 191, 275
Nixon, Richard: criticism of Kennedy,
    247 n.2; Kennedy's criticism of, 240;
    Kissinger on, 116–18, 123–24, 128;
    presidential debates, 35, 150–52. *See
    also* Watergate
Nondominant leaders. *See* Stigmatized
    leaders

Nonverbal communication, 80, 89–90.
    See also Emotional intelligence (EI)
Norms and values of groups, 33
Norm theory, 104
Norton, M., 161
Nye, J. L., 118, 121–22

Obama, Barack, 166, 167
Obedience to authority: authority
    independence and litmus test
    hypotheses, 304–8; destructive power
    of, 300–302, 309–10; Milgram's
    experiments, 300–301, 303, 309–10.
    See also Followers
Obertynski, M. A., 202–3
Objectification by the powerful, 290–91
Ochsmann, R., 49
Offerman, L. R., 118
Ogilvie, D. M., 52–53
Ohio State University, 14, 127
O'Keefe, D. J., 206
Ones, D. S., 140
Openness, 23
Optimism, 288
Oratory skills. *See* Speaking and
    communications skills
Orchestras, 170
Organizational adaptation, 23–24
Organization decision making. *See* Bay
    of Pigs invasion; Decision making
Otten, S., 293–94
Outgroups, 65–66
Overbeck, J. R., 291
Overconfidence, 291–92

Paddock, L., 225
Paglis, L. L., 255
Palestinian suicide bombers, 190, 192
Park, B., 291
Parks, Rosa, 285
PAS (physician-assisted suicide), 306–7
Pattern approach to leadership and
    personality, 20, 24
Peoples Temple, 31, 34, 36, 38
Perceiving leaders: age of leaders, 276;

competence of leaders, 5, 106–11, 210; core dimensions in person perception, 106–11; exemplars, 101, 104–5; implicit leadership theories (ILTS), 116–29; leader image-maintenance, 125–26; moderated by culture and gender, 108; overview of, 4–6; performance cue effect, 123; roots of conferred influence, 116–29; schemas, 101, 102–6; warmth, perceptions of, 5, 106–11. *See also* Presidents (U.S.), predictors of "greatness" ratings; Prototypes; Situational moderators; Social cognitive perspectives; Social identity theory; Stigmatized leaders

Perceptions by leaders, 67, 127–28, 258, 289–90

Performance cue effect, 123

Performance goals and levels, 15, 18–19, 218. *See also* Evaluation of leaders

Performance of followers, 192–93, 223–24

Personal appearances of leaders, 123, 204, 210

Personal characteristics of leaders, 13–25; born leaders, 3, 7, 218, 257; five-factor model of personality and leadership, 16; historical review of research on, 13–17; innate temperamental dispositions as foundations of, 84; leader role occupancy, 19, 20–22; leadership effectiveness and, 22–24; likability, 7, 204, 210; multiple personality attributes, 19–24; nature of leadership situations, 17–20; overview of, 3–4; personality vs. situation typology, 17 (*see also* Situational moderators); poise, 7; self-assurance, 7; in small groups, 15. *See also* Charisma and charismatic leadership; Emotional intelligence (EI); Social identity theory

Personality measures. *See* Mayer-Salovey-Caruso Emotional Intelligence Test (MSCEIT)

Perspective taking, 295–96

Persuasion, 199–210; elaboration likelihood model, 201; implications for leaders, 209–10; message characteristics that increase, 205–10; Need for Cognition (NFC), 156, 158–59; repetition as principle of, 6–7; source characteristics that increase, 203–5; types of, 201–3. *See also* Motivators/motivation; Speaking and communications skills

Peter the Cruel, 57

Petty, R. E., 201–2

Physician-assisted suicide (PAS), 306–7

Pillutla, M. M., 296

Pinker, S., 271

Platow, M. J., 72

Plea bargaining, 202–3

Pleistocene period, 269–70

Poise, 7

Polite forms of speech, 205, 210

Political prisoners, 181, 182

Political social cognition, 5

Porteus, J., 49

Postman, L., 150

Power and leadership, 283–97; distinguishing from leadership, 284–86; harnessing to become an effective leader, 295–97; leadership, defined, 284, 285–86; moderating the effects of, 293–95; as motivation to obtain leadership roles, 21; overview of, 283–84; pernicious psychological effects of, 289–93; positive psychological effects of, 204, 288–89; presidential greatness ratings corresponding with, 142, 143; psychological construct of, 286–88; as source characteristic that increases persuasiveness, 209. *See also* Dominance; Motivators/motivation

Powerful speech, 205, 209, 210. *See also* Speaking and communications skills

Powerless speech, 204–5, 210

Predecessors, 35

Predictors of leader role occupancy, 13
Prejudice. *See* Stigmatized leaders
Presidential Greatness (Bailey), 134
Presidents (U.S.): "accidental
    presidents," 142–43; assassinations,
    5, 105, 132, 136–41, 142–45, 188;
    debates, 5, 149–63; debates,
    ambiguity of, 150; debates,
    evaluations of, 150–51; debates,
    importance of, 150; debates, media
    coverage of, 150–52, 156–57, 162, 163;
    debates, primaries vs., 160–61;
    debates, trait-focused spin (TFS),
    156–60; debates, interactions of pre,
    160–63; debates, simple conformity
    and debate perceptions, 152–55; elec-
    tions, predictions of, 58; elections,
    primaries, 160–61; elections, shared
    prototype of being an American by
    polarized political groups, 73; idea
    leader trait studies, 109; perspective
    taking of presidents presiding over
    divided governments, 295–96; pre-
    dictors of "greatness" ratings, 132–
    46; predictors of "greatness" ratings,
    1980s studies, 136–39; predictors of
    "greatness" ratings, 1990s studies,
    139; predictors of "greatness" rat-
    ings, 2000s studies, 139–41; predic-
    tors of "greatness" ratings, charisma
    correlating with, 142; predictors of
    "greatness" ratings, greatness ratings
    of First Ladies corresponding to, 139;
    predictors of "greatness" ratings,
    individual vs. situational factors,
    142–44; predictors of "greatness" rat-
    ings, methodological issues, 141–42;
    predictors of "greatness" ratings,
    objective performance vs. subjective
    attribution, 144–46; predictors of
    "greatness" ratings, overview of, 5,
    132–33; predictors of "greatness" rat-
    ings, power motivation correlating
    with, 142; predictors of "greatness"
    ratings, six variable prediction
    equation, 132, 139–41, 142–46; pre-
    dictors of "greatness" ratings, theo-
    retical interpretation, 142–46;
    predictors of "greatness" ratings, cri-
    terion and methods of assessing, 134–
    36; scandals, 5, 9, 33, 140, 143, 160,
    296; social cognitive perspectives
    applied to, 102–3, 104–5; as viewed
    by inner circles, 35; wartime leaders,
    ancestral environments, 274; wartime
    leaders, as charismatic leaders, 30–
    31, 35, 275; wartime leaders, greater
    support for leaders during, 35, 50,
    275; wartime leaders, greatness pre-
    dictors, 136–37, 138, 140, 141, 143,
    144. *See also specific presidents by
    name*
Prestige theory, 273–74
Price Waterhouse v. Ann Hopkins, 172
Problem solving, 22–24, 81. *See also*
    Crisis conditions; Decision making
Procreation by leaders, 8
Prospect theory, 245
Protection motivation theory, 207–9, 210
Prototypes: described, 4, 65–66, 101,
    103–4, 105; factors representing, 110;
    gender and ethnic stereotypes used
    in judging the degree of, 169; group
    members, 4; influence and
    effectiveness of leaders, 66, 70; lack of
    perfect leader image, 104, 107; mixed
    and unclear research results on, 107–
    8; provided by ILTs, 121–22, 124–25;
    role requirements, 254–55; schemas
    vs., 103, 104; shared prototype of
    being an American by polarized
    political groups, 73; social identity
    theory and, 67–69, 251. *See also* Social
    identity theory
Prototypical Band Leadership, 272
Psychological security. *See* Terror
    management theory (TMT)
Psychologie des Foules (Le Bon), 2
Psychology, 1–3. *See also specific
    disciplines by name*

Public speaking. *See* Speaking and
   communications skills
Pygmalion effect, 36–37
Pyszczynski, T., 49–50, 52–53, 55, 188

Quayle, Dan, 150, 160, 162

Race. *See* Minorities
Radio. *See* Media
Ranney, A., 151
Readings in Social Psychology, 2
Reagan, Ronald: as charismatic leader,
   30, 32–33; death of, 187–88; Gallup
   poll ranking, 187; media coverage of,
   187–88; presidential debates, 150,
   153–55, 162; as the "Teflon
   president," 33
Reedy, G. E., 243
Reeves, R., 234, 236, 240
Reichard, R. J., 255–56, 257–58
Reid, S. A., 72
Relational identity, 253
Religion, 47, 190. *See also* Beliefs
Religious cult leaders, 31, 34, 35
Remote Associates Test, 174
Reputations, 193, 225
Resources, 8
Responsibility. *See* Accountability
Reverse discrimination, 173
Reynolds, K. L., 202–3
Rice, Condoleezza, 173
Rice, T. W., 138
Richardson, Bill, 166
Ridings, W. J., Jr., 135, 139–40
Riggio, R. E., 37
Risk-taking behavior, 39, 225–26, 292,
   296
Rivalries, 8
Rogers, R. W., 207
Role modeling, 33, 34
Role schemas, 103. *See also* Schemas
Roman culture, 189–90
Roosevelt, Eleanor, 173
Roosevelt, Franklin Delano, 31, 134, 275
Roosevelt, Theodore, 104

Rossiter, C. L., 134, 135
Rothschild, Z., 55
Rotundo, M., 20
Rubenzer, S. J., 140
Rusk, Dean, 237, 242
Russell, E., 70, 71f

Sacrifices by leaders, 33–34, 39, 189–92.
   See also Deceased leaders
Saints. *See* Martyrs
Salovey, P., 78–79, 81–82. *See also*
   Mayer-Salovey-Caruso Emotional
   Intelligence Test (MSCEIT)
Sanger, D., 50
Santayana, George, 181
Sashkin, M., 16
Satis, 190
Saturn cars, 226
Scandals, 5, 9, 33, 140, 143, 160, 296. *See
   also* Morality/moral convictions
Scapegoats, 47
Schein, Virginia, 169–70
Schemas, 101, 102–6
Schlenker, B. R., 125–26
Schlesinger, A. M., 135, 137, 230, 238,
   240, 242
Schneider, B., 20
Scientific psychology, 2
SCM (Stereotype Content Model), 106–7
Selection of leaders, 123, 273. *See also*
   Presidents (U.S.), elections
Self, cultural definitions of, 294
Self-assurance, 7
Self-awareness, 35–36, 91–92, 254, 258–
   59. *See also* Self-judgments
Self-categorization, 65–67
Self-development, 252–54, 256–57
Self-discrepancy theory, 256–57
Self-efficacy, 22, 254–55, 257–58
Selfishness, 273
Self-judgments, 81–82, 83, 88, 91, 127,
   258, 259. *See also* Evaluation of lead-
   ers; Self-regulation
Self-management strategies, 255
Self-monitoring dispositions, 21, 22

Self-oriented behaviors, overview of, 7–8

Self-preservation, 47

Self-regulation, 250–61; Bandura's theory, 8; defined, 252; developing perceptions of self-schema and leader identity, 252–54; implications for research in social psychology and leadership, 259–61; leader identity strength, 257; leader performance and, 254–55; the self and motivation to develop leadership, 255–58. *See also* Evaluation of leaders; Perceiving leaders; Self-awareness; Self-efficacy

Self-report measures of emotional intelligence (EI), 81–82, 83, 88, 91

Self-schema, 8, 251–54

Self-transcendence, 16

Senate, 166

September 11 terror attacks, 35, 50, 191, 275

Sexual indiscretions, 33, 140, 160, 296

Shakur, Tupac, 188

Shamir, B., 34, 36

Shoshone, 269–70

Silicon Valley, 34–35

Similarity, 204, 210

Simmel, M., 185–86

Simon, L., 49

Simonton, D. K., 136–37, 138–40, 141

Sisyphus, King, 184

SITL (Social Identity Theory of Leadership), 251. *See also* Social identity theory

Situational moderators: ambiguous situations, defined, 18–19; crisis conditions, 32; fundamental attribution error, 32, 275; historical review of research on, 14–15; ILT influenced by, 119–20; leader effectiveness and, 87; leadership role seeking precluded by, 22; lower level leadership, 17–18; overview of, 5; personality vs. situation typology, 17; presidential greatness predictors,

142–44; self-schema and, 251–53; strong situations, defined, 18–19; upper level leadership (executive), 17–18; weak situations, defined, 18–20

Sivanathan, N., 291–92, 296

Skills approach, 87

Skitka, L. J., 306–7, 311

Small groups, 15

Smith, J. A., 22

Snakes, 271

Snyder, M., 40

Sociability, 23. *See also* Warmth, perceptions of

Social cognitive perspectives, 101–12; Bandura's theory, 254; core dimensions in person perception, 106–7; described, 251; focus on beliefs, 102; implicit leadership theories (ILTs), 105; lack of universal leader image, 107–9; leader images in trait studies, 109–10; situation-contingent leadership research and, 110–11. *See also* Perceiving leaders; Self-regulation

Social exchange concepts, 33, 111

Social identity theory, 62–74; appearance of influence, 67; components of, 64–65; described, 64–66, 169; emotions as contagious, 80; empirical evidence, 70–72; followership as focus of, 64; Freud's approach, 4; gender and ethnic stereotypes used in judging the degree of prototypicality, 169; historical review of research on, 64–66; identity strength, 257; leaders as entrepreneurs of identity, 68–69; leadership across multiple groups, 73; legitimacy, trust, and innovation, 67–68; prototypes and, 67–69, 251; salience raised or lowered by leaders, 69; social construction of charisma, 68; Social Identity Theory of Leadership (SITL), 251. *See also* Prototypes

Social judgment skills, 87
Social potency, 20, 21
Social problem solving, 22–24
Social psychology: evolutionary social psychology (ESP), 268; history and development of discipline, 1–3; roadblocks to full utilization in current leadership theorizing, 260–61; Social Psychological Constructs Involved in Charismatic Leadership, 40t
Social Psychology (Ross), 2
Social-role theory (Eagly), 124
Social scientific analyses, 31–32
Social stigma and leadership. *See* Stigmatized leaders
Social vs. emotional skills, 84
Socioemotional leaders, 109–11
Socrates, 189–90
Sokolsky, E., 134, 135
Solomon, S., 49–50, 52–53, 188
Solon, 188
Sophocles, 188
Sopory, P., 207
Sorensen, Ted, 235
Sorenson, G. J., 63
Sosik, J. J., 259
Source credibility, 202, 203, 209
Spangler, W. D., 35
Speaking and communications skills: of charismatic leaders, 39–40, 204–5, 210; disclaimers, 205, 210; emotional intelligence (EI) and, 80; hedges, 205, 210; motivated communicators, 24; polite forms, 205, 210; powerful speech, 205, 209, 210; powerless speech, 204–5, 210; repetition as principle of powers of persuasion, 6–7; selection of talkative leaders, 123; speech hesitations, 205, 210; of women, 277. *See also* Motivators/motivation; Persuasion
Spencer, S. J., 173–74
Spiders, 271
Spin, 156–62

Stakeholders, 308
Stalin, Joseph, 275
Stanford Prison study, 296
State of Oregon, Gonzales v., 306–7
St. Catharines, Ontario, Canada, 202–3
Steele, C. M., 173–74
Steele, Shelby, 175–76
Steeper, F. T., 151
Steinbrenner, George, 185
Stereotype Content Model (SCM), 106–7
Stereotypes, 5–6, 65, 173–74, 175. *See also* Prototypes; Stigmatized leaders
Sternberg, R. J., 246
Stigmatized leaders, 5–6, 165–78; experiences of stigmatized leaders, 173–77; the glass ceiling turned labyrinth, 166–67; perceptions of and responses to stigmatized (subordinated) leaders, 168–73; social stigma, described, 167–68; stereotypes, 5–6, 65, 173–74, 175; underdogs, 6, 183–87, 191, 193. *See also* Gender; Minorities; Perceiving leaders
Stockdale, James, 160
Stogdill, R. M., 284
Stranger anxieties, 271
Strategic risk. *See* Risk-taking behavior
Stress, 254
Stroebe, W., 207–8
Strong speech. *See* Powerful speech
Subordinated leaders. *See* Stigmatized leaders
Subordinates. *See* Followers
Succession, 35
Suffering. *See* Sympathetic figures as inspirational leaders
Suicide, 190, 191–92. *See also* Martyrs
Supino, A., 171
Svensson, A., 70, 71f, 72
Sympathetic figures as inspirational leaders, 181–93; characterization of, 182; deifying the dead, 182, 183–89; empathy, defined, 183; martyrs,

189–92; underdog leaders, 6, 183–87, 191, 193. *See also* Stigmatized leaders

Sympathy. *See* Emotions

Systematic Multiple Level Observation of Groups inventory (SYMLOG), 121–22

Tabor, J., 189

Tacit knowledge, 246

Task leaders, 109–11

Taylor, Zachary, 134

Television. *See* Media

Teresa, Mother, 46

Terror management theory (TMT), 3–4, 46–58, 188–89

Tetlock, P. E., 245, 247

TFS (trait-focused spin), 156–60

Thatcher, Margaret, 69

Thomas, Clarence, 172–73

Thompson, L., 216–17

Thomson, J. C., 241–42

Thoughtful innovators, 24, 67–68, 111, 273

Threatening messages, 207–9, 210

360-degree Assessments, 83, 91, 258, 259

Thucydides, 188

Time Magazine, 51

TMT (Terror management theory), 3–4, 46–58, 188–89

Tolerance for ambiguity, 23

Top-down selection of leaders, 273

Toxic leaders, 57–58

Trait-focused spin (TFS), 156–60

Traits, 292–93. *See also* Implicit leadership theories (ILTS)

Transformational leaders, 86, 90, 308. *See also* Charisma and charismatic leadership

Transgressions by leaders. *See* Idiosyncrasy credit model; Scandals

Trewhitt, Henry, 153–54

Truman, Harry S., 38

Trump, Donald, 185

Trust, 67–68, 111, 259, 271. *See also* Warmth, perceptions of

Tsongas, Paul, 160

Tyranny, 273

Underdog leaders, 6, 183–87, 191, 193. *See also* Sympathetic figures as inspirational leaders

University of Michigan, 14

Unjust laws and legal decisions, 307–8

Upper level leadership (executive), 17–18, 24. *See also* Chief executive officers (CEOs)

U.S. Civil War, 143. *See also* Wartime leaders

U.S. Congress, 166

U.S. presidents. *See* Presidents

U.S. Supreme Court, 306–7

Utility theory, 245

Values, 33, 189, 309. *See also* Morality/moral convictions

VandeWalle, D. M., 223

Van Kleef, G. A., 290

Van Knippenberg, D., 72

Van Vugt, M., 70–72

Verbal communication. *See* Speaking and communications skills

Vice presidents, 5, 105, 142–43, 153, 157, 160. *See also* Presidents (U.S.), debates

Vietnam War, 117, 141, 143, 231. *See also* Wartime leaders

Villaraigosa, Antonio, 167

Virgin Group, 279

Visionary leaders, 39, 68

Volkerpsychologie, 2

Voter behavior. *See* Presidents (U.S.), elections

Vroom, V. H., 17

Waldman, P., 156–57

Walumbwa, F. O., 16

Warmth, perceptions of, 5, 106–11. *See also* Trust

War on terror. *See* Bush, George W.

Warren Harding Effect, 123

Wartime leaders: ancestral

environments, 274; as charismatic leaders, 30–31, 35, 275; greater support for leaders during, 35, 50, 275; greatness predictors, 136–37, 138, 140, 141, 143, 144. *See also* Presidents (U.S.), predictors of "greatness" ratings

Washington, Booker T., 183

Washington, George, 134, 138, 143

Watergate, 231

Watson, C. B., 255

Weber, Max, 31–32, 34, 45, 46, 51, 56, 57, 127

Weeden, K., 72

Weise, D. R., 53, 55

Weld, William, 161–62

Wendt, H. W., 136

West Point, 171

White, R., 2

Whittier, John, 188

Whittington, J. L., 252–53

Whyte, G., 244, 245

Wicklund, R., 258

Williams, C. J., 151

Williams College, 153

Winfrey, Oprah, 175, 185

Winter, D. G., 142, 296

Wirtz, P. W., 118

Wofford, J. C., 252–53, 260

Women: bias attributions vs., 172–73; as chief executive officers (CEOs), 166; competition for status benefits, 279; empathy and communication skills of, 277; evaluation of women as leaders, 123, 124–26, 170–72; expectations as leader, 108; female leadership prototype activated by intragroup conflict, 279; Gallup poll on women as presidents, 169; "glass ceiling," 166; ILTs of, 120, 122, 124–26; leader image–maintenance by, 125–26; leadership style of, 277; as members of U.S. Congress, 166–67; negotiation skills of, 216–17; as nondominant leaders, 5–6; objectification by the powerful leaders, 290, 291; preferential treatment for, 176; rarely at top of lists of charismatic leaders, 41 n.1; self-efficacy ratings, 255; traits associated with, 170. *See also* Gender

Wood, G. M., 16

World Trade Center. *See* September 11 terror attacks

Worldviews. *See* Cultural worldviews

Woycke, J., 35

Wundt, Wilhelm, 2

Wurf, E., 254

Yammarino, F. J., 258, 259

Yanomamö, 269–70, 276

Yukl, G. A., 21, 49–50

Zaccaro, S. J., 14, 17, 21, 22–23, 24

Zhang, Z., 20

Zhong, C., 294